Located throughout REVEL, **quizzing** affords students opportunities to check their understanding at regular intervals before moving on.

D0222543

REVEL enables students to read and interact with course material on the devices they use, **anywhere** and **anytime**. Responsive design allows students to access REVEL on their tablet devices, with content displayed clearly in both portrait and landscape view.

Highlighting, **note taking**, and a **glossary** personalize the learning experience. Educators can add **notes** for students, too, including reminders or study tips

REVEL's variety of **writing** activities and assignments develop and assess concept **mastery** and **critical thinking**.

Superior assignability and tracking

REVEL's assignability and tracking tools help educators make sure students are completing their reading and understanding core concepts.

REVEL allows educators to indicate precisely which readings must be completed on which dates. This clear, detailed schedule helps students stay on task and keeps them motivated throughout the course.

REVEL lets educators monitor class assignment completion and individual student achievement. It offers actionable information that helps educators intersect with their students in meaningful ways, such as points earned on quizzes and time on task.

Understanding the Political World

A Comparative Introduction to Political Science

Twelfth Edition

James N. Danziger
University of California, Irvine

Charles Anthony Smith
University of California, Irvine

PEARSON

Boston   Columbus   Indianapolis   New York   San Francisco   Amsterdam
Cape Town   Dubai   London   Madrid   Milan   Munich   Paris   Montréal   Toronto
Delhi   Mexico City   São Paulo   Sydney   Hong Kong   Seoul   Singapore   Taipei   Tokyo

Editorial Director: Dickson Musslewhite
Publisher: Charlyce Jones Owen
Editorial Assistant: Maureen Diana
Marketing Managers: Tricia Murphy, Brittany Pogue-Mohammed
Media Project Manager: Tina Gagliostro
Program Manager: Rob DeGeorge
Project Manager: Gail Cocker

Project Coordination, Text Design, and Electronic Page Makeup: Integra
Cover Designer/Manager: Maria Lange
Cover Photo: wong yu liang/Shutterstock
Operations Specialist: Mary Ann Gloriande
Printer/Binder: Courier/Kendallville
Cover Printer: Courier/Kendallville

Acknowledgements of third party content appear here: page xv, which constitutes an extension of this copyright page.

This work is solely for the use of instructors and administrators for the purpose of teaching courses and assessing student learning. Unauthorized dissemination or publication of the work in whole or in part (including selling or otherwise providing to unauthorized users access to the work or to your user credentials) will destroy the integrity of the work and is strictly prohibited.

Library of Congress Cataloging-in-Publication Data

Danziger, James N.
  Understanding the political world : a comparative introduction to political science/James N. Danziger, University of California, Irvine, Charles Anthony Smith, University of California, Irvine.
    pages cm
  ISBN 978-0-13-394147-0 (alk. paper)—ISBN 0-13-394147-7 (alk. paper)
1. Political science. 2. Comparative government. I. Title.
  JA66.D36 2015
  320—dc23

                                                                2014036594

10 9 8 7 6 5 4 3 2 1—V011—15 14

Student Edition
ISBN 13: 978-0-133-94147-0
ISBN 10:   0-133-94147-7

A la Carte Edition
ISBN 13: 978-0-134-12519-0
ISBN 10:   0-134-12519-3

Instructor's Review Copy:
ISBN 13: 978-0-133-97903-9
ISBN 10:   0-133-97903-2

Detailed Contents

Preface

During early 2014, opposition to Ukrainian President Yanukovich escalated from demonstrations, to protests, to bloody confrontations and more than 200 deaths. On a February night in 2014, opposition leaders took the stage in Kiev to announce triumphantly that a deal had been reached with the president to end the increasingly violent conflict. The deal, brokered by the European Union, called for elections in the fall. A 26-year-old protester named Volodymyr Parasiuk climbed onto the stage, took the microphone, and gave an impassioned impromptu speech criticizing the peace deal and chastising the opposition leaders for "shaking hands with this killer." The crowd of thousands, and then many Ukrainians, turned against the peace accord, and that night President Yanukovich fled the capital. After several days, the legislature stripped him of his power. One young man had commandeered a microphone and altered the course of Ukrainian, Crimean, Russian, and even interstate politics, despite the extensive efforts and agreements of high-ranking diplomats in the European Union and the Ukraine.

Our theories and research findings in political science cannot predict this sort of event. Yet that does not frustrate or embarrass us on behalf of political scientists everywhere. One endlessly fascinating aspect of the study of politics is that there are always new challenges to our explanations. This makes politics intriguing. Albert Einstein commented that politics is more difficult than physics. The political phenomena that we attempt to study and explain include many variables and can spin in unexpected directions, especially while unpredictable humans try to control them. Yet all is not chaos. There are patterns, and some actions and outcomes are much more likely than others.

A central goal of political scientists is to identify and communicate what happens and why it happens and then to offer generalizations that capture the broad processes and underlying dynamics of politics. This is how political science attempts to enhance our understanding of the political world: hence the title of this book.

The book provides you with some of the tools—key concepts, research findings, explanations—to help you better understand both politics and how political science approaches its subject matter. It offers you a path. After a brief consideration of how we decide what we know, the book explores what we do know about the political beliefs and actions of individuals. It then advances to the country level of analysis, examining political institutions and political processes. This is followed by a consideration of politics at the level of the global system. The final chapters draw together all the themes of the book while examining the politics of three broad clusters of countries around the world.

We hope the events that are unfolding in the political world have persuaded you that it is essential to understand it and to act sensibly within it, because politics is arguably the most critical domain in which our futures are being shaped. In this book, you will be encouraged to consider whether the information, insights, and concepts of political science are useful. Can they help us understand the political world? Can they inform our value choices and normative judgments about public policies? Can they guide our policies and actions in ways that improve the quality of our lives, individually and collectively?

New To This Edition

Given the extraordinary rate of change in the political world, there is a systematic and thorough update of the quantitative data in almost every figure and table and extensive updates to most of the in-depth examples that are embedded throughout the text. Professor Tony Smith is the most notable addition in this edition. He brings broad political science knowledge, with particular strengths in international relations, political institutions, and judicial politics (he was a practicing lawyer before he returned to academia). Here are some additional significant differences from the previous edition:

- Among the vignettes that open every chapter by introducing a major theme of that chapter are new ones. One explores the financial crisis associated with the euro and the European Union, with particular attention to Greece, and another discusses Canada as an example of the complexity of the contemporary developed countries of the Global North.

- Chapter 4 has been revised substantially to include an extensive new discussion of explanatory approaches associated with political psychology, including rational choice, cognitive psychology, intergroup relations, personality approaches, and biopolitics.

- Chapters 6 and 7 contain an expanded discussion of institutionalism and revised sections on judicial politics, constitutions, and regime types.

- Chapter 8 reworks the analysis of political economy, with a new section on state capitalism, significant revision of the discussion of statism and corporatism, and a pared down treatment of communism.

- Chapter 10 now incorporates and updates the analytic framework (previously in Chapter 13) employed to classify the world's countries into the groupings examined in Chapters 13–15.

- Chapter 11 brings in current debates and approaches in international relations, including revised sections on international law, globalization, and transnational systems.

- Chapter 12, on political violence, reflects the evolving role of terrorism and its causes and consequences and expands the discussion of separatist violence.

- Chapters 13 and 14 have been revised to reflect the emerging challenges to both the Global North and the Global South, including such topics as the impact of the global economic crisis and the apparent "rise of the South."

- Chapter 15, on the transitional developed countries, has been significantly revised to emphasize the recent evolution in both the post-communist developed countries and the newly industrialized countries in Latin America, and it includes a completely new discussion of the five BRICS countries.

- New data and graphical analyses are presented to illuminate such issues as the crossnational measurement of the level of democracy, the comparative rates of economic growth in transitional developed countries across two decades, and the relationship between level of democracy and level of economic development.

- On the Web, a list of useful and relevant Internet sites, and For Further Reading suggestions at the end of each chapter have been updated and expanded.

REVEL™

Educational technology designed for the way today's students read, think, and learn

When students are engaged deeply, they learn more effectively and perform better in their courses. This simple fact inspired the creation of REVEL : an immersive learning experience designed for the way today's students read, think, and learn. Built in collaboration with educators and students nationwide, REVEL is the newest, fully digital way to deliver respected Pearson content.

REVEL enlivens course content with media interactives and assessments— integrated directly within the authors' narrative—that provide opportunities for students to read about and practice course material in tandem. This immersive educational technology boosts student engagement, which leads to better understanding of concepts and improved performance throughout the course.

Learn more about REVEL
www.pearsonhighered.com/revel/

Features

The twelfth edition of *Understanding the Political World* retains the conceptual framework of previous editions, focusing on politics at every level, from the individual person to the global system. To enrich the reader's understanding, it employs a comparative perspective, considering evidence and examples from many countries in all regions of the world. This approach is guided both by Aristotle's wise observation that all thinking begins in comparison and by a recognition that the political world is now truly global.

As noted above, the book is organized to provide the reader with a brief characterization of how political scientists study politics in a comparative framework. It then uses such a framework to focus on how to understand politics at the level of the individual and the group, the different ways in which political institutions are organized, the dynamics of important political processes, and the key patterns of politics in major clusters of countries.

Chapter 1 and the Appendix introduce the logic of political science and the methods of comparative political analysis.

Chapters 2–4 examine both normative political theory and the empirical study of political behavior at the individual and group levels, describing and explaining the causes of political beliefs and actions.

Chapters 5–8 emphasize the structural and institutional elements of political systems, offering concepts and examples that characterize the different ways in which people organize themselves politically.

Chapters 9–12 analyze crucial political processes, such as public policymaking and the exercise of power, political and economic development, politics across national borders, and political violence.

Chapters 13–15 explain in detail how important groups of countries try to achieve their broad goals of prosperity, stability, and security within the complex international environment. These chapters provide specific analyses of the developed countries, the developing countries, and

three sets of transitional developed countries—the postcommunist developed countries, the newly industrializing countries in Latin America, and the BRICS countries.

In addition, the twelfth edition retains most key features of the previous edition:

- Many discussions and debates provide memorable applications of key concepts, such as power, democracy, political violence, equality, and globalization, and key issues, such as whether terrorism is ever justifiable and whether interest groups are good for democracy.

- Continual use of country-based examples grounds every topic in relevant, specific realities.

- Numerous presentations of current data, often in graphical form, facilitate analysis and comparisons on many topics.

- Captioned photographs illuminate themes in a way that complements the textual discussions.

- A recurring focus on political economy emphasizes the significance of linkages between the political system and the economic system.

- Eight excellent, full-color maps display the geographic relations of countries in all areas of the world.

- An engaging, readable style draws in the reader.

Supplements

Pearson is pleased to offer several resources to qualified adopters of *Understanding the Political World* and their students that will make teaching and learning from this book even more effective and enjoyable. Several of the supplements for this book are available at the Instructor Resource Center (IRC), an online hub that allows instructors to quickly download book-specific supplements. Please visit the IRC welcome page at www.pearsonhighered.com/irc to register for access.

INSTRUCTOR'S MANUAL/TEST BANK This resource includes learning objectives, chapter overview and lecture suggestions, multiple-choice questions, essay questions, and discussion questions for each chapter. Available exclusively on the IRC.

PEARSON MYTEST This powerful assessment generation program includes all of the items in the instructor's manual/test bank. Questions and tests can be easily created, customized, saved online, and then printed, allowing flexibility to manage assessments anytime and anywhere. Available exclusively on the IRC.

POWERPOINT PRESENTATIONS Organized around a lecture outline, these multimedia presentations include photos, figures, and tables from each chapter. Available exclusively on the IRC.

LONGMAN ATLAS OF WORLD ISSUES (0-205-78020-2) From population and political systems to energy use and women's rights, the *Longman Atlas of World Issues* features full-color thematic maps that examine the forces shaping the world. Featuring maps from the latest edition of *The Penguin State of the World Atlas*, this excerpt includes critical thinking exercises to promote a deeper understanding of how geography affects many global issues.

GOODE'S WORLD ATLAS (0-321-65200-2) First published by Rand McNally in 1923, *Goode's World Atlas* has set the standard for college reference atlases. It features hundreds of physical, political, and thematic maps as well as graphs, tables, and a pronouncing index.

Acknowledgments

Many sources of ideas and information constitute the basis of my understanding about politics. Broadly, you should know that I was born and have been educated primarily in the United States. I have also studied, lived, and/or spent significant periods of time in more than 70 countries in Western and Eastern Europe, Central and South America, Asia, the Middle East and North Africa, and Sub-Saharan Africa.

I have circumnavigated the globe twice as part of five global voyages on Semester at Sea. The people I met and the events I experienced in all these places certainly have influenced my perceptions about politics.

More direct contributions to this book have come from the work of my colleagues in political science and from the many students and others in the political world with whom I have interacted. I have drawn deeply and often from the ideas of these groups. By the publication of the twelfth edition, the layers of contributions and ideas to the construction of this book are deep, rich, and indescribable. In every edition, there is a list of people who added positively to that edition, and I continue to be grateful to them all. Explicit guidance and advice regarding the writing of this particular edition have come from several valuable sources: scholarly colleagues who have offered useful suggestions, especially Richard Coldwell, C.B.E., and students who have provided feedback on the book, including Sanaa Khan and Aaron McCullough. The reviewers, who offered very thoughtful and constructive commentaries for this edition, include Charles Ellison, University of Cincinnati; Daniel Masters, University of North Carolina, Wilmington; Brian Anderson, Mississippi University for Women; and Kurt Messick, Ivy Tech Community College.

I am very grateful for the help provided by all these (and many unnamed) sources. Regarding the roads not taken and the missteps in this book, the responsibility is mine.

James N. Danziger

The privilege of using the earlier editions of this book to bring political science and the world to thousands of students has been a true joy. I am now honored to join Professor Danziger in his quest to bring the next edition to fruition. I echo his gratitude to the many colleagues, friends, family, and students who provided feedback and support along the way.

Charles Anthony Smith

From the Reviews:

"Danziger and Smith have written the perfect book for an introduction to political science. Presenting a full range of domestic and international issues plus detailed scenarios that make students think critically, they balance the academic approach to political science with the practical need to be fluent in real world politics."

—Krista Wiegand, University of Tennessee, Knoxville, Tennessee

"This book remains the gold standard for introduction to the breadth of topics that animate political science. Encompassing topics such as political ideology, democracy, protest, domestic and interstate politics, and newly industrializing countries as well as developed, the book takes the student on a journey through the discipline itself as well as its subject matter. Because it is accessible to beginning undergraduates and because of its explicit application of comparative methods of inquiry, this book remains the key recommendation I always offer to my colleagues."

—Matthew Shugart, University of California-Davis, Davis, California

"Danziger and Smith bring a fresh and exciting pedagogical approach. Their terrific book presents cutting-edge topics with current data in a compelling narrative."

—Heather Smith-Cannoy, Lewis & Clark College, Portland, Oregon

"Danziger and Smith have written a current and impressive textbook. It is empirically rich, but still accessible and engaging."

—Royce Carroll, Rice University, Houston, Texas

"This is an innovative approach to teaching introductory level political science. It challenges the students with up-to-date information presented in an analytical framework that helps lay the foundation for a comprehensive understanding of how the political world actually works."

—Shawn Schulenberg, Marshall University, Huntington, West Virginia

To the Reader

The aim of this book is revealed by its title: It is meant to help you understand the political world. It assumes that you are willing to think about politics. It does not assume that you have substantial knowledge about politics or political science or even that you know the difference between politics and political science. We hope that when you complete the book and any course in which you are reading it, you will feel that you have increased your knowledge about the contemporary political world.

The study of politics is full of fascinating questions. First are the questions about *what is*, such as: Who exercises political power, and what values and purposes guide them? Why do people accept political authority? How do people organize themselves politically? What factors are associated with political violence? A second set of questions concerns *what ought to be*: Who should exercise political power, and what values should they pursue? Why should people accept political authority? How should political structures be organized? When is political violence justifiable?

People disagree sharply about answers to both these descriptive (what is) and normative (what ought to be) questions. In addition, the study of politics provokes a third set of questions regarding *what we can actually know* about the political world. Here also there are major disagreements about the appropriate methods for describing and understanding politics.

Although this book cannot resolve the underlying disputes, it offers you the basis for making sense of politics at all three levels. As the authors, we make some basic assumptions: that you can think systematically about politics and make general statements about how politics works; that you will learn more about politics by considering the politics of many different places; that every observer of politics (certainly including you and us) has biases, only some of which can be understood; that you need a variety of sources of ideas and information before you can make informed and sensible decisions about the value disagreements pervading politics; and that this book is one such source that can be helpful to you. Our efforts will be successful to the extent that *you* ultimately judge our assumptions to be correct (especially the last one).

It is inevitable that you will be frustrated with the treatment of politics at some (many?) points in this book. We would say: Reader, be merciful! The study of politics is very complex. Gather bits of understanding where you can find them.

Maps

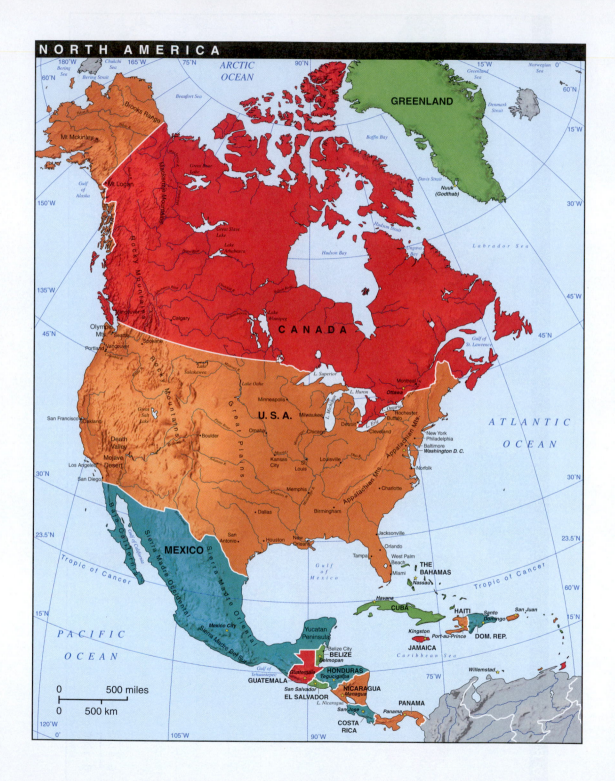

NORTH AMERICA

GREENLAND

CANADA

U.S.A.

MEXICO

ARCTIC OCEAN

ATLANTIC OCEAN

PACIFIC OCEAN

Caribbean Sea

CUBA

THE BAHAMAS

HAITI

DOM. REP.

JAMAICA

BELIZE

GUATEMALA

EL SALVADOR

HONDURAS

NICARAGUA

COSTA RICA

PANAMA

Tropic of Cancer

SOUTH AMERICA

80°W · 70°W · 60°W · 50°W · 40°W · 30°W

Caribbean Sea

Barranquilla

Maracaibo · Valencia

Barquisimeto

VENEZUELA · **GUYANA**

SURINAME

Medellín · Georgetown · Paramaribo

Cayenne

Bogotá · *Río Orinoco* · **FRENCH GUIANA (France)**

Cali

COLOMBIA

10°N

ATLANTIC OCEAN

Quito · 0°

ECUADOR

Guayaquil · *Amazon Basin*

Gulf of Guayaquil

Río Negro · Manaus · *Amazon R.* · Belém · Marajó Island

Fortaleza

Río Madeira

PERU

Río Juruá · *Río Purus* · Teresina

10°S

Lima · *Río Madre de Dios*

Río Tapajos · *Río Xingu* · Recife

BRAZIL

BOLIVIA

Mato Grosso Plateau · Salvador

La Paz

Lago Titicaca · Sucre

20°S

Goiânia · Brasília · Belo Horizonte

Río Paraguay

PARAGUAY · Río de Janeiro

Campinas

CHILE · Asunción · São Paulo · Curitiba · Cabo Frio

Tropic of Capricorn · 23.5°S

Atacama Desert

Río Paraná

PACIFIC OCEAN

Porto Alegre

30°S

ARGENTINA · **URUGUAY**

Cerro Aconcagua · Rosario

Río Uruguay

Santiago · *Pampas* · Buenos Aires · Montevideo

Río Colorado

Andes Mountains

Patagonia

40°S

Isla Grande de Chiloé · *Gulf of San Matías*

Valdés Penninsula

Gulf of San Jorge

ATLANTIC OCEAN

Taitao Penninsula

50°S

FALKLAND ISLANDS

SOUTH GEORGIA ISLAND

Strait of Magellan

Port Stanley

Tierra Del Fuego

0 — 500 miles

0 — 500 km

70°W · 60°W · 50°W · 40°W · 30°W

AFRICA

THE MIDDLE EAST

EAST AND SOUTH ASIA

45°N   30°N   15°N   0°   15°S

165°E   150°E   135°E   120°E   105°E   90°E   75°E   60°E

Pacific   Ocean

Sea of
Okhotsk

MICRONESIA

Marshall
Islands

Gilbert
Islands

GUAM

PALAU

SOLOMON
ISLANDS

Honiara

PAPUA
NEW
GUINEA

NEW GUINEA

Port Moresby

EAST TIMOR

INDONESIA

Dili

Kupang

Semarang

Jakarta

Surabaya

Bandung

Palembang

Medan

Ujungpandang

BRUNEI
Bandar Seri
Begawan

MALAYSIA
Kuala Lumpur   Singapore

PHILIPPINES

Quezon City

Manila

Davao

Sea of
Japan
(East Sea)

Sapporo

Sendai

JAPAN

Tokyo
Yokohama

Nagoya
Osaka
Fukuoka

NORTH
KOREA

P'yongyang

SOUTH
KOREA

Seoul
Inch'ŏn

Pusan

Taejon

Dandong

Dalian

East
China
Sea

Shanghai

TAIWAN

T'aipei
Kao-hsiung

Yellow
Sea

Qingdao

Jinan

Nanjing

Hangzhou

Wenzhou

Ningbo

Xuzhou

Kaifeng

Zhengzhou

Luoyang

Wuhan

Changsha

Nanchang

Fuzhou

Xiamen

Shantou

Hong Kong

South China
Sea

Shenzhen

Guangzhou

Zhanjiang

Nanning

VIETNAM

Hanoi
Hai
Phong

LAOS

Vientiane

THAILAND

Bangkok

CAMBODIA

Phnom Penh

Ho Chi Minh City

Bay
of Bengal

Rangoon

MYANMAR

BANGLADESH

Dhaka

BHUTAN

NEPAL

Kathmandu

Mt. Everest

CHINA

Harbin

Jilin

Changchun

Qiqihar

Liaoyuan

Fushun

Fuxin

Jinzhou

Beijing

Tianjin

Tangshan

Hohhot

Baotou

Yinchuan

Lanzhou

Xi'an

Chongqing

Chengdu

Guiyang

Kunming

Xining

Ürümqi

Mianyang

Shiquanhe

Lhasa

MONGOLIA

Ulaanbaatar

INDIA

Delhi

New Delhi

Jaipur

Kanpur

Lucknow

Patna

Dhanbad

Kolkata
(Calcutta)

Nagpur

Indore

Bhopal

Surat

Mumbai
(Bombay)

Pune

Hyderabad

Bangalore

Chennai (Madras)

Tiruchchirappalli

Coimbatore

Cochin

Colombo

SRI
LANKA

Vishakhapatnam

PAKISTAN

Karāchi

Hyderabad

Mūltan

Faisalabad

Lahore

Rawalpindi

Islāmābād

Peshāwar

AFGHANISTAN

Kābul

TAJIKISTAN

Dushanbe

KYRGYZSTAN

Bishkek

Arabian
Sea

Indian   Ocean

1000 miles

1000 km

0

xxv

AUSTRALIA AND OCEANIA

Java Sea

Timor Sea

Indian Ocean

Arafura Sea

Aru

Gulf of Carpentaria

Wellesley Islands

Arnhem Land

Darwin

NEW GUINEA

PAPUA NEW GUINEA

Port Moresby

Torres Strait

Solomon Sea

New Britain

Bougainville

SOLOMON ISLANDS

Honiara
Guadalcanal

Coral Sea

Great Barrier Reef

New Hebrides

VANUATU

Port-vila
Efate I.

Loyalty Islands

Nouméa
NEW CALEDONIA (France)

FIGI
Vanua Levu
Viti Levu
Suva

Tropic of Capricorn

Pacific Ocean

Norfolk Island
Kingston

Tasman Sea

NEW ZEALAND

Great Barrier Island
Auckland
North Island
Wellington
South Island
Stewart Island

AUSTRALIA

Brisbane
Fraser

Great Dividing Range

Great Artesian Basin

Simpson Desert

Macdonnell Ranges

Musgrave Range

Tanami Desert

Great Sandy Desert

Kimberley Plateau

King Leopold Range

Gibson Desert

Great Victoria Desert

Nullarbor Plain

Hammersley Range

Darling Range

Perth

Great Australian Bight

Kangaroo Island

Adelaide

Melbourne

Murray River

Murrumbidgee River

Darling River

Sydney
Canberra
Mt. Kosciuszko

Hobart
Tasmania

Southern Ocean

10°S
20°S
23.5°S
30°S
40°S

120°E 130°E 140°E 150°E 160°E 170°E

500 miles
500 km
0

xxvi

Chapter 1
Politics and Knowledge

 ## Learning Objectives

1.1 Define politics within a public context.

1.2 Analyze three types of political knowledge.

1.3 Evaluate the strengths and weaknesses of different sources of political knowledge.

1.4 Identify techniques and approaches used to gain political knowledge and assess whether they constitute a science.

Imagine you have a 13-year-old sister in eighth grade. She has quite the day at school: The vice principal comes into her math class unexpectedly and asks her to bring her backpack and accompany him to his office. In his office, she sees a planner, a knife, a lighter, and some white pills on his desk. The vice principal lectures her about the importance of telling the truth, then asks which of the items belong to her. She tells him that she had lent the planner to another girl a few days earlier but that the other items are not hers. The vice principal responds that the other girl had reported your sister for giving her the pills, which students are not allowed to possess at school.

The vice principal asks if he can look through your sister's backpack, and she agrees. A female secretary enters the office and searches the backpack. Your sister is then told to follow the secretary to the nurse's office, where she is asked to remove her jacket, socks, and shoes. She follows their directions. They next ask her to take off her pants and shirt, and again she follows their directions. These clothes are searched, and when nothing incriminating is found, they order your sister to stand up, pull her bra away from her body and shake it, then pull her underwear loose and shake it. No pills drop out when she complies. She is allowed to put her clothes back on and sits outside the principal's office for several hours. Finally, she is sent back to class.

What do you think of the events just described? Is this situation *political*? Do the actions of the vice principal seem appropriate? What about the actions of the school's secretary and nurse? Did your sister do the right thing by complying with each of their requests? Did she have a choice? What would you do in a similar situation?

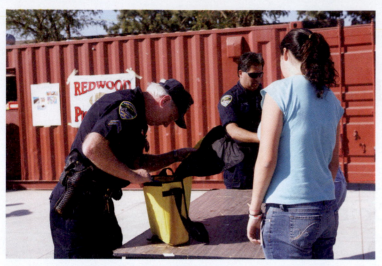

Search me? Are there fundamental political issues when a school searches its students? When is a search legal?

Stop and think about these questions briefly before you continue reading. You will be asked many such "reflection questions" as you read this book. Your attempt to answer them, either with a quick note in the margin or at least a mental note, will help you better grasp your own understanding of issues that are raised. As E. M. Forster commented: "How do I know what I think until I see what I say?" So, what do you think about this situation?

Of course, this did not happen to your little sister (if you have one), but it did happen to 13-year-old Savana Redding of Safford, Arizona, in 2003. Here are some additional facts in this case. This public school has a responsibility to ensure the safety and health of all its students. The previous year, a student nearly died from drugs taken without permission at the school. The school district has a zero-tolerance policy for all drugs—no student is allowed to possess any drugs at school, whether over-the-counter, prescription, or illegal. The vice principal acted on information from another girl who reported that Savana had given her pills that day. It was not really a "strip search" because Savana never took off her underwear. All of these considerations seem to justify the actions that occurred.

However, there are valid points on the other side of the issue. The Fourth Amendment to the U.S. Constitution seems to protect Savana from this kind of search unless significant evidence indicates that something illegal is occurring (probable cause). The vice principal's actions were taken based on questionable information from another girl who was already in trouble for possessing the pills. And the search occurred despite Savana's claim that she had no pills, without parental approval, and before any further investigation of the situation was attempted. Then there is common sense: The pills are merely extra-strength ibuprofen (pain killers). Is this really a legitimate reason for adults in authority positions to force a 13-year-old girl to submit to a humiliating strip search?

Savana's mother was outraged. With the assistance of a lawyer from the American Civil Liberties Union (ACLU), she sued the school officials on the grounds that they had subjected her daughter to an "unreasonable search." Savana's lawyer argued that, while a search of her backpack might be reasonable, a strip search was not, given the flimsy evidence of guilt and the minimal threat associated with ibuprofen. The school district's officials responded that the vice principal's actions were justified and consistent with numerous court cases that uphold the rights and responsibilities of schools to prevent dangerous behavior among their students, including searches for drugs or weapons.

Initially, a judge in Tucson ruled in favor of the actions by the school officials; however, on appeal, the circuit court reversed the decision by the narrowest of margins (6–5). The court concluded that the strip search of an eighth grader while looking for prescription drugs was a violation of her constitutional rights, and it held that the family could sue the school officials for damages. The school's lawyers then appealed the case to the U.S. Supreme Court. In 2009, the court majority (8–1) held that the search of Savana was unconstitutional. The majority reasoned that the particular drugs suspected in this case were not sufficiently threatening to justify the search. However, the court did not allow the family to sue school officials, leaving open the question of how it might rule if school officials suspected a student of possessing something more dangerous than ibuprofen.

Toward a Definition of Politics

1.1   **Define politics within a public context.**

The first step in our journey toward a better understanding of the political world is to establish what we mean by politics. The Savana Redding search captures some of the crucial themes related to politics:

> Politics is the competition among individuals and groups pursuing their own interests.
>
> Politics is the exercise of power and influence to allocate things that are valued.
>
> Politics is the determination of who gets what, when, and how.
>
> Politics is the resolution of conflict.

All of these definitions share the central idea that **politics** *is the process through which power and influence are used in the promotion of certain values and interests.* (The **bold** type indicates a Key Concept; these terms are listed at the end of the chapter and are included in the Glossary beginning on page 461.) Competing values and interests are clearly at the heart of the search of Savana Redding. The values that guide a zero-tolerance policy regarding drugs at the school are balanced against values that protect a student against an illegal search. Other groups might have a stake in this conflict, as did the ACLU, which intervened to promote its views about individual liberty, and the courts, which asserted their responsibility to interpret the laws.

As individuals, groups, and governmental actors make decisions about what is good or bad for society, and as they try to implement their decisions, politics occurs. Every individual holds an array of preferred values and interests, and that individual cares more about some of those values than others. What values is each individual willing to promote or yield on? If the values of different individuals come into conflict, whose values and rights should prevail? And, if people cannot work out their conflicting values privately through discussion and compromise, must the government intervene? How does the government exercise its power to resolve the conflict? Who benefits and who is burdened by the policies of government? These are all *political* questions.

For our purposes, politics is associated with those aspects of life that have *public* significance. Other aspects of life, in contrast, are understood to be private and thus are beyond the domain of politics. However, what is considered "private" in one country may be considered "public" in another. It is relevant that the search of Savana occurred in the United States. There are many other countries (e.g., Cuba, Iran, Zimbabwe) where the kind of search conducted on Savana would be well within the standard practices of government authorities and few, if any, citizens would publicly challenge the action.

In the political context of the United States, the school board—a political body elected by the citizens—has the right to establish policies regarding which behaviors will be unacceptable by the students (e.g., possessing drugs, using profane language) and by its employees (e.g., using corporal punishment, teaching creation science). The vice principal, as a public employee, exercises power when he implements those policies. The courts—another political institution—are active in the case as its judges, also public employees, attempt to resolve the conflict in values and interests between Savana's family and the school's employees. The court's judgments are based on interpretations of politically created rules, including the U.S. Constitution, which ensures each citizen of certain rights but also grants government certain powers.

Even your choice about the job you take, the religion you practice, or what you read on the Internet can be either a private choice or one within the public domain. Can you see why a government might conclude that each of these choices has public significance and is thus political? Within each country, there is a constant debate about the appropriate areas for governmental action and the domains of life that should remain private and unrestrained by political action. Sometimes the term *politics* is used even more broadly than in this book to refer to competition over values in domains that are not truly public, such as the "politics of the family" or "office politics."

In almost every contemporary society, the domains that are subject to politics are very large. Politics, usually via government, determines how much education you must have and what its content will be. Politics establishes the words you cannot utter in a public place, how much of your hard-earned income you must give to government, and how various governments spend that money to provide different groups with a vast range of benefits (e.g., education, roads, fire protection, subsidized health care, safe food, national defense, and aid to another country). Politics determines whether you are allowed to use a certain drug; the amount of pollutants that your car can emit; how secure you feel against violence by others within your neighborhood and within the global system; and whether you receive unequal treatment in the allocation of benefits because of your ethnicity, gender, ideology, or some other factor.

On Political Knowledge

1.2 **Analyze three types of political knowledge.**

Types of Political Knowledge

Clearly, politics can affect your life in many ways. Yet people differ greatly in their understandings about the nature of politics, the uses of political power, and the distribution of political benefits and burdens. If you have discussed politics with your friends, you probably have noticed that they differ, both in how much they know about politics and in their opinions about what constitute good and bad political actions. Your understandings about politics and your decisions about whether to undertake specific political actions are grounded in your knowledge of politics. Every individual's understanding of politics is composed of three general types of political knowledge: (1) *descriptions* of political facts; (2) *explanations* of how and why politics occurs as it does; and (3) *prescriptions* of what should happen in the political world.

Description

Many bits of political knowledge offer a ***description***, which focuses on *what* questions and is usually based on one or more "facts." (The **bold and italic** type indicates a Key Concept; these terms are listed at the end of the chapter but are not in the Glossary at the back of the book.) Descriptive political knowledge is mostly composed of relatively straightforward political facts such as these:

> The date Hosni Mubarak resigned as President of Egypt: February 11, 2011
>
> The number of states in Nigeria: 36
>
> The country with the highest GDP (gross domestic product) per capita (PPP) in the world in 2014: Qatar at $102,100

But on many questions about the political world, there are no indisputable answers. On some questions, it is difficult to get precise information. Suppose you want to know which countries have operational nuclear weapons. Six countries acknowledge having operational nuclear devices: France, India, Pakistan, Russia, the United Kingdom, and the United States. However, the precise number of such weapons in each country is a state secret. China clearly has nuclear weapons but claims that none are operational. Experts conclude that Israel has nuclear weapons, although Israel does not confirm this. North Korea claims to have operational nuclear weapons, but there is no publicly available evidence about this capability, and Iran is suspected of having a secret nuclear weapons program. Twenty other countries, including Algeria, Argentina, Belarus, Brazil, Kazakhstan, Libya, South Africa, and Ukraine, are "potential proliferators" that had or were close to having nuclear weapons but are now assumed to have backed away from nuclear ambitions (Federation of American Scientists 2014). Thus, even the experts cannot reach consensus on the straightforward issue of which countries belong to the so-called nuclear club.

On other questions about politics, description requires assessments that raise complicated issues about power, interests, and values, making it difficult to reach agreement about the facts. Here are two examples:

> Do nonwhites and whites in the United States experience equal treatment before the law?
>
> Can a country legally invade another country that has not used military force against it?

This discussion on "Description" briefly refers to 21 countries on five continents. Do you have a clear sense of where they are? There will be detailed discussions of many countries in this book. Knowing the location of a country and its geographic relationship to other countries in its region is sometimes extremely important for understanding its political choices and actions. When a country is discussed and you are not sure where it is, you are strongly encouraged to locate the country on a map. For this purpose, a set of maps is included in this book. Several recent studies have shown that students in the United States are more ignorant of world geography than students in most other countries. If that applies to you, help change the situation by referring frequently to the maps.

Explanation

A lot of political knowledge is more complicated than just description because it is in the form of *explanation,* which attempts to *specify why something happens* and to *provide the reason or process by which the phenomenon occurs.*

Why is one in seven people "poor" in the wealthy United States? What causes a country (e.g., Zimbabwe) to have inflation higher than 10,000 percent in a single year? Why does a popular uprising rapidly overthrow the government in one country (e.g., Tunisia) but not in another (e.g., its neighbor, Syria)? Responses to these kinds of questions require explanation, not just descriptive facts. Such questions can be among the most fascinating in politics, but adequate explanation is often difficult because patterns of cause and effect can be extremely complex.

Prescription

Statements about politics often include claims or assumptions that certain choices and actions are more desirable than others. These represent a third form of political knowledge: prescription. A **prescription** is *a value judgment that indicates what* should *occur and* should *be done.* Thus, a prescription deals with answers to questions about what ought to be, not merely description and explanation of what is.

For example, there are many possible prescriptive responses to this question: What should be the government's role in the provision of health care? Answers vary from the viewpoint that government should take absolutely no action that interferes with the private provision of health care to the viewpoint that government should meet the full range of health care needs at no direct cost to patients. You can probably think of many positions between these two extremes.

The prescriptive position that you select on a political issue is an element of your **normative political knowledge**—*your value judgments.* Notice that normative political knowledge combines three types of understanding: (1) your descriptive knowledge of certain facts (e.g., the alternative ways that health care could be provided in a particular society); (2) your explanatory knowledge about why certain outcomes occur (e.g., the reasons why people don't receive equal health care); and most important, (3) your priorities among competing values (e.g., your preferences regarding equality, lower taxes, and limited government).

Throughout this book, you will be encouraged to clarify your own understandings about politics. You will be offered a variety of descriptive, explanatory, and prescriptive knowledge claims. It is hoped that as you absorb more of this information, you will become more knowledgeable about politics! Let's explore some of your views about politics by means of a thought experiment we term "the acid test".

Assume you were born 20 years ago in either the country of Gamma or the country of Delta. You do not know about your personal situation: whether you are male or female; your ethnicity, education level, and social class; your parents' wealth; whether you reside in a city or a rural area; your religion; your mental or physical skills; and so on. Table 1.1 provides a variety of indicators of some *current* conditions in Gamma and Delta with regard to each country's prosperity, security, and stability. Here is the "acid test" question: *Now that you know the current conditions in Gamma and Delta, into which country would you prefer to have been born 20 years ago?* The Compare in 1 (there will be a Compare box in each chapter) considers some of the issues regarding this acid test. Make your choice from the data in Table 1.1 *before* you read the Compare in 1!

Table 1.1 The Acid Test I

	Gamma	Delta
Governmental type	Nondemocracy	Liberal democracy
Democracy index (148 countries)	142nd	38th
Political rights (1–7; 1 = most extensive)	7 (very low)	2 (high)
Civil liberties (1–7; 1 = most extensive)	6 (low)	3 (moderately high)
Press freedom (among 194 countries)	181st: Not free	72nd: Partly free
Economic freedom (among 177 countries)	136th: Partly free	119th: Partly free
Government restrictions on religion	Very high	Low
Social hostilities involving religion	High	Very high
% women in national legislature	21%	11%
Gender Equality (186 countries)	35th	132nd
Political stability	High	Medium
Rate of crimes against the person	Low	Medium
Life expectancy	74 years	66 years
Literacy rate (adults)	94%	63%
Infant mortality/1,000	16	48
% population with access to essential drugs	85%	35%
Internet users/100	28.8	5.0
% below the national poverty line	2.8%	22.9%
Unemployment rate	6.5%	8.5%
Wealth (GDP: gross domestic product) per capita	$9,300	$3,800
GDP per capita annual growth: 2000–2012	10.6%	7.7%
Inflation rate	2.3%	9.3%
Public debt as % of GDP	31.7%	49.6%

Compare in 1

The Acid Test I

As you examined the indicators in Table 1.1, you perhaps noticed significant differences between Gamma and Delta. The economic prosperity (indicated by measures such as the country's wealth per capita and its economic growth rate) is noticeably higher in one country. The probability you would be poor, uneducated, and live a shorter life is higher in one country. Your likely freedom of action, in domains such as politics, religion, and access to information, varies considerably. There also seem to be differences in gender equality between the two countries. What differences are most striking to you?

The acid test asks you to decide, after considering all the data provided about Gamma and Delta, into which country you would prefer to be born. Which one did you choose?

Gamma and Delta are pseudonyms for two real countries, and the data are recent. Both countries have a variety of broad similarities—population, climate variability, social history, period of time since independence, violent interactions with neighboring countries, and so on. These are arguably the two most important countries in the developing world. Each country has a rich history, including a remarkable ancient culture; extensive colonial exploitation; a fickle climate; deep social cleavages, especially those based on religion, gender, and class/caste; and each has more than 1 billion people.

However, since the independence of India in 1947 and the communist victory in China in 1949, the two countries have followed very different paths. Under the long and tumultuous rule of Mao Zedong (in power from 1949–1976), China (Gamma) attempted to implement a pervasive system of communism with a command political economy and totalitarian one-party government. The Chinese leadership after Mao engaged in a steady introduction of market economics, transforming China into a global economic power while still retaining tight Communist Party rule over the government. Initially, India (Delta) attempted to implement strong government control of key sectors of the economy, and it introduced democratic politics, although one party was very dominant. Eventually, both experiments evolved in India as the economy shifted much more to private firms and the political system became more competitive with multiple parties.

Some results of these two different approaches to government and policy are reflected in the measures in Table 1.1. The strong commitment under Mao to egalitarianism and providing benefits to all citizens led to public policies that reduced inequalities based on gender and social class with broad improvements in literacy and health for most of the population. The Indian government did not provide extensive policies to address inequalities based on caste, gender, and urban–rural differences; thus, these inequalities have lessened much more slowly in India, resulting in continued disparities in domains such as literacy and health. China has sustained remarkable levels of economic growth for several decades as it has become a global power, while India's growth has been more sporadic but high since 2000. India proudly proclaims itself the "world's largest democracy" with a rough-and-tumble political system characterized by broad political rights, a relatively free media, a professional apolitical military, and an independent judiciary. In contrast, China's leadership continues to use a combination of state military and security forces, political socialization, severe censorship, and rewards to those who conform to sustain its oppressive Communist Party domination of political and social life.

Despite many similarities in their resources and history, China and India have significantly different current profiles. While many explanations can be offered for these differences, it is reasonable to claim that the most powerful explanation is *politics*—the decisions and actions taken by those with political power and authority in each country. As you develop your understandings of politics in this book, some of the key points underlying this acid test will be persistent themes.

First, a people and its government can pursue numerous desirable goals. While every country (and you) might like to have very positive scores on every indicator in Table 1.1, you will discover that the reality is starker: Most countries cannot have it all. Various trade-offs must be made due to limited resources, the incapacity of people and their institutions to control their environment fully, and other factors related to human failures and impacts of the global system.

Second, the acid test challenges you to decide what aspects of political, social, economic, and personal life are more important to you. The book will assist you in clarifying your own thinking about what you value and what role you think government should play in helping you achieve those values.

And third, your choices and your values will not be the same as everyone else's—even among your peers and certainly among people around the globe. You will gain greater awareness of the different mixes of approaches and values that are part of the debate about how government can help individuals and societies pursue a variety of desirable life conditions such as security, prosperity, stability, freedom, equality, justice, democracy, and well-being. Disagreements about ends and means are at the heart of politics in every country.

Further Questions

1. Which broad value seemed to most influence your choice between Gamma and Delta?

2. Did your knowledge of the identities of Gamma and Delta change your evaluation at all?

3. What assessment(s) might cause another person to select the country that you did not select?

Sources of Political Knowledge

1.3   **Evaluate the strengths and weaknesses of different sources of political knowledge.**

This chapter has already made many knowledge claims—statements about what is accurate or correct. Table 1.1 and the Compare in 1 are loaded with such claims. When you are confronted by such claims, how do you decide what you know and what you believe? That is, where does your political knowledge—your unique combination of descriptive facts, explanations, and prescriptions about politics—come from? This section describes three important sources of your knowledge: (1) authority; (2) personal thought; and (3) science.

Authority

The method of **authority** involves *the appeal to any document, tradition, or person believed to possess the controlling explanation regarding a particular issue.* Knowledge about politics can be based on three kinds of authority sources: (1) a specific authority; (2) a general authority; or (3) "everyone."

SPECIFIC AUTHORITY SOURCES A particular individual (but few others) might place great confidence in the knowledge he derives about politics from a specific authority source such as a parent, teacher, friend, or famous person. Young people and those minimally interested in politics are especially likely to rely on specific authorities for much of their political knowledge. Chapter 4 will argue that specific authority sources powerfully influence some important political beliefs of most individuals. Can you think of a significant piece of your own political knowledge that you derived primarily from a parent, an influential teacher, or a public figure you admire?

GENERAL AUTHORITY SOURCES A general authority source is one that has substantial influence on a large proportion of people in a society. Examples include constitutions, revered leaders, widely respected media or books, and religious teachings. General authorities are especially evident as a basis for normative political knowledge. Consider, for example, the issue of the role of women in politics. While this can be a descriptive issue, how do we determine the normative question of what the role of women should be? In some societies, there is disagreement about this question, and many look to an authority source to provide the answer.

- In the United States, the crucial source of authority for such questions is a *legal document*—the Constitution. Despite the claim that "all men…are endowed by their creator with certain inalienable rights…" not every citizen was allowed to vote in 1787. Indeed, women were not granted this fundamental political right until the Nineteenth Amendment to the Constitution in 1920—130 years into the American Republic. Advocates of women's rights argue that women still do not have full and equal political rights and proposed another constitutional amendment, the Equal Rights Amendment; but it was never ratified by the 38 states necessary for its passage.

My Little Red Book: Young girls recite and memorize sayings from Chairman Mao Zedong during China's Cultural Revolution (circa 1968).

- In Iran, the key source of authority on women's political rights is also a document, but it is a *religious document*, the Koran. During the political regime of Shah Reza Pahlavi (1941–1979), women were encouraged to participate much more fully in politics than what Iran's religious conservatives thought was consistent with the Koran. When the Ayatollah Khomeini (in power 1979–1989) replaced the shah, he insisted on a strict interpretation of the Koran that significantly limited the political roles of women. The political rights and activities of Iranian women remain a contentious issue between those who advocate an expanded role and those, like the current top leader Ayatollah Khamenei, who insist on enforcing a more conservative interpretation of the Koran.

- In contemporary China, the political rights of women were established by the authoritative pronouncements of a *person*, Mao Zedong (in power 1949–1976). Prior to the revolution of 1949, the role of women in China was defined by the traditions of Confucianism. Most women were essentially the property of men, and they had few political rights. As part of Chairman Mao's efforts to transform Confucian tradition, he granted women full equality under the law, and women were encouraged to participate actively in all aspects of political life. (The conflict between Mao's views and those of Confucianism are explored further in the Focus in 4.)

"EVERYONE" AS AUTHORITY Sometimes we are convinced that something is true because it is a belief strongly held by many other people. If almost everyone (i.e., the reference group to which you look for information and knowledge) seems to agree on a "fact" about politics, there is little reason for you to disagree with or challenge that fact. One reason to place confidence in a belief that is strongly held by many people is the assumption that it is unlikely so many people could be incorrect. Such knowledge has stood the test of time because it could have been challenged and repudiated in the marketplace of ideas. For example, you will probably find that almost everyone you know agrees that political terrorism is bad.

PROBLEMS WITH AUTHORITY AS A SOURCE OF KNOWLEDGE There are fundamental problems with using authority as a way of knowing. This should be most obvious with *specific authorities*. You might think that your parent or best teacher or favorite celebrity has the correct view on an important political issue, but few of the other 7.2 billion people in the world have any confidence in this source of your political knowledge.

And even though "everyone knows that X is true," there is no guarantee that everyone is correct. First, as "Honest Abe" Lincoln observed, you can fool all of the people some of the time. Indeed, a political belief that is widely held might be particularly immune to careful assessment. Experiments in psychology have revealed that some of a person's beliefs can be altered by the beliefs of others. For example, if a subject hears several respondents (collaborating with the experimenter) all give identical wrong answers to a question, the subject can usually be persuaded to change his mind about what he knows—even when he is correct. Second, "everyone" often consists mainly of people whose cultural background we share. If you reexamine the above example about terrorism with a different "everyone," it is unlikely that almost everyone living under an oppressive political regime believes that political terrorism is bad. It is common for citizens in most political systems to believe that the citizens of rival political systems have been brainwashed. We know that some beliefs of our rivals are incorrect. Isn't it likely that they are equally convinced that some of our strongly held beliefs are wrong?

There are even problems with *general authorities*. Sometimes even the most competent general authorities might not have access to crucial information or might rely on inaccurate data, as when they list the countries with nuclear weapons. And sometimes, despite a group's acceptance of a single authority, there are still ambiguities and problems of interpretation.

Consider again the normative issue of the political role of women. In interpreting gender equality, all branches of government in the United States continually debate and interpret the rather limited framework outlined in the Constitution. The appropriate

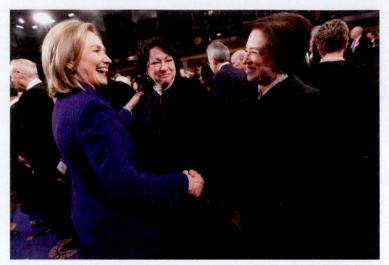

Powerful women: A chat between former Secretary of State Hillary Clinton and Supreme Court Justices Elena Kagan (right) and Sonia Sotomayor (center), who are among those with key roles in defining the evolving role of women in American politics.

role of women in Iran's politics remains a highly contested issue, despite the Koran. Indeed, there is considerable difference of opinion within the broader Muslim world regarding how to interpret the Koran's authoritative prescriptions regarding women's roles in political life. In some Muslim countries, such as Saudi Arabia and Sudan, women's roles are greatly restricted. Yet Bangladesh, Indonesia, Pakistan, and Turkey are Muslim-majority countries that recently selected female heads of government (prime ministers). And in China, Mao Zedong's pronouncements on many topics, especially on economic matters, are now rejected by the leadership, even as his general views about gender equality remain a key authority source.

In short, it is common, and perhaps inevitable, for authority sources to offer inconsistent or conflicting knowledge claims about the political world. It is extremely difficult to differentiate among alternative authorities or even to establish widespread agreement on precisely what political knowledge a particular authority source provides.

Personal Thought

Have you ever insisted that some fact is correct because it seemed so obvious to you? It is possible to feel confident that you know something on the basis of personal thought—your own reason, feelings, or experiences. This second source of knowledge does not rely on outside authorities; rather, it assumes that the individual can use his own rationality, intuition, or personal experience to assess a knowledge claim.

RATIONALITY On occasion, you probably have decided that a certain claim is true because it is logical or obvious—it "just makes sense." The available information fits together in a coherent framework that, it seems, would lead to agreement among all people who think clearly. Or it is assumed that the knowledge claim is verified because it is self-evident to reasonable people and needs no further justification. For example, the Preamble to the U.S. Declaration of Independence claims that there are "self-evident" truths—that all men are created equal and that they have inalienable rights to life, liberty, and the pursuit of happiness.

INTUITION Another form of personal thought is intuition. Here, one's knowledge is based on feeling, on a sense of understanding or empathy, rather than on reason. You have probably been convinced that something is correct because it *feels* right. For example, the key slogan of Barry Goldwater, the Republican presidential candidate in 1964, was an explicit appeal to intuition: "In your heart, you know he's right!" And Barack Obama's 2008 campaign incantation "Change we can believe in!" was essentially an appeal to feeling and hope.

PERSONAL EXPERIENCE You can also be convinced that something is true because of your personal experiences. For example, you might be convinced that government bureaucracies are inefficient because a specific agency handled your inquiries so ineptly. Or you might believe that different ethnic groups can live together in harmony based on your own positive experience in a multiethnic setting. Personal involvement in a dramatic event, such as witnessing a handgun murder or being physically harassed by the police, can have a particularly powerful impact on one's political beliefs.

PROBLEMS WITH PERSONAL THOUGHT AS A SOURCE OF KNOWLEDGE There is a major problem with all three forms of personal thought as a source of knowledge: There is no method for resolving "thoughtful" differences of opinion among individuals. This is most obvious with personal experience: Because people have different personal experiences, they are unlikely to reach the same conclusions about what is true. Similarly, there is no reason to assume that different people will share the same intuitive feelings regarding what is true. Goldwater's poor electoral showing (he received only 39 percent of the vote) suggests that many people concluded (intuitively?) that he was not right, or perhaps they decided (rationally?) that he was too far right—too conservative ideologically. And, after a few years of Washington's rough-and-tumble politics, many of Obama's supporters had lost confidence in "change you can believe in."

Even rational thought will not necessarily enable people to agree on political facts. We do not all employ the same logic, and it is rare to find a knowledge claim that everyone agrees is obviously correct. Consider again the key knowledge claim cited earlier: "We hold these truths to be self-evident—that all men are created equal." This seems a clear appeal to rationality, a political fact that is self-evident to all thinking people. But what exactly does this claim mean? Do all men have equal physical or mental traits at birth? Do they grow up with equal opportunities? Are they equal before the law, regardless of the quality of legal help they can purchase? We have noted the historical disagreement about how women's equality is to be interpreted. Many legal and political struggles in the United States during the more than two centuries since this "self-evident" truth was proclaimed have concerned precisely what equal rights *are* assured to every person in the U.S. political system, with particular regard to race, gender, and age.

Science

In contrast to the two other sources of knowledge, science uses explicit methods that attempt to enable different people to agree about what they know. The goal of any science is to describe and explain—to answer *what, why,* and *how* questions. There are four essential characteristics of the **scientific method**:

1. Science is *empirical* in the sense that it is concerned with phenomena that can be observed or at least measured.
2. Science entails a *search for regularities* in the relationships among phenomena.
3. Science is *cumulative* because it tentatively accepts previously established knowledge on a subject as the foundation for development of further knowledge. One can challenge existing knowledge, but it is not necessary to reestablish the knowledge base every time.
4. The method of science is *testable.* Its practitioners, scientists, specify the assumptions, data, analytic techniques, and inference patterns that support their knowledge claim. Other scientists look for some analysis or evidence that would invalidate (falsify) the claim. They evaluate all aspects of the claim and can repeat the analysis to ensure that the claim should be part of the accumulated knowledge.

These four characteristics are supposed to give the scientific method some major advantages over the methods of authority and personal thought in determining whether we can agree on a knowledge claim. This can be helpful because you are surrounded by competing claims regarding the political world. There are many sources of statements about politics—family, friends, television, books, newspapers, teachers, politicians. When you hear or read any claim about politics, you might take one of the following actions:

Ignore it.

Accept that it is correct.

Reject it.

Try to assess it.

If you decide to assess it, you would probably ask questions such as: Is it based on accurate information? Is it consistent with other things I know about politics? Does it influence any political actions I might take? When you begin to ask assessment questions, and especially when you try to answer them, you are engaged in political analysis. At its core, **political analysis** is *the attempt to describe (to answer the* what *questions) and then to explain politics (to answer the* why *and* how *questions).* This book attempts to enhance your ability to engage in political analysis—to answer the *what, why,* and *how* questions about politics.

Political Science

1.4   **Identify techniques and approaches used to gain political knowledge and assess whether they constitute a science.**

Political science is one approach to political analysis. As you will discover in reading this book, **political science** applies *a set of techniques, concepts, and approaches whose objective is to increase the clarity and accuracy of our understandings about the political world.*

That is, it is an attempt to apply the logic of the scientific method to political analysis. You will learn how some political scientists try to think systematically about political phenomena to describe "political reality" and to explain how politics works. You will also be introduced to some of the findings about politics that have emerged from the work of political scientists and other social scientists.

Doing Comparative Analysis

Aristotle observed: All thinking begins in comparison. This book is called "a *comparative* introduction to political science" because it emphasizes how to utilize comparative thinking to enhance our understanding of politics. Comparisons will guide many of the discussions throughout the book, and each chapter will also have a specific feature called "Compare in…" to illuminate the comparative method in action. You were introduced to some aspects of the comparative method in the "acid test" that was the focus of the Compare in 1.

Political Science and Political Knowledge

Not everyone agrees that it is appropriate and desirable to apply the scientific method to politics. Some insist that a "real" science must utilize strong applications of the four elements set out in Thomas Kuhn's book *The Structure of Scientific Revolutions* (1996): (1) central **concepts**, which *identify and name crucial phenomena* (specifically, such as "the Iraq War," or generally, such as "war"); (2) **theories**, which are *sets of systematically related generalizations that provide explanations and predictions about the linkages between certain concepts* (in the form "If A, then B under conditions C and D"); (3) *rules of interpretation,* which indicate the methods that will establish whether the explanations and predictions posited by the theory are right or wrong; and (4) a list of questions or *issues* that are worth solving within the area of inquiry.

Few would claim that political science is fully developed on any of these four elements. Thus, is it possible to engage in political science? Each chapter in this book will offer you a debate about an issue relevant to the attempt to understand the political world. Where better to start than with the Debate in 1: Is political *science* possible?

The discussion about the value of political science raises important questions that you should assess throughout this book. In general, this book will make the case that, despite the complexity of politics, generalizations are possible—each political phenomenon is not unique. If political science means the attempt to apply the scientific method to understand the political world better, it seems desirable to use such systematic and analytic thinking. And, if we are to share *any* knowledge about the political world, we need methods to reach some interpersonal agreement about political facts. Although political science lacks precise concepts and theories, it does enable us to develop better concepts, improved methods, and sounder generalizations, and thereby it makes the study of the political world an exciting intellectual challenge.

This book assumes that understanding politics is extremely important. As Austrian philosopher of science Karl Popper (1963: 227) suggests, "We must not expect too much from reason; argument rarely settles a [political] question, although it is the only means for learning—not to see clearly, but to see more clearly than before." In the face of fundamental value conflicts and the potential for massive political violence among individuals, groups, and countries, enhanced political knowledge might reduce our misunderstandings and misconceptions. It can also be the grounds for greater tolerance and wiser value judgments about normative political issues. Enhancing *what* we know about politics and what we *value* should make us more effective in knowing *how* to behave politically—as voters, political activists, and political decision makers. The study of the political world is of crucial importance to the creation of humane social life. Ultimately it is up to you, as you read this book, to decide what can be known about politics and whether you think political science is feasible.

The Debate in 1

Is Political *Science* Possible?

Science and Politics Do Not Go Together Well

- The analysis of politics cannot be objective and unbiased in the way assumed by the scientific method. The issues chosen for study and the manner in which variables are defined, measured, and analyzed are all powerfully influenced by the analyst's social reality (e.g., by the analyst's own culture, ideas, and life experiences). In this view, no person—whether Sunni Muslim or agnostic, rural Nigerian or cosmopolitan Parisian, international lawyer or migrant farm worker—can be totally objective and unbiased in the way he tries to analyze political phenomena.

- The subject matter of politics defies generalization. The political world is far too complex and unpredictable for systematic generalizations. Politics is based on the actions and interactions of many individuals, groups, and even countries. Politics occurs in the midst of many changing conditions that can influence those actions. The range of variation in what people might do and in the conditions that might exist is so vast that clear "if A, then B" statements about politics are impossible.

- Political science is not a "real" science, in comparison to natural and applied sciences (e.g., chemistry, physics, engineering). The four key elements described by Kuhn (as listed above) are well developed and widely shared within the research communities of every natural and applied science. In contrast, researchers in political science (and other social sciences) have not agreed on a coherent set of concepts, theories, and rules of interpretation. As you will discover throughout this book, many different methods are used in political science. There is disagreement regarding the important issues that ought to be solved, little consensus on what theories or generalizations have been proven, and even great difficulty in operationalizing key concepts such as power or democracy.

- The "scientific" study of politics cannot adequately address the most crucial questions about politics, which are normative. Since the time of Aristotle (384–322 B.C.E.), classical political theorists have insisted that the ultimate aim of political analysis is to discover "the highest good attainable by action." In this view, political analysis is a noble endeavor because it helps determine what government and individuals *should* do so that valued goals (e.g., democratic politics, a good life, a just society) can be achieved. Max Weber (1864–1920), the influential German social scientist, approvingly quoted Russian novelist Leo Tolstoy's assertion that science can provide no answer to the essential question, "What shall we do, and how shall we arrange our lives?" (1958a: 152–153).

Political Science Is Possible and Worthwhile

- Every person, including those who study politics, has biases. But the scientific method encourages individuals to be very aware of their biases and to counteract those biases by making their assumptions as transparent as possible. The method of science requires the analyst to be extremely clear in describing his assumptions, in characterizing how evidence is gathered, in displaying the techniques used to analyze the data, and in exploring threats to the validity of the knowledge claims that are made. This transparency limits bias and exposes the analyst's thinking to scrutiny. (As authors, we have attempted to be aware of our own biases—as Americans, men, baby boomers, etc.—that influence every aspect of this book. As you read, try to become more conscious of *your* biases, which will affect your assessments of claims about the political world.)

- While the political world is complex, few events are truly random—there are patterns and linkages among political phenomena. The challenge for the political scientist is to specify these patterns. Rather than assuming that all is chaos and nothing is related, the political scientist assumes that, by employing systematic techniques of gathering and analyzing empirical data, it is possible to present knowledge claims that help clarify that complex reality. Tendency statements—"if A, then a tendency to B"—might seem imperfect, but they can significantly increase our confidence regarding what we know to be true or untrue about politics.

- Although some sciences come closer to Kuhn's ideal than others, no science is pure. Scholars who study the way in which a scientific community operates conclude that every scientific discipline can be characterized by disagreements over concepts, methods, and theories and that the theories of every science include subjective elements. It is certainly true that political science is less scientifically pure than astronomy or chemistry, but this does not negate the value of applying the scientific method to make our thinking more precise and our knowledge claims more transparent, testable, and reliable.

- Even those who use the scientific method to study politics do not assume it can provide a compelling answer to every important normative question. However, if it does provide more reliable knowledge, it enhances our capacity to reason about the questions of what should be done. Whether at the individual level or at the national government level, decisions about what actions should be taken in the political world will be improved if they are informed by empirical evidence and sound knowledge claims that are based on the scientific method.

More questions…

1. Can you identify any of your own biases about political issues? What might be the main sources of those biases?

2. Can you think of examples where you have gained useful political knowledge from nonscientific sources such as literature, music, personal experience, or general authorities?

The Subfields of Political Science

Political science is composed of certain subfields that are usually defined by their specific subject matter rather than by their mode of analysis. While there are different ways to categorize the subfields, four are prominent:

1. **Comparative politics.** This subfield *focuses on similarities and differences in political processes and structures.* As noted above, much of empirical political science is comparative. Thus, comparative politics covers a huge domain within political analysis, and it has many sub-subfields (e.g., public administration, political parties,

development, individual political behavior, and public policy). Comparison might be crossnational (e.g., comparing the legal systems of Iran and Italy or comparing the voting patterns in 40 countries), or it might compare actors within a single country (e.g., comparing the political beliefs about democracy among different religious groups in Nigeria).

2. **American politics.** To the rest of the world, the study of American politics is merely a subfield of comparative politics. While this is quite sensible (and appropriate), American politics is treated as a separate subfield in the United States. In terms of issues and approaches, American politics covers the same types of topics as comparative politics.

3. **International relations.** The *focus is on the political relations among countries, the behavior of transnational actors, and the dynamics within the worldwide system of states and groups.* Subjects within international relations include war, interstate conflict resolution, international law, globalization, neocolonialism, regional alliances (e.g., the European Union), international organizations (e.g., the United Nations), and transborder political organizations (e.g., Amnesty International). The study of foreign policy is also within this subfield.

4. **Political theory.** More precisely called political philosophy, this subfield *focuses on the ideas and debates dealing with important political questions.* Some of this work attempts to characterize and interpret the writings of major political theorists (e.g., Plato, Thomas Hobbes, Karl Marx, John Rawls), whereas other work is original explorations of the political questions themselves (e.g., What is the nature of a just society? What is the appropriate relationship between the citizen and the government?). Political **theory** is *the source of many of the normative knowledge claims made by political scientists.* Much of the work in political theory is based on the methods of rationality or authority or on an appeal to moral truths rather than on the scientific method.

BOUNDARY-SPANNING HYBRIDS Political science is an eclectic field that often links with other fields of inquiry or at least borrows and adapts ideas from other disciplines. Some work actually spans the boundary between political science and another discipline. While the subject matter of this work fits within one of the preceding four major subfields, these hybrids include political anthropology, political economy, political psychology, political sociology, and biopolitics.

Where Is This Book Going?

Just as there are different approaches to political science, there are different ways to introduce you to the political world. This book is organized to lead you along one route to understanding. It uses a comparative approach; it builds from the politics of the individual to the politics of countries and the international system and concludes with chapters that bring all the topics together for each of three large groups of countries. Fundamentally, the book aims to help you create an increasingly sophisticated analytic framework for the study and analysis of the political world that surrounds you.

The book is organized in five parts, each with its own chapters. You have nearly completed Part One, which offers an initial discussion of the nature of political knowledge and the approach political scientists take to understanding, analyzing, and evaluating that knowledge. Each chapter includes a Debate on a political topic, a Compare analyzing two or more political actors, and a Focus on a chapter-relevant topic for a single country. Since this chapter has focused on political knowledge, the Focus in 1 shows you how the scientific method has been applied to explore whether political knowledge varies across age groups within the United States.

The remaining four parts of the book build from studying the individual in the political world to analyzing countries in the global system. "Man is the measure of all things," observed ancient Greek philosopher Protagoras (ca. 490–421 B.C.E.). In that spirit, Part Two begins its exploration of the political world at the most personal and individual level. It initially examines what individual men and women think about politics and how they act politically. After Part Two, the book moves on to the politics of large collectivities of people that we call states and that are organized politically as governments. Thus, Parts Three, Four, and Five offer perspectives and explanations from political science regarding how states and governments are organized for political action, how political processes occur, and how countries are attempting to fulfill their political goals in the challenging conditions of the global system.

Part Two, "Political Behavior," begins in Chapter 2 with an assessment of the kinds of *political beliefs* that people hold and a description of normative political theories. It continues in Chapter 3 with a consideration of the *political actions* that people and groups undertake. Chapter 4 moves from description to explanation: Can we explain *why* people think and act politically in certain ways?

Part Three, "Political Systems," is about the politics of large numbers of people— how the political world is organized and the *structures of government.* Chapters 5 through 8 address questions such as: What is a state? How are the political system and the economic system linked? What features distinguish democracies from dictatorships? What are the responsibilities of political structures such as the judiciary or the legislature?

Part Four, "Political Processes," emphasizes the *key dynamics of politics.* Chapter 9 characterizes the public policy process and details three major explanations for how political power is distributed and how policy decisions are made. Chapter 10 explores the processes of political change and development. The vital issues of politics across borders and the manner in which states and other transnational actors cooperate and compete are central to Chapter 11. The various forms and causes of political violence are analyzed in Chapter 12.

Part Five, "Politics among States," focuses on the actions and challenges facing *countries in the contemporary political world.* Chapters 13 through 15 consider countries at different levels of development as they pursue the general goals of prosperity, security, and stability in the complicated global system. Finally, the Appendix explains some major concepts in political science, including four important frameworks for engaging in political analysis: taxonomic, formal, functional, and relational.

Our hope is that, by the time you complete reading and studying this text, you will think more like a political scientist in the sense that *you will have more confidence in your knowledge about politics and you will have developed a more informed and systematic approach to understanding the political world.*

Focus in 1

The Political Knowledge of Different Age Groups in the United States

You might have heard the claim that younger adults are less knowledgeable about politics than older adults. The Pew Research Center for the People and the Press uses sophisticated social science methods to regularly assess what the people know about a host of issues. To illustrate how the scientific method is used to explore a political question, this Focus very briefly describes the steps the researchers utilize as well as a few of their results and conclusions.

1. *Examine existing evidence* that is relevant. Initially, you should look at existing research by political scientists or other social scientists that offers evidence and conclusions on the topic. Pew used the available research on age and political knowledge as the foundation for designing and conducting the study.

2. With this background, *state the issue* in a precise manner. This particular issue can be stated in the form of a *hypothesis* (i.e., a proposition about a political fact): Younger people have less political knowledge than older people.

3. *Operationalize key concepts* by specifying exactly what each concept means and how it will be measured. In this study, operationalizing the concept of political knowledge begins with the recognition that it could cover many things. Political knowledge could be defined in terms of descriptive, explanatory, and/or prescriptive information about various aspects of politics such as policies, institutions, events, or people. It could also include how-to knowledge, such as how to vote or how to circulate a petition. For simplicity, the Pew analysis focuses on a few descriptive political facts.

Specifically, Pew examines people's knowledge of the names of key political leaders and the central facts in current political issues. While cross-national comparisons are interesting, this analysis looks only at people in the United States and only at a single point in time (2010). Another key concept in this research is age. Pew uses a simple taxonomy of four age groups among adults, as listed in Table 1.2. (If you don't know what a taxonomy is, consult the discussion of this concept in the Appendix.)

In any scientific research, you should consider whether there might be problems with the validity of the data. In this case, for example: Was the set of individuals selected for study a reasonable one? Were the questions well-constructed, minimally biased, properly asked, and accurately recorded? Was sufficient data gathered to explore the core question?

4. *Gather appropriate data.* You need a strategy for collecting evidence that is valid (i.e., it measures what it is supposed to measure) and reliable (i.e., it is accurate). You also decide what specific cases you are going to examine. In the empirical work by Pew, the data were collected from a U.S. national sample of 1001 adults, selected randomly and interviewed by means of a telephone survey using numbers from both cell phones and landlines. Respondents were asked eleven multiple choice questions about their political knowledge and about certain personal characteristics (including age). You can take Pew's most recent News IQ Quiz at: http://www.pewresearch.org/politicalquiz/

5. *Analyze the evidence.* The data in Table 1.2 simply report the percentage in each age group who correctly answered the question. A more thorough analysis might use computer-based statistical techniques to assess the explanatory power of multiple variables, rather than just age, or it might combine multiple responses into an index score of knowledge.

6. *Decide what, if any, inferences and conclusions can be made* about the issue on the basis of your evidence. This is where your analytic skills become especially important. The Appendix in this book discusses some of statistical techniques that can be utilized to help you judge whether the age-group differences in the data are greater than might be expected by chance. Without engaging in these statistical tests, what do you think from assessing Table 1.2? Do these data indicate differences in political knowledge across the age groups? The data do seem to suggest that the youngest group knows less about most of the questions asked. However, notice the results for the last question. Are there issues on which younger people may be just as aware or even more informed than older people?

Is this evidence sufficient to conclude whether younger adults are less politically knowledgeable? Can you have confidence in a generalization about age and political knowledge in the United States based on only these questions in a single study at one point in time? Defensible conclusions often require extensive data, thorough analysis, and consideration of several alternative explanations. Sometimes the phenomena are so complicated or the evidence is so mixed that no generalization is possible. Any conclusion based only on Table 1.2 would be very tentative.

Other research on this topic contains more extensive data analyses. For example, a book-length study by Cliff Zukin and his colleagues (2006) analyzed a large database with sophisticated techniques. They concluded that there is a positive relationship between higher age and greater political knowledge in the United States. Their study, like most good research, attempts to address the deeper questions and the ultimate goal of the scientific method, explanation and broader generalization (theory). Does increased age cause increased political knowledge? If so, why and how does this occur? In trying to explain the relationship between age and political knowledge, has some other important variable been overlooked?

To deal with this possibility, Zukin's group identify and analyze factors other than age that might affect political knowledge. Among other explanatory factors that seem relevant are the individual's: income level; education level; gender; political

Table 1.2 Political Knowledge among Adults in the United States, by Age

Age Group	18–29	30–49	50–64	65+	Old-Young Difference
New House Speaker? (Boehner)	14%	39%	48%	51%	+37%
Republicans have majority in? (House)	27	45	55	57	+30
India-Pakistan relations? (Unfriendly)	27	42	46	46	+19
Current unemployment rate? (10%)	43	52	57	60	+17
Int'l trade: U.S. buys/sells more? (Buys)	54	63	74	68	+14
Prime Minister of Great Britain is? (Cameron)	10	14	16	19	+9
U.S. gov't spends most on…? (Defense)	45	41	35	33	−12

Each column contains the percentage providing the correct answer in the age group identified at the top. These are abbreviated versions of the multiple choice questions asked, with the correct answers in parentheses after the question.

SOURCE: Pew Research Center (2010). http://www.pewresearch.org/2010/11/18/ public-knows-basic-facts-about-politics-economics-but-struggles-with-specifics/

party affiliation; the political issues that matter most to each age group; and the political climate at the time of the study. Do you understand why these types of factors might provide a better explanation than age does for the cause of variations in political knowledge? Zukin's group did conclude that age mattered, even when considering other variables.

Political phenomena are rarely straightforward and they can change—sometimes quite rapidly. These are among the reasons that the study of politics is so fascinating (and perhaps frustrating). For the political analyst, this means that generalizations must be made with care. If you wanted to establish a broad generalization about age and political knowledge, you would want data on more measures of political knowledge, from several time periods, and probably not just from the United States. In the spirit of the scientific method, every aspect of the analysis is open to criticism by other analysts. And the conclusions stand only as long as other analysts are unable to challenge successfully any aspect of stages 1–6 in this process. In exploring political questions, further analyses are always appropriate to strengthen our knowledge claims.

Further Focus

1. What political knowledge would you measure if you did a comparative analysis across different age groups? Why? (Always assume there is an implicit "why" question when these questions are raised in the book.)

2. What do you think is the most compelling explanation for the apparent differences in political knowledge across age groups in the United States? Would this differ in another country? What countries come to mind?

Key Concepts

authority (as a knowledge
    source), p. 9
concept, p. 15
description, p. 5
explanation, p. 6

normative political knowledge,
    p. 6
political analysis, p. 14
political science, p. 14
politics, p. 3

prescription, p. 6
scientific method, p. 14
theories, p. 15
theory, p. 18

For Further Consideration

1. What do you think is the most serious obstacle to a "science" of politics?

2. Which authority have you relied on most extensively as a source of your knowledge about politics? What is the biggest shortcoming of this source?

3. What is the most important question that political science should attempt to answer? What might prevent political scientists from answering this question adequately?

4. Many people insist that most of their political knowledge is based on their own rational thought processes. What might be wrong with this claim?

5. Do you think political scientists can play an important role in government, or are they just intellectuals who should only stand on the sidelines and analyze politics?

For Further Reading

Almond, Gabriel. (1989). *A Discipline Divided: Schools and Sects in Political Science.* **Newbury Park, CA: Sage.** One of the major scholars of comparative politics assesses the diversity of approaches to political science and the possibility of a science of politics.

Brians, Craig, Lars Willnat, Richard Rich, and Jarol B. Manheim. (2011). *Empirical Political Analysis: Research Methods in Political Science.* **8th ed. New York: Pearson.** A very effective and understandable presentation of the primary methods that political scientists utilize in the attempt to understand politics and develop defensible generalizations, focusing on a full range of qualitative and quantitative approaches.

Goodin, Robert E., ed. (2011). *The Oxford Handbook of Political Science.* **New York: Oxford University Press.** Almost seventy top political scientists contribute articles summarizing the key issues, findings, and emerging developments in all the subfields of political science, selected from the ten Oxford Handbooks focusing on each subfield of political science.

Katznelson, Ira, and Helen Miller, eds. (2004). *Political Science: State of the Discipline.* **Centennial ed. New York: W. W. Norton.** In only(!) 993 pages, a diverse group of political scientists offers essays (sponsored by the American Political Science Association) on the current insights and debates on central issues related to core concepts in the discipline such as the state, democracy, political institutions, participation, and modes of political analysis.

King, Gary, Kay L. Schlozman, and Norman Nie, eds. (2009). *The Future of Political Science: 100 Perspectives.* **London: Routledge.** One hundred mini-essays (in 304 pages), many by distinguished political scientists, which explore a broad array of interesting questions about politics and political science.

Kuhn, Thomas. (1996). *The Structure of Scientific Revolutions.* **3rd ed. Chicago: University of Chicago Press.** A short, understandable, and enormously influential discussion of how sciences develop and overturn paradigms; first published in 1962.

Kurian, George, James E. Alt, Simone Chambers, Geoffrey Garrett, Margaret Levi, and Paula D. McClain, eds. (2011). *The Encyclopedia of Political Science.* **Washington, DC: CQ Press.** This five-volume reference resource provides helpful essays on more than 1,200 concepts that are significant in the study of politics as well as hundreds of valuable overview essays.

Monroe, Kristen Renwick, ed. (2005). *Perestroika: The Raucous Rebellion in Political Science.* **New Haven, CT: Yale University Press.** These essays reflect on a strong reform movement that emerged among some political scientists who demanded a broader and more methodologically diverse discipline, a democratization of the profession's governance and journals, and a broadening of graduate student education.

Pollack, Philip H. (2011). *The Essentials of Political Analysis.* **4th ed. Washington, DC: CQ Press.** Using many interesting examples, the book explains how to use empirical data and quantitative analysis (especially the Statistical Package for Social Sciences—SPSS) in the study of political phenomena.

Popper, Karl R. (2002). *The Logic of Scientific Discovery.* **London: Hutchinson.** A major and widely respected statement of the philosophy and application of the scientific method; first published in 1959.

On the Web

http://www.apsanet.org

This Web site for the American Political Science Association, the major organization for political scientists in the United States, provides links to a variety of activities and opportunities associated with political science professionals, including online papers from the national conference and articles from *PS: Political Science and Politics*.

http://www.psqonline.org

Political Science Quarterly is the United States' oldest, continuously published political science journal and brings you the world of politics.

http://www.etown.edu/vl

The rich and extensive set of links on this Web site, "WWW Virtual Library: International Affairs Resources," includes numerous sites

for each region as well as links to many key international topics as varied as international organizations, environmental issues, world religions, media resources, health, and human rights.

http://www.realclearpolitics.com

This Web site is a daily compendium of many of the most interesting stories about politics available on the Internet, including blogs, with a primary focus on U.S. politics.

http://www.politicsresources.net

Richard Kimber's Political Science Resources page includes an extensive listing of sites on topics such as political theory, political thought, constitutions, elections, political parties, international relations, and British politics.

Chapter 2
Political Theory and Political Beliefs

Learning Objectives

2.1 Compare conservatism, classical liberalism, and socialism.

2.2 Distinguish cognitive, affective, and evaluative beliefs.

2.3 Compare belief systems of the mass and the elite.

2.4 Determine the extent to which political culture explains political behavior.

On your way to campus one day, you stop by Burger King for lunch. As you get your food, you notice a group of your classmates engaged in a very heated debate over the recent war in Afghanistan, a topic that hasn't interested you much. You decide to sit with them.

As you eat, Julie says, "The U.S. invasion of Afghanistan was totally immoral. The United States has no right to cause all that suffering, and it has cost America $80 billion a year that should be spent dealing with issues at home, like poverty and education! This is even worse than what we did in Iraq! Don't you agree?"

She looks directly at you, searching for support. As you stare at your cheeseburger, you realize you are in the hot seat. You think: Do I support the U.S. action? Did the United States "invade"? Is it costing $80 billion?

When you do not respond, Glen interjects, telling Julie, "You have no right to say that. Those in power are our most politically knowledgeable decision makers and have information we don't know about. As citizens, we shouldn't question their authority on complex issues such as deciding when to use our military!"

Julie replies, "It is not fair that I work so hard every day of the week so that the government can funnel my tax dollars into buying more tanks, guns, and airplanes to fight a war I do not support. Our government should focus on our own poor people and should do more to create jobs for us. I have every right to protest government action." You see Julie's point when you think about problems at home while your family's tax money is being used for a costly, distant war.

What march would *you* join? These college students express their strong political beliefs on an important issue.

"I sort of agree," says Byron. "The United States is in a huge budget crisis. Our government is way too big. We should be cutting way back on spending on everything. Cut taxes. Give the money back to people who earned it!"

Frustrated with Julie's challenges to the government, Glen says, "By not supporting our leaders and criticizing their actions, you are threatening our country's political stability with your lack of patriotism. For your information, that money has not been wasted. By expanding our military power, we make our country more secure from people who threaten our way of life, and we are able to promote positive values such as democracy and freedom." Supporting democracy and U.S. military strength do seem worthwhile to you.

Then Elene joins in: "You both miss the point. The real reason the United States went to war is because of the men who led the countries in the conflict. Obama decided to risk many lives in Afghanistan, just like Bush did in Iraq, because he wanted to demonstrate his manliness and power. If women had more authority in these countries, they might have figured out a solution without so much violence and death. I'm not saying it's all about gender, but a lot of women do see things differently than many men do, and if women had more political authority, they might come up with less violent approaches."

Amir, whose family is from the Middle East, cannot resist speaking. He says, "I agree with Julie. American leadership has caused great pain and suffering for many innocent Muslim families. In Iraq the reports of weapons of mass destruction were just a sham to allow the United States to force its values upon the Iraqis. George Bush even called the war a crusade! Then Obama caused more mass destruction in Afghanistan!

What's next? Syria? Iraq again? We are marching tonight on campus to protest any more U.S. military involvement in the region. Join us!"

You decide that everyone has made some good points. You wonder if you should spend more time gathering knowledge about political issues like the conflicts in the Middle East. This discussion has made you reflect on your own values: When are war and violence acceptable? What should the government spend money on? Should your country push other countries to adopt American values? Should you attend the protest rally?

How would you (the real you!) react to this conversation? What are your views on these questions?

This conversation is richly political—full of many knowledge claims. Some of the comments seem factual, while others mix fact, feeling, and evaluation. Some include strong prescriptive statements about what should be. There is a call for action. Your responses to this incident and to the questions it raises offer interesting evidence about your reactions to the political world. Some of your responses might involve what you think (your political beliefs and your political ideology), and others might involve what you do (your political actions). This combination of *an individual's beliefs and actions* is the essence of the domain of political science called **political behavior**. It is also sometimes called **micropolitics** because *the key object of study is the smallest political unit*—the individual as a thinker and actor in the political world. Micropolitics can also include the study of the political beliefs and actions of small groups such as families, committees, and juries.

Part Two of this book develops your understanding of the political world by examining major themes in the study of political behavior. This chapter explores individuals' political views, ranging from *core values to specific beliefs*. Initially, it examines normative political theory—the assumptions and broad beliefs that guide political ideologies. The primary focus is on three political ideologies prevalent in Western political thought: conservatism, classical liberalism, and socialism. The chapter then details what empirical analyses reveal about the basic elements of an individual's *political beliefs*. Third, the chapter considers the configuration of beliefs held by an individual—a cluster of beliefs called a *political belief system.* The final section attempts to characterize the dominant patterns of political behavior for an entire society—its *political culture.* The two other chapters in Part Two will extend our exploration of political behavior. Chapter 3 examines the political actions taken by individuals and groups. Chapter 4 assesses alternative explanations for the sources of people's political beliefs and actions.

Normative Political Theory

2.1   **Compare conservatism, classical liberalism, and socialism.**

Should an individual resist a government policy on drug use with which she disagrees? Why? By what means? With what goals? Should government provide for the poor? Why? By what means? With what goals? As each of us attempts to answer such questions, we must grapple not only with the facts and realities of the situation, as we understand them, but also with our underlying beliefs about topics such as the appropriate role of government and the rights and duties of the individual in society. Political questions are often very difficult to resolve because they can be embedded in underlying values and core beliefs that are subject to deep disagreement.

Notice that the preceding questions are essentially *should* questions. The subfield of political science called **normative political theory** *offers explicit arguments and proposes answers to the significant "should" questions in the political world,* based on fundamental claims about the individual, the society, and the state. Normative political theorists develop their ideas about the "should" questions by blending their observations about the world with the detailed articulation and defense of one or more basic values, principles, or norms that shape their viewpoint. So, for example, a normative theorist's response to whether the government should provide for the poor would require an elaboration on several key issues, such as whether society has a political or moral obligation to assist individuals, how this applies to the particular case of poverty, and how government is implicated in any such obligation. Such theorizing usually invokes fundamental themes like justice, fairness, equality, and freedom.

Although there are overlaps between the two general approaches, normative political theory can be broadly contrasted with **empirical political theory**, which *relies upon observation and analysis of real-world data as it attempts to apply the methods of science in order to develop descriptive and explanatory knowledge claims about the political world.* Later sections of this chapter offer information and generalizations about people's cognitive, affective, and evaluative beliefs based explicitly in an empirical approach. But the formulation of an evaluative belief or a prescriptive knowledge claim will also draw upon normative thinking. Thus this chapter about political beliefs initially explores some key themes in normative political theory and describes several major political ideologies.

Some of the core issues of normative political theory are associated with the basic question: Why do we need a government? Theorizing about this can provoke further questions about human nature, about why and how people associate with one another, about how government should function, and about how people and government should interact. Plato, Aristotle, Confucius, Thomas Hobbes, John Locke, Karl Marx, and John Stuart Mill are among the many important thinkers who have offered profound, provocative, and influential ideas about these basic normative questions regarding the relationships among individuals, the state, and society. Such political questions remain important and fascinating. This section describes some of these questions and a few of the many answers that are proposed.

You will notice that many of the knowledge claims made by normative political theorists are based on more than their values. Most political theorists include descriptive statements (claims of how things actually are) as part of their arguments regarding what should be and why it should be. As they articulate their normative claims about the political world, they are influenced by the same factors that surround those engaged in empirical political analysis—their personal experiences and education, the nature of the time and place in which they live, and other key forces in their lives. Focus in 2 briefly considers how the socioeconomic context contributed to the hugely influential writings of three major political theorists.

Focus in 2

Great Britain as a Context for Some Great Political Theorists

What influences the thinking of the great political theorists? Of course, the answer is complex and variable. Chapter 4 will suggest that most people's political beliefs are influenced by an array of factors, including their personal experiences and upbringing, their teachers and other individuals whose ideas engage them, and the sociopolitical contexts that provide evidence guiding their assumptions and inferences about human nature, the role of the state, and other key topics. It is probably not surprising that most of the great political theorists of the last four centuries selected for major English-language anthologies were substantially influenced by their lives in the sociopolitical context of Great Britain (see, for example, Goodin and Pettit 2006; Love 2010; Ryan 2012). Even many modern thinkers who did not live in the British Isles were substantially influenced by Britain's unique institutional innovations and political culture in the seventeenth through nineteenth centuries. Here are very brief examples of three major theorists directly affected by their lives in Britain.

Thomas Hobbes. Englishman Thomas Hobbes (1588–1679) studied classics in school and at Oxford. After traveling in Europe, Hobbes became embroiled in the social turmoil, civil war, and serious succession problems in England after the death of Queen Elizabeth, as several different hereditary lines claimed the throne. One king (Charles I) attempted to reign absolutely over a resistant parliament through two civil wars and then was executed for high treason in 1649 as Cromwell's Puritans took over government. The chaos in England certainly influenced Hobbes's ideas about the brutal behavior of humans in the "state of nature." In 1640, Hobbes had written a tract to lawmakers urging that the sovereign (king) must exercise absolute power to reduce such disorder. He then fled England, fearing that he would be executed for his support of the monarchy. While abroad, Hobbes wrote his masterpiece, *Leviathan* (1651), in which he elaborated on his ideas, arguing that a powerful monarch should be established and obeyed. Recognizing the growing political influence of business in England, he also suggested that the

"voice of the people" should be heard through representatives of the business class. However, no one has any right to challenge the complete power of the monarch to make and enforce laws, as long as the monarch preserves social order.

Adam Smith. Adam Smith (1723–1790) left his small village in Scotland to study in Edinburgh and then Oxford, where he focused on philosophy and European literature. Smith served as chair in logic and moral philosophy in Glasgow and then traveled in Europe as tutor to a wealthy English duke. Smith had developed a strong opposition to the British government's interventions in its economy—a view reinforced when he saw similar problems in France. He retired to Scotland to write his classic *An Inquiry into the Nature and Causes of the Wealth of Nations* (1776). Shaped by his training as a philosopher, his work explored how humans could best interact to produce the most efficient economic system. He emphasized the benefits of a division of labor, in which economic actors—generally unhindered by government—pursue their own rational self-interest while the "invisible hand" of the market guides the economy (see Chapter 8 of this book). However, Smith's life in Britain and his work as a customs agent persuaded him that there were some limitations to the free market, and he began to advocate certain important roles for government in the economy, such as enforcing contracts, protecting intellectual property rights, and acting in areas where the decisions of private economic actors would not produce necessary goods (e.g., roads and bridges). He also entered a contemporary policy debate, arguing that Britain should abandon its American colonies due to the high costs of sustaining imperialism.

Karl Marx. Although Karl Marx (1818–1883) was born in Germany, he lived the second half of his life (34 years) in England, where he researched and wrote his major work, died, and was buried. The moral and philosophical bases of his theories (especially French socialism and German philosophy) were established during his time as a student, journalist, and political agitator in Germany, France, and Belgium. His activism led to his expulsion from all three countries, and thus in 1849 he moved to England and found refuge in London. His earlier ideas were blended with his experiences in England: a detailed study of English corporate records and other research in the British Museum; his projections of the future of capitalism based on his analysis of English capitalism, the world's most sophisticated economic system; and his observations of the hardships of the English working class. Indeed, Marx's own life was substantially shaped by the severe hardships suffered in London by his own family, which lived in poverty and disease and included the painful deaths of three of his children. His writing in England culminated in his monumental work, *Capital: A Critique of Political Economy* (1867). As stated by his disciple, Wilhelm Liebknecht, "[I]n England Marx found what he was looking for, what he needed: the bricks and mortar for his work. *Capital* could only have been written in London. Marx could only become what he did become in England" (Mclellan 1983).

Further Focus

1. Based on these brief discussions, which of the three theorists seems to have been most influenced by the context of life in Britain?

2. Could you make a case that most major political theorists would probably have developed their ideas regardless of the country in which they lived?

Political Ideology

The political theories of Thomas Hobbes, Adam Smith, and Karl Marx are among the several dozen most famous and widely studied in the Western world. Some would describe the work of each of them as a political ideology. We can define a **political ideology** as *a comprehensive set of beliefs about the political world—about desirable political goals and the best ways to achieve those goals.* Thus, a political ideology characterizes what is and what should be in the political world, and it might also offer strategic ideas about how to make changes in the direction of that preferred situation. Many relatively coherent belief systems in the contemporary world might be classified as political ideologies.

This section characterizes three of the fundamental concerns that are addressed by most political ideologies and help us distinguish analytically among them. These three fundamental concerns are their assumptions and value judgments about: (1) individual human nature; (2) the proper relationship among the individual, state, and society; and (3) the desirability of establishing equality among individuals. Then it details three broad ideologies that are widely discussed in contemporary Western societies: conservatism, classical liberalism, and socialism. There are short explanations of the ideologies of fascism and political Islam as well as brief characterizations of some other "isms."

THE INDIVIDUAL The "nature versus nurture" debate centers on disagreements about whether a person's fundamental beliefs and behaviors are determined primarily by innate needs and values with which she is born or are mainly a product of her environment and experiences. Chapter 4 provides an empirical assessment of the implications of nature and nurture for political beliefs and actions. Here, our focus is on key assumptions that a political ideology makes about an individual's innate nature (e.g., the extent to which individuals are selfish or sharing, violent or nonviolent, emotional or rational) and about the adaptability of individuals (the extent to which they can be taught or induced to act and think in a way that is against their innate nature). For example, Thomas Hobbes grounds his theories in the assumption that people are essentially motivated to serve their own interests and that they will use whatever means necessary, including violence, to protect themselves.

INDIVIDUAL, STATE, AND SOCIETY What is the proper relationship among the individual, the state, and society? One view is that the highest value in social arrangements is to maximize individual liberty and freedom of action. A different view is that the collective good of society is most important and individual freedom must be constrained by the state (the government, broadly understood—see Chapter 5) to achieve the results that most benefit the overall society. For example, Adam Smith emphasizes the benefits both to individuals and to the "wealth of the nation" from allowing economic actors to operate with a very high level of freedom from government controls, because their pursuit of enlightened self-interest will result in a good society with an efficient and effective economy.

EQUALITY To what extent should there be equality in terms of what individuals do and the benefits they acquire? One position is that there should be legal equality— that every person should be equal before the law, have equal political rights, and enjoy equality of opportunity. An alternative position is that there should be material equality—that every person should enjoy a comparable level of benefits and goods. This second position places a high value on equality of conditions, adding social and economic equality to legal equality. A third position posits that people and situations are intrinsically unequal and that it is neither possible nor desirable to legislate any kind of equality. Karl Marx is among those who argue most fervently that a good society is achieved only when there is substantial equality in the material conditions of all individuals.

Three major Western ideologies are described below—conservatism, classical liberalism, and socialism. Although there is broad agreement about the core beliefs within an ideology, it is subject to varying interpretations across individuals and across cultures. And an ideology can have distinct versions, such as the differences within socialism between its Marxist–Leninist form and its democratic socialist form.

Conservatism

Conservatism *attempts to prevent or slow the transition away from a society based on traditional values and the existing social hierarchy.* As the word suggests, the essence of conservative ideology is to conserve the many valued elements of the system that already exists. What the conservative wishes to preserve depends on the time and place, but certain underlying elements are highly valued. Particular importance is placed on stability, tradition, and loyalty to God and country. The relationship of the individual to society and an antipathy to egalitarianism (i.e., equality of conditions) are at the core of conservatism.

THE INDIVIDUAL Conservatism makes two key assumptions about human nature. First, individuals are not consistently rational. In many situations, people are emotional and are unable to reason clearly. Thus, tradition and religion, rather than reason, are viewed as the most reliable sources for guiding society because they support stability and moderate change. In the words of one British conservative, "The accumulated wisdom and experience of countless generations gone is more likely to be right than the passing fashion of the moment" (Hearnshaw 1933: 22). Second, individuals are inherently unequal in intelligence, skills, and status. Some individuals and groups are superior to others, and those who are superior should be in positions of power in society and in government.

INDIVIDUAL, STATE, AND SOCIETY Individuals have a basic need for order and stability in society. They belong to different groups that are unequal in power, status, and material possessions. Social harmony is maintained when these various groups cooperate. Traditional values and ethics provide the guidelines for group cooperation as well as individual behavior. And it is the role of societal institutions such as the family and the church, as well as government (the state), to communicate and enforce these values.

Individual liberty is valued and individual rights should be protected, but only within a framework of mutual responsibility. No individual or group has absolute freedom to do whatever it wants; rather, each should behave in a manner consistent with society's traditional values. The superior groups should be allowed to enjoy the benefits and exercise the responsibilities associated with their position, but they should also protect the weak from severe hardships, a responsibility that the French call *noblesse oblige*—"the obligations of the nobility." And government should use its power to maintain social order; to preserve traditional values, especially regarding family life, religion, and culture; and to protect private property rights. State military and economic power should also promote the country's interests abroad and defend against intervention by other states.

EQUALITY Because inequality is a natural aspect of society, it is foolish and even dangerous to seek egalitarianism. Forced equality is unwise because it disrupts the natural, cooperative hierarchy among groups, causes social conflict, and endangers the fundamental goal of order and stability. Attempts to force equality are also unacceptable because they directly undermine individual liberty, which is of greater importance than equality.

Thomas Hobbes, Plato (427–347 B.C.E., who proposed rule by philosopher kings), and Confucius (551–479 B.C.E., who celebrated rigid social hierarchy; see Focus in 4), all reflect core values of conservatism. Other important advocates of conservatism include Edmund Burke, a British member of Parliament; British prime ministers Benjamin Disraeli and Winston Churchill; and, to a lesser extent, American Founding Fathers James Madison and Alexander Hamilton. In the conversation at Burger King at the beginning of this chapter, Glen's views were generally consistent with conservatism.

Most contemporary conservatives are pragmatic. They are less concerned about the form of government than about the use of government to promote order and stability. The conservative perspective is sympathetic to government intervention when the objective of the policy is to maintain or return to traditional values such as patriotism, family, morality, piety, and individual responsibility. In every era, conservatives resist current threats to the traditions they value. Today, those threats often include multiculturalism; expansion of the welfare state; and forced equality across class, race, and gender. A conservative government might actively support a state religion, expand its military power to influence other countries, suppress disorderly protest, provide minimal relief to those in poverty, or make abortion illegal. Some new policies are supported, but the rationale is always "to change in order to preserve," as the British Conservative Party has put it. Many of the contemporary political leaders who come closest to the spirit of conservatism are in certain countries in Asia and the Middle East (e.g., Brunei, Kuwait, and Saudi Arabia) where social hierarchy, order, and traditional values are celebrated.

Classical Liberalism

The ideology of **classical liberalism** *places the highest value on individual freedom and posits that the role of government should be quite limited.* In part, this ideology emerged in the sixteenth through eighteenth centuries as a response to rigid, hierarchical societies, such as those in feudal Europe. Intellectuals and those in commerce, among others, desired to be free from the constraints imposed by the dominant political, economic, and religious institutions in their society. They posited that each person should live responsibly but also should be allowed to live in the manner dictated by her beliefs and to enjoy fully the benefits of her efforts with minimal limitations from these stifling, conservative institutions.

THE INDIVIDUAL John Locke (1632–1704), a primary theorist of classical liberalism, describes individuals in a "state of nature" prior to the existence of government (see his *Second Treatise of Government*, 1690). Each person enjoys natural rights to life, liberty, and property. Each person is rational and has the ability to use reason to determine the sensible rules (the "laws of nature") that shape how she should live in pursuit of her own needs and without harming others. Classical liberalism contrasts with conservatism in several important ways: (1) the freedom of each individual to pursue her natural rights is the highest value; and (2) each individual is rational and responsible and is the best judge of what is in her self-interest. (Notice also that the classical liberal's view of the state of nature is far more benign than the one described by conservative Hobbes as "solitary, poor, nasty, brutish, and short.")

INDIVIDUAL, STATE, AND SOCIETY A person's full capabilities can be realized only if she is not limited by a conservative social order in which tradition and hierarchy are dominant. The social order celebrated in conservatism not only restricts individual freedom but also stifles progressive change and growth. In the classical liberal view, no one is forced to accept the authority of the state (government). Individuals can consent to be governed—choosing to "contract" with a minimal government, the main roles of which are limited to clarifying the laws of nature and enforcing the occasional violations of those laws. The state should mainly be a night watchman, a low-profile police officer who ensures the basic safety and freedom of every individual. Thomas Paine's (1737–1809) slogan captures this perspective: "That government is best which governs least."

For similar reasons, classical liberals celebrate a laissez-faire economy, a view particularly associated with the writings of Adam Smith noted briefly in Focus in 2. Each person should be free to pursue her economic goals by any legal activity and to amass as much property and wealth as possible. Individual actors are guided by enlightened self-interest, and the overall economy is structured by the "invisible hand" of the market and free trade. There are only a few circumstances in which the state should act to constrain this freedom of economic action. This vision of a market political economy will be further explored in Chapter 8.

EQUALITY Equality before the law (equality of opportunity) is important, but government should not attempt to create material equality (equality of outcomes). People pursue their interests in different ways and with different levels of success. Even in situations of hardship, government action is undesirable because it undermines individual initiative and independence. Thus, government should have no significant role in addressing inequalities.

Among the many political thinkers associated with classical liberalism, in addition to John Locke and Adam Smith, are Jeremy Bentham (1748–1831) and John Stuart Mill (1806–1873). More contemporary advocates of classical liberalism (some of whom are labeled neoconservatives) include economists F. A. Hayek (1899–1992) and Milton Friedman (1912–2006) and political commentator William F. Buckley (1925–2008). At Burger King, Byron was most aligned with this perspective. Part Five of this book will reveal that many contemporary political regimes are powerfully influenced by classical liberalism. Its emphases on limited government, individual liberty, and laissez-faire economics are among the central themes in many ongoing debates about public policy and government action.

A brief aside: If you are an American, you might be confused by these characteristics of liberalism because, in the United States, a *liberal* is someone who supports substantial government intervention and public policies that increase equality of outcomes. This confusion of terminology emerged during Franklin Delano Roosevelt's tenure as U.S. president (1933–1945). Faced with a devastating economic depression, Roosevelt argued for a "New Deal" in which the national government had a clear duty and responsibility to assist actively in economic recovery and in social action. This expanded government would regulate business, create jobs, and distribute extensive welfare services to the citizens, including cash payments and increased public provision of education, housing, health care, and so on. Roosevelt's political opponents labeled his policies "socialism." He knew this was a very negative label in the United States, so he called himself and his policies "liberal," contrasting them with the "conservative" policies of others (mainly Republicans, such as the previous president Herbert Hoover) who emphasized limited government, laissez-faire economics, and individual freedom. Notice that, in the general language of political ideologies, what

Roosevelt was calling conservatism was mostly classical liberalism, and what he was proposing as liberalism was a very modest version of democratic socialism (described below). Roosevelt's meanings of liberals versus conservatives were adopted in the United States, but not in most other countries. In this book, the traditional ideology of liberalism will be called classical liberalism to distinguish it from the American understanding of liberalism as an ideology of extensive government and reduced inequality.

Socialism

For **socialism**, *the most important goal is to provide high-quality, relatively equal conditions of life for everyone, with an active state assisting in the achievement of this goal.* Many people were still impoverished and exploited in the nineteenth-century world, despite the emergence of industrialization and democracy. Socialism evolved as a distinctive ideology among theorists concerned about the plight of people who had relatively little economic, social, or political power. They were dissatisfied that neither conservatism nor classical liberalism revealed much concern for improving the conditions of these groups. Socialism articulated a vision through which economic and political power could be directed to benefit all groups in society.

THE INDIVIDUAL In the socialist perspective, people are social and caring by nature. They are not innately selfish and aggressive, although negative social conditions can produce such behavior. Every individual's attitudes and behaviors are largely determined by the environment of family, community, and work. Thus, it is crucial to create an environment that encourages individuals to place the highest value on cooperation and sharing and to act in ways that increase the collective good.

INDIVIDUAL, STATE, AND SOCIETY Because the good of the society as a whole is the most important goal, some of an individual's interests must be subordinated to, or at least coordinated with, the overall interests and needs of everyone in the society. All groups, from national organizations (e.g., trade unions) to local organizations (e.g., workplaces, social clubs) to the family, must encourage everyone to act in ways that result in cooperation and service to the common good. The state has a crucial role, both through policies that provide every citizen with good material living conditions and through education and civic training. Thus, government must take an expansive role in society, ensuring that every citizen has access to high-quality education, shelter, health care, and jobs, as well as financial security against economic uncertainty. The state is also much more active in controlling powerful actors and self-interested groups whose behavior will harm the collective good of the society, and thus it engages in extensive regulation of both the economic sphere and the social sphere. When everyone enjoys comfortable material conditions, there is much greater willingness to work for the common good and to subordinate one's acquisitiveness and greed.

EQUALITY Both the organic, hierarchical world of conservatism and the individualistic, self-serving world of classical liberalism result in societies with huge disparities of material conditions, wealth, status, and power. From the socialist perspective, these disparities and inequalities cause misery, deep alienation, and pervasive conflict in the society. Thus, the ideology of socialism centers in a deep commitment to use the power and policies of the state to increase the material, social, and political equality of all its members. It is assumed that such equality transforms people into fulfilled, happy citizens and creates a society in which alienation and conflict are greatly reduced.

There are significant variations within the ideology of socialism. Among these, two major variations should be distinguished: Marxist–Leninist socialism and democratic socialism.

MARXIST–LENINIST SOCIALISM Marxist–Leninist socialism is a variant of socialist ideology that begins with three assumptions regarding the *forceful actions necessary to produce equality and social justice.* First, the entrenched socioeconomic elite, supported by the state that it controls, will resist change by every means available, and thus change will require violent overthrow of the existing order. Second, the transformation to socialism will be complex and face many obstacles in the existing system. Thus, a powerful government must be established and allowed total control of the process of change. Among the government's most important tasks is the restructuring of the economic system, with public ownership of all the major resources in the society and the production and distribution of goods and services for human need. Third, a small, dictatorial leadership group must be empowered to manage the government and to effect the complex changes in the economy and society. Once relative equality is achieved, both this leadership group and the powerful government supporting it can be eliminated. They will, in the words of Marx, "wither away" and be replaced by decentralized, citizen-run politics and an efficient administration. (See Chapter 9 on the class approach and Chapter 8 on the command political economy for a more complete discussion of these points.)

The core elements of this version of socialism are the theories of Karl Marx and its modified practical applications by V. I. Lenin in the Soviet Union and by Mao Zedong in China. These variations of socialism are often called communism, Marxism, or revolutionary socialism as well as Marxist–Leninist socialism. In the last 70 years, this version of socialism has been attempted in more than 60 countries, ranging from A (Albania, Angola, Algeria) to Z (Zimbabwe). Most of the major regimes that implemented Marxist–Leninist socialism have since abandoned it (see especially Chapter 15 on postcommunist developed countries). Some conclude that the Marxist ideology of communism has been totally discredited. Debate in 8 will consider whether communism is, in fact, dead.

DEMOCRATIC SOCIALISM The other major variation within socialist ideology is **democratic socialism**. This variant also has egalitarianism as its primary goal, and it assumes that the changes can be effected by a government that comes to power and rules by democratic means. It rejects the idea that a society based on justice and equality can be created only through violence and repression. This government's authority is democratic, derived from consent of the governed in fair elections. In democratic socialism, the state's policies emphasize the substantial reduction of inequalities in material conditions, power, and status, but the state does not attempt to achieve complete equality of material conditions. The approach to change is gradual, placing continued importance on the protection of individual rights and freedoms even as it transforms the socioeconomic order. The government might own some of the major economic resources in the society and it strongly regulates much of the economy, but it does not attempt to plan and control all aspects of the economic system (Przeworski 1985, 1993).

The ideology of democratic socialism is rooted in utopian socialists such as Thomas More (1478–1535), Robert Owen (1771–1856), and Claude-Henri St. Simon (1760–1825), who envisioned voluntaristic communities based on cooperation. Twentieth-century variations include the Fabian socialists such as George Bernard Shaw, Sydney Webb, and Beatrice Webb, who were convinced that the people would elect democratic governments that gradually created socialist societies, and the revisionist Marxists such as Karl Kautsky, who argued that violence and repression by the state was not a legitimate means for achieving lasting change. At Burger King, Julie was probably the person closest to this ideology.

One vision of democratic socialism was articulated by the British economist Sir William Beveridge in a major policy statement commissioned by the British government in 1941. This statement was prompted by the dismay among British leaders regarding the very poor education and health of many young British working-class men who were drafted for World War II (this is another British example of political ideas shaped by socioeconomic conditions). In response to these circumstances, Beveridge argued that in a society operating according to the tenets of classical liberalism, there are five tragic effects on some people. Thus, the government should act as a **"welfare state"** (Castles et al., 2010), implementing policies to overcome each of these five effects:

1. **Disease:** to be combated by public provision of subsidized or free health care services, including doctors, treatment, hospitals, and medicines.
2. **Want:** to be eliminated by public provision of sufficient money and other services to raise people above poverty.
3. **Squalor:** to be reduced by state provision of publicly owned and subsidized housing affordable to all.
4. **Ignorance:** to be eliminated by universal, free public education.
5. **Idleness:** to be overcome by government policies that ensure meaningful work for every person.

The principles of democratic socialism have substantially shaped the current governance, social life, and material conditions in some contemporary social market systems present in countries such as Denmark, Germany, and Sweden (see Compare in 13). This socialist ideology is also advocated by some of the political elites in the postcommunist countries of Central and Eastern Europe (see Chapter 15).

Some Further Points About "ISMS"

To advance your knowledge regarding particular belief systems, you might take a course in political theory, political ideology, or world cultures, or you might pursue the "ism" of interest at the library or via the Internet. The preceding section identified three major political ideologies that influence the political belief systems of many citizens in Western countries. There are many other significant political ideologies in the contemporary political world, at least some of which are "isms." Table 2.1 briefly characterizes the essence of some of the political "isms" that you might encounter. Broader systems of religious-social beliefs also have great political importance, including Christian fundamentalism, Islamic fundamentalism, Confucianism, and Hinduism. Chapter 4 will indicate that it is almost impossible to understand politics in the contemporary world without considering the influence of these religious "isms" on beliefs and actions.

Some "true believers" adhere almost totally to a particular ideology, and these people are the genuine ideologues. But only a few individuals have a complete grasp of the details and subtleties of any ideology, and even fewer are prepared to accept without reservation every element of an ideology. A larger set of people is substantially influenced by one or more ideologies. They have developed their own system of political beliefs, in which they combine basic principles from particular ideologies with ideas from other sources. It will be suggested later in this chapter that many people have only rudimentary and inconsistent political beliefs.

Yet a particular "ism" can be a powerful force influencing people and shaping history. In the twentieth century, for example, both communism and fascism had particularly strong impacts. The role of communism will be explored later, especially in Chapters 8 and 15. Table 2.1 provides a basic definition of fascism. **Fascism** is antisocialist—it emphasizes an organic social order and thus opposes the idea of class struggle among groups. And it is antidemocratic—it views competitive, multiparty politics as divisive and destabilizing. While several twentieth-century regimes included strong elements of fascism, it is most closely associated with Italy under Benito Mussolini (1922–1943) and Germany under Adolf Hitler (1932–1945). In Germany, Hitler's particular version of fascism was driven by several key ideological elements. First, it held that the top leader is the embodiment of the national will and must be obeyed. Second, it inspired nationalistic fervor with powerful loyalty to the homeland. The German leadership combined these ideas with a celebration of the superiority of the German race. This produced a virulent racism that became a justification for the brutal treatment of Jews, gypsies, gays, and other "undesirable" groups, including the extermination of more than 6 million in the concentration camps of Europe. All of these ideological elements, under Hitler's charismatic leadership, resulted in Germany's expansion beyond its borders, provoking a war (World War II) that spread across three continents and caused more than 51 million deaths. Groups or political parties that embrace core ideas of fascism, especially nationalism and ethnic purity, continue to be active in many contemporary societies.

In the early twenty-first century, considerable attention has focused on the rising political importance of *Islamism*, also known as "political Islam" (and less accurately characterized as Islamic fundamentalism). Islam is one of the world's great religions, with more than 1.3 billion adherents across its many variations. Chapter 1 noted that there are deep disagreements within *dar al Islam* (the world of Islam) about how to interpret its crucial authority sources, especially the Koran, the teachings of Mohammed, and the analyses of Islam by venerated scholars of an earlier era. Islamic

Table 2.1 A Brief Primer on Political "Isms"

In politics and political theory, there are many "isms"—systems of beliefs that address how societies should function, how people should live and what they should value, and how political systems should operate. Entire books are devoted to each of the "isms" below, but here they are characterized in 40 words or less to give you an orienting (dangerously simplified?) idea about the core vision regarding any "ism" with which you are unfamiliar. The references in parentheses indicate the chapters in this book where some of these "isms" receive greater attention.

Anarchism—a moral–political ideal of a society that is untouched by relationships of power and domination among human beings; there is an absence of organized government.

Authoritarianism—a system in which the political rights and interests of individuals are subordinated, usually by coercion, to the interests of the state (see Chapter 7).

Capitalism—linking politics to the political economy, it is a system dominated by a (laissez-faire) market economy in which economic actors are generally free from state interference (see Chapter 8).

Collectivism—a doctrine holding that the individual's actions should benefit some kind of collective organization such as the state, a tribe, or the like, rather than the individual.

Communism—based on the theories of Karl Marx, the essential goal of this system is the socialization of societal resources with the state owning land, labor, and capital and using them to promote the equal welfare of all citizens (see Chapters 8 and 15).

Conservatism—a belief in the virtue of preserving traditional values and social institutions and of promoting loyalty to country, reliance on family, and adherence to religion.

Corporatism—a political economy in which there is extensive economic cooperation between an activist state and a few groups that represent major economic actors such as large industry, organized labor, and farmers (see Chapter 8).

Environmentalism—advocacy of the planned management of a natural resource or of the total environment of a particular ecosystem to prevent exploitation, pollution, destruction, or depletion of valuable natural resources.

Fascism—a system in which the unity and harmony of government and society are of central importance and forces that might weaken that unity are repressed; a top leader is usually viewed as the embodiment of the natural will, and all individuals are expected to obey the leader's will.

Feminism—a diverse social movement promoting equal rights and opportunities for women and men in their personal lives, economic activities, and politics; it is also an influential analytic perspective on political science topics from the perspective of feminist theory.

Islamism—guided by a rigid and conservative interpretation of Islam, this "political Islam" encourages active, even violent, opposition against any who undermine its beliefs about the appropriate way of living, both public and private.

(Classical) Liberalism—an emphasis on the primacy of the freedom and rights of the individual, relative to any constraints imposed by the state.

Libertarianism—an extreme version of classical liberalism, advocating the right of individuals to act freely and unconstrained by the state as long as they do not harm other people.

Marxism—a set of ideas based on the writings of Karl Marx, who argued that society is composed of competing classes based on economic power, that class struggle and change are inevitable, and that the desired goal is the equal distribution of welfare in the society (see Chapter 8).

Nationalism—a deep commitment to the advancement of the interests and welfare of the core group (based on location, ethnicity, or some other crucial factor) with which an individual identifies powerfully (see Chapter 5).

Pacifism—a belief that the highest political and social value is peace and the absence of violence.

Socialism—a system committed to utilizing the state, the economy, and public policy to provide a high-quality, relatively equal standard of living for all and, usually, to support democratic political processes (see Chapters 8 and 13).

Totalitarianism—a system in which the state possesses total control over all aspects of people's lives, including their economic, social, political, and personal spheres (see Chapter 7).

Sieg heil! Fascism under Adolf Hitler, with its extreme nationalism, antisocialism, and leader veneration, became one of the most effective and destructive mass mobilization ideologies in modern history. Here, Hitler prepares to speak to 700,000 followers in 1934.

fundamentalists tend to embrace the most rigid and assertive beliefs regarding the interpretation of their holy authorities and the guidelines for their way of life, both personal and public. The political implications of this perspective can include an intolerance for what is viewed as deviant behavior by other Muslims, antagonism among different sects of Islam (e.g., Shi'a and Sunni), and hostility toward those non-Muslims who appear to challenge Islamic rule or to practice other religions within Muslim countries. Most Islamic fundamentalists participate in personal, social, and political activities to further their beliefs. However, a minority of this population (the Islamists) believes it is necessary to engage in violent struggle against those other groups to protect the *Umma*, the community of all Muslims. Some of these Islamists have gained considerable notoriety for their violent actions and terrorism (see Chapter 12), including such groups as al-Qaeda, Hamas, Hezbollah, Islamic State in Iraq and the Levant (ISIL), and the Taliban. The death and suffering associated with communism, fascism, Islamism, and other extreme ideologies during the last 100 years are compelling evidence that political ideologies can be much more than bundles of ideas debated by intellectuals.

Individual Political Beliefs

2.2   **Distinguish cognitive, affective, and evaluative beliefs.**

Types of Political Orientations

Can you describe your thought process when you were asked how you would respond to the issues raised at Burger King? Your reaction might have been determined by fundamental and consistent principles you have about society and government—what has been characterized above as a political ideology. But if you are like most people, your thought processes in reaction to such political phenomena are probably best described in terms of a less structured combination of your factual knowledge, your feelings, and your assessments. These components of your political beliefs are termed cognitive, affective, and evaluative orientations.

Cognitive orientations are *an individual's knowledge about the political world*—what the person believes are political "facts." Cognitive orientations include descriptive knowledge such as: the names of political leaders; the policies supported by particular politicians, political groups, or countries; events in political history; the features of a constitution; or the procedures and actions of a governmental agency. They also include explanatory ideas, such as why the United States' military is in Afghanistan or why the stability of the eurozone is linked to the Greek economy. A person's cognitive orientations might be correct and accurate, or they might be totally wrong. (Recall the survey questions about facts in Compare in 1.)

Affective orientations include *any feelings or emotions evoked in a person by political phenomena.* For example, what (if any) feelings are stimulated in you when you come across the following?

You see someone burning your national flag.

You read about a deadly terrorist attack in an area where you have friends.

You are faced with the option of voting in an election, and you don't like any of the candidates.

You are present at a political demonstration supporting a policy you strongly support.

The nature and intensity of your feelings in reaction to each of these situations are instances of your affective orientations.

Finally, an *evaluative orientation* involves your *synthesis of facts and feelings into a judgment about some political phenomenon.* For example, you might decide whether to vote for a candidate. You might determine whether an individual has a free speech right to make negative comments on the Internet about a racial group. You might assess whether Palestine should be granted full member status in the United Nations General Assembly.

A particular situation might generate a variety of political beliefs. For example, if your government has proposed a policy that restricts the right of a woman to have an abortion, this might stimulate many different thoughts and feelings—your knowledge about the constitutional rights of an individual to freedom of action and of the state to limit those rights; your religious, moral, or scientific beliefs about the status of a fetus; your personal knowledge of the experiences of people who have made decisions about abortions; your emotional response to the idea of abortion; and your judgment of what you conclude should be government policy on abortion. In short, on any topic you can hold a variety of cognitive, affective, and evaluative political beliefs. It is likely that many of the attitudes that you might identify as your fundamental political beliefs are based on evaluative orientations grounded in cognitive and affective orientations.

Identifying Specific Beliefs

When employing the methods and assumptions of empirical political theory, we build our conceptual understanding of political beliefs in several stages. If we want to understand *one* person's political orientations, we might begin by collecting empirical data by means of an interview or questionnaire. A telephone interview was the basis for the data in Table 1.2, for example. There are hundreds of politically relevant questions that enable us to identify some of the specific beliefs that a person holds: Does she know the name of the country's chief executive? How does she react to news that

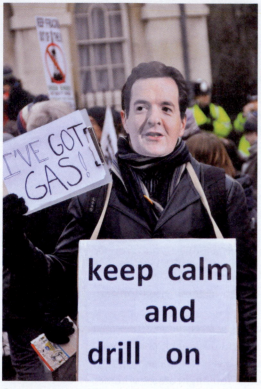

On every issue involving government policy, there are individuals who hold strong political beliefs.

her state's governor has just prevented the execution of a convicted murderer? Does she support the use of foreign troops in Afghanistan?

A similar analytic strategy can be used to determine what *many* people think about a specific issue. When *the attitudes of many people are gathered, aggregated, and summarized,* they constitute the most widely available data about people's political orientations: **public opinion polls** (also known as **survey research**). Almost every day, the media provide data on the percentage of people who hold a certain opinion regarding a political issue. For example, a public opinion poll might report data about how Canadians respond to the question, "On the whole, should your government be responsible to reduce income differences between the rich and poor?" On the basis of this survey research data, you might decide you know what Canadians think about the issue. This information seems to be a stronger basis for a knowledge claim than a discussion with a few Canadian friends or even a statement by a Canadian political leader. Table 2.2 provides examples of the types of political questions that appear on such polls, offering comparative data on the responses from

Table 2.2 Selected Political Beliefs of People in Six Countries*

Country	On the whole, should your government be responsible to reduce income differences between the rich and poor?		How successful is the government in your country in controlling crime?		Suppose your government suspected a terrorist act was about to happen. Do you think the authorities should have the right to stop and search people in the street?		How often do public officials deal fairly with people like you?	
	Definitely	Probably	Very	Quite	Definitely	Probably	Always	Often
Canada	36%	31%	4%	30%	13%	26%	11%	34%
Japan	34	32	2	16	11	36	2	22
Russia	53	33	2	9	6	21	3	10
South Africa	41	43	4	12	30	28	5	21
Sweden	37	31	1	11	26	32	25	36
United States	27	24	5	31	17	24	11	22

*Only the two most positive of the four or five possible responses are indicated in this table, so the totals do not equal 100 percent.

SOURCE: World Values Survey (2006).

Canadians, Japanese, Russians, South Africans, Swedes, and Americans (from a major comparative survey research project conducted by political scientists in more than 80 countries). According to these data, about 67 percent of Canadians say that government should reduce income differences.

Public opinion polls should be interpreted with care. In assessing the information, you should consider questions such as these: Did those who conducted the poll have a bias toward a particular result? Were the questions or the possible responses worded in a way that might distort people's opinions? Did those who responded seem a representative sample of the entire group to whom the opinion is attributed? Are different interpretations of the data possible? Even when the survey researchers are unbiased, there are numerous reasons why their findings might be somewhat inaccurate. For example, there can be errors in their predictions, based on public opinion polls, of how the population will vote in an election. Why might this happen?

Belief Systems

2.3   **Compare belief systems of the mass and the elite.**

Beyond the identification of specific beliefs of individuals, other interesting analyses can focus on the array of their political beliefs. The term **political belief system** refers to *the configuration of an individual's political orientations.* This network of cognitive, affective, and evaluative beliefs serves as a basic framework (also termed an opinion schema), guiding a person as she organizes her existing political knowledge and processes new information to establish a viewpoint on a particular subject (Dalton 2013; Niemi, Weisberg, and Kimball 2011).

To examine a person's belief system, you can ask a series of analytical questions:

1. What is the *content* of the beliefs—that is, the subject matter and the nature of the beliefs?
2. What is the *salience* of the beliefs—that is, the importance or significance the person attaches to the beliefs?
3. What is the level of *complexity* of the beliefs?
4. Is there a *consistency* among subsets of beliefs that suggests a series of general principles from which specific beliefs are derived?
5. How *stable* are the beliefs over time?
6. Do the beliefs *motivate* the person to undertake any political action(s)?

The early empirical research on the nature of belief systems was particularly influenced by the analyses of Philip Converse (1964), who focused on people in the United States. In general, Converse argues that a belief system has two levels of information. One level includes relatively straightforward *facts or opinions* such as a person's opinion about whether American public schools should allow Christian prayer during class time. The second level is *constraint knowledge,* in which more abstract and overarching concepts (such as one's ideological or religious values) operate to shape and link ideas. In the school prayer example, a person might base her opinion on constraint knowledge about the constitutional separation of church and state or about free speech issues.

Studying the beliefs of individual Americans in the 1950s, Converse concluded that only about 15 percent of the population had a sophisticated, "elite belief system" characterized by extensive political knowledge and abstract ideas that were well organized by constraint knowledge. The rest of the population lacked detailed political knowledge, operated with minimal constraint knowledge, and thus had a belief system that lacked coherence. He termed this the belief system of the "mass public." Converse reported that almost half of the U.S. public revealed either a set of "simplistic political beliefs" or "political ignorance."

More recent research has challenged some of Converse's conclusions, particularly the distinction between belief systems of a mass public and an elite. Many empirical studies reveal that the extent of individuals' political knowledge ranges in a more normal curve from the highly informed to the uninformed (Delli Carpini and Keeter 1996). Other studies conclude that even those with a modest level of political knowledge *are* able to fashion reasonable political opinions and make good judgments about politics (Sniderman, Brody, and Tetlock 1993; Zaller 1992). In this view, members of the mass public use simple rules of thumb to make sense of issues, particularly in issue areas that interest them (Dalton 2013; Lupia and McCubbins 1998; see also Chapter 4). Another perspective argues that individuals develop structured ways of thinking about the world but that these ways are not similar for everyone. Thus, if the analyst studies how a particular person structures her thoughts—rather than merely asking questions about specific beliefs—her political attitudes might be generally consistent and coherent within this structure (Rosenberg 1988, 2002).

Despite continuing debate regarding the precise nature of political belief systems across the full range of people, most researchers agree on certain generalizations that are broadly accurate for most people in most countries. Like nearly every generalization about politics, these are subject to many qualifications and some exceptions.

1. Political issues have low salience compared with other concerns in people's lives. Although Aristotle called the citizen *homo politicus,* or "political man," most people do not locate political issues in the center of their interest and attention space.
2. People tend to focus attention on concrete issues and have minimal grasp of the abstract political concepts that serve as constraint knowledge.
3. Interest and knowledge are greater on immediate, short-term issues than on longer-term ones.
4. While people's fundamental beliefs are relatively stable, there can be considerable volatility in their short-term political opinions, which tend to shift when subjected to modest changes in political information. This volatility might be due to limited interest or to the sheer difficulty of trying to understand complicated political questions.

5. Significant inconsistencies can exist across political beliefs, in the sense that a person can hold contradictory positions. For example, an American might express support for the First Amendment right to free speech but deny the right of an Islamic fundamentalist to speak at a public meeting or the right of the Knights of the Ku Klux Klan to hold a public rally in a predominantly African American community.

6. The content of beliefs is often inaccurate. In one survey, for example, half the Americans questioned did not know how many U.S. senators serve their state.

Individuals with more sophisticated belief systems tend to differ on all six of these factors. Their belief systems are generally characterized by high levels of salience, abstraction, breadth, stability, consistency, and accuracy. While they employ constraint knowledge extensively to inform their beliefs, they do not all share the same core beliefs (Higley and Burton 2006). For example, some people might have a coherent system of beliefs that supports the protection of an individual's civil liberties, while other people's constraint knowledge and specific opinions consistently support the right of the government to limit individual liberties substantially in the protection of social order (Sniderman et al. 1991).

While the political beliefs of every person can affect the political world, those who have more sophisticated belief systems are particularly significant. First, the most sophisticated and active political thinkers can influence the views of many others. They absorb and analyze complex events and issues in the political world and then communicate them to a broader audience. This "two-step communication flow" is viewed by some to be crucial in shaping the understandings of many people. Second, many of those with more sophisticated belief systems hold positions of power and authority in society, and thus the actions they take on the basis of their political views can have substantial impact.

Political Culture

2.4   **Determine the extent to which political culture explains political behavior.**

Some analysts attempt to identify broadly shared patterns of political orientations that characterize a large group of people. The objective is to develop generalizations about the political culture of the group. **Political culture** is normally defined as *the configuration of a particular people's political orientations*—that is, the generalized belief system of many. For this reason, political culture is not precisely a topic in micropolitics, but it is examined here because it is embedded in individual-level analyses.

The composition of the group whose political culture is studied depends on the interests of the researcher. It might be the people of a geographic community (e.g., Londoners, English, British, or Europeans) or of a community of shared identity (e.g., Sikhs in the Indian state of Punjab, Sikhs in the Indian subcontinent, or all Sikhs in the world) or of a community of shared meaning (e.g., French Canadians or all French-speaking peoples). Most studies have focused on the political culture of a country or of a major (ethnic or religious) community within a country.

National Character Studies

Some research, generally termed *national character studies*, *attempts to capture the essence of a people's political culture* in terms of broad adjectives (Inkeles 1997). When someone is described as being "soooo French," you might think of her as sophisticated, romantic, and volatile. At one level, we recognize immediately that such a characterization is a stereotype that does not fit the majority of individual subjects. Yet most of us, including people in the political world, use these kinds of labels (at least occasionally) as a shorthand method of describing groups or nations. Indeed, Franklin Delano Roosevelt (U.S. president from 1933 to 1945) observed that "the all-important factor in national greatness is national character."

Some political analysts have tried to specify the national character of a certain country and then to predict or explain the population's political behavior on the basis of such characteristics. Typically, these studies do not claim that everyone fits the national character profile, but they maintain that the profile significantly affects many politically-relevant actions. For example, Jorge Castaneda (2011: xi) analyzes how "the very national character that helped forge Mexico as a nation now dramatically hinders its search for a future and modernity." He defines a bundle of traits that includes a mistrust of others, fear of outsiders, and resistance to change. These combine with an unwillingness to engage in a vigorous debate on current political and economic issues, especially among the more powerful groups in Mexican society. Most importantly, the Mexican national character is dominated by "a premodern individualism" that, he argues, results in a fundamental rejection of collective action and collective solutions that must occur for Mexico to evolve into a vigorous democracy and respond effectively to the challenges of the global economy (Castaneda 2011: 32).

A controversial analysis based on a very broad notion of supranational character is Samuel Huntington's (1998) description of nine global "civilizations." These civilizations are the highest level of cultural identity among humans, with the nine groups differing in history, language, culture, and especially religion. The groups, which are also somewhat regionally based, are African, Buddhist, Confucian, Hindu, Islamic, Japanese, Latin American, Orthodox (Russian), and Western. Huntington predicts that clashes among these civilizations are now the fundamental source of international political conflict and are the most likely cause of the next global war. The Debate in 2 considers Huntington's claims.

Many analysts criticize national character studies as impressionistic and loaded with gross generalizations that greatly oversimplify political reality. Consequently, most scholars dismiss national character studies as caricatures with little capacity to account for the complex actual political behaviors within a country. However, the more thoughtful analyses of national character, based on dominant patterns of beliefs and behaviors, can provide fascinating insights into both the political culture and the political actions taken in a society, and such culture-based explanations are evident in recent research (Moisi 2009; Wiarda 2013).

The Debate in 2

Is There a Clash of Civilizations?

Although national character studies are no longer in vogue, Samuel Huntington's (1998) controversial analysis is based on the concept of broad differences across supranational character types. Huntington defines nine distinct civilizations. He then predicts that tensions and conflict are more likely to occur *among* these nine civilizations rather than within them, and he specifies which civilizations are most opposed. Huntington's claims about the crucial impact of these supranational character groups on current global affairs have been a source of heated debate among policymakers and academics. Is there a clash of civilizations?

A Clash of Civilizations Exists

- There is considerable empirical evidence that fundamental differences exist among civilizations. For example, analyses from the World Values Survey indicate that Muslims and Westerners disagree profoundly on numerous social issues like gender equality and homosexuality (Norris and Inglehart 2012).

- While ideologies and political regimes may change, underlying civilization identities are the product of centuries and will not disappear. Most people can choose to embrace or shed a particular political ideology, but few reject the fundamental ethnoreligious identity of their birth. These broad ethnic and religious identities have a major and growing significance in a global society in which violent conflicts over ideas and resources are unavoidable.

- The empirical evidence also reveals that since the end of World War II, there has been a continual rise in the number of ethnoreligious conflicts within states in which the cleavages are related to the civilizations described by Huntington (Eriksson et al. 2003). Examples include the struggles between: the United States' Western alliance and Muslim groups in Afghanistan, Iraq, and Iran; Tamils (Hindus) and Sinhalese (Buddhists) in Sri Lanka; the Tibetans (Buddhists) and the Chinese; and Israelis (Jews) and regional Muslim groups.

- The humiliation and lack of respect experienced by many in the Islamic culture and the fears of danger and decline experienced by many in the Western culture have resulted in increasing hostilities between these two civilizations, which generally blame each other for these conditions (Moisi 2009).

- As Huntington predicted, there have been particularly extensive and intensive clashes between the Islamic civilization and adjacent civilizations in recent decades, such as Russian Orthodox (Chechnya, Kazakhstan), African (Sudan, Nigeria), Sinic (Western China), and Hindu (India).

- Leaders of many Latin American countries have expressed open opposition to the ideology, policies, and values that guide the United States, as the leader of the Western bloc of developed countries. While major conflict is unlikely, there is clearly a volatile clash between the West and Latin American opinion leaders such as Evo Morales in Bolivia.

There Is No Clash of Civilizations

- Like other discredited national character studies, "civilizations" as an organizing principle vastly oversimplifies reality. Each category collapses countless cultures, languages, and histories (Said 2001). For example, there are substantial differences within the Islamic civilization, like those between Shi'a and Sunni; among Saudi, Indonesian, and Turk; and so on. Such differences are also clear among the many ethnic groups within the African civilization's Congo, Ghana, South Africa, and so on. Overall, there is as much variation *within* each civilization as there is among civilizations.

- The argument of value differences among civilizations on issues like gender ignores the compelling empirical evidence of deep divisions within Western countries; for example, on issues such as gay marriage, abortion, and the need for an equal (gender) rights amendment.

- More broadly, the empirical facts show no evidence of a systemic clash of civilizations. Statistical analyses demonstrate that "pairs of states split across civilizational boundaries are no more likely to become engaged in disputes than are other states" (Russett et al. 2000). Even disputes arising between the West and Islam (a friction point predicted by Huntington) are no more likely than conflicts between any other two states, *ceteris paribus*.

- For civilizations to exist as Huntington describes them, they must resist the penetration and influence of other civilizations. Yet globalization has dramatically increased the penetration across cultures, the convergence in values and behaviors, and the blurring of differences.

- Individuals and thus societies are not solely defined and motivated by their religious and ethnic identities (Sen 2006). National and regional identities that crosscut Huntington's civilizations can also create powerful ties that bind. Indians' national pride, for example, is a strong counterbalance to Hindu–Muslim distinctions within India.

- Stephen Walt (1997) argues that the clash of civilizations argument is merely an attempt by some in the West to build up a new "bogeyman"—to find a new set of enemies after the fall of the Soviet Union and the end of the Cold War. If policymakers behave as if civilizations will inevitably clash, it will provide political leaders on both sides with justifications for certain military and foreign policy actions and might even result in an artificially induced civilizational conflict.

More questions…

1. Which of Huntington's nine civilizations seems most plausible to you? Which seems least plausible?

2. What empirical evidence would you find sufficient to resolve the question of this debate?

Survey Research Analyses

The section above described how survey research is used to gather empirical data about individuals' political beliefs, as in Table 2.2. Thus, a more systematic and scientifically acceptable method for establishing the nature of a political culture is the use of carefully gathered empirical data on individuals' political beliefs and actions. Such *survey research analyses then aggregates these empirical data, searching for patterns or configurations that profile the political culture* of the sample and, by inference, that characterize the political culture of the population from which the sample is taken.

The first major study of this type is *The Civic Culture* by Gabriel Almond and Sidney Verba (1963). Lengthy interviews were conducted with a large sample of citizens in each of five countries. The data were then aggregated and analyzed in diverse ways to provide rich descriptions, as the study contrasted the different political cultures of Italy ("alienated"), Mexico ("alienated but aspiring"), the United States ("participant"), the United Kingdom ("deferential"), and (West) Germany ("detached"). Another of the notable early studies found widespread similarities in the social and political concerns among citizens in many democratic countries. Personal desires for a happy family life, a decent standard of living, and good health were most important, and political concerns centered on fears about war and political instability (Cantril 1965).

The most comprehensive recent comparative surveys of political culture are the World Values Survey (WVS). Ronald Inglehart and collaborating scholars have conducted six "waves" of this survey (in 1981, 1990, 1995, 2000, 2006, and 2014), and the survey now includes individuals from more than 80 countries that contain more than 85 percent of the world's population. Large samples of adults in each country are asked many questions about their opinions regarding politics, societal needs, personal values, and so on. Table 2.2 presented a few examples of the questions on the survey. Do you think the data in Table 2.2 are evidence that there are differences in the citizens' political beliefs across the selected countries? Compare in 2 describes recent research from the WVS that attempts broad crossnational comparisons of political orientations.

Compare in 2

Value Differences across Countries

The World Values Survey is a major attempt to compare social and political values in more than 80 countries. The survey attempts to measure an extensive array of each individual's political orientations. The researchers then aggregate those beliefs for the respondents in each country to specify "people's prevailing value orientations" (Inglehart and Welzel 2005). The result of one of their most ambitious efforts to map the values across countries is shown in Figure 2.1. The responses to numerous questions were combined to create individual-level and then country-level values on two broad dimensions. The *self-expression versus survival* value dimension measures the priority placed on subjective well-being values such as tolerance versus security values. The *secular-rational versus traditional* value dimension reflects how strongly individuals embrace the norms associated with religion, family, and country. Figure 2.1 is one of the comparisons that can be made using the country-level scores on these two dimensions. A brief look at several countries suggests how these collective value scores seem reflected in each country's actual politics. We focus in particular on the issues of homosexuality and obedience to authority, which, according to Inglehart's group, are especially significant reflections of the level of tolerance and propensity to democracy in a society (Norris and Inglehart 2012; Inglehart and Welzel 2005, 2010).

Switzerland's population scores very high on both secular-rational values and self-expression values. The Swiss value personal freedom and independence, with minimal state control over their actions and lives. Theirs is one of the most orderly and nonconflictual societies in the world. It is a wealthy country that has generally avoided many of the economic fluctuations that have plagued many other advanced countries, and most of its citizens enjoy considerable prosperity and have less immediate concerns about economic insecurity. Religion's lack of influence on Switzerland is also a factor regarding the views of the Swiss on individual rights, including homosexuality and divorce. Although some in Switzerland disapprove of homosexuality, the general population is tolerant of the gay community. In fact, Switzerland remains one of the most progressive countries regarding gay rights. Homosexuality was decriminalized as early as 1942, and in 2007 Switzerland began recognizing same-sex partnerships with the Partnership Act. Switzerland actively encourages its gay citizens to reveal their homosexuality with the annual "Coming Out Day."

Uganda, in contrast, has been torn apart by political instability, poverty, and conflict among social groups. These conditions are consistent with a political culture characterized by survival values and a very clear orientation to traditional values. Traditional values and a low level of tolerance are evident in Uganda's approach to gays and lesbians. Since its colonial era, Uganda has outlawed homosexuality and conviction currently carries a 14-year

Figure 2.1 Dimensions of Human Values at the Collective Level

SOURCE: Inglehart and Welzel 2010.

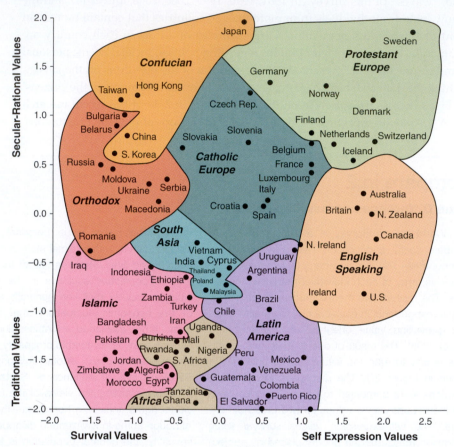

prison sentence. In 2014, a new law specified that certain forms of homosexual behavior are punishable by life imprisonment, a sentence reduced from the death penalty only in response to harsh criticism from the global community. Also, a person can even be imprisoned for counseling gays or lesbians.

In another example, Morocco has a population that generally exhibits strong traditional and survival values. Most Moroccans live in tight-knit extended families and identify strongly with their kin group. The emphasis on obedience and acceptance of authority seems linked both to the power of the hereditary king and a somewhat repressive regime and also to the influence of the Muslim religion over the lives of

most Moroccans. It is perhaps not surprising that the country was not among the first or the second wave of countries in rebellion against their leaders during the "Arab Awakening" that began in the summer of 2011.

In contrast, the citizens of the Czech Republic are particularly high on secular-rational values. Nearly 60 percent of the Czechs report they are atheists—one of the world's highest proportions. Both their break with religion and the harsh experiences under communism from the late 1940s to the late 1980s seem associated with their skepticism regarding those in authority and the value of obedience. While there is some Czech nationalism, their identities are diluted by regional ties and residual links to the Czechoslovakia prior to 1989 as well as their growing identity as Europeans within the EU.

While you might find the blobs of countries in Figure 2.1 a bit odd, the researchers claim that most countries can be grouped, based especially on region and/or religion, into the nine political cultures that are labeled in Figure 2.1 (Inglehart and Welzel 2010). This is an admirable attempt to use solid empirical data to compare the broad value systems of people in many countries. While the analyses are more sweeping than many other studies, most scholars of political behavior conclude that the citizens of different nationality groups have social and political orientations that can be measured and compared.

Further Questions

1. The location of which country in Figure 2.1 most surprises you? Why?

2. Do the clusters in Figure 2.1 make sense to you? Can you suggest a different way to categorize the countries?

3. Where do you think *you* might be located in Figure 2.1?

4. Does the analysis in Figure 2.1 seem to provide any support for Huntington's ideas about a clash of civilizations?

The extensive empirical research on political culture—as it has become more precise in its methods and more cautious about cultural biases—has revealed the considerable variability in political culture within a country, across individuals, among groups, and over time. Chapter 4 will examine some of the factors that might account for differences in the political beliefs of individuals within a society. But it is also evident from the survey research that many countries have a political culture that can be distinguished from the political cultures in some, perhaps most, other countries.

Looking Ahead

Chapter 2 has introduced you to the systematic analysis of political behavior. This chapter has described key topics in the empirical study of political beliefs—what individuals know, feel, and think about politics. Analysis can focus on a single person, a group, or even a culture, and it can assess a single belief or an array of beliefs across many issues. The chapter has also examined normative political theory—the exploration of how individuals, government, and society *should* operate. Normative theory is arguably the oldest subfield in the study of politics, and its perennial questions about the good society and the appropriate role of government remain as intriguing and as contested as they were during the time of Plato.

The next step in the analysis of political behavior is to move our focus from political beliefs to political actions. Thus, Chapter 3 explores the array of political actions in which an individual or group can engage.

Key Concepts

affective orientation, p. 41	Islamism, p. 38	political behavior, p. 27
classical liberalism, p. 33	Marxist–Leninist socialism,	political belief system, p. 43
cognitive orientation, p. 40	p. 36	political culture, p. 45
conservatism, p. 31	micropolitics, p. 27	political ideology, p. 30
democratic socialism, p. 36	national character studies,	public opinion polls, p. 42
empirical political theory, p. 28	p. 46	socialism, p. 35
evaluative orientation, p. 41	normative political theory,	survey research, p. 42
fascism, p. 38	p. 28	welfare state, p. 37

For Further Consideration

1. What are your general beliefs about human nature? Are these beliefs consistent with your most important beliefs about how people ought to behave and do behave politically?

2. What do you think is the most sensible assumption and the most questionable assumption of conservatism? Of classical liberalism? Of socialism?

3. Can you characterize your own political belief system? For example, what are your three to five most salient political beliefs? Do they deal with the same general content area?

4. If you were to analyze the political belief system of another person on the basis of five questions, what questions would you ask?

For Further Reading

Almond, Gabriel, and Sidney Verba. (1963). *The Civic Culture.* **Princeton, NJ: Princeton University Press.** This is a landmark empirical, comparative study of the political cultures of different countries.

Bryson, Valerie. (2003). *Feminist Political Theory: An Introduction.* **2nd ed. New York: Palgrave Macmillan.** This provides an accessible introduction to some of the variations in the complex set of theoretical approaches and debates in this increasingly influential set of perspectives on analyzing politics at all levels.

Carlisle, Rodney, ed. (2005). *Encyclopedia of Politics: The Left and the Right.* **Newbury Park, CA: Sage.** This clever and comprehensive (1,100 pages) two-volume set (the "left" volume examines progressive/socialist thinking and the "right" examines conservative and classical

liberal perspectives) contains more than 450 readable and interesting articles that concentrate on the "isms" and many, many other interesting themes, as elaborated by historical and contemporary thinkers from many parts of the world.

Fromm, Erich, ed. (1965). *Socialist Humanism.* **New York: Doubleday.** Prominent social scientists and political philosophers expound the virtues of socialism.

Griffin, Roger, ed. (1998). *International Fascism: Theories, Causes, and the New Consensus.* **London: Bloomsbury Academic.** A diverse and thorough selection of writings on fascism, by both fascists and antifascists, exploring the strong appeal of this ideology to many individuals and groups during the mid-twentieth century and also at the beginning of the twenty-first century.

Huntington, Samuel P. (1998). *Clash of Civilizations and the Remaking of the World Order*. New York: Simon and Schuster. As described in this chapter (see Debate in 2), the author offers a sweeping and controversial analysis of major cultural groupings at the global level, where identity, especially religious and cultural, is the dominant force shaping both the beliefs and actions of individuals and also the patterns of world politics.

Inglehart, Ronald, and Christian Welzel (2005). *Modernization, Cultural Change and Democracy: The Human Development Sequence*. New York: Cambridge University Press. Building on his important earlier work (Inglehart 1989, 1997), the author and his co-author further develop detailed analyses based on the World Values Survey that characterize the nature of and shifts in political culture across more than 75 countries (see Compare in 2).

Lebow, Richard Ned. (2012). *The Politics and Ethics of Identity: In Search of Ourselves*. New York: Cambridge University Press. An exploration of how an individual establishes personal identity, showing that such identities are fluid and fragmented, and how distinct political orientations emerge that are associated with conservatism, totalitarianism, liberalism and anarchism.

Love, Nancy S., ed. (2010). *Dogmas and Dreams: A Reader in Modern Political Ideologies*. 4th ed. Washington, DC: CQ Press. A solid reader that includes important writings by many key theorists of the three major "isms" as well as others including anarchism, fascism, and feminism.

Mayer, Lawrence, and Erol Kaymak. (1998). *The Crisis of Conservatism and the Rise of the New Right in Western Democracies: Populist Revolt in the Late Twentieth Century*. Armonk, NY: M. E. Sharpe. An interesting exploration of the activities of ideologically driven and rather alienated populist groups that have their roots in traditional conservatism but have diverged

substantially from it in both their attitudes and their political styles.

McLellan, David, ed. (2007). *Marxism after Marx*. 4th ed. New York: Palgrave. An excellent set of readings exploring the many versions of Marxism that have continued to wield great significance in the field of political theory.

Moisi, Dominique. (2009). *The Geopolitics of Emotion: How Fear, Humiliation and Hope are Reshaping the World*. New York: Random House. In a variation on the clash of civilizations perspective, Moisi argues that there are broad, regionally based cultures that differ. He claims that the driving emotion of the Western cultures is fear, of the Islamic cultures is humiliation, and of the Asian cultures is hope, and that the evolution and interplay of these patterns will have critical impacts on global society.

Murray, Charles. (1997). *What It Means to Be a Libertarian*. New York: Broadway Books. A brief, readable application of libertarian ideology to many contemporary issues (e.g., abortion, education, drugs, economic regulation, free speech), written by one of America's most controversial social critics.

Nisbet, Robert. (2001). *Conservatism: Dream and Reality*. Piscataway, NJ: Transaction. A short, illuminating discussion that traces the development of conservative thought and its significance in contemporary politics.

Putnam, Robert D. (1993). *Making Democracy Work: Civic Traditions in Modern Italy*. Princeton, NJ: Princeton University Press. Using communities in northern and southern Italy as his cases, the author develops a significant and widely cited argument about the role of political culture in sustaining democracy, and especially about the crucial importance of "social capital"—the citizens' willingness to engage and interact with each other.

Ryan, Alan. (2012). *On Politics: A History of Political Thought: From Herodotus to the Present*. New York: Liveright. A long (1, 150 page) but readable and exceptional exploration of the great political thinkers and the continuing importance and insights they provide.

Sabet, Amr G. E. (2008). *Islam and the Political: Theory, Governance and International Relations*. **London: Pluto Press.** A serious attempt to explore ideas such as development, human rights, and democracy from the perspective of Islam and to compare those views to political theories dominant in Europe and the United States.

Tucker, Robert, ed. (1978). *The Marx–Engels Reader*. **2nd ed. New York: Norton.** An extensive selection of the important writings, with commentaries, from the major theorists of revolutionary socialism, Karl Marx and Friedrich Engels.

On the Web

http://www.nationalgeographic.com
National Geographic has offered rich information and photographs from locations around the world for nearly a century. Some of this material is informative about culture and society in many places, including insights about political culture.

http://www.americanprogress.org/issues/2009/03/progressive_quiz.html
One of several Web sites where you can respond to a series of questions about your political beliefs and receive an analysis of your political ideology. Try it!

http://turnabout.ath.cx:8000
This site offers an interesting, quirky, and very diverse array of links to materials associated with "traditionalist conservatism worldwide." Links range across political perspectives from various countries, from conservatism in many of the world's religions to extreme-right fringe groups.

http://www.intellectualtakeout.com
This site promotes individual freedom and limited government and targets college students.

http://www.libertarianism.com
This portal for the libertarian belief system provides clear policy positions and many sources guided by this ideology.

http://internationalsocialist.org
The site of the International Socialist Organization, an association promulgating the Marxist–Leninist perspective, and publisher of the *Socialist Worker* newspaper and the *International Socialist Review* journal.

http://socialistinternational.org
The site of the international democratic socialist movement, it contains information about the people, ideas, and events important to the movement.

http://www.keele.ac.uk/depts/por/ptbase.htm
This rich website hosted by Keele University in England provides many links to key political theorists and political theories.

http://www.independent.org
The Independent Institute, a libertarian organization, provides access to a comprehensive list of various online opinion articles, policy analyses, and book reviews tied to political ideology.

http://www.fordham.edu/halsall/mod/modsbook.html
The Internet Modern History Sourcebook includes numerous links related to important works on major political philosophies as well as key historical documents.

http://www.liberal-international.org
This Web site serves as the electronic home of Liberal International, a worldwide federation of liberal and progressive political parties.

http://www.feminist.com
Feminist.com is an online community designed to promote feminism and women's rights. The site contains a number of articles and speeches related to feminist thought.

Chapter 3
Political Actions

Learning Objectives

3.1 Classify the modes of conventional and less conventional individual political action.

3.2 Distinguish between interest groups and political parties.

3.3 Summarize interest group strategies.

3.4 Identify the types of interest groups and the constraints under which they operate.

3.5 Analyze the roles of political parties.

Imagine that you are walking in a crowd of peaceful protesters. Your group is asking for the basic political right to vote for the candidate of your choice for national office. Ahead of you is a line of heavily armed troops who are blocking your march. Although you are engaged in a nonviolent protest, you know that brutal force has been used against groups like yours in similar situations. What is *your* next step?

In this politically charged instant, one tiny woman moves forward. She walks alone up to the armed troops who aim their weapons directly at her and warn they will shoot. But no one fires or seizes her, and she walks through the troops. You and the others are emboldened to follow her. Do you step forward now?

In a country with a repressive and abusive military regime, one person stands tall, although she is only 5 feet 4 inches and weighs less than 100 pounds. Aung San Suu Kyi is a powerful voice for human rights and democratic freedom in Myanmar (some, including the United States, still call it Burma), a country of 56 million in Southeast Asia. This woman has been classified as a national security threat by the military junta that has controlled the government of Myanmar since 1962. How can one woman stir up so much anxiety within a military leadership that seems all-powerful and uses extensive violence to subjugate its citizens?

Suu Kyi's first major public speech occurred in 1988 when she addressed nearly 500,000 protesting citizens who had begun a prodemocracy movement that year. Thousands of students participated in these protests, and many citizens risked their

Fearless activist. Aung San Suu Kyi has consistently been a strong voice promoting democracy and opposing the repressive regime in Myanmar. Here, she addresses a rally shortly before one of her lengthy periods under house arrest.

jobs and personal security to join her party, the National League for Democracy. When the party won control of the legislature in a 1990 election, Suu Kyi was designated as the prime minister–elect. However, the military dictatorship refused to turn over power to her and the democratically elected representatives. Suu Kyi was awarded the 1991 Nobel Peace Prize for her efforts, although the government would not allow her to travel from Myanmar to accept it.

To intimidate and weaken the members of the opposition movement, the military placed Suu Kyi under house arrest. For 16 of 21 years, she was confined to her own house and prevented from making public speeches or meeting other political leaders. Suu Kyi has been attacked by a mob of government goons and accused of tax evasion, leading to brief imprisonment. But she refused to give up the struggle for political and human rights. Even the prime minister was arrested in 2004 after proposing a "road map to democracy" and allowing Suu Kyi to speak in public.

Many citizens in Myanmar lived quietly, intimidated by the ruthless actions of the military, and hoped to go unnoticed. But some did engage in courageous actions. The Karen people, an ethnic minority, have resisted violently for 60 years, demanding autonomy in eastern Myanmar. Opposition politicians speak out for change and call for fair elections. Massive demonstrations for democracy were held again throughout the country in 2007, drawing more than 100,000 peaceful protesters, which included large numbers of Buddhist monks. The government responded with troops who arrested, beat, and bullied those who were demonstrating, even raiding pagodas to arrest monks. Some protesters were sentenced to 65 years in prison. In response to the continuing resistance and international pressure, the regime finally began to open the political system in 2010. Thousands of political prisoners were freed and legislative elections were held in 2012 with multiple parties competing. Suu Kyi was elected to the legislature and now leads the major opposition party group in government.

Most political actions by individuals and groups have complicated and complex motivations. The political actions of the military junta, Aung Sun Suu Kyi, and other prodemocracy protesters in Myanmar are prime examples of attempts to control or shape agendas and events in a society. If you were a citizen of Myanmar, would you have the commitment and courage to stand up against a repressive system? More realistically, have you taken *any* meaningful political actions within the last year? What is the most risky political action you have ever taken?

In Chapter 2, we began our analysis of political behavior by examining the political beliefs of individuals and groups. The next step in our understanding of political behavior is to consider what people *do* politically—not merely what they think. For those people opposed to the regime in Myanmar, political beliefs must be converted into action before they will have any meaningful effect. And in the discussion at Burger King described at the beginning of Chapter 2, the most relevant questions from the perspective of the political world, even more than what you knew or what you thought, are: What did you *say*? What did you *do*?

In this chapter, we examine **political participation**—*all of the political actions by individuals and groups.* The explicit objective of most political participation is *to influence the actions or selection of political rulers*. We focus on the prominent modes of actual political behavior in which people engage, and we consider groups as well as individuals because many individuals, such as Aung San Suu Kyi, realize that they can be more effective politically if they act with others rather than alone. Thus, instead of engaging in a lone act of protest, a person could join a huge demonstration; instead of writing a letter requesting a change in public policy, a person could join an organization that speaks for thousands of people.

What is the range of behaviors that a person might undertake in the political world? At one extreme are people who are obsessed with politics, see political implications in most of life's actions, are constantly involved in political discussion and action, and want to make political decisions for others. At the other extreme are people who have absolutely no interest in politics, pay no attention to political phenomena, and engage in no politically relevant actions. (In some instances, such as not voting in an election to indicate dissatisfaction, not doing something can also be a type of political participation.)

In the first half of this chapter, we examine this full range of individual political actions. In the second half, we analyze the nature and activities of two major forms of political groups: interest groups and political parties. Both individuals and groups share some modes of activity, but the actions of groups can also be analyzed in some additional dimensions because of their size and structure.

Individual Political Actions

3.1 **Classify the modes of conventional and less conventional individual political action.**

Modes of Political Activity

There are various ways to classify the modes of individual political action. Empirical studies of political participation consider both the more conventional forms of activity, such as voting, campaigning, contacting officials, and participating in civic groups, and the less conventional actions, such as protesting and even terrorism (Dalton 2013; Verba, Nie, and Kim 1978).

Figure 3.1 classifies the modes of individual political action in terms of two dimensions. The first (vertical) dimension reflects the extent to which the individual engages in the political action, ranging from never to occasional to frequent to pervasive engagement. The second (horizontal) dimension considers the extent to which the political action is more or less conventional. While there are differences in what various people would consider conventional, there is clearly variation across an array of actions. Figure 3.1 suggests labels for those associated with certain domains of political actions. At the four extremes (corners) are those who are totally apathetic about politics, those who have made a full-time vocation of politics as elected officials, those revolutionaries who are passionately committed to transforming the existing political system, and those who are provoked into a rare but highly unconventional action. While we will explore some of these types of political actors and actions throughout this book, we can characterize a few of the main types here. Although most individuals can be labeled by their dominant activity, a particular individual might operate in different action domains at various times (Dalton 2013; Schlozman, Verba, and Brady

Figure 3.1 Some Modes of Individual Political Action

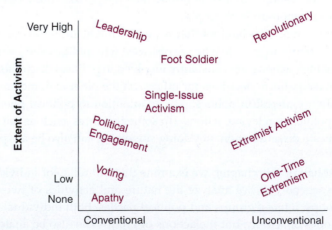

2013). For example, an elected official will almost certainly vote, while a revolutionary might vote; and a conventional voter might at some point be mobilized to participate in an unconventional action such as a violent demonstration.

The categories in Figure 3.1 are elements of a *taxonomy*. When you attempt to classify units by some criteria, you are engaged in **taxonomic analysis** (as discussed in the Appendix). Recall Aristotle's comment that all thinking begins in comparison. In political science, many comparisons begin in taxonomies. Developing a taxonomy is often the first stage in political analysis because it sorts cases into a small number of groups to reduce complexity, facilitate comparative analysis, and aid the development of generalizations. Because the categories in a strong taxonomy do not overlap, Figure 3.1 is only a loose taxonomy. You will find numerous taxonomies in this book (e.g., the types of party systems, democracies versus nondemocracies, the Global North and Global South). No single taxonomy is used in all political analyses because each taxonomy emphasizes different aspects of the political world. It will be your decision whether any particular taxonomy seems useful.

Political Activists

Although the more routine modes of political action (listed in the middle and bottom of the left side of Figure 3.1) constitute the vast majority of actual political behavior, many of us are particularly interested in the extraordinary actions of the *political activists, who seem to "live politics."* Political activists might hold government office, or spend many hours furthering a political goal or leader, or even risk their freedom and life in the pursuit of a political objective. At least four different types of political activists can be identified: foot soldiers, single-issue activists, extremist-activists, and political leaders.

FOOT SOLDIERS *Foot soldiers* are *activists who do the basic work of politics.* They link the masses to the government and the top political leadership by performing tasks such as communicating with citizens to promote an issue or a political leader, volunteering in a campaign, or regularly attending political rallies. In most countries, many foot soldiers are members of political parties or groups with a political mission. Most political organizations could not function effectively without foot soldiers.

SINGLE-ISSUE ACTIVISTS Another group of political actors engage in political behavior more sporadically than foot soldiers. These people normally do not participate very actively in the political world, but an issue emerges that mobilizes them into a period of high-level action. For example, some residents in a neighborhood might become agitated when they oppose a plan for a new development that will have negative impacts on their community. They might spearhead a petition drive or organize a disruptive activity such as picketing or a protest march. The new social media, such as the Internet, Facebook, and the blogosphere, have provided individuals with an extraordinarily rich new array of tools for engaging in political activism, enabling them to communicate their viewpoints and network with others who share their interests (Loader and Mercea 2012). Also, people who are dissatisfied with the existing leaders or regime gather in public spaces for what are initially peaceful protests. However, if the regime responds with repression rather than policy change, these individuals can become more mobilized and more aggressive in their demands and their own actions, transforming them into political activists. In recent years, these "people power" movements, primarily composed of individuals who normally engage only in very conventional political behaviors, have become more frequent. As in the Myanmar example, many individuals in such countries as Egypt, Peru, Syria, Tunisia, and Ukraine have recently "taken it to the streets" in modes of political action that, for most of them, are exceptional. Such actions often last for only a short period, and then most return to more conventional modes of political action.

EXTREMIST-ACTIVISTS *Extremist-activists* are *those who are willing to engage in extensive, unconventional political action in pursuit of their vision of an ideal political outcome* that is substantially different from the existing situation. "Extremism" is a subjective and relative concept—a person is politically extreme only in comparison with some standard position, typically the broad center of the existing political order. Like foot soldiers and single-issue activists, extremist-activists might participate in conventional political activities. However, what distinguishes them is their willingness to engage in very intensive modes of unconventional political action and to sustain their actions over a long period of time. Some individuals can be classified as extremist-activists if their political goals or tactics locate them on the margins of the existing political culture. For example, members of the Earth Liberation Front are linked to violent acts promoting environmentalism in almost 20 countries. Another example is the Libyans who mobilized to fight for the overthrow of Muammar Gadaffi—during their armed insurrection, fewer than 1,000 of the thousands who fought Gadaffi's regime had ever fired a weapon before they participated in the armed rebellion.

Political analysts have focused considerable attention on individual extremist-activists who are the most unconventional and fully engaged: the revolutionaries. A *revolutionary* is a person who attempts to overthrow the existing political order and to replace it with a very different one, using political violence if necessary (see Chapter 12). Some well-known revolutionaries, such as Mao Zedong (China), Fidel Castro (Cuba), Ayatollah Khomeini (Iran), and Nelson Mandela (South Africa), eventually attained leadership roles in their political system after years or even decades of struggle. Others, including Che Guevara (Cuba, then Bolivia) and Steve Biko (South Africa), died in the struggle and became martyrs to those committed to revolutionary change. (Two other examples are featured in Compare in 4.)

Many extremist-activists are radical versions of foot soldiers, serving as the members of organizations such as the Revolutionary Armed Forces of Columbia (FARC); the worldwide al-Qaeda ("the Base") network; and ETA, the Basque separatist group in Spain and France. But an increasing proportion of the extremist-activists operate as members of small, relatively independent groups, and occasionally as a "lone wolf" extremist who acts almost completely alone (Sageman 2008). There is strong contemporary interest in extremist-activists who are willing to use *any* tactics and *any* level of violence to achieve their goals. These individuals are often labeled as terrorists because of their extreme tactics, particularly their willingness to direct violence against those who are not actively engaged in political struggle (for more details, see Chapters 4 and 12). Most extremist-activists operate in relative obscurity. Eventually, they burn out and drop out, are captured by the state, or die as a result of political violence.

POLITICAL LEADERS Many of us are fascinated with ultimate political activists such as Angela Merkel, Robert Mugabe, Barack Obama, and Vladimir Putin. These top political leaders are distinctive because they suc-

A youthful and charismatic Enrique Peña Nieto campaigns successfully for a Mexican state governorship in 2004. He was elected President, Mexico's top leadership position, in 2012.

ceed in capturing supreme political power within a government and using it with extraordinary energy and effect (whether good or bad). Their titles vary by country and level of government and include chairman, chancellor, dictator, governor, king, mayor, president, prime minister, and supreme leader, among others. A top political leader might put his substantial political power and position to admirable purposes, might implement reprehensible policies, or might accomplish almost nothing. These political leaders have been the subject of more descriptions, analyses, and evaluations than any other type of actors in the political world. They will frequently be the subjects in this book.

Political Participation Studies

After categories of political action are established, a basic research question is: How many people participate in each category, both within and across various national political contexts?

The most reliable comparative empirical data on political participation across many countries measure voting in national elections. Table 3.1 provides these data for selected countries. A striking observation about these figures is the huge variation in voting levels, ranging from a reported 99 percent in Vietnam to only 29 percent in Nigeria. Notice the very high voter turnout in countries such as Vietnam and Cuba. In such countries, voting is primarily a symbolic act that is supposed to express support for the existing political leadership, not an action in which citizens select their leaders. In some countries, voting is mandatory (e.g., Australia, Singapore, and Uruguay). In some, those in power either engage in election fraud to ensure victory (Afghanistan, Zimbabwe) or repudiate the vote if the outcome is not favorable (as in Myanmar when Aung San Suu Kyi won in 1990). These variations in voting alert us to a general

Table 3.1 Voting Participation in Selected Countries: Percentage of Eligible Adults Voting in Most Recent National Legislative Election

Percentage Turnout	Countries
95–100	Vietnam
90–94	Australia, Cuba, Singapore, Uruguay
85–89	Denmark, Turkey
80–84	Brazil, France, Ghana, Malaysia, Sweden
75–79	Argentina, Italy, Myanmar, Palestine (territory), Taiwan
70–74	Belarus, Germany, South Africa
65–69	Cambodia, Costa Rica, Finland, India, Indonesia, Israel, Mongolia, Spain, United Kingdom, United States
60–64	Canada, Egypt, Hungary, Iran, Iraq, Mexico, Philippines, Russia
55–59	France, Japan, Portugal, Uganda, Ukraine
50–54	Bangladesh, Pakistan, South Korea, Syria
45–49	Chile, Morocco, Poland, Switzerland
40–44	Algeria, Colombia, Romania, Zimbabwe
35–39	
30–34	
25–29	Nigeria
0-24	

SOURCE: *International Institute for Democracy and Electoral Assistance,* www.idea.int/vt

problem in crossnational analyses of individual-level political data—the same action or belief might have quite different meaning and significance in different settings.

It is even more difficult to do empirical, crossnational comparisons for modes of individual political participation other than voting. The same act can vary in meaning in different political and cultural environments. For example, the significance and potential personal risk of a public political protest are far greater for a person in North Korea than in South Korea and greater in both those countries than for someone in Sweden.

The most consistent finding in recent comparative research on participation is clear: Apart from voting, which *is* a political act done by many/most citizens, high levels of persistent political activity tend to be uncommon in most political systems. Research reveals that political activists who engage in a high level of the more demanding forms of political action such as top leadership, protest, or extensive partisan political work make up less than 10 percent of the population (and in many countries, considerably less) (Dalton 2013; World Values Survey 2006). In contrast to these political "gladiators," even in an open democracy like the United States, about one-fifth of the adult population engages in no political activity and another one-fifth does little more than vote (Verba, Schlozman, and Brady 1995: 50–54, 72–74).

A second broad finding is that some citizens are willing to engage occasionally in more activist modes of political participation. While very few citizens participate in violent protests against people or property, there is evidence that a significant number of people do perform certain less conventional political acts, including some actions that require considerable effort or risk. For example, in about half of the countries for which World Values Survey (2006) data are available, 15 percent or more of the citizens have engaged in at least one "challenging act" (e.g., a lawful demonstration, boycott, or building occupation). Compare in 3 and Table 3.2 examine the levels at which the citizens of 10 countries engage in a range of more and less conventional forms of political participation. The empirical evidence is still unclear on whether the new communications technologies, such as social media, have drawn new individuals into political activity in democratic countries (Anduiza, Jensen, and Jorba 2012; Loader and Mercea 2012).

Although systematic, comparative data on less democratic and nondemocratic countries are limited, it seems that the reliance on nongovernmental channels and the incidence of unconventional political behavior are greater (and vary more substantially) in those countries than in democratic systems. In some less democratic countries, state repression deters the great majority of citizens from participation. And there are also countries characterized by "de-participation" because the political leadership has weakened or even eliminated the mechanisms that enable citizens to engage in political actions (Nelson 1987: 116–120). However, the dramatic expansion of new media and social networking capacities noted above have introduced a new avenue for political participation and lowered the costs of organizing group activities,

Table 3.2 Recent Political Actions by Citizens in 10 Countries

Country (Number of Respondents)	Discuss Politics Often	Often Attempt to Convince Friends on Political Issues	Contact a Politician or Civil Servant to Express Views*	Donate Money to Politician or Issue*	Boycott or "Buycott" Products for Political or Ethical Reasons*	Attend Political Meeting or Rally*	Took Part in a Demonstration*
Brazil (2,000)	8.0%	17.3%	3.7%	2.3%	3.2%	7.3%	3.6%
Canada (1,211)	10.7	6.7	19.0	27.5	32.4	11.2	5.6
Chile (1,505)	7.0	5.5	6.1	17.0	3.2	2.5	2.9
Mexico (1,201)	10.4	11.3	10.6	23.3	8.5	12.6	7.4
Philippines (1,200)	11.3	9.8	6.5	3.5	2.4	14.3	3.0
Poland (1,277)	9.0	6.3	2.5	12.2	3.0	1.0	0.8
Russia (1,789)	13.0	8.1	3.7	3.9	3.0	3.3	2.8
South Africa (2,784)	5.0	4.5	3.0	5.2	2.8	10.9	4.0
Sweden (1,295)	9.6	7.4	7.2	24.6	36.1	8.2	6.7
United States (1,472)	15.6	12.3	21.9	30.8	24.1	12.5	5.3

*Respondent reports behavior within the last 12 months.

SOURCE: International Social Survey Programme (2004).

Compare in 3

Extent of Political Actions in Mexico and Poland

An individual might engage in a variety of political actions, and Figure 3.1 suggests that these actions range in frequency and conventionality. How much do individuals engage in various political actions? Are there differences in levels of participation across different countries? Table 3.2 presents comparative data on such questions from the International Social Survey Programme, in which 1,200–2,800 individuals in each of 37 countries reported their recent political actions to survey researchers. What observations do you think are supported by the data? Let's briefly assess the political actions of people in Mexico and Poland.

The proportion of individuals engaging in politics in Mexico is greater than the proportion in Poland for every type of political action in the table. Compared to the Poles, Mexicans are 9 times more likely to take part in a political demonstration, 12 times more likely to attend a political rally, and 4 times more likely to contact a politician to express their views. Voter turnout is higher in Mexico (Table 3.1). It seems clear that Mexicans engage in political actions at substantially higher levels than Poles. Why do you think this is? While the data in the table cannot explain differences, might this be a reflection of the countries' recent histories?

Even before the Mexican Revolution that began in 1910, Mexicans had a history of political uprisings against their rulers. In the years following 1910, there was a complex set of armed struggles for control of the government. Under activist leaders such as Pancho Villa and Emiliano Zapata, ordinary citizens were encouraged to take part in demonstrations and political violence, with a promise of social and economic justice. Political action was widespread, with civil war and force replacing six governments in just the period from 1911 to 1928. These uprisings mobilized diverse social classes from both rural and urban areas. The ideas of resistance and revolution became a powerful part of most Mexicans' understandings about governance. Indeed, the dominant political party for seven decades—and still a major party—is called the Institutional *Revolutionary* Party

(PRI), and the other two major parties are called the Party of the Democratic *Revolution* (PRD) and the National *Action* Party (PAN).

While Poland also had a tradition of regime change in the twentieth century, the situation is different from Mexico. Despite recurrent resistance movements, most Polish regimes were established by outside powers that, especially after 1930, did not allow the Poles much freedom of political action or dissent. The borders of Poland were drawn by the great powers after World War I and substantially redrawn by the victors of World War II. Germany and Russia (and then the Soviet Union) were particularly repressive in controlling the Polish government's policies and ensuring that any serious political opposition by citizens was crushed. After the Communists took control in 1944, political dissent and any forms of antigovernment activism were dealt with harshly by the Polish regime. There was a notable three-day protest in Poznan in 1956, but it was quickly crushed by authorities, with support from the Soviet Union. When an independent trade union movement (Solidarity) emerged, martial law was declared in 1981, thousands were jailed, and the extent of activism was limited considerably. In general, the citizens' calculus for anti-regime activism through this period was high costs with minimal benefits.

As noted above, these data cannot prove the reasons for higher or lower levels of participation. However, it is notable that the three countries in Table 3.2 that seem least participatory (Russia, South Africa, and Poland) all have recent histories as highly repressive regimes that ruthlessly punished political dissent. In contrast, the three countries that seem the most participatory (United States, Canada, and Mexico) all have a strong tradition of rebellion, protests, and activism. It is also interesting that the data suggest that Americans are more politically active than might be expected from recent discussions of the low level of political participation in the United States. The United States is one of the top three countries on the level of participation for six of the seven modes of political activity in Table 3.2. These data about the United States recall a conclusion in the classic book, *The Civic Culture* (Almond and Verba 1963), which termed the United States the most "participatory political culture" in the study.

Like many studies using comparative political data, the data in Table 3.2 can be analyzed in different ways and can lead to somewhat different knowledge claims. For example, Table 3.2 only reports those who *often* discuss politics, but it might also consider those who occasionally discuss politics. In another example, the table focuses on a single year instead of several years or another year in which the political dynamics in certain countries might be different. Also, might the crossnational differences be greater or smaller if other countries were selected for

analysis? The analyst makes a variety of decisions about how data like these are selected, presented, and interpreted. This does not mean that the data can be manipulated to produce any conclusion you want, but it should caution you that it is important to evaluate the data and consider multiple alternative interpretations.

Further Questions

1. Do the data in Table 3.2 seem to support the generalization that most people in these countries are *not* very active in politics?

2. What types of political actions seem to be the best measures of the level of political participation by average citizens?

even in countries with more repressive regimes (Siegal 2011). In recent years, a combination of encouragement from the actions in other countries, use of social networking technologies, and coverage by global media has increased the willingness of individuals to join in public protests against unpopular regimes, leaders, and policies (Schmidt and Cohen 2010). From Egypt, Tunisia, and Libya to China and Brazil, social networks like Facebook have allowed individuals to become aware of, and thereby choose to participate in, protests and other activities even when state-run media have attempted to hide these citizen-level activities.

Group Political Actions

3.2 **Distinguish between interest groups and political parties.**

The actions of Aung San Suu Kyi offer a compelling example of the impact that one extraordinary person can have on the political world. However, even this totally dedicated political activist understood that there is power in numbers. Thus, she worked with many other citizens to establish and build the National League for Democracy, a movement that steadily gained supporters and organized into a political party that stands up against the military dictatorship. College students and Buddhist monks have been among the other individuals in Myanmar demanding change, emboldened by the willingness of their peers to join them in the streets. In almost every situation, a political agenda is furthered most effectively when many people form a group.

As an analytic concept, a *group* can be defined as *an aggregation of individuals who interact in order to pursue a common interest* (see also Chapter 9). It is the pursuit of a common interest that is most crucial to this definition because the individuals do not necessarily interact directly with one another. The factor that distinguishes a *political interest group* from other groups is that *the common interest the group pursues is a political objective*—an interest in a particular area of public policy where action might be taken. A political interest group can be any coalition that forms and interacts politically. The members of a political interest group might agree on an action even if they disagree about why they choose that action. For instance, a group which advocates that government should purchase and distribute food to the poor might be made up not only of people who are concerned about the well-being of the poor but also of people who want to promote the economic benefits to farmers and others in the agricultural sector.

A distinction is usually made between political interest groups and political parties, although both types fit our general definition of political group. A political group enters the special category of *political party* when the group seeks not only to influence political decisions but also to place its members in the actual roles of government such as chief executives and legislators. Although this distinction can become rather fuzzy among the most politically active groups, we shall treat political parties as a category different from other types of political interest groups. Winning elections, building the party, and actually altering policy may be among the cluster of goals of a political party; but a political party may also have more modest goals like bringing a topic into the public agenda or a broad goal such as challenging the existing power structure.

Most people tend to feel that they are relatively powerless in politics when acting alone. But if a person joins with many others in a political group, it is possible that the group can exercise influence in the political world because of the group's numbers, organization, and capabilities. This chapter has provided examples of the impacts on a country's politics when many individuals join in unconventional political behavior, as in the recent populist uprisings in Egypt and Syria. And extremist groups, such as ISIL, might have few members but can generate major effects as they pursue extensive, radical agendas. Group political action in more conventional modes can also have significant consequences. The mobilization of individuals into the Tea Party movement in the United States has enabled this loosely structured array of groups to use the ballot box to elect many new members to national and state office and to pressure many elected officials to shift their policy positions in the directions advocated by the movement.

Groups are also extremely important in politics because they are often the major mechanism through which individuals are linked to the political system—hence their label as "linkage institutions." Some political groups, such as Mothers Against Drunk Driving (MADD) or the German Farmers Association, are narrowly focused in their objectives and have limited membership. Other groups, such as a major political party like Myanmar's National League for Democracy, have wide-ranging goals and a huge membership. The rest of this chapter describes the nature and activities of various kinds of political groups and political parties.

Political Interest Groups

3.3 **Summarize interest group strategies.**

Activities of Political Interest Groups

All political interest groups share the common objective of attempting to influence the allocation of public values. But such groups can employ a variety of strategies to achieve this purpose (Cigler and Loomis 2013; Grossman 2012).

POLITICAL ACTION The most direct methods to achieve political objectives involve some form of political action. Such action might be taken by all group members or by some members who formally or informally represent the entire group. Depending on the political system, this might entail voting and campaign activities to influence the selection and action of political authorities. Or the group might attempt to communicate its interest to political actors by techniques such as letters, personal contacts, petitions, rallies, or political violence. Groups often raise money from their members or provide other resources, like volunteers, to help politicians who support their causes.

PROVISION OF MATERIAL RESOURCES Political interest groups can also provide goods or services to political actors. Such a strategy assumes that providing goods and services will influence decision makers to be more favorably disposed toward the interests of a group or that providing goods and services to policymakers who share the values of the group makes it more likely those values will be taken into account as policy is made. Each political system develops its own rules about the amounts of money or goods that can be given legitimately to political actors and the legal methods for giving these resources. The line between legal and illegal provision of money and goods varies dramatically across political cultures. In some political systems, all it takes to shock people is the revelation that an interest group has given a political actor a small gift, but in many political systems, it requires a multimillion-dollar kickback to a politician to upset citizens and provoke action. In other words, what might be judged an improper act of bribery in one political system might be an expected and perfectly acceptable payment in others.

In most countries where there is some transparency in political contributions by private groups, the amount of money involved is substantial. From 2008 to 2013, for example, interest groups spent $19.4 billion on direct lobbying of government officials and candidates in the United States (Center for Responsive Politics 2013). Most such contributions are legal, although some are problematic; for example, in 1997 the Democratic Party returned more than $1 million to questionable donors, and President Clinton was widely criticized for "renting the Lincoln Bedroom" for overnight visits in the White House by big contributors. In South Korea, it is estimated that legislative candidates in contested seats spend 10 times more money on their campaigns than is allowable under the law (Plasser 2002: 149).

The ethics of a system in which political interest groups can make huge contributions is increasingly questioned. It is obvious that interest groups give money in the expectation of influencing public policies. Although cause-and-effect relationships are hard to establish, there are striking linkages between groups' campaign contributions and beneficial legislation (Phillips 2003). In the 1996 election in the United States, for example, tobacco companies contributed $11.3 million; soon after, legislation was passed directing a 15-cent-per-pack cigarette tax to a fund offsetting lawsuits—a $50 billion benefit to the tobacco companies. The broadcasting industry contributed $5 million to members of Congress and soon gained digital TV licensing rights worth $70 billion (Parenti 2010: 200–203). Oil, energy, and natural resource firms contributed $18.3 million and then gained $18 billion in exemptions from the passage of an alternative minimum tax law (O'Connor and Sabato 2007: Figure 16.3).

No one knows the amount of illegal resources that are distributed, although in most countries, scandals regarding bribes and kickbacks seem to be reported with increasing frequency (Johnson 2006). In 2007, for example, former Philippine president Joseph Estrada was found guilty of taking more than $85 million in bribes during his presidency. Among other recent top leaders linked to corruption are Alberto Fujimori, former president of Peru, in prison for (among other crimes) embezzling $600 million, and Hosni Mubarak, former president of Egypt, accused of accumulating as much as $30 billion in illegal wealth during his administration. Evidence surfaced that Samsung executives distributed $205 million in payoffs to South Korean government officials and journalists in 2008 (Bloomberg.com 2009). Halliburton executives were imprisoned for paying more than $180 million in bribes to Nigerian officials for oil and gas contracts (U.S. Department of Justice 2008). As China's president declared a war on corruption, powerful politician Bo Xilai was given a life sentence in 2013 for accepting bribes and embezzling millions of dollars of state funds. One estimate reports that the total annual cost of corruption in China is more than $800 billion (Hayoun 2013). This is not a new phenomenon. Indeed, it is hard to imagine a system in which those with substantial stakes in the policies implemented by a government do not try to influence that government.

EXCHANGE OF INFORMATION Providing data and information to those within the government is another activity performed by some interest groups. The interest group may have specialized or expert information that policymakers would find difficult or impossible to collect themselves or obtain from other sources. These private groups are stakeholders with a vested interest in the public policies that emerge, so they most actively provide data that support their own interests. For example, in the early 1980s, the U.S. Congress began considering a law requiring mandatory air bags as a safety restraint in automobiles. In determining whether to pass such a law, legislators were particularly influenced by information provided by automobile manufacturers (whose data indicated that air bags were costly, would reduce fuel economy, and would not substantially reduce overall injury levels in automobile collisions). This critical information, from a highly interested party to the decision, was an important reason behind the refusal of Congress to require air bags (Reppy 1984). Later in the decade, a barrage of counterinformation from another powerful interest group, the insurance industry, persuaded Congress and the public that air bags could save lives and lower insurance premiums. This resulted in laws requiring air bags.

In many countries, as the scale of government and the reach of public policy have expanded, many organizations in society need detailed, inside information about what the government is doing or intends to do that might affect their organization. Thus, Salisbury (1990; Salisbury et al. 1991) has concluded that American interest groups in Washington, DC, now spend more time gathering information *from* the government that is relevant to their organizations' interests (e.g., changes in rules or laws) than they do providing information *to* the government that might influence its policies.

COOPERATION Major interest groups can also exert influence through their compliance or noncompliance with the government policy process. In many countries, government actors understand that policy is implemented more successfully when it is acceptable to the affected interest groups. There are many countries (especially industrial democracies such as France, Japan, South Korea, and Sweden) in which government cultivates a special relationship with the interest group representatives of major economic organizations such as business, labor, and farmers. When such interest groups interact directly with the government to formulate and implement policy, they enjoy a privileged position. Governance based on *close cooperation between government agencies and these major sectoral interest groups* is called **corporatism**. For example, the shortcomings regarding the 2011 Fukushima (Japan) nuclear plant meltdown have been linked to the fact that the government regulatory agencies allowed the nuclear industry to establish and monitor its own safety procedures. Obviously, an organization benefits greatly when its interest group persuades the government to allow the organization to regulate itself. On the one hand, the industry would have the most complete information about how best to regulate; but on the other hand, the interests of the industry might be in conflict with the interests of society—for example, additional product safety might be sacrificed for additional profit.

Constraints on a Group's Behavior

3.4 **Identify the types of interest groups and the constraints under which they operate.**

Each interest group must decide what mix of activities is most likely to serve its political agenda. This mix depends on many factors, including the nature of the group's political resources, the objectives it pursues, and the political environment in which it operates.

POLITICAL RESOURCES A group's **political resources** are *those elements, controlled by the group, which can influence the decisions and actions of political actors.* The political resources that are most effective differ according to the situation and the political system. The preceding section emphasized the potential impact of financial resources and information, but certain other political resources can also be influential: control of factors of production, social status, legality, special knowledge or skills, ability to mobilize large numbers of people who pressure the government, capacity for social disruption, and access to decision makers. Various groups usually have dramatically different levels of all these political resources. An interest group's behavior depends on the kinds of resources it has available and its decision to use a particular mix of resources.

OBJECTIVES The *objectives* that interest groups pursue in the political world are as diverse as the different policy issues on which the government might act. One group might want one specific goal, such as a subsidy for growing wheat, while another group might have very broad objectives, such as a set of policies to eliminate poverty. An interest group's strategies and the probability that it will be successful are related to the group's political objectives. In general, an interest group has an advantage to the extent that its objective (1) is similar to existing policy and (2) is a decision that the political system has the capacity and motivation to make. For example, the Greenpeace groups in France and Poland are more likely to influence government policies on safer disposal of nuclear wastes than on stopping the development of new nuclear power stations, and these groups have little chance of achieving their broader goal of world-wide nuclear disarmament.

POLITICAL ENVIRONMENT At the most basic level, the demands that groups can make and the actions they can take depend on the boundaries of acceptable political action within the particular *political environment*. Every example of interest group action given thus far in this chapter has focused on a group operating in a democratic political system. An essential feature of democratic systems is that interest groups have extensive rights to make political demands and engage in political actions. Yet there is some disagreement about the extent to which interest groups contribute to healthy democratic processes (see Debate in 3).

The Debate in 3

How Interested Are Interest Groups in Democracy?

For as long as democratic governments have existed, there has been ambivalence about political interest groups. On the one hand, democratic theory is grounded in the idea that individuals can and should form political interest groups to influence the selection of officials and to promote public policies that serve their goals. On the other hand, the press, the public, and even some governmental officials are often heard blaming a country's problems on "special interests," which are effective in influencing government to enact policies that serve the interests of specific groups but are not in the public interest. Do interest groups hinder the democratic process or facilitate it?

Interest Groups Facilitate Democracy

• Interest groups are fundamentally important actors in a democratic system because they

enable citizens to organize into groups of sufficient size to communicate their concerns and demands in a clearer, more amplified voice to policymakers (Baumgartner and Leech 1998).

• Interest groups are especially valuable in representing and supporting those groups whose views are not effectively represented by any of the political parties (Berry 2000).

• In a single country, thousands of interest groups can operate at the same time, representing the interests of different groups of people. Because there are so many groups whose voices are heard, no one interest group will go unchecked and become too powerful and influential relative to the others (Dahl 1971).

• Financial contributions from interest groups enable candidates to purchase the expensive media that allow them to communicate their ideas to many citizens and thus enhance the citizens' capacity to participate knowledgeably in the democratic process.

- Interest groups play a beneficial role in the public policy process. They provide public officials with an enormous amount of relevant, specialized information that public agencies might not be able to gather efficiently and that supports improved policymaking.

- Interest groups serve as an expert watchdog over legislation or policies that public officials might try to implement but that are based on error or are self-serving. By articulating such concerns, interest groups add a valuable level of accountability and monitoring to the process of democratic governance (Berry 2000).

Interest Groups Hinder the Democratic Process

- Most interest groups work to garner support for a single or narrow set of goals, often at the expense of the interests of the broader society (Parenti 2010).

- Many interest groups have large professional staffs that work 24/7 to promote their goals. Ordinary citizens rarely have this level of expertise and time commitment for political action, and thus the interests of these ordinary citizens are not as well promoted in the policy process as those of special interests (Schlozman, Verba, and Brady 2013).

- Interest groups have specialized information and data that they provide to government officials. Such information can be influential in the policy process, but it also tends to be heavily biased in favor of the interest group's position on issues (Baumgartner et al. 2009).

- Interest groups are the major supplier of personal resources to many political actors. Campaign contributions and other "goodies" can be the source of considerable corruption because they purchase special access to and influence with public officials (Cigler 2013; Johnson 2006).

- Interest groups form an unnecessary layer that insulates citizens from their government and discourages citizens from engaging in direct democracy (Barber 2004).

More questions...

1. Can you think of any effective interest groups whose actions are a positive force in making your government work in a more democratic manner? Can you think of any effective interest groups that actually undermine democracy? Are your choices of interest groups closely linked to *your own* interests and values?

2. Does a system of strong and active interest groups increase or decrease the effectiveness of political parties?

3. Can you imagine an effective political system that has no organized interest groups?

In democracies such as Great Britain, Italy, and Japan, professional representatives of interest groups (lobbyists) are as much a part of the accepted set of governmental actors as elected legislators and their staffs. In Japan, it is common for a senior government official to "descend from heaven" (*amakudari*), leaving his position for a high-paying lobbyist's job for a major corporate interest. In the United States, over 12,000 full-time professional lobbyists are registered in Washington, DC, and one analyst contends that the total number of people engaged primarily in lobbying activities is more than 80,000—that is, more than 140 lobbyists per member of Congress (Birnbaum 2005; Center for Responsive Politics 2013).

In contrast, repressive political systems tolerate only a very narrow range of interest group activities that are in opposition to the leadership. In general, one of the key factors ensuring the survival of a repressive political system is its capacity to stifle or crush opposition interest groups. In these environments, such groups operate on the margins of the political system, and they range from small revolutionary cells such as FARC in Columbia to organized groups such as the Buddhist monks in Myanmar to mass movements such as the recent democracy demonstrations in Hong Kong and Syria. Such groups, and especially their leaders, usually face extensive harassment and punishment from the authorities, especially when they "go public." From 2011 through the beginning of 2014, for example, the Syrian government killed more than 100,000 people, arrested tens of thousands more who publicly protested against or opposed the Assad regime, and caused over one million people to flee the country (Genocide Watch 2014).

Nonetheless, groups periodically emerge to articulate demands for political, social, and economic changes. Sometimes, the state responds positively to these demands, and occasionally the group protests become so extensive that they drive the regime from power as occurred in the "velvet revolutions" in Europe in 1989 and the uprisings in Tunisia and Egypt in 2011 (see Chapter 12 for more examples). Some interest groups are eventually granted a major role in the political process. This happened in South Africa to the African National Congress, which began in 1912 as an interest group to promote the human rights of black South Africans, was later a government opposition movement, was then an outlawed violent protest group (in 1961), and finally became the country's major political party whose leaders (from Nelson Mandela to Jacob Zuma) have become presidents of the country.

Types of Interest Groups

A relatively simple taxonomy distinguishes four types of political interest groups: (1) associational; (2) institutional; (3) nonassociational; and (4) anomic (Powell et al. 2012).

ASSOCIATIONAL INTEREST GROUPS The first type, the **associational interest group**, is *organized specifically to further the political objectives of its members.* One example is the British Medical Association (BMA), a professional organization promoting public policies that support the goals of its members, 151,000 doctors. The BMA makes major contributions to political parties, provides expert information to government agencies, and guides the doctors' willingness to cooperate with government health policies. Another example is MADD, a primarily volunteer organization whose central goals are to stop drunk driving and underage drinking and to support the victims of drunk drivers. It utilizes its Web site, its network of more than 3 million members in five countries, and a professional lobbying staff to persuade policymakers and judges to impose stringent laws and harsh penalties on drunk drivers. It has trained 1,400 victim-advocates to provide counseling and legal support to victims of drunk drivers.

INSTITUTIONAL INTEREST GROUPS These groups have been formed to achieve goals other than affecting the political system, but they also pursue political objectives. Most occupational and organizational groups recognize that the decisions of the political system sometimes have major impacts on their own interests. Thus, they have a formal or informal subunit whose primary purpose is to represent the group's interests to the political system. For example, the University of California is a large institution of higher education, but its interests are strongly affected by local, state, and national policies on educational funding, research funding, regulation of research, discrimination in admissions and hiring, tax law, patent law, collective bargaining, and many other policies. Consequently, the university has full-time professional and student lobbyists on each campus, in Sacramento (the state capital), and in Washington, DC.

NONASSOCIATIONAL INTEREST GROUPS These groups are fluid aggregates of individuals who are not explicitly associated with a permanent organizational entity but who share some common interest regarding certain issues and become politically active on an issue. A loosely structured organization might temporarily emerge to plan and coordinate political activities, but the group is temporary and relatively informal and, once the issue has lost its immediate salience, the group disappears. If an interest group emerges in your community to stop a building development, to recall a public official, or to promote a particular law, it can be categorized as a nonassociational interest group. Such an interest group can be also termed a *social movement* when its *activities on an issue of social change become more sustained*, its supporters increase in number and loyalty, and its form becomes more of *an organized campaign spread over a broader geographic area*. Examples include the women's rights movement, the civil rights movement, the indigenous peoples movements, the pro-choice and antiabortion movements, and the U.S. Tea Party movement (Castells 2012; Givan, Soule, and Roberts 2010; Smith 2007).

ANOMIC INTEREST GROUPS These groups are short-lived, spontaneous aggregations of people who share a political concern. These people participate in a group political action that emerges with little or no planning and then quickly stops after the action is completed. A riot is the clearest example of an anomic interest group—the participants tend to share common political interests or grievances that they express through a generally disorganized outpouring of emotion, energy, and violence. A political demonstration is a somewhat more organized version of this type of interest group activity, and this characterizes the initial period of many of the recent "people power" actions described above.

Many taxonomies, like these four types of interest groups, present what Max Weber called ideal types. An **ideal type** is *a set of distinctive forms of a phenomenon defined in order to reveal the different ways in which key*

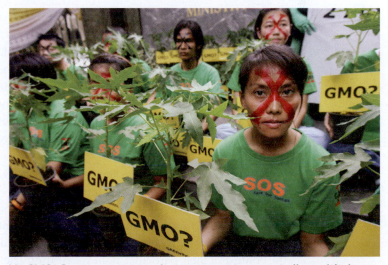

No GMO! Greenpeace activists demonstrate against genetically modified papaya outside the Thai Ministry of Agriculture. In most countries, thousands of interest groups engage in political action in the attempt to influence public policy decisions.

characteristics can be combined. There are usually no actual cases that are precisely like one of the ideal types, and most actual cases blend elements of the different ideal types. Ideal types are analytic constructs that are pure forms meant to facilitate our comparative thinking and our understanding. There will be many sets of ideal types offered in this book in addition to the four ideal types of interest groups, including types of legislative-executive relations, administrative systems, party systems, political economies, public policies, and political violence.

Political Parties

3.5   **Analyze the roles of political parties.**

An interest group is transformed into a **political party** when *the group attempts to capture political power directly by placing its members in governmental office.* The political party is the broadest linkage institution in most political systems because most parties are overarching organizations that incorporate many different interests and groups. While countries can have thousands of political interest groups, most have only a handful of political parties.

Activities of Political Parties

Political parties in most countries engage in six broad activities, functioning to: (1) broker policy ideas; (2) engage in political socialization; (3) link individuals and the political system; (4) mobilize and recruit activists; (5) coordinate governmental activities; and (6) organize opposition to the governing group.

BROKERS OF IDEAS The first, most central activity of political parties is to serve as major brokers of political ideas. Many individuals and political groups have interests and demands regarding the policies of government. A crucial function of political parties is to aggregate and simplify these many demands into a few packages of clear policy alternatives. To the extent that political parties are effective in this activity, they dramatically reduce the complexity and scale of the political process for the decision maker, who must perceive and respond to the individual and group demands, and for the voter, who must select political leaders whose overall policy preferences are closest to his own.

While all political parties are brokers of ideas, parties can be differentiated into two broad categories—ideological and pragmatic—on the basis of their intensity of commitment to those ideas. *Ideological parties* hold major programmatic goals (e.g., egalitarianism, ethnic solidarity, Islamic fundamentalism) and are deeply committed to the full implementation of these goals. Ideological parties are usually extreme within the context of their particular political culture. The German Green Party, described in Focus in 3, is an example of an ideological party. Others include the Islamic Salvation Front (FIS) in Algeria, the North Korean Communist Party, Sínn Fein in Northern Ireland, and the American Libertarian Party.

In contrast, *pragmatic parties* hold more flexible goals and are oriented toward moderate or incremental policy change. To achieve electoral success, pragmatic parties might shift their position or expand the range of viewpoints they encompass. Parties of the center are characteristically pragmatic parties. Examples include the Christian Democrats in Germany, the Congress Party in India, the Institutional Revolutionary Party (PRI) in Mexico, and the Democratic Party in the United States.

Focus in 3

Let's Party! The Rise of the Green Party in Germany

Few political interest groups transform into successful, modern political parties. The Green Party in Germany has achieved this transformation. It began as a diverse set of loosely affiliated interest groups in the 1960s and declared itself a political party in 1980. Its electoral fortunes in the national legislature have gone up and down (starting with 3.7 percent of the seats in 1983, dropping as low as 0 percent of the seats in 1990, and currently holding 10 percent of the seats).

Where did the Green Party come from? Like all political groups, it began with people who wanted to influence politics. In the late 1960s, some West Germans were displeased with their government's support of U.S. actions in Vietnam and Southeast Asia. Some believed that their government, and the entire "establishment" in their society, had been corrupted in its quest for ever-expanding power and wealth. And some had other policy concerns, including the huge inequalities in wealth and welfare within their society and among countries, the discrimination against certain groups such as women and ethnic minorities, the frightful build-up of nuclear weapons by the superpowers, and the degradation of the environment.

People with these various political beliefs, energized mainly by young countercultural Germans, demonstrated, marched, and formed local protest groups. These groups began to elect some of their members to local office, especially in larger cities. The most dynamic people in these local groups developed a national network, and in 1980 they formed a national political party, *Die Grünen* (the Greens).

The common concern that attracted many individuals to the Green Party was its commitment to preserving the environment. In Europe, the Greens became the first important party representing the "self-expressive, postmaterialist values" discussed in Chapter 2.

The Green Party remains an ideological party, and its party platform includes strong antiestablishment elements. The party ideology emphasizes the transformation of Germany: from a leading postindustrial society to one that uses only those technologies that do not damage the environment; from elite domination to broad democratic participation; from capitalism to a system in which workers own and control industry; from a militaristic, NATO-based country to one that becomes neutral, eliminates nuclear weapons, and stops preparing for war.

The Green Party had a substantial impact on German politics in the 1980s but struggled for electoral support in the early 1990s. In 1993, it merged with three East German progressive parties and is now called Alliance 90/The Greens. This merged party was a somewhat uneasy junior partner in a governing coalition with the large Social Democratic Party (1998–2005). It did not participate in either of the conservative-led "grand coalitions" of parties (2005–2009 and currently) or the previous government, all three under Chancellor Angela Merkel.

The future of the Alliance 90/Green Party at the national level remains uncertain. Germany is both the largest economy and the political leader within the European Union. Although the country is still attempting to improve the economic conditions in the formerly communist East Germany, which merged with West Germany in 1990, the German population is generally prosperous and enjoys a high standard of living. Recent economic problems associated with the global economic slowdown and hostility toward the large immigrant population are among the policy issues that have created electoral swings toward more conservative political parties. However, the German citizenry is one of the world's most secular and self-expressive in terms of political culture (recall Figure 2.1), and thus a portion of the electorate might continue to support the progressive policies of the Alliance 90/Green Party. Will it be outflanked by the more radical Left Party or absorbed by the large Social Democratic Party in the left center? Can it avoid self-destruction caused by the strong ideological differences among its moderate and more radical factions? Some analysts suggest that this party is too wild to last much longer.

Further Focus

1. What condition(s) might substantially increase or decrease the support for Germany's Green Party?

2. What policy positions are most likely to benefit and harm electoral support for "green" parties in most countries?

AGENTS OF POLITICAL SOCIALIZATION A related activity of political parties is their socialization of people into the political culture (see Chapter 4). In some countries, most people develop a clear party identification, which means that a person has a strong attachment to one political party he trusts to represent his political interests. The person's political beliefs and actions are influenced by information that a political party provides or by the person's perceptions of what the party supports. Even if a person does not have a strong party identification, political parties can be an important source of his political knowledge because they provide easily understood reference points regarding politically relevant information.

LINKS BETWEEN INDIVIDUALS AND THE SYSTEM In its role as a linkage institution, a political party connects individuals and the political system. Most individuals rely on political groups to represent their interests within the political system. More than other groups, political parties function to formulate, aggregate, and communicate a coherent package of demands and supports. If the party gains political power, it can attempt to implement those demands on behalf of the individuals whose interests it serves. Thus political parties greatly facilitate the individual's sense of integration into the political process.

MOBILIZATION AND RECRUITMENT OF POLITICAL ACTIVISTS The political party offers a well-organized and obvious structure within which a person can direct his political interests. It is a source of political information, of contact with other politically relevant individuals and groups, and of effective access to the political system. In many political systems, involvement with a political party is the primary mechanism through which individuals are drawn into roles as political foot soldiers and, ultimately, as political leaders. Often, political parties select the candidates for political positions or have the power to place people directly in positions within the political system. Whether one is considering a highly democratic polity such as Great Britain or an extremely nondemocratic one such as China, most individuals in key executive and legislative positions have achieved these positions through recruitment and selection by a political party.

COORDINATION OF GOVERNMENTAL OPERATIONS The fifth major activity of political parties is coordinating the actions of the government. The political party can encourage or require its members to work together to achieve shared policy goals. It can establish an internal hierarchy, with party leaders (e.g., in the U.S. Senate, majority and minority leaders, whips, and committee chairs) controlling the actions of party members in the conduct of government. The parties can also provide mechanisms for facilitating cooperation and regulating conflict among different parties. Leaders of several parties might form a coalition to secure majority support for certain policies. Such coalitions are especially important in legislatures in which no single party commands a majority. Political parties can also establish forms of power sharing in the conduct of government business. For example, the parties can agree to formulate executive or legislative committees in a manner that reflects the political strength of the various parties.

ORGANIZED SOURCES OF OPPOSITION Finally, in a political system that has more than one party, the parties not participating in the governing group can serve as an explicit and organized source of opposition. The function is fully institutionalized in Great Britain, where the major out-of-power party in parliament is explicitly designated as "Her Majesty's Loyal Opposition." This party should oppose, but never obstruct, the actions of the governing party because the opposition party remains loyal to crown and country. In Britain, the opposition party is guaranteed control of a specified amount of time during legislative sessions. The opposition leaders receive salaries to serve as a "shadow government," with a member of the opposition serving as the alternative and potential future replacement for each top official in the government. Hence, there is a shadow prime minister, a shadow minister of defense, and so on, who articulate what they would do if they held ministerial positions as the governing party.

Doing Politics

Politics comes alive when people engage in political action. Participation in a protest march, the attempt to persuade a friend to share your political perspective, and even the act of voting can be a moment of heightened experience. Acting alone or with others, the individual who takes political action might seek to serve his own interests, a national goal such as democratic governance, or an altruistic goal such as global peace.

This chapter should increase your awareness of the diverse modes of political action as well as the rather modest levels of such actions usually reported by most people. Some people are shocked that so many citizens do not even bother to vote in a country such as the United States. Others are surprised that anyone really thinks that one person's involvement in politics, whatever the level of commitment, will make any difference in the grander scheme of things. Yet events, such as recent ones in the Middle East, might challenge some assumptions about the limited impact of group political action. Political participation is a crucial topic in our developing understanding of the nature of the political world because people's actions are at the heart of the political process.

In this chapter, you have been introduced to methods and findings from the study of individual and group political actions. To this point, our treatment of political behavior has focused mainly on description and taxonomy—what people believe about politics and what political actions people undertake. For a richer analysis, however, we must at least attempt to answer the *why* questions: Why do people engage in a particular political action? Can we explain the apparent differences in people's political beliefs? Explaining political beliefs and actions is the central topic in Chapter 4.

Key Concepts

associational interest group, p. 72

corporatism, p. 69

extremist-activists, p. 60

foot soldiers, p. 59

group, p. 65

ideal type, p. 73

ideological party, p. 74

political interest group, p. 66

political activists, p. 59

political environment, p. 70

political participation, p. 57

political party, p. 74

political resource, p. 69

pragmatic party, p. 75

social movement, p. 73

taxonomic analysis, p. 59

For Further Consideration

1. Why might the absence of a political action be viewed as an act of political participation?

2. Apart from voting, what political action do you think is most important?

3. Imagine that you could engage in a conversation with the political activist—contemporary or historical—who most fascinates you. Whom would you choose? Why? What would you ask him or her?

4. Should there be any limits on a group's actions to influence political decision makers? What principles can you offer to justify any such limitations?

5. What is the most unconventional political action in which you have engaged? If the same circumstances arose now, would you behave any differently? Why?

For Further Reading

Ackerman, Peter, and Jack DuVall. (2001). *A Force More Powerful: A Century of Non-Violent Conflict.* **New York: Palgrave.** A series of engaging case studies set in many countries (e.g., Chile, Denmark, Poland, Serbia) reveals how political activism grounded in strategies of nonviolence (e.g., strikes, protests, boycotts) has achieved major political change in the face of repressive regimes and dictatorial leaders.

Ahmed, Shamima, and David Potter. (2006). *NGOs in International Politics.* **Bloomfield, CT: Kumarian Press.** A sensible description of the actions and impacts of major NGOs (nongovernmental organizations) that operate as global citizen activists and service providers as they work with and around national governments.

Aung San Suu Kyi and Alan Clements. (2008). *Aung San Suu Kyi: The Voice of Hope:*

Conversations. **Updated and rev. ed. New York: Seven Stories Press.** Former Buddhist monk Clements presents moving conversations secretly recorded in Myanmar with Aung San Suu Kyi (recall the chapter opener). Her extraordinary blend of spirituality, love, courage, and defiance are reflected in her approach of activist Buddhism.

Baumgartner, Frank, Jeffrey Berry, Marie Hojnacki, David Kimball, and Beth L. Leech. (2009). *Lobbying and Policy Change: Who Wins, Who Loses, and Why.* **Chicago: University of Chicago Press.** Based on an extensive study of cases, the authors argue that most lobbies, even well-funded ones, tend to be less effective in shifting U.S. policy than most people assume.

Beah, Ishmael. (2008). *A Long Way Gone.* **New York: Farrar, Straus and Giroux.** A dramatic and remarkable autobiography of a Sierra Leone boy who is captured and trained as a child soldier. He describes his violent world and how he escapes it and establishes a new life for himself.

Bohlen, J. (2000). *Making Waves: The Origins and Future of Greenpeace.* **Montreal: Black Rose.** The fascinating history, written by one of its founders, of an international interest group committed to fighting governments and huge corporations to protect the environment.

Chan, Stephen. (2011). *Southern Africa: Old Treacheries and New Deceits.* **New Haven, CT: Yale University Press.** Richly textured analyses are offered for five men who have dominated the politics of South Africa and Zimbabwe in recent decades: Mandela, Mbeki, Mugabe, Tsvangirai, and Zuma.

Cigler, Allan J., and Burdett Loomis, eds. (2013). *Interest Group Politics.* **8th ed. Washington, DC: CQ Press.** Thoughtful essays on how interest groups operate in the American political context during an era characterized by a huge infusion of money into the policy process, single-interest politics, social movements, and the Internet.

Givan, Rebecca Kolins, Sarah Anne Soule, and Kenneth Roberts, eds. (2010). *The Diffusion of Social Movements: Actors, Mechanisms, and Political Effects.* **New York: Cambridge University Press.** A series of studies explore how social movements regarding such issues as creationism science, human rights, and genetically modified foods emerge, spread, and affect the public policy domain.

Greenwood, Justin. (2011). *Interest Representation in the European Union.* **3rd ed. Basingstoke, England: Palgrave Macmillan.** An exploration of the roles, behaviors, and impacts of various types of interest groups (e.g., business, "the public," professional groups, and labor) in the context of the European Union (EU) as a supranational policymaking body that also must link with national governments and a multitude of interest groups.

Hoffman, Abbie. (1989). *The Best of Abbie Hoffman.* **New York: Four Walls, Eight Windows.** A selection of the funny, irreverent writings on radicalism and revolution by one of the key leaders (now deceased) of the student radical movement of the late 1960s and a member of the Chicago 7, tried for conspiracy after the riots at the 1968 Democratic Party convention in Chicago.

Jensen, Jane. (2008). *Women Political Leaders: Breaking the Highest Glass Ceiling.* **New York: Palgrave Macmillan.** An exploration of the pathways to power and the challenges facing 60 women (e.g., Benazir Bhutto in Pakistan, Michelle Bachelet in Chile, Kim Campbell in Canada, and Ellen Johnson Sirleaf in Liberia) who have achieved the highest positions in their governments.

Loader, Brian D., and Dan Mercea, eds. (2012). *Social Media and Democracy: Innovations in Participatory Politics.* **New York: Routledge.** Focusing primarily on Europe and North America, these essays explore how the new social media platforms, such as Facebook, YouTube, and Twitter, provide powerful means of political communication and mobilization and how these media interact with traditional media. See also: Loader, Brian D., Paul G. Nixon, Dieter Rucht, and Wim van de Donk, eds. (2004). *Cyberprotest: New Media, Citizens, and Social Movements.* London: Routledge.

Lowi, Theodore. (2009). *The End of Liberalism: The Second Republic in the United States.* **40th anniversary ed. New York: Norton.** An incisive critique of the shortcomings of politics dominated by interest groups.

Ma Bo. (1995). *Blood Red Sunset: A Memoir of the Chinese Cultural Revolution.* **New York: Viking.** A harsh, gripping autobiography of a young person drawn into the fervor of Mao Zedong's Cultural Revolution. A Red Guard working on a hopeless program to create farmland in Mongolia, Ma Bo is transformed from a true believer into an embittered man fighting to clear himself from charges that he is a reactionary.

Meisner, Maurice, and Gareth Schott. (2006). *Mao Zedong: A Political and Intellectual Portrait.* **London: Polity Press.** An illuminating biography of one of the most remarkable leaders of the twentieth century, emphasizing both his personal qualities and his enormous impact on the evolution of politics and economics in China.

Schlozman, Kay, Sidney Verba, and Henry Brady. (2013). *The Unheavenly Chorus: Unequal Political Voice and the Broken Promise of American Democracy.* **Princeton, NJ: Princeton University Press.** Based on extensive interviews and survey data, the authors argue that the actions of organized interest groups and the more affluent individuals have substantially more influence on American politics that the less advantaged.

Till, Brian Michael. (2011). *Conversations with Power: What Great Presidents and Prime Ministers Can Teach Us about Leadership.* **New York: Palgrave Macmillan.** Till, a recent U.S. college graduate, manages to interview many of the most fascinating top leaders of our era, including Gorbachev, de Klerk, Carter, Musharraf, Barak, Havel, and Clinton. The book includes his narratives about each leader and their answers to his pointed questions.

Volgy, Thomas J. (1999). *Politics in the Trenches: Citizens, Politicians, and the Fate of Democracy.* **Tucson: University of Arizona Press.** A political science professor offers a brief, highly readable, and revealing description of the challenges and actual experiences of political leaders in U.S. local politics, based on his many years as a local government elected official and his interviews with more than 300 elected officials.

Zaeef, Salam. (2010). *My Life with the Taliban.* **New York: Columbia University Press.** A fascinating inside look at the thinking and actions of the leadership in the Taliban through the eyes of an Afghan who became a top official in the movement.

On the Web

http://www.politics1.com/parties.htm
This site offers a directory and description of U.S. political parties.

http://www.ifex.org
The International Freedom of Expression Exchange represents more than 80 organizations in 50 countries committed to human rights and civil liberties and describes current situations of concern.

http://www.idea.int
The International Institute for Democracy and Electoral Assistance (IDEA) provides information about current democratic practices and various relevant databases for more than

100 countries, including comparative data on voter turnout for both presidential and parliamentary elections since 1945.

http://www.greenpeace.org/usa

Greenpeace's U.S. Web site describes some of the key initiatives taken by this global, action-oriented interest group.

http://www.uschamber.com/default

This Web site of the U.S. Chamber of Commerce, the world's largest business federation, representing more than 3 million large and small businesses and, according to some, the most powerful lobby group in the United States.

http://pol.moveon.org

The site for a progressive citizen action group in the United States that mobilizes its 3.3 million members to engage in political activism.

http://www.protest.net

This Web site provides a comprehensive calendar of upcoming protests and political rallies taking place around the world. The site lists upcoming protests by both geographic region and political issue.

http://www.internationalanswer.org

This Web site serves as the electronic home of International ANSWER, a coalition of antiwar and antiracism groups, providing information about movements taking place throughout the international community.

http://www.sociosite.net/topics/activism.php

This site, developed by Washington State University, provides a number of links and articles related to both U.S. and global social movements.

http://www.amnesty.org

Amnesty International has been dedicated to human rights causes for more than 40 years, with 2.2 million members in 150 countries. The site provides information on a variety of topics ranging from refugees to arms control.

http://civicyouth.org

The Center for Information and Research on Civic Learning and Engagement (CIRCLE) promotes research on the civic and political engagement of Americans between the ages of 15 and 25. The organization's Web site offers a variety of interesting data and studies on this topic, including research papers on youth participation and strategies for mobilizing young adults into political participation.

Chapter 4
Influences on Beliefs and Actions

 Learning Objectives

4.1 Assess how the context in which individuals live impacts their political beliefs and actions.

4.2 Characterize the different agents of political socialization.

4.3 Illustrate how demographic characteristics are linked to political beliefs and actions.

4.4 Consider how approaches from political psychology help us understand politics and political processes.

The following five excerpts are from school textbooks used in different countries. In each, what subject is being taught, and from what country might each textbook come?

1. Add "not" to the following sentence: "The Iranians are brave."

2. Our forefathers believed, and we still believe today, that God himself made the diversity of peoples on earth....Interracial residence and intermarriage are not only a disgrace but also forbidden by law. It is, however, not only the skin of the Betas that differs from the Alphas. The Beta stands on a much higher plane of civilization and is more developed. Betas must so live, learn, and work that we shall not sink to the cultural level of the Alphas. Only thus can the government of our country remain in the hands of the Betas.

3. Imperialism knows no other type of relations between States except domination and subjugation, the oppression of the weak by the strong. It bases international relations on abuse and threat, on violence and arbitrariness. Between January 3 and June 10, 1961, Gamma military airplanes violated Delta airspace 3 times in the month of January, 15 in February, 17 in March, 9 in April, 8 in May, and 10 in June. What was the average monthly number of violations of Delta airspace by Gamma military airplanes?

Our hero! Belarus children (literally) sing the praises of their President. Schools provide the state with a powerful setting in which to teach (indoctrinate?) children about the state's version of appropriate political beliefs and actions.

4. Which of the following descriptions of the United States is incorrect?
   (a) The world's leading arms-exporting country.
   (b) The world's most heavily nuclear-armed country.
   (c) The world's leader in chemical weapons research.
   (d) The world's most peace-loving country that never once was at war with other countries.

5. The instinctual state of the ants corresponds to the leadership state among mankind…the principles of a perfect insect state give people cause to think. They have preserved bees and ants in the struggle for survival and thereby proved their validity. We earlier noted the following truths . . . :
   • The work of the individual has only one purpose: to serve the whole group.
   • Major accomplishments are possible only by the division of labor.
   • Each…risks its life without hesitation for the whole.
   • Individuals who are not useful or are harmful to the whole are eliminated.
   • The species is maintained by producing a large number of offspring.

   It is not difficult for us to see the application of these principles to mankind:…The ethnic state must demand of each individual citizen that he does everything for the good of the whole, each in his place and with his abilities. And if a person acts against the general interest, he is an enemy of the people and will be punished by the law. A look at our history proves that we as a people must defend our territory to preserve our existence.

Many factors can influence an individual's political beliefs and political actions. The educational system certainly can be one of those influences. To most observers, each of the examples above might be characterized as a crude form of indoctrination. In each case, those controlling the state also controlled the content of the educational system. And that content is created and taught in certain ways in the attempt to shape the behavior of the people raised in that society.

Do you have an idea of the source of any of the textbook excerpts above? Example 1 is from an Arabic language arts textbook for sixth-grade Iraqi students (Robinson 2003). Example 2 is from a South African high school textbook on race relations during the era of apartheid (1948–1988, substitute "whites" for "Betas" and "nonwhites" for "Alphas") (Thompson 1966: 100). Example 3 is mathematics as it is framed for Cuban middle school students (substitute "Cuban" for "Delta" and "North American" for "Gamma") (Fagen 1964: 68). Example 4 is an item on a history test for South Korean eighth graders (Demick 2003). And Example 5 is from a biology text for fifth-grade German girls during World War II (Harm and Wiehle 1942).

The textbook examples above lack subtlety. Even as a young child, you would have recognized and resisted such manipulation…right? Is it possible that your own education presented you with ideas that manipulated your thinking about politics—perhaps in much more subtle ways? Who or what shaped your ideas and actions in the political world? The attempt to answer that question is the central theme of this chapter and the next step in our journey toward becoming more informed political thinkers.

In analyzing political behavior in Chapters 2 and 3, we focused on *describing* the political beliefs and political actions of individuals and groups. In this chapter, we explore some of the interesting *why* questions in this analysis of political behavior and political identity. Can we *explain* why individuals hold particular political beliefs and why they engage in certain political actions? Figure 4.1 indicates four broad types of explanatory factors that might account for individual political behavior: (1) the environment; (2) agents of political socialization; (3) demographic characteristics; and (4) personality and human nature. This chapter considers these four types of influences on the political beliefs and actions of individuals, from apathetics to activists.

The Environment

4.1   **Assess how the context in which individuals live impacts their political beliefs and actions.**

In the 2011 national election in Vietnam, it was reported that 99.5 percent of the adults voted, whereas in the United States, 54.6 percent of the voting-age population voted in the 2012 national election. What best accounts for this difference? In Vietnam, voting is an obligatory act, a required gesture of support for the current political leadership rather than a genuine selection among candidates—indeed, there is no choice. Most Vietnamese vote because someone who does not vote risks unwanted scrutiny by Communist Party authorities. In the United States, voting has always been a voluntary act, and there are no sanctions for not voting. Thus, the citizen decides whether her

Figure 4.1 A Framework for Explaining Individual Political Behavior

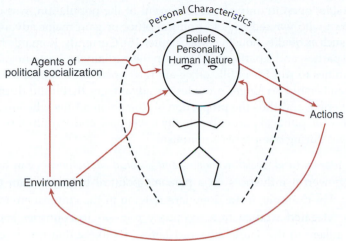

sense of civic responsibility or her desire to affect the outcome on ballot choices merits the effort of going to vote.

The example of voting in Vietnam and the United States is suggestive of how a person's *environment*—*the broad context in which an individual lives*—can powerfully influence her political behavior. In its most comprehensive form, the environment includes everything outside the individual. It obviously includes political elements (e.g., governmental procedures, political and governmental institutions, public policies, specific political events, and political actors), but it also includes elements of the social and cultural system (e.g., religious foundations and attitudes toward ethnicity, gender, and class), elements of the economic order (e.g., level of economic prosperity and development), and the physical features of the environment (e.g., topography and natural resources).

For any particular political belief or action, there are various possible effects from an environmental stimulus. An element of the environment might activate, repress, transform, or amplify a person's political behavior. Most elements of the environment are likely to have little or no effect at any given moment, so the task of the political analyst is to identify those few environmental elements that do have especially significant effects on political belief or action and to explain how these effects occur. Because the environmental context is—at least in theory—of enormous scope, it is helpful to consider different ways in which the environment might affect behavior. Here are two examples regarding the *political environment*:

1. **Effects on information about politics.** In Myanmar, the government strictly limits the information available about politics so many citizens have minimal knowledge of the current politics—even of their own country. In the United States, the interested citizen has access each day to information about worldwide political events from hundreds of hours of television and radio programming and almost unlimited access to information through Internet sites and other reading materials.

2. **Effects on individuals' political party involvement.** From the late 1940s to the late 1980s, Romania had only one legal political party, the Communist Party. Party membership, open to only about 10 percent of the population, was essential for any citizen who wanted to hold political office or gain major advantages in the society, such as quality housing (see Chapter 15). Currently, Romania has 17 active political parties, and 8 parties hold seats in the parliament. Party membership and opportunities to run for public office are now open to all Romanians. However, party membership no longer provides the advantages that it did during the communist period, and thus the proportion of Romanian adults who are active party members of *all* political parties is actually lower now under multiparty democracy than it was during one-party communism.

The broader *cultural, social, economic, and physical environments* can have indirect but no less powerful influences on a person's political behavior than the political environment. For example, if the dominant religion in the cultural environment has traditionally relegated women to a secondary role—as in countries such as Saudi Arabia that adhere to the sharia laws of Islam—it is likely that few women will be political activists. If the social environment has an undercurrent of racism, this will affect the voting behavior and political participation of both the majority and minority racial groups. If the economy has very high unemployment, this will influence policy decisions about job creation. Can you think of ways in which even a country's physical environment could influence politics? (Read the Compare in 11 if you cannot).

The impact of the environment on political behavior is sometimes hard to predict. If poverty is widespread in an economic system, will this influence the probability of political rebellion? On the one hand, such poverty might produce a frustrated population that will be responsive to a revolutionary movement promising future prosperity, and it might inspire a particular person to become very active in such a movement. On the other hand, the people might be too concerned about basic survival to have the time and/or energy to engage in political action.

It should be evident from these examples that many aspects of the environment might influence political beliefs and actions. The analyst must be sensitive to possible environmental effects when attempting to provide an adequate explanation for a particular political behavior.

Agents of Political Socialization

4.2 **Characterize the different agents of political socialization.**

Each person has a complex blend of political beliefs—cognitive, affective, and evaluative orientations regarding political phenomena. (These three kinds of orientations were defined in Chapter 2.) Even individuals who live in the same environment can hold very different political beliefs. Political socialization research attempts to explain the sources of individuals' political beliefs.

Political socialization can be defined as *the processes through which individuals acquire their beliefs and values about the political world.* An understanding of how this process works is of importance not only to political analysts but also to those who wish to influence people's political beliefs and actions, especially political leaders. Plato (ca. 428–347 B.C.E.) observed that society's most important function is civic training and instructing citizens regarding the nature of their social and political world and their proper roles in that world. The appropriate content and style of such political socialization are subject to debate because one person's vision of proper civic training might be viewed by another person as indoctrination and brainwashing.

Political scientists attempt to analyze the *agents of political socialization—the major sources of political training and indoctrination shaping an individual's political beliefs and values.* The main focus has been to explain the processes through which the key agents of socialization affect political beliefs. There has been considerably less attention paid to, and very limited empirical success in, demonstrating a link between the activities of a specific agent of socialization and individuals' actual political actions. In this section, we discuss some of the most important agents of political socialization: the family, schools, social networks, the media, religion, culture, and events.

The Family

The family is the first—and often most powerful and lasting—agent of political socialization. The political orientations of most individuals are deeply influenced by the behaviors and beliefs they experience in the family environment. Before individuals are capable of making judgments for themselves, they have absorbed perceptions about the political world from conversations overheard within the family. For example, most seven-year-old children in the United States already identify with one political party and have affective orientations toward both major parties. Children are very likely to adopt the same political orientation as their parents if the families are very interested in politics and provide consistent cues over time (Jennings, Stoker, and Bowers 2009).

Even the pattern of interactions between parents and children can have political implications. If the family is very hierarchical—with the father or mother ruling with an iron hand, preventing discussion, and using strong sanctions for disobedience—the child might conclude that this is the appropriate pattern of authority relationships in the society. If the family tends to discuss issues before it makes rules or decisions, the child might feel more strongly that she has the right to participate actively in decisions, even in the political world. The political leadership usually has minimal control over the political socialization that occurs in the family. Indeed, the family can transmit values that are at variance with those preferred by the state and its leaders. The Focus in 4 describes how Mao Zedong used the other agents of political socialization to counteract the influence of the family in China.

Schools

The excerpts from textbooks that opened this chapter are extreme examples of the use of schools for political socialization. From the perspective of political authorities, schools can be the state's most valuable agent for political socialization. Schools offer the opportunity for sustained and highly controlled contact with youth at the

Focus in 4

Political Socialization in China

Contemporary Chinese political culture is shaped by many forces. Historically, the most critical influence on the cultural norms in China is Confucianism. Based on the teachings of a fifth-century B.C.E. Chinese intellectual, **Confucian culture** stresses that *individual action must be based on what is best for the group and for society as a whole*. Harmony and cooperation are always to be sought, and disunity and conflict must be avoided. Confucianism places the highest value on *order, stability, and discipline* within a framework of hierarchical authority. Society is shaped by a series of superior–subordinate relationships in which obedience must be offered: by subject to ruler, by child to parent, by younger to elder, and by female to male.

Such principles powerfully support a political system in which authoritarianism is natural and acceptable. The political elite is justified in taking any action that maintains harmony and order or that serves the broader interests of the society—regardless of the costs to individuals or groups (e.g., political parties, unions, and students).

When Mao Zedong came to power in China in 1949, his commitment to egalitarianism and a revolutionary restructuring of Chinese society placed him in direct conflict with Confucian values. He deeply opposed the Confucian ideals valuing tradition over change, males over females, and older people over younger people. To transform China into a new society associated with his interpretation of Marxism, Mao dealt aggressively with all the key agents of political socialization.

Mao attacked all forms of *religion*—including Confucianism—and used the power of the state to suppress religious practices and to force all the people to embrace atheism. He viewed the *family* as the most important agent of socialization in Confucian norms. He tried to eliminate the nuclear family through collective child-rearing. When that failed, he demanded that the family must "revolutionize itself," but he soon concluded that families would continue to be a "citadel of oppression." Thus, he emphasized other agents of political socialization to shift cultural norms from Confucianism to communism.

He utilized the *schools* as the primary agent of socialization. Students were relentlessly drilled on the values of the new communist social order and taught that the norms of Confucianism constituted reactionary, unacceptable thinking that would be harshly punished. Every aspect of the curriculum and textbooks were grounded in Marxist thinking, whether it was history, literature, or science. Students were also given a book of Mao's political comments, *The Little Red Book*, which many memorized completely and recited at school, at home, and in public marches.

Mao altered *peer relations*. He promoted gender equality, placing women in positions of authority within the Communist Party, major organizations, and government councils. He enacted the Marriage Law of 1950, which gave a woman rights to take legal recourse against bodily harm by her husband, to initiate a divorce, and to own property. These rules were a direct repudiation of Confucian norms, in which a wife was the property of her husband, who could exploit or dispose of her as he wished. He outlawed foot binding, a practice in which many young girls had their feet wrapped tightly with cloth every day so that their toes did not develop properly, preventing them from walking freely (and making them more dependent on males).

Mao also mobilized young people as active participants in the revolution. They were encouraged to report any counterrevolutionary action, even by their parents or friends, and many did so. He established the Red Guards, a grassroots organization composed primarily of teenagers. The Red Guards were empowered to attack "the four olds" of society—old ideas, cultures, manners, and customs. For example, the Red Guards destroyed 5,000 of China's 7,000 temples. They would parade "capitalist roaders" (anyone accused of lacking enthusiasm for the revolutionary changes in society) through the streets, ridicule them, and beat or kill them.

Mao used Communist Party membership to grant power and authority to those loyal to his ideology. At every level in society—whether a large collective farm, a factory, a school, or a village—real power was held by members of the party who enforced the "mass line" on all others. Those who deviated from Mao's vision were subjected to intense criticism from their peers and, if peer pressure and "re-education" failed to make them recant and behave properly, they would lose privileges (like good jobs and housing), be tortured and imprisoned, or even be executed.

Also, the *media and modes of cultural expression* became instruments of absolute support for Communist Party viewpoints. Television, newspapers, and other media were all owned by the state. No independent perspectives were allowed. Plays, music, artworks, and all other forms of culture were required to reflect "socialist realism"—a celebration of the glorious revolution, the heroic struggle of the workers and peasants in overthrowing the feudal regime under the emperor and the privileged classes, and the new utopia of communist egalitarianism and abundance shared by all. The state engaged in extensive censorship, destroyed counterrevolutionary cultural works, and punished any who used artistic expression to criticize the party or the state.

Few modern societies have controlled the agents of political socialization with such intensity and pervasiveness as in Mao's China. In the face of extensive coercion and socialization, very few were willing to challenge the new norms publicly. Most behaved in accordance with those norms and some became true believers—political activists in support of the revolution. However, there was always some resistance to the new values, especially in villages, and Confucian values were never fully extinguished. Indeed, one of the dominant explanations for the recent explosion of economic development and productivity in China—as well as in other East Asian countries such as Singapore, South Korea, and Taiwan—is the norms of order, hard work, education, and financial acquisitiveness associated with Confucianism (Compton 2000; Meisner 2006).

Further Focus

1. What can a state do to try to counter the influence of the family or religion as an agent of political socialization?
2. Which agent of political socialization has had the biggest influence on you? Why?

extremely impressionable age when many political beliefs can still be molded. Apart from the family, the classroom is the most important microcosm of society that most young people experience. The teacher is the authority figure who rewards thinking and behavior that conform to what is deemed desirable by the society and who sanctions or withholds rewards from those who fail to conform. In most societies, students are taught to accept the authority of the teacher, to control their behavior, and to value the symbolic rewards offered by the education system. Every school system has rituals that support the political system. These might include songs, chants, or activities that express allegiance to political leaders or symbols. The photo on page 83 shows students in Belarus singing a daily song that celebrates the virtues of their country's president.

The school curriculum can be extremely powerful in shaping the students' understanding of the political world. Educational authorities control what subjects are taught, what textbooks contain, what content is tested, who teaches, and even what teachers say and do. An extreme form of this central control over education was achieved during the French Fourth Republic (1946–1958). It was said that the minister of education in Paris could look at her watch and specify exactly what chapter in what textbook the children of a certain age were studying at that moment all over France. While most subject matter in the schools of most countries is not openly political, school systems in *every* country present materials that are supportive of that country's politics and dominant cultural norms. All textbooks and all lessons in school are selective and thus contain biases in what is emphasized, what is ignored, and how meaning and value are established.

Have you noticed anything unusual about the use of the pronouns *he* and *she* in this book? To counter the male dominance in the language of many American textbooks, we alternate masculine and feminine pronouns in odd and even chapters, respectively. If you were aware of the gender pronouns in Chapter 2 and this chapter, your reaction may be indicative of the subtle ways in which you have been affected by cultural norms that are reinforced by language and education.

Social Networks

Persistence is the rule for the political attitudes and behaviors an individual learns from parents and schooling–that is, what you learn early tends to have deep and long-lasting effects. However, according to the *life cycle* interpretation of political socialization, learning never stops. As the importance of parents and formal schooling diminishes, social networks become an increasingly significant influence on many people's political socialization. **Social networks** include friends and colleagues from peer groups such as work, school, church, and clubs. A social network can also emerge from a person's interactions on social media, such as Facebook. A person tends to be influenced by what "people like me" think. People bring their ideas and values into closer conformity with those of their social networks since this makes the relationship more comfortable (Agnew 2003; Campbell 2013).

In many cases, peers and others influence a person's political views via a *two-step communication flow* (Bennett 2012; Katz and Lazarsfeld 1955). People with greater interest in and knowledge of politics absorb new information from various sources (*step one*). Then they relay what they have learned to others (*step two*), especially those in the mass public whose political beliefs are less salient and developed (recall Chapter 2). Direct communications from peers allow for a rich exchange of political information because such political messages have the immediacy, credibility, and power of personal interaction. Focus in 4 describes how China has used the peer group as a major mechanism for political socialization, especially during the period under Mao Zedong.

The influence of social networks can also be a powerful factor in the radicalization of the "homegrown" terrorists who are becoming a significant threat in many countries. There is considerable evidence that individuals, especially young adult males who feel alone and alienated as part of a cultural and religious minority, find encouragement and direction from a small group of peers who gather informally. As they share their ideas and frustrations, they begin to radicalize one another and to discuss how they could strike out at those in their country who antagonize them (King and Taylor 2011). In some cases, these ideas move from imagination to action, usually in the form of violent acts. Often, these acts are the result of small social networks rather than a central plan directed by the leadership of a large organization (Sageman 2008). These small peer groups, which usually have no direct connection with the larger, known terrorist organizations such as al-Qaeda, are emerging in many countries, from Europe and North America to Asia, North Africa, and the Middle East. An example of this type of small-group terrorism is the September 2014 suicide car bombing in Anbar Province, Iraq in which 37 were killed and individuals affiliated with no known group were the suspects.

The Media

Very few of us directly experience most of political phenomena about which we claim knowledge. For most adults, *the media*—especially television, radio, the press, and the Internet—are the major sources of political information. Dan Nimmo and James Combs (1990: xiii) argue: "Few people learn about politics through direct experience. For most persons, political realities are mediated through mass and group communication, a process that results as much in the creation, transmission, and adoption of political fantasies as it results in independently validated views of what happens." They claim that each of us creates a personal vision (a "fantasy") of political reality based mainly on what is communicated to us by information sources such as other people, the mass media, and popular culture. Regardless of how fantastic our political visions are, it is important to understand that the media can be a crucial agent of political socialization for either stability or change.

These information sources really do *mediate* between the individual and most political reality. While most media content is not explicitly political, much of it does contain subtle information that influences how one thinks about politics and society. Exposure to television and radio is extensive in most countries. Thus, the individual is bombarded with messages about values, lifestyles, and so on. While sweeping generalizations about the impacts of the media on people's political beliefs and actions are not possible, two broad observations can be offered.

First, there is considerable evidence that the media are especially significant in *drawing people's attention to some political phenomena rather than to others*—an impact called *agenda setting*. The media signal what is important by their selection of what topics to cover and the depth of coverage, and the media influence the individual's interpretation of political phenomena by the manner in which information is presented. In general, the media (over?) simplify political topics by personalizing stories, focusing on single events, and glossing over the complex nature of most political issues (Bennett 2012; Iyengar 2011).

Second, however, the research concludes that few people absorb media information in a way that significantly changes most of their political attitudes or actions. Rather, people interpret and retain media information selectively to reinforce their existing attitudes. Many people, especially those with less sophisticated political belief systems and minimal political knowledge (see Chapter 2), do not pay much attention to the media that provide explicit political information. Moreover, with the proliferation of media outlets through cable and Internet sources, people can easily select news outlets that they perceive share their views (Iyengar and Hahn 2009). The media-based information for such people often comes indirectly from a politically knowledgeable peer or their broader social network through the two-step communication flow described on page 90.

Newspapers are still credited with having the greatest effect on knowledge about politicians and issues among the most educated people (Graber 2009; Johnson and Kellstedt 2013). However, television is now regarded as the most important source of political information for the largest number of people in Western democracies (Dalton 2014). In the more technologically developed societies, the many forms of Internet content—which includes not only online television and news media but also search engines, blogs, and online videos—have become a key source of political information (Chadwick 2013; Loader and Mercea 2012). An increasing amount of this digitized political information is actually transmitted through peer-to-peer networks, enhancing its power. There is some debate whether the shift from broadcasting to narrowcasting, especially via the Internet, social media, and partisan media sites, will enable individuals to focus almost exclusively on sources that reinforce their existing political viewpoints, and whether this selective exposure is dangerous for a healthy democracy (Iyengar and Hahn 2009; Sunstein 2009). The Debate in 4 assesses whether the new ICTs (information and communications technologies) are dramatically altering the impact of media on political beliefs and political actions.

Much of what you know about the political world from the mainstream media is contingent on what topics the media choose to cover and what content the media select to report. Like textbooks, the media are not neutral; someone has selected the subjects and content. In many countries, the major media are owned and controlled by the government or by members of the wealthy, dominant class in that society (Bagdikian 2004). Even in democratic countries, most media are not free of ideological bias. Most media are owned by private interests, and those owners have biases—the broad conservatism of News Corp.'s media mogul Rupert Murdoch is one example (Folkenflik 2013). At least, most media in free societies are oriented to please those who advertise with them and their core audience and thus have a profit-based bias.

The print and broadcast media are free of substantial government censorship in less than one-third (32 percent) of all countries, and these countries include only 15 percent of the world's population. Governments severely censor the media for 43 percent of the world's people (Freedom House 2013). Through their ability to control the media, most governments have a significant resource for political socialization, exposing people to news and information that reinforce the government's view of the political world. And there is empirical evidence of a global decline in freedom of the press the last decade (Freedom House 2013). Moreover, an analysis of freedom on the Internet concludes that such freedom has recently declined in 34 of the 60 countries examined (Freedom House 2013). Google has also identified a dramatic increase in governmental efforts to censor the Internet around the world (Malcolm 2013).

Of course, you are not completely passive in the process. In most countries, people can choose among alternative media sources and can attempt to evaluate the truth of what they read, hear, and see in the media. And the recent explosion of telecommunications technologies (such as satellite television transmissions and the Internet) has made it increasingly difficult for a government to control all the sources of information

The Debate in 4

Do the New ICTs Substantially Change Our Political Beliefs and Actions?

With the enhanced global communication through cell phones, satellites, peer-to-peer networks, and the Internet, many societies have become information-rich and communication intensive (Chadwick and Howard 2009). From the globalized 24/7 news to the extensive political blogging to the tweets reporting revolution in the streets of repressive regimes, the impacts of all these information and communications technologies (ICTs) seem extraordinary (Cropf and Krummenacher 2011). Thus, some argue that these ICTs are dramatically changing the nature of individual political beliefs and actions. Others insist that these ICTs are important but merely add incrementally to the existing array of agents of political socialization that influence political behavior. Are these new social media truly game changers?

New ICTs Are Powerfully Shaping Political Beliefs and Political Actions

- As the impacts of parents and schools as agents of political socialization fade by an individual's teenage years, the media often become the critical agent. For younger generations, the Internet is increasingly the primary platform for acquiring and sharing knowledge about the political world. The diversity, speed, anonymity, and shrill nature of political information circulated on these ICTs have substantially altered the content and impacts of this information on both citizens and political officials (Chadwick 2013; Graham and Dutton 2014; Pew 2011).

- While collective norms might still be shaped by mainstream broadcast media outlets, the Internet and new social media are critical in the creation of the individual's identity. Through the Web, people rely on themselves and their own resources to solidify an identity and self-awareness, including the formation of their cognitive, affective, and evaluative political beliefs (Anduiza et al. 2012; Papacharissi 2010).

- Information is power. ICTs such as search engines, online news, and political Web sites allow individuals to access far more information than in the past. Access is easier and less costly, and the user can rapidly explore multiple sources and control her analysis of information and knowledge claims about politics (Brookings 2011).

- Social media ICTs such as YouTube and blogs enable those with minimal resources to reach a large, possibly global audience, giving expression and potential influence to those who previously had no capacity to communicate their political messages to a broad audience (Loader and Mercea 2012).

- These social media and digital technologies such as cell phones have become critical tools providing political activists with new modes for cooperation, mobilization, and coordination of their political actions, as in the Arab Spring 2011 uprisings in Egypt and Tunisia (Ritter and Trechsel 2011).

New ICTs Have Not Dramatically Changed Political Beliefs and Political Actions

- While the utilization of online sources of political information has increased dramatically, most people primarily seek this information from online modes of traditional, dominant news sources (e.g., CNN, BBC, Al Jazeera). The mere digitizing of information from conventional sources will not result in major changes in the content or even the impact of these agents of political socialization (Chadwick 2013; Garrett and Danziger 2011).

- More broadly, most empirical research has concluded that ICTs in the political world are essentially power-reinforcing. Those elites and groups who already exercise substantial political power and influence have been able to capture a disproportionate share of the power and benefits associated with the use of ICTs (Bimber 2003; Schmidt and Cohen 2010).

- Despite the presence of all these ICTs, most citizens exhibit no greater knowledge about or interest in the political world, and political participation has not increased significantly as a result of these technologies. Most research on participation has not yet found a positive correlation between the greater use of ICTs and increased levels of citizen engagement in politics (Boulianne 2009; Garrett and Danziger 2011).

- Social media seem mainly to facilitate "slacktivism" instead of activism (Gladwell 2010). That is, many casual participants and bandwagoners seek social change through low-cost activities such as joining a digital social movement (e.g., a "Save Darfur" Facebook group). Such forms of virtual political action translate into minimal effects in the real world of political action (Shirky 2011).

- Those who use ICTs to focus and narrow their exposure to sources consistent with their existing political views experience little more than a modest strengthening of those views (Sunstein 2009). Those who expose themselves to the multiplicity of perspectives and the huge number of contradictory knowledge claims about politics from the nonmainstream ICTs tend to be overwhelmed. As with other agents of socialization in conflict, the dominant effects are to increase uncertainty and reduce political action.

More Questions...

1. As governments are increasingly unable to control the information that citizens access through the new ICTs, will there be generally positive changes in pursuit of the goals of democracy, tolerance, and a shared community of meaning in a society?

2. Are you persuaded that the content of political information that most individuals are influenced by will change as they become more reliant on ICTs as a crucial source?

reaching its citizens. Consequently, most governments are becoming less effective in shaping people's political beliefs through the media, even as the media are an increasingly important source of people's political "reality."

Religion

For some individuals, religion is a powerful agent of political socialization. First, political beliefs and actions can be influenced by religious beliefs that individuals should act to correct the failures of secular society and should promote religious views on issues on which the government has enacted unacceptable public policies, such as abortion, school curriculum, gender relations, and even policy choices about economic development (McDuie-Ra and Rees 2010). Second, people in some environments are so disillusioned with the conditions of their society that they look to religion for a framework of beliefs and actions to improve those conditions. This is especially the case in societies in which people perceive substantial negative effects due to the shift from traditional to modern life (Haynes 2007, 2010). And third, some religious belief systems make no distinction between religious life and public life, and thus it is natural that religious values—not public policies—always have precedence. This acceptance of the dominance of religious prescriptions over secular authority is evident in certain fundamentalist groups within all the major religions, particularly Christianity, Judaism, and Islam.

In all these situations, religious authorities—whether texts or the pronouncements of religious figures—can guide and motivate their followers. Arguably more than any of the other agents of political socialization, it is possible to link the content communicated by religion as a socializing agent with both political beliefs and political actions. Even the impact of family socialization, as discussed above, can be shaped by and reinforce religious beliefs if the family is devout. In many instances, one person's piety can be another person's intolerance and bigotry. The current era is one in which there are huge differences in the impacts of religion as an agent of political socialization on those who are generally unaffected by religious beliefs, those who separate their religious beliefs from their political beliefs, and those whose political views are substantially shaped by their religious values (Putnam and Campbell 2012).

Culture

In every country, most mainstream culture, which ranges from product advertisements to cinema to music to public monuments, is supportive of the society's dominant values, including its political values. (Consider, for example, whether there is variation in the main ethnicities of villains in films produced in your country over the past 70 years.) Moreover, culture—like the media—can be extensively controlled by the dominant political order in a society and can be used to reinforce the state's view of the political world. Cuba, like many of the communist states in the past, has generally insisted that culture must meet the standards of socialist realism, which means that no art, theater, or cinema should be allowed if it fails to celebrate the virtues of socialism—Cuban style.

However, culture does not necessarily reinforce the dominant order. Culture can inform and criticize subtly, by means of metaphor and symbol, in ways less likely to be interpreted as a direct challenge to the established authorities. This is especially true in societies in which there is considerable censorship of the media and state control of most sources of public information. During the 1980s, for example, an extensive body of fiction, cinema, poetry, theater, art, and music emerged with political content critical of the state's views in countries such as East Germany and Poland that were still communist (Larkey 1990). Culture can also be openly subversive, directly attacking mainstream values or advocating opposing values. For example, Jamaican reggae music offers a revolutionary vision of an alternative social and political world for its people. While most contemporary American music has little explicit political content, overt political content can be found across a spectrum of music in songs by performers such as the Dixie Chicks, Green Day, Kanye West, Macklemore & Ryan Lewis, Toby Keith, and Bruce Springsteen (Coles 2003; Fisher and Flota 2013).

Events

The general effects of the environment on political beliefs and action have already been discussed. While the context of everyday life has slow, evolutionary effects on a person's political behavior, a specific event can act as a sudden and powerful agent of political socialization. For example, Sarah Brady shifted from being a politician's wife to being a tireless political activist on behalf of gun control legislation after her husband, James Brady, President Reagan's press secretary, was shot and paralyzed in a 1981 assassination attempt on the president. Another example of mobilization after a dramatic event is the transformation of Sonia Gandhi, an apolitical spouse, into the leader of the Congress Party in India after the assassination of her husband, Prime Minister Rajiv Gandhi, in 1991. It is also suggested that many recruits for extremist movements such as political Islam are motivated to avenge a traumatic experience in which a family member or close friend was injured or killed by the domestic or foreign military.

Demographic Characteristics

4.3 **Illustrate how an individual's demographic characteristics are linked to political beliefs and actions.**

In our explanation of political beliefs and actions, we should also analyze the influence of an individual's *demographic characteristics*. Sometimes called *personal characteristics*, these include both visible characteristics, such as age, gender, and ethnicity, and less visible ones, such as education, income, social class, and occupation. These characteristics, when taken together, might be thought of as an individual's identity. What underlying dynamic might link these personal characteristics and an individual's identity with political behavior?

Demographic characteristics can be thought of as *filters* that influence how the environment and the agents of political socialization affect an individual's political behavior. For example, the current impact of parents as agents of political socialization is likely to be far greater for their offspring of age 4 than those of age 44. Similarly, an environmental context of Islamic fundamentalism in Saudi Arabia will have very different effects on the political beliefs and behaviors of Saudi men and women.

Much of the empirical research on political behavior attempts to establish and clarify the relationships between demographic characteristics and specific political beliefs or actions. Recent scholarship embraces the idea that these characteristics combine to create the identity of the individual. No single demographic characteristic is a certain predictor of political behavior, but empirical research (based on relational analysis) in many countries indicates that some demographic characteristics are associated with certain political beliefs and actions. Often, a person's identity can provide insights into her political behavior. And when key demographic characteristics seem to reinforce one another or be especially critical for the formation of an identity, you might have greater confidence in a correct prediction about a particular political behavior.

For example, can you think of any demographic characteristics that might inform your prediction of whether a particular person voted for Barack Obama or Mitt Romney in the 2012 U.S. presidential election? Table 4.1 uses relational analysis (like Table A.4 in the Appendix) to explore those linkages. Do any demographic characteristics seem to be associated with a tendency to vote for either candidate?

Table 4.1 Voting Choices in the 2012 U.S. Presidential Election, by Demographic Characteristics

			Obama 51%	Romney 47%
Gender	Male	47%*	48%	52%
	Female	53	55	45
Ethnicity	Caucasian	74	39	59
	African American	13	93	6
	Latino	10	71	27
	Asian American	3	73	26
Age	18–29	19	60	37
	30–44	27	52	45
	45–64	38	47	51
	65+	16	44	54
Family Income	Less than $50K	41	60	38
	$50–100K	31	46	52
	More than $100K	28	44	54
Education	Not high school grad	3	64	35
	High school grad	21	51	48
	Some college	29	49	48
	College grad	29	47	51
	Postgraduate	18	55	42
Religion	Protestant	53	42	57
	Catholic	25	50	48
	Other	7	74	23
	None	12	70	26

*Percentage of total electorate
Note: Due to rounding, not all categories total 100 percent.

SOURCE: Based on data from Roper Center 2012

In addition to comparing the overall percentage of voters in a category (e.g., high school graduates) for each candidate, another useful technique for answering this question is to determine whether there are instances in which the candidate's percentage for a category is noticeably different from the candidate's percentage of the total vote.

While most of the differences are not dramatic, some demographic characteristics do seem to correlate with support for Obama or Romney. Notice, for example, that the probability of voting for Obama was substantially higher among those who had any of the following characteristics: 18 to 29 years old; African American, Latino, or Asian American; "other" religion; not a high school graduate; and family income below $50,000. People's probability of voting for Romney was especially high among Caucasians, Protestants, and those over age 65.

Although there are some clear associations among variables, we cannot conclude that any demographic characteristic actually *caused* a person to vote for a particular candidate (see the distinction between correlational and causal analysis in the Appendix). And when several demographic characteristics are associated with voting choice, we cannot determine which of them are the most powerful predictors of candidate choice without statistical analysis (such as regression analysis, a statistical technique that identifies how much variance in the dependent variable—vote choice, in this case—can be attributed to each subject's level on various independent variables). Nonetheless, Table 4.1 provides reasonable support for our assumption that demographic characteristics are sometimes associated with political behavior.

While generalizations are always difficult, there is some consistency in the empirical research on the demographic characteristics of those who do vote (in political systems in which there are genuine voting choices). In general, a higher probability of *voting* is correlated with characteristics such as membership in organizations that have explicit interests in politics (e.g., political parties and unions), higher education, higher income, higher social class, greater age, and male gender. Incidence of voting is also associated with the person's political beliefs, especially a strong identification with a party; a greater sense of personal capacity to influence the political world (political efficacy); and deeper knowledge about the available political choices.

Research findings on *other modes of political behavior* are less extensive and less consistent. As in the taxonomies of participation, the crossnational studies by Verba and his colleagues (Verba, Nie, and Kim 1978) remain among the most influential in identifying the individual characteristics that correlate with each mode of conventional political action. Participation in campaign activities is especially linked with higher education, higher income, and male gender. Communal activities are generally associated with higher socioeconomic characteristics and with identification with a particular social group (religious, ethnic, or linguistic) that has a political perspective. Contacting government officials personally is least clearly related to demographic characteristics, and some research suggests that the decision to engage in personal contacts depends more on whether the person has an effective private means to gain her objective or must rely on contacting public officials to achieve this objective. Contacting officials might be the type of political action that has increased most during recent decades and it is increasingly facilitated by e-mail and other digital communications innovations (Anduiza, Jensen, and Jorba 2013; Marien et al. 2010).

In studying *extremist-activists,* many analyses attempt to specify the demographic characteristics that typify a particular type of activist relative to the general population. For example, many of the Muslims who have engaged in terrorist acts are young adult males who are well educated, married with children, and come from middle-class families (Berrebi 2007; Sageman 2008). The rural extremist-activists engaged in a struggle for control over land in Asia and Latin America tend to be male, poor, and have limited education. Urban activists who promote leftist ideologies (e.g., Marxism, environmentalism) are generally characterized as well educated, middle class, young,

Compare in 4

You Go Your Way, I'll Go Mine

The two young men have some common roots. Both are born into societies grounded in traditional social systems of hierarchy and male domination and strong, fundamentalist religion. Both are sons of prosperous professional fathers who are deeply religious. Each young man displays high intelligence and receives an excellent education.

As young adults, each trains successfully for a professional career and enters that career. Each is shocked when he witnesses religious or racial discrimination and the severe deprivation that characterizes the lives of the substantial majority of people in his society. Each becomes a deeply devout follower of his religion. Each develops a powerful commitment to the independence of his people from foreign powers, which are seen as the source of oppression and injustice. Each chooses a life of political activism and decides to engage in extreme political acts, as necessary, to achieve his vision of social justice. But the two men follow very different paths.

The first man travels to another country to join the revolutionary struggle against a major colonial power. He is trained and supported in guerrilla warfare tactics (see Chapter 11) by the U.S. Central Intelligence Agency and becomes an effective leader. After successfully defeating the foreign power, he returns home to Saudi Arabia to work in the family business. However, he is deeply offended by the presence and influence of foreigners in his religion's holiest lands. His open demands to expel the foreigners and establish a pure religious state result in conflict with the authoritarian regime in his homeland. He is harassed by the regime, his citizenship is revoked, and he is forced to leave the country. He eventually returns to the country where he had fought on behalf of the revolution.

By this time, he is convinced that his righteous cause can be advanced only by extreme acts of violence. He uses his considerable personal wealth ($300 million) to organize a loosely connected international network of highly trained extremist-activists living in more than 60 countries. He calls on all his followers to use any means necessary to free their lands from foreign rule. Members of his network commit many acts of international terrorism, including a massacre of tourists in Luxor, Egypt, in 1995 and the bombings of the U.S. embassies in Kenya and Tanzania in 1998. Many plots are unsuccessful, including an attempt to fly a hijacked airplane into the Eiffel Tower and assassination attempts on the leaders of Egypt, Jordan, and Pakistan. His network commits the most brutal terrorist attack ever undertaken in the United States, with two hijacked passenger airplanes crashing into the twin towers of the World Trade Center and another into the Pentagon on September 11, 2001. These attacks resulted in more than 3,000 deaths as well as worldwide fear and disruption of both travel and financial markets. In response to criticism that he targets innocents and supports terrorism, he comments:

> American history does not distinguish between civilians and military, and not even women and children. Americans are the ones who used the bombs against Nagasaki. Can these bombs distinguish between infants and military?...Your situation with Muslims in Palestine is shameful....[T]he American-led sanctions resulted in the death of over 1 million Iraqi children. All of this was done in the name of American interests. We believe that the biggest thieves in the world and the terrorists are the Americans. The only way for us to fend off these assaults is to use similar means. We do not differentiate between those dressed in military uniforms and civilians; they are all targets in this fatwa [death decree]. (*Source:* http://abcnews.go.com/sections/world/dailynews/terror_980609.html)

The Central Intelligence Agency (CIA) labels his al-Qaeda organization "the most dangerous terrorist organization in the world," and he becomes the prime target in the "war on international terrorism" initiated by then–U.S. president George W. Bush. He is hunted relentlessly for nearly a decade and is finally killed in 2011 by U.S. Special Forces in a raid of the home in Pakistan where he had been hiding.

Osama bin Laden and Mohandas Gandhi are two extraordinary extremist-activists who had similar backgrounds but chose fundamentally different paths of political action.

The second man witnesses the whites' racism against Indians while serving as a lawyer in South Africa. To resist such injustice, he develops a strategy of civil disobedience inspired by Henry David Thoreau as well as by his own religious beliefs. His fundamental principle is *ahimsa*—nonviolence in thought as well as in action. He advises his followers: "Not to submit; to suffer." He is repeatedly jailed for his nonviolent resistance to laws that he believes are unjust. He assumes that the opposition will discredit itself by its repressive responses to nonviolent protest.

Returning to his native India, he begins to organize protests demanding independence from the British imperialists. His protest techniques continue to be based on nonviolence and *satyagraha*—soul force. In contrast to brute force, soul force produces constructive change through positive action and reconciliation, not through harming and angering the enemy. He observes, "My experience has shown me that we win justice quickest by rendering justice to the other party." He becomes an extraordinarily powerful and inspirational leader through his theatrical acts of civil disobedience and his personal sacrifices, including extended fasts, lengthy marches, and sexual abstinence. His nonviolent activism captures world attention, and his Indian followers

expand to the tens of thousands. His supporters call him *Mahatma*—great soul. His tireless political activism over three decades contributes greatly to Britain granting independence to India. His life of struggle is not a complete success, however. He fails to prevent the division of India into separate countries dominated by Hindus and Muslims, a struggle bloodied by 1 million deaths. He fails to persuade Hindus to repudiate the divisive and unjust social caste system, and he is assassinated by a Hindu extremist within months of India's independence.

Despite their early similarities, Osama bin Laden (1957–2011) and Mohandas K. Gandhi (1869–1948) diverged onto nearly opposite paths of extreme political activism in the pursuit of their personal visions of social justice and human liberation.

Further Questions

1. Given the similar upbringings of bin Laden and Gandhi, how might you explain their different paths of activism?

2. Is it ironic that both died violently?

3. Which of *your* demographic characteristics has had the biggest impact on your political beliefs and actions?

and only slightly more likely to be male than female. Right-wing urban activists are more varied. Those promoting an ethnic or racist position (e.g., neo-Nazism) tend to be young, male, working or lower class, and somewhat lower in education (Schain, Zolberg, and Hossay 2002). Those promoting conservative causes such as the anti-abortion movement tend to be middle aged, female, middle class, and relatively well educated (Dalton 2013).

Overall, what do you expect to be the demographic characteristics most likely among *top political leaders* in a given society? Perhaps the broadest generalization is that leaders' demographic characteristics tend to be consistent with the characteristics of the socially dominant groups within their society. Why do you think this occurs? Among the most common shared characteristics across many societies are high education, upper-middle-class or upper-class background, association with the society's dominant religion and ethnicity, and male gender.

Given our general fascination with extraordinary political actors such as presidents, charismatic leaders, and revolutionaries, it is interesting to assess whether particular environments, socialization experiences, or demographic characteristics seem to account for the political behavior of these individuals. Compare in 4 briefly describes the environment, socialization, and demographic characteristics of two remarkable political activists. Do these factors seem relatively similar for the two men? Do these factors seem to produce similar political behavior?

Political Psychology

4.4   Consider how approaches from political psychology help us understand politics and political processes.

Why does one person vote and another abstain? Why does one ethnic group engage in a killing rampage against another group? Why does a political activist follow the path of bin Laden rather than Gandhi? These are examples of the modes of political behavior that political science attempts to explain. The three types of explanatory factors we have discussed to this point are either outside the person (the environment and agents of political socialization) or are surface characteristics (e.g., age, ethnicity, wealth). However, you might find yourself agreeing with those political scientists who insist that an adequate explanation of political behavior requires analysis that probes inside a person. This is broadly understood as the field of **political psychology**—*study of the deeper psychological dynamics within the individual that affect that person's response to political stimuli.*

Political psychology uses the theories and tools that have been developed in psychology to explain political behavior. It draws on such fields as neuroscience, evolutionary psychology, social psychology, cognitive psychology, and biopsychology, among others. Political psychology brings emotions, cognitive processes, and social interactions into our attempts to understand the politically relevant thoughts and actions of individuals and groups (Huddie, Sears, and Levy 2013). It includes the study of political orientations (Chapter 2) and of social network relations (discussed above as an agent of socialization). The subject of study might be an ordinary citizen—for example, why does a person vote for a particular candidate or hold anti-immigration sentiments? The focus might be members of the political elite—why does a leadership group make a decision like starting a war? Or the subject might be mass political behavior—what causes many people to join a huge public protest against a regime? (Tesler and Sears 2010; Sniderman and Hagendoorn 2007; Crenshaw 2000; Lerner et al. 2003).

There are several alternative (and sometimes complementary) frameworks of analysis that guide the work in political psychology. Here are brief descriptions of five of these approaches.

- *Rational choice* approaches base an explanation of individual or group political actions on the claim that people have relatively stable preferences and that they will try to think through how to achieve outcomes consistent with those preferences. There is no presumption that a person will be totally rational or will choose the "correct" decision and action. But the approach does assume that a person will attempt to make an assessment of the costs and benefits of alternative choices, estimate the probability of different outcomes, and then act on the choice with the most favorable expected outcome. The Appendix details a classic example of a paradox tackled by the rational choice approach: Why should a person put in all the effort (costs) associated with voting in a national election when her vote has so little probability of affecting the outcome and producing direct benefits? (Downs 1957; Green and Shapiro 1994; Shepsle 2010).

- *Cognitive and affective psychology* approaches suggest that the brain often makes decisions more rapidly than deliberative rational thought can manage. In essence, individuals use shortcuts based on their cognitive and affective orientations (recall these orientations from Chapter 2) to make many decisions quickly and with very little information. Analyses attempt to specify the content of these shortcuts regarding what a person knows and feels about a particular situation, and then this content is applied to explain how it shapes political behavior. For example, in many countries one of the key shortcuts that guides political behavior is party identification, which helps voters interpret policy positions by candidates and informs their voting decisions (Sniderman and Stiglitz 2012). Interestingly, research has demonstrated that rapid, low-information decision making on electoral choices (e.g., Should I vote for or against this ballot proposition?) can result in mass political outcomes that are no worse than those resulting from reasoned political deliberation (Lau and Redlawsk 1997).

- *Intergroup relations* analyses offer an explanation of group dynamics and collective behavior. Such group-based behavior has a central role in politics. For example, an understanding of intergroup dynamics provides insights about how groups compromise (e.g., how countries negotiate a peace treaty) and how people cooperate in groups to enhance their situation (e.g., forming an effective social movement) (Aguilar and Galluccio 2010; Sullivan, Snyder, and Sullivan 2008). This approach can also explain how groups end up in conflict. One group's sense of psychological threat and hostility toward another group might be based on perceived or actual competition over resources (e.g., jobs or goods), on conflict over values, beliefs, and identity (e.g., religion), or on a sense of different levels of status (Kinder and Sears 1981; Plant and Devine 2003; Pratto et al. 1994; Rick, Mania, and Gaertner 2006). Once a group is identified as constituting a threat, having undesirable values, or being of lower status, political elites could exploit these elements to persuade a group's members to join in violent actions against the targeted group. This might help explain such intergroup conflicts as the brutal interethnic violence in the 1990s in the Balkans or Rwanda (see Chapter 12) (Green et al. 2009; Staub 2011; Smith 2012).

- *Personality and psychodynamics* approaches explore aspects of the formation and effects of personality. Work in psychobiography explains adult political behavior on the basis of formative childhood experiences or critical life experiences (Erikson 1969; Schultz 2005). An interesting recent example from the political world is the contrasting psychobiographies of former U.S. President Bill Clinton (Fick 2000; Gartner 2009). Other analyses emphasize important needs, drives, and experiences embedded in a person's psyche to explain political thoughts and actions (George and George 1956; Post 2004). A related group of studies explains the significance for political behavior of certain personality characteristics, such as openness to experience, extraversion, need for security, desire for praise, conscientiousness, narcissism, and so on (Feldman and Stenner 1997; Woshinsky 1995).

- *Biopolitics* focuses on biological processes to explain decision making, information processing, and preference formation that have implications for political behavior. It builds on important work that has considered the essential elements of *human nature* and how human behavior has evolved over time within its social and environmental contexts (Wilson 1978). Neuroscience, which considers the neural processes of individuals, is the basis for explanations ranging from the reduction of intergroup violence over generations to the rulings about individual responsibility for human rights violations by the International Criminal Court (Pinker 2011; Shniderman and Smith 2014). John Hibbing and his colleagues present experimental evidence that individual genetic factors and brain biology are connected with a person's predisposition to certain ideological orientations (Hibbing, Smith, and Alford 2013; see also Fowler and Dawes 2009). Other research suggests that one's willingness to cooperate is "hard-wired" into our psychological processes, as are the tendencies to define groups to which we belong and groups we see as rivals (Kurzban, DeScioli, and Fenn 2012).

It should be evident that political psychology approaches offer explanations for many aspects of people's political beliefs and actions. Some of these explanations blend aspects of various approaches to political psychology. For example, Steven Pinker (2011), a distinguished neuroscientist, has offered a wide-ranging explanation of why violence has declined over many generations. Starting with our hunter-gatherer ancestors, Pinker blends the long evolution of our human nature with social history, the emergence of modern social institutions, the rise of science and rationality, and advances in individuals' cognitive content. He identifies the ways in which "the better angels of our nature" (the title of his book), such as empathy, reason, and a heightened moral sense, have slowly prevailed over sources of violence in human nature, such as sadism, dominance, and vengeance. He explores how "groupthink" has enticed people to accept ideologies and engage in actions that are repugnant to those outside the group. But he also describes social advances that have mitigated humans' violent tendencies, such as the emergence of controlling states and social institutions, the constructive interdependencies from commerce, and the increased reliance on secular reasoning.

Among the intriguing questions raised by political psychology is whether citizens are equipped to carry out their duties under a democratic system (Le Cheminant and Parrish 2010). For some people, the array of cognitive and affective biases that underpin political preferences may distort collective reasoning and deliberation. Resistance to new information that conflicts with partisan predispositions, negative reactions to immigrants, and positive reactions by voters to biological characteristics of candidates (like facial features or height) are all examples of psychological mechanisms that can override rational deliberation (Lenz et al. 2010). If citizens and leaders process political stimuli through such psychological mechanisms, stable democracy is at risk because it functions best with open dialogue, reasoned contestation over ideas, tolerance, and trust in political institutions (Pharr and Putnam 2000).

Recently, there has been particular interest in analyzing the psychology of those who engage in terrorist acts. While the backgrounds and even the personalities of terrorists vary, it has been suggested that many share some traits. They can be troubled by high levels of loneliness, alienation, and isolation and a sense that their identity group is not respected. As noted above regarding the impact of social networks, they can seek to overcome this through the sense of belonging provided by a small, strong network of friends. These individuals can also be very frustrated because they feel that the political and social conditions they value have been denied them by others whose actions are illegitimate and against whom they are willing to retaliate with violence. Some recent terrorists also have very strong religious convictions and are prepared to engage in any necessary actions to protect and promote their religion (Post 2008; Sageman 2008; Smelser 2007; Staub 2011; Victoroff 2005).

Concluding Observations

Our exploration of political behavior has continued with a consideration of primary explanations for individuals' political beliefs and political actions. The research and theories that attempt to answer the *why* questions about political behavior emphasize four types of explanatory factors: environmental context, agents of political socialization, demographic characteristics, and political psychology. The basic assumption is that some combination of these factors influences the kinds of political stimuli to which people are exposed, the manner in which they interpret these stimuli, and their responses to the stimuli.

The *environment* presents the individual with stimuli and opportunities as well as obstacles to certain political beliefs and actions. While a person can ignore or misperceive these broad environmental constraints, they do constitute a framework that guides, and to some extent determines, political behavior. In most political behavior research, the analyst can (and should) identify the major features of the environment that might affect the probability that an individual will manifest certain political beliefs or actions.

In a similar manner, an individual's *demographic characteristics,* such as age, gender, social class, and education, can have a powerful cumulative influence. First, they can serve as a set of filters that influence the kinds of political phenomena to which the person is exposed. Second, they can influence the expectations that others have regarding how the person ought to think and act politically. The empirical evidence is sometimes quite clear (as are the data on voting in the 2012 U.S. presidential election) that certain demographic characteristics (in a given environmental context) correlate significantly with particular political beliefs and actions. Demographic characteristics, rather like the environment, are best understood as a set of forces that influence the nature and intensity of individual political behavior but do not determine that behavior.

The inadequacy of either the environment or demographic characteristics as a complete explanation for most individual political behavior is reflected in the fact that people with comparable demographic characteristics or people who operate in a similar environment do not necessarily manifest identical political beliefs or actions. For example, of two sisters, one might be an activist deeply involved in Democratic Party politics and the other might be politically apathetic. Similarly, consider the divergent paths of political activism pursued by Mohandas Gandhi and Osama bin Laden, despite notable similarities in their characteristics and environments. While the environment and demographic characteristics might not provide a total explanation, a strong case can be made that these factors tend to set the boundaries within which much political behavior occurs.

The attempt to build an empirically validated causal theory of the effects of *political socialization* on political behavior is intriguing. A major analytic shortcoming in most of the political socialization research has been the difficulty of demonstrating empirically that there is a clear causal linkage from a specific agent of socialization to a particular belief and then to a politically relevant action. In most instances, researchers lack the methodologies and the data-gathering instruments to measure how the messages of various agents of political socialization are absorbed, interpreted, and responded to by people. Rather, the researchers must attempt to infer what socialization agents have been important by asking individuals to recall the major sources of their own political beliefs.

Despite these empirical difficulties, the study of political socialization is a useful tool/strategy in increasing our understanding of the major forces that influence how people learn about and evaluate political phenomena. In their attempt to use the agents of political socialization, political regimes display their own belief that these socialization processes can either create and preserve popular support for the existing political order or create a new political consciousness. Research suggests that where the agents of political socialization are ineffective or provide contradictory messages, a person's political behavior will tend toward apathy or, in a few cases, toward producing the totally committed political activist. While the precise linkages among agents of political socialization, political beliefs, and political behavior have yet to be empirically verified, this area of inquiry remains an important one for political scientists.

The explanation of political behavior by *political psychology* is perhaps the most intriguing of the four sets of factors. The psychology-based work examines the mechanisms for decision making that lead to both individual and group actions. The emerging work on the biological bases of political psychology focuses primarily on the political beliefs and political actions of the mass public. Some aspects of political psychology approaches are difficult to isolate from the other forces—the environment, demographic characteristics, and political socialization and learning—that intervene between human nature and political behavior and that shape psychological responses. The recent research linking political beliefs and actions to biological mechanisms is mainly based on laboratory experiments whose results are interesting but far from conclusive.

We began this chapter by asking whether it is possible to explain political beliefs and actions. In general, analyses can rarely prove that any of the four types of explanatory factors we examined is almost always *the* basic causal factor for a particular individual's political belief or action. Nonetheless, the evidence we explored in this chapter suggests that relevant knowledge about each of these four sets of explanatory factors can provide significant insights that can further your understanding of political behavior.

Key Concepts

For Further Consideration

1. Which agent of political socialization has been strongest in influencing *your* key political beliefs? Which of your key beliefs have been least influenced by this agent? What accounts for the agent's minimal influence on these beliefs?

2. Under what conditions are demographic characteristics likely to have particularly powerful effects on an individual's political beliefs or actions?

3. To what extent are people either a blank page on which political beliefs can be written ("nurture") or genetically determined actors ("nature")? In what ways is this overall assessment valid for *you*?

4. Can you identify any examples in which your own schooling might be viewed as politically biased by someone from another culture?

5. Can you predict the political behavior of a friend or family member based on what you know about the individual's demographic characteristics or identity? Try it and then check to see if your predictions are correct!

For Further Reading

Calderisi, Robert. (2007). *The Trouble with Africa: Why Foreign Aid Isn't Working.* **London: Palgrave.** A controversial explanation, which focuses particularly on a national character analysis, for the difficulties that most African countries have faced in achieving economic development.

Campbell, David E. (2008). *Why We Vote: How Schools and Communities Shape Our Civic Life.* **Princeton: Princeton University Press.** This demonstrates the connection between the fostering of strong civic norms and subsequent civic and political engagement. The early influence on civic engagement can be seen decades later.

Erikson, Erik. (1969). *Gandhi's Truth.* **New York: Norton.** Applying his rich psychobiographical approach, Erikson explains the crucial points of development shaping the personality and political style of Mohandas Gandhi.

Evans, Geoffrey and Nan Dirk de Graaf, eds. (2013). *Political Matters: Explaining the Strength of Class and Religious Cleavages in Cross-National Perspective.* **New York: Oxford University Press.** The analyses document the continuing (although declining) influence of social class on party choice and the extent to which secularization has reduced the impact of religious beliefs on political positions, especially for many Europeans.

Gobodo-Madikizela, Pumla. (2003). *A Human Being Died That Night: A South African Story of Forgiveness.* **Boston: Houghton Mifflin.** A psychologist who was a member of the Truth and Reconciliation Commission in South Africa explains the importance of this public acknowledgment process in creating a new peace and reducing the likelihood of future ethnic and racial atrocities.

Hancock, Ange-Marie. (2013). *Solidarity Politics for Millennials.* **New York: Palgrave-Macmillan.** This is a current and provocative look at intersectionality (how several different systems of identity, especially systems of oppression) can reinforce one another, influencing behavior.

Hayhoe, Ruth. (1992). *Education and Modernization: The Chinese Experience.* **New York: Pergamon.** A classic, insightful analysis of the effects of education on the political socialization process and on culture and modernization in China, from Confucianism to Marxism.

Hibbing, John, Kevin Smith, and John Alford. (2013). *Predisposed: Liberals, Conservatives, and the Biology of Political Differences.* **New York: Routledge.** Based on a series of experiments, the authors attempt, in an engaging read, to utilize biological, genetic, and brain behavior approaches to explain political beliefs and actions related to topics such as leadership styles, tolerance, aggression, and racial attitudes.

Huddy, Leonie, David O. Sears, and Jack C. Levy, eds. (2013). *Oxford Handbook of Political Psychology.* **New York: Oxford University Press.** This award-winning book employs the insights of psychology to examine issues in the political world such as the impact of personality, political socialization, information processing in opinion formation, emotion and politics, gender and political behavior, and styles of conflict resolution.

Huxley, Aldous. (1932). *Brave New World.* **London: Chatto and Windus.** A chilling vision of a society in which the state effectively uses socialization and material conditions to control the thoughts and actions of citizens.

Khadra, Yasmina. (2007). *Sirens of Baghdad.* **Trans. John Cullen. London: Heinemann.** A compelling novel that describes the conversion of a gentle, idealistic Iraqi college student into a disillusioned survivor in war-torn contemporary Iraq and then into a violent, nonreligious radical activist.

Lawrence, Bruce, ed. (2005). *Messages to the World: The Statements of Osama bin Laden.* **London:** Verso. The known commentaries by the late leader of al-Qaeda provide insights into his worldview and strategies.

Mandela, Nelson. (1995). *Long Walk to Freedom.* **Boston: Little, Brown.** In his autobiography, the late Nelson Mandela provides a compelling narrative of his extraordinary life of political activism against racial injustice and apartheid, culminating in his election as president of South Africa.

Mearsheimer, John J. (2011). *Why Leaders Lie: The Truth about Lying in International Politics.* **New York: Oxford University Press.** This always-controversial political scientist examines the different strategies and motivations when top leaders lie about the reasons for their foreign policy actions.

Monroe, Kristen. (2011). *Ethics in an Age of Terror and Genocide: Identity and Moral Choice.* **Princeton, NJ: Princeton University Press.** In studying why people engage in altruistic acts (e.g., putting oneself at risk by harboring Jews from persecution in Nazi Germany), this book links the power of identity, the role of basic values, and problems with the rational choice explanation.

Nixon, Richard M. (1962). *Six Crises.* **New York: Doubleday.** Richard Nixon, one of the most controversial U.S. presidents, provides a revealing self-assessment of his reactions to six critical events in his early political career.

Norris, Pippa, and Ronald Inglehart. (2011). *Sacred and Secular, Religion and Politics Worldwide.* **Second ed. Cambridge: Cambridge University Press.** Using evidence generated by the World Values Survey, the volume considers the role of religiosity and religion for political behavior in the contemporary political world.

Pinker, Steven. (2011). *The Better Angels of Our Nature: Why Violence Has Declined.* **New York: Viking.** A readable, widely discussed book by a neuroscientist who claims that violence, including political violence, has declined because humans have evolved over many centuries into a less violent species, in part due to the role of state institutions, interdependency, and education, as well as human reason.

Post, Jerrold. (2004). *Leaders and Their Followers in a Dangerous World: The Psychology of Political Behavior.* **Ithaca, NY: Cornell University Press.** A distinguished psychiatrist analyzes the crucial role of personality and the psychological bases of political behavior, focusing on both top leaders such as Saddam Hussein and radical political activists. See also Post's 2008 book, *The Mind of the Terrorist*.

Putnam, Robert D., and David E. Campbell. (2012). *American Grace: How Religion Divides and Unites Us.* **New York: Simon & Schuster.** A rich (and very readable, if lengthy) study, based on extensive survey data, of the power of both religion and secularization on the thinking and actions (including political) of different generations of citizens of the United States.

Rolfe, Meredith. (2013). *Voter Turnout: A Social Theory of Political Participation.* **New York: Cambridge University Press.** The case is made that standard demographic variables are not sufficient explanators of variation in political participation. Instead, systematic variation in social ties among potential voters explains why some choose to participate while others do not.

Sinclair, Betsy. (2012). *The Social Citizen.* **Chicago: University of Chicago Press.** Evidence is provided to show that political choices are shaped by social interactions. Political behavior is shaped and altered by the political opinions and actions of our peers.

Skinner, B. F. (1948). *Walden Two.* **New York: Macmillan.** A renowned behavioral psychologist presents his conception of a setting in which socialization is used to create a benign and cooperative community. An intriguing counterpoint to Huxley's *Brave New World*.

Wattenberg, Martin. (2011). *Is Voting for Young People?* **3rd ed. New York: Pearson.** This short book uses empirical data from the United States in comparison to other democracies to assess the political inactivity of young Americans, relative to their European peers and older Americans, and to argue for more political activism.

Wolfenstein, E. Victor. (1967). *The Revolutionary Personality: Lenin, Trotsky, Gandhi.* **Princeton, NJ:** Princeton University Press. A classic study of three major revolutionary leaders from a psychoanalytic perspective.

Zuckerman, Alan S., Josip Dasovic, and Jennifer Fitzgerald. (2007). *Partisan Families: The Social Logic of Bounded Partisanship in Germany and Britain.* **Cambridge: Cambridge University Press.** Using longitudinal data, the authors demonstrate the impact of family on partisan political attitudes. The comparative analysis presents generalizable evidence about the persistence of family in the shaping of attitudes.

On the Web

http://america.aljazeera.com
A somewhat alternative perspective of a network based in Qatar, Al Jazeera claims that it offers "unbiased, fact-based stories of U.S. and international news."

http://www.americanrhetoric.com/ informationindex.htm
The News and Information Index from American Rhetoric is an extremely rich set of links to newspapers from around the world and other online news sources, magazines, search engines, polling databases, and legal databases.

http://www.electionstudies.org
Data (that can be downloaded) and analyses from the American National Election Study, the major survey of U.S. political opinions and behavior (1948–2008). The material on the Web site addresses topics such as the role of demographic characteristics, ideology, and partisanship in relation to political beliefs and actions.

http://www.cddc.vt.edu/feminism
The Feminist Theory Web site, hosted by the Center for Digital Discourse and Culture at Virginia Tech University, provides a large

number of links to information on beliefs as well as groups and movements inspired by a feminist perspective on political and social issues in many countries.

http://culturalpolitics.net

This site offers numerous links that explore the role of culture in shaping our political, economic, and social lives.

http://www.cnn.com/WORLD

The site for CNN, the 24-hour, U.S.-based international news organization.

www.google.com/transparencyreport/

This is a comprehensive report containing data about governments related to the search engine company, including requests to remove content and information about users.

http://www.itn.co.uk

World news and British news from Independent Television News, based in London, are provided.

http://www.nytimes.com

This is the site for key articles and information from one of the premier newspapers in the United States.

http://wn.com

WorldNews provides an extensive electronic news portal with international sites in multiple languages categorized by geographic region, country, and subject.

http://news.bbc.co.uk

The Internet home of the British Broadcasting Company, this site offers world political, business, scientific, and entertainment news from a British perspective.

http://news.google.com

Using the same technology as in the Google Internet search engine, this site provides access to thousands of different news sources.

Chapter 5
Political Systems, States, and Nations

 ## Learning Objectives

5.1 Characterize the alternative definitions and goals of the state.

5.2 Contrast the concept of nation from that of the state.

5.3 Outline the key components of the political system.

They inhabit a region of 74,000 square miles, most living inside the current borders of Turkey, Iraq, and Iran. But they are not Turks, not Arabs, not Persians (Iranians). These kin-based, mountain nomads have always had their own language, a distinctive culture, and a powerful sense of shared identity. They want to be recognized as their own country; instead, they have experienced centuries of discrimination, cultural destruction, massive violence, and even genocide.

They continue to dream of Kurdistan—the land of the Kurds. Kurdistan was briefly recognized by a few other countries (e.g., the former Soviet Union) after World War I, but the Kurds' land was successfully claimed by other countries. Great Britain held colonial control of some of the area, where substantial oil deposits were discovered in 1920. The British gave most of the oil-rich areas inhabited by the Kurds to Iraq, whose new leaders the British installed and assumed they could control. At the same time, Atatürk was establishing the modern state of Turkey (see Focus in 10). Atatürk launched a major military and cultural offensive against the 19 million Kurds inside Turkey. He insisted they were not Kurds, but "mountain Turks." Kurdish language, names, schools, and cultural traditions were forbidden, and when the Kurds resisted, the Turkish military killed 250,000 of them.

In Iran, Shia Muslims took power after the Iranian Revolution of 1979. They have extensively persecuted the Kurds within Iran's borders because the Kurds are Sunni Muslims. Then, Iraq's Saddam Hussein—frustrated by the Iran–Iraq War (1980–1988) turned his wrath on the Iraqi Kurds. In the military campaign known as *Al Anfal*, meaning "The Spoils," the Iraqi military were given orders to kill every Kurdish male between

A stateless nation. Kurds in Iraq protested in 2011, demanding greater autonomy. They now employ political and military power to promote their larger goal, a state of Kurdistan.

the ages of 18 and 55. Between 1986 and 1989, *Al Anfal* included mass executions of tens of thousands of noncombatants; the destruction of more than 4,000 villages; the use of chemical weapons, such as mustard gas, in more than 60 villages; the destruction of civilian buildings like schools and mosques; and the arbitrary jailing of tens of thousands, including women, children, and elderly people accused only of sympathizing with the Kurdish cause. More than 180,000 Iraqi Kurds were killed during this genocide.

Although as many as 35 percent of the Kurds fled the area to escape the violence, about 36 million Kurds still live in the region, including about 19 million in Turkey, 9 million in Iran, 6.5 million in Iraq, and 1.5 million in Syria. The granting of partial autonomy to the Kurdish region in Iraq after the fall of Saddam Hussein has raised the hopes of Kurds throughout the region that—through negotiation, political activism, and armed resistance—Kurdistan will one day become a reality.

The desire of the 36 million Kurds for a state of their own highlights one of the most significant causes of conflict in the modern world: the existence of nations— groups of people with a powerful, shared sense of identity—who live in areas that are not coterminous with the boundaries of states, which are the legal political entities in the international system. Sometimes, as in the case of the Kurds, the Masai in Kenya and Tanzania, and the Palestinians in Israel and Jordan, the nation spills over across the boundaries of two or more states. Other times, the nation is a subgroup that exists within a single state but wants autonomy or independence. This is the situation of groups such as the Quebecois in Canada, the Tamils in Sri Lanka, and the Catalans in Spain, among many others.

In Part Two (Chapters 2–4), we focused on improving our understanding of the political beliefs and actions of individuals. In Part Three, we substantially expand our analysis, examining the politics and political behavior of very large collectivities of people. This chapter explains and distinguishes two crucial concepts characterizing these large groupings: *state* and *nation.* States are arguably the most important actors in the international system. However, nation-based identities are powerful, and the disjunction between state boundaries and peoples with shared identities might be the greatest cause of violence and death in the contemporary political world. The chapter concludes with a focus on a more abstract model that can help us grasp how these large groups operate as a political entity—the concept of the *political system.*

The State

5.1   **Characterize the alternative definitions and goals of the state.**

In discussing the politics of large groups of individuals, one of the core concepts is the state. Anthropological evidence suggests that early social organization among humans was probably based on small groups. As suggested by humanistic psychologist Abraham Maslow (1954), human groupings formed so that people were better able to meet their physiological, safety, love, and belonging needs. As groupings became larger, tribes or bands were formed on the basis of more extensive kinship and economic ties. It might be argued that the "state" emerged in ancient times, when a large collectivity had distinctive leadership roles, accepted rules for social interaction, and a set of organizational arrangements that identified and served collective needs.

A Legal Definition of the State

However, the social scientific concept of the state is a relatively modern one. It is based on the legal notion that the **state** is *a territorially bound sovereign entity.* The idea of sovereignty emerged in the sixteenth and seventeenth centuries. In current interpretations, **sovereignty** is *the premise that each state has complete authority and is the ultimate source of law within its own boundaries.* Sovereignty is the key element in the legal concept of the state. It is a basic assumption of international politics and is reflected in a fundamental principle of the United Nations—the sovereign equality of all member states. This means that, before the law, Cambodia is equal to China, Bolivia is equal to Brazil. While sovereignty has legal standing and moral force in international law, the reality of international politics is that a state's sovereign rights depend ultimately on whether the state has sufficient power to enforce its position (Sassen 1996; 2008). Thus, it is not likely that, when major national interests are at stake, China will yield to Cambodia merely on the basis of Cambodia's sovereign rights.

State is among the most extensively used concepts in political science, and it has various meanings. Notice that in the general language of political science, the word state usually refers to the set of organizational units and people that performs the political functions for an entire national territorial entity, such as France, Indonesia, or Nigeria. In some countries, including the United States, the concept of state also refers to subnational governmental units (e.g., the State of Alabama). In this chapter and throughout this book, the term state will normally denote the full array of governmental units that act on behalf of a sovereign country.

You should also be aware that the language of political science often treats the state as though it were a single actor. For example, consider the statement that "each state has complete authority...." In reality, the state is composed of many people who behave as individuals but whose combined behaviors are characterized as if they were performed by a single actor. This book also examines other collectivities of individuals (e.g., the group, the political party, the judiciary) that are discussed as though they operate as a single actor.

Associated with the idea of sovereignty in the legal definition of the state is the doctrine of **territorial integrity,** which holds that *a state has the right to resist and reject any aggression, invasion, or intervention within its territorial borders.* As with the more general notion of sovereignty, a state's actual protection of its territorial integrity depends on the state's capacity and political power.

It might seem that there are many relatively clear examples of a state's territorial integrity being violated, such as the Iraqi army's invasion of Kuwait in 1990, but there is often considerable disagreement over claimed violations of territorial integrity. First, territorial integrity is a fuzzy concept when there is a *dispute over borders.* There are numerous current disputes among countries regarding ownership of offshore waters and their resources (e.g., Canada, Denmark, Russia, and the United States regarding the Arctic). Such disputes are sometimes settled by adjudication by an international agency. But border disputes can precipitate fighting, as did an ongoing land border dispute between Cambodia and Thailand that began in 2008.

Second, attempts to exercise sovereignty can be disputed when there is *disagreement about who the legitimate rulers are.* In Angola, for example, three contending groups each claimed to be the legitimate ruling group of the resource-rich country at independence in 1975. Each group controlled parts of the country, and each had outside assistance (money, arms, troops) from actors such as Cuba, South Africa, the former Soviet Union, the United States, and the United Nations. This struggle over sovereignty resulted in a devastating civil war that ravaged the country for more than 25 years (1975–2002). The toll included complete collapse of the economy, 4.5 million refugees, tens of thousands who lost limbs to millions of land mines, and the death of more than 1.5 million Angolans. Similar conflicts over sovereignty have arisen recently in Ivory Coast, Somalia, and the Spanish Sahara.

Third, the international community has become less sensitive to the protection of sovereignty when there is strong evidence that the government is committing *serious human rights violations* against its own citizens. This can lead to intense controversies about whether sovereignty has been violated. One recent example is Libya. After substantial numbers of Libyans openly protested against the rule of Muammar Gaddafi in 2011, opposition groups seized control of considerable territory, especially in Eastern

Libya. Gaddafi responded aggressively, sending his military forces against the rebels. Some major actors in the international community, including the United Nations, Britain, France, and the United States, insisted that Gaddafi stop the violence against his own people. A NATO-led coalition then intervened, claiming its goal was a humanitarian intervention to prevent Libya from using its troops to engage in widespread, deadly violence against the regime's opponents. Airplanes and missiles destroyed some of Libya's military capabilities but also attacked Libyan troops and other sites, including Gadaffi's residence. Gaddafi claimed that these actions were a clear violation of Libya's sovereignty. Whose claim is most compelling? By late 2011, the external and internal opposition forces overthrew Gaddafi's government. Gaddafi was found hiding and was brutally executed by rebels. Similar disputes over sovereignty versus intervention are becoming more common as the international community embraces the doctrine of R2P—the "responsibility to protect." This issue is explored in the Debate in 5.

A Structural–Functional Definition of the State

As an alternative to the legal definition, the state can be defined by the key organizational *structures* that operate as "the government" and the key *functions* that the state performs. In this structural–functional perspective, the **state** is defined as a country's *organized institutional machinery for making and carrying out political decisions and for enforcing the laws and rules of the government.* Chapters 6 and 7 take a more in-depth look at institutions and consider how variations in institutional design can affect politics and policy.

Max Weber (1864–1920), the great political sociologist, emphasizes one specific function that distinguishes the state from all other organizations: The state has a monopoly on the legitimate use of force and coercion in the society. That is, only the state has the right to use violence to enforce the society's laws and decisions.

In the broader state-centered definition, the state is an autonomous actor, composed of public officials making decisions. The state's essential functions are to maintain order and to compete with other actual or potential states (Levi 2002). In this view, the state pursues "the national interest," which it attempts to achieve against resistance or competition from both domestic and international actors (Morgenthau 2005; Kahler 2003). The particular way in which a state's structures are configured is crucial in shaping the content of public officials' policy preferences and the state's effectiveness in implementing those policy preferences in the society.

A widely used structural–functional approach, based on the work of the late Gabriel Almond and his colleagues (e.g., Powell, Strom, and Dalton 2012), centers on two questions:

1. What *functions* must be performed if the state is to persist?
2. What *structures* perform these necessary functions within a given state?

Chapters 6 and 7 will detail many of the major political structures and institutional arrangements (e.g., legislatures, judiciaries, and electoral systems) that handle the

The Debate in 5

Does Humanitarian Intervention Violate State Sovereignty?

A controversial issue in recent years is whether it is acceptable for states and international actors to use force (or the threat of force) against a state that is suspected of or is abusing the human rights of its own citizens. This is sometimes justified as humanitarian intervention by those taking the actions (Holzgrefe and Keohane 2003). However, the state that is the target of such an intervention can object that this is a clear violation of its sovereignty and hence of international law (Jackson 2007). Indeed, this policy has been termed "the most significant adjustment to national sovereignty in 360 years" (Gilbert, quoted in Pattison 2012: 4). Disputes over the clash between these principles have recently been serious issues regarding countries such as China, Congo, Libya, and Syria. Is humanitarian intervention an acceptable action if it violates a state's sovereignty?

Protecting Human Rights Takes Precedence over State Sovereignty

- The international society of states now defines sovereignty in terms of a bundle of both rights and obligations. Respect for human rights to "life, liberty, and security of person" is among those

obligations, by virtue of the Universal Human Rights Declaration (adopted by the United Nations in 1948) and other treaties. Thus, a state that inflicts gross and widespread atrocities on its own population has forfeited some of its rights, including its claim that humanitarian intervention violates its sovereignty (Pattison 2012).

- The United Nations General Assembly (in 2005) and Security Council (in 2011) explicitly asserted a collective "responsibility to protect" (R2P) people by humanitarian intervention when a government does not safeguard its own peoples' lives, particularly in cases of large-scale state violence against its population such as ethnic cleansing, violent repression of peaceful protest, or extensive use of imprisonment without due process (Evans 2009).

- The global community of states has a clear responsibility to "take all necessary measures" to prevent any state from abusing individuals' human rights because this demonstrates the states' responsibility and willingness to act beyond national self-interest (Weiss 2012).

- Outside states, acting in concert, also have a responsibility to intervene in situations of a

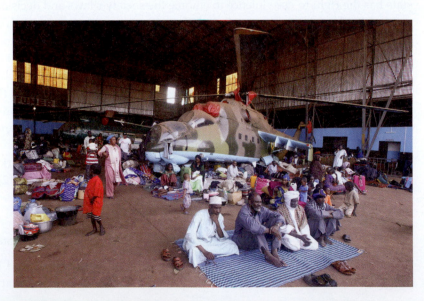

When a political system breaks down in violence and political decay, thousands die and even more seek food, shelter and to escape their state. These refugees in the Central African Republic seek such humanitarian intervention in 2014.

severe humanitarian crisis, including actions to prevent a deepening of the crisis, to direct reactions to it, and to engage in rebuilding efforts in the aftermath, regardless of objections from the "sovereign" state (Pattison 2012).

- If no outside group intervenes to stop a state from serious violations of human rights, the state might engage in even more extensive and unacceptable acts of violence against its own citizens. Similarly, in the absence of such action by interveners, other states might be emboldened to violate the human rights of their own citizens.

State Sovereignty Takes Precedence over Outsiders' Concerns about Human Rights

- State sovereignty and territorial integrity are a central premise of international law and have been repeatedly restated by the United Nations. This core principle provides a state with almost complete authority to implement policy decisions within its own borders. A state's right to this exclusive internal jurisdiction is violated if another state or group intervenes within its borders without its consent. In accordance with international law, the state can respond by any means necessary to defend its territory (Bajoria and McMahon 2013; Jackson 2007).

- Despite the idealized notion of universal human rights, different cultures have significantly different interpretations of individual rights and the conditions under which such rights have been violated. It is not appropriate that a predominantly Western conception of human rights should necessarily take precedence over a country's own standards.

- It can be very difficult for outside actors to determine the precise level of the purported violations of human rights within another country.

Even more important, there are no universally accepted standards regarding the level at which human rights violations become so gross (that is, so extensive, severe, and persistent) that outside intervention is justified (Evans 2009).

- States accept the principle that, in the absence of full procedural support from the UN, external actors cannot intervene within a state that opposes such an action. Yet such interventions do occur (e.g., NATO in Kosovo and Libya). Such actions are often better understood as an assertion by powerful states of the right to intervene (R2I) in the affairs of weaker states that they wish to control—even if under the cover of UN support (Bajoria and McMahon 2013).

- Humanitarian intervention, when associated with severe economic sanctions and military invasion, can cause more harm to the population than the human rights violations that prompted these actions. Military intervention can produce disproportionate levels of violence, and the situation after intervention can be highly unstable and dangerous (Pattison 2012).

More questions...

1. How severe and extensive must a violation of human rights be to justify the intervention of other countries in the internal affairs of a sovereign state? Who can legitimately judge the level of violation?

2. Is R2P more compelling if there appear to be human rights violations by several groups within a country, not just the government?

3. Is it acceptable for external interveners to cause widespread suffering and destruction within a country in the attempt to end the perceived human rights abuses?

---

various political functions. The classic version of Almond's structural–functional approach identifies eight functions that must be performed in every state:

1. **Political socialization** is the processes through which individuals acquire their cognitive, affective, and evaluative orientations toward the political world.

2. **Political recruitment** is the processes through which people are drawn into roles as political actors.

3. **Political communication** is the mechanisms by which political information flows through society.

4. **Interest articulation** is the low-level communication by individuals and groups of what they need or want from the state.

5. **Interest aggregation** is the transformation of all these political needs and wants into a smaller number of coherent alternatives.

6. **Policymaking** is the process by which the state establishes laws, policy decisions, and value allocations.

7. **Policy implementation** is the actual application of such laws and policy decisions.

8. **Policy adjudication** is the interpretation and resolution of disagreements regarding what the policies mean and how they should be implemented.

While it might seem obvious at first glance that a certain structure always performs a particular function, more reflection (and later chapters) will suggest that the situation is usually more complex. In most contemporary societies, almost every political function is performed by a variety of structures. Many of these structures are part of the state, but others are nonstate actors such as interest groups, religious organizations, media, social groups, private businesses, and international organizations. For example, it is not the case that only Congress performs the policymaking function in the United States. Many policy decisions are also formulated by the president, by cabinet departments, by the bureaucracy, by the courts as they both interpret and reshape laws, by structures at the local levels of government, by special interest groups, and by citizens through electoral initiatives. Thus, the central focus in structural–functional research is to illuminate the key processes performed by each important structure and the subtle relationships among structures as they contribute to a given function.

Major Goals

Another core question is: What major goals does a state pursue? Each state assigns different levels of relative importance to a wide variety of goals; however, most can be subsumed under three overarching goals: **security**, **stability**, and **prosperity**. Each of these goals includes component goals that the political system might act to serve. The significance of each component goal and the capacity of the state to achieve each goal depend on many factors such as the state's resources, strategic location, history, political culture, leaders, political structures, and the behavior of actors outside the political system. While many of these factors depend primarily on dynamics inside the state's borders, others are substantially affected by the actions of other global actors. Figure 5.1 illustrates this framework of basic goals. In the descriptions that follow, the major components of each overarching goal are presented in the general order of their priority for most states.

Security

1. *Survival* is the fundamental element of security. It entails the very existence of the state, such that other states do not conquer it and that internal forces do not destroy it.

2. *Autonomy* refers to the capacity of the state to act within its own boundaries without intervention in or control of its affairs by external actors.

Figure 5.1 Basic Goals of States

3. *Influence* involves the state's ability to alter the actions of external actors in desired ways by means of persuasion or inducements.
4. *Prestige* is the desirable situation wherein external actors admire and respect the state.
5. *Dominance* is the use of power or violence to enable the state to impose direct control over external actors.

Stability

1. *Order maintenance* is the capacity of the state to ensure social peace for its citizens through the prevention of individual and group violation of societal norms, especially those involving violence.
2. *Political development* refers to the concentration of political authority in a state that has strong capabilities to make and enforce effective policies and to gain support from its citizens.
3. *Democratization* is the process of institutionalizing a democratic system of governance, which is achieved by allowing free elections, limiting the actions of the rulers, and guaranteeing civil and political rights.

Prosperity

1. *Economic growth* refers to the increasing scale, complexity, and specialization of the productive system and of the goods produced.

2. *Economic development* is the capacity of the political economy to obtain, manage, and transform resources into valued goods.

3. *Welfare distribution* refers to the private or public allocation of adequate and increasing levels of valued goods to enhance the quality of life of the citizenry.

Notice that, in Figure 5.1, stability and prosperity rest on the foundation of security because survival must be an essential goal of every country. In most states, certain prosperity goals and stability goals are more important than some of the other security goals, such as dominance. No state can fully achieve its desired level on all of these 11 major goals. Thus, a state must make difficult trade-offs when pursuing multiple goals. For example, when a state makes a costly increase in the welfare goods and services allocated to its citizens, it uses resources that it might otherwise have reinvested in its economic system to facilitate economic growth. This trade-off is often referred to as the fundamental policy choice of *growth versus welfare*. In another example, resources that the state allocates to the military for major security goals are not available for either welfare or the production of consumer goods. This policy trade-off is characterized by the phrase *guns versus butter* (Norpoth 1987). Of the 11 major goals listed in Figure 5.1, which ones do you think are most complementary? Most incompatible?

Throughout this text, we will frequently examine the pursuit of the goals of security, stability, and prosperity through the state's actions within its own boundaries and the state's interactions with actors outside its borders. There are crucial normative questions that each state confronts regarding how much priority to give to each goal, what strategies it should employ in the pursuit of its goals, and how extensive state action should be. Moreover, there are strong disagreements within each state regarding how expansive its domain of action should be. Everyone agrees that the boundaries of state activity should be limited to **res publica**, a Latin phrase meaning *"things of the people."* But what things should be included? And how expansive should the state's involvement with these things be? For example, each of the major "isms" outlined in Chapter 2—conservatism, classical liberalism, socialism, fascism, Islamism, and so on—has a fundamentally different prescription for the extent of legitimate state action. A central topic in Chapter 8 is the role of the state in the economic system.

We shall see throughout this book, and especially in Part Five, that some states are active in almost every aspect of their citizens' lives, while other states intervene in only limited spheres and to a limited extent. One state might provide a total health care delivery system to all citizens, with no direct charges for doctors, hospitals, or treatment, whereas another state might subsidize only hospitalization for the very poor. One state might require schools to provide daily religious instruction, while another state might forbid schools from engaging in even the general discussion of religious philosophies. In every society, there are persistent, and sometimes very contentious, political debates about the appropriate boundaries of state action and about the best means to achieve a particular aspect of one of the 11 major goals.

The Nation

5.2   **Contrast the concept of nation from that of the state.**

In the political world, the concept of the nation has a psychological and emotional basis rather than a legal or functional basis (as the concept of the state does). A **nation** is defined as *a set of people with a deeply shared fundamental identification*. Different factors might be the basis of such identification: shared descent (belief in a common kinship or history), shared culture, shared geographic space, shared religion, shared language, or shared economic order. The nation is a community of understanding, of communication, and of trust (Smith 2010). The Kurds are an example of a nation that fulfills all these conditions.

Most people identify with a variety of different reference groups or communities such as a religion, local community, ethnic group, social club, or sports team. A person's self-described identity might be based on one or more of the factors, such as shared culture, and it might also be shaped by some combination of the demographic characteristics described in Chapter 4. In the usage here, what distinguishes a nation from other reference groups is that the nation is a major group, beyond the family group, with which a person identifies very powerfully. It is an essential division between "us" and "them."

A related concept is *identity politics*. This means that some key shared trait(s) lead a significant group of people to see themselves as being distinctive, with a shared political agenda that might shape their political beliefs or motivate their actions (Hoover, Marcia, and Parris 1997; Parker 2005). Identity politics characterizes a group defined by one of the major nation-based factors described above, such as ethnicity or religion. Some suggest that the concept of identity politics particularly applies to groups that perceive themselves to be marginalized or oppressed within their social order. In this sense, it has been applied to groups based on markers such as ethnic minority status, caste, gender, or sexual orientation.

Another broad class of nation-based groups that is sometimes given special consideration is *indigenous peoples*—a term for more than 370 million people in about 70 countries. Each of these 5,000 distinct nations is understood to be a "first people" who originally inhabited a geographic area as "natives," but who were then subjugated by an invading nation. In nearly every case, these nations have almost no political or social power and their culture is marginalized or suppressed by the dominant culture. Since the early 1970s and most recently with the Declaration on the Rights of Indigenous Peoples (2007), the United Nations has been concerned about protecting such groups against discrimination and against efforts to destroy their national identity and culture. Some of these nations have become more politically assertive, demanding autonomy, although most countries resist providing their indigenous peoples with special political rights.

The strength of a person's primary nation-based identity depends on the relative importance he places on various identities and the extent to which the most important identities reinforce the basic conception of "us" versus "them." When there is a strong identity with a large group, it can be termed **nationalism**—*a powerful commitment to the advancement of the interests and welfare of an individual's own nation*, usually with minimal concern about benefitting the conditions of those outside the nation. Nationalism can be a positive force when it brings people together to cooperate and achieve collective benefits, or it can be negative when it mobilizes a population to oppress or do violence to others outside the nation.

Nation and State

The best situation for effective governance is a ***nation–state***, which is *an area that has both the territorial borders of a single state and a citizenry who all share the same primary national identity*. Only a few modern states have the combination of common culture, history, ethnicity, religion, and language that results in a strong sense of shared nationality among nearly all the citizens governed by the state. Japan is an example of a relatively homogeneous nation–state.

However, the most common situations are what might be termed stateless nations. Occasionally, one nation is split into two states, such as North and South Korea. In such cases, the citizens often dream of reunification, even when their governments and ideologies differ fundamentally. This occurred in Germany, which was split into communist East Germany and capitalist West Germany after World War II. In 1990, citizens of the German nation were reunited in a single country after nearly half a century of antagonistic separation into two very different states. The example of the Kurds at the beginning of the chapter illuminates the more severe form of a stateless nation, with one nation distributed across multiple states.

The reality of the contemporary world is that most countries are ***multinational states***, which *include significant groups whose fundamental identities are associated with different nations*. While it can be difficult to define when a state is truly multinational, it is evident that the great majority of current states contain nation-based groups with distinctive identities (Stojanovic 2010). When identity and region are relatively similar, it is possible to provide greater autonomy to major groups or to reorganize states and borders. For example, substantial political autonomy has been granted to nation-based regions such as Catalonia within Spain, the Kurds in Iraq, and the Scots in the United Kingdom, whose vote for sovereign independence failed in 2014. When the former Soviet Union—the world's most multinational state—collapsed in 1991, it was replaced by 15 sovereign states that were generally organized on nationality grounds. The 2011 split into Sudan and South Sudan is another recent attempt to better align borders and national identities.

However, there are far more instances in which the problems in multinational states persist. When these nation-based identities are very strong, they can produce intense animosity and violence between groups within (and among) states (Laitin 2007; Miller 2007; Taras and Ganguly 2010). Russia acted illegally in 2014 to reclaim the Crimea, a region in Ukraine whose majority population has strong nation-based identity with Russia. The agitation by the Quebecois in Canada, the Basques in Spain, and the Irish Catholics in Northern Ireland is testimony to the possibility that even centuries-old states can struggle with nationality conflict. The bloody nationality violence in Eastern Europe during the 1990s was based on devastating ethnic battles among the Bosnians, Croatians, Serbs, and others in the former Yugoslavia. These types of conflicts are considered in more detail in Chapter 12, Political Violence.

These problems have been particularly evident in many of the states that gained independence after 1945 with borders that were based on the arbitrary administrative decisions of colonial powers, not nationality differences. The horrendous ethnic conflict in Rwanda and Burundi between the Hutus and the Tutsis resulted in the slaughter of more than 100,000 (mostly Tutsis) in Rwanda in only 100 days in 1994, and more than 300,000 Hutus and Tutsis were killed in ethnic conflict in Burundi between 1994 and 2006. There are reports every day of struggles within countries by groups that do not share the nation–state's dominant identity, such as the Palestinians in Israel, the Tibetans and Uighurs in China, the Nuer in South Sudan, and the pro-Russians in eastern Ukraine. Thus some scholars predict that the current reorganization of states based on national identities will produce more than 50 new states and that nation-based conflicts might remain the world's major cause of violence and instability (Barber 1996; Miller 2007). The example of the Indian subcontinent in Focus in 5 illustrates many of these issues regarding the challenges of balancing states and nations.

The Political System

5.3 **Outline the key components of the political system.**

As the Appendix explains, formal models are abstractions that can sometimes be very helpful in enabling us to better visualize how something works. A formal model that has influenced the way many political scientists (including us) understand the dynamics of politics is based on a concept called "the political system." You might also find it useful, perhaps as a metaphor for thinking about politics.

The political system concept was developed in the work of David Easton (1965), whose idea was to adapt general systems theory from biology. Any system is a series of components that operate together and are interrelated, such that change in any one component can affect other components. For example, an engine is a mechanical system composed of such interrelated components as pistons, carburetor, spark plugs, and so on. A jazz band is an example of a human system whose components can be more improvisational but no less interrelated. A political system is also a system of human behavior with multiple components. The political system model identifies these components and the linkages among them as they perform certain activities.

For Easton, the unique nature of the **political system** is that it performs a particular function: *the authoritative allocation of values for the collectivity*. This means that the political system makes policy decisions (allocations) that are binding (based on its authority) with regard to things that have importance (values) to the people it serves (the collectivity). Each part of this definition is important for our general understanding of politics, so the next few paragraphs elaborate on each.

Focus in 5

State and Nations: The Indian Subcontinent

The problem of discontinuities between nations and states is often most severe in states that have gained independence since 1945. The Indian subcontinent exemplifies these problems. The vast Indian subcontinent was a feudal society divided into many small kingdoms ruled by kings (maharajahs). Starting in the sixteenth century, the riches of India were pursued—and often exploited—by many traders, including the British, Dutch, French, and Arabs. The states from which these traders came began to struggle for dominance over the Indian trade, and the British gained hegemony in the eighteenth century after defeating the French. From that time until 1947, the Indian subcontinent was the major jewel in the British imperial crown, treated as a single territory under colonial rule.

After a lengthy and often violent campaign of political and social action by Indian nationalists, the British granted the subcontinent independence in 1947. Despite the desires of the British and the efforts of some Indian leaders, such as Mohandas Gandhi (recall Compare in 4), the subcontinent was deeply split on the basis of religion between Hindus and Muslims. Because it seemed impossible to fashion a single state out of these two nations, two states were formed in 1947: India, which was predominantly (82 percent) Hindu; and Pakistan, which was predominantly (90 percent) Muslim.

Many Hindus in Pakistan and Muslims in India were forced to leave their homelands and migrate to the new state sharing their religion. The hostility and bloodshed associated with the partition resulted in 1 million deaths. There have been periodic violent boundary conflicts ever since. The ownership of nuclear weapons by India and Pakistan since 1998 accentuates the need to resolve the conflicts between the two states.

While the major religious difference on the Indian subcontinent was generally resolved by this partition, many other nationality problems remained. For example, since 1947 India and Pakistan have disagreed about which country should control the region of Jammu and Kashmir. At independence, India was given control of the region, although the majority of the population was and remains Muslim. Disputes over control of the region have resulted in more than 60 years of military conflicts and intermittent guerrilla war, despite persistent United Nations involvement.

The situation was further complicated by the concentration of Muslims in two geographically distinct areas in the northeast and northwest regions of the subcontinent. As a consequence, Pakistan was composed of two parts at independence, separated by more than 1,500 miles of rival India's territory. The two parts of the country engaged in a protracted nationality dispute between the two major ethnic groups, the Punjabis, who were dominant in West Pakistan, and the Bengalis, who were dominant in East Pakistan. The Bengalis felt discriminated against both economically and culturally by the Punjabis, who controlled the government and the military. When the Bengalis won a national election in 1970, the Punjabis in West Pakistan attempted to retain political power and refused to allow the elected Bengali leaders to take the reins of government. The Punjabis launched a brutal military operation to suppress the Bengalis, who decided that victory in the struggle would enable them to form their own independent nation–state. After a brutal civil war in 1971, which resulted in 3 million deaths from violence and starvation and 10 million refugees fleeing Pakistan, the Bengalis of East Pakistan won the civil war and created a new sovereign state, Bangladesh.

Major nation-based cleavages continue to plague India, creating substantial barriers to forging a single identity as a nation–state. There are 21 official languages in addition to the two national languages, Hindi and English, each understood by only about one-third of the population. In all, there are about 1,650 different dialects spoken in India, most of which are mutually unintelligible.

India has at least five major religious groupings: Hindu, Muslim, Sikh, Christian, and Buddhist.

Hindu nationalism has increasingly been expressed through a political movement, resulting in the growing power at the regional and national levels of Hindu parties, particularly the Bharatiya Janata Party (BJP). The BJP, which dominated the government from 1998 to 2004 and rules as the majority since 2014, is the most serious threat to a secular Indian government since independence. With the increase in Hindu nationalism, violence against Christians and Muslims has risen significantly.

Another religion-based nation that has been a source of political unrest in India is the Sikhs, who are concentrated in the northwest part of India called the Punjab. The Sikhs have a very strong identity as a religious community and an ethnic group. Their sense of nationality is heightened by their belief that they are discriminated against politically by the Hindus. The Sikhs have occasionally been militant in demanding greater political autonomy, and since the early 1980s some have insisted on full independence to create the nation–state of Khalistan. Prime Minister Indira Gandhi was assassinated in 1984 by two Sikhs among her private guard in retaliation for an Indian army attack on rebels inside the Sikhs' holiest shrine.

Rajiv Gandhi succeeded his mother as prime minister, only to be the victim of another nation-based dispute. The Indian army had intervened on the neighboring island-country of Sri Lanka in an attempt to limit the extremely violent, ethnically based civil war between the native Sinhalese and the Tamils, who had migrated to Sri Lanka from southern India. Tamils in Sri Lanka were angry that India did not support their independence struggles and by the treatment they received from the Indian army. In 1991, Rajiv Gandhi was assassinated by a Tamil woman who had strapped a bomb to her body.

In sum, the many deep cleavages on the Indian subcontinent, based on religion, ethnicity, culture, and region, have exposed the (now five) states to persistent instability, conflict, and nation-based carnage.

Further Focus

1. What strategies can a state like India use to overcome the many nation-based cleavages?

2. Might the current problems in the region have been even greater if Gandhi's vision of a single state had been fulfilled, rather than the split into Bangladesh, India, and Pakistan?

VALUES *Values* are those *things that have great significance and importance to people.* *Political values*, those within the domain of *res publica*, have a variety of other forms. They can be *broad ideals* like liberty, equality, freedom, and justice. They can be *material goods*, such as a decent house or road system; they can be *services*, such as quality health care or a good education; or they can be *conditions*, such as clean air or security from national enemies. Values can also be *symbolic goods*, such as status. In addition to positive values, there are negative values such as coercion or imprisonment, polluted water, epidemic disease, and so on. (Notice that this social scientific concept of values is broader than the notion of values as moral judgments that people use to guide their actions.)

Most values are scarce resources—either there is an insufficient amount of a given value to satisfy everyone or the enjoyment of one value by some requires a loss of value to others. For example, a state's vast arsenal of nuclear weapons may make one person feel secure and at the same time make another person feel extremely insecure. One person might favor more government expenditures to fight global terrorism, while another would prefer the government to spend more resources on providing quality health care, and a third might prefer lower taxes rather than either of these forms of government spending. Every possible value distribution entails trade-offs among different values as well as some inequality in the benefits and burdens linked to each person. Thus, there are always disagreements, competition, and even violent conflict over whose values will be served and whose will not. What are *your* top two values for your society? For yourself?

ALLOCATION Pierre Mendes-France, a distinguished French premier (1954–1955), observed that "to govern is to make choices." *Allocation* refers to such choice making— the process by which decisions and actions are taken to grant values to some and deny values to others. Value allocations occur at every moment when decisions are made to alter or even to sustain the existing distribution of values. Making these decisions and actions in the face of competition and conflict over values is a central aspect of politics.

AUTHORITATIVE Value allocations are *authoritative* when the decisions are accepted as binding by those people affected by the decisions. One of the most fascinating questions in political analysis is: Why do people accept the authority of the political system to allocate values in a manner that is not to their direct advantage? That is, why do people accept the imposition of taxes, policies, and laws that they judge to be undesirable for themselves? Compare in 5 suggests some of the reasons people accept the decisions of the political system, comparing authority relations with the exercise of power.

FOR A COLLECTIVITY The domain of activity for the political system is all those areas in which it makes authoritative decisions that affect people's lives. In Easton's classic definition, a political system functions "for a society." His definition serves the purposes of this book well because the book focuses primarily on states—country-level political systems. But a political system can exist at any level. This concept could certainly apply to subnational political systems (including such U.S. examples as states, counties, and municipalities). It could also apply to a supranational political system that encompasses more than one country (e.g., the European Union, which includes 28 separate countries). Thus, this book offers a more generalized definition of the political system as "the authoritative allocation of values *for a collectivity.*"

Conceptualization of the Political System

In Easton's (1965) conceptualization, the political system can be viewed as a gigantic processing mechanism that converts inputs into outputs (Figure 5.2). The political system exists within a larger environment that includes other systems, such as the economic system, the cultural system, the physical resource system, and many others. This broader environment generates many *inputs*, called demands and supports, which the actors in the political system consider. The political actors then produce outputs, the decisions and actions that allocate values. If these outputs have an effect on the environment, this might produce new demands and supports. This processing system becomes a continuing cycle.

The *environment of the political system* is the name given to *all those activities that are not part of the political system's activity domain.* Do not think of the environment as a separate physical area, but rather as those things that occur around the political system and provide both opportunities and constraints on its functioning. This environment could include anything anywhere in the world, although most of the global environment has little direct relevance to any action by a particular political system. So, for

Compare in 5

Power and Authority

Few discussions about politics can occur without direct or indirect reference to power or authority. Both concepts imply the capacity of A (one actor) to control the behavior of B (another actor). What is the difference between power and authority?

Power. *Coercive* **power** *is exercised when A induces B to behave in a manner in which B would not otherwise behave, based on the use of force or the threat of force.* In some cases, A actually inflicts direct bodily harm on B using an instrument of force (e.g., guns, bombs, or torture) or A imposes undesirable conditions on B (e.g., imprisonment or discriminatory treatment). However, there are many cases of power exercise in which B's behavior is controlled when B believes there is a credible threat that A will administer coercive power.

Some scholars distinguish a second form of power, economic power (Boulding 1993). In *economic power*, A alters B's behavior by manipulating resources that B wants or needs. A might refuse to sell or give to B an important resource (e.g., oil, economic aid, or military protection) that B wants unless B meets A's demands. Alternatively, A might promise to provide B with a resource (e.g., a trade agreement or a bribe) only if B does what A desires.

Of course, A is not necessarily successful in the threat or use of coercion or the manipulation of economic resources. B could decide not to alter its behavior in the way that A wants by ignoring a threat, by refusing the economic resources offered by A, or by responding with its own coercive power, which could result in violence between A and B. When actors have competing values, the option of employing coercive power or economic power is always a possibility.

A third form of power is **"soft power"** (Nye 2009). Soft power is evident when B is persuaded to accept what A wants because B greatly admires A's virtue and qualities and because B believes that it shares important values with A. Thus A exercises its soft power when B accepts A's demand, even if it is not in B's evident self-interest, without any explicit threat or the promise of the provision of a resource. (For other views of power, see Bachrach and Baratz 1962; Boulding 1989; Dahl and Stinebrickner 2003; Lukes 2005; and Wrong 1996.)

Authority. B's compliance in an authority relationship with A is not based on power. B behaves in the manner consistent with A's demands on the basis of **authority** when *B willingly accedes to what A wants because of B's belief that A has a legitimate right to demand compliance.* Authority is voluntaristic. B accepts the decision or demand of A because it is "the right thing to do," not because of coercive, economic, or soft power. The judgment of B that A's authority is legitimate might be grounded in one or more of the following (see Weber 1958a: 295–301):

Law. B believes that the laws or rules enforced by A are rationally established, purposeful, and enacted by a legitimate process, and thus compliance with those laws is proper behavior.

Tradition. B is influenced by a long-standing habit among most people to accept patterns of authoritative action by A. Socialization is typically an element in this form of convincing (indoctrinating?) B to accept the authority of A.

Charisma. B accepts the actions of a dynamic leader whose personal qualities are so extraordinary that the leader wins B's trust and unquestioning support. This seems an extreme form of soft power.

Contract. Acceptance of A's authority is based on B's belief that there is a contract between A and B in which A enforces a social order that protects B's interests. When actor A is the state, a broad version of this is the concept of the social contract proposed by classical political theorists such as Thomas Hobbes (1588–1679; recall Chapter 2) and John Locke (1632–1704).

Notice that the dynamics of power and authority relationships cover a vast number of situations that involve competing values and agendas and thus are political. There are many instances in which the behaviors of both actors A and B are a complex mix of power and authority patterns. As with other actors, even the power and authority of the state can be challenged. Consider: Antigone, in Sophocles' (496–406 B.C.E.) classic play, who challenges a law by the king, her uncle Creon; Mohandas Gandhi's campaign of resistance to British rule in India; the civil rights movements in South Africa and in the United States; and the citizens' resistance to tainted political leadership in many countries, such as the challenge to Syria's Bashar al-Assad. Of course, not all challenges to a state's power and authority are legitimate and desirable. Creon tries to persuade Antigone that a danger of defiance is social disorder: "He whom the State appoints must be obeyed to the smallest matter, be it right or wrong....There is no more deadly peril than disobedience" (Sophocles 1967: 144). The balance between compliance and resistance to power and authority is at the heart of politics.

Further Questions

1. In general, is it more sensible for the state to rely on power or authority to achieve its goals of security, stability, and prosperity?

2. Consider Lord Acton's cynical aphorism that "all power corrupts." Do you agree with this gloomy appraisal?

3. American philosopher Henry David Thoreau (1817–1862) writes: "If [the law of the state] is of such a nature that it requires you to be the agent of injustice to another, then I say, break the law" (Thoreau 1849: 92). What injustice would persuade you to break the law? What law would you be willing to break?

Figure 5.2 Conceptualization of the Political System

SOURCE: Based on Easton 1965: 31.

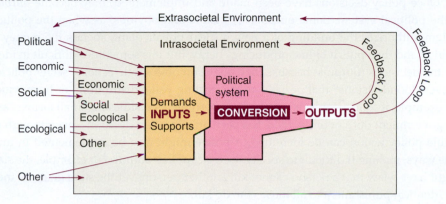

example, if the physical resources environment inside the country (or the relevant parts of the physical resources environment outside the country) contains few energy resources, that has an effect on the challenges facing those making political decisions. If the internal cultural environment is permeated by religious conflict, that matters. If a neighboring country is taking actions perceived as a threat to security, that will affect the demands and supports that the political system must deal with. You can see that many aspects of the environment can shape the inputs to the political system's actions.

Demands are *wants or desires for particular value allocations.* Demands might come from individuals, groups, or systems either within or outside the society. For example, when a citizen or interest group expresses a preference for lower taxes, more expenditure on health care, or greater regulation of corporations, this becomes a demand on the political system.

Supports are *actions by individuals or groups that indicate either favorable or unfavorable orientations toward the political system.* These actions can be directed toward any *actor* in the political system, from a major figure like the president to a low-level bureaucrat to a governmental body like the legislature to a political symbol like the country's flag. Support can be positive, as when a person pays taxes, serves in the state's military, salutes the flag, or votes. Support can also be negative, through actions that criticize or oppose the political system such as when a person refuses to pay taxes, avoids military service, burns the flag, or defaces a ballot.

At the heart of the political system framework is *conversion*—the process by which political actors assess demands and supports within the context of the relevant environmental forces and then determine what values will be allocated to whom. Many political analysts have been especially interested in studying this process. Chapter 9 will describe an analytic model of the public policy process that defines a series of key stages, from problem definition to implementation and evaluation. Chapter 9 also compares three general explanations of how the political system makes policy decisions: the *class approach,* the *elite approach,* and the *pluralist approach.* You will find that in each of these three approaches, a different mix of groups wields power and influence as the political system converts demands and supports into policy decisions.

Once policy decisions have been made and implemented, they become *outputs* of the political system. Some outputs are visible and obvious, as when the political system authorizes the building of a new nuclear power plant, spends the money to build it, and then puts it online producing energy. But it is sometimes difficult to identify the decisions (outputs) because they might involve subtle actions, secret policies, or even "nondecisions" that perpetuate the existing value distribution or bury issues. For example, if some people demand new government subsidies for small farmers and the government does nothing, there has been an allocation decision—even though no visible policy action can be identified. A policy might also be implemented in multiple ways, making it difficult to specify the exact policy output. For example, the state might have a law that a person cannot kill another person, yet the state does not mete out identical punishment to all those who do kill.

Most analysts distinguish outputs from *outcomes—the impacts of the decisions taken and implemented by the political system.* Ultimately, it is the impacts of the political system's policy choices that really affect people's lives. The essential question is: What difference did that policy choice (that value allocation) make? That is, how does the implemented policy affect people's health, welfare, security, freedom, knowledge, self-worth, or other values? Even more than in the analysis of outputs, it can be extremely difficult to identify with precision the overall outcomes of a policy and its effects on particular individuals and groups.

The final component in the systems approach is the feedback loop. Decision outputs result in outcomes that alter aspects of the environment and thus affect the next round of demands and supports reaching the political system. *Feedback* is the dynamics through which information about those changes in the environment are monitored by the political system. As changes alter both the environment and the demands and supports, political actors might decide to revise the value allocations they have previously made. As Figure 5.2 indicates, feedback is drawn as a loop to emphasize the continuous circular process among components in the system.

For Easton (1965), a crucial question is: How does a political system persist in a world of challenges and change? Political decision makers must maintain a delicate balance of forces: The environments must be prevented from constraining or overwhelming the political system and must be exploited for the resources and opportunities they present; political actors must be sensitive and accurate in their perceptions and policy decisions; demands must be managed so that they are not irreconcilable and do not overload the resources available; and positive support must be nurtured and negative support discouraged or suppressed. In short, the actors in the political system must operate with political skill and political will. If the political system's performance is poor, there can be serious consequences: a substantial decline in the quality of citizens' lives; major social disorder, as in Syria since 2013; a "failed state" such as Somalia; even the "death" of the political system, as occurred in the Sudan in 2011 (when it broke into two countries). Later chapters, especially Chapters 10 and 12, will develop these themes more fully.

Three Major Concepts: A Reprise

This chapter has furthered our understanding of the political world by exploring three major concepts that characterize large political entities: state, nation, and political system. First, *state* emphasizes the legal standing and power of sovereign entities, the necessary functions that they perform, and the domain of their actions. The discussion also identified an array of goals that most states pursue, centering on the core goals of security, stability, and prosperity.

Second, *nation* indicates a mental state characterized by a sense of shared identity among a set of people, distinguishing "us" from "them" in the sociopolitical world. Multinational states face particularly strong challenges from the instability that can result from different nation-based identities. The Indian subcontinent is among the many examples of the problem of disjunction between state and nation.

Third, *political system* attempts to provide political scientists with a basic analytic concept for building a general theory of political entities and processes. It is useful as a metaphor for thinking about the dynamic processes among the crucial components in an open, dynamic, and adaptive system whose essential function is the authoritative allocation of values for its collectivity. In Chapters 6 and 7, our discussion of political units will become more concrete as we examine the actual political institutions and structures in contemporary states.

Key Concepts

authority, p. 127
demands, p. 129
environment of the political
   system, p. 126
feedback, p. 130
identity politics, p. 121
indigenous peoples, p. 121
inputs, p. 126
multinational state, p. 122

nation, p. 121
nationalism, p. 122
nation–state, p. 122
outcomes, p. 130
outputs, p. 130
political system, p. 123
political values, p. 125
power, p. 127
prosperity, p. 118

res publica, p. 120
security, p. 118
soft power, p. 127
sovereignty, p. 113
stability, p. 118
state, p. 115
supports, p. 129
territorial integrity, p. 114
values, p. 125

For Further Consideration

1. Do you think there are circumstances in which a country's sovereignty should be violated? What is the most serious problem with your position on this question?

2. Do you identify with more than one nation? Is there any conflict between these identities? Under what types of circumstances might a person's multiple national identities produce serious internal conflicts?

3. To what extent is it possible to align states and nations in the contemporary world? Would doing this be desirable?

4. Develop a dialogue between person A, who believes that the authority of the state must be obeyed under almost all conditions, and person B, who believes that the authority of the state can be disputed in any situation in which B substantially disagrees with the state's decision.

5. Describe several situations in which the decision-making capacity of the most powerful actors in the political system is almost completely constrained by factors in the extrasocietal or the intrasocietal environment.

For Further Reading

Barber, Benjamin R. (1996). *Jihad vs. McWorld.* **New York: Random House.** An incisive analysis of current world trends, in which there is a simultaneous globalization of culture and economics and a breakdown of peoples into distinct and hostile nationality groups.

Bell, Stephen, and Andrew Hindmoor. (2009). *Rethinking Governance: The Centrality of the State in Modern Society.* **Cambridge: Cambridge University Press.** Challenges arguments that the state has been undermined by globalization and presents empirical support connecting the role of the state to governance and civil society.

Connor, Walker. (1994). *Ethnonationalism: The Quest for Understanding.* **Princeton, NJ: Princeton University Press.** A detailed analysis of the nature of and the imperatives driving a people's strong identity with nation as opposed to state, enriched by many illuminating examples.

El Ouali, Abdelhamid. (2012). *Territorial Integrity in a Globalizing World.* **Berlin: Springer Berlin Heidelberg.** A reimagining of the bounds of territorial integrity as a cornerstone of international law in light of globalization.

Evans, Gareth. (2009). *The Responsibility to Protect: Ending Mass Atrocity Crimes Once and for All.* **Washington, DC: Brookings Institution Press.** Linked to the Debate in 5, this is a vigorous justification of the obligation of a state to protect its own citizens from atrocities and, if it fails, the necessity (R2P) of international intervention.

Hutchinson, John, and Anthony Smith, eds. (1995). *Nationalism.* **New York: Oxford University Press. Hutchinson, John, and Anthony Smith, eds. (1995).** *Ethnicity.* **New York: Oxford University Press.** These two Oxford Readers offer an exceptional selection of short excerpts relevant to understanding each concept. Each book includes perspectives from a wide variety of social scientists, historians, social theorists, and others.

Jackson, Robert. (2007). *Sovereignty: The Evolution of an Idea.* **Malden, MA: Polity Press.** A thoughtful exploration of the concept of sovereignty, including its historical development and its contemporary implications for interstate relations, human rights, and global society.

Kaufman, Stuart J. (2001). *Modern Hatreds: The Symbolic Politics of Ethnic War.* **Ithaca, NY: Cornell University Press.** The manipulation of ethnonationalist sentiments to serve the political goals of leaders is described in a set of intriguing case studies.

Kesey, Ken. (1962). *One Flew Over the Cuckoo's Nest.* **New York: New American Library.** A funny, gripping novel (also made into a film) that, at its core, considers the virtues and costs of defying institutional authority.

Marx, Anthony W. (2003). *Faith in Nation: Exclusionary Origins of Nationalism.* **New York: Oxford University Press.** This study emphasizes the way in which nation-based identity is created mainly by excluding groups, especially based on religious differences, as an intentional strategy to establish nationalism and consolidate governmental power.

Miller, Benjamin. (2007). *States, Nations, and the Great Powers: The Sources of Regional War and Peace.* **New York: Cambridge University Press.** An explanation of why some regions are peaceful and others are war prone based on different patterns of balance or imbalance between nations and states in the region, using case studies from Europe, South America, and the Middle East.

Pattison, James. (2010). *Humanitarian Intervention and the Responsibility to Protect: Who Should Intervene?* **New York: Oxford University Press.** Based on the conventions of international law and an analysis of recent examples, the author offers an argument for the conditions under which intervention by those outside a sovereign state is legitimate and likely to be beneficial.

Paul, T. V., John Ikenberry, and John Hall, eds. (2003). *The Nation–State in Question.* **Princeton, NJ: Princeton University Press.** These essays explore the continuing power and central importance of the state, despite the enormous forces undermining the state from both nation-based identities and globalization.

Pierson, Christopher. (2011). *The Modern State.* **3rd ed. New York: Routledge.** What defines a state and what role does the state play in modern times? The author attempts to answer these questions while also placing the evolution of the state in the context of a globalizing world.

Rashid, Ahmed. (2002). *Jihad: The Rise of Militant Islam in Central Asia.* **New Haven, CT: Yale University Press.** Author of the widely discussed *Taliban* (2010, Yale University Press), Rashid offers a rich account of the rapid emergence of religious nationalism in the "stans" of Central Asia (e.g., Tajikistan and Kazakhstan), driven particularly by poverty, corruption, and a reaction to the suppression of Islam in the region.

Snyder, Jack. (2000). *From Voting to Violence: Democratization and Nationalist Conflict.* **New York: W. W. Norton.** In exploring four different types of nationalism (civic, ethnic, revolutionary, and counterrevolutionary), the author examines the relationship between nationalism and other dynamic forces, especially democratization, political leadership, and political violence.

Sorensen, Georg. (2001). *Changes in Statehood: The Transformation of International Relations.* **New York: Palgrave.** A useful taxonomy of states (modern, postmodern, and postcolonial) is the basis for an exploration of how states attempt to achieve their security goals as they respond to pressures from external and internal forces.

Taras, Raymond, and Rajat Ganguly. (2010). *Understanding Ethnic Conflict: The International Dimension.* **4th ed. New York: Longman.** In addition to a helpful conceptualization of the nature of ethnic conflict, revealing case studies discuss the problems of nation and state in settings such as Canada, Eritrea and Ethiopia, Sri Lanka, and the former Yugoslavia.

Thoreau, Henry David. (1849/1981). *Walden and Other Writings.* **Ed. J. W. Krutch. New York: Bantam.** These essays, especially "Civil Disobedience," constitute one of the most influential arguments in English for resisting authority.

On the Web

http://www.atlapedia.com

Atlapedia provides diverse statistical information and various maps for each country as well as recent political history.

http://cwis.org

The Web page of the Center for World Indigenous Studies, an independent, nonprofit organization emphasizing the distribution of knowledge about the issues and status of indigenous peoples (nations not coterminous with states) and promoting greater autonomy of power to such peoples.

http://www.ipl.org

The Internet Public Library provides links to numerous reference books, newspapers, and magazines about various countries.

https://www.cia.gov/index.html

The Web site of the U.S. Central Intelligence Agency includes the CIA World Factbook, a detailed and relatively up-to-date compilation of information about the political, economic, geographic, and demographic characteristics of every country.

http://www.un.org/esa/socdev/unpfii

The official site of the United Nations Permanent Forum on Indigenous Issues.

http://www.state.gov

Operated by the U.S. Department of State, this site has country reports and information on international organizations, human rights, and numerous other topics related to foreign policy and international relations.

http://www.countryreports.org

Country Reports provides comprehensive reports for most countries and includes access to international news and reference maps.

http://www.nationsonline.org

This site offers an encyclopedic array of portals with details of states and many aspects of their governmental, cultural, and economic forms.

http://www.economist.com/countries

This site, produced by the publishers of *The Economist,* a respected British newsmagazine, contains detailed country profiles and links to international news resources.

Chapter 6
Political Institutions I: Institutional Structures

 Learning Objectives

6.1 Analyze the structure and roles of political executives.

6.2 Summarize the roles of the legislature.

6.3 Compare the functions and powers of political administrative systems.

6.4 Outline the major elements within judicial systems.

There was trouble on the Korean peninsula. Troops from communist North Korea had invaded noncommunist South Korea in 1950. U.S. President Truman authorized a "police action" and sent U.S. troops to South Korea to stop the invasion. As the conflict escalated into a major war, the Truman administration concluded that a stable U.S. economy was important for the war effort. However, a wage dispute resulted in a major strike by the steelworkers' union against the steel mill industry. Truman feared this strike would seriously disrupt the steel supply and war-related production of many defense contractors and harm the U.S. economy as a whole.

Given these concerns, Truman seized the steel mill industry, placed it under the control of federal administrative agencies, and ordered the workers to end their strike. However, President Truman's bold steps to control the industry did not follow the proper procedures outlined in acts of Congress. The president argued, with the support of the steelworkers, that he had inherent powers to seize the steel mills, especially in a time of crisis. The steel companies, led by Youngstown Sheet and Tube Company, challenged Truman's justification and filed suit against President Truman and Secretary of Commerce Charles Sawyer. The companies claimed that the president did not have the authority to seize the steel mills without following the procedures that were specified in the legislation.

After hearing the case, the United States Supreme Court supported the position of the steel companies by a vote of 6 to 3. In the majority opinion, Justice Black wrote

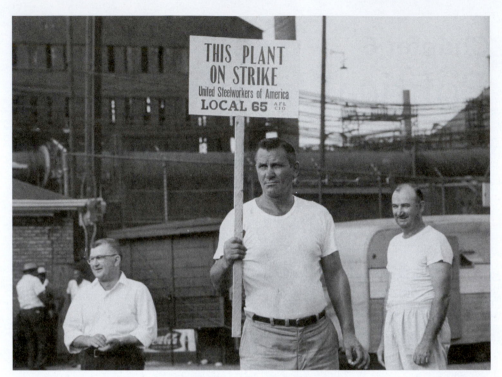

On strike! Union members of the United Steelworkers of America picket outside a U.S. steel plant in support of their goals of higher wages and improved working conditions.

that the inherent power to order seizure of the steel mills would need to be based on either executive authority provided for in the U.S. Constitution or a statute passed by Congress. The court majority ruled that there was no such constitutional provision or statute. Chief Justice Vinson disagreed. In a dissenting opinion, Vinson argued that President Truman's actions were justified because Congress had not passed legislation expressly prohibiting this kind of action by the president and because previous presidents, including Abraham Lincoln, had taken similar actions in the past. Faced with the Supreme Court decision, Truman's administration withdrew its control of the steel mills, and the workers went back on strike. At that point, Congress became very concerned about the impacts of the strike on the Korean War effort. Congress then quickly passed legislation specifically providing the president with the power to seize the steel mills. In response, the workers ended their strike.

In this famous case, all the major political institutions of the U.S. national government were actively involved: the executive (the president), the legislature (Congress), the judiciary (the Supreme Court), and the administration (federal agencies). These four political institutions exist in every modern state. And every political system has grappled with serious questions regarding how to design, modify, and manage its set of political institutions and political arrangements to maintain an effective government that can achieve valued goals. As James Madison noted during the writing of the

U.S. Constitution: "In framing a government which is to be administered by men over men, the great difficulty is this: You must first enable the government to control the governed; and in the next place, oblige it to control itself."

Political institutions are the established roles, rules, procedures, and structures through which government operates. Political systems with well-developed institutions are more likely to be stable over time. To the extent that the institutions in any given country are easily replaced or ignored, the government will be more vulnerable to political, social, or economic upheaval.

Studying the institutional structures of the state raises questions such as: Which institution dominates a given policy sphere? How independent are the different institutions? How are the preferences of the citizens represented in the institutions? How are these roles allocated to specific people? What are the relationships among the executive, the judiciary, the administration, and the legislature? How powerful is the legislature? Are the courts independent of the other branches of government? How do the political system and the economic system intersect? What is the role of the constitution? How does the national government interact with sub-national governments?

Exploring these kinds of questions in Chapters 6 , 7, and 8 helps us identify and compare the government structures and processes of political systems around the world. Initially, Chapter 6 provides an analysis of the four major institutional structures that are the basic components of contemporary political systems: *executives, legislatures, administrative systems*, and *judiciaries*. Chapter 7 will compare different institutional arrangements regarding matters such as executive–legislative relationships, the party system, and citizen democracy. Chapter 8 will analyze the ways in which the political system and the economic system are linked. The discussions in these chapters will emphasize broad patterns and generalizations. The usual qualifications apply: There are exceptions and variations across political systems and even within each political system as it is influenced by many factors such as forces in the environment, personalities, political culture, policy area, and so on. Let's begin with a discussion of executives.

Executives

6.1 Analyze the structure and roles of political executives.

The historical evidence indicates that as long as there have been political systems, there have been individuals or small groups who assume top leadership roles. Such leaders have the responsibility to formulate and especially to implement public policy, and they can be broadly called the *executive structure*. The word *executive* comes from the Latin *ex sequi*, meaning "to follow out" or "to carry out." Thus, the particular role of the **executive** is *to carry out the political system's policies, laws, and directives*.

One might be tempted to assume that a few individuals generally emerge as the leadership cadre in *every* political order. But there are some historical counterexamples, especially from Africa and Asia, of societies that are *acephalous*—that is, "without a head." In such systems, many people in the community share power somewhat equally as a collective leadership. Nonetheless, in most systems, a few people do assume the positions of executive power.

At the apex of the executive structure, there is usually an actor who can be called the chief executive. In a national political system, this might be a single person with a title such as president, prime minister, chief, premier, supreme leader, or queen. Or the top executive leader can be a role filled by two or more people. In this case, there might be a president and a prime minister (as in the French example described in Compare in 7) or a group exercising shared executive leadership (e.g., a junta).

A broader definition of the executive includes not only the chief executive but also the entire administrative system. Such a definition derives from the notion that the policy implementation function (the execution of policy) is shared by the chief executive and the administration. The top executive group cannot survive without the continuing support of an extensive system of people who interpret, administer, and enforce its policy directives. However, we examine the chief executive and the administration in separate sections of this chapter so that we can differentiate analytically among the major structures in most political systems.

Roles of Executives

LEADERSHIP ROLES In the contemporary political world, political leadership is almost always associated with chief executives. The leadership role entails taking the initiative in formulating, articulating, and implementing the goals of the political system. The effective chief executive becomes the spokesperson for the aspirations of the people, attempts to galvanize the people's support for these goals, and develops strategies that facilitate their accomplishment.

To a large extent, the chief executive takes the initiative in policy formation. Executive policy leadership is especially crucial during times of crisis because the executive structure has the potential for a level of coherence and unanimity of action that is often lacking in the legislature. The basic logic is that the top executive is usually one person or a very small group that can make a decision and implement a plan of action more easily and rapidly than a large group. In most political systems, the chief executive also has the capacity to veto, either directly or indirectly, the bills that the legislature initiates. Increasingly, even the drafting of legislation is a function dominated by the executive because many major bills require the expertise and policy direction of the chief executive and its staff.

SYMBOLIC AND CEREMONIAL ROLES The actors in the executive role usually function as the unifying symbol of the entire society, becoming the ultimate mother/ father figures for the people. This is especially true when the chief executive has a strong image, such as Thailand's King Bhumibol and King Mswati III in Swaziland (see Focus in 9). The executive's presence becomes central to many of the society's rituals and ceremonies, whether it is the Japanese emperor's wedding, the Kenyan president's official send-off of the national team to the Olympic Games, or the British queen's Christmas Day televised message to her subjects. The executive is often the mourner-in-chief in times of sorrow, the primary cheerleader in times of triumph, and the one who articulates the hopes and dreams of the country.

SUPERVISION OF THE ADMINISTRATION In almost all contemporary political systems, the executive has primary responsibility for implementing the policies and laws of the political order. At the apex of this administrative hierarchy, which might include millions of public employees in the state's departments, bureaus, and agencies, is the top group of the executive structure. Most systems have an executive cabinet, with each member directly and personally responsible for some major area of administration. Given the scale and complexity of the activities in each area, these top executive actors can neither know nor control all of the actions that occur within their domain. Nonetheless, they are supposed to set the broad guidelines for policy implementation, and in many political systems, they are accountable for any major failures that occur. In parliamentary systems, for example, the minister of a department will probably resign if there is a serious shortcoming or blunder in her area of responsibility.

SUPERVISION OF THE MILITARY AND FOREIGN AFFAIRS Given the state's monopoly of the legitimate use of force, the top political executive usually has direct control over the military (including internal security forces). In such cases, the top executive is the commander in chief of the entire military system of the state, including personnel and other resources (aircraft, nuclear weapons, military intelligence, and so on). The chief executive must set policy and supervise the organization and utilization of the state's military capabilities, a task that can have the most serious consequences for the security and well-being of the country.

Associated with control of the military is the executive's responsibility for foreign affairs—the state's relations with other states. As Chapter 12 will describe more fully, the relations among states involve complex patterns of cooperation and conflict as each state attempts to accomplish its goals in the international environment. The chief executive (or the chief executive's delegates) represents the state in its dealings with other countries. Particular significance is often attached to situations in which the chief executives of different states meet directly, as in a state visit or a summit conference. In reality, such meetings among heads of state typically are symbolic gestures of cooperation or occasions for ratifying agreements that have been reached by the chief executives' representatives. But the concentration of the states' political power in the chief executives is so great that such meetings can provide opportunities for major breakthroughs in the relations among the states.

Structural Arrangements

FUSED VERSUS DUAL EXECUTIVE Many political systems have a **dual executive**. One actor, the *head of state, performs the more ceremonial aspects of top leadership*, while another actor, the ***head of government***, *is responsible for the more political aspects of governance.* The main advantage of the dual executive is that citizens can be angry or hostile toward the head of government while remaining loyal to the nation and to the political system through their affection and support for the more ceremonial head of state.

Constitutional monarchies are obvious examples of political systems with a dual executive. In these systems, there is a ruling king or queen (e.g., Queen Elizabeth II in Britain, Queen Margrethe II in Denmark, or Emperor Akihito in Japan) and a prime minister or other head of government. The monarch has little or no power to make authoritative policy decisions and serves mainly symbolic or ceremonial functions, as an embodiment of the nation and the people. Monarchs with limited powers also operate in some less democratic countries, such as King Norodom Sihamoni in Cambodia where the king is head of state but Prime Minister Hun Sen commands dominant political power as head of government.

Some countries have attempted to create a dual executive without a monarch, establishing a second executive office as head of state (such as the presidency in Germany, India, and Ireland) that is typically insulated from the daily struggles of politics and thus can be a symbol of national unity. In countries where the culture is deeply grounded in a religious belief system, the head of the religion can function like a head of state, as in Iran, where the president (Hassan Rouhani) and legislature lead the political system, but the religious leader, Ayatollah Ali Khamenei (the Leader of the Islamic Republic and of the Nation), has formidable power over most aspects of political life.

Most political systems have a *fused executive*. Here, *a single actor fulfills both the ceremonial roles associated with the head of state and the political functions associated with the head of the government*. In such cases, it can be difficult or impossible to distinguish (dis)loyalty to a partisan political leader from (dis)loyalty to the nation. Clever chief executives use this fusion of roles to their advantage, "wrapping themselves in the flag." Such executives criticize or even punish their opponents by claiming that they are traitors to the political society (even though the opponents are usually criticizing only the political actions of the leader). For example, Zimbabwe's President Robert Mugabe used this tactic very effectively to intimidate and eliminate his rivals and to justify using violence against political opponents.

Some political systems have two actors who perform parts of the chief executive role but are not really dual executives in the sense described in the preceding paragraphs. For example, there are countries (e.g., France and Russia) where

Queen Elizabeth II, the head of state, opens Parliament each year by delivering a speech written by the prime minister, the head of government. The speech outlines the legislation the prime minister's government will introduce. The queen comes to Britain's House of Lords, whose members sit behind the Law Lords (the highest judiciary group, wearing the wigs). By tradition, the now powerful House of Commons members, including the prime minister, symbolically "demand" entry into the chamber and stand in the back (not visible in the photo).

both a prime minister and a president perform essentially political functions, although one usually has a stronger claim to the head-of-state role (see Focus in 7). Some political systems have both a political executive and a monarch who, in addition to serving as head of state, is a powerful political actor. Bhutan, Kuwait, Morocco, and Swaziland are examples where the monarch is the head of state and has greater political power than the prime minister.

THE EXECUTIVE While the term *chief executive* refers to the one person or small group at the top of the executive structure, **the executive** is a broader term, including *all the people and organizational machinery that are below the chief executive in the executive structure.* Thus, the executive encompasses high-level decision makers in all the departments, agencies, and other administrative units that are in the chief executive's chain of command. As was noted earlier, a definition of the executive far broader than the one in this book might include the entire administrative system.

In theory, and usually in practice, this is a hierarchical system of political control, in the sense that the actors in the executive structure are supposed to follow the directives of the chief executive. But the chief executive's power over the rest of the executive is rarely absolute. There are many reasons why the chief executive's directives might not be carried out:

- Units within the executive might be too disorganized or corrupt to act effectively.
- Units within the executive might lack the resources to carry out policies in the manner desired by the chief executive.
- Some units might be more involved in competing against other units than in coordinating their actions to meet the chief executive's policies.
- Units might misunderstand, resist, or defy the chief executive.
- Can you think of other reasons?

The Age of the Executive?

Although chief executives have nearly always been evident, and usually ascendant, in political systems, some analysts call the twentieth century the "age of the executive." This label reflects the apparent concentration of power in executives and the relative decline of legislatures' powers. What might account for this concentration of power? To some extent, this is a chicken-and-egg issue: The reduced capacity of many legislatures to take coherent and decisive state action is linked to the emergence of more coherent and decisive executives.

In comparison with legislatures, the executive structure tends to be more streamlined and less prone to stalemate and inaction. Also, the executive, centered in a single person or small group, can offer a unified focus for a mass public that either desires simplicity and clarity in an age of great complexity or wants a form of heroic leadership. The chief executive typically speaks with one voice and, when effective, can assure the people that political power will be exercised with purpose and efficiency to respond to the pressures and demands in the society and in the international environment. Even if a chief executive cannot deliver, she can at least promise decisive leadership in a manner that no other political structure can.

Can you suggest any conditions under which a state might be dominated by a structure *other* than the political executive?

Legislatures

6.2   **Summarize the roles of the legislature.**

Nearly every country has a legislature as one of its basic structures of governance (Derbyshire 2000). Legislatures might have one or two "houses." Examples include the Senate and the House of Representatives (United States), the Senate and the Chamber of Deputies (Chile, Mexico, and Venezuela, among others), the Legislative Assembly (Costa Rica), the National People's Congress (China), the Majlis (Iran), the National Assembly (Egypt and Tanzania, among others), the Lok Sabha and the Rajya Sabha (India), the Knesset (Israel), the House of Representatives and the House of Councillors (Japan), and the House of Commons and the House of Lords (United Kingdom). The names differ, but most perform the same essential functions.

Roles of the Legislature

Legislatures are *structures in which representatives of the people discuss, assess, and enact public policies.* Indeed, the root of the name of the first modern legislature, the British Parliament, suggests this crucial function—the French word *parler* means "to talk." Most early legislatures were created to provide advice to the political executive, typically a monarch, and to represent politically relevant groups. Legislatures also became responsible for enacting public policies. The roots of the word *legislature* are the Latin words *legis*, meaning "law," and *latio*, "bringing or proposing." Some of the earliest legislatures, such as the Roman Senate (ca. 500 B.C.E.–100 C.E.), had great power to discuss and enact laws. Thus, most modern legislatures have three broad roles: (1) enacting legislation; (2) representing the citizenry; and (3) overseeing the executive.

ENACTMENT OF LEGISLATION It might seem obvious that legislatures draft, modify, and then ratify public policy in the form of legislation. In some political systems, many laws are initiated and written by the legislature. However, most contemporary legislatures do not play the dominant role in policymaking; this role has passed to the executive and the administration. Although executives often set the policy course, most legislatures retain the right to investigate, legislate, and appropriate. They need the authority to investigate in order to determine what they ought to legislate about, and they need the power to appropriate to ensure that what they legislate can be implemented. Indeed, appropriation, the power to enact laws that raise revenue and authorize its expenditure, is one of the most significant responsibilities a legislature has.

The source of the legislature's power in the policymaking process is, in most political systems, a constitutional provision that a majority vote of the members of the legislature is required to authorize the passage of any law (legislative enactment). In some systems, legislatures have special committees that thoroughly assess and can amend all proposed legislation under the committees' jurisdiction. Each step of the legislative process provides an opportunity for those opposed to legislation to derail it. Although citizens might feel their legislature moves too slowly, legislatures are slow by design. Collective decision making usually takes more time than the decision of one person, and legislatures are designed as institutions of collective decision making. There are many members of the legislature, and each member can face complicated issues of representation.

REPRESENTATION OF THE CITIZENRY   The second major role of the legislature is to represent the opinions and interests of the citizenry. One of the many institutional puzzles for every political system is how to convert the votes of citizens into a legislature that reflects the voters' preferences. Focus in 6 explores these issues of the electoral system and legislative representation with a case study of South Africa.

Another complicated issue is how the legislator determines whose interests she represents. The concept of *representation* is not straightforward because there are at least six different views of the broad interests that a legislator might represent: (1) all of the citizens in the legislator's constituency (geographic area); (2) the people within her constituency who voted for her; (3) the group that is most dominant in the legislator's constituency, possibly a social class, religious group, or ethnic group; (4) the political party to which the legislator owes loyalty; (5) the country as a whole, whose broad interests might transcend those of any area, group or party; or (6) the legislator's own conscience, which provides moral and intellectual judgment about appropriate political action (a position made famous in a brilliant justification by British parliamentarian Edmund Burke in his 1774 "Address to the Electors of Bristol" [1790/1955: 219–222]).

Is it possible for a legislator to represent all six interests simultaneously? Most contemporary legislators do not do so, for reasons such as these:

- In the Burkean ideal, a legislator could act against the views of her constituents, those who voted for her, or her party to follow a policy she believes is in the country's best interest.
- A legislator could deliver specific benefits to her own constituents (e.g., "pork barrel politics"), even though these are not the best use of resources to meet the needs of the country as a whole.
- The legislator could vote for a policy that is not the preference of her constituents but is part of a vote trade with other legislators to gain support for another policy she prioritizes.
- A legislator could vote on an issue primarily in exchange for financial or other support from a particular interest group.
- A legislator holding office in some systems must follow the dictates of the political leadership and acts as little more than a "rubber stamp." This is the position of a legislator in an undemocratic regime like North Korea, for example.

- Some legislators are deeply committed to adhering to their political party's line, or they must obey the party to survive politically. Such party discipline is usually the situation for members of the British House of Commons, for instance.

- Some legislators have such deep loyalty to a particular ideology or group that they rarely feel obligated to consider how they might represent other groups among the electorate. Members of religious parties, such as Shas in Israel, can have this perspective, as do members of extremely ideological factions, including some Tea Party Republicans in the United States.

Focus in 6

Electoral Systems and Legislative Representation: South Africa

Even before South Africa began dismantling the system of apartheid in 1990, there were extensive discussions about how to transform the political system into an effective democracy. Given the deep social cleavages and widespread citizen mistrust of the government, one critical issue was how to establish an **electoral system** that *translates the citizens' votes into a fair and representative legislature.* During apartheid, South Africa had elected its legislature by a form of ***plurality voting***: *the candidate who receives the largest number of votes is elected* in each constituency. The plurality system is most often used in single-member districts, where just one legislator is elected to represent each region.

To ensure that each nation-based group in South Africa received legislative seats that approximated the group's electoral strength, the 1994 constitution implemented a system of ***proportional representation (PR)***: *The seats are allocated to a party's candidates in close proportion to a party's share of the total votes.* Thus, when the African National Congress Party received 62.1 percent of the votes in 2014, it was allocated 249 (62.0 percent) of the 400 seats in the National Assembly. Although there are nearly 50 countries that utilize plurality voting for their legislatures (including Great Britain and the United States), the majority of countries now utilize some form of PR (Reynolds, Reilly, and Ellis 2005: 31). The box (on page 145) offers a simple example of how plurality and PR would work in the mythical countries of Zeta and Theta.

The PR system requires that legislative districts be multimember, meaning that two or more legislators are elected to represent a region. South Africa is divided into nine multimember regions, which each sends between 4 and 46 representatives to the National Assembly. Two hundred (of the 400) seats are distributed proportionately, based on the votes in each of these nine regions. The other 200 seats are filled with candidates elected for the entire country. For both these groupings of seats, the South African electorate chooses from "closed lists." This means that each party determines its own priority list of candidates, indicating to voters the order in which candidates will be elected if the party wins seats.

South Africa differs from most PR countries that have large districts because there is no minimum threshold of votes that a party must win nationally to win seats in the legislature. Thus, South Africa currently has seven small parties that received less than 1 percent of the national vote but have one to three members in the National Assembly. In other PR systems, minimum electoral thresholds are implemented (for instance, a party gets no seats unless it receives at least 5 percent of the national vote in Germany). The higher the minimum threshold requirement, the more difficult it is for smaller parties to obtain seats (Klingemann 2009).

There is an active debate in South Africa about whether to modify this electoral system. Some argue that the problem with PR in general, and especially with closed lists, is that the parties have too much control over the specific candidates who will be elected because the parties produce candidate lists. Some countries (e.g., Finland) utilize an "open list" PR system, which allows the voters to select (from the parties' lists) the specific candidates they want to elect. Others object to the multimember districts, arguing that there is very little connection between the individual voter in a particular district and the numerous legislators who represent the district. For instance, South Africa averages more than 20 legislators per district. This limits the direct representational link between a legislator and a specific constituency of people to whom she provides services. Thus, some South Africans propose that some or all of the members of the National Assembly should be elected in single-member districts with plurality voting.

The debate in South Africa mirrors the discussion in many countries about how to establish an electoral system that blends several goals. Plurality systems have the virtue of increasing the electorate's control over the legislator who serves them, increasing *accountability*. In contrast, PR systems generally produce a distribution of seats across parties that closely approximates the overall distribution of votes, increasing *fair representation*. Regarding *effective governance*, plurality systems tend to reduce the number of significant parties in the legislature, resulting in a more adversarial democracy—a system of majority government and minority opposition. In contrast, PR produces multiple successful parties, encouraging a more consensual democracy because more parties usually must cooperate to produce a legislative majority (Norris 2004: Ch. 2). South Africans continue to debate changes in their electoral system to increase its effectiveness for both representation and governance.

Zeta and Theta each have a 250-member national legislature. Zeta uses a plurality electoral system. Assume that in each of the 20 individual legislative seats in one region of Zeta, the candidate for Party A garners 31 percent of the votes, more votes than the candidate of any other party. Party A wins all 20 seats. In Theta, the same region utilizes PR and has the same 20 seats. Here, Parties A and B would each send six legislators, D would send four, B would send three, and E would send one. While the example for Zeta is probably unrealistic (some other party might get the plurality of votes in some of the individual seats), it is not uncommon that, in a plurality system, the largest parties win far more seats than their share of votes in the election, and small parties tend to get few or no seats.

	Percentage of Votes	Zeta: Plurality (of 20 single seats)	Theta: PR (of 20 seats in district)
Party A	31%	20 (wins in every constituency)	6
Party B	15%	0	3
Party C	29%	0	6
Party D	19%	0	4
Party E	6%	0	1

Further Focus

1. Which aspect of the South African electoral systems seems least desirable? How would you alter it?

2. What would guide your decision about whether to implement a plurality or PR electoral system in a particular country (given your specification of conditions relevant to that decision)?

Most legislators are elected by a set of voters, and it is generally assumed that a key responsibility of a legislator is both to reflect and to serve the interests of those voters. But the different interests that are described above can sometimes place a legislator under serious cross pressures. Even the attempt to reflect the views of one's constituents can be complicated. Some groups in the district might express their views loudly,

Voting matters. In a township near Johannesburg, South Africans wait for hours to cast votes for their representatives to the national legislature.

because they care passionately about the issue or because they have the resources to amplify their voices, while there is a "silent majority" whose views are different or unclear. And in a multimember electoral system like the one in South Africa, it can be difficult to determine exactly who one's constituents are. For the conscientious legislator, the challenges of representation can be daunting.

OVERSIGHT OF THE EXECUTIVE AND ADMINISTRATION The third major role of legislators concerns their interactions with the executive and the administration. In general, the legislature is responsible for overseeing the political executive's actions. Legislative powers to investigate, legislate, and appropriate are also the mechanisms for oversight. The legislature might have the constitutional right to select the executive, to approve the chief executive's selection of key appointments, and to authorize major policy decisions by the executive. In the steel industry case, for example, the U.S. Congress resisted presidential action that went beyond executive powers they had authorized but then authorized the actions the president had taken for those circumstances only. In parliamentary systems, the cabinet and prime minister hold office and make policy only if they have the "confidence" of the majority of the members of the legislature (see Chapter 7). In some systems, such as in India, the president is actually chosen by the legislature (although it is the prime minister, not the president, who is the most powerful executive officer).

Many legislatures have the right to approve the executive's selection of major appointments. The Israeli legislature must approve the cabinet as a whole. The U.S. Senate has the right to "advise and consent" on presidential appointments such as cabinet members, ambassadors, and Supreme Court justices. The Senate's 1987 rejection of Judge Robert Bork, President Reagan's nominee for the Supreme Court, is an example of a legislature asserting its power over a top-level executive appointment.

The right of the legislature to scrutinize executive performance might include regular procedures by which the legislature can question and investigate whether the executive has acted properly in implementing public policies. At a minimum, the legislature serves as a discussion and debating chamber. Subjecting the political executive's plans and actions to public debate serves as a modest check on executive power. This investigative function can also shape the public debate about policy. Many legislatures have a regular opportunity, during their legislative sessions, to question the specific plans and actions of key members of the executive. In Britain, Italy, and South Africa, for example, ministers in the executive cabinet must appear before the legislature and respond to legislators' questions or criticisms about any actions taken by their department.

Most legislatures also have formal investigatory powers on a continuing or a case-by-case basis. The 2003 parliamentary investigation of British Prime Minister Tony Blair regarding the basis of his claims that Iraq had weapons of mass destruction and whether this justified Britain's military intervention is an example of such oversight. In addition, some legislatures have followed Sweden's innovative idea, setting up an *ombudsman—an independent agency that investigates complaints regarding the actions of the executive branch and its administrative units.* If legislative questioning, committees, or the ombudsman discovers inappropriate behavior by an administrative unit, the legislature can usually oblige the unit to alter its behavior. If the problem is with the executive, significant political pressure is exerted on the executive to correct it. Of course, if the executive resists such pressure, the ultimate resolution of the dispute entails either resolution through the courts or, in most cases, a power struggle between the executive and the legislature (DiPaolo 2010).

The most fundamental power of oversight held by some legislatures is their capacity to overturn the government. In a parliamentary system, the legislature can require or pressure the executive to resign from office by a vote of censure or of no confidence or by defeating a major bill put forth by the executive (see Chapter 7). In Italy, for example, the legislature forced the executive to resign about once a year—on average—between 1951 and 1994. Even in presidential systems, the legislature has the power to overturn the executive by means of extraordinary processes like impeachment or recall elections (Marsteintredet and Berntzen 2008). In 1992, Brazilian President Fernando Collor de Mello resigned after being impeached by the National Congress on corruption charges. And in 2008, Pakistan's President Musharraf resigned as the legislature began impeachment proceedings for treason. In the United States, no president has been removed from office because of impeachment and conviction. However, in 1868, President Andrew Johnson was acquitted on the House of Representatives' impeachment charge by only one vote in the Senate, Richard Nixon avoided an impeachment trial in 1974 only by resigning, and Bill Clinton was acquitted by the Senate on two articles of impeachment brought by the House in 1998.

Legislative Structures

NUMBER OF HOUSES There is one very visible difference in the structural arrangements of various legislatures—the number of houses (often called *chambers*). There are **unicameral** (*one-chamber*) **legislatures** in more than half of the countries that have legislatures (Derbyshire 2000). The presumed advantages of a unicameral system are that political responsibility is clearly located in one legislative body and that risks of duplication or stalemate between parallel bodies are eliminated. More than two-thirds of the countries with a strong central government (see Chapter 7 on these "unitary states") have unicameral legislatures, including Algeria, Bulgaria, China, Costa Rica, Denmark, Finland, Greece, Hungary, Israel, Kenya, New Zealand, South Korea, Sweden, Taiwan, and Tanzania.

Since 1990, there has been a considerable increase in the proportion of countries that have **bicameral legislatures**—those with two separate chambers. Bicameral systems are especially prevalent in countries that are federations (states in which a central government and regional governments share power). Bicameral federations include Australia, Brazil, Canada, Germany, India, Mexico, and the United States. There are bicameral systems in one-third of the unitary states, including France, Great Britain, Italy, and Japan (Derbyshire 2000).

Although passing laws is generally easier in a unicameral system, a bicameral system can be defended on several grounds. First, two legislative houses provide more careful deliberation on issues and laws. One body can act as a check on the other to ensure more broadly acceptable policy is implemented. Second, the two houses make it easier to accommodate different desirable models of representation. In about two-fifths of the bicameral legislatures (e.g., Germany and the United States), one house represents the regional governments and the other house more directly represents the numerical and geographic distribution of citizens. A few upper houses also represent functional groups in the society, as in the Republic of Ireland, where members are appointed as representatives of sectors such as agriculture, labor, industry, culture, and public services.

Over time, some bicameral systems have evolved toward unicameral systems, especially in cases in which the need for extensive checks and balances within the legislative branch has not seemed compelling and in which the problems of overlap and stalemate between the two chambers have become severe. Some political systems, such as those of Sweden and Costa Rica, have constitutionally abolished one chamber. In others, such as Norway, Japan, and Britain, the powers of one chamber have been so reduced that it can delay, but cannot veto, the decisions of the more powerful chamber. In fact, the United States is now the only bicameral political system in which the regional upper chamber (the Senate) is more powerful than the popularly based lower chamber (the House of Representatives) (Derbyshire 2000).

SIZE OF LEGISLATURES The number of members in legislatures varies enormously, with some houses having fewer than 10 members and others having thousands of members (e.g., the National People's Congress in China has 2,987 members). The single house, or the lower house, typically represents "the people." Each legislator is elected from a constituency of roughly the same size. In general, there is a positive correlation between a country's population and its number of legislators (a ratio defined mathematically as a "cube root law" by Taagepera and Shugart 1989: 174–179). Among the more populous countries, however, there is no obvious principle for determining the optimal number of legislators. In the U.S. House of Representatives, 435 members are elected, a ratio of 1 member per 729,000 people. Of the 165 countries with a legislature, only India has a higher ratio of population to members than the United States. The United Kingdom, with less than one-third the U.S. population, has 650 elected members in its House of Commons, a ratio of 1 member per 97,000 citizens. More than half of all countries have a ratio of fewer than 65,000 people per representative (Derbyshire 2000).

Can you think of an appropriate criterion for deciding the number of members in a country's legislature? For example, are there good reasons why the upper house in the United States (the Senate) has two rather than three—or four or more—representatives from each state?

The Decline of Legislatures

Many observers claim that for more than 100 years, there has been a general decline in the power of legislatures relative to executives and administrations. While it is very difficult to measure power relations over time with precision, several types of circumstantial evidence suggest legislative weakness. First, national budgets are often structured by the executive rather than the legislature (Schick 2012). Controlling the finances is one of the most powerful aspects of governance.

Second, most legislatures do not provide a coherent structure within which power can be concentrated and exercised effectively. Many legislatures have relatively slow and cumbersome procedures for the lawmaking function, especially when there are regular legislative committees that amend legislation. This complexity in the legislative process is even more evident in bicameral systems because there is often disagreement between the two chambers.

Third, most legislatures react to policy initiatives from the executive more than they create policy. The legislatures almost never have the level of support services that is available to the executive. Their budgets, facilities, staff sizes, and even the legislators' own salaries are significantly lower than those of top members of the executive and administrative structures. Similarly, the technical expertise and knowledge resources available to legislatures are far less than those available to the executive and administrative structures, a major liability when legislators attempt to deal with the complex subjects facing governments in modern societies.

Fourth, some analysts also suggest a social–psychological weakness of legislatures: Most citizens desire clear, dynamic, identifiable, and singular political leadership, but legislatures are composed of many people, and most citizens feel the legislators are either indistinguishable (when party discipline is very strong) or offer too many different identities. In the United States, for example, it is usually possible to answer this question: What does the president think about issue Y? But there is no easy answer to the question: What does the legislature think about issue Y?

Not only are there two chambers and two parties, there also is a great diversity of opinions among the individuals and factions within the legislature. As discussed in Chapters 2 and 4, even the parties, which send cues to voters about their views on issues, sometimes have open disagreement in their ranks. Thus, although legislatures usually have spokespersons and leaders, no one can truly speak for all the individual members of the legislature. One might conclude that the legislature in a democratic society tends to fulfill one of its roles *too* well: Its members too accurately represent the diversity of political beliefs among the society's population, and thus they speak with many voices.

Although the power of legislatures has not kept pace with that of other institutions, especially the executive and the administration, not all legislatures are weak or diminished institutions. Certain national legislatures remain extremely powerful political structures, such as those in Italy, Japan, Sweden, and the United States. In most other relatively democratic political systems, legislatures have significant impacts on the governing process through their roles in enacting legislation, in representation, in framing the issues for the public, and in oversight. And in almost all societies that have a legislature, its members can exercise political power in many subtle ways. At the least, members of the legislature have much more political power than most other citizens.

Administrative Systems

6.3   **Compare the functions and powers of political administration systems.**

Administration is the general term used to describe *the machinery and the processes through which the state's rules and policies are applied and implemented.* While the executive (discussed above) denotes the top managers of the policy implementation function, the administrative system consists of the thousands, or even millions, of public employees who do the ongoing business of interpreting and implementing the policies enacted by the state. These employees are divided into organizational units called departments, ministries, agencies, and bureaus. Administrative units perform important activities such as providing publicly provided goods and services (e.g., national security, roads, education, solid-waste disposal, health care, monetary aid for the needy), maintaining order, collecting revenues, keeping records, and regulating or controlling aspects of the economy (e.g., the power grid, provision of transportation, finance system, growth and distribution of food).

Administrative Functions and Power

The scale of activity of a state's administrative structure depends on the political system's definition of *res publica* (recall page 119). In political systems that penetrate a larger sphere of the society and economy, there is a corresponding need for more extensive administrative structures because the administration is the basic apparatus through which the state interprets, implements, and monitors all of its policies and activities. The administrative structures in contemporary political systems perform five broad functions:

1. **Provision of public goods and services.** The essential work of the actors in the administrative structure is the constant interpretation and application of policies that provide public goods and services to individuals and groups.

2. **Regulation and enforcement of behavior.** Administrators are also responsible for interpreting and applying many public policies that set guidelines for the behavior of individuals or groups. These can vary greatly, from monitoring collusion among corporations to enforcing traffic laws to protecting the civil rights of ethnic minorities.

3. **Provision of knowledge.** Many administrators develop great expertise within their specialized areas. This knowledge can be of enormous utility for almost every decision and action undertaken in that area by the political system.

4. **Information management.** Administrators are responsible for the collection, storage, and analysis of huge amounts of information about the people and processes in the society. This information provides a crucial database—for recording activities and conditions in the society and for providing information relevant to every stage of the policy process (see Chapter 9).

5. **Resource management.** In roles such as collector of revenues from citizens and businesses or operator of state-owned companies producing goods and services, the administrative structure is in charge of many tasks that extract and utilize resources for the political system.

This brief list of functions suggests the enormous breadth and depth of the administrative structure and its activities. Some observers argue that in the complex, extensive, and knowledge-based political systems of the early twenty-first century, the power of administrative institutions is supreme. Although the administrators are, in theory, "servants" of their political masters and their clients, in reality these roles might be reversed. Civil servants have such unmatched knowledge and experience in their specialized domains that generalist politicians rarely have sufficient expertise to question their information, recommendations, or actions (Weber 1958a). Also, their power to grant or withhold benefits provides them with considerable leverage over clients. And most administrators are career employees who have quasi-permanent tenure, while politicians and clients come and go. The modern administrative structure has such wide-ranging power and competence that it is typically credited with keeping the political system functioning when executives and legislatures are ineffective, as in the Third and Fourth Republics in France and in many modernizing states in Africa and Asia. Indeed, Max Weber, the great German sociologist, observed that "in the modern state, the actual ruler is necessarily and unavoidably the bureaucracy" (Weber 1958a: 211).

Bureaucracy as One Form of Administration

Weber's quote about bureaucracy is a reminder that administration and bureaucracy are often treated as synonymous concepts; but in the attempt to clarify our language of political analysis, it is helpful to distinguish them. Weber provided the definitive definition of bureaucracy: a particular structure and set of processes through which the administration can operate. Structurally, **bureaucracy** is an *organization that is hierarchical and specialized, by means of an elaborate division of labor.* Weber also defined the concept of bureaucracy by a key process: its members (1) apply *specific rules of action* to each case; therefore, the resulting treatment of each case is (2) *rational; (3) non-discretionary; (4) predictable; and (5) impersonal* (Weber 1958a: 196–244).

In some countries, governments have deeply incorporated this rational bureaucratic style of administration. A well-structured bureaucracy can help citizens navigate their government and can act as a deterrent to corruption (Dahlstrom et al. 2012). But there are also many contemporary political systems, and even more examples historically, in which public administrators treat people unpredictably or with clear biases. Compare in 6 characterizes five different forms of administration.

In complex societies, calling an organization "bureaucratic" is not usually intended to be a compliment. Some criticisms of bureaucracy are really directed at all large administrative structures that exercise increasing control over people's lives and that seem too large and too powerful. Fundamentally, the bureaucracy label has come to connote a system that is too inflexible and impersonal. And the bureaucrats themselves are seen to be relatively free of political accountability because they are protected by professional norms and employment rules that give them job security and insulate them from political pressure. Despite criticisms of its occasional excesses in practice, most people conclude that they would prefer a Weberian bureaucracy to one that is arbitrary, discriminatory, or corrupt. Every country is a mix of the five styles described in the Compare in 6, but the variations in that mix are huge. Personal contacts and bribes (in various societies called *chai, baksheesh, mordida*, or *dash*) are still essential for success in dealing with the administrative system in many countries.

Compare in 6

Five Styles of Administration

For many people in the most advanced democracies, the words *bureaucracy* and *bureaucratic* have a negative connotation, as in "that is so bureaucratic!" Bureaucracy is only one style of the administrative function. While its rigid, rule-following approach can seem mechanical and inefficient, let's compare it to four alternative styles of administration by exploring variations on a single scenario:

You are driving in another country and are given a ticket for speeding—driving 80 kilometers per hour (kph) in a 40 kph zone. You plead your case to the traffic officer: You are unfamiliar with the metric system, you don't understand how to read the traffic signs, you can't figure out the speedometer in this rental car, you are sorry, and you are a friendly tourist! What happens next? Here are five alternatives:

1. The officer listens patiently. Your pleading makes no difference. She explains that Rule 3.207 of the Vehicle Code governs this case—you are traveling more than 10 kph over the posted limit. The rules state that you must follow her to the local judge's office, pay a fine of 125 rupesas, and you will then be free to continue your journey. The judge is also unmoved by your arguments, repeating that the law is clear. You pay the 125 rupesa fine and you leave. This is a classic case of *Weberian bureaucracy* in action: There are explicit rules, and you

are merely a case in which all the representatives of the organization apply the rules exactly and with no consideration of your personal circumstances.

2. When you plead your case, the officer seems sympathetic. She says that she understands how tourists might be confused by the rules in her country and that she will reduce the reported speed on the ticket from 80 kph to 60 kph, which will result in only a 50 rupesa fine. You try your pleas again with the judge, promising to obey the all the country's laws. The judge senses your contrition and suspends the fine, after giving you a stern warning. You leave quickly, before anyone reconsiders. This is *humane administration* because those with authority do not merely apply the rules—they try to understand your personal circumstances and adjust their actions to be responsive to your particular situation. Humane administration seems preferable to the bureaucratic style; however, once the rules are no longer applied impersonally and predictably, other styles (numbers 3–5 below) are much more likely.

3. When none of your arguments work with the officer, you point out that other cars were passing you just before you were stopped. Why you? The officer just shrugs. At the judge's office, your arguments again are ineffective. The judge then announces your fine is 200 rupesas. You are shocked and say that the traffic officer said that the fine would be about 125 rupesas. The judge looks sternly at you, and responds that the fine is whatever she decides it should be. Did you want to question her decision? If so, she might have to increase the fine even further. Or perhaps you'd like to spend the night in jail, thinking about your dangerous driving? You flinch, pay, and get out of the building as fast as you can. This is *arbitrary administration.* You are singled out for ticketing among others who are equally guilty. Why? You are given a higher fine than stated in the rules. Why? The answer is that those with authority can use their discretion to decide when and how to administer the rules. Discretion worked in your favor under humane administration, but in arbitrary administration, you are just as likely to be placed at a disadvantage by flexible, unpredictable and non-rule-following actions.

4. When you try your arguments on the traffic officer, she notices your foreign accent. Where are you from, she asks? You say, I am from the United States! She frowns and mutters that Americans need to be taught a lesson. In front of the judge, you are asked your religion, and reply that you are a Protestant. The judge responds: "Do you know this is a Catholic country and we believe in following the rules? Your fine is 175 rupesas." You have a sense that if you had been from a different country or were Catholic, you might have gotten off easier. In this situation of *discriminatory administration,* you might be right. In cases of discriminatory administration, the authorities treat people differently on the basis of their ethnicity, religion, gender, social class, or some other marker that distinguishes among groups. Unfortunately, in this situation, you are in groups that are not favored.

5. After the officer listens impassively to your pleadings, she tells you that things will not go well with the judge. You will pay a very big fine of about 250 rupesas and might go to jail because you were traveling over 150 kph. You are stunned by these "facts" and scared, but decide to take a risk. As you hand your license to the officer, you also fold a 50 rupesa note underneath the license. The officer examines your license and hands it back to you, but the 50 rupesa note is gone. She says if you pay a 60 rupesa fine on the spot, you will not need to go before the judge. You hand over another 60 rupesas. She returns to her motorcycle and rides off. This is *corrupt administration.* There are many ways in which bribes are solicited, collected, and distributed in such systems. If you are lucky, you'll handle the bribe transaction successfully and not end up in jail.

Further Questions

1. How could a non-Weberian bureaucracy operate like number 2 above without significant risk of becoming one of the less desirable approaches (3, 4, or 5)?

2. Why is corrupt administration probable in many countries, especially those with lower levels of individual wealth?

Judiciaries

6.4 **Outline the major elements within judicial systems.**

In a Hobbesian state of nature (see Chapter 2), disputes among people would normally be resolved by force or the threat of force. In such a setting, "might makes right." Thus, a primary reason for the social contract is to authorize the state to intervene in the potential and actual disputes among individuals and groups by creating and enforcing rules regarding proper forms of behavior. Every society holds that those who violate its rules and laws (i.e., its policies) must be sanctioned. The specific rules in a given society emerge from its unique culture, history, and politics. However, in all legal systems there are usually ambiguities regarding the rules:

What does the rule mean?

Has a rule been violated?

Who are the "guilty" actors?

How serious is the offense?

What sanctions are appropriate?

These kinds of ambiguities are resolved through the adjudication function in every political system. Most political systems have established judicial structures whose primary role is adjudication.

Aspects of Adjudication

The **adjudication** function attempts to *interpret and apply the relevant rules or laws to a given situation,* addressing the five questions above. There are several different types of laws. When the issue involves *civil law*—the rules regarding relations between private actors (individuals or groups)—the main objective of adjudication is to *settle the dispute.* Examples include the rules dealing with divorce, contracts, and personal liability litigation.

The situation involves *criminal law* when an individual or group behaves in a manner interpreted as an offense against the social order. Here, adjudication can be an important mechanism of *social control.* Examples of offenses are murder, substance abuse, theft, bribery, extortion, and environmental pollution. The state represents the public interest and enforces the social contract, ensuring that the relations among actors are within the boundaries of acceptable social behavior. Just as the definition and scope of *res publica* differ greatly across political systems, the definition of acceptable social behavior varies dramatically. In some countries, social control entails little more than regulation of violent behavior among people. In contrast, other countries might enforce rules that prohibit spanking one's child or wearing certain clothing.

Adjudication can also consider cases involving *constitutional, administrative,* or *statutory law.* Here, the activities center on *arbitration regarding the behavior of the political system itself.* The main issues for adjudication involve questions about the legitimate domain of action by a governmental actor in its relations with other governmental units or private actors. Such a dispute might concern a highly technical disagreement over the implementation of a specific policy (e.g., is a person with vision correctable to 20/400 qualified to receive state-subsidized services intended for the "visually impaired"?), or it might raise fundamental constitutional questions about the distribution of political power (e.g., can the chief executive seize control of an industry in the absence of authorization from the constitution or legislature?).

Finally, **international law** is comprised of the *rules that attempt to prevent and resolve disputes between states or other global actors.* Adjudication entails interpreting written agreements about interactions that cross state borders or laws formulated by international legal bodies such as the International Court of Justice within the United Nations. As Chapter 11 will detail, there are substantial difficulties in enforcing international law, especially when a state determines that the law is not in its national interest.

Judicial Structures

Most political systems have specialized structures of the **judiciary**—*the system of courts and personnel that determines whether the rules of the society have been transgressed and, if so, whether sanctions ought to be imposed on the transgressor.* (Some broad definitions of judicial structures even include agencies of law enforcement, such as police and security forces, as well as agencies that apply sanctions against rule breakers, such as prisons, although in this book these are considered administrative structures.)

While there are significant crossnational variations, most political systems have a hierarchical system of judicial structures, with appeal processes possible from lower- to higher-level courts. The United States has one of the world's most complex judicial structures, with its Supreme Court and extensive system of federal, state, and local courts, including judges, prosecuting attorneys, defense attorneys for the indigent, court clerks, and so on. Most judicial systems also have subsystems that are responsible for different aspects of adjudication. For example, the French judicial structure separates the criminal and civil law system from a second system that handles administrative law. In Ukraine, one major system handles criminal and civil law, and a second major system is composed of special prosecutors who monitor actions in all types of cases and who can challenge, retry, or even withdraw cases from the regular courts. In Great Britain, one major judicial system is responsible for criminal law and a second handles civil law.

Among the contemporary countries that do not have judicial structures as part of the government are the Islamic countries that adhere to sharia law. Sharia is the divine law, detailed in the Koran and further elaborated in the *hadith*, the teachings of Muhammad. It is sharia, not the laws of humans, that is the dominant judicial framework in countries such as Iran, Saudi Arabia, and Sudan. The Koran prescribes all aspects of social, spiritual, and moral life. As part of that prescription, the sections on law provide the details of what in Western jurisprudence includes criminal law, civil law, and administrative law. Sharia is applied by religious courts, and the punishments for many violations of the law are specified in the Koran.

The constitutions of many states include provisions meant to create an independent judiciary. The notion that a judicial system is independent means that the judicial actors are not under the direct control of any other political structure. It does not mean that the judiciary is *apolitical.* The legal system and the set of judicial structures in *every* political system are political. Adjudication, by its very nature, entails crucial decisions that distribute values and shape meanings for a society. Also, the judicial officials in most systems are either appointed by those with political power or elected in a political process by the voters.

The judiciary in some political systems has the substantial power to exercise **judicial review**, whereby *judicial structures establish the final interpretation of what the constitution and the laws mean,* including the right to reinterpret, revoke, or overrule the policy decisions of the other political structures, including the executive, the legislature, and the administrative branches. About 1 in 10 states has a strong system of judicial review, including Canada, Colombia, Germany, India, Israel, Italy, Mexico, Norway, Switzerland, and the United States. Research has revealed that judicial structures in many advanced democracies have exercised increasing power to redefine and overturn the actions of the other branches (Koopmans 2003: Ch. 4). Increasingly, international courts, like the European Court of Justice, are also exercising this type of institutional power and growth (Stone Sweet 2004; Stone Sweet and Brunell 2012). The Debate in 6 questions whether such judicial review is consistent with democratic premises.

However, even when judicial structures do strive to maintain some political independence, they still might respond to external pressure. First, the judiciaries in nearly all contemporary states are ultimately dependent on other political

The Debate in 6

Is Judicial Review Democratic?

In essence, judicial review means that the judiciary has the right not only to interpret what a particular rule means but also to assess the constitutional legitimacy of any law enacted by the legislature or any policy action implemented by the executive or the administration. The judiciary can uphold the authority of the government regarding the policy, or it can rule that the government's action violates fundamental laws, especially the constitution. Currently, more than half the world's democratic countries have some form of broad judicial review. It can be a key method of ensuring there is a strong countervailing power that prevents the legislature, executive, and administration from overstepping their authority. However, some critics argue that essential features of judicial review are actually inconsistent with the basic values and principles of a democratic society. Is judicial review democratic?

Judicial Review Is Undemocratic

- The hallmark of representative democracy is that those who have great power over the laws of the society should have a direct mandate from the people by means of election. Yet in most countries, the judges who exercise the extraordinary power of judicial review are not elected by the people. Thus, Alexander Bickel (1962), a distinguished professor at Yale Law School, argues that judicial review is undemocratic because "it thwarts the will of representatives of the actual people of the here and now; it exercises control, not on behalf of the prevailing majority, but against it."

- High court judges making these decisions cannot be held accountable because they usually serve for life and cannot be removed from office except in extraordinary circumstances (i.e., impeachment). Thus citizens have almost no capacity to replace the judges who make fundamental decisions about the restraints on the rulers or the rights of the ruled, a hallmark element of democracy (see Chapter 7). Indeed, "the people" have no significant influence on either what cases the judges consider or the decisions that the judges make.

- Crucial interpretations and decisions can hinge on a bare majority vote by a tiny number of people. The highest constitutional court in most countries makes decisions by simple majority, with fewer than 15 judges. In the United States, for example, fundamental judicial rulings are made by only five members of the Supreme Court, even when four of their colleagues on the court completely disagree with them.

- Even if the judges truly are independent (which is questionable), the grounds for a decision in cases of judicial review can be highly subjective. There can be deep disagreements among the judges about how the basic legal documents of the society should be interpreted and applied to specific cases.

- In short, crucial rulings about actions by the government are made when a handful of unelected and unaccountable individuals use their subjective reasoning to offer a contested interpretation of documents and statutes that can be generations old. And "the people," the elected chief executive, and the elected national legislature have no recourse but to accept this judgment (Waldron 2006). What could be more undemocratic in a democratic society?

Judicial Review Supports Democratic Processes

- In representative democracies, supreme power rests with the citizens, who then exercise that power to elect officials to serve them. Those officials, in turn, appoint many others to play important roles in governance. Even in countries where top judicial officials are appointed, their authority is derived directly from the elected officials, whose power is based on popular consent. Thus, empowering appointed judges is fully consistent with democratic principles.

- Once appointed, high court judges are independent of those in other powerful roles in the political system. Unlike most other political actors in a democracy, judges engaged in judicial review do not need to curry favor to raise money for reelection and they have no need to compromise their positions to make deals with others in the political system. Thus, they are able to make reasoned interpretations of the fundamental laws of the land and rule on specific actions by the other branches of government, based solely on the constitutional merits of the case.

- A just democracy must be guided not only by majority rule but also by a commitment to protect the rights of the individual and minorities against a "tyranny of the majority." An independent judiciary, including judicial review, is a key element in such protection. In making decisions on constitutional rights of the weak as well as the strong, these judges are not pressured or constrained by the current whims of the electoral majority because they do not need to stand for reelection.

- In *Federalist Paper No. 78*, Alexander Hamilton (2007) explains that judicial power does not "by any means suppose a superiority of the judicial to the legislative power. It only supposes that the power of the people is superior to both; and that where the will of the legislature, declared in its statutes, stands in opposition to that of the people, declared in the Constitution, the judges ought to be governed by the latter rather than the former. They ought to regulate their decisions by the fundamental laws."

- In most democracies, the judges engaged in judicial review are highly qualified legal experts. They generally have years of experience in the legal system, and their judicial decisions are bound by the statutes and by precedent. While they might occasionally disagree on the interpretation of a constitutional issue, most of their decisions are by clear and unambiguous majorities and reflect shared analyses.

More questions…

1. In a democracy, is it acceptable to have powerful decision makers who are neither elected by nor directly accountable to the citizens?

2. Might there be any serious problems if the binding interpretation of the constitution is made by elected officials?

3. If courts could not engage in judicial review, would judges simply become the agents of the other political actors in the system?

4. How does the considerable distance between the people and the highest judges in the judicial branch serve as an advantage? A disadvantage?

structures, especially the executive and the administration, to enforce their decisions. Second, when judicial officials displease the dominant power group, they can often be ignored, replaced, diluted, or even eliminated. In an extreme example, more than 150 high-level Argentine judges "disappeared" during the 1970s, and it is speculated that the Argentine government ordered their executions. In the United States, President Franklin D. Roosevelt became frustrated with decisions by the U.S. Supreme Court in the 1930s when it blocked his New Deal legislation expanding government policies in response to the Great Depression. He threatened to add members to the nine-member Supreme Court to get favorable decisions, but Congress did not support his threat. However, the Court did begin to rule favorably on his legislation. While it cannot be proven empirically that Roosevelt's threat to increase the size of the Court changed the judicial reasoning of the justices, it was punned at the time that "a switch in time saved nine."

Third, because the people in top judicial positions have usually been socialized by those in the culture's dominant socioeconomic groups, they are likely to share the values of those groups when they make judgments. Thus, one key consideration regarding an *independent* judiciary is assessing the extent to which the judicial structures make decisions and take actions that are *not* substantially influenced by their shared political orientations with and dependence on other powerful social, economic, and political structures in the society. While the rituals of the judicial structures offer the appearance of protecting impartial justice, the reality is that the judicial structures in many, perhaps most, countries serve the interests of the political and economic elite and that a truly independent judiciary is a rarity.

Styles of Adjudication

Among the many styles of adjudicating disputes, several are prevalent. The **common law** tradition is grounded in the general laws and rules that have been enacted by legislatures and have evolved over time. The key goal of the legal system is to interpret existing precedents from previous judicial rulings. Innocence is presumed until evidence indicates guilt. The court system is adversarial, with the disputing sides making their points and the judge acting as a referee to ensure that the proceedings are fair. The common law style emerged in England and was generally adopted in countries strongly influenced by Britain or the United States.

In the **civil law** tradition, the key goal is the precise application of extremely detailed legal documents to the specific case. The court system is more inquisitional, with the judge asking critical questions under the assumption that the party on trial is guilty of violating the law unless innocence can be proven. This system is associated with the legal approaches of ancient Rome and also France, with its development of the Napoleonic code. It is generally adopted in Continental Europe and the countries emerging from its colonial influence as well as many former communist countries. It is arguable that Sharia law is similar to civil law in its style of adjudication, although the laws of Sharia, as noted above, were promulgated by religious authorities, not legislatures and administrations as in civil law.

A third style of adjudication might be termed *dispute resolution*. Here, the goal is to find a ruling that is generally acceptable to all sides. Such an outcome might be based on negotiations led by a third-party arbitrator who works to develop a satisfactory compromise between the disputants. This third party might be appointed by the political system or might be respected members of the community. This style has been especially effective in some Arab and sub-Saharan African societies, and many countries attempt to handle some legal cases through dispute resolution approaches.

Concluding Observations

Traditional political science assumed that a detailed description of political structures is the best way to explain how politics works. But empirical research revealed considerable diversity in the roles of particular political structures. Key political functions might occur in a wide variety of structures inside and outside the formal governmental arrangements. In response, there was a period during which political structures were viewed as so malleable that most analyses treated them as secondary elements, merely forming one of the contexts in which various political, economic, and social groups maneuver as they pursue their interests. More recently, many scholars have reemphasized the importance of institutional arrangements. For these "new institutionalists," the particular configuration of political structures and rules can powerfully shape political actions and outcomes (March 2006; Bell 2011). And for the "neostatists," the structures of the state—its institutional arrangements, the actors who have major roles in its institutions, and its policy activities—are autonomous and have fundamental impacts on political, economic, and social processes.

Thus, precise, behaviorally oriented and process-based analyses of politics now treat political structures more richly. In brief, institutions matter because they set the rules and roles of political behavior and interaction. A full understanding of the political world requires a clear grasp of the essential features of executive, legislative, administrative, and judicial structures. Institutional structures are the skeleton and organs of the body politic. Just as one could explain certain biological functions and processes of the body without explicit reference to the skeleton and organs, one could explain certain functions and processes of the political system without reference to structures. But such an abstract description of a biological organism would be incomplete without indicating the way in which the structures constrain and shape the functions. Similarly, attempts to describe or explain politics, especially in actual settings, are much richer and more complete if they include a characterization of how key political institutions constrain and shape the political process (March and Olsen 1989; Lewis and Steinmo 2012). The next chapter will take us further in understanding political institutions as it analyzes how some of the key institutional structures interact to produce different forms of the body politic.

Key Concepts

adjudication, p. 154
administration, p. 150
bicameral legislature, p. 148
bureaucracy, p. 152
civil law, p. 159
common law, p. 158
dispute resolution, p. 159
dual executive, p. 139

executive, p. 137
fused executive, p. 140
head of government, p. 139
head of state, p. 139
international law, p. 155
judicial review, p. 156
judiciary, p. 155
legislature, p. 142

ombudsman, p. 147
plurality voting, p. 144
political institutions, p. 137
proportional representation, PR,
   p. 144
representation, p. 143
unicameral legislature,
   p. 148

For Further Consideration

1. Whom should a legislator represent on policy decisions? Develop an argument justifying the order of importance you attribute to representing the following entities: those groups who voted for the legislator, the constituency, the legislative coalition, the political party, the party leader, the nationality group, the country, the legislator's own best judgment.

2. Evaluate whether, on balance, it would be desirable to have an administrative system

that is flexible and is sensitive to unique, individual circumstances in the handling of each case (that is, does not follow the principles of a Weberian bureaucracy).

3. The discussion of the judiciary asserts that every set of judicial structures is political. Is the notion of an independent judiciary a sham?

4. What are the benefits and shortcomings of a political system that has a weak chief executive? A fused chief executive?

For Further Reading

Bishin, Benjamin G. (2009). *Tyranny of the Minority: The Subconstituency Politics Theory of Representation.* Philadelphia: Temple University Press. Why do minorities sometimes get their way over majority preferences? This careful and methodologically

sophisticated book presents a vigorous exploration of the logic of representation.

Derbyshire, Denis, with Ian Derbyshire. (2000). *Encyclopedia of World Political Systems.* New York: M. E. Sharpe. A useful inventory (circa 2000) of the forms of contemporary political institutions, as well as detailed descriptions of each national political system.

Ginsburg, Tom, and Rosalind Dixon. eds. (2013). *Comparative Constitutional Law.* **Northampton, MA: Edward Elgar.** This comprehensive (780 pages) and costly volume offers thoughtful essays on the nature of constitutional law, including current debates regarding such topics as constitutional design, human rights, and judicial review.

Gormley, William T., and Steven J. Balla. (2012). *Bureaucracy and Democracy: Accountability and Performance.* **Washington, DC: Sage.** How can you evaluate the accountability of the bureaucracy? The authors explore how democracies ensure proper administration, using approaches such as bounded rationality, principal–agent theory, interest group mobilization, and network theory.

Helmke, Gretchen. (2012). *Courts under Constraints: Judges, Generals, and Presidents in Argentina.* **Cambridge: Cambridge University Press.** This case study asks: When a democracy is unstable or collapsing, how do courts secure their institutional capacity to sustain the rule of law?

Jackson, Donald W., Michael C. Tolley, and Mary L. Volcansek, eds. (2010). *Globalizing Justice: Critical Perspectives on Transnational Law and the Cross-Border Migration of Legal Norms.* **Albany, NY: SUNY Press.** This edited volume examines the effect of globalization on judicial systems and courts in both the Global North and Global South.

Kelleman, R. Daniel. (2011). *Eurolegalism: The Transformation of Law and Regulation in the European Union.* **Cambridge: Harvard University Press.** The EU's fragmented institutional structure and prioritization of market integration has led to political incentives and functional pressures to enact transparent and judicially enforceable rules. This has opened a floodgate of public and private litigation as the rules are framed as rights.

Koopmans, Tim. (2003). *Courts and Political Institutions: A Comparative View.* **Cambridge: Cambridge University Press.** Koopmans, a former law professor and judge in the European Union, offers a persuasive analysis of the increasing power of the courts to engage in judicial decision making and to exercise influence and control over the actions of other political structures. The cases of Britain, France, Germany, and the United States are at the center of the study, but other constitutional court systems are also examined.

Martin, Shane, Thomas Saalfeld, and Kaare Strøm, eds. (2013). *The Oxford Handbook of Legislative Studies.* **Oxford: Oxford University Press.** A comprehensive set of recent analyses of legislative systems and processes with comparative and case study examples from many countries.

Norris, Pippa. (2004). *Electoral Engineering: Voting Rules and Political Behavior.* **Cambridge: Cambridge University Press.** A creative scholar considers the impacts of the various electoral systems with survey data and other empirical evidence from 32 countries. She assesses whether, given political culture, such engineering of institutional arrangements can influence such political behaviors as voting, the building of social capital, and democratic accountability

Osborne, David, and Ted Gaebler. (1993). *Reinventing Government.* **New York: Penguin.** An influential critique of large, bureaucratic government and a framework (using examples from the United States) of how to make government (and especially the administrative system) more responsive and entrepreneurial.

Peters, B. Guy. (2015). *The Politics of Bureaucracy: A Comparative Perspective.* **7th ed. New York:** Routledge. A rich, analytic comparison of the behavior and power of bureaucracies in many countries.

Pitkin, Hannah F. (1972). *The Concept of Representation.* **Berkeley: University of**

California Press. A thorough descriptive and normative exploration of political representation.

Sparrow, Malcolm K. (2000). *The Regulatory Craft: Controlling Risks, Solving Problems, and Managing Compliance.* **Washington, DC: Brookings Institution.** Writing as much for those who work in the public service as for scholars, Sparrow offers a positive and persuasive argument in support of administrative regulation, detailing the role of regulators as important innovators and protectors of the public interest within the policy process.

Toobin, Jeffrey. (2008). *The Nine: Inside the Secret World of the Supreme Court.* **New York: Anchor.** A readable and fascinating description of the inner workings, politics, and personalities of the U.S. Supreme Court during the recent period.

Von Mettenheim, Kurt, and Bert Rockman, eds. (1997). *Presidential Institutions and Democratic Politics: Comparing Regional and National Contexts.* **Baltimore: Johns Hopkins University Press.** A collection of essays, some written from a comparative perspective and others focused on a single country, that examines the behaviors and institutional frameworks of top executives.

Wilson, James Q. (1991). *Bureaucracy: What Government Agencies Do and Why They Do It.* **New York: Basic Books.** An interesting analysis of the performance of the U.S. national administration, identifying both the values and the flaws of the system.

On the Web

http://www.gksoft.com/govt/en
Governments on the Web provides a comprehensive database of governmental institutions on the Internet. The site contains 17,000 entries from 220 different countries. Most of the information is accurate, although there have been no updates for a decade.

http://www.gov.uk/en/index.htm
Directgov is the official Web portal of the government of the United Kingdom, and it provides extensive details about all the major political institutions and government agencies. The majority of the world's countries now have an official Web portal like this. They can usually be located by entering "Countryname" and "government portal" on a search engine. (For example, Canada is: http://www.canada.gc.ca/home.html.)

http://thomas.loc.gov/home/legbranch/cis.html
http://www.loc.gov/rr/news/fedgov.html
http://www.uscourts.gov
These three Library of Congress sites provide information about the legislative, executive,

and judicial branches of the U.S. government, respectively.

http://www.fedworld.ntis.gov
This site provides a huge central information network of the U.S. federal government, with searchable access to agencies and departments, documents, databases, and so on. It is a comprehensive site for searching for, locating, ordering, and acquiring government and business information.

http://www.thisnation.com
This electronic textbook provides an in-depth look at U.S. politics and includes links to other U.S. government–related Internet resources.

http://www.usa.gov
The U.S. government's official Web portal provides a wealth of government-related material, including access to the Internet sites of every major U.S. government agency.

http://lcweb.loc.gov/rr/news/extgovd.html
This site allows you to browse through Library of Congress electronic government resources.

Chapter 7
Political Institutions II: Institutional Arrangements

Learning Objectives

7.1 Assess the impact of written constitutions on regimes.

7.2 Distinguish between democratic and nondemocratic political systems.

7.3 Compare and contrast unitary, federal, and confederal systems.

7.4 Differentiate between parliamentary, presidential, and other types of executive-legislative systems.

7.5 Characterize the different types of political party systems.

Thomas Jefferson once observed that true democracy can only grow on fertile soil. The "soil" needs to be enriched with certain elements. There needs to be tolerance (and ideally cooperation) among different factions in the country; there needs to be an effective structure of authority and governance; and perhaps most importantly, the people need to trust in government and in one another. It might be that a reasonable level of economic prosperity is also an important nutrient. Without these elements—without a fertile soil—a democracy cannot thrive. Iraq is among the countries currently struggling to find that mix of elements.

Iraq was fashioned out of parts of Mesopotamia and Kurdistan by the British, who faced an immediate rebellion and installed an outsider from Mecca to be king in 1921. Deeply split into three nations (the Shias, the Sunnis, and the Kurds), Iraq was the first Arab state to overthrow its leader by a military coup, in 1936. Despotic political leadership continued during the brutal rule of President Saddam Hussein, from 1979 to 2003. When the United States led an invasion into Iraq searching for weapons of mass destruction and overthrew Hussein, Iraq was left without a government. The

The family that votes together…Iraqis show their inked fingers signifying they have voted in the parliamentary elections in April 2014.

United States insisted that the Iraqis establish a democratic government. But could a country with a history of nationality differences and tyranny be rapidly transformed into a democracy?

Having no recent experience with government transparency, free elections, competitive political parties, or peaceful turnovers of power, the Iraqis had no foundation upon which to build a Western-style democracy. The democratic institutions like those discussed in Chapter 6 were not in place. The United States established a transitional government in 2003 and pressured the Iraqis to move forward with a version of democracy envisioned by the foreign power by offering substantial aid and military support. Despite continued violence and volatile relations among different groups in Iraq, a constitution was ratified by a national vote in October 2005. The new Iraqi government is defined in the constitution as a parliamentary democracy, with a legislature elected by proportional representation. The executive branch is a hybrid headed by a prime minister, a president, and a presidency council. Iraq is a federation with 18 provinces and a system of local governments. There is a national judiciary guided by both civil law and sharia law (since Islam is the state religion).

In the 2010 election for the 325-member legislature, more than 450 candidates were not allowed to run because they were linked to the banned Ba'athist (Sunni) Party and the election was tainted by considerable voter fraud. It then took eight months to fashion a governing coalition due to continued disagreements among the major parties. That government was controlled by the Shias, who used their majority status to marginalize the Sunnis, the group who had dominated and repressed them during the

Saddam Hussein regime. But the new national government could not deliver on security or economic growth. In the face of continuing violence and political instability, the Kurds successfully pushed for regional autonomy.

The violence was further complicated by the emergence of Islamic State, a brutal insurgency group whose goal is to establish a fundamentalist state (a caliphate) in Iraq, Syria, and beyond. Armed resistance to IS comes from the Iraqi army, Shia militias, and Kurdish militias.

In the 2014 elections, nearly 400 candidates were prevented from running and more than 250 political groups ran candidates. After the election, the politicians did produce an inclusive coalition government that includes Shias, Sunnis and Kurds. Yet Iraq remains a troubled land of guerrilla warfare, suicide bombings, executions, and other forms of brutality.

Most see a half-full, half-empty glass of democracy in Iraq. On the one hand, the Iraqis have a sound constitution and have implemented all the appropriate political institutions for democratic governance, including elections. On the other hand, the government lacks credibility with many citizens and has not been particularly effective in enacting and implementing policies, and intergroup violence continues to (literally) explode in Iraq on almost a daily basis. This complex "soil" of instability, ongoing group strife, difficult living conditions, economic stress, and poor government performance has not resulted in the levels of trust, tolerance, and well-being that seem necessary to nurture the young democracy in the near future.

Chapter 6 provided us with a clearer grasp of each of the four major institutional structures in political systems. While all are in place now in Iraq, they have not yet delivered prosperity, stability, or security. It is evident that it is valuable to seek a deeper understanding of how these institutions and other structural elements interact in the pursuit of fundamental goals. Thus, this chapter takes us further in exploring the various ways in which these institutional structures and other key elements of governance are arranged across different countries. We will examine the role of the constitution, the continuum from democratic to nondemocratic regimes, the distribution of power between central and peripheral governments, the various patterns of executive–legislative relations, and the types of party systems.

Constitutions and Constitutional Regimes

7.1   **Assess the impact of written constitutions on regimes.**

Constitutions

In Iraq, a central element in framing the government's institutional arrangements is a **constitution**, *a set of statements describing the fundamental rules of the political system.* The constitution declares the existence of the state, and it expresses three crucial sets of rules. First, the constitution allocates governmental activities, defining what actions are within the domain of *res publica* and what political structures will perform these various functions. Second, it establishes the formal power relationships among the major political institutions, indicating the conditions under which each is independent of or dependent on the actions of the others. Third, the constitution limits the power of the rulers and guarantees the rights of the ruled by defining the maximum extent of the state's authority over its citizens and by enumerating citizens' freedoms and benefits from the state.

The drafting of every constitution is either directly or indirectly controlled by those with political power in the society. Constitutions reflect the political bargains that are struck at the time of their drafting. Many groups in a society—leaders, courts, political parties, interest groups—might offer interpretations of what the constitution means and how it ought to be applied to particular circumstances. Ultimately, the force of the constitution depends on the will of those with political power to enforce its provisions and the willingness of the citizenry to accept it as a legitimate blueprint for governance.

Most constitutions are a single written document, like the Iraq Constitution. However, a few political systems do not have such a document; their fundamental rules are embedded in major statutes, precedents, and legal decisions, as in Great Britain's "unwritten constitution" or in Israel's "basic laws." While early constitutions tended to be relatively short and general, some postcolonial constitutions are quite detailed. The Nigerian Constitution has 320 articles, and the Indian Constitution has 395 articles. The language of constitutions is also becoming increasingly similar because drafters liberally borrow ideas and even specific language from other countries. For example, more than three dozen countries have borrowed Abraham Lincoln's felicitous phrasing regarding government "of the people, by the people, and for the people."

Although the idea of a constitution has a certain timeless quality, the constitutions of political systems are always changeable. Most countries periodically alter their constitutions. For example, India has added more than 100 amendments to its constitution since 1950. And at some point, many countries have abandoned their existing constitutions and ratified new ones in an attempt to rejuvenate their political systems. In a typical year, between three and seven countries ratify a new constitution. In 2013, it was Fiji, Vietnam, and Zimbabwe. The process does not always succeed. In 2005, Kenyan citizens rejected a new constitution proposed by then-President Mwai Kibaki. In 2007, Venezuelans rejected a bundle of 33 major amendments to the constitution proposed by then President Hugo Chavez. And, although the parliament of the European Union adopted a new constitution in 2004, some key member states (e.g., France and the Netherlands) have subsequently voted against ratification.

A country's constitution does not necessarily provide a description of how the political system actually works. As you will read below, the reality of politics in many countries is dramatically at odds with the vision in their constitutions. Yet a constitution can be a very significant document. Even if the state makes major diversions from its constitution's provisions, the constitution remains a moral yardstick against which to measure actual performance, and it is a persistent reminder of the high ideals and goals that have been set for the political system.

Constitutional Regimes

It is useful to analyze the extent to which a political system generally abides by the provisions in its constitution. A **constitutional regime** *operates in terms of the rule of law and ensures effective restraints on the power holders*, as defined within the constitution. The defining feature of a constitutional regime is that the state attempts to fulfill the provisions of its constitution. A political system becomes more fully a constitutional regime to the extent that it abides by the three sets of crucial rules described above. In the short run, at least, those who have political power in the society greatly influence the interpretation of the constitution and how the constitution's provisions will be implemented (Law and Versteeg 2011). In constitutional regimes, these interpretations are generally reasonable and judicious, and the implementation is fair (Sunstein 2001).

Among constitutional regimes, it is not always the case that compliance with the rules is complete. Disagreements over interpretation of the constitution occur, practice and precedent can result in a gap between the rules and standard practice, and political actors sometimes willfully bend the rules to serve their agendas. Even the limits on the rulers and the rights of the citizens are not absolute and are not absolutely implemented. For example, Article 10 of the French Constitution guarantees freedom of religious practice, but the courts have ruled that current legislation preventing French (Muslim) women from wearing a burqa in public is an acceptable limit on their rights. Also, some states implement a "temporary" suspension of major constitutional provisions in response to circumstances that seriously threaten the stability of the society.

Thus, regimes range on a continuum and are less constitutional when the disparity becomes larger between the provisions in the constitution and the actual politics of the society. In theory, at least, a state could scrupulously follow a repressive and undemocratic constitution imposed by the political leadership and be labeled a constitutional regime. Saudi Arabia might be an example of this, given its adherence to authoritarian "basic laws" and sharia.

Nonconstitutional Regimes

Hence, in a **nonconstitutional regime**, *the structural arrangements of the constitution are not generally upheld and there are few restraints on those with political power*. Almost every political system occasionally violates or ignores some principle in its constitution. But the regime can be called *nonconstitutional* when there is persistent nonenforcement or disregard of constitutional provisions, especially those regarding the rights of the ruled or crucial limits on the rulers.

Various sets of conditions can result in a nonconstitutional regime. First, leaders in some political systems simply ignore with impunity the basic rules in the constitution (e.g., Myanmar, Vietnam). Second, in some countries (e.g., Congo, Somalia), the rule of law collapses because the social order disintegrates through severe political violence or natural catastrophe. And third, there are instances when either the entire constitution or major constitutional rights are suspended "temporarily" but then are not restored for a lengthy period. In Israel, for example, this temporary suspension of constitutional rights (there is no written constitution) has persisted since its independence in 1948.

Democracies and Nondemocracies

7.2 **Distinguish between democratic and nondemocratic political systems.**

Another taxonomy for classifying political systems is to specify the extent to which their institutional arrangements are democratic. "Democracy" is arguably the most ideologically loaded concept in any discussion about politics and governance. How do we define democracy? Here is a multiple-choice question version:

We know that all political systems are not democracies. But what does constitute a democracy? From our education, as well as from our other socialization and experiences, most of us have an intuitive sense about which countries are democracies and which are not. However, the concept can become slippery when we try to apply it. North Korea calls itself the *Democratic* People's Republic. Is it? Sri Lanka calls itself the *Democratic* Socialist Republic. Is it? Egypt, France, Kenya, and Venezuela also consider themselves democracies. Are they? Democracy has become such a highly valued label that most states, except a few systems ruled by a

Democracy is:

(a) an agreeable, lawless…commonwealth, dealing with all alike on a footing of equality, whether they be really equal or not.

—*(Plato, ca. 427–347* B.C.E., *Greek philosopher)*

(b) the theory that the common people know what they want, and deserve to get it good and hard.

—*(H. L. Mencken, 1880–1956, U.S. journalist [Mencken 1916: 19])*

(c) a system where no man is good enough to govern another man without that other's consent.

—*(Abraham Lincoln, 1809–1865, U.S. president)*

(d) the substitution of election by the incompetent many for appointment by the corrupt few.

—*(George Bernard Shaw [1903/2001], 1856–1950, Anglo-Irish playwright)*

(e) all of the above.

(f) none of the above.

hereditary monarch, claim that they are democratic. Is almost every contemporary political system to be called a democracy? If not, what general label do you give to countries that are not democratic? Dictatorship? Tyranny? Totalitarian regime? Authoritarian system?

Suppose you were to determine which of a group of countries were democracies. How would you proceed?

One approach is to distinguish democracies from nondemocracies. While we work toward acceptable definitions and labels, let's start by considering dictatorship as the opposite of democracy. To begin to clarify your thinking, use your current understanding of democracy and dictatorship to classify these seven political systems: Algeria, Cuba, Japan, Kuwait, Singapore, the United States, and Zimbabwe. If you have been raised in the United States or Western Europe, you might view Japan, the United States, and possibly Kuwait and Singapore as democracies and Algeria, Cuba, and Zimbabwe as run by dictators. Why might it matter where you were raised? Recall that Chapter 4 attempted to persuade you that how one understands and uses political labels depends on one's own political socialization and political environment. It might be argued that this problem regarding interpersonal differences in assessments underscores the virtue of the scientific method. The scientific method requires the analyst to specify what a particular concept means with great precision and in an empirically measurable manner. This method might be the only way in which people with fundamentally different ideological views could agree on which states are democracies and which are dictatorships. The discussion in this chapter will proceed in the spirit of the scientific method, although the authors acknowledge their own lifetime socializations, which are grounded in the political conceptions of the American and Western world.

How might individuals with dramatically different political worldviews attempt to agree on the accuracy of the classifications suggested earlier? For example, consider these issues:

- In Cuba, a far greater proportion of the citizens vote in elections than in either Japan or the United States. The government provides far more extensive social benefits to all its citizens than either Japan or the United States. Aren't those the best features of a democracy?

- Algeria calls itself the Peoples' Democratic Republic. Elections for the president were held in 2004, 2009, and 2014.. Abdelaziz Bouteflika was elected each time by substantial majorities and, despite his failing health, led the ruling National Liberation Front party in the 2014 election with 82% of the vote. Elections for the national bicameral legislature occurred in 2002 and 2007, with 22 different parties winning seats. Under these conditions, is Algeria a dictatorship?

- By what criteria is Zimbabwe not a democracy when President Robert Mugabe defeated other candidates in five straight elections (in 1990, 1996, 2002, 2008, and 2013) and his party won 160 of the 210 seats in a 2013 legislative election?

- By what criteria is Singapore a democracy when almost every member of the national legislature and every prime minister has, in every election since its independence in 1959, been from a single political party?

In asking and responding to such questions, you begin to establish the standards that must be applied when you attempt to distinguish between democracy and dictatorship. These kinds of questions also underscore the importance of defining with precision the concepts that we use in political analysis.

Defining Democracy

What are the necessary and sufficient conditions for democracy? In its classic sense, true ***direct democracy*** (also known as **participatory democracy**) is government of and by the people—*all the citizens are active, direct participants in making public policy decisions.* Realistically, there is no such political system; indeed, Jean-Jacques Rousseau (1712–1778) claimed that only a society of gods could be a true democracy. If our definition is less stringent, democracy might entail the relatively equal capacity of *every* citizen to influence the policy process. It would be difficult to make a persuasive case that this condition holds in *any* political system, including Japan or the United States. In every political system, "some are more equal than others." In every political system, some make public policy decisions and others observe them.

An alternative concept is **representative democracy**, a system in which the *citizens periodically elect people who represent them in the political process and make policy decisions on their behalf.* Another general term used to describe a representative democracy is a *republic.* In fact, the majority of the countries in the world, in their formal title, call themselves republics (examples, from the *A*s: Republic of Albania, People's Democratic Republic of Algeria, People's Republic of Angola, Argentine Republic, Republic of Armenia, Republic of Austria, and Republic of Azerbaijan). You might think some of these *A* "republics" are not particularly democratic.

Kuwait seems to meet this criterion for representative democracy because its citizens periodically elect representatives. Yet few would classify it as a democracy because about half of its resident adult population (those who cannot trace their Kuwaiti ancestry to 1920) are not allowed to vote in legislative elections, and the chief executive, the emir, is appointed from the ruling Al-Sabah family. Thus, the definition needs to be refined to specify that the elections for representatives must be held under conditions of *universal (adult) suffrage.*

Cuba meets all these conditions, but few would consider it a democracy because, among other reasons, there are very limited choices for governmental office. There is only one candidate per district, and this person is chosen by a local committee based on "patriotism" and "revolutionary history" as well as merit. In practice, nearly every candidate is a member of the single (Communist) party. Thus, an adequate definition of democracy should also stipulate that the elections provide voters with *alternative choices.*

Even with this clarification, there are cases, such as Singapore, where numerous parties offer candidates but more than 90 percent of legislators are always elected from one party. Thus, even the notion of a contest among alternative candidates can be ambiguous. However, these conditions do seem to define an *electoral democracy*:

a political system in which virtually all citizens have the right to periodically vote to select political leaders from among alternative contenders.

Additional conditions might seem appropriate in refining our definition of democracy. It is also important that the people have the genuine capacity to retain or reject those serving as their political leaders. This additional condition, called the **limited mandate**, means that the electorate grants the authority to govern (the mandate) for only a short, fixed (limited) period of time, and then the electorate has the opportunity to select representatives again. And it means that if political leaders do not gain sufficient votes (that is, if they lose), they relinquish office voluntarily and peacefully. This condition can be harder to demonstrate because it is not clear if the top leaders in several of these countries would peacefully step down if they lost an election. This is problematic in Singapore, and there are instances in both Algeria and Zimbabwe in which an election that would have turned out the leaders was ignored. It is hard to imagine that the leaders in Cuba or Kuwait would step down even in the unlikely situation they were outvoted.

Are we there yet? Perhaps. But shouldn't a full democracy not only ensure voting rights among alternative choices and a limited mandate but also allow the citizens and the media to exercise freedoms such as freedom of speech, assembly, the right to petition government for action, and political opposition at all times? Zimbabwe, for example, loosely meets the conditions for electoral democracy, but opposition groups and media are harassed, arrested, and subjected to violence by those loyal to President Robert Mugabe. Thus, scholars classify a political system as a **liberal democracy** when *citizens enjoy not only electoral democracy but also substantial political rights and civil liberties regarding participation, personal freedoms, and opposition.* And if a country is *an electoral democracy, but its citizens' political rights and civil liberties are significantly limited*, some analysts describe that country with yet another term, *illiberal democracy* (Zakaria 2007; Rhoden 2013).

Now we have established one possible set of sufficient, as well as necessary, conditions for a **democracy**: *governance by leaders whose authority is based on a limited mandate from a universal electorate that selects among genuine alternatives and has some rights to political participation and opposition.* This is a modest notion of democracy because it guarantees the people little more than political rights and the occasional opportunity to select among the competing elites who govern them. Some scholars include even more elements, such as an electoral system that does not substantially skew the conversion of votes to seats (recall Focus in 6 on electoral systems), an independent and neutral judiciary, and civilian control of the military (Diamond and Plattner 2009).

Our definition is clearly less than a full participatory democracy, in which there would be active, direct rule by all the people, who would be empowered to make policy decisions themselves by referenda or some other means (see Barber 2004; Dahl 1971, 2006; Schumpeter 1950). Even with our modest definition, only two (Japan and the United States) among the seven political systems are clearly classified as democracies. Singapore is more problematic because the extent to which there is genuine contestation is unclear. Not only does one party win nearly all the legislative seats and control the government, but also the last several presidents of Singapore have been

Zimbabwe's President Robert Mugabe is very popular with his supporters, whom he rewards; but most observers inside and outside the country judge him to be a ruthless and corrupt dictator who suppresses opposition and rigs the elections.

elected by default because a governing panel declared that only one candidate was qualified to run. While all seven systems encourage some forms of political participation and allow some political opposition, the authority of the political leadership in Cuba and Kuwait is not based on its electoral selection, by universal suffrage, among genuine alternatives, or for a fixed period of time. And the leaders in Algeria and Zimbabwe have so manipulated the electoral process (harassing and arresting opponents, controlling the media, engaging in electoral fraud) that neither country meets the spirit of the definition.

Most definitions of democracy focus on *the process*, as discussed above. However, some analysts go even further, arguing that a genuine democracy not only must guarantee appropriate processes of empowering and replacing leaders but also must deliver desirable *policy outputs*. In such a process-plus-output conception of genuine democracy, the political system might ensure that all citizens have access to quality education, employment, good health care, and decent housing and enjoy such conditions of life as a sense of personal safety and a healthy environment. While it might seem reasonable that a democracy should "deliver the goods," there is substantial disagreement about the nature of this package of goods, and thus the policy decisions about these goods are part of the political process but do not define democracy (see Chapter 9).

This extensive discussion might help you identify the criteria that *you* think are necessary for an adequate definition of democracy. (It is certainly possible that your definition will differ from any of those suggested here. You should, however, be able to justify your criteria.) Could you now articulate a conceptual definition of democracy and use it to classify a set of political systems? Do you think your friends will accept your definition and classifications? Would a Singaporean or Cuban student accept it? You might be surprised by how difficult it is to develop a generally accepted definition of this most widely used political concept.

Defining Nondemocracy

How about *nondemocracies*? What concepts can be used to characterize those political regimes that are not democratic? Several are widely employed.

AUTOCRACY One conventional concept for some nondemocracies is *autocracy*. A stringent definition might be that a single ruler exercises absolute power and authority without any legal constraints or citizen mandate. An autocrat would likely acquire power through birth or force. Some might classify North Korea under Kim Jong-un or Swaziland under King Mswati III (see Focus in 9) as autocracies. However, you might consider whether any one person could successfully exercise absolute power in any country in the contemporary political world. It might be that even in an autocracy, at least some sectors of the country must support the ruler.

DICTATORSHIP Related to autocracy is the concept of *dictatorship.* A dictator might be a single individual or small group that has nearly absolute power and authority. **Dictatorship** might be better defined in terms of *rulers who hold power in the absence of a limited mandate*—a critical factor in our definition of democracy. That is, if the citizens have no regular and realistic opportunity to replace the political leadership, then the political system is a dictatorship. This applied to the military dictatorship in Myanmar that ruled from 1989 through 2011. However, even a political leadership that has popular support from the majority but does not provide genuine opportunities for the population to renew the mandate for governance in competition with alternative leaders could be defined as dictatorial (Escriba-Folch 2013). This conception of dictatorship might characterize the situation in Cuba under Raul Castro and perhaps the situation under some hereditary rulers, such as Bashar al-Assad in Syria.

AUTHORITARIAN REGIME A concept that political scientists often apply to a nondemocratic system is *authoritarian regime*. Many authoritarian regimes, like dictatorships, lack a limited mandate. But what distinguishes **authoritarianism** is another dimension: The political actions and decisions of the ruler are not constrained, while the political rights and freedoms of the citizens are significantly limited. In other words, an authoritarian regime places severe restrictions on the activities of individuals and groups who desire to understand and influence the political system. The flow of political information is strictly controlled by the government. And the great majority of the population is not allowed to participate in any political activities except those expressly encouraged by the regime, such as mass rallies and voting in support of the leaders (Linz 1993; Wiarda 2004). Citizens are not permitted to question the political institutions, procedures, or public policies of an authoritarian regime. However, the nonpolitical aspects of people's lives, such as their occupation, religion, and social life, are not generally under the direct control of the political system. Many current nondemocratic regimes, ranging from Algeria to Zimbabwe, could be characterized as authoritarian regimes.

TOTALITARIAN REGIME In a *totalitarian regime*, the definition of *res publica* becomes total. Thus, under **totalitarianism**, the political system's decisions and its control penetrate into almost every aspect of its people's lives. The totalitarian regime demands complete obedience to its extensive rules regarding culture, economics, religion, and morality. The state attempts to dictate the behavior and even the thoughts of its population in almost every domain of existence. Every political system intervenes occasionally in such domains, but the defining characteristic of the totalitarian regime is its constant and pervasive efforts to totally control the lives of its population. All organizations are subordinated to the totalitarian state. Every activity of the individual citizen is subject to scrutiny by the state, which claims it is protecting what is best for the society as a whole. The state might define the acceptability of films and plays, determine what job each individual will have, prohibit the activities of organized churches, prevent families from moving without approval, and so on.

Totalitarian regimes, even more than authoritarian regimes, depend on the use of extensive coercion for their survival. The state employs its military, internal security forces, and other instruments of violence to suppress any citizen or group that challenges its authority. To sustain its pervasive control, the totalitarian regime also makes extensive use of the agents of political socialization, especially the media, educational system, and cultural forms. Often the totalitarian state is dominated by a single leader, venerated in a cult of personality, and by a single political party. The people have no control over the policies or the mandate of the leadership. George Orwell's novel *1984* (1949/1967) is a literary vision of the totalitarian state, and recent examples include Afghanistan under the Taliban (1996–2001), Cambodia under Pol Pot (1975–1979; see Compare in 10), and North Korea (since 1948).

Most nondemocracies can be located on a continuum between totalitarianism and authoritarianism. That is, some regimes extend their control beyond basic authoritarianism into important nonpolitical domains but do not exercise the totality of control associated with absolute totalitarianism. Belarus, Congo under Mobutu Sese Seko (1965–1997; see Focus in 11), Indonesia under Suharto (1966–1998), Iran, and Saudi Arabia are examples along this continuum of countries that are not totalitarian regimes but do assert extensive control over culture, religious practice, and social life.

Not all political analysts are consistent in how they employ these concepts. In this book, autocracy, dictatorship, authoritarianism, and totalitarianism will all be treated as modes of politics that contrast with democratic regimes. *Autocracy* will be applied if there is near-absolute one-person rule. *Dictatorship* will especially emphasize the absence of a limited mandate for the political leaders. *Authoritarianism* will connote a more encompassing array of nondemocratic practices and significant controls over citizens' political behavior. And *totalitarianism* will be used to describe systems whose oppressive control goes far beyond the political sphere into personal and social life. Many authoritarian or totalitarian regimes are dictatorships. However, there are instances in which people elect their leaders (electoral democracies) but the political system substantially limits the people's personal and political freedoms, as in Singapore and Iran.

A Democracy–Nondemocracy Measure

This discussion of democracy suggests that there are gradations along a democracy–nondemocracy continuum. Can we measure how democratic national political systems are? Can we identify the number of countries that are democratic? The precise number of countries in the current "wave of democracy" (a key theme in Chapter 10 and in Part Five of this book) ebbs and flows yearly as some countries establish democratic systems while others retreat or revert to nondemocratic systems (Diamond 2009; Schedler 2013; Smith 2013).

Freedom House (2014) is an international organization that analyzes these questions. First, Freedom House identifies those countries that meet the minimal conditions for an electoral democracy. Second, those countries that do not meet these conditions can be classified as nondemocracies. Third, Freedom House analyzes the extent to which each country grants its citizens the *political rights* (e.g., to form political parties that promote genuine alternatives, to campaign and vote in free and fair elections) and *civil liberties* (e.g., religious and ethnic freedom, press freedom) that define a liberal democracy.

Freedom House has developed a widely cited scale, with each country scoring from 1 to 7 points on political rights and from 1 to 7 points on civil liberties. A country's combined average score on the two measures can range from 1.0 points, the most extensive liberal democracies, to 7.0 points, the world's most repressive regimes. Based on actual conditions, a country is classified as "free" (1.0–2.5 points), "partly free" (3.0–5.0), or "not free" (5.5–7.0) (Freedom House 2014).

According to the analysis of Freedom House, 45 percent of all countries (and just over 40 percent of the world's population) are "free." However, 30 percent of the countries are only "partly free," and 25 percent of the countries are "not free." Even more striking, 35 percent of the world's population is not free, living under highly repressive political regimes. There are clear regional variations, ranging from 88 percent of European countries being classified as free, compared to only 6 percent in the Middle East and North Africa, where 66 percent of countries are not free. Table 7.1 reports the Freedom House classifications of selected countries on both political rights and civil liberties, circa 2014.

There are other useful measures of the level of democracy in countries. For example, the Economist Intelligence Unit (2013) calculates a yearly Democracy Index for each country. It measures such factors as the nature of the electoral process, the level of genuine political participation, the extent of civil liberties, and the effective functioning of government. It calculates an index score for nearly 170 countries on a scale from 10.0 (most democratic) to zero. Currently, 25 countries are "full democracies," 54 are "flawed democracies," 37 are "hybrid regimes," and 51 are "authoritarian regimes." Norway is the highest ranked country, with a score of 9.93, and North Korea is lowest, with a score of 1.08. Figure 14.4 reports the Democracy Index scores of selected countries of the Global South.

Table 7.1 Classification of Selected Countries by Level of Freedom and Regime Type, circa 2014

	Freedom Score	Liberal Democracy	Electoral Democracy	Nondemocracy
Free	1.0	Costa Rica 1,1*		
		Sweden 1,1		
		Poland 1,1		
		United States 1,1		
		Japan 1,1		
	2.0	South Korea 2,2		
		South Africa 2,2	Argentina 2,2	
			Brazil 2,2	
			Serbia 2,2	
	2.5	India 2,3	Indonesia 2,4	
Partly Free	3.0		Indonesia 2,4	
	3.5		Mexico 3,3	
			Sierra Leone 3,3	
			Turkey 3,4	
	4.0		Thailand 4,4	
	4.5			Singapore 4,4
				Nigeria 4,4
	5.0			Venezuela 5,5
Not Free	5.5			Cambodia 6,5
				Egypt 6,5
				Myanmar 6,5
				Russia 6,5
	6.0			Congo 6,6
				Swaziland, 7,5
				Vietnam 7,5
	6.5			China 7,6
	7.0			Saudi Arabia 7,7
				Syria 7,7
				North Korea 7,7

*Scores: The first score is political rights, the second score is civil liberties, with 1 = the highest score and 7 = the lowest score. A country's Freedom Score is the average of these two component scores.

SOURCE: Freedom House 2014.

Areal Distribution of Power

7.3 **Compare and contrast unitary, federal, and confederal systems.**

With the exception of small political systems serving only a few thousand citizens, most political systems have found it desirable or necessary to create governmental structures at several levels. Thus, another type of institutional arrangement is the *areal distribution of power*—the allocation of power and functions across the levels of government. National political systems are organized into one of three major forms: (1) unitary states; (2) federations; and (3) confederations.

Unitary State

In a **unitary state**, *a central government holds all legitimate power.* The central government has indivisible sovereignty, although it usually delegates some power to regional units such as provinces, departments, or counties. These subnational governments serve at the convenience of the central government, which can revoke their power or functions at any time. Currently, more than 70 percent of the countries are unitary states. Examples include most African, Asian, and Latin American countries, as well as China, France, Japan, South Africa, and the United Kingdom.

Why are most contemporary states unitary? The major advantage is that there is clear, hierarchical authority—all power is controlled by the central government. Even if there were a disagreement between the central government and the peripheral governments, the center's superior constitutional power is clear, and center–periphery stalemates are uncommon. Also, control from the center should provide a more uniform implementation of policy throughout the country. And primary citizen loyalty tends to be mainly attached to the national political system, reducing the risk of divisive regionalism.

Federation

A **federation** has *a constitutional division of power and functions between a central government and the set of regional governments.* In contrast to a unitary state, the central government and the regional governments share power in a federation. Each level has primary control of certain functions, and neither level has legal power to dominate the other level in all policy domains. The central government usually controls policy in at least such areas as national defense, finance, commerce, and foreign affairs. The essence of a federation is coordination, not hierarchy. Federations require a complex balancing of the power between the central government and the regional governments and thus are more prone to disagreements, power struggles, and stalemates than a unitary state. Nonetheless, there are five major rationales for a federation:

1. **Large size.** Many states become federations to distribute governmental power where there is a huge area to be governed. Currently, 25 states are federations and Iraq and Sudan are in transition to federal systems. This group includes nearly half the land area of the world and about 40 percent of the global population. Most of the largest states are federations, including Brazil, Canada, India, Mexico, Nigeria, Russia, and the United States. During the constitutional debate in the United States, Thomas Jefferson observed, "Our country is too large to have all its affairs directed by a single government."

2. **The prior existence of strong states.** A federation can be an acceptable compromise when strong peripheral governments create a central government. In the formation of the United States, for example, the already strong state governments were unwilling to give up all of their power to a central government, as in a unitary state. Rather, they agreed to delegate certain functions to the new central government while retaining all other "residual" powers for themselves.

3. **The attempt to create unity or accommodate diversity.** Chapter 5 described the serious problems of conflict between states and nations, especially in the newer states. Federations attempt to bond diverse nations into a unified state while still recognizing the different nations' diversity and desire for power at the regional level. The regional governments can represent a major ethnic, linguistic, religious, or other nation-based characteristic dominant in the region. India is a federation with 28 states, most of which are related to the linguistic, ethnic, or religious majority in the area.

4. **The desire to disperse political power.** A federation can be established to prevent the overconcentration of power in the central government. After the trauma of Hitler's rule, West Germans formed a federation to prevent the emergence of another overly powerful central government. The bulk of legislative power was granted to the central government, but most power to administer and adjudicate the laws is held by the Länder (regional) governments.

5. **The desire to concentrate power and resources.** In contrast to the preceding rationale, a federation can be created to combine several states into a stronger political system. For example, in the effort to create Arab unity and to expand the political and economic power of the state, Egypt has several times formed federations with its neighbors: Syria, Yemen, Iraq, and Jordan.

Confederation

A **confederation** is *an association in which states delegate some power to a supranational central government but retain primary power.* It is a loose grouping of states in which each state's membership, participation, and compliance with the supranational central government are conditional, depending on the state's perception of its own national interest. Confederations are usually created when states decide that the performance of certain functions is enhanced by structured cooperation with other states. To facilitate such cooperation, the states establish permanent supranational machinery. The United Arab Emirates is a confederation of ministates, and the United Nations is a confederal structure containing more than 190 member states. Confederations can emphasize economic cooperation, such as the European Union (EU), or military cooperation, such as the North Atlantic Treaty Organization (NATO).

Although confederations can serve many useful functions for member states, their activities and even their very survival are always contingent on the members' continuing support. A member state might refuse to comply with confederation

Table 7.2 Relative Strengths and Weaknesses of Areal Distributions of Power

Form of Areal Distribution	Strengths	Weaknesses
Unitary state	Clear authority Decisive control No stalemates between center and periphery	Hyperconcentration of power Weak representation of diversity and minorities
Federation	Representation of diversity Checks on center's power Creates unity	Duplication and overlap of power Conflicts over ultimate power Sluggishness; compromises
Confederation	Facilitates cooperation Power retained by subunits	Conditional compliance Instability

policies that conflict directly with the state's definition of its own national interest. Disagreements among the members can necessitate negotiation and compromise, as in the periodic adjustments within the EU regarding issues such as farm subsidies to member states and a common monetary policy. A confederation can wither if the supragovernment is ineffective, as in the case of the Articles of Confederation in colonial America, or if members refuse to support its directives, as in the League of Nations after World War I.

Table 7.2 summarizes some of the major advantages and shortcomings of each approach to the areal distribution of power. While each has relative advantages under certain conditions, none is without considerable drawbacks, and none can ensure the effective functioning or even the survival of a political system. Due to the general trend toward the centralization of political power within states, the distinctions between unitary states and federations are less clear than in the past and confederations have become particularly fragile.

Forms of Executive–Legislative Relations

7.4 **Differentiate between parliamentary, presidential, and other types of executive–legislative systems.**

Another conventional method of classifying and especially of describing political systems is by defining the pattern of power and interaction between the executive and legislative structures. The taxonomy in this section emphasizes the three most common patterns through which these two structures interact to perform the functions of policymaking and policy implementation: the presidential, parliamentary, and hybrid forms of government. Two other types of executive–legislative arrangements are also briefly examined: the council and assembly systems.

Presidential Government

The crucial feature of **presidential government** is the *separation of executive and legislative structures.* Figure 7.1 portrays the electoral chain of command that is supposed to define the relationships between citizens and these major political structures. In separate electoral decisions, the citizens select the chief executive (usually called the president) and the members of the national legislature. This electoral process provides both the president and the legislature with independent mandates to represent the citizens in the governing process. The term length of each is predetermined, and thus the tenure in office of each is not dependent on the other (except in the rare case of impeachment of the chief executive).

The separation of executive and legislative powers is explicit and intentional to ensure a system of checks and balances in the policymaking and policy-implementation processes. Primary responsibility for policymaking (debating, modifying, and enacting policies as law) resides in the legislature. Although the chief executive can veto legislation, the legislature can override that veto. Primary responsibility for the implementation of policy is with the president, who has control of the government's administrative departments. The president also appoints and manages a cabinet, and its members are responsible for overseeing policy in the government's administrative departments.

In practice, it is common to find considerable interdependence and blurring of functions between the executive and legislative structures and especially for the president to have substantial involvement in policymaking. The United States is the model example of presidential government, which is also found in many Latin American and some African and Asian states, including Brazil, Ivory Coast, Kenya, Mexico, Sri Lanka, Venezuela, and the Philippines.

Parliamentary Government

In contrast to the presidential system, the crucial element of **parliamentary government** is the *fusion of executive and legislative functions and structures.* As is indicated in Figure 7.1 , the people elect the legislature (the parliament), whose majority empowers a cabinet, which then empowers one of its members to be the chief executive, typically called a prime minister or premier. The maximum length of the legislature's mandate

Figure 7.1 Presidential and Parliamentary Systems of Government is often five years, but its term can be shorter under the circumstances described next. The complex relationships among cabinet, legislature, and prime minister merit further detail.

CABINET AND LEGISLATURE The cabinet is a collective leadership group of 6 to 30 people who are, in most systems, also members of the legislature. The cabinet is "responsible" to the legislature. This means that the cabinet serves only as long as it can retain the confidence of the majority of the members in the legislature. The cabinet has primary responsibility for both the policymaking and policy-implementation functions. Although policies must be voted into laws by the legislative majority, it is the cabinet that devises, drafts, and implements most policies.

In an intriguing manner, the cabinet and the legislature are at each other's mercy. At *any* time, the legislative majority can pressure the cabinet to resign, either by a negative vote on a major piece of legislation proposed by the cabinet or by a general motion of "no confidence" in the cabinet. Also at *any* time, the cabinet can dissolve the legislature, requiring immediate new elections. In the subsequent election, voters select a new legislature, whose majority then identifies a cabinet it will support, and the process begins anew. Thus, the cabinet and the legislature are rather like two gunfighters standing gun-to-gun in an old Western movie: Each has the power to eliminate the other, but each might also be destroyed in the exchange. In 2013, the governments of Greece and Thailand survived no-confidence votes, but the Lebanese cabinet resigned due to the loss of legislative support.

LEGISLATURE AND PRIME MINISTER In the parliamentary system, the prime minister (or premier or chancellor or whatever the chief executive is called) is not directly elected by the citizens. The prime minister is the member of the legislature who is supported as chief executive by the majority of the legislature. The prime minister can be removed at any time by a no-confidence vote of the legislature, and he might also be obliged to resign if the legislature defeats a major legislative initiative he proposes. In 2013, the prime ministers of the Czech Republic, Libya, Slovenia, and Somalia lost no-confidence votes and were removed from office.

CABINET AND PRIME MINISTER The balance of power between the cabinet and the prime minister can be subtle, although both depend on majority support of the legislature. Traditionally, a cabinet that had legislative support could select one of its members to serve as prime minister. The prime minister was *primus inter pares*—"first among equals"—in the cabinet. The prime minister exercised broad policy leadership within a collective decision-making body. If a cabinet majority no longer supported a prime minister, the prime minister either resigned or attempted to reconstitute a cabinet that did support him and was supported by the legislative majority.

In many contemporary parliamentary systems, however, there has been a substantial shift of power from the cabinet to the prime minister. In these systems, the electorate selects legislative candidates from a party committed to support a particular prime minister. If a legislative majority can be formed, its leader becomes prime minister. The prime minister then appoints the members of the cabinet and clearly dominates the cabinet in the governmental process. In Figure 7.1, the two-headed arrow between cabinet and prime minister indicates these alternative patterns of power.

Thus, the parliamentary system is characterized by the fusion of executive and legislative functions because the cabinet and prime minister formulate policies, guide their passage through a legislature that they control, and administer policy through the administrative departments. However, the actual policy process in a parliamentary system depends on whether there is a coherent majority group in the legislature. There are both "stable" and "unstable" parliamentary systems.

In a stable parliamentary system, there is a clear majority in the legislature. Such a majority could be composed of either one party or a coalition. This majority provides the prime minister and cabinet with sufficient legislative support to enact their policy program, without the problems of stalemate and confusion of accountability that can result from the separation of powers in the presidential system. Australia, Denmark, Great Britain, and Japan are examples of parliamentary government systems that are usually stable.

In contrast, an unstable parliamentary system often emerges when there is no coherent legislative majority. Instead, policymaking requires agreement within a coalition composed of multiple parties that tend to disagree on some important policy issues. If the legislature votes no confidence in the cabinet or defeats it on a major bill, the cabinet usually resigns. Then the media report that a parliamentary government has "fallen" or that there are efforts to form a new government (actually, a new cabinet). The new cabinet might have almost all the same people as members, or it might have a different set of people from the legislature. In general, prime ministers in unstable parliamentary systems are weaker than those in stable parliamentary systems. Unstable parliamentary systems have been prevalent in contemporary legislatures that have strong ideological differences and multiple political parties, such as Israel and Poland. Great Britain currently has a somewhat unstable government due to the uneasy coalition between the Conservatives and the Liberal Democrats.

Hybrid Systems

An increasing number of political systems attempt to blend desirable aspects of the presidential and parliamentary systems. These **hybrid systems** *have a prime minister and an elected legislature that can both enact and implement policies, but they also have an independent president,* who is elected for a fixed term, has some executive functions, and can act with decisiveness (Elgie 2004; Shugart and Carey 1992; Samuels and Shugart 2013).

Some hybrid systems function more like parliamentary systems: The president has limited power, and the prime minister and cabinet exercise most of the control. In India, for example, the president is elected by the legislature for a five-year term and has notable responsibilities, including the appointment of state governors and the right to take over governance of the states during emergencies. However, the prime minister is the dominant political power in the system, while the president performs mainly ceremonial roles, such as appearances on national holidays. Germany, Austria, Iraq, and Ireland are other examples of this style of the hybrid.

Who's on first? Vladimir Putin (right) has dominated Russia's hybrid political system since 2000, moving from president to prime minister to president again, while Dmitry Medvedev is second in command, holding the other position.

In other hybrid systems, there is a more balanced sharing of power between the president and the parliament. In Finland, for example, the president controls the administration, has oversight powers, and must cosign legislation. However, the prime minister, cabinet, and legislature are in charge of most policymaking. Finally, there are some hybrids in which the president is the most powerful political actor. While the prime minister and the cabinet have primary responsibility for day-to-day policymaking and administration, the president tends to dominate the policy process when he chooses to do so, and he is the main focus of public attention and expectations regarding the leadership function. Focus in 7 describes the French hybrid system, in which the president is the key actor. Hybrids with a strong president have been implemented in almost all the postcommunist countries that emerged from the Soviet Union and in Central and Eastern Europe.

Council Systems

In **council systems**, *a small group shares collective leadership and is responsible for both executive and legislative functions.* Although one member of the group might be deemed the leader for symbolic reasons, all members of the council are equal in constitutional terms, and they make decisions and actions based on the will of the council majority or, ideally, on council consensus. In U.S. local government, the weak-mayor–council system and the boards of commissioners/supervisors (prevalent in many counties, school districts, and special districts) are council systems. Also, many tribal societies in Africa were traditionally ruled by a council of elders who collectively made decisions that were binding on the members of the tribe.

Focus in 7

A Hybrid System in Action: France

Many recent constitutions establish a hybrid model in which both a president and a prime minister have significant political power. A central issue for hybrids is whether two independent executives can share power effectively. An early example of this system is the French Fifth Republic, established by the "de Gaulle Constitution" of 1962. France created this hybrid to overcome the highly unstable parliamentary system of the Fourth Republic, in which governments averaged less than one year. In the hybrid, the premier (prime minister) and cabinet are responsible for the day-to-day functioning of the government, as in a parliamentary system, but the president (an office Charles de Gaulle fashioned for himself as a condition for his return to government) has extensive power and the freedom to exercise it. The president is elected popularly for a fixed term, and he selects a premier, who selects a cabinet. The cabinet controls the budget and legislative agenda as in a normal parliamentary system; however, the president can dissolve the legislature while retaining the cabinet. And Article 16 in the constitution provides that the sweeping powers of the presidency may be exercised whenever the president *alone* deems the political situation to be dangerous for the country.

De Gaulle served as the first president of the Fifth Republic from 1958 to 1969. He was an extraordinarily powerful man, and he demanded extraordinary power. He established a precedent that the president can act far more extensively than the constitution allows. He dominated every premier who served during his presidency. The presidents after de Gaulle (from Pompidou to Hollande) have continued to follow the de Gaulle precedent, exercising considerable power. The president is so strong that the French hybrid is also termed a "semi-presidential" system.

Many people felt that the French "dyarchy" (dual rule) would lead to a constitutional crisis as soon as a premier and cabinet challenged the president's extensive power. The first strong test of the French hybrid occurred between 1986 and 1988, when Socialist President François Mitterrand was faced with a legislative majority dominated by conservatives. But Mitterrand accepted the situation, appointing the conservatives' leader, Jacques Chirac, as premier. Despite strong ideological differences between the president and the premier–cabinet–legislature majority, there was a reasonable sharing of power and authority, which the French call *cohabitation*. President Mitterrand continued to be very active in foreign policy but allowed the premier to control the domestic policy agenda. From 1993 to 1995, a conservative legislative majority produced a second period of cohabitation. A weakened Mitterrand acknowledged that "it is not the task of the president of the Republic to govern" (Safran 2008).

In 2000, the French shortened the presidential term from seven years to five years, ostensibly to increase the political accountability of the president. The shorter term also makes it considerably more likely that the elected president will be from the same part of the political spectrum as the legislative majority that empowers the premier and cabinet.

Since 2002, there has been no cohabitation. From 2002 until 2011, both the president and the prime minister were from the coalition of conservative parties. In 2012, Francois Hollande was elected president as a member of the Socialist Party and fellow socialist Manuel Valls is prime minister. After several periods of cohabitation, the power relationships between the president and the premier in the French hybrid system seem to be sufficiently limited and institutionalized to survive the conflict inherent in dyarchy and in a future situation where strong ideological differences exist between the two executives.

Further Focus

1. What seems to be the greatest benefit of the French hybrid, in comparison to a parliamentary system?

2. If the president and prime minister are from opposing parties in a hybrid, would this usually be a desirable check-and-balance feature?

In many situations in which a small collective group forcefully removes the top leader, the group initially shares power. When the group that has taken power is from the military, this council-type group is called a *junta*. There were numerous juntas in Latin America and Africa in the latter half of the twentieth century (e.g., in Algeria from 1992 to 1999; in Argentina from 1976 to 1983), and Egypt was briefly ruled by a junta after the ouster of President Mubarak in 2011. In most cases, council rule evolves into more dictatorial rule as a single political leader increasingly dominates the others.

Assembly Systems

In **assembly systems**, *collective leadership is exercised by a large group, usually constituted as a legislature.* There might be an executive officer, but the legislature is clearly dominant. Switzerland has an assembly system in which the legislature dominates the collective seven-member executive council that it elects. Most confederations, such as the United Nations and the European Parliament (the elected legislative wing of the EU), are assembly systems in which legislatures delegate administrative power to an appointed executive. The New England town meeting, a form of U.S. local government, is an extreme version of the assembly system because all citizens can directly participate in key decisions and oversee the administration of policy.

In theory, most communist states are assembly systems because the constitution grants most power for policymaking to the legislative body. In reality, however, the legislatures in such states have traditionally rubber-stamped the policies and administration of a single leader or a small collective leadership group, as in China and North Korea. In fact, few, if any, national political systems operate as true assembly systems because power for policymaking and policy implementation rarely remains dispersed among a large group of relatively equal rulers.

Which Form Is Optimal?

Which form of executive–legislative relations is best? If there were agreement on this question, we might reasonably expect most states to have adopted the same form of government. In fact, each form has its strengths and weaknesses, as reflected in the Debate in 7.

Political Party Systems

7.5   **Characterize the different types of political party systems.**

The system of political parties is another institutional arrangement that can be explored. **Party systems** are generally classified according to *the number of political parties* and *the interactions among the parties in the governing process.* In the comparative study of political parties, there are usually four main types of party systems: (1) two-party systems; (2) multiparty systems; (3) dominant-party systems; and (4) one-party systems. The distinguishing features of each type are described in this section, and representative examples are identified in Figure 7.2 and discussed in Compare in 7.

The Debate in 7

Which Form of Government Is Preferable: Parliamentary, Presidential, or Hybrid?

A central normative question regarding government institutions is: Which arrangement of executive–legislative relations is preferable? Countries vary in the manner in which they organize executive–legislative relations. Initially, most modern countries established either the parliamentary form or the presidential form, yet many of the countries that have dramatically transformed their governmental structures in the last several decades have opted for a hybrid. The current diversity suggests that no one form is clearly preferred in all cases. Moreover, other factors such as the nature of the party system and the electoral system can be crucial in shaping the effectiveness of any of the forms (Cheibub 2007; Mainwaring and Shugart 1997; Svolik 2013). Nonetheless, it is useful to consider the key arguments regarding the strengths and weaknesses associated with each of the three major forms of executive–legislative relations.

The Parliamentary Form Is the Most Effective Institutional Arrangement

- The fusion of executive and legislative powers eliminates potential executive–legislative conflicts that can result in deadlock in presidential or hybrid systems. This singular authority structure ensures that, as long as the governing majority (party or coalition) maintains its cohesiveness, this group is responsible for every stage of the policy process and there are few roadblocks to the passage and implementation of any policy (Strøm 2004).

- This concentration of political control also ensures that there is a clear system of accountability. The successes or failures of policy can be associated directly with those who are part of the governing coalition. If citizens are dissatisfied, they know which parties to vote against in the next election, and citizens know whom to reelect if they are satisfied (Linz 1994).

- The chief executive position does not concentrate such a dangerous level of power as in the presidential system. And if the chief executive loses the support of the governing majority, he can be replaced at any time and in a relatively rapid political process that does not require a national election or the trauma of an impeachment trial.

The Parliamentary Form Has Serious Problems

- A coherently organized majority exercises great, unchecked power: It can steamroll policy through almost all opposition because it controls both the legislative process and the agencies that administer policy. Even in its most benign form, the system is not well structured to encourage compromise, to protect against a tyrannical majority, or to ensure that minority concerns are represented in the public policy process (Horowitz 1990).

- The electorate does not directly choose the chief executive because he can be selected and changed by a vote of the legislature at almost any time, without any direct input from the citizens. It is possible for the citizens to be stuck with a chief executive for whom they did not vote and whom the majority does not support.

- Parliamentary systems are often plagued by uncertainty and instability, which stems from the chief executive's capacity to dissolve the legislature at any time and the legislature's ability to vote no confidence in the executive at any time. This perpetual vulnerability of the executive and the legislature can result in extensive strategic game-playing, despite the apparent fusion of executive and legislative actors (Tsebelis 2002).

The Presidential Form Is the Most Effective Institutional Arrangement

- In presidential systems, citizens have the power to elect their top executive leader directly. The voters explicitly choose a president, who serves for a fixed term in office without legislative intervention (except in the extraordinary circumstances of impeachment).

- This directly elected president can act as a singular leader and an embodiment of the political will of the national majority; he is not someone who emerged from a backroom deal in the legislature. And the president can take strong positions, even in the face of short-term disfavor in public opinion.

- Presidential systems are more stable because presidential and legislative elections occur in regular, fixed intervals, so everyone knows exactly when the next election will occur and new mandates for power will be given.

- The separation of executive and legislative power provides a healthy system of checks and balances, preventing abuse of power and ensuring more careful consideration of policy before it is adopted and implemented (Horowitz 1990).

The Presidential Form Has Serious Problems

- Presidential systems often obscure which policymaking structure is responsible for the impact of a particular policy. Executive and legislative power can be exercised by different groups that can, rightly or wrongly, accuse each other of policy failures. Thus, accountability is often unclear, even if the executive and legislative majorities are from the same political party and especially when there is a partisan split between the two branches.

- The separation of power enables the legislature and the executive to block each other's actions if they do not fully share a political agenda. The legislature can refuse to pass executive-supported legislation, while the executive can veto policies adopted by the legislative majority and can use its control over all administrative agencies to distort or even block the intent of legislative policy. Such circumstances can produce interbranch conflicts, policy stalemates, and governmental paralysis (Tsebelis 2002).

- The fixed terms of both the executive and the legislature provide predictability at the cost of flexibility and responsiveness. An ineffective legislature cannot be forced to face the electorate

until the end of its term. And, short of a traumatic impeachment, a highly unpopular chief executive cannot be replaced before the end of his lengthy, fixed term and can hold onto power with minimal support from either the legislature or the citizenry (Linz 1994).

The Hybrid Form Is the Most Effective Institutional Arrangement

- The hybrid combines the best of both the parliamentary and presidential systems. It takes advantage of the parliamentary form's fusion of executive and legislative power to ensure greater policy coherence, from conception to adoption to implementation.

- The hybrid also provides an independently elected presidential-type executive who can represent the national will and can act decisively when the cabinet and legislature fail to respond to a critical situation (Elgie 2004).

The Hybrid Form Has Serious Problems

- As with presidential systems, a significant risk with hybrids is the potential for major power struggles, especially between the cabinet and prime minister on one side and the president on the other side. The situation is made worse by the fact that the constitution is usually ambiguous about the conditions in which one or the other is dominant in the policy process.

- The hovering presence of the president does not usually reduce the inherent problems of the parliamentary form, such as excessive concentration of power in the majority and the uncertainty and instability due to the constant threat of dissolution.

And in Case You Were Wondering...

A *council system* has the virtue of distributing power among a manageable number of people, but there is a strong tendency for collective leadership to result in persistent internal power struggles as one or a few members attempt to assert their dominance. And while *assembly systems* are the best approximation of a genuine representative democracy, they lack the clear and decisive executive leadership that people in most contemporary states seem to want and that complex modern political systems seem to need.

More questions…

1. Which system makes most sense to you?
2. Can you think of any conditions (e.g., the party system, aspects of the political culture, and so on) that might make different forms preferable?

Two-Party Systems

A *two-party system* is characterized by two major political parties that alternate in governmental power. Each party has a realistic possibility of forming a governing majority, although the electoral success of each party varies over time. Minor third parties exist in a classic two-party system like Honduras, but these parties have limited power. At the moment, there are only a few countries, such as Jamaica and the United States (Figure 7.2), where only two parties hold virtually all of the seats in the national legislature. Although either the Conservative or Labour Party had been a majority party in Great Britain for many decades, neither won a legislative majority in the 2010 election. Regional parties (e.g., the Scottish Nationalist Party) won some seats, and the Liberal Democratic Party held enough seats to become a necessary coalition partner, aligning with the Conservatives to achieve a parliamentary majority. When a country has two large parties, but third parties consistently prevent either party from achieving an outright majority, it is termed a "two-plus" party system.

Multiparty Systems

As you might expect, a *multiparty system* has more than two parties that can win enough seats to be potential partners in creating a legislative majority and enacting legislation. In parliamentary systems, this means that a coalition of two or more parties might be necessary to form a government. Most contemporary political systems have some form of multiparty system.

WORKING MULTIPARTY SYSTEMS In some "working" multiparty systems, a cluster of parties usually cooperates to form a governing majority. For example, several center- and right-oriented parties might form one group, with social democratic and socialist left parties constituting another. This is the case in Sweden, which has a relatively stable system of eight major parties which form coalitions. Currently, the Social Democratic Party leads a multiparty center-left coalition (Figure 7.2).

There are also some multiparty systems in which parties have organized themselves into two blocs that compete for power. Citizens are reasonably confident that, even when they vote for a party that cannot win a majority of seats, their party is committed to cooperating with particular parties to form a governing group. Italy, which had experienced decades of highly volatile multiparty government, introduced a new electoral system in 1996 in an attempt to create more party coherence. After some initial turbulence (a total of 251 parties put forth candidates in the 1996 election), the system seemed to stabilize with two major alliances, each led by the major party in

Figure 7.2 Examples of Party Systems (Governing Parties in Bold)

One-Party System
Cuba, National Assembly (2013), 614 seats

Communist
100%

Two-Party System
United States, House of Representatives (2015),
435 seats

Republican
57%

Democrat
43%

Multiparty Systems

Sweden, Riksdag (2014) 349 seats

Centre 6%   Christian Democrat 5%
Social Democrat 32%
Moderate 24%
Liberal People's 5%
Green Environment 7%
Sweden Democrat 14%   Left 10%
Left 6%

Germany, Bundestag (2013), 622 seats

Christian Social Union 9%
Social Democratic 30%
Christian Democrat 40%
Green 10%
Left 10%

Mexico, Chamber of Deputies (2012), 500 seats

New Alliance 2%
Ecologist Green 6%
Citizen's Movement 3%
Institutional Revolutionary (PRI) 42%
Democratic Revolution (PRD) 21%
National Action (PAN) 23%
Labour 3%

Canada, House of Commons (2011), 308 seats

Bloc Quebecois 1%
Liberal 11%
Conservative 54%
New Democrat 33%

Dominant Party Systems

Singapore, Parliament (2011), 87 seats

People's Action 93%
Worker's 7%

South Africa, Parliament (2014), 400 seats

African National Congress 62%
Democratic Alliance 22%
Economic Freedom Fighters 6%
Inkatha Freedom 2%
National Freedom 2%

the bloc: the People of Freedom group (victors in the 2008 election) and the Democratic Party group (victors in the 2013 election). Chile is another example, where six parties each have a substantial proportion of seats but these parties have formed two dominant coalitions, meaning that this multiparty system currently operates almost like a two-party system.

It is also possible, although uncommon, to have a working multiparty system in which parties across the ideological spectrum cooperate in a long-standing governing coalition. A notable example of this situation is Switzerland, where four major parties, ranging from right wing to center left, have shared governing power in every election since 1959, and the general viewpoint is that it is undesirable for any one of the parties to govern independently. A more distinctive form of this broad array of parties was Germany's "grand coalition" from 2006 to 2009. When neither multiparty coalition gained a majority of seats, the leading parties of the two blocs agreed to create a governing cabinet including nearly all the major rival parties (the two leftist parties refused to participate) under the leadership of Angela Merkel, leader of the Christian Democrats. Merkel's conservative coalition ruled with a majority in the legislature from 2009 to 2013. However, when her coalition did not win a majority of the seats in 2013, she forged another broad center-left coalition between her Christian Democratic Union/Christian Social Union and the main opposition party, the Social Democrats (Figure 7.2).

UNSTABLE MULTIPARTY SYSTEMS Multiparty systems are often unstable. In these cases, no party is close to a majority and differences in party ideology prevent temporary coalitions from forming long-term blocs. In such party systems, there is usually a point at which the government's policy on an issue induces a coalition partner to withdraw its support, in turn causing a crisis for the government. In parliamentary systems, such a crisis often leads to the resignation of the government or the dissolution of the legislature. In presidential or assembly systems, this situation tends to produce paralysis in the legislature. Clearly, the difficulty of forming a governing majority among multiple parties increases because different parties are more firmly committed to their unique ideological orientations. Smaller parties often demand more influence than their vote total merits if they are crucial to the coalition majority. Instability is especially high in multiparty systems with a minority governing coalition that controls less than half the seats.

Israel presents an extreme example of the challenges in some multiparty systems. In the 2013 election, the 120 seats in the Knesset were shared among 12 parties, and only 1 party had more than 20 seats. The largest party, Likud Yisrael Beiteinu, is a center-right party that won 31 seats, was able to form a governing majority—a complex coalition of parties including an ultrareligious party, a centrist secular party, and a progressive party. Any of these parties might bolt at any point if their views are not supported by the government. The largest party in the previous government, Kadima, dropped from 28 seats to 2, an example of the dramatic loss of power by one party that does occasionally occur in multiparty systems.

New democracies seem especially prone to a proliferation of political parties. In 2005, more than 300 parties competed for votes in Iraq. And in the initial years (after 1989) of democratic politics in the postcommunist states of Central and Eastern Europe, as many as 200 parties ran candidates. While there has usually been a significant reduction in the number of effective parties in the postcommunist states (Hungary, for example, now has only four), many are still dealing with somewhat unstable multiparty systems. When many parties win representation, it has been difficult to form the stable coalitions necessary for coherent policymaking. Even more established political systems grapple with the challenges of achieving stability in situations with multiple competing parties. Canada has had multiple parties and minority governments in four of the prior five elections, but elected a Conservative Party majority in 2011 (Figure 7.2).

Dominant-Party Systems

In a *dominant-party system*, the same party repeatedly captures enough votes and seats to form the government, although other parties are free to compete. In Figure 7.2, South Africa and Singapore are clear-cut examples of a dominant party. In Singapore, the People's Action Party wins nearly all the contested seats in the legislature in every election (since the first full general elections in 1959), although as many as 20 other parties put up candidates. Typically, a dominant party eventually loses support and becomes a competitor in a multiparty system. This happened to the Congress Party in India and to the Institutional Revolutionary Party (PRI) in Mexico. Japan's Liberal Democratic Party (LDP) was a dominant party in Japan from 1947 to 1993. Due to scandals, leader defections, and changing voter attitudes, LDP has been voted out of power several times since then, although it regained a strong majority in 2012.

One-Party Systems

In a *one-party system*, a single party is controlled and protected by the government elite. Some authoritarian regimes do not tolerate the existence of any political parties other than the single party that represents the state and its vision of political order, as in North Korea. Any party that expresses opposition to the ruling party is viewed not as the "loyal opposition" but as disloyal or even seditious (in other words, it is seen as stirring up resistance or rebellion against the government). There are currently few absolute one-party systems in a technical sense, given the high ideological premium associated with the appearance of democratic processes. Thus, some form of party competition is introduced, although the ruling party maintains near-total control. In Cuba (Figure 7.2) and China, for example, the Communist Party allows other parties to elect a few representatives.

No-Party Systems

The taxonomy should have a category for those political systems that have no political parties. Historically, many political systems had no organized parties, but only a few contemporary political systems do not allow political parties. Countries such as Kuwait, Oman, and Swaziland have banned political parties, either because the rulers do not want any organized bases of opposition to their authority or on the grounds that parties divide people's loyalty and do not focus on what is best for everyone. The latter argument is a primary justification given for the nonpartisanship (lack of political party affiliations or organization) of candidates for public office in many U.S. local governments.

Compare in 7

Party Systems in Four Countries

As indicated in this chapter, party systems can range from multiparty systems to one-party systems. Figure 7.2 displays the distribution of parties in eight countries, reflecting the various types of party systems. While each country's situation is unique, this comparison focuses on four of the examples to reflect how different party systems function.

The political elite in *Cuba*, a *one-party system*, attempts to sustain the total domination of the Cuban Communist Party. Unlike some one-party states, candidates can run for the National Assembly without the direct approval and support of the party. The party was created under Fidel Castro's leadership in 1965 through the merger of several revolutionary groups. Although other political parties are banned, some of the members of the Cuban legislature are not members of the party when they are elected. But because all candidates are selected by bodies (e.g., trade unions, women's groups) dominated by the party, all candidates are approved by the party. To offer at least the appearance of popular control, if the proposed candidate in a district does not win a majority of votes (almost everyone 16 or older votes), a new candidate must be proposed.

South Africa is a *dominant-party system*. Numerous parties put up candidates for the parliament, and seats are distributed through a mix of single-member and multimember PR districts (Focus in 6). Since the end of apartheid, the African National Congress (ANC) has won a clear majority of seats in every election. Other parties try to challenge the dominance of the ANC, but no combination of parties has yet made a serious dent in the ANC's huge majority of parliamentary seats. However, the first serious split within the ANC occurred before the 2009 election, over a rancorous conflict between current President Jacob Zuma and the man he outmaneuvered within the ANC, former President Thabo Mbeki, whose followers have created a breakaway party. Although the 2014 election brought a continuation of the erosion in the strength of the ANC—down to 62 percent of the vote from 69 percent in 2009—it is still the dominant party, with the Democratic Alliance coming in at a weak second with 22 percent of the vote.

The *United States* is a clear example of a *two-party system*. While candidates from other parties are usually on the ballot in most districts, it is rare that the individual winner by plurality will be from any party other than the Democratic or Republican parties. This produces a legislature in which only the two parties have a major role. In 2012, the Republicans won 234 seats in the House of Representatives, the Democrats won 201 seats, and not a single member was from any other party. Only 2 of 100 Senate seats are held by Independents. Why are other parties unsuccessful? It is partly a tradition among the large majority of voters to select either a Democrat or a Republican. Even more importantly, the electoral system is based on plurality voting in single-seat districts, making it extremely hard for a third-party candidate to win. This leads many voters to conclude that a vote for a third party is either a wasted vote or serves only as a protest vote because such a vote will not influence the outcome.

Like almost all *multiparty systems*, *Mexico* has a proportional representation (PR) electoral system with more than one member elected from each district. The Mexican system is similar to the mixed PR system in South Africa, which was described in Focus in 6. There are 300 single-member districts, which elect the person with the highest vote total, and 200 PR seats based on party lists. To prevent a proliferation of small parties in the legislature, a party must get at least 2 percent of the national vote to get any seats from the PR lists. Only in the 1990s did Mexico's Chamber of Deputies become a true multiparty system. Two parties (PAN, a conservative party, and PRD, a leftist party) began to garner enough votes to prevent the centrist PRI (the Institutional Revolutionary Party) from winning the majority of seats, as it had done for five decades. Since the 2000 election, there has been active competition among the three major parties and considerable change in the composition of the legislature in each election. During this period, no single party has come close to a majority in the Chamber of Deputies, although PRI won 212 of the 500 seats in 2012. Because the three major parties are always competing with one another and do not share a common political agenda, it is often difficult to fashion a majority to pass legislation.

Further Questions

1. If multiparty systems are more prone to instability, why are they present in so many countries?

2. Can you explain why PR electoral systems tend to produce multiparty systems?

Classification and Clarity

Most theorizing about political systems begins with some classification scheme. Classifying political systems into a taxonomy can be straightforward, especially when the categories are based on clear institutional characteristics (e.g., federations, confederations, and unitary states). But many of the most interesting classifications (e.g., democracies and dictatorships) are challenging because political systems tend to be complex mixtures of characteristics that do not fit tidily into any category. In addition, any classification is time-specific because evolutionary and revolutionary processes can change the nature of a political system.

There are at least three important reasons for classifying political systems. First, such classification can provide us with useful descriptive information about political systems. Most people have a vague sense that other political systems are different from their own, and by describing how various political systems are organized between central and peripheral units or between the executive and legislative functions, we expand our grasp of alternative forms of governmental structures.

Second, the classification of political systems helps us undertake political analysis—to identify patterns of similarities and differences among the political systems of the world. Rather than positing that every political system is unique, the analyses in Chapters 6–8, as well as throughout this book, assume that some generalizations can emerge from comparative analysis. Sets of political systems that share important characteristics can be compared with one another or compared with sets that do not share those characteristics. Such comparisons provide us with a basis for thinking more clearly about the kinds of generalizations that we can articulate and can then increase our confidence regarding what we know about the political world.

Third, the taxonomies in this chapter might encourage us to specify with greater precision what we mean by value-laden terms such as *democracy* and *dictatorship*. In this manner, the analytic study of political institutions improves our understanding of how these terms are most appropriately used as thoughtful descriptors rather than as mere rhetorical labels.

Ultimately, developing greater precision in our use of key political concepts and increasing our knowledge about the political world can do more than clarify our thinking. They can also enhance our ability to evaluate the nature and desirability of the political structures in our own nation and in other countries and to decide whether there is a "best" form of government.

Would you argue that one form of areal division of power, one form of executive–legislative relations, and the same constitution are best for *all* states? Or might the best institutional arrangements be contingent on the major goals and key characteristics of the particular political society? As a closing puzzle, if your country were to convene a constitutional convention now, would you argue in favor of retaining all of the governmental forms that currently exist in your political system? Why or why not?

Key Concepts

assembly system, p. 185
authoritarian regime, p. 173
authoritarianism, p. 173
autocracy, p. 173
confederation, p. 178
constitution, p. 165
constitutional regime, p. 167
council system, p. 183
democracy, p. 171

dictatorship, p. 173
direct democracy, p. 170
electoral democracy, p. 170
federation, p. 177
hybrid system, p. 182
illiberal democracy, p. 171
liberal democracy, p. 171
limited mandate, p. 171
nonconstitutional regime, p. 167

nondemocracy, p. 173
parliamentary government, p. 180
participatory democracy, p. 170
party system, p. 185
presidential government, p. 180
representative democracy, p. 170
totalitarianism, p. 174
totalitarian regime, p. 174
unitary state, p. 177

For Further Consideration

1. What is your definition of a democratic political system? What are the minimal conditions necessary for a country to be classified as a democracy? If you opt for the definition used in this chapter, explain which elements of the definition are the most essential and the least essential for democracy.

2. In the late eighteenth century, the United States opted for a federal, presidential, bicameral, two-party system with plurality elections. Given the situation in the early twenty-first century, what are the major shortcomings of each of these decisions?

Speculate what politics in the United States might be like if the country became a unitary state with a parliamentary government or a multiparty system based on proportional representation.

3. Some analysts argue that democracy is not possible unless there are at least two political parties. Provide a critical evaluation of this viewpoint. In theory, might we expect any relationship between the number of parties and the extent to which the political system is democratic?

For Further Reading

Arendt, Hannah. (1973). *The Origins of Totalitarianism.* New York: Harcourt. The classic study of the forces underlying totalitarian regimes.

Chhibber, Pradeep, and Ken Kollman. (2004). *The Formation of National Party Systems: Federalism and Party Competition in Canada, Great Britain, India, and the United States.*

Princeton, NJ: Princeton University Press. The evolution of party systems in the four countries are examined over three centuries to illuminate the importance of the areal distribution of governmental power in shaping the party systems, despite similar electoral systems.

Cheibub, Jose Antonio. (2007). *Presidentialism, Parliamentarianism, and Democracy.* **New York: Cambridge University Press.** Using many cases over several decades, the author analyzes whether the presidential or parliamentary form is more likely to be successful in achieving stability and in sustaining democracy.

Collier, Paul. (2010). *Wars, Guns, and Votes: Democracy in Dangerous Places.* **New York: Harper.** The always-controversial Collier argues that democracy has been pushed with the wrong incentives in many of the developing countries, generating more violence and instability. He suggests that the key promises given to countries engaging in democratization should be security from coups and aid that goes to NGOs, not government agencies.

Dahl, Robert, Ian Shapiro, and Jose Antonio Cheibub, eds. (2003). *The Democracy Sourcebook.* **Boston: MIT Press.** This very strong collection of readings covers critical topics, from the definition of democracy to issues of representation, constitutional regimes, and the impacts of democracy on individual countries and the global system. The (generally short) excerpts include both major historical thinkers (Locke, Rousseau, Madison) and important contemporary scholars (Dworkin, Pzeworski, Sen).

Diamond, Larry. (2009). *The Spirit of Democracy: How to Build Free Societies Throughout the World.* **New York: Holt.** A compelling, highly readable (and optimistic) exploration, full of engaging examples, of the strategies that can help countries in all areas of the world establish and sustain democracy.

Elgie, Robert, (2011). *Semi-Presidentialism.* **New York: Oxford University Press.** An exploration of the strengths and weaknesses of hybrids, based on numerous case studies.

Kollman, Ken. (2013). *Perils of Centralization: Lessons from Church, State, and Corporation.* **New York: Cambridge University Press.** Using the United States, the European Union, General Motors, and the Roman Catholic Church as cases, the author examines the dynamics of federal systems. Critical issues of governance and centralization are explored on the basis of these examples.

Lawson, Kay, ed. (2010). *Political Parties and Democracy.* **Santa Barbara, CA: ABC-CLIO.** Lawson is the general editor of a series of five volumes, each of which offers illuminating case studies of political parties in specific countries from a region of the world (Americas, Europe, Post-Soviet and Asian, Africa, Arab World).

Mainwaring, Scott, and Anibel Perez-Linan. (2013). *Democracies and Dictatorships in Latin America: Emergence, Survival, and Fall.* **New York: Cambridge University Press.** Why do some democracies and dictatorships persevere while others fail? This book uses a rich theoretical and rigorous empirical approach to answer those questions.

Rosenfeld, Michel, and Adras Sajo, eds. (2012). *The Oxford Handbook of Comparative Constitutional Law.* **Oxford: Oxford University Press.** This edited volume provides the theories and tools necessary to conduct comparative constitutional analysis. It presents current debates, concepts, and developments in the field of comparative constitutional law.

Schrad, Mark Lawrence. (2014). *Vodka Politics: Alcohol, Autocracy, and the Secret History of the Russian State.* **Oxford: Oxford University Press.** Alcohol has long been used as a means of social control by the Russian government. This volume tells the intertwined history of Russia and vodka and demonstrates that the politics of vodka have helped ensure autocratic rule.

Sorensen, Georg. (2008). *Democracy and Democratization: Processes and Prospects.* **3rd ed. Boulder, CO: Westview Press.** A useful exploration of central issues associated with the diffusion of democracy to many countries, including the attempts at promotion by outside powers, the rise of electoral authoritarianism, and the consequences for the international system of the trends toward democratization.

Tudor, Maya. (2013). *The Promise of Power: The Origins of Democracy in India and Autocracy in* *Pakistan.* **Cambridge: Cambridge University Press.** Why did India institutionalize democracy while Pakistan institutionalized an autocracy? The author demonstrates how two of the world's most populous countries emerged from a similar colonial legacy in radically different ways.

Wheare, K. C. (1980). *Modern Constitutions.* **2nd rev. ed. London: Oxford University Press.** Although first written in 1951, this description of the content and impacts of constitutions is still insightful.

On the Web

http://confinder.richmond.edu

Constitution Finder at the University of Richmond provides links to the constitutions and other key documents for most countries.

http://portal.clinecenter.illinois.edu/cgi-bin//rview?REPOSID=1

This site provides the texts of more than 720 national constitutions written since 1789 as well as rich discussions of many of the issues and themes addressed in constitutions.

http://www.servat.unibe.ch/law/icl

The International Constitutional Law (ICL) project provides English translations of constitutions as well as other textual material related to constitutions from more than 90 countries. It also cross-references those documents for quick comparison of constitutional provisions.

http://freedomhouse.org

The site of Freedom House, which includes current ratings for every country and topical discussions regarding the levels of political and civil rights and press and religious freedom in those countries.

http://www.systemicpeace.org/polity/polity4.htm

The Polity IV Project provides current and longitudinal trend data and generates scores for each country, which is classified along a 21-point continuum ranging from "consolidated democracy" to "hereditary monarchy."

http://mirror.undp.org/magnet/Docs/parliaments

This site explores a variety of issues regarding the functioning of legislatures and their relations with other branches of government and covers governing systems and executive–legislative relations within presidential, parliamentary, and hybrid systems, along with information about political parties.

http://www.politicalresources.net

This is a very useful and accessible site with information on many countries, including current data on party systems and links to the Web sites of most parties from each country.

https://www.cia.gov/index.html

This part of the U.S. Central Intelligence Agency Web site presents the World Leaders database that lists the chiefs of state and cabinet members of all foreign governments.

http://m.state.gov/mc36886.htm

A site sponsored by the U.S. State Department that provides basic details of the governments of every country.

Chapter 8
Political Economy

Learning Objectives

8.1 Explain the role of the state in a nation's economy.

8.2 Determine the relationship among the separate elements that make up the political economy.

8.3 Assess the different measures of economic prosperity.

8.4 Compare the ideal-type political economies.

8.5 Identify the challenges faced by market, command, and mixed economies.

8.6 Contrast political economy "isms", real-world examples and ideal-type political economies.

Eleven countries in the European Union (EU) officially replaced their national currencies with the euro—a common EU currency—on January 1, 1999. By 2002, euro paper money and coins replaced the national currencies in all 11 countries: French francs, German Deutschmarks, and so on, were eliminated. Although Greece had joined the EU in 1981, it was not allowed to join the first wave of countries adopting the euro because Greece did not qualify under the Maastricht criteria: An EU country could participate in the eurozone (the area that would share the common euro currency) only if its government maintained low inflation, low government debt, and low government deficits. However, by the time the paper euros were circulated in 2002, Greece had qualified to join the eurozone because the Greek government had imposed a series of tough economic policies that cut spending and reduced both its overall debt and its annual deficit.

After Greece joined the eurozone, the international business community assumed Greece was a safer place to invest than previously. One result of this new confidence was that the interest rate the Greek government had to pay to borrow money dropped significantly, from as high as 25 percent in the early 1990s to as low as 4 percent in 2006. Greece was now able to borrow a lot more money at a much lower interest rate. Extensive borrowing between 2002 and 2007 helped generate substantial annual economic growth. The borrowed money helped build infrastructure and stimulate business development. Greece also spent billions to host the 2004 Summer Olympics, which brought tourism but left a generally unused Olympics complex. The

Supply and demand: Dockworkers in Athens strike and protest their government's extensive privatization and spending cuts in response to the severe economic crisis in Greece.

government also hired many more employees and promised them generous pensions when they retired at age 55.

The Greek government's borrowing led to an explosion of its level of debt, which nearly doubled between 2001 and 2011, reaching 1.7 times the total annual output of the entire Greek economy. The public sector now employed one out of every four workers in the country. Unfortunately, toward the end of this period, there was a severe slowdown in the world economy, and a global financial crisis emerged in 2008. Economic growth in Greece fell sharply. Unemployment rose, tax revenues shrank, many more Greeks needed government assistance, and the government had big debts to repay.

Lenders insisted that the Greek government reduce its spending and pay off its debts. No one would loan the Greek government additional money except at prohibitively high interest rates. Under these pressures, the government introduced austerity policies. It drastically cut spending on social programs, fired many government workers and cut the pay of others, cut pensions, and raised the retirement age. These policies generated a firestorm of anger among Greeks and widespread protests against the government. But the policy measures that the beleaguered government implemented were not sufficient to get the debt under control. As the financial crisis deepened, there was fear that Greece would default on its debt, plunging the world economy into greater peril. Thus there were several rounds of major "bailout" loans from the EU, the European Central Bank, and the International Monetary Fund to help Greece pay its bills. In exchange for more than 220 billion euros (nearly $275 billion) in loans, the Greek government was required to deepen its austerity programs and sell off many government-run corporations. Most Greeks were angry at their political leaders, at the EU, and at the lenders. Protests and pressure on the Greek government continued to grow, resulting in political turmoil. And the populations of other EU countries such as Germany were also angry—at the Greeks for their overspending and underachievement and at their own governments for bailing out Greece with their money. Currently, Greece continues to struggle despite the bailouts.

If one needed evidence that the economic system and the political system are intertwined in a modern society, the recent history of Greece offers a compelling case. Government policies in Greece and the EU determined the conditions under which Greece: joined the eurozone; borrowed and spent huge amounts of money; achieved economic growth and then suffered a debt crisis; and introduced austerity programs that caused suffering, protest, and government instability.

Indeed, both the economic difficulties and the economic policy challenges currently facing most countries in the EU, including Great Britain, Ireland, Portugal, and Spain, and many other countries around the world, are directly associated with their governments' policies. Thus, the distinguished scholar Charles Lindblom (1977: 8) observes: "In all the political systems of the world, much of politics is economics and most of economics is also politics… For many good reasons, politics and economics have to be held together in the analysis of basic social mechanisms and systems."

This book is about the *political* world. But if Lindblom is correct, your understanding of contemporary politics requires an understanding of its pervasive linkages with economics. This *combination of politics and the economy* is called **political economy**. This chapter explains this concept. First, it describes the connections between the economic system and the political system. Then it characterizes three different types of political economies: (1) the *market economy*; (2) the *command economy*; and (3) the *mixed economy*. Finally, it examines how these political economies are related to major "isms" in the political world, especially capitalism, state capitalism, socialism, communism, and corporatism.

Politics and the Economy

8.1 **Explain the role of the state in a nation's economy.**

Many decisions made by the political system have significant impacts on the economy. Can you think of how the following government policies might affect the economy?

- The government does not construct or repair any highways or roads.
- The government bans the sale of any automobile with gasoline fuel efficiency less than 45 miles per gallon.
- The government collects very high taxes on the profits of businesses.
- The government fully finances the provision of all medical services for all citizens.
- The government places no restrictions on the right of foreigners to enter and work in the country.
- The government controls the prices of all basic foods.

Similarly, the actions of major economic actors and the performance of the economic system can have major impacts on the political system, which depends on the economic system to generate income, goods, and services for the survival and prosperity of its citizens. For example, what policy responses might you predict from the U.S. government to the following economic situations?

- A lengthy nationwide strike by air traffic controllers
- Exceptionally high unemployment over many months
- The proposed sale of the country's largest automaker to a Chinese corporation
- The discovery that there is less than five years' worth of petroleum reserves within the country's boundaries
- Bankruptcy filings by two of the country's largest financial institutions

The more one reflects on modern societies, the clearer it becomes that "much of politics is economics and most of economics is also politics."

Understanding political economy requires a grasp of some basic economic concepts. This chapter describes a conceptual framework for the economic system that is similar in spirit to Easton's framework for a political system (see Chapter 5). The framework presents only some core ideas that have been simplified considerably. However, this discussion does involve complicated abstractions, so hang in there! (If you want the full treatment, take an introductory economics course or read an introductory economics book such as Heyne, Boettke, and Prychitko [2013]. For a political science perspective, see Wilensky [2002: Ch. 2]).

A Political-Economic Framework

8.2 **Determine the relationship among the separate elements that make up the political economy.**

The abstract model of an economic system presented in Figure 8.1 is our starting point for understanding the idea of a political economy. The figure offers an extremely simple characterization of the way in which extraordinarily complex systems of production and exchange operate (see Baumol and Blinder 2012: Ch. 8; Miller 2014: Part II).

Factors, Firms, and Households/Consumers

In the beginning (according to this model), there are three kinds of important productive resources—the three major *factors of production* (A) (see Figure 8.1). *Land* means the ground plus any raw materials (commodities such as coal and bananas) on or in the ground. *Labor* is human productive input (our common understanding of "work"). *Capital* is the nonhuman productive input from other resources (especially financial resources, machinery, and technology). Each factor of production is controlled by an owner who, in the language of economics, is referred to as a *household* (B).

Figure 8.1 An Economic System Framework: The Income-Expenditures Model

Some actor called a *firm* (C) attempts to acquire a combination of these productive resources (factors of production) to produce a *good* (D1). A good can be a product (e.g., a pencil, a nuclear missile) or a service (e.g., a lawyer defending you in court, transportation on an airplane).

A firm (in this book, the terms *firm* and *producer* are used interchangeably) might be a single person who produces a good from her own resources. For example, a lawyer represents you in traffic court through her own labor skills. Or a firm might be a large organization that uses many productive resources (of land and commodities, labor, and capital). For example, a firm that produces something as simple as pencils needs productive resources such as wood, graphite, rubber, machines, and workers. The firm transforms these factors of production into the final good—here, pencils. Often some intermediate goods (D2) are acquired to make more complicated goods. The pencil firm, for example, has probably acquired intermediate goods such as graphite (which it acquires from another firm that has mined and refined this chemical element) and wood (which has come from a firm that owns, cuts, and mills trees).

A household has a second role, as a *consumer*, when it wants to acquire a final good (e.g., a pencil, a legal defense, whatever). A consumer offers something of value to the firm in exchange for the good that the consumer wants. What emerges between the household/consumer and the firm is a system of payments (E1 and E2 in the figure). A firm must pay something to a household that controls a productive resource necessary for the firm to produce goods. And a household, in its role as a consumer, must pay something to the firm to get a final good that it wants. Notice that any individual or group can act as a household, a consumer, or a firm, depending on whether the individual or group is selling a factor, transforming productive resources into goods, or acquiring a final good. Of course, many actors both produce *and* consume goods and services.

The size of a payment (the price) is established when there is an agreement between a consumer who is willing to exchange (give up) something to get the good and a firm who is willing to give up the good for what the consumer offers. In the language of economics, each actor increases her **utility** (her overall happiness) in such an exchange because each has higher utility after the exchange than before it. So, for example, the actor who has grown a dozen tomatoes might exchange them for a shirt. Both the tomato grower and the shirt maker have a higher utility after the exchange because each values the other's good enough to give up her own good for the trade.

In every system, there are some good-for-good exchanges, called *barter trading* (e.g., the dozen tomatoes are traded for a shirt). But most economies are dominated by good-for-money exchanges, in which the consumer gives the producer some amount of money in exchange for the final good (e.g., a tomato might be exchanged for $1, or the shirt might be exchanged for $20).

If firms want to sell more shirts than customers want to buy, the price of a shirt is likely to come down. This is how **supply and demand** operates: If demand is low relative to supply, the price comes down; if demand is high relative to supply, the price goes up. In theory, with enough producers and consumers making exchanges, the price of a good reaches a perfect balance point between supply and demand, known as the *equilibrium point* (see Figure 8.2).

The payment by a consumer to a firm (E2) is usually a different amount from the payments by the firm for the productive resources used to produce that good (E1 in Figure 8.1). A firm is successful if it can sell the good for more than it paid to produce the good. This excess of payments over costs is **profit**. If the firm must sell the good for less than the cost of producing it, the firm suffers a *loss*. Obviously, firms normally try to increase their profit and to avoid loss.

Figure 8.2 The Relationship Between the Supply of a Good and the Demand for the Good

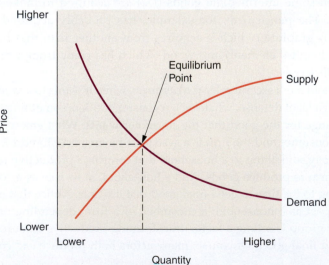

Getting and Spending

This system of exchanges goes around and around. Households expend their resources on goods, and firms provide the households with income as they pay for productive resources. Ideally, everyone is exchanging things of value for other things that they value even more. As the system becomes more complex, many actors are involved in the production and distribution of goods. Some additional actors operate as brokers, organizing and facilitating exchanges. For example, the grower of tomatoes might sell them to a broker, who then sells them to a market that sells them to the ultimate consumer. If more and more goods are produced, bought, sold, and consumed by all the actors in the economic system, there is *economic growth*.

The complexity of the actual exchanges in most economic systems is beyond comprehension. As an example, see how long a list you can quickly develop of the different people who contributed some fraction of the value (the one dollar) that you pay for a can of tomatoes at the supermarket. Think about all the actors involved in the production and distribution to you of that can of tomatoes. The chain of production includes the labor and materials to grow the tomatoes, manufacture the can and label, process the tomatoes, ship the finished product, manufacture the truck and containers in which the product was shipped, pay store employees, and so on. You could easily identify hundreds of people involved in the process who then share the dollar you paid.

The richest merchant in a Bedouin market in Morocco displays the goods she is selling, proudly wearing the chains of gold coins that attest to her entrepreneurial skills as a "firm" in a market economy.

Presumably, you (like every other actor) attempt to pursue a strategy that maximizes your utility (i.e., that results in your most preferred mix of goods and resources) and hence enhances your life. Individuals (and groups) have very different sets of preferences. One person might want to hoard money, food, or precious metals; another might want to spend everything on consumption for personal pleasure. One person might work hard to gain the resources to own a mansion and a Mercedes-Benz, while another person might be happiest with minimal work and no possessions other than the bare necessities she carries in a backpack.

Of course, it is a tough world, and all people are not equally capable of maximizing their value preferences. A person's success in getting her preferred mix of goods and resources can be affected by realities such as the types and amounts of resources she already controls, her skills in producing goods, the demand for her goods, the actions of other producers, and even luck. Over time, there are likely to be huge differences in the mix of goods and resources controlled by different individuals and groups.

The State Joins In

We now have our first approximation of an abstract model of the economic system. One very important addition to this simplified model is the political system. As noted at the beginning of the chapter, the modern economic system is inextricably connected to the political system. Why might the state decide to intervene in the economy? Here are a few of the most important reasons:

- there is a certain good that is socially important but no firm can produce it for a profit (e.g., a clean water supply);
- there is a good that requires a scale of production beyond any firm's capacity (e.g., national defense);
- the state is needed to enforce legal behavior by households and firms (e.g., contracts);
- the state must protect people from dangerous or illegal goods or production techniques;
- the state has a policy goal of providing a good to some individuals who cannot afford it (e.g., health care);
- the state's goal is to redistribute goods and wealth from some individuals to others.

Notice that each subsequent rationale for state intervention on the previous list is driven more fully by a *political* value relative to an economic necessity (Lindblom 2003).

When the state (F) is added in Figure 8.3, the interactions between the economy and the state result in the dynamic processes we call the *political economy*. The state can powerfully affect the economic system in the six general ways, labeled F1 through F6 in Figure 8.3. The state can

- be a consumer, purchasing any good from a firm. (F1)
- replace (that is, be) a household, in the sense that it controls certain factors of production. (F2)
- replace (that is, be) a firm, producing a good. (F3)

Figure 8.3 A Political Economy Framework

- regulate the manner in which either households or firms operate by enacting policies that encourage or prevent certain behaviors by those economic actors. (F4)
- tax (extract resources from) the payments to any actor. (F5)
- transfer payments or goods to any actor. (F6)

The state's patterns of action on these six dimensions distinguish different types of political economies.

The World Joins In

The second important addition to our simplified model of political economy is nothing less than "the rest of the world." While Figure 8.3 could represent an economy at any level (e.g., a city), it is most commonly understood as the national economy of a state. Many exchanges of goods and factors of production cross the boundaries of the state. *All those goods and factors of production that are sold to actors outside the state's boundaries* can be considered **exports**. Thus, if the tomatoes or automobiles produced in the United States are sold to households in Mexico, these exports generate revenue for U.S. firms (hence the plus sign in Figure 8.3). Exports are generally viewed as a positive for the economy, assuming the goods are sold for a profit, because they inject additional money into the system. Conversely, *the goods that a country's actors purchase from firms in another country* are **imports**. Thus, if the United States imports tomatoes or automobiles produced in Mexico, these imports result in money leaving the U.S. economy (although the U.S. households and firms do get the goods).

Each country has major policy choices as it decides whether to influence the economic transactions that cross its borders. The state might be genuinely committed to free trade and thus make no effort to influence import and export activity. However, many countries do intervene in economic transactions that cross their borders in an attempt to serve their own national interests. The state can discourage imports by taxing them on entry (tariffs) or by limiting how much of an import is allowed (quotas). In some cases, the state might even encourage certain imports. Similarly, the state can implement policies that either facilitate or obstruct exports by its own firms. Can you think of reasons why a state might restrict certain exports or encourage certain imports?

There have always been economic exchanges that cross state borders. In the last few decades, however, the scale and complexity of interstate exchanges have become extraordinary. There is now a vast "global economy," and 60 percent of world economic value is now international trade—exchanges that cross state borders (UNDP 2013: 2). Chapter 11 will detail the forces of globalization, but the key point here is that states find it increasingly difficult to control their own economy. First, many firms now operate multinationally—that is, they operate in multiple countries and can move their production from country to country, often very rapidly. Second, even more firms utilize factors of production and intermediate goods they have acquired from other countries. And third, most large firms now sell their goods in multiple countries. Thus, many consumers purchase goods whose productive factors are not primarily from their home country and, conversely, many firms do not produce goods with an expectation that they will be consumed in the country of production. For example, consider whether the clothes you are wearing or your electronics gear are goods in which the majority of components were produced by firms inside your country. Probably not.

The global economy has many consequences for the national political economy. States have much less capacity to regulate the behavior of firms, to control the balance of imports and exports, and even to tax many economic transactions. Thus, for most countries, the actions of firms and households outside the state's borders are very significant for the functioning of their political economy. The key impacts of such external actors will be emphasized in Chapters 13– 15.

The Economy Strikes Back

The previous discussion described how the state can implement a variety of policies that affect the economy. It is equally important to consider how the economy affects the state. A fundamental goal of every country is prosperity, and a healthy economy is the essential provider of resources to serve that goal. The state depends on the economic system to generate the goods and revenue that enable the state to function and its citizens to prosper. More than any other policy domain, governments flounder and fall when there are serious problems with the economy, because the economy has a direct impact on the quality of life for most of the citizens in a country.

In most political economies, a substantial proportion of the activity in the economic system is not under the direct control of the state. Rather, there are many economic actors whose behaviors are of fundamental importance to economic health. The political economy is in trouble if unemployment is high, or a major firm is struggling, or state regulation is stifling economic growth, or high taxes are discouraging investment or consumption. Thus, those private sector actors with economic power can wield substantial, sometimes massive, influence on the decisions and actions of the state. Moreover, some of those actors are among the most active and well-funded political groups, and they contribute money and employ lobbyists to shape public policies in ways that benefit their operations (Parenti 2010).

Who are the major sets of economic actors? First, there are the *large corporations* operating in the country. These firms are especially concerned about such policies as taxation, regulations on business practices and labor relations, and investment incentives. This group includes the flagship companies in the national economy, and their prosperity is directly linked to the prosperity of the country, psychologically as well as financially. There are also the multinational corporations with significant activity in the country. They have particular leverage with government officials because they can threaten to shift their productive activities outside the country if policies do not favor their operations. A second group is the country's *small businesses*. In most economies, these firms are the source of most job growth and are the heart of the overall functioning of the economic system because they produce and distribute the bulk of the goods. A third set of actors is the *interest groups* that represent these various business communities and engage in substantial lobbying on their behalf. These interest groups are well funded and highly influential with government in almost every country, and in some countries (described below as corporatist political economies), the representatives of these organizations are actually direct participants in the policy process.

A fourth group of economic actors that are very powerful is composed of organizations in the *global financial community*. Some operate within a country—the banks and a broad array of institutions that have been termed the "shadow banking system" and that control financial capital (Lanchester 2010). Others are international financial institutions like the International Monetary Fund, the European Central Bank, and the World Bank, which can force major policy decisions on many governments, particularly those in the developing world and in countries that are struggling financially, like Greece. During the recent global recession and the financial crises in countries from Greece to the United States, these global financial actors, in concert with the banks, insurance companies, and brokerage houses, have been increasingly visible as the players whom governments placate and protect. In analyzing the collapse of bubble economies, the extent to which governments have allowed these actors to operate in dangerous ways and the willingness of governments to offer them protection (e.g., bailouts) has become much more evident than in the past (Roubini and Mihm 2011). Some critics argue that in almost every country, some combination of these powerful economic actors dominates governments far more than they are controlled by governments and its economic policies (Blustein 2006; Ritholtz 2009). At least, the deep intertwining of the economic system and the political system is indisputable.

Measuring Economic Prosperity

8.3   **Assess the different measures of economic prosperity.**

How can you determine if the economy in a country is doing well? How can you measure the economic prosperity of a country? The most widely used indicators are based on one of two monetary figures that summarize "gross product"—the total value of all the final goods produced by a state's economic actors during a certain time period, adjusted for exports minus imports. *Gross domestic product (GDP)* is the total value of all final goods produced by all people within a state's boundaries, whether or not they are citizens (see Figure 8.3). The *gross national income (GNI)* includes the production of all citizens of the state, whether or not they are inside the state's boundaries. For crossnational comparisons, these amounts are typically measured in U.S. dollars. International economic actors have mainly utilized GDP as the primary indicator of a country's economic vitality, but in recent years some have begun to emphasize GNI. Each has certain strengths as a measure of a country's prosperity in a global economy in which there are increasing numbers of noncitizen workers and multinational firms.

Because both measures are greatly influenced by the size of the country, attempts to compare the relative prosperity of the people in different countries typically divide the productive total by the number of citizens (per capita). However, as measures of a country's prosperity, both GDP per capita and GNI per capita have at least three important flaws:

1. They do not measure how the prosperity is distributed among the country's economic actors, and thus many citizens have an individual level of prosperity that is sharply different from their country's average production per capita. The level of wealth inequality *within* countries is a perennial hot topic, with some analysts claiming that it is a critical problem and others viewing it as an inevitable condition of a vibrant economic system. Compare in 8 and Figure 8.4 examine the level of inequality in selected countries.

2. Only the goods that actually enter the society's monetary sector are measured, while many other valued goods are ignored. These unmeasured goods include both household work and goods in the "underground economy," particularly trade in illegal goods, barter trade, and the black market. In some countries, GDP and GNI are particularly misleading because such unmeasured goods are a significant proportion of total economic activity.

3. GDP per capita and GNI per capita are often used to compare the prosperity of one country to that of another. However, there are huge between-country disparities in the exchange value of money. In two different countries, the same amount of money (converting local currencies into an international exchange currency, usually U.S. dollars) can buy much more or much less of the same specific goods (e.g., a pound of rice in Japan might cost 20 times as much as in India).

Due to these crossnational disparities in the value of money, there is increasing use of a third prosperity measure that attempts to establish equivalent value across countries, an index based on *purchasing power parity (PPP)*—that is, *correcting monetary indicators to reflect the amount of currency required in that country to buy certain standard goods.*

An understanding of the average wealth of citizens in a country, especially in comparisons between richer and poorer countries, is somewhat different depending on which measure is presented. If we use PPP indexing, Cambodia's GDP per capita of only $946 per year equates to $2,360 per capita in purchasing power, more than two and a half times higher (World Bank 2013). In some countries, PPP lowers the wealth measure because the cost of living is high. Norway's GDP per capita based on purchasing power parity ($65,639), for example, is only two-thirds of its GDP per capita ($99,600). In purchasing power dollars, the economic gap between the wealthier countries and the poorer countries usually decreases. Thus in the case of Norway and Cambodia, the ratio drops from about 105:1 to 28:1 when corrected for PPP. Indeed, for many of the poorer countries, GDP per capita (PPP) dollars are more than double the GDP per capita dollars because of the low cost of living in the poorer countries. However, it is important to note that when a country attempts to participate in the global economy, and especially when it attempts to import goods, the purchasing power of its currency is directly tied to international exchange rates, not to the price of rice at home (or PPP dollars), and its relative wealth or poverty remains.

More broadly, is there a better measure of the general prosperity in a society than GDP (or GNI) per capita (PPP)? Some scholars now argue that GDP-type measures give value to many economic activities in our collective lives that should not be valued, such as the cost of cleaning up environmental damage (e.g., oil spills) or expenditures on crime (e.g., maintaining prisons), and also that GDP does not account for many things that do provide us with a higher quality life, such as volunteer service and environmentally sustainable activities. They also cite the recent findings of economists and other social scientists who conclude that beyond a limited level of wealth, human well-being correlates more with conditions such as physical and mental health, quality of social life, and level of education rather than with increases in GDP per capita and material consumption (Easterlin 2006; Layard 2011; but see Wolfers and Stevenson 2013).

Thus, some propose an alternative measure, such as the Genuine Progress Indicator (GPI). The GPI adds the economic value of those things that enhance our quality of life and increase environmental sustainability and subtracts the costs of those economic activities that reduce quality of life. While GDP per capita in the United States rose about 240 percent during the period from 1950 to 2005, the Genuine Progress Indicator per capita rose only about 25 percent (Costanza 2008; Redefining Progress 2007). Another group proposes the Happy Planet Index (HPI), a measure for each country that combines individuals' reported satisfaction with their lives, longevity, and the country's ecological footprint (to protect resources for future generations) (Abdallah et al. 2011). Do you think there is a case for a different measure of prosperity instead of GDP? What approach do you find better for comparing two societies?

Compare in 8

Wealth Inequality

Chapter 2 identified the normative disagreements, especially between conservatives and socialists, about the desirability of equality. Many discussions focus on the inequalities in wealth between the "rich" countries and the "poor" countries. However, others focus on the wealth inequalities *within* countries. These can be masked by general measures of national economic prosperity per capita, such as GDP per capita (PPP). Are there significant inequalities within many countries? How are we to make sense of this?

Economic inequality (or equality) can be measured in various ways. One widely used measure is a statistic called the Gini index. When used as a measure of income inequality, the Gini index computes a score in which a perfectly equal distribution of wealth in the population would have an index score of 0.00 and a completely unequal distribution would have an index score of 100. Higher Gini index scores, especially those greater than about 45, indicate very unequal wealth distribution. The index also provides a way to compare the relative inequality across countries. Another form of measuring wealth within a country is the ratio of the country's personal income that is held by the top X percent of the population relative to the lowest Y percent.

Figure 8.4 provides Gini index scores for selected countries among the 136 countries for which there are data. Inequality in the distribution of family income ranges from the most unequal country,

Figure 8.4 Wealth Inequality/Equality in Selected Countries (Gini Index)

SOURCE: CIA World Factbook 2013
https://www.cia.gov/library/publications/the-world-factbook/rankorder/2172rank.html

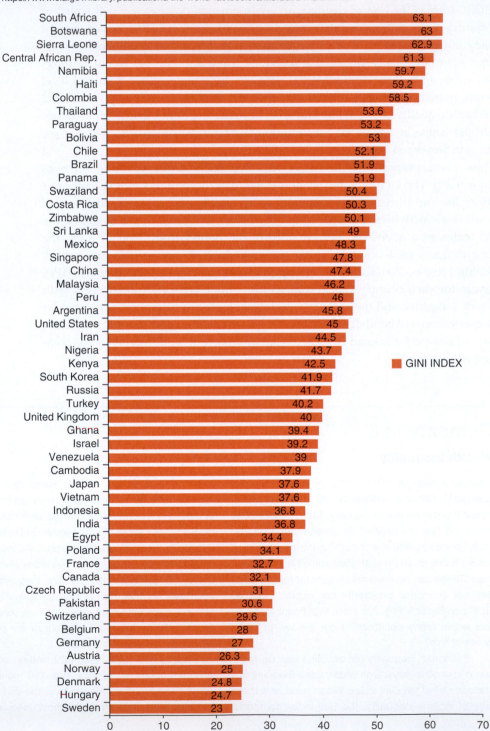

Lesotho, with a Gini index score of 63.2, to the most equal, Sweden, at 23.0. There are considerable cross-national differences in the extent of wealth inequality. About 28 percent of the countries have Gini indices of 45 or higher. Less than 4 percent of the countries have scores above 60.0, 13 percent score in the 50s, 28 percent are in the 40s, 40 percent are in the 30s, and 15 percent are below 30 (CIA 2013). Of the 10 most unequal income distributions, 6 are in sub-Saharan Africa and 4 are countries in Latin America. Of the 10 countries with the most equal distributions, 6 are in Europe and 4 are in Scandinavia.

In general, the rich countries (discussed as the "developed countries of the Global North" in Chapter 13) have relatively less inequality in the distribution of wealth than most of the poorer countries (the "developing countries of the Global South" in Chapter 14). Most of the countries with the greatest wealth inequalities are extremely poor countries. And most of the countries with the greatest equality

in wealth distribution are countries that are either European social democracies or European countries that were under communism until 1989. There are exceptions to this general pattern. Two rich countries (Singapore and the United States) have rather high inequality scores, while some poor countries (e.g., Ethiopia, Kazakhstan, and Pakistan) do have substantial equality in income distribution. Two important issues to be addressed in later chapters are what general factors might account for greater or less equality in income distributions and why inequality might be politically significant.

Further Questions

1. Does the location of any country in Figure 8.4 surprise you? Why?

2. Why might there generally be more wealth inequality in poorer countries than in richer countries?

Two Ideal-Type Political Economies

8.4   **Compare the ideal-type political economies.**

Based on the framework in Figure 8.3, we can distinguish two ideal-type political economies: *market economy* and *command economy*. Remember that an *ideal type* is a description of what a certain phenomenon might be like in its pure form, but it does not necessarily correspond exactly to any real-world example.

In distinguishing the market economy from the command economy, it's useful to consider five fundamental questions:

1. Who controls the factors of production?
2. Who determines what goods are produced?
3. Who establishes the value attached to different resources and goods?
4. Who decides how resources and goods will be distributed?
5. What is the role of the state?

The next two sections consider these questions for each ideal-type political economy. Table 8.1 summarizes the responses to each of these key questions. The table also provides answers for a "mixed" economy, which is less an ideal type than a real-world compromise between the two. (For other approaches that explain political economy, see Heyne, Boettke, and Prychitko [2013] and Lindblom [1977, 2003].)

Table 8.1 Comparing Command, Market, and Mixed Political Economies

	Command	Market	Mixed
Who controls the factors of production?	The state owns all significant factors (land, labor, and capital).	Every private actor (household) controls her own factors.	The state and private actors each control some factors.
Who determines what goods are produced?	The state devises a detailed economic plan that specifies what level of each good will be produced.	All actors (firms) make their own separate decisions about production in an attempt to maximize their own utilities.	Some firms are under direct state control, but most make decisions in the market. The state regulates some actions of many firms and households.
	The system is supply-oriented.	The system is demand-oriented.	The system is mainly demand-oriented.
Who establishes the value attached to different productive factors and goods?	The state sets the value (price) in all exchanges.	The market (via the "invisible hand") sets the value, based on the equilibrium of supply and demand.	The market sets the value. The state regulates some prices to serve national priorities.
Who decides how factors and goods will be distributed?	The state's plan indicates who will receive which goods and in what amounts.	Distribution is based on a summation of the actions of all consumers and producers in the market.	The market is the main decision maker. The state intervenes in some cases to ensure that certain actors have access to particular goods.
What is the role of the state?	The state is dominant, controlling almost all aspects of the political economy.	The state plays a minimal role in the political economy. The state enforces the "social contract," protecting all from violence and lawbreakers.	The state attempts to strike a balance between: (1) state control and competition; and (2) private profit and a sharing of societal resources.

The Market Economy: Total Private Control

1. **Who controls the factors of production?** In the ideal-type **market economy**, there is *total private control.* The state has almost no significant role in the political economy. Thus, every actor has direct, personal control over the use of all the factors of production that she owns. The laborer, the landowner, or the owner of capital decides with whom, if anyone, she will exchange her resources and the amount of resources she will accept in that exchange. And each firm acts to maximize its profits through acquiring productive resources and then producing goods that can be sold to consumers.

2. **Who determines what goods are produced?** All the firms' decisions about what goods to produce are based on their own assessments of how they can achieve maximum profit. If one thinks of an economy in terms of the supply and demand for goods, the market economy is demand-oriented. The most important consideration for a firm that is deciding what to produce is this: What good can I offer that others will demand and that will generate the highest profit for me? Overall, production is guided by what the famous Scottish economist Adam Smith (1723–1790, Compare in 2) called the "invisible hand" of the market. This invisible hand is a summation of the self-serving actions of every household and every firm regarding their uses of the factors of production.

3. **Who establishes the value attached to different factors and goods?** Similarly, the invisible hand of the market establishes value. Every factor of production and every good that is produced is valued at its *opportunity cost*—the resources that someone will give to acquire it. Value is determined in the competitive market of supply and demand (recall Figure 8.2) as every household and firm tries to gain the maximum payment from others in exchange for its productive factor or good. Competition is particularly intense where supply and demand are very unequal. For example, if a firm needs five workers who can program in Python (demand) and only two workers are available with this skill (supply), the workers can bid up the resources that the firm will offer (this is usually a wage rate, but it can also include other resources such as work conditions, benefits [e.g., housing, health care], or shares of the firm's profits). Conversely, if five workers offer the skill and the firm needs only two workers with this productive factor, the firm can lower the resources it must pay for the work.

    A basic economic assumption in a market economy is the continual adjustment of supply and demand toward an equilibrium point. For example, some workers might move to a different place or offer a different labor skill if the wages for programming get too low or there are too few jobs. And a firm might find a substitute for the labor it needs if the labor is too expensive or too scarce to enable the firm to make a profit (e.g., outsourcing). Can you think of other supply–demand adjustments that the workers or the firm might make?

4. **Who decides how productive factors and goods will be distributed?** Again, it is the invisible hand of the market, rather than anyone in particular, that determines who gets which factors and goods. As each person pursues her own individual utility, economic actors accumulate dramatically different bundles of factors and goods, depending on their preferences, the resources they control, and their skill and luck in exchanging and transforming resources in the market.

5. **What is the role of the state?** The state is passive in the productive system, allowing private actors to operate in a relatively unconstrained manner. The state's primary obligations, under the social contract, are to prevent private actors from doing violence to one another, protect private property rights, enforce contracts, and defend the state's sovereignty. In meeting these responsibilities, the state might purchase some goods and productive factors, might levy minimal taxes, and might affect firms' import and export activities. Otherwise, state intervention in the economy is extremely limited.

The Command Economy: Total State Control

1. **Who controls the factors of production?** In the ideal-type **command economy**, *the state assumes total control of almost all the significant factors of production.* The state eliminates private ownership of labor, land, and capital. The state owns the land, the natural resources, the factories, the machines, and so on. The state even owns labor, in the sense that the state decides the form in which all individuals will provide their labor.

2. **Who determines what goods are produced?** The state devises a detailed *economic plan* that specifies what goods will be produced, in what quantity, and from what combination of productive factors. The production decisions in the

state's plan are supply-oriented (in contrast to the demand orientation of the market economy). The state-as-firm attempts to use all productive factors optimally to maximize the supply of goods that it has determined are most appropriate to produce.

3. **Who establishes the value attached to different factors and goods?** Because the state controls all the factors of production and is the firm producing all the goods, it can also set the values (i.e., establish the payments) for all exchanges within its boundaries. Competition is eliminated because the state, rather than the market, establishes the payments for every factor of production and every good in the society. Thus, the state tells a group of farmers to produce 1 million tomatoes and then sets the exchange value (i.e., the price) of those tomatoes. Similarly, the state decides which individuals will have jobs programming Python, and it establishes the wages and benefits they receive for their work.

4. **Who decides how productive factors and goods will be distributed?** The state is particularly active in the decisions about the distribution of goods to the population. The state's plan aims to distribute an optimal bundle of goods to every citizen, given the resources available. Thus, the plan indicates who will receive which goods in what amounts. The plan could specify, for example, that automobile-producing factory X will receive 46 tons of steel each month and that town A will receive three tomatoes per family per week. The plan can even indicate where these goods will come from (i.e., steel from factory Y and tomatoes from farm B).

5. **What is the role of the state?** Clearly, the answers to the preceding four questions indicate that the state has a dominant—even an overwhelming—role in this ideal-type political economy. The state controls almost all the important factors of production, plans the manner in which they will be utilized in the production of goods, establishes the official value of all resources and goods, and decides how the resources of the society will be distributed among individuals. In the command economy, profit is accumulated by the state, not by individuals. The state then determines how this profit will be used to serve its objectives of prosperity, security, and stability.

Key Problems of Each Ideal-Type Political Economy

8.5   **Identify the challenges faced by market, command, and mixed economies.**

Table 8.2 lists several important virtues for each of the two types of political economy. These benefits stem from the logic of each approach. In theory, the market economy is efficient and dynamic because profit-driven, self-serving behavior in a highly competitive environment encourages high levels of productivity and innovation. In theory, the command economy is effective and humane because society's resources are managed and distributed so that everyone benefits from the most desirable set of goods and services possible. These virtues are valid, at least in theory. However, there are significant potential shortcomings in the functioning of both the market economy and the command economy. These problems are also summarized in Table 8.2 and are characterized below.

Table 8.2 Benefits and Problems of Market and Command Economies

	Benefits	Problems
Market Economy		
Competition	Energetic and efficient production	Ruthless interactions; huge inequalities in wealth and resources
Demand orientation	Goods' cost and quality responsive to consumers' desires	Creation of demand for and proliferation of goods that have limited social value
No central plan	Local decision and "invisible hand" stimulate innovation, facilitate freedom	Economic cycles of boom and bust, inflation and recession
Command Economy		
No competition	Work for common good; relative equality of wealth and income; minimal conflict	Little initiative; shoddy products; low productivity; limited innovation
Supply orientation	Production and distribution for social and individual needs	Oversupply and shortages; lack of coordination
Central plan	Rational use of societal resources	Overcentralized control; lack of responsiveness to changing circumstances

Market Economy

RESOURCE INEQUALITY AND HARDSHIP Substantial resource inequalities tend to emerge in a market economy. Competition is everywhere, and it tends to become ruthless. In the economic marketplace, some are extremely successful and others are complete failures, and the market system is indifferent to the hardships of those who do not succeed. Neither the successful actors nor the state intervenes to protect those who have minimal success. Over time, the rich tend to get richer (especially if they cooperate with one another), while the less successful increasingly lack the resources for a secure and decent life.

PRODUCTION FOR PROFIT, NOT NEED A demand-oriented system of private production does not necessarily produce goods that best meet human needs. Rather, production decisions are dominated by actors who produce those goods that they believe will result in maximum profit. Such goods might be inessential or extravagant or even dangerous. The state does little to regulate the economic actors or to provide for those who cannot afford important goods, like health care. More broadly, the aggressive pursuit of profit in the absence of state regulation can result in economic behavior that is unethical or dangerous. And short-term profitability ("greed is good") trumps longer-term considerations of societal benefits, such as environmental sustainability.

SEVERE ECONOMIC CYCLES A third problem is that a market economy can experience major economic cycles. There is no guarantee that the very large number of private decisions about production and consumption (the "invisible hand") will mesh in a manner that ensures steady growth and prosperity for the economic system as a whole. The economy is prone to large swings toward either hyperactivity (causing inflation and scarcity) or serious economic slowdown (causing recession or depression), and the state does not intervene to counteract these swings. Fluctuations between boom and bust, even if infrequent, can be deeply disruptive to the productive system, and the bad times can result in substantial hardship.

Command Economy

LIMITED INCENTIVES FOR EFFICIENCY The absence of competition in the command political economy can result in problems as serious as those resulting from excessive competition. First, if the state controls wages and prices, there are no major economic incentives for firms to be efficient, for managers to be innovative, or for individual workers to work hard. Second, if there is no competitive market of alternative goods, there is minimal incentive to produce goods of high quality. People are obliged to accept goods that are unexciting or poorly made.

UNRESPONSIVE PRODUCTION The state's emphasis on a supply orientation means that production decisions are not directly responsive to consumer demand. The central planners' ideas of what people should want are not necessarily what consumers actually want and will purchase. Thus, the plan typically results in substantial oversupply of some goods and severe shortages of others.

OVERCENTRALIZATION AND INFLEXIBILITY Command economies are so centralized that they lose touch with the differences and complexities of individual firms and consumers. The central planners usually do not receive and react effectively to information regarding miscalculations and mistakes in either the development or the implementation of the state's overall plan. Such rigidity and unresponsiveness make the efficient use of productive resources unlikely. In short, the political economy that combines minimal competition, a weak demand mechanism, and inflexibility is prone to low productivity, inferior goods, and inefficient use of resources.

Cubans rally in Havana's Revolution Square in support of one of the few remaining communist, command economies.

The Mixed Economy

In reality, no economy is actually identical to either ideal type. Rather, economies develop somewhere along the continuum between the command and market types, and most shift somewhat over time to respond to particular challenges and political agendas. For example, in response to the Great Depression of the 1930s, the United States moved further from the market economy end and closer to the command end of the ideal-type continuum. An expansive set of new government policies provided many new social welfare benefits to less-advantaged citizens, implemented vast public works programs, and introduced extensive new regulations on many aspects of the economy, such as agricultural prices. An example of the opposite shift occurred during the 1990s in most previously communist countries that had been in the Soviet bloc. These countries shifted substantially from the command economy end of the continuum, allowing many features associated with a market economy. These changes included privatizing most factors of production, enabling firms to pursue maximum profitability, and allowing the market to determine the prices of goods. Some, like Poland, flourished. Others, like Russia, had trouble breaking away from elite control of the economy (See Chapter 15 for a discussion of the postcommunist states).

Because almost every contemporary political economy lies somewhere between a market economy and a command economy, it might be helpful to describe a political economy that is in the middle of the continuum as a **mixed economy**, which can be understood as *an attempt to blend the strengths of the two ideal-type economies while minimizing their shortcomings.* As a hybrid, the mixed economy is not a "pure" ideal type. It compromises on each of the five major issues considered earlier (see Table 8.1).

1. **Who controls the factors of production?** Control of the means of production is shared between the state and private actors. The state owns or directly controls some of the major factors of production, such as those relating to key commodities (e.g., coal, oil, steel), key infrastructure systems (e.g., transportation, telecommunications), and key financial resources (e.g., banks). Sometimes the state determines who will control key factors of production, even when the state itself does not. However, many firms are private and private actors (households) control a substantial share of the factors of production.

2. **Who determines what goods are produced?** Production decisions are primarily demand-oriented, driven by the market mechanism. Half or more of all production is done by private firms. Most public-sector firms (those owned and managed by the state) must interact and even compete with many private firms when acquiring productive resources and when selling goods to consumers. However, private firms and households are constrained by the state, which regulates the behavior of private actors and can implement an economic plan that specifies broad guidelines for all actors in the economic system.

3. **Who establishes the value attached to different productive factors and goods?** The value of most goods is established, as in a market economy, through the processes of supply and demand. But the state does intervene to ensure that national priorities are protected. For example, the state might set guidelines to control the prices of key goods (e.g., basic foods, energy) and of certain factors of production (e.g., wages); it might regulate the manner in which firms and households

collaborate and compete; and it might employ taxing and expenditures (purchases [F1] in Figure 8.3) to influence the economic system.

4. **Who decides how factors and goods will be distributed?** Decisions on the distribution of productive factors and goods are the most complicated element of the mixed economy. Private actors are allowed to take actions that maximize their profits. The state then intervenes through taxation mechanisms (F5 in Figure 8.3), extracting resources from firms and households. The state uses these taxes to purchase goods (F1) or to provide transfer payments (F6), both of which the state redistributes to certain actors in the social order. The state undertakes only a partial redistribution of resources, leaving private actors with considerable resources and freedom to make their own decisions about production and consumption.

5. **What is the role of the state?** The state is far more active than in the market economy but far less in control than in the command economy. The system blends a demand orientation and a supply orientation. The state acts to facilitate some competition while mitigating the effects of ruthless competition. It allows private actors and the economy to benefit from their skillful use of resources while ensuring a certain level of material well-being for the less successful actors. The great challenges for the state in a mixed economy concern striking a proper balance between competition and control, between a free market and a managed economy, and between private property and a sharing of society's resources.

All real-world political economies are mixed in the sense that each country is constantly attempting to find the best balance of market forces and state interventions. The process is contentious because those with different ideologies disagree on answers to all five of the questions above. Moreover, the state's economy not only is subject to all the complexity and change within its borders but also is nested in the economies of the region and the world. Thus the state's capacity to manage the economic health of the country at any given moment might be limited, whatever its policies regarding the political economy. Focus in 8 describes some of the challenges facing the Mexican political economy.

Focus in 8

Mexico's Political Economy

Since the Mexican Revolution of 1917, the economy of Mexico has experienced dramatic highs and lows as it has transformed from an agrarian system to a more diversified economy. Currently, about 62 percent of the Mexican labor force is engaged in the provision of services, 24 percent is in manufacturing, and 13 percent is in agriculture. The economy now generates about $15,600 per person (in PPP), ranking eighty-eigth among all countries (CIA 2014). The evolution of the economy is shaped by many forces, but two have been most critical.

The first force is Mexico's geopolitical situation—its natural resources and its geographic location (on geopolitics, see Compare in 11). Mexico has discovered abundant oil and other minerals, has considerable land suitable for farming, and has a long coastline on two oceans. Also, Mexico's economy operates under the looming presence of the United States, which is the largest and most influential economic system in the world as well as a political and military superpower. And to Mexico's south are the small countries of Central America, which have lower GDP per capita than Mexico and more commodity-based economies.

The second critical force shaping the economy has been the policies of the Mexican national government. Policy was dominated by a single party (PRI, recall Chapter 7) from the Revolution of 1917 until the 2000 election of Vicente Fox. PRI policies shifted the Mexican economy from a reliance on agriculture toward more balance and diversification first through industrialization and then through provision of services. State control and intervention in the economy were relatively high. The government owned large shares in major industries (e.g., energy, telecommunications) and regulated most key economic sectors. Its policies of high tariffs and subsidies to domestic firms protected both agriculture and industry from external competition. Labor was controlled to keep wages low, although some PRI leaders did promote state spending on social programs for the poor as well as some redistribution of land to the peasants. PRI was accused of extensive corruption that funneled considerable wealth from the economy to its members and to wealthy Mexicans.

During the 1980s and 1990s, the government shifted away from state control and ownership of the economy and toward more market-based policies, encouraging private entrepreneurs and opening the economy to foreign capital and imported goods. These policy changes were driven by severe economic crises in Mexico, including the near collapse of the peso, and by the general trends in the global economy.

The evolution of the Mexican political economy was accelerated when Mexico joined Canada and the United States in the North American Free Trade Agreement (NAFTA) in 1994. Mexico gained much greater access to the huge market for goods in the United States. More than 80 percent of its exports go to the United States. This includes oil, vegetables and fruits, and manufactured goods, many of which are produced in plants (*maquiladoras*) located near the U.S. border. Most of these plants import components (intermediate goods) from the United States and then complete the assembly of final goods that are exported, such as automobiles and televisions.

The Mexican economy has grown in most recent years, with increasing rates of job creation, home ownership, and business start-ups, and with many families rising to the middle class. Greater prosperity has been associated with reduced birth rates and improved tax collection by the government.

NAFTA has also resulted in some negative effects in Mexico. For example, many agricultural products are now imported from the United States because they are cheaper (due to more efficient technology and U.S. government subsidies to its producers). This has increased unemployment and poverty among Mexican farmers. Also, the Mexican economy has become so dependent on the health of the U.S. economy that the recent economic problems in the United States have generated even deeper problems in Mexico, in areas such as job losses, difficulty obtaining financial capital, and decreasing currency value.

Illegal immigration, high levels of violent crime, and a burgeoning drug trade are also linked to Mexico's stronger economic ties to the United States. And while the areas close to the U.S. border have enjoyed most of the benefits from trade within NAFTA, many people in central and southern Mexico have experienced a decline in their living standards. Inequality has grown in Mexico with the market-based economy of the NAFTA period. But the recent national governments led by fiscally conservative presidents Fox (2000–2006) and Calderon (2006–2012) did not promote increases in government aid to the poor and others affected by the economic decline. PRI might direct more resources to the less-advantaged groups now that the party has regained the presidency (Pena Nieto 2012–) and power in the Chamber of Deputies (recall Figure 7.2). However, his government has also privatized oil resources and limited the control of powerful unions. The evolution of Mexico's political economy will be a key factor in its progress as a transitional developed country (see Chapter 15).

Further Focus

1. What seems to be the most serious problem for the Mexican political economy? How might it be dealt with?

2. Does it seem more beneficial or harmful for Mexico to have the United States as its neighbor?

Politics and Political Economy: The Other "ISMS"

8.6 Contrast political economy "isms", real-world examples and ideal-type political economies.

The Three-Plus "Isms"

One set of great "isms" in political analysis includes the Western ideologies of conservatism, classical liberalism, and socialism (see Chapter 2). Another set of "isms" explicitly links politics to political economy: capitalism, communism, and socialism. In twentieth-century politics, these were extremely emotive labels, endowed with powerful ideological content. In their most straightforward form, capitalism, communism, and socialism correspond loosely to market economy, command economy, and mixed economy, respectively. These three classic "isms," along with three others in some contemporary societies—state capitalism, statism, and corporatism—are described below.

Capitalism is *a system in which private economic actors are quite free from state constraints, private property rights are fundamental, and the state engages in few actions that might shift resources among private actors.* It is founded on the philosophy of laissez-faire economics celebrated by Adam Smith, and it imposes the severe limitations on government activity that are associated with classical liberalism and the market political economy. The freedom of private economic actors is paramount, and the state should not intervene to benefit either winners or losers in the economic competition. It is praised for its economic dynamism, innovativeness, and responsiveness to market demand. There is no assumption that capitalism requires any particular form of political processes (e.g., on the democracy–nondemocracy continuum) to function efficiently (Thurow 1997). Chile, Switzerland, and Uganda are examples of mainly capitalist systems. Capitalism is maligned by its critics as a system of self-interested individualism that denies the need for collective action to protect the disadvantaged, to nurture society as a whole, to promote social values and culture, or to protect the ecology (Heilbroner 1994).

Communism has as its centerpiece *the socialization of resources—the notion that the state must actively control society's land, labor, and capital to achieve substantial equality for all citizens.* Consistent with the command political economy model, the state guides the utilization of all these major means of production with a central plan so that the production and distribution of goods serve the best interests of the entire population. However, communism also emphasizes a strong ideological commitment to economic and social equality among all its citizens. And it typically posits that government and politics, like the economic system, must be guided powerfully by a unified leadership, at least until equality is achieved. Communism is generally associated with the theories of Karl Marx and with the economic systems that were developed in countries such as China (1949 to about 1990), Cuba (since 1959), North Korea (since the early 1950s), and the former Soviet Union (1917–1991). Its critics disparage communism as an inefficient economic system with a nondemocratic government that denies individual freedoms and rights. In recent decades, most countries have abandoned the command economy that is central to communist principles, leading some to suggest that communism is dead. The Debate in 8 considers this proposition.

Socialism is in the middle of the three "isms," and thus it is not precisely differentiated from the other two. It seeks *a complex balance between state involvement and private control of the economy, and a key policy goal is a relatively equitable distribution of benefits to all citizens.* As in the mixed political economy, some major productive resources are owned or controlled by the state, and the state actively intervenes in planning and regulating the economy; but most production decisions are private, and value is established primarily by supply and demand (Przeworski 1985). Socialism is distinguishable from communism because the state only controls a few important factors of production in the society, allows private actors considerable freedom of action, and does not aim to achieve total economic equality among all citizens. Finland and Denmark are examples of what are known as democratic socialist systems (or "social market" systems; see Chapter 13) because they blend socialist economics with democratic politics.

State capitalism is a political economy in which the *leaders of the political system assert extensive control over who is allowed to compete in the key sectors of the economy, and the primary goal of the economy is to serve state power.* State capitalism is also referred to as "political capitalism." The state is a very active participant in the political economy, supporting and controlling major firms in a marketplace that is based on competition. Although economic activity seems to resemble laissez-faire capitalism, the core principle guiding economic decisions is not to maximize profit but to ensure that major firms and critical assets enhance the power of the state and its leaders. Political leaders allocate management of those firms and assets either to "friends of the government" or to government officials themselves. Most small firms are allowed to operate relatively freely in pursuit of private profit within a strong regulatory framework. The politics of most state capitalist countries tends to be nondemocratic. This includes some countries that shifted away from a command political economy but retained centralized political power, such as China, Russia, and Vietnam (see Chapter 15). Numerous other authoritarian regimes, such as Saudi Arabia and Venezuela, have also adopted forms of state capitalism (Bremmer 2010).

Statism is a political economy variation of state capitalism. **Statism** also has *a highly active state, which manages the system of production and distribution of goods, with a primary goal of economic growth and development.* Firms compete in the marketplace, although the state attempts to nurture and protect them from external competition. The main distinction between statism and state capitalism is that in a statist political economy the primary motivation for state involvement is to develop the economy as rapidly and strategically as possible. Economic growth and economic vitality, guided strongly by the profit motive, drive the policy choices. The state extensively regulates the actions of firms and households. Many important areas of production (e.g., transportation, power, banking) might be publicly owned and operated as state enterprises. The state also controls the prices of certain basic goods (e.g., foods, fuel). State policies support the firms that are targeted for success in the domestic and global market, but there is far less concern than in state capitalism with exploiting the economy to protect the power of a particular political elite or to benefit "friends of the government."

Statist systems have tended to be authoritarian or somewhat democratic. Japan was an early innovator of the contemporary form of statism, which was then adopted in many developing countries, including Brazil, India, Mexico, Singapore, and South Korea (Johnson 1995; Woo-Cumings 1999).

Corporatism is a system characterized by a political arrangement that facilitates *extensive economic cooperation between an activist state and large organizations representing major sectors of economic actors.* The corporatist state attempts to consult, cooperate, and coordinate with the representatives of several key groups that control major productive resources in the society. These "peak associations" (organizations that represent these big groups) usually include large industries, organized labor, farmers, major financial institutions, and the military. The peak associations have some autonomy from the state, but they are supposed to work together for common national interests. Thus, corporatism blends features of capitalism (e.g., private ownership, private profit), state capitalism (e.g., selecting and supporting key economic actors), and socialism (e.g., extensive state economic planning, coordination of major factors of production with the state's conception of the national interest). While the boundaries between corporatism and the other isms can be blurry, some scholars would include Japan, the Netherlands, Peru, Portugal, and Sweden among the contemporary states that have significant corporatist tendencies (Crouch and Streeck 2006; Molina and Rhodes 2002; Schmitter 1989).

The Debate in 8

Is Communism Dead?

In the decades after World War II, many thought that Marx's prediction of the inevitable success of communism was correct because more and more countries adopted its main guidelines for their political economies. Soviet Union leader Nikita Khrushchev famously announced in 1956 that communism would bury capitalism. However, the Cold War between the communist Soviet bloc and the capitalist bloc led by the United States ended in the late 1980s with almost every country abandoning the command political economy, even the Soviet Union. While many note the triumph of capitalism over communism (Fukuyama 1992; Heilbroner 1994), the global economic meltdown has revitalized the Marxist perspective (Panitch 2009). Is communism, as a model for a political economy and a society, dead?

Communism Is Dead...

- The command political economy that drives communism has stifled the incentives for productivity,

innovation, and flexibility in every country that has implemented it. These fundamental weaknesses resulted in failure and abandonment of this approach almost everywhere, from the Soviet Union and Eastern Europe to wherever it was attempted in Africa, Asia, or Latin America.

- Even most countries that are still nominally communist actually practice capitalism. For example, although China protects its one-party political system, it has freed its markets and many of its firms to benefit economically from global trade. In a radical departure from Marxist ideas, the Chinese "Communist" Party protects property rights and promotes wealth accumulation. Of more than 180 countries, the only countries that still practice something close to communism in political-economic terms are a very few small, economically backward states like Laos and North Korea.

- The attempt to create a population that truly believes in the communist ideology of collective sharing of societal resources and the equal distribution of benefits has repeatedly failed. Despite massive efforts at political socialization and substantial use of coercion by the state, human nature seems to prevent people from genuinely embracing the ideals of collectivism and egalitarianism.

- In retrospect, it is clear that the viability and spread of communism during the Cold War (1945–1990) occurred primarily because communist countries could wield extensive coercion against their own populations and possessed formidable military power to promote communism abroad.

- Consider the well-known European aphorism: If you are not a communist at 20, you have no heart; if you are still a communist at 40, you have no brain (an observation even repeated by Russia's top leader Vladimir Putin in 2007). Political and economic power in the world is clearly dominated by older and wiser people who, almost without exception, completely reject communist ideas.

Communism Is Alive and Well...

- Numerous countries still operate under the general principles of a command political economy or state capitalism. While they might not call themselves "communist," they have retained a strong, one-party state that controls the political economy and opens it to the market only to the extent that the market furthers the key communist aims of using society's key resources to increase the broad sharing of benefits. This is the case in countries in European Central Asia (e.g., Belarus, Tajikistan, Turkmenistan, Uzbekistan), Asia (e.g., Cambodia, Nepal, North Korea, Laos, Vietnam), and Latin America (e.g., Cuba).

- In countries that have "abandoned" communism, a substantial proportion of the population still prefers their circumstances under communism to those in the postcommunist period. In Russia, for example, two-thirds of those surveyed in 2013 still view communism favorably and a majority have a positive attitude toward life under the old communist system (Carden 2013). Similarly,

some of China's rural population not only oppose the effects of state capitalism in their country but also support the communist principle of equal property distribution (Nadiri 2007).

- Democracy and communism are not incompatible. In fact, several democratic countries have or recently had majority communist party governments—Cyprus, Moldova, and Nepal. In democratic India, three states have recently been dominated by the communist party, including West Bengal for 34 straight years (Williams 2008).

- The key principles of communism, especially the collectivization of major societal resources and redistribution of wealth toward the less advantaged, are very evident in the political philosophies of leaders such as Evo Morales in Bolivia, Daniel Ortega in Nicaragua, Jacob Zuma in South Africa, and Nicolas Maduro in Venezuela, as well as some European leftist parties with solid electoral support.

- Insurgency movements inspired by Neo-Marxist communist ideals are still active in some countries that suffer from economic underdevelopment and severe inequalities. This includes movements in Colombia, India, Peru, the Philippines, and Turkey.

- Reconsider: If you are not a communist at 20, you have no heart....The majority of the world's population is young, poor, and suffering from the severe inequalities in their own societies. It is not surprising that many of them are attracted to the fundamental values of an ideology that promises economic and social justice.

More questions...

1. Is it possible that the ideals of communism will always appeal to at least a minority of people in countries experiencing high levels of poverty and inequality?

2. Is the repeated failure of the command political economy due to clumsy implementation or its inherent flaws?

3. Is a relatively classless society possible, or will there always be inequality?

The Real World

As noted above, because they are ideal types, no contemporary country has a political economy that corresponds exactly to either the market economy or the command economy. While it is possible to place countries generally along a continuum from a "pure" market economy to a "pure" command economy, all actual political economies are mixed and move on that continuum depending on political fortunes and economic necessities. This does not mean that all political economies are basically the same—the mix of elements varies a great deal from country to country. Every state engages in some activities as a firm, some regulation of economic actors, and some redistribution of resources. Every state favors some economic actors over others. Politics and values play a powerful role in establishing exactly what kinds of interventions the state will undertake and what values and interests the state will serve.

Thus, understanding the mixed nature of actual political economies entails more than simply comparing the proportion of the GDP controlled by private actors with that owned by the state or even assessing the bundle of state-provided goods and services. The five examples that follow—Switzerland, South Korea, Denmark, Cuba, and Russia—briefly suggest some of the features of actual political economies relative to the ideal types grounded in the major "isms" presented above (data sources are CIA 2014; Heritage Foundation 2014; Transparency International 2013; UNDP 2013).

GENERALLY MARKET AND CAPITALIST: SWITZERLAND The fourth wealthiest major country in the world (measured as GDP per capita in purchasing power parity), Switzerland has a relatively weak central government. This decentralization of political power is linked to a political economy that strongly emphasizes private control and limited government involvement. Switzerland is ranked third among 176 countries on a measure of freedom of the economy from state regulation. Nearly all factors of production are privately owned, and most decisions and actions regarding the use of those resources are in private hands. Apart from defense expenditures and education, relatively few resources are allocated to the provision of public goods, given the wealth of the society. Central government spending is less than 15 percent of GDP, and total expenditure by all levels of government is 34 percent of GDP, among the lowest of all developed countries.

GENERALLY MIXED AND CAPITALIST: SOUTH KOREA In South Korea, the state has little commitment to use the political economy for direct improvement of its citizens' quality of life. Apart from education, the state does not provide many welfare goods and services to its citizens. Government expenditures (by all levels) are only about 27 percent of GDP, the lowest among all relatively developed countries. It is not a purely capitalist system, however, because the state is extremely interventionist in promoting economic development. The state bureaucracy works very closely with firms to implement a comprehensive, collaborative strategy for economic growth, helping it rise to twenty-ninth in the world on GDP per capita. This strategy has particularly favored the development of a few major Korean companies. Government loans, tax credits, and other subsidies are channeled to these companies, which are expected to operate and diversify in directions suggested by the government. In turn, the government has assured the companies that they will enjoy high profits and a labor force that is well educated, disciplined, and unable to organize effectively for higher wages. The state has also used many hidden subsidies and import restrictions to provide competitive advantages in the international market to its export-oriented firms. Thus, South Korea ranks twenty-ninth on the measure of economic freedom. (This "developmental state" approach, a variation of statism, will be discussed further in Chapter 10.)

GENERALLY MIXED AND SOCIALIST: DENMARK Denmark is ranked twenty-second in terms of GDP per capita (PPP). The great majority of productive resources in Denmark are privately owned, and the state allows entrepreneurs considerable freedom of action, with a ranking of ninth on the economic freedom measure. However, the state is very active in guiding the Danish political economy. First, it enforces strong policies that regulate private economic actors in a generally corporatist approach, especially policies that control working conditions and environmental quality. Second, the state provides an extensive array of welfare services to the population, including: income supplement programs; a comprehensive, free health care system; state-subsidized housing for the elderly and for low-income groups; free child care; free education from infancy through university; and an extensive public transportation system. Third, it has one of the world's most equal income distributions and is ranked the world's least corrupt country. More than 58 percent of GDP is spent by all levels of government, the second highest among developed countries. To finance these programs, the government collects various forms of taxes equal to more than 50 percent of the GDP.

GENERALLY COMMAND AND COMMUNIST: CUBA In response to the global movement toward more market-oriented systems, Cuba has reduced its level of centralized state control over the economy. People can now buy and sell houses and cars and run small, for-profit businesses. However, the state still owns and controls Cuba's major means of production, and there is a detailed central economic plan. Cuba is ranked 175 among the 176 countries on economic freedom. Agriculture and manufacturing operations remain collectivized, and the state controls many prices. The state promises work for all (although there is unemployment), and it sets workers' wages. Consistent with the ideals of communism, the state retains a fundamental commitment to control and allocate societal resources to serve human needs. There has been a strong emphasis on state spending on education and health care and on policies to equalize the distribution of land and income and to increase equality among races, between genders, and between urban and rural citizens. Despite its modest GDP per capita (it ranks ninety-fourth in the world), government policies result in Cuba ranking in the top 25 countries in the world on the UN's non-income measure of quality of life that emphasizes health and education (see Chapter 13).

GENERALLY STATE CAPITALIST: RUSSIA Most of the key principles of the command political economy and the communist redistribution of resources to create greater equality have been abandoned in Russia since 1989. The political leadership controls major economic assets and firms, either through state-run enterprises or through its control of the owners and managers of large privately owned firms. Russia has replaced central planning with market-based pricing and production decisions as firms compete in the global market environment, and it has joined the World Trade Organization. But the decisions of all major economic actors must support the goals and power of the authoritarian political leadership headed by Vladimir Putin. The greatest economic gains are reserved for those associated with the political elite. Strong state control and regulation result in an economy that ranks only one hundred thirty-ninth in economic freedom. But by exploiting its vast natural resources (e.g., oil, natural gas, minerals) and its educated labor force, Russia's annual economic growth since 2000 has averaged a healthy 4.8 percent, the current GDP/capita/PPP has risen to $18,100, and real disposable incomes of Russians have doubled. Entrepreneurs who are successful in marketing goods and serving the agenda of the state can become very wealthy, and inequality of income in Russia has increased substantially since 1990. The state has cut back dramatically on its provision of social goods, such as subsidies for housing, food, education, and health care, resulting in considerable hardship for those who are unsuccessful in the state capitalist system.

Concluding Observations

This chapter has introduced you to an approach to political analysis that classifies and characterizes countries in terms of their political economies. These concepts are abstract and require the fusion of political science and economics. They are important concepts because the linkages between the political system and the economic system are fundamental and pervasive in the contemporary world. Indeed, the two systems have become so interrelated in most states that it is difficult to separate them except in an analytic sense. There is substantial variation in the extent to which the state intervenes in the economy. In some countries, the state's role is limited, while in others the state is deeply involved in most aspects of the production and distribution of goods. Regardless of the form of the political economy, the health of its economy is crucial to every state and the impacts of the economy and economic interests on government and politics are enormous.

In considering variations in economic systems, you might find it difficult to avoid strong normative judgments due both to your political socialization and to your tendency to identify an "ism" with particular states for which you have definite positive or negative feelings. In the United States, Tea Party activists are outraged by the "socialist" policies of President Obama. In Bolivia, President Morales claims that "(t)he worst enemy of humanity is U.S. capitalism." It is certainly reasonable that you will make both analytical and normative judgments about the virtues and shortcomings of every form of political economy and every "ism."

Indeed, assessing the appropriateness of a country's political economy might be the most crucial issue in understanding its effectiveness in the contemporary political world. In recent years, the support for communism and the command political economy has substantially declined among the leaders and citizens in many countries.

As you will see in Part Five, however, the rejection of communism has not led to a complete embrace or full implementation of a market economy. It has not even meant that most political leaders and most citizens have abandoned their support for all of the principles associated with a more command-oriented political economy or more extensive redistribution of wealth.

Despite your own political socialization, you might reflect on a fundamental question: Is every state, regardless of its current economic and political development, best served by exactly the same political economy? If you allow for variations in the most appropriate form of political economy for countries in the current global system, you leave open many challenging and important questions about political choices, questions that will be considered from a variety of perspectives in the remainder of this book. This exploration will begin in Part Four, with chapters that examine crucial issues associated with political decision making; political, social, and economic change; and political violence.

Key Concepts

capitalism, p. 220
command economy, p. 213
communism, p. 220
corporatism, p. 222
economic growth, p. 203
exports, p. 205
factors of production, p. 200
firm (producer), p. 201
good, p. 201

gross domestic product (GDP), p. 207
gross national income (GNI), p. 207
household (consumer), p. 200
imports, p. 205
market economy, p. 212
mixed economy, p. 217

political economy, p. 199
profit, p. 202
purchasing power parity (PPP), p. 208
state capitalism, p. 221
statism, p. 221
socialism, p. 221
supply and demand, p. 202
utility, p. 202

For Further Consideration

1. The economic productivity of command political economies has always been inferior to that of market political economies in comparable countries. What, then, might have been the attraction of this approach to many groups and to many countries between the 1950s and 1970s?

2. What would be the greatest benefit to individuals if the state played almost no role in its political economy? What would be the most serious problem with such a system?

3. Are there measures, other than the growth in GDP per capita, that might indicate the success of a political economy? Why are leaders in most states so worried if there is no growth in GDP per capita?

4. Do you agree with those who contend that capitalism is so individualistic that it fails to protect the collective good?

5. Why might some analysts argue that state capitalist systems have competitive advantages over more purely market-based systems?

For Further Reading

Courtois, Stephane, Nicholas Werth, Jean-Louis Panne, Adrzej Paczkowski, Karel Bartooek, and Jean-Louis Margolin. (1999). *The Black Book of Communism: Crimes, Terror, Repression.* Trans. Jonathan Murphy and Mark Cramer. Cambridge, MA: Harvard University Press. A detailed and profoundly critical analysis of the history of communism in the twentieth century. Its core argument is that a series of regimes and ruthless dictators (e.g., Lenin and Stalin in the Soviet Union, Mao Zedong in China, Pol Pot in Cambodia, Kim Il Sung in North Korea) have led communist regimes that engaged in brutal "class genocide" in their societies, resulting in as many as 100 million deaths.

Friedman, Milton. (1981). *Capitalism and Freedom.* Chicago: University of Chicago Press. The major contemporary explication of the classical liberal preference for a strong market economy with limited state intervention.

Garson, Barbara. (2003). *Money Makes the World Go Around.* New York: Penguin. The controversial social critic offers a wonderfully readable exploration of the global economy by tracking the money in two small investments and revealing how that money has various effects on people around the world.

Heilbroner, Robert. (1994). *Twenty-First Century Capitalism.* New York: W. W. Norton. An economist and social critic outlines the challenges facing capitalism and the continuing need for the state to guide the market economy and serve the social good.

Judt, Tony. (2011). *Ill Fares the Land.* New York: Penguin Press. Writing to young people, this major scholar of social history offers an eloquent argument for the values of social democracy—collective action for collective good—in contrast to the ideology of capitalism and self-interest that dominates current thinking in the most prosperous countries and is, he argues, dangerous and destructive.

Van Kersbergen, Kees, and Barbara Vis. (2013). *Comparative Welfare State Politics: Development, Opportunities, and Reform.* New York: Cambridge University Press. The authors consider how capitalist democracies have chosen to reform their welfare state structures and provide insight into the variations and challenges of economic planning.

Kristol, Irving. (1978). *Two Cheers for Capitalism.* New York: Basic Books. A leading U.S. neoconservative argues that capitalism is superior to alternative forms of political economy.

Levitt, Steven D., and Stephen J. Dubner. (2010). *Super Freakonomics: Global Cooling, Patriotic Prostitutes, and Why Suicide Bombers Should Buy Life Insurance.* New York: William Morrow. And now for something completely different: Like the earlier *Freakonomics* (2008), this book offers a playful and interesting wander through microeconomics, revealing how economic thinking can explain the impacts of incentives and public policy on individual and group behavior and (often) generates unexpected outcomes.

Lindblom, Charles E. (1977). *Politics and Markets: The World's Political-Economic Systems.* New York: Basic Books. A rich, comparative analysis of the relative merits of the political economies of modern socialism and capitalism.

Reisman, George. (1998). *Capitalism: A Treatise on Economics.* A lengthy (1,100 pages) but powerful and readable defense of laissez-faire capitalism, debunking myths about its weaknesses and critiquing rival theories, from Keynesianism to communism. Available free online at www.capitalism.net/Capitalism/CAPITALISM_Internet.pdf.

Ritholtz, Barry. (2010). *Bailout Nation: How Greed and Easy Money Corrupted Wall Street and Shook the World Economy.* New York:

Wiley. Blogger and money manager Ritholtz offers a scathing and highly controversial indictment of both government policy and the behavior of profit-driven financial actors that led to the recent global economic crisis.

Roubini, Nouriel, and Stephen Mihm. (2011). *Crisis Economics: A Crash Course in the Future of Economics.* **New York: Penguin.** A reasoned analysis of the interplay between the economic system and the political system that explains how problematic behavior of actors in both domains caused recent financial crises in many countries and must be altered or there will be an even bigger crisis soon.

Royo, Sebastian. (2002). *"A New Century of Corporatism?" Corporatism in Southern Europe—Spain and Portugal in a Comparative Perspective.* **Westport, CT: Praeger.** Detailed case studies of the last three decades in Spain and Portugal are the basis of an exploration of how technological and postindustrial changes have created the conditions for a resurgence of corporatism in European settings.

Stiglitz, Joseph E., and Mary Kaldor, eds. (2013). *The Quest For Security: Protection Without Protectionism and the Challenge of Global Governance.* **New York: Columbia University Press.** This collection presents a series of analyses about how the well-being and security of citizens, especially the less advantaged, can be protected in a globalized world by enlightened economic and social policies.

Walter, Stephanie. (2013). *Financial Crisis and the Politics of Macroeconomic Adjustments.* **New York: Cambridge University Press.** This book demonstrates the connection between economic policy and the preferences and risks of the electorate. The options available to policymakers are limited by the economic and social vulnerabilities of the population.

Wallerstein, Immanuel, Randall Collins, Michael Mann, Georgi Derluguian, and Craig Calhoun. (2013). *Does Capitalism Have a Future?* **New York: Oxford University Press.** Five progressive scholars each present a provocative argument about how capitalism's shortcomings are likely to result in substantial changes in the political economies of individual states and the global system.

Yunus, Mohammed. (2011). *Building Social Business: The New Kind of Capitalism that Serves Humanity's Most Pressing Needs.* **New York: PublicAffairs.** Nobel Prize winner for his innovative microcredit strategy (see Focus in 14), Yunus offers his vision of a model of "social business" that blends free market entrepreneurialism with a focus on meeting social needs.

On the Web

http://imf.org

The key documents and agreements among all states and for particular members of the International Monetary Fund (IMF), an organization that includes more than 180 countries that cooperate to sustain a smoothly functioning system of interstate trade and to provide loans and other financial assistance to countries.

http://freetheworld.com

A site containing reports and data from the Economic Freedom Network, a congeries of researchers "committed to bringing economic freedom and growth to all the countries of the world."

http://www.marxists.org

The Marxists Internet Archive offers links to numerous sources that make the case against capitalism as an economic system.

http://worldbank.org

The official site of the World Bank, an international consortium of banks and other major financial institutions, includes extensive economic data regarding the structure and performance of the economies of more than 180 countries.

http://www.wto.org

The World Trade Organization (WTO), which coordinates trade policy for about 150 countries, offers this Web site to provide key documents and agreements as well as sections that articulate and justify the WTO philosophy of open trade relations among countries.

http://globalexchange.org

Dedicated to a progressive agenda, this Web site includes links to articles and a section on the global economy that emphasizes fair trade, fair loan practices, and greater equality among countries and people.

http://www.cato.org

From the Cato Institute, this site offers evidence, including various online studies and articles, for the benefits of free trade and the costs of protectionism.

www.economywatch.com

Brief characterizations of many national economic systems are provided, including data and graphics, as well as links to other sites.

http://www.weforum.org

The site of the World Economic Forum, an organization designed to allow world leaders to address global issues, contains a substantial amount of information on a variety of international economic issues (e.g., sustainable development, globalization).

http://www.capitalism.org

This libertarian-inspired site describes the core principles of a system of unconstrained, free market capitalism, including a useful glossary, links to articles, a newsletter, banners, and the unique "Capitalism Tour."

http://www.economist.com

The electronic home of *The Economist*, a leading British-based news magazine, provides access to economic data and selected articles examining issues of political economy and world finance.

Chapter 9

Public Policy, Power, and Decision

 Learning Objectives

9.1 Differentiate among the types of public policy and outline the stages of public policy.

9.2 Identify three major approaches that explain public policymaking.

9.3 Characterize the elite approach.

9.4 Characterize the class approach.

9.5 Characterize the pluralist approach.

9.6 Evaluate the similarities, differences, and usefulness of the three major approaches to public policymaking.

"Mapuche"—their name means "people of the land." This indigenous people of Chile has sustained its nation-based identity for many centuries. They fought the Inca Empire to a standstill in the 1400s, and drove back the Spanish conquistadores from their land in the 1500s. But in the late nineteenth century, a substantial part of the land claimed by the Mapuche in southern Chile was acquired by outsiders, especially large agricultural barons, small farmers, and multinational logging companies.

Since the middle of the twentieth century, the Mapuche have persistently urged the Chilean government to enact policies that respond to their claims regarding their land rights, the protection of their cultural identity, and their desire for greater political autonomy. The Mapuche do have some resources for influencing government policy. With 800,000 people, they hold some electoral clout. Chile is one of only 22 countries that have ratified the United Nations' Indigenous and Tribal Peoples Convention (1989), which pledges to promote the rights of groups like the Mapuche. Also, the center-left coalition that dominated Chilean politics from 1988 to 2010 expressed some sympathy for the Mapuche claims. And in 1998, the Mapuche

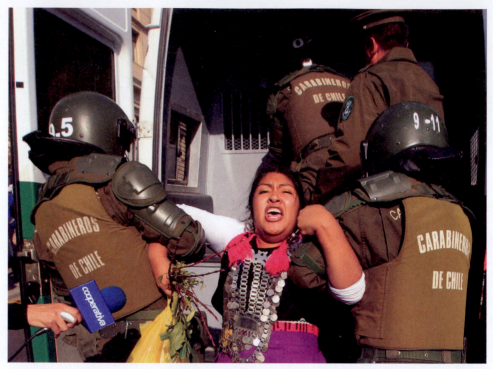

Outside Chile's Supreme Court, police arrest a Mapuche woman protesting the long sentences imposed on four Mapuche activists who had attacked police while asserting their land rights on a settler's farm.

established Coordinadora Arauco-Malleco (CAM), an interest group to coordinate their political actions.

However, the political forces lined up against the goals of the Mapuche are formidable. There are some elites in Chile who are directly opposed to the Mapuche's land claims. In particular, the wealthy landowners and multinational logging interests who currently hold Mapuche lands have considerable influence with key elected political leaders in the executive and legislative branches and with senior appointed officials in the administration. More broadly, the general Chilean population is not particularly sympathetic to the Mapuche claims that the national government should grant them political autonomy. Although they are a sizeable subgroup, the Mapuche constitute only 5 percent of the Chilean population, and most of them are poor, landless peasants who lack political skills or the will to mobilize into political action.

Thus, proposed legislation to expropriate land and return it to the Mapuche generated substantial opposition and was defeated in the legislature. Chile's president, who initially supported their claim, dropped his advocacy. As a concession, the government did purchase a small amount of land (20,000 acres), which was distributed to the Mapuche, but not the one million acres the Mapuche claim as their native lands. And the redistribution program was very limited, because most landowners demanded high prices to sell their land to the Mapuche and the government was unwilling to pay that amount or to force them to lower their price. Similarly, the government allocated only a modest amount of funds to support the maintenance of Mapuche cultural traditions.

Then in 2010, the coalition that gained a majority of the seats in the national legislature shifted to include several conservative groups, including Alianza por Chile, that promote a single national identity for all Chileans and insist that the government should aggressively punish the illegal activities of the Mapuche. Thus, the Mapuche remained frustrated by their lack of success in persuading government to respond favorably to their policy agenda. Since their policy demands have not been achieved through normal political channels, some of their activists continue to engage in unconventional political actions (Carruthers and Rodriguez 2009). This has included hunger strikes, demonstrations, and some violence. For example, a group of Mapuche occupied a farm that was being minimally used. When they refused to leave, the government was pressured by local landowners to intervene, and its security forces were dispatched to reclaim the property. The confrontation became violent, and an unarmed 22-year-old Mapuche student was shot in the back by the police. Between 2009 and 2013, the reported acts of violence in this conflict have increased tenfold (Henao 2013).

The center-left Chilean government elected in 2013 has attempted to calm the volatile situation. It has appointed special commissions to investigate the issues, proposed new policy initiatives, and returned a small amount of land. The government has made such decisions to satisfy the policy agendas of both the Mapuche and those who oppose their demands. But the Mapuche simply do not have as much political clout as their opponents. Thus, the political goals pursued by the "people of the land" remain largely unfulfilled and unpromising.

Recall from Chapter 1 that the core definitions of politics focus on the competition among individuals and groups who utilize power and influence to pursue their interests on issues controlled by public authorities. The attempts by the Mapuche to regain their lands and preserve their cultural autonomy are clearly within the domain of *res publica* in Chile. As the Mapuche engaged in politics, other groups that had a competing agenda also mobilized. Policy decisions were made by the government. The Mapuche got some of what they sought, but not much. Other groups seem to have been more successful.

Considering the story of the Mapuche raises one of the most obvious yet fascinating general questions in political science: *How does politics actually work?* That is, how does a political system handle the incredibly difficult and complicated issues and the competing demands that are the stuff of politics? How and why do actors in the political system decide to deal in one way or another on issues like these? Who has political power and influence, and how are they exercised?

If someone from another country asked you how major public policy decisions are made in your country, what would you say? What key points would you emphasize? Presumably, your response would include a discussion of certain important actors and how they utilize power and influence within the context of the key political institutions that make such public policy decisions.

Earlier chapters introduced many of these actors and institutions—political activists, interest groups, executives, legislatures, legal systems, and so on. And they characterized concepts such as power and analytic models such as the political system framework. This chapter expands the discussion by focusing explicitly on several fundamental approaches for analyzing public policy and the exercise of political power. Initially, the chapter explicates the concept of public policy, with a consideration of taxonomies and frameworks that characterize the public policy process. It then describes three basic theories (elite, class, and pluralist) that provide alternative explanations of how public policy decisions are made and how the distribution of power shapes that decision process.

Public Policy

9.1 **Differentiate among the types of public policy and outline the stages of public policy.**

A **public policy** is *any decision or action by a governmental authority that results in the allocation of something that is valued*. Earlier chapters indicated that each political system establishes how extensively and in what forms its public policies will define *res publica* and impact its environment. These public policy decisions range enormously: in substantive area, in scale, in significance, in the number of people affected, and in the role of the policymakers. A national government can decide to declare war on a rival country or to commend a victorious sports team. A local government employee can decide to fill a pothole or to issue a building permit to a homeowner. The government representatives of many countries can hammer out a joint treaty to limit greenhouse gases. A security unit can arrest a suspected terrorist. A government can pass a law making sex between certain consenting adults illegal. The Chilean government can decide to allocate some land to the Mapuche or to use force to drive them off someone's private property. Each of these actions is an example of a public policy.

Table 9.1 and Compare in 9 offer some representative examples of current public policy decisions made by seven national political systems. The Compare claims that there is considerable policy variation across these countries. Do you agree? Beyond these kinds of direct comparisons of public policies, there are several other approaches to the study of public policy. One approach is to classify and compare various *types* of public policies by means of a taxonomy. A second approach analyzes the various stages of the policy *process* and attempts to explain the dynamics at each stage. A third approach studies the *impacts* of a particular public policy because what matters, ultimately, is how (if at all) the policy makes a difference in the lives of individuals and groups. Finally, a fourth general approach is more *prescriptive*, evaluating what public policy ought to be implemented, given existing goals, conditions, and resources. We can start by considering the types of public policies.

Types of Public Policies

Several criteria are used to classify different types of public policies. For example, a straightforward classification of policies is based on the *functional area* that is served, such as education, health, transportation, trade, public safety, the environment, or

Table 9.1 Selected Public Policies in Seven National Political Systems

	Brazil	China	D.R. Congo	India	Russia	Sweden	United States
Policy on abortion	Only to save life or after rape	Yes, on multiple grounds	Only to save life	Yes, on multiple grounds	Yes, on multiple grounds	Yes, on multiple grounds	Yes, on multiple grounds; varies by state
Policy on death penalty	No, since 1889	Yes, for 60 crimes, ~2,000/year	Yes, but only 2 since 1995	Yes, but only 3 since 1995	Yes, for 30 crimes, ~10/year	No, since 1921	Yes, in 32 of 50 states, ~16/year
Mandatory military service	Yes	Yes, but not enforced	No	No	Yes	No	No

Sources: World Bank (2013);
http://www.un.org/esa/population/publications/abortion/doc/unitedstates.doc;
http://www.icj-cij.org/icjwww/ibasicdocuments/ibasictext/ibasicdeclarations.htm.
http://blog.foreignpolicy.com/posts/2013/01/03/india_is_a_death_penalty_country_again

defense. Alternatively, policies can be distinguished by the broad *objective of the policy*: (1) *Distributive* policies provide particular goods and services (e.g., the building and maintenance of a system of streets and highways); (2) *redistributive* policies explicitly transfer values from one group to another group (e.g., a policy that provides subsidized housing to those with limited financial resources); (3) *regulatory* policies limit actions (e.g., a policy that prohibits a woman from having an abortion); (4) *extractive* policies take resources from some actors (e.g., a sales tax on purchases); and (5) *symbolic* policies confer honor or disrepute on certain actors (e.g., a medal awarded to a soldier for bravery).

Compare in 9

Selected Public Policies in Seven Countries

Over time, do different political systems make substantially different public policy decisions? To explore this briefly, Table 9.1 provides examples of broad public policy decisions made by seven national political systems. The expenditure data are reported as the percentage of each country's total GDP (gross domestic product) that is allocated to a policy domain by all levels of government. This is an indicator of policy effort, given the country's overall wealth. The tax revenue measure is an extractive policy, while the other expenditure measures are distributive policies. The three non-monetary policies are regulatory, regarding certain rights and freedoms of individuals relative to state power.

The broadest conclusion from these data is that there are considerable differences in public policy decisions across the seven countries. On every specific policy domain, the country with the highest proportion allocates at least three times as much as the lowest. Each country has developed its own distinctive pattern of public policies, which are particularly grounded in the country's needs, wealth, and dominant political ideologies. For example, Sweden is a wealthy country that has a long tradition of democratic socialism and the provision of social welfare goods to its population (see Compare in 13). Thus, Sweden allocates a substantially higher proportion of its societal wealth through government spending than any of the other countries, with a particular focus on education and health care. To pay for all these public services, Sweden also collects the highest proportion of taxes. Sweden has progressive policies on abortion and capital punishment and stopped requiring military (or community) service in 2010.

It is also interesting to compare Brazil, Russia, India, and China, four of the five BRICS countries that are advancing toward global power status (see Chapter 15). Although each is attempting to project its power within its region and globally, the policy choices vary. Russia, which aims to reassert its military might, allocates far more of its total societal wealth to the military than the others. Brazil's government, in contrast, has decided to direct more national wealth to education and health spending than the other three countries.

The level of funds allocated is one way to compare policy decisions. It is also important to consider how the money is spent. For example, what are the key targets of health care spending (e.g., disease prevention, infant health, medical training, care for HIV-positive people, hospitals)? Is public spending on education emphasizing teachers' salaries or student-teacher ratios or educational technologies or...? The manner in which a public policy is implemented is also significant for policies that are not primarily measurable in terms of money. For instance, the Chinese government not only allows abortion, it has also aggressively encouraged and facilitated abortion in an attempt to control population growth. In contrast, legal abortion is severely limited in nominally Catholic Brazil and is a deeply controversial policy domain in the United States.

And while comparing policy outputs is meaningful, the most important comparisons might be of the *impacts* of policies. That is, what is the effect of public spending on health care on indicators such as life expectancy and infant mortality rates? Does an increased level of military spending seem to increase a country's security? Which groups carry the burden of taxes and which do not? Does spending in one policy area (e.g., health care) provide indirect benefits to another policy area (e.g., education)? What is the effect of the policy of capital punishment on crime if it is rarely used (as in India)? Table 9.1 and these kinds of questions should help you to see the rich and complex considerations that are relevant when you attempt to compare public policies within and across political systems.

Further Questions

1. On what public policy do you think it would be most interesting to study crossnational differences in policy implementation? Why? What might you learn?

2. Which two countries in Table 9.1 seem to have the most similar configuration of policy allocations?

Analysis of the Stages of the Policy Process

A different approach to policy analysis examines the *stages of the policy process—the sequence of actions from the inception of an idea for policy to the point at which the policy ceases to exist.* A policy can be analyzed at each stage: what actors participate, how they interact, how the policy is defined, and so on. Such an analysis might emphasize the generally rational weighing of evidence and arguments to reach a reasoned decision, or it might focus on the complex interactions among different actors who engage in a process of competition and compromise to reach a more political decision (Stone 2011). Many public policy analyses focus on one specific stage and explore the dynamics of that stage of policymaking in detail (Andersen 2011; Bardach 2011). Six stages are usually distinguished, as characterized in Figure 9.1 and described below. And to provide

Figure 9.1 The Stages of the Public Policy Process

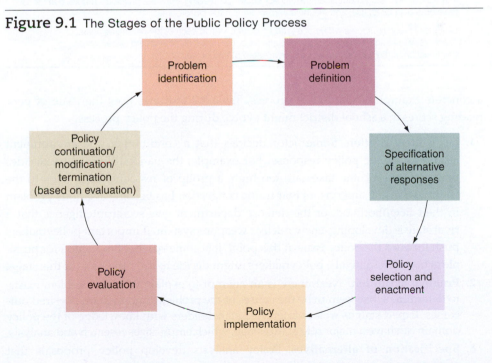

Table 9.2 An Example of Each Stage of the Policy Process: Reading Skills of Children

Stage	Action
Problem identification	Data indicate reading scores of children are too low.
Problem definition	Set goal: Raise mean reading scores of sixth-grade children by 10 percent in three years. Reading scores decline steadily from national average in grades 2–5. Low reading scores are especially associated with families in which English is not the first language. Lowest average reading scores are in seven schools where more than 20 percent of students come from such families.
Specification of alternatives	Target seven lowest-scoring schools or apply programs to all schools? Policy options: • Intensive reading instruction in grades 3–5. • Provide teachers with training in reading pedagogy. • Provide reading specialist teachers. • Provide computer-aided learning software. • Require an extra 30 minutes of reading instruction per day. • Or…
Policy selection	Local school board decides: • Focus only on seven lowest-scoring schools. • Provide three new reading specialists to work with students. • Allocate funds to seven target schools for computer-based reading instruction software.
Implementation	School superintendent meets with principals of target schools and they decide how to distribute the time of the reading specialists across the schools and classrooms. Committee of principals will select and hire specialists. Interschool technology committee trains teachers to use reading software, principals require teachers to develop a plan for its use, and teachers implement it in the classrooms.
Evaluation	Changes in reading scores will be analyzed by district staff in each of the next three years. Teachers will provide written report on the effects of the new initiatives on the classroom. Continuation of the two policies will be reevaluated at end of year 3.

a concrete example of the policy process, Table 9.2 indicates how the issue of poor reading scores in a school district might evolve during the policy process.

1. **Issue identification.** Some actor decides that a condition in the environment requires a public policy response. For example, the national legislature decides that personal income taxes are too high, a group of residents complains to the county board of supervisors that traffic congestion has become a serious problem in their neighborhood, or the defense department gets secret intelligence that a rival state is developing a new nuclear weapons system. If important policymakers push forward the policy issue at this point, it becomes part of the agenda for possible action. Alternatively, policymakers might decide to drop the issue at this stage.

2. **Problem definition.** Next, there is an attempt to explain why the problem exists, to determine what seem to be the causes of the problem, and to define desired outcomes. Expert staff as well as interested stakeholders with knowledge of the policy domain can have a major role at this stage, which emphasizes research and analysis.

3. **Specification of alternatives.** Policy analysts develop policy proposals that seem to respond to the problem, given the causes, the preferred outcome, and the likely obstacles. In addition, the resources necessary to implement each policy

alternative are identified. The costs (e.g., financial, political, organizational) of each alternative policy must be estimated, as well as the level of expected benefits.

4. **Policy selection.** Decision makers study the alternatives, trying to assess the possible costs and benefits from the options. At this stage, the process will be some mix of political, financial, and technical considerations. The decision might be to enact a particular policy, to delay, or to do nothing and see if the policy issue disappears from the public agenda. Considerable negotiations, lobbying, compromises, and adjustments to the proposed policy might occur during this stage.

5. **Implementation.** The policy is now interpreted and applied in specific contexts. Those in relevant administrative positions typically take the lead role, determining how to translate the new policy into actual programs and activities, organize the necessary resources, and then deliver those programs.

6. **Evaluation.** After some period of time (or never), new information is gathered to ascertain whether the policy has had any of the anticipated impacts, whether conditions (related to the policy domain or the political situation) have changed, and whether any unintended effects of the policy must be considered.

At any stage, but especially after implementation or evaluation, the policy might be continued, modified, or terminated. This is best understood as a variation of stage 4, since it is a version of policy enactment rather than a distinct stage. It is also possible that the circumstances might trigger another cycle of the policy process outlined above, possibly beginning with a new stage of problem identification.

Policy Impact Analysis

The last stage of the policy process described above, evaluation, is an especially significant mode of policy analysis. As noted in the Compare in 9, a crucial question is: What difference did the policy make? This can be considered in different ways. What have been the direct effects of the policy? Have there also been notable indirect effects? Who benefits and who experiences negative effects from this policy? What are the nature and extent of those benefits and burdens? What have been the actual costs compared with the anticipated costs? On balance, has the policy improved the overall situation? These questions about the impacts of a policy might be addressed by policymakers and their staffs or by various other actors, such as interest groups, affected publics, and political rivals.

Policy Prescription

Every public policy affects someone's interests. Thus, there are always actors (stakeholders) trying to influence and shape public policy decisions at every stage and to influence policymakers to make some decisions and not others. As actors define and then pursue a policy goal, they are also engaged in *policy prescription*. Their policy goal might be based on careful policy analysis and policy impact studies, derived from ideological principles, or influenced by an agent of political socialization or an authority source such as a political party or political leader (recall Chapters 2– 4). Whatever the basis of their policy prescriptions, policy advocates propose what public policies *should* be adopted and how policy *should* be implemented: The Chilean government should respond to the land claims of the Mapuche by policy A; the U.S. government should implement policy B to respond to job losses; the government of India should adopt policy C to improve the health of its millions of rural poor.

A key analytic question regarding the public policy process is: How does the process lead to certain decisions and not others? The next section explores this question from three very different perspectives that attempt to explain how political power is distributed and wielded by various groups who participate in the policymaking process.

Explaining Public Policy Decision Making

9.2   Identify three major approaches that explain public policymaking.

The first part of this chapter described analytic concepts that specify the stages in the public policy process. This section details three political explanations of the public policy process: (1) the elite approach; (2) the class approach; and (3) the pluralist approach. Each approach provides a different explanation of how politics works, how influence is exercised, and what forces seem to shape the decisions that result in public policy. Each focuses on the interactions among aggregations of individuals who use the political system to pursue their own particular interests. No actual country or political system is likely to operate exactly like any of these three approaches. Rather, each approach is a rich illustration of a pattern of power and decision making that is prevalent in some systems. Our discussion begins with the elite approach.

The Elite Approach

9.3   Characterize the elite approach.

Key Concepts

Two key concepts are central to the **elite approach**. First, *politics* is defined as *the struggle for power to control policy*. Second, the political world is characterized by *political stratification*; that is, *the population is segmented into separate groups that are in layers (or "strata") with higher or lower amounts of power*. In the elite approach, there are only two major strata. The stratum that *does more of what there is to do* (in the public policy process) and that *gets more of what there is to get* (in valued impacts from policy decisions) is called the **political elite**. The stratum that *does less and gets less* is called the *mass*.

Elite theory can be visually represented by a power pyramid, as shown in Figure 9.2. Such a depiction emphasizes that the elite is composed of a relatively small number of individuals who are in a dominant position on top of the large mass. Notice that there is a third stratum between the elite and the mass. This is the *political understructure*, composed of *political officials and administrators who carry out the elite's policy directives*.

Figure 9.2 Characterization of an Elite System

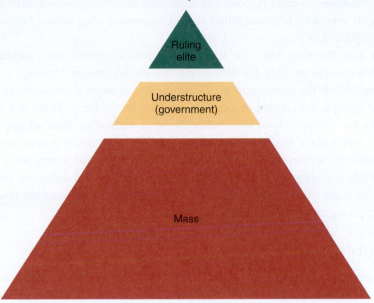

Major Theorists

The elite approach is particularly grounded in the writings of European political theorists of the late nineteenth century, especially the Italians Roberto Michels, Wilfredo Pareto, and Gaetano Mosca. In *The Ruling Class* (1896/2011), Mosca analyzes the political histories of a variety of political systems and concludes that they all have two strata: the political class (the elite) and the nonpolitical class (the mass). The political class controls all political functions, holds almost all political power, and dominates the public policy process. The basis of elite power has varied across time and location, but Mosca identifies broad historical stages during which the primary basis of elite domination has been military power, then religious control, then economic power, and most recently, technical knowledge. According to Mosca, the major role of the political system is as an instrument of the political class, serving the elite's interests in making and implementing public policies.

A well-known U.S. application of the elite approach is *The Power Elite* (2000) by C. Wright Mills. Mills concludes that the power elite in U.S. society is composed of those who control society's most powerful institutions: (1) the "warlords" in the military establishment; (2) the "corporation chieftains" in the economic sector; and (3) the "political directorate" in the top positions in the political system. Mills observes that the members of the elite share crucial values about how society in general, and the political system in particular, ought to operate. The members of the elite tend to come from similar social and educational backgrounds, to circulate among major positions in each of the three key institutional structures, and to have long-standing personal relationships with one another. Like other elite theorists, Mills does not claim that the elite operates as a conspiracy that continually plots to retain control. But some of its active members do meet periodically to discuss common interests, and most of its members act in concert to protect their shared interests during times of crisis (see also Domhoff 2005, 2013).

Most elite theorists focus on the elite itself—the identity and socialization of elite members—and on how the elite maintains its domination through a variety of techniques, such as the manipulation of symbols, the strategic distribution of resources to various groups, the control of the state, and the use of force. There is a normative element in the discussions of many elite theorists, indicating their disapproval of a system in which there is such a high concentration of political power serving only a small minority within society. But others respond that elite theory merely reveals the inevitable tendency for a few people to take control of and dominate the political order, while those in the mass willingly subordinate themselves to the few who are capable of giving coherence to political society.

The Public Policy Process

The process through which values are allocated is explained primarily in terms of the elite's actions. Some members of the elite decide that a particular public policy decision is in the elite's interest. They then discuss whether this policy should be enacted and how it should be implemented. When there is general consensus among those members of the elite who are concerned about the decision, representatives of the elite instruct the relevant members of the understructure (the government) to perform the policymaking and policy-implementation activities that serve the elite's interests.

In the elite explanation of the policy process, the active elites are subject to very little direct influence from the mass or even from the understructure of governmental officials. The mass is politically apathetic and impotent, and this large proportion of the population passively accepts whatever policies are imposed upon them. The members of the understructure follow the elite's directives because they believe that their survival in positions of authority depends on the power and support of the elite.

The Prevalence of Elite-Based Political Systems

How many countries have elitist political systems? More than half of the countries have nondemocratic systems (Economist Intelligence Unit 2013, and recall Chapter 7). It seems reasonable to infer that most of these systems are dominated by an elite in the manner described by the elite approach.

However, the issue might be more complicated. Is it true that all the key conditions of elitism are met in every nondemocratic country? This empirical question could be examined in specific political systems (e.g., Cuba, Saudi Arabia, and Zimbabwe) by assessing these kinds of analytic questions:

- Does the political leadership act with unanimity on all major issues?
- Is there active and effective political participation by nonelite groups?

Focus in 9

Elite Politics in Swaziland

A contemporary example of elite politics is Swaziland, a small African country between Mozambique and South Africa. While Swaziland was a British colonial protectorate (1902–1968), a local king (Sobhuza II) became a hero of his people by leading the movement for independence (starting in 1921). After independence in 1968, Sobhuza became the ruling monarch of the new country. A British-style parliament with competing parties was installed. Parties competed in three parliamentary elections, although the king's party dominated in each election.

In 1973, the king banned all opposition groups and declared that European government forms were "un-Swazi." The king personally appoints two-thirds of the members of the Senate and one-fourth of the members of the House. Indeed, according to Swaziland's official publications, even the method for selecting the next king is "a secret," except it is stipulated that he must be a young, unmarried prince. When Sobhuza II died in 1982, the private power struggle among members of the royal family and the king's council resulted in the selection of King Mswati III. He has been termed "the world's last absolute monarch," and although a few concessions to opposition activities were made in recent years, political parties are still essentially banned and the nonpartisan parliament essentially affirms the king's decisions.

Everyone in Swaziland (population 1.4 million) has always understood that real political power is concentrated in the king and his elite group of advisers, known as the National Council. Young King Mswati III quickly removed many of his rivals from positions of authority and elevated his own set of trusted advisers to positions of decision-making power. Under King Mswati III, as under King Sobhuza, both policymaking and the major sectors of the economy (the mines and most farmlands) are directly controlled by a king's council. Thus, one key criterion of elite politics is clearly met: Almost all major political decisions are made by a small group, and the mass of people in Swaziland have little direct impact on the policies or politics of the state.

A day after being called back from high school in England and being crowned as the ruler of Swaziland, King Mswati III attends a party in the palace. The 18-year-old king moved quickly to establish rule under his personal control.

Most of the benefits of policy are enjoyed by this elite, a second key criterion of an elite system. The richest 10 percent of the Swazi population have one of the world's highest shares of total income (40 percent), and the country has a high level of income inequality (recall Figure 8.4). In contrast, 69 percent of the Swazi population is below the poverty line and 40 percent of adults are unemployed. Swaziland has the world's highest incidence (one in four) of adults with HIV/AIDS, and the average life expectancy is only 50 years, among the bottom five among all countries (CIA 2014).

Further Focus

1. Is inequality or nondemocracy likely to be a more serious problem for maintaining stability in Swaziland?

2. Are there any reasons why a country might be better off if it is governed by a small elite?

- Are some major political decisions responsive to nonelite demands, even when the decisions are contrary to the elite's interests?
- Is there dramatic inequality in the distribution of resources between the elite and the mass?

While definitive answers to these questions are difficult, our knowledge of political systems suggests that many contemporary states are generally characterized by elite rule. (Consider the brief description of Swaziland in Focus in 9). The power to make crucial political decisions and most of the benefits from those decisions seem predominantly concentrated in the hands of a small elite.

It is also possible to ask whether a country classified as a democracy is actually run by an elite. That is, even if a political system meets the basic criteria of democracy such as a limited mandate and freedom to criticize and oppose the leadership (recall Chapter 7), does this necessarily mean that the system is not elitist?

This question underlies a fierce debate among analysts regarding whether the elite approach best describes politics, even in many democratic political systems. Some, such as C. Wright Mills (2000; see also Parenti 2010), provide arguments and evidence that there is elite rule even in most democracies. In this view, a small proportion of the population dominates most significant political decisions and enjoys a hugely disproportionate share of the benefits from the truly important policy decisions made by the government.

Such empirical assessments of the elite approach, whether for a single city or an entire country, are highly controversial and ideologically charged because they represent a direct attack on whether the place is a democracy. Conclusive verification of the elite approach in most political systems would be a massive undertaking, requiring the documentation of systematic elite dominance on a large number of key decisions across a variety of issue areas.

The Class Approach

9.4 **Characterize the class approach.**

The **class approach** shares certain fundamental concepts with the elite approach, but it offers a very different explanation of the continuing dynamic processes of politics. The most important shared concept is *stratification*, the basic fact of *structured inequality* in the distribution of values in society.

The strata identified in the class approach are called classes, the second key concept. *Class* denotes *a large group of individuals who are similar in their possession of or control over some fundamental value*. The most fundamental value that distinguishes classes differs for different class theorists. Karl Marx (1818–1883), the best-known class theorist, differentiates classes primarily on the basis of a group's relationship to the major factors of production in the economic system (Marx 1867/1981: Ch. 52). At the simplest level, Marx divides society into two classes: (1) the *capitalist class*, which includes those who own significant amounts of the major factors of production (especially financial resources, raw materials, and capital—the elements to produce goods and accumulate wealth); and (2) the *proletariat class*, which includes those who own little more than their own labor.

Some contemporary analysts suggest various modifications to Marx's ideas about class. First, most class theorists identify more than two major class strata, with each class characterized by its particular levels of social, political, and economic power. Second, some argue that it is *control* (rather than ownership) of the means of production that is most important. Third, others observe that in certain social systems, the key elements that distinguish different class strata are status, kinship, ethnicity, religion, or tradition-based authority (rather than ownership of the means of production). And fourth, still others posit that possession of information resources and knowledge has become the crucial resource distinguishing classes in postindustrial, high-tech societies (Castells 2009). In general, these analysts assert that there is strong empirical evidence for the continuing prevalence of class politics, even in developed countries and even in the twenty-first century (see, for example, Poulantzas 1973; Wright 2005; Wright and Rogers 2010).

Figure 9.3 provides two models characterizing class systems. Part A shows a characterization similar to the elite approach in its hierarchical and pyramidal form, and it emphasizes a clear separation between multiple classes. Alternatively, part B highlights the overlap among classes. Here the boundaries between classes are permeable rather than distinct, there is more interdependence among classes, and some members of a "lower" class have as much or even more political power than those in the class

---

Figure 9.3 Two Different Characterizations of Class Structures

SOURCE: Based on Bill and Hardgrave 1981: 181.

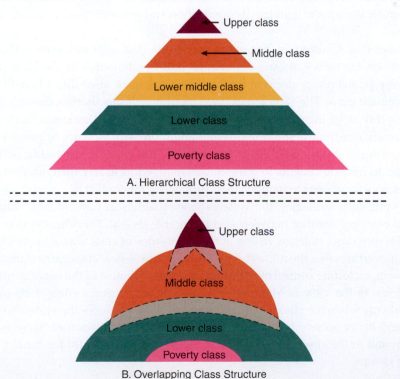

A. Hierarchical Class Structure

B. Overlapping Class Structure

above them. However, class domination continues to be the basic form of political and social relations (see Lenski 1984).

The third crucial concept of the class approach is *class conflict*. It is assumed that classes lower in the class system can increase their share of key values only at the expense of the classes above them. Given the fundamental inequalities in the distribution of values, struggle between classes is inevitable. The higher classes employ various strategies, and ultimately coercion, to prevent a significant loss of values (and of relative advantage) to the classes below them. Lower classes find that only violence enables their class to increase its relative share of values. Thus, class conflict is systematic and ubiquitous, although its most visible and violent manifestations (such as strikes, riots, and rebellion) might be suppressed for periods of time if the higher classes are effective in the ways they distribute benefits and use coercion.

The Public Policy Process

Most class analysts do not explain in detail how policy decisions are actually made. They assume that the common interests shared by members of a class will result in general consensus within that class regarding what public policy decisions should be enacted. Like elite theorists, class analysts view the political system as a set of structures that are subordinate to the dominant class. Thus, members of this dominant class either hold key positions of governing authority or directly control those who do. The interests of this class are well understood by those who can enact public policy. Consequently, the policies and actions of the state serve the interests of the dominant class, which attempts to maintain its domination and preserve the existing distribution of values.

Rather than focusing on the policy process, the class approach centers its analytic attention on the tactics of class domination and the dynamics of the class struggle. Not every public policy decision by the state is coercive or of direct benefit to only the dominant class. The state might implement policies to shorten the length of the working day or to increase health care benefits to the middle classes. Such policies either ameliorate the worst conditions that might provoke violence or provide certain classes with advantages over classes below them. The goals of such public policies are strategic: to provide benefits to some classes in an effort to buy their support or their acquiescence, or at least to dampen their propensity for conflict.

Despite such strategies, the systematic inequalities in fundamental values generate continuing conflict between classes in the society. Periodically, this conflict explodes into class violence. In one of these episodes of class war, a lower class succeeds in overthrowing the highest class. At this point, a new class gains dominance in the system, including control over the government and most of the benefits from public policies. In the view of Marx and many other class theorists, major class conflict will end only when the elimination of dominant classes reduces the system to a single class, and hence society becomes classless. The state's policies then serve everyone equally, and in the absence of class inequalities, there is no cause for further conflict among groups.

The Pluralist Approach

9.5 Characterize the pluralist approach.

Pluralism offers a very different account of the political process, in which *multiple groups compete actively in the pursuit of their political interests*. The pluralist approach is grounded in the concept of the ***group***, which is defined as *any aggregate of individuals who interact to pursue a common interest*. A political group, as an analytic concept, exists whenever individuals have a shared interest regarding some allocation of values by the political system.

The pluralist explanation of politics as a complex web of group interactions has many historical roots but is particularly identified with American social scientists, especially political scientists Arthur Bentley (1908/1967), David Truman (1951), and Robert Dahl (1961, 1971, 1991), who is most strongly associated with the development and defense of pluralism (which is also sometimes termed polyarchy or the group approach).

Pluralism begins with the assumption that an individual's *group memberships are multiple and nonoverlapping*. That is, any particular individual can belong to many different groups. Individuals are not stratified into large, permanent groups as described by the elite and class approaches because the aggregation of people who share a common identity on one political interest is not the same as the people who are part of groups formed for other political interests. Table 9.3 shows six hypothetical people whose group memberships overlap in different ways, depending on the issue.

The second important assumption is that *many different* **political resources** *might influence those who make public policy decisions*. As discussed in Chapter 3, the kinds of resources that might be used to influence political stratification include money, numbers of supporters/voters, monopoly of expertise, political skill, access to information, legal rights, and status. It is also assumed that every individual (and hence every political group) has some political resources with which he can attempt to influence policy decisions.

Table 9.3 Group Memberships of Six Hypothetical Individuals in the United States*

Groups	Person 1	Person 2	Person 3	Person 4	Person 5	Person 6
Democratic Party	✓				✓	
Republican Party		✓	✓			
AFL-CIO union	✓					
Family Research Council			✓			✓
Mothers Against Drunk Driving		✓			✓	✓
NARAL Pro-Choice America	✓	✓				
National Rifle Association	✓		✓			
Parent-Teacher Association	✓	✓				

*Each checkmark indicates a group with which the individual is affiliated. This distribution supports the concept of nonoverlapping (nonreinforcing) group memberships. An individual shares membership with different people across various groups and policy domains.

In pluralism, **politics** can be understood as *the interaction among groups that are pursuing their political interests*. The role of the government is to manage the interactions within this giant system of interacting groups. Thus, **public policy** is defined as *the balance point of the competition among groups on an issue at the time when government makes a policy decision*.

The Policymaking Process

Figure 9.4 provides a visual model of how a policy decision is made according to pluralism, using health care policy in a country such as the United States as the example. There is a continuum of possible policies, ranging from free state provision of all health care services to every citizen at one extreme to total private provision based on fee-for-service to each recipient of health care at the other extreme.

The analytic framework of the policy process in pluralism can be summarized in five major steps:

1. Identify the key groups that have an active interest in decisions in this policy area.
2. On a continuum of possible policy outcomes, locate the preferred policy decision of each group.
3. Estimate the level of political resources each group employs to influence the decision regarding this policy (represented as a "weight" on the continuum, based on the total impact of the political resources that the group utilizes).
4. The government establishes the equilibrium point that balances the "weights" of the political resources mobilized by all groups.
5. This equilibrium point on the policy continuum is authorized by government as a public policy decision.

Figure 9.4 A Group Approach Model of the Policy Process: A Hypothetical Policy Decision

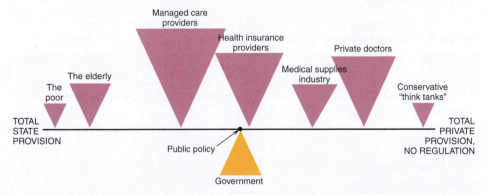

Symbols:
— = Continuum of possible public policies regarding health care policy
▼ = Interest group mobilized on this issue, with volume of triangle representing the group's political resources applied to the issue
▲ = Government, which determines the equilibrium point and ratifies that point as public policy
• = Public policy position, which is the equilibrium point in the competition among groups, given each group's political resources

In the pluralist model, the particular functions of the government are to (1) establish rules of the game for the group struggle; (2) determine the interests of competing groups and the levels of political resources mobilized by those groups; (3) find a public policy that approximately balances the positions of all active groups in terms of their interests and resources; (4) enact these balance points as public policy decisions; and (5) implement the resulting policy. Government, as an analytic construct in pluralism, is best understood as a referee (a neutral arbiter) in the competition among groups.

Can we talk?: In many societies, local policy decisions are made through discussion and group voting, as in this jirga (tribal meeting) in southeastern Afghanistan.

In a more realistic interpretation, however, government is not merely an automatic weighing machine that totals the value of each group's influence resources. The government might have an ideological position and thus place greater emphasis on some objectives rather than others. For example, the government might enforce rules that help or hinder some groups in using their political resources, it might value some political resources more substantially than others, it might allow certain groups greater access to important information, or it might be more or less willing to find the financial resources necessary to implement a certain policy. In addition, certain elected and career governmental actors have their own personal and institutional interests (e.g., for political support, growth of their unit's power, personal wealth). When such interests are relevant, these actors can become active as groups that participate in the decision process (with obvious advantages because they are inside "the system").

Like all models, Figure 9.4 substantially simplifies reality. But it should help you understand the logic of pluralism. A policy decision can change at any time if a different distribution of group interests is mobilized and the issue is taken up by policymakers. Pluralism explicitly rejects the notion that a small elite or a single class dominates the public policy process. Rather, many different groups become active in politics, but only on the narrow range of issues relevant to their interests. Mobilized groups use their political resources to affect the decision. While a group might not always win, its participation can affect the policy decisions on which it is active. In the case that opened the chapter, for example, it seems that although the Mapuche only got a small part of what they wanted, they did utilize their political resources and the Chilean government did grant them some land rights. And, pluralist theorists would argue, the Mapuche achieved some success against strong opponents (including major political parties) and will have more opportunities to pursue their goals at the next round of policymaking.

Critics of pluralism argue that some groups *are* likely to win almost every time they play the game of politics because they have a huge advantage in their political resources, such as wealth, access to decision makers, and political skill. Further, some challenge the pluralist assumption that no one resource always dominates, arguing that money trumps all other resources. This argument is the subject of the Debate in 9. The critics also claim that the government/state, far from being neutral, is guided by a strong ideology and is almost always responsive to those upper-strata groups with most economic and social power in the society. Thus, even though "the little people" might occasionally win a particular episode, the powerful groups in the system are persistent winners, and big winners, and the system perpetuates very substantial inequalities in the distribution of benefits (Bachrach and Baratz 1962; Parenti 2010). While the relatively poor Mapuche were appeased with a small amount of land, the big winners were the rich and powerful landowners and logging companies, who continued to profit from land that should have been returned to its original owners.

The Debate in 9

Does Money Dominate the Policymaking Process?

Some are convinced that money dominates politics, even in the most properly run democracies. Class theory is particularly pointed in its arguments that the power and actions of the dominant economic class ensure that government and policy decisions serve its interests (Domhoff 2013). In contrast, pluralist theory argues that while money is one important resource that can influence the policy process, no one resource dominates. Other key political resources that can shape policy decisions include large numbers of people who can use their votes, the media, and the legal system. Everyone can form interest groups to promote their political goals. Everyone can win in the competition over policy decisions (at least some of the time), and the wealthy do not get everything they want (Dahl 1961, 1991). If we consider the country celebrated as the inspiration and model of pluralist democracy, the United States, does money dominate policymaking?

Money Dominates Policymaking

- Most of those in positions of substantial power in the government, whether in the executive,

legislative or judicial branch, are among the wealthiest 3 percent of the society. Government cannot be understood as a neutral referee in the policy process when so many of those who make policy decisions are from and share the interests of the monied class (Parenti 2010: 197–200).

- Politicians at all levels depend on increasingly large amounts of money to finance their (re)election campaigns. Those who contribute significant funds to elected officials have the greatest access to elected officials and can make successful demands on their decisions.

- Corporations and wealthy individuals far outspend others in society in hiring lobbyists, funding policy advocates, sponsoring think tanks, and purchasing media content that both promote their interests and influence the beliefs and actions of government officials and voters (Bagdikian 2004; Phillips 2003).

- The ultimate test of public policy is: Who benefits most? Whenever financial considerations are a key factor in a policy debate, it is almost always the wealthy who enjoy the greatest benefits from the enacted policy. For example, between 1979 and 2007, the richest 10 percent of Americans gained 91 percent of all income growth, and favorable government tax policies are a key to this disproportionate distribution of benefits (Economic Policy Institute 2011).

- Justice might seem blind, but seeking justice is not free. Most legal disputes on matters of public policy involve interpretation of laws and discretionary decision making. The balance is typically weighted in favor of those who can afford the best legal representation (Parenti 2010: Ch. 9).

Money Does Not Dominate Policymaking

- In a pluralist democracy, votes and elections count (Dahl 1961). As median voter theory posits, the policies of government officials will generally be responsive to the interests of those with sufficient votes to determine their electoral success. And it is voting coalitions of the numerous citizens from the middle and lower classes that determine the outcome of elections, not the votes of the relatively small number of rich people (Stone 1989).

- Prolific spending in a campaign or in lobbying the government does not guarantee victory. There are a significant number of instances in every electoral cycle in which a candidate or a ballot proposition is victorious despite being outspent during the campaign. Similarly, heavy spending by interest groups is not always correlated with policy success (Baumgartner et al. 2009; Edwards, Wattenberg, and Lineberry 2014).

- There are many political interest groups that are composed largely of members who are not part of the wealthiest 10–20 percent. But these groups organize, aggregate their political resources, and prevail on policy issues of major importance (e.g., education, equality, abortion, immigration, workers' rights, and social welfare programs) (Dahl 1991).

- Many powerful elected and appointed policymakers, including seven of the last nine U.S. presidents, are from modest backgrounds. Some of them, as well as some political leaders with considerable wealth, have been powerful advocates for those with limited wealth and social standing (e.g., Bill Clinton, L. B. Johnson, the Kennedys, Barack Obama).

- In the U.S. legal system, justice is "money blind." The interpretation of law is based on the principles of justice and fairness. If an actor has legality on his side, he will usually prevail in protecting his interests, regardless of his economic situation. Litigation often protects the less advantaged against those with "deep pockets" in numerous policy domains (e.g., civil rights, environmental protection) (Robinson 2009; Schmalleger 2011).

More questions…

1. Can you think of compelling examples of policy decisions in which, as pluralist theory posits, groups utilize other political resources to defeat groups who deploy substantially more financial resources?

2. Is there any potent political resource that money can't buy?

The Three Approaches Compared

9.6 Evaluate the similarities, differences, and usefulness of the three major approaches to public policymaking.

Which Approach Is Correct?

The three approaches offer compelling answers to the basic political questions of who gets what, why, when, and how. Which of these three approaches is correct? Is one the most accurate explanation of politics for all political systems? For most political systems at a given historical moment? Do different approaches best account for the politics of particular systems? For particular types of issues?

Advocates of each position offer both theoretical and empirical evidence to show that the politics of actual systems correspond to the description provided in their approach. As an indirect method of providing support for their approach, advocates also cite considerable evidence indicating the inaccuracies and contradictions of the other approaches. As you might suspect, the debate has been most acrimonious between supporters of pluralism and supporters of the elite and class approaches, which both assume persistent stratification and deep inequality. Some scholars contend that almost all political systems, even democratic ones, are elitist in the sense that the policy process is guided by and generally supports the interests of a dominant elite (Domhoff 2013). In the United States, the debate has been most intense among those who study power at the local level, prompted by the dispute five decades ago between "elitists" such as sociologist Floyd Hunter (1953) and "pluralists" such as political scientist Robert Dahl (1961).

Political scientists and other social scientists have yet to establish a critical test that reveals which of the approaches best describes or explains politics. After hundreds of studies in various political systems at the local, regional, and national levels, the disagreements among the advocates of the three approaches remain as deep as ever. To decide which approach provides the greatest insight into the politics of a particular political system, you might consider numerous conceptual and empirical questions, a few of which follow:

- For the *elite approach*, look for: evidence of actual collaboration among the elite in the formulation of public policy; the frequency with which the elite seems to lose on policy decisions of significance to its members; whether there really is a mass of citizens who are uninformed, politically inactive, and impotent regarding policy choices.

- For the *class approach*, analyze: whether the state almost always operates to serve the interests of one dominant class group; whether most people's interests and behaviors can be defined in class terms; whether most significant social changes are attributable to violence grounded in class conflict.

- And for *pluralism*, assess: whether there are persistent winners and persistent losers on policy decisions; whether the state applies rules and policies fairly and equally to all groups; whether competition among groups can be fair if there are huge inequalities in the levels of political resources available to different individuals and groups.

Essential Similarities and Differences

The elite and class approaches share certain crucial premises. For both approaches, the fundamental feature of society is stratification—the unequal distribution of values across distinct groups. Also in both approaches, the government is one of the key mechanisms controlled by the dominant group, and the government's policy decisions are intended to maintain that group's domination.

But the elite and class approaches differ in their conceptions of the nature of the groups and of group interactions. For the elite approach, there are two broad groups:

the elite and the mass. Elite theorists mainly focus on the elite—its membership, the basis of elite domination, and the strategies employed by the elite to maintain its control. The mass is assumed to be inactive politically and is rarely analyzed in detail.

In contrast, most class theorists identify more than two distinct class groups and emphasize the dynamic interactions among the classes. There is substantial political energy inherent in the lower classes, who are the active agents of major political change. The class approach attempts to explain why class conflict is inevitable, how it manifests itself, and how it produces transformations in the sociopolitical system. In short, the elite approach tends to provide a top-down perspective in a two-group system, whereas the class approach often takes a bottom-up perspective that emphasizes the dynamic processes of conflict and change among multiple groups.

Pluralism differs fundamentally from both the elite and class approaches, beginning with its rejection of the notion of social stratification. It conceptualizes a sociopolitical world composed of many groups, with each individual belonging to a variety of groups. Different groups emerge on each particular political issue, and each group has an array of resources that it can organize to influence decisions on that issue. As groups compete to shape a public policy decision, the government is a relatively neutral referee that ensures the competition is fair; it is not the instrument of any particular group or class. There is a dispersion of power, resources, and benefits from policy decisions, not a pattern of structured inequality. Everyone wins some and loses some, but the losers can always win on the next issue.

Vigorous and often hostile debate has persisted among the advocates of these three conceptions of how politics works. This debate is deep and serious because it reflects fundamental disagreements about the very nature of society and politics. The elite and class approaches are based on a *coercive view of society*. Conflict is a fundamental feature of the relations among groups. Social coherence is maintained by means of power and constraint, evident in domination by the most powerful class and its agent, the state. In contrast, pluralism reflects an *integrative view of society*. Society is essentially stable and harmonious in the sense that there is a moving equilibrium maintained by a "fair" competitive game, refereed by the state and played by many groups who accept the rules and the outcomes. Social coherence is grounded in cooperation and consensus (see Dahrendorf 1959).

The analytic taxonomies and stage model presented in the first part of this chapter offer a different way of understanding the public policy process. Those approaches tend to focus on providing an in-depth, empirical account of the dynamics during a particular stage of the process (e.g., implementation of health care policy) or the analysis of a specific policy domain (e.g., the impacts of tax policy, the case for military action in a particular setting). There is an attempt to define how political institutions shape the process and to explore the behavior and interactions among various stakeholders.

The various approaches to public policy analysis presented in this chapter provide you with a rich set of alternatives for responding to Harold Lasswell's (1960) classic question about politics: Who gets what, when, how, (and why)? Public policy analysis provides some additional useful tools in the political science quest to better understand the actions of any particular political system, its power structure, and its decision-making processes. Policy analysis can also be employed to determine the most desirable response to a given problem, providing a prescriptive policy recommendation. These descriptive, explanatory, and prescriptive insights about the public policy process will be helpful as we consider countries' pursuit of prosperity, stability, and security in the remaining chapters of this book.

Key Concepts

class, p. 244
class approach, p. 244
class conflict, p. 246
elite approach, p. 240
group, p. 247

mass, p. 240
pluralism, p. 247
political elite, p. 240
political resources, p. 247
political stratification, p. 240

political understructure, p. 240
politics, p. 248
public policy, p. 248
stages of the policy process, p. 237

For Further Consideration

1. What do you think is the single most important flaw in the assumptions or knowledge claims of the elite approach? The class approach? Pluralism?

2. How might someone who embraces the class approach and someone who accepts the pluralist approach debate the public policy decisions associated with the Mapuche presented in the chapter-opening case? How might the pluralist approach account for a case like Swaziland, described in Focus in 9?

3. In a sense, all political systems are elitist because a few govern and many are governed. Does this observation seem accurate? Is it a persuasive basis for confirming the validity of the elite approach?

4. List six groups that have a political agenda and with which you have a membership or a strong identity. Ask a variety of friends to provide you with a similar list. How much overlap is there in your group affiliations? Does this seem to support the pluralist tenet of nonoverlapping memberships? (To undertake a more complete test, you would need to survey many individuals from a variety of backgrounds.)

For Further Reading

Allison, Graham, and Philip Zelikow. (1999). *The Essence of Decision: Explaining the Cuban Missile Crisis.* **2nd ed. New York: Longman.** This revised edition of Allison's seminal case study of the Cuban missile crisis in 1961 offers a superb presentation of three important models of the policy decision process that differ from those described in this chapter. These models emphasize: (1) "rational choice" by decision makers who engage in a dispassionate cost–benefit analysis of the expected utilities of different actions (see the Appendix); (2) "organizational processes" by which institutional routines shape policy due to actors' adherence to simple problem-solving strategies and standard operating procedures; and

(3) "bureaucratic politics," whereby stakeholders' behaviors and choices are based on their personal values and the imperatives of their particular roles.

Anderson, James E. (2015). *Public Policymaking: An Introduction.* **8th ed. Kentucky: Cengage.** A solid text introducing the field of public policy analysis, with chapters focusing on the stages of the policy analysis framework presented in the first part of this chapter.

Balulis, Joseph, and Vickie Sullivan, eds. (1996). *Shakespeare's Political Pageant: Essays in Politics and Literature.* **Lanham, MD: Rowman & Littlefield.** These articles offer a rich exploration of how the interplay of politics, power, and human nature is illuminated in the extraordinary plays of William Shakespeare.

Burki, Shahid J. (1991). *Pakistan Under the Military: Eleven Years of Zia ul-Haq.* **Boulder, CO: Westview.** A detailed description of elite rule in Pakistan under an authoritarian regime.

Castles, Francis. (1999). *Comparative Public Policy: Patterns of Post-war Transformation.* **Northampton, MA: Edward Elgar Publishers.** A careful comparison of the development of 12 key public policy domains in many of the advanced democracies, spanning 30 years.

Chadwick, Andrew, and Philip Howard, eds. (2008). *The Routledge Handbook of Internet Politics.* **New York: Routledge.** An excellent selection of analyses regarding the interplay between politics and the Internet, considering the links of the Internet to political behavior, government institutions, public policy, and the law.

Dahl, Robert. (1961). *Who Governs?: Democracy in an American City.* **New Haven, CT: Yale University Press.** This remains the classic theoretical and empirical statement of pluralism as an explanation of politics and the policy process.

Domhoff, G. William. (2013). *Who Rules America?: The Triumph of the Corporate Rich.*

7th **ed. Boston: McGraw-Hill.** The author updates Mills's *The Power Elite*, using more data and an elaborated theoretical base and reaching similar conclusions that an elite governs the United States. See also his interesting Web site at http://sociology.ucsc.edu/whorulesamerica/power/wealth.html

Evans, Geoffrey, ed. (1999). *The End of Class Politics?: Class Voting in Comparative Context.* **Oxford: Oxford University Press.** In a series of revealing country-based studies, the contributors to this volume present a data-based case, grounded particularly in analyses of elections, that class politics continues to be a powerful force in certain developed countries and postcommunist developed countries.

Glazer, Amihai, and Lawrence S. Rothenberg. (2005). *Why Government Succeeds and Why It Fails.* **Cambridge, MA: Harvard University Press.** This readable analysis emphasizes the economic conditions that influence public policy in domains such as the regulation of personal behavior, welfare policy, and economic growth.

Ibsen, Henrik. (1882/1964). *Enemy of the People.* **In** *Six Plays by Ibsen.* **Trans. Eva Le Gallienne. New York: Random House.** A classic Norwegian play revealing the political processes by which self-interest and greed overwhelm the efforts of a good citizen to prevent his town from making a policy decision that will result in grave environmental damage and a risk to public health.

Kingdon, John. (2010). *Agendas, Alternatives, and Public Policies. Update edition with Epilogue on Health Care.* **2nd ed. New York: Pearson.** The classic work that most fully explains the idea of agenda setting: how an issue emerges from many and becomes an important item drawing attention and action in the policy process.

Moran, Michael, Martin Rein, and Robert Goodin, eds. (2006). *The Oxford Handbook of Public Policy.* **New York: Oxford University**

Press. A comprehensive (780 pages) treatment of public policy analysis, including all the major analytic approaches and all stages of the policy process.

Rothkopf, David. (2009). *Superclass: The Global Power Elite and the World They Are Making.* **New York: Farrar, Straus and Giroux.** In a supercharged version of elite theory, this lively book identifies the 6,000 members of the global elite and explains how they exercise enormous power and control over the economic and political systems of the contemporary world.

Stone, Deborah. (2011). *Policy Paradox: The Art of Political Decision Making.* **3rd ed. New York: Norton.** A readable and insightful description of the nuances and complex interaction of multiple perspectives and agendas, in combination with a more analytic approach, in the policymaking process, using the United States as context.

Wildavsky, Aaron. (1979). *Speaking Truth to Power.* **Boston: Little, Brown.** One of the most perceptive scholars of the public policy process, the late Aaron Wildavsky offers many insights in this exploration of policymaking and policy analysis.

Yang, Benjamin. (1997). *Deng: A Political Biography.* **Armonk, NY: M. E. Sharpe.** A compelling characterization of Deng Xiaoping, the shrewd leader who followed Mao Zedong to power in China. This book also provides an intriguing and illuminating account of an elite political system in action.

On the Web

http://www.trinity.edu/mkearl/strat.html
This site provides a comprehensive look at the study of social inequality and contains links to many lively Web sites on inequality as well as information on related topics such as gender stratification and homelessness.

www.mapuche-nation.org
This site highlights the culture, history, and political plight of the Mapuche Nation.

http://www.marxist.com
In Defense of Marxism is a comprehensive site that argues for the relevance of class theory and Marxism in the contemporary world, with essays and research on many political topics.

http://www.ncpa.org
The conservative National Center for Policy Analysis provides material, blogs, and links to many current policy issues on its Web site.

http://www.urban.org
The Urban Institute describes itself as a non-partisan economic and social policy research organization that focuses on policy analyses in domains such as education, health, crime, the economy, and international affairs.

http://www.care2.com/causes/politics
The Care 2 Make a Difference Policy Network offers numerous links to ideologically progressive material, think tanks, and blogs that address current policy issues.

http://www.angelfire.com/or/sociologyshop/CWM.html
This site offers a variety of links that explore the works and theories of elite theorist C. Wright Mills.

http://www.publicpolicypolling.com
Details of current public policy issues in the United States, including current polls regarding proposed legislation and candidates.

http://www.ifpa.org
From the Institute for Foreign Policy Analysis, a nonpartisan group, this site focuses on foreign policy issues.

Chapter 10
Change and Political Development

Learning Objectives

10.1 Compare alternative perspectives on social, political, and economic change.

10.2 Identify the attributes of development and summarize economic development strategies.

10.3 Classify states by developmental characteristics.

10.4 Outline the characteristics and stages of political development.

10.5 Analyze how political systems respond to environmental challenges through political institutionalization and system transformation.

As you sail up the Huangpu River into Shanghai, you are struck by many things. The huge cranes loading container ships along both sides of the river seem to go on for miles. You enter a city of massive, modern skyscrapers and more construction cranes than any other city in the world. The roads suffer from such pervasive gridlock and the air is so thick with pollution and noise that you wonder why so many people stay in this huge metropolis. But what is perhaps most noteworthy is what this city represents—the rapid and extensive development of a country that was, until only three generations ago, weakened for centuries by internal conflicts, famines, corruption, and foreign intervention. And that this country, whose recent development occurred under the iron hand of communism, has become the world's largest manufacturing economy and a global economic powerhouse. What accounts for these remarkable changes in such a relatively brief period?

The transformation began in 1949, when communist forces under Mao Zedong gained power in China after a lengthy civil war. The next three decades under Chairman Mao were a blend of chaos and rapid development. Mao wanted to revolutionize the country by destroying the burdens of its feudal, rural, impoverished, and disorganized past. He established a strong, centralized political system between 1949

257

The New China: Shanghai is dominated by a skyline of skyscrapers and construction cranes and a river full of commercial shipping traffic.

and his death in 1976, using harsh totalitarian controls over political and cultural life under the guardianship of the oppressive Communist Party. Mao directed his political power to transform China's economic and social systems. His regime implemented an extensive command political economy, with state ownership of almost all productive means. Population growth was aggressively limited, and there was a shift from rural to urban areas. The Focus in 4 described some of Mao's attempts to use the agents of socialization to undermine Confucian values.

Mao's time in power was also wracked by chaos and conflict. Mao's policies led to more than 30 million state-caused deaths through brutal treatment of opponents, "permanent revolution" movements, and recurrent famines. Despite the turbulence of Mao's rule, this period also laid the foundations for economic development. Among the many important changes were the establishment of an effective central government; land reform; weakening of the rigid Confucian hierarchy of gender, age, and class; great improvements in health, education, and infrastructure; and the transformation from an agrarian to an industrial nation.

Under Deng Xiaoping, Mao's successor (and China's top leader from 1978 to the 1990s), the political system remained authoritarian, firmly under the control of the Communist Party. However, Deng abandoned the command economy and quietly embraced many aspects of the free market. Chided that he had adopted capitalism, the pragmatic Deng mused: "It doesn't matter if a cat is black or white, so long as it catches mice." Profit became not only an acceptable motivation but also a highly desirable one (another of Deng's famous comments is "to get rich is glorious"). Under Deng, the share of industrial output under state ownership dropped from 78 percent to 26 percent, and almost the entire agricultural system shifted from state communes to private control. China moved aggressively into the global economy, including a rapid shift to manufacturing for export and to more sophisticated goods. China's total GDP and foreign trade each rose more than twelvefold, and both rural and urban income per capita increased more than tenfold.

Since Deng stepped down in the early 1990s, the political leadership has continued to actively manage the Chinese economy, and it has sustained a very high growth rate, due particularly to strong gains in labor productivity and great success in exporting goods. Overall, GDP has steadily increased, at an annual rate of 8 percent since 1978. China now accounts for one-fourth of all global economic growth. A larger proportion of Chinese enjoy a high standard of material living than at any point in the history of the country. Yet millions of Chinese still live in relative poverty, especially in rural areas, and increasing urban–rural inequalities in the distribution of wealth are creating substantial tension. Citizen dissatisfaction with corruption is rising. Environmental degradation has been severe, especially in urban areas. As China has become "the world's largest…"—in terms of exports, industrial output, holder of foreign currencies, and purchaser of commodities (e.g., energy, food)—many believe that the continuing path of development in China is the most significant factor in the evolution of the world's economy in the near future (CIA 2014; Meisner 1999, 2006).

Change

10.1   **Compare alternative perspectives on social, political, and economic change.**

The recent history of China is a dramatic example of social, economic, and political *change*, the processes of becoming different occurring in every contemporary society. Chapter 15 takes a closer look at China, among other countries that are in rapid transition. For now, China illustrates how the political system can be a major source of change. Exploring the links between the processes of change and the political world is the focus of this chapter.

There is typically a tension between continuity and change. Even with the strong forces of globalization, some cultures are changing more slowly than others. For example, many of the Masai on the Serengeti Plain in East Africa live in a manner that is similar to the ways of their ancestors of 50 generations ago. They continue to raise their cattle, ignoring the Kenya–Tanzania border and resisting the attempts of the Kenyan government to alter their long-standing cultural patterns of family and tribal life. But even the Masai have been affected by the modernization surrounding them. It has brought health care and disease; money from tourists and reduced land for grazing herds; education and cultural confusion.

There seems nowhere to hide from the forces of change. The Greek philosopher Heraclitus articulated this view in the fifth century B.C.E. His famous dictum, "You can never step in the same river twice, for fresh waters are ever flowing in upon you," is an extreme version of the viewpoint that everything is in constant flux, that change is inevitable. Just as individuals move through a developmental process of birth, growth, maturity, decline, and death, social organisms (groups, organizations, and societies) also have some form of evolutionary development.

On the opposite side of the debate about the inevitability of change is the wry French observation: *Plus ça change, plus c'est la même chose.* This translates loosely as "The more things change, the more they remain the same." This view suggests that even if the specifics in a society alter, the fundamental human dynamics and the challenges that any state faces remain relatively constant. Do you believe this? Is this a wise commentary about the human condition? An erroneous cliché?

There are also ongoing disagreements about the desirability of change as well as its inevitability. One normative position, most aligned with modern rationalism, is that change is generally a positive force in human society. Change is the mechanism of growth, development, and progress, all of which are assumed to increase knowledge, extend control over the environment, and thus improve the human condition. Change is the result of the rejection of the status quo in favor of a preferred status. This view is reflected in the ideas of thinkers such as Isaac Newton (1642–1727), Immanuel Kant (1724–1804), and Charles Darwin (1809–1882). In the contemporary world, it is especially prevalent among those who believe in the benefits of science and technology.

A contrasting position is that change and development have significant negative effects, perhaps so many negatives that change is undesirable. Plato (ca. 428–347 B.C.E.), Jean-Jacques Rousseau (1712–1778), and Sigmund Freud (1856–1939) are among those who argue that knowledge, civilization, and excessive control over the environment result in a loss of innocence, goodness, and happiness and create the capacity for great harm and destruction. In this view, humans have achieved material progress at the cost of moral and spiritual decline. Moreover, our capacity to increase our supply of food and material goods cannot be separated from our development of harmful behaviors and technologies (e.g., weapons, chemicals) that degrade the environment and eliminate certain species of life—including, possibly, human beings. Most people now recognize the paradox that change and development simultaneously increase *and* reduce the quality of life. Change can be good, bad, or, most often, both. And most accept the serious problems and dangers associated with progress to enjoy the material benefits that change brings.

Development

10.2   **Identify the attributes of development and summarize economic development strategies.**

Characteristics of "More Developed" Systems

Contemporary changes of social, economic, and political systems are usually discussed in terms of development or modernization. While both of these concepts can be slippery, social scientific research often avoids the concept of *modernization* because it is particularly fuzzy. What is "modern" depends very much on the particular histori-cal moment and even on the values and culture of the analyst. Beethoven, the Beatles, and Avicii all created "modern" music. In the world of rapid social and technological change, what seemed modern in the United States 40 years ago, before the Internet, social media, smartphones, and GPS, does not seem so modern today.

The concept of **development** is also fluid, but it is more measurable. Development refers to *the processes through which certain key dimensions become more pronounced*. There are no agreed-upon measures for distinguishing sharply between systems that are developed/modern and those that are not. Broadly, a more developed human system exhibits relatively high levels on three key dimensions that tap social, cultural, eco-nomic, political, and personal characteristics (Bill and Hardgrave 1981: 63):

1. The *organizational* dimension: behaviors and actions by groups, institutions, and societies that are based on specialization, interdependency, and differentiation of roles and functions
2. The *technological* dimension: the use of increasingly complex and sophisticated artifacts to produce useful goods and services and to control the environment
3. The *attitudinal* dimension: cognitive, affective, and evaluative orientations that are dominated by scientific knowledge, rationality, secular values, and individualism

The *technological* dimension is the core driver of **economic development**, *an increase in the amount, complexity, and value of the goods produced by an economic system*, a goal of great importance to every state (recall Figure 5.1). Thus, states attempt to identify and implement strategies that facilitate economic development, which they usually define by some measure of national economic production such as GDP per capita or the rate of growth in GDP (described in Chapter 8). The expansion of avail-able goods and services in the society offers the promise of a life that is more secure and more comfortable for at least some citizens.

Advances on the *organizational* and *attitudinal* dimensions are reflected by social indicators such as greater urbanization, expanded communications, more extensive social networks, improved efficiency, higher education levels, higher literacy rates, and greater social mobility. Most people assume that there are societal benefits associated with increases on each of these dimensions, but there are some individuals and groups that argue that increases on these dimensions are not necessarily desirable (Kenny et al. 2013). They believe that such changes can have negative effects on deeply revered social and cultural values. In some countries, these negative changes are referred to as **Westernization** and are evident in attitudinal changes that shift toward *greater secular-ism, individualism,* and *materialism*. Groups that are strongly committed to sustaining traditional cultural and religious values, such as those of Islam or Hinduism, can be very concerned about these types of changes within their countries.

Indeed, even economic development is questioned by those alarmed about the negative effects on the environment of unrestricted economic growth. Concerns for the environment center on both the *depletion of Earth's resources* (e.g., the destruction of the forests, shortages of water, overfishing, and the overcultivation of the land to increase food production) and the *degradation of the environment* (e.g., climate change, air pollution, soil erosion, and solid waste associated with industrial processes and consumerism) (Meadowcraft 2013).

The Process of Development

STAGE TYPOLOGIES Scholars have attempted to define the process(es) through which development and modernization occur. One approach is to define a series of stages or phases through which each society passes (Rostow 1960). Best known are the simple typologies, many of which have only two stages, such as *traditional* and *modern, less developed* and *more developed,* or *mechanical* and *organic.* These labels are so broad that they do not provide much conceptual clarity.

Karl Marx proposed a more complex typology in which most societies pass through six stages of development, each based on how its major productive resources are controlled. Marx posited that there is an initial stage of *primitive communism*, in which all individuals jointly share control over any available productive resources. The development process then continues through a series of stages in which there are increasingly subtle forms of domination by some classes over others: *slavery*, then *feudalism*, and then *capitalism.* Marx claimed that capitalist systems are eventually transformed into *socialist* and finally to *communist* systems, the ultimate stage of development in which all citizens blend into a single class that shares control of resources (recall Chapters 2, 8, and 9 on communism and class theory).

RESPONSE TO KEY CHALLENGES Most explanations of the process of development do not assume, as Marx does, that there is a single, inevitable sequence of stages. Rather, analysts identify a series of key challenges in the development process (Black 1966). These challenges include the tension between traditional values and modern ones; the transition from a rural, agrarian society to an urban, industrial society; the transfer of social and political power from traditional elites to modernizing ones; and the convergence of geographical territory, nation-based identities, and state boundaries.

A country's development process depends on the sequence in which the challenges occur, how the society responds to the challenges, and crucial features of the society and its environment. For example, Barrington Moore (1966) uses detailed historical analyses of eight countries to define four different models of development based on how relationships evolved among key social groups, especially the landed aristocrats and peasants in the rural areas and the entrepreneurs and government employees in the urban areas. One of Moore's most powerful conclusions is that all forms of development are essentially revolutions from above, implemented by a ruthless minority and causing great hardship to the large majority of the population, which does not want these changes.

INDIVIDUAL-LEVEL CHANGE Most analyses of development focus on the macro level—that is, on the organizational and technological dimensions of systems such as economic and political systems. But attention to the attitudinal dimension shifts the analysis to the social-psychological characteristics of individuals that might account for variations in rates and patterns of development (Inglehart and Welzel 2005, 2010;

Inkeles and Smith 1999). You might understand individual-level change intuitively if you think about what happens to people when their existing values are challenged by education, other religions, or different cultures. The Koran recognizes the importance of personal values in shaping society, noting, "Lo! Allah changeth not the condition of a people until they first change what is in their hearts." These analyses of individual attitudes and change are related to the political behavior studies described in Chapters 2–4, although the focus here is on a broader array of beliefs (not just political beliefs).

In the attempt to establish the attitudinal traits associated with modernity, the work of Alex Inkeles and his colleagues (Inkeles and Smith 1999) is noteworthy. This group gathered extensive survey data from men in six developing countries (Argentina, Bangladesh, Chile, India, Israel, and Nigeria). Statistical analyses produced a set of seven qualities that the researchers believe constitute a "syndrome of modernity"— that is, the general attitudinal traits of a modern person in a developing society:

1. Openness to new experiences regarding both people and behaviors
2. A shift in allegiance from those individuals in traditional authority structures (e.g., parents, religious leaders) to those representing modern institutions (e.g., government leaders)
3. Confidence in modern technologies (e.g., science, medicine) and a less fatalistic attitude about life
4. Desire for social mobility for oneself and one's children
5. Belief in the value of planning and punctuality
6. Interest in local politics and community affairs
7. Interest in news, especially national and international affairs

Inkeles and his colleagues conclude that there is remarkable similarity in these clusters of beliefs among the modern men in all six societies they studied and perhaps among modern individuals in almost all cultures. Some posit that such an emerging commonality of beliefs is part of a broader set of forces that are homogenizing everyone into a global culture, a global information network, and a global economy (Barber 1996; Friedman 2007). However, it is unclear whether most people are equally exposed to and changed by global culture. In most developing societies, some people and groups enthusiastically embrace the new beliefs and new behaviors, while others cling tenaciously to the old ones. Indeed, in some cases of religious fundamentalism, it seems that leaders who display the activist and outward-oriented psychological traits associated with the syndrome of modernity are actually working to return the society to more traditional patterns of attitudes and actions (Hansen and Postmes 2013; Sahoo 2013).

EMERGENCE OF CIVIL SOCIETY The attitudinal changes in individuals are especially important when they result in new patterns of social interaction. Thus, one key consideration in assessing development is the extent to which a *civil society* has emerged. Attitudes particularly associated with the existence of civil society include tolerance of differences in opinions and behaviors, social trust, willingness to negotiate and to avoid violence in resolving differences, and a sense of shared identity with others. Some analysts conclude that, while a society can be "developed" without being a civil society, these values of civility are crucial for sustaining effective community and democracy (Diamond 2009; Linz and Stepan 1996; Putnam 1993, 2001).

CULTURE AND CHANGE Some studies of development emphasize the importance of the culture in the processes of change (Hall and Lamont 2013). Since Max Weber's classic study (1958a) of the link between the culture of Protestant religions and the rise of capitalist political economies, there have been continuing efforts to clarify the relationship between broad cultural systems and economic development. Some, like Weber, argue that Protestantism motivated people to make substantial, even irrational, sacrifices of material consumption and the pleasures of life, inciting them to work extraordinarily hard and accumulate wealth rather than spend it. A society infused with such values is associated with the transformation to a modern society and economy.

Weber (1951, 1958b) also applied an analysis of culture and religion to India and China to explain the absence of development there. But since the 1980s, there has been a dramatic surge of economic development among the newly industrializing Asian countries (to be discussed later in this chapter). Because these Asian countries have had substantially higher levels of development than most other countries employing similar development strategies, more recent explanations have emphasized how Asian culture has *facilitated* development (Fukuyama 2009; Huntington 1991; Wiarda 2013).

A Development-Based Taxonomy of States

10.3   **Classify states by developmental characteristics.**

As you discovered in Part One, a central goal of political analysis is to develop general descriptions and explanations of political phenomena. To attempt the near-impossible task of generalizing about more than 180 countries, it seems that comparative analysis would be more manageable if it is based on an appropriate taxonomy that distinguishes only a few groups of countries. What categories would you suggest to create just a few distinct groups of countries? Given your categories, how, for example, would you classify Malaysia?

If you tried to classify Malaysia using social statistics, many alternatives could emerge. You might economically classify Malaysia as an upper-middle-income country—given its GDP per capita (PPP) of $17,500. You might classify it in a regional group as one of the countries in East Asia. Or you could utilize a cultural taxonomy in which it is a predominantly Muslim country, although it has substantial Buddhist and Christian minorities. Ethnically, it is majority Malay, but there is tension with the large number of ethnic Chinese. Historically, it is a postcolonial country, after nearly two centuries of British rule ended in 1963. Geopolitically, it is a significant country, rich in commodities and in a strategic location between the Strait of Malacca and the South China Sea. You might use a political criterion, such as classifying Malaysia as a parliamentary system, or as a multiparty system (with a governing coalition of 13 parties), or as a flawed democracy in transition after 22 years under a single leader. The list of possible taxonomies is long.

However, if you put your boots on the ground in Malaysia, you might be perplexed about how to classify Malaysia in terms of its development. Flying into KL (Kuala Lumpur), you would be dazzled by arguably the most architecturally cutting-edge, high-tech airport in the world. Every aspect of your arrival, baggage handling, and customs would be facilitated by the most advanced technologies, as would your ride into the center of the capital on a sleek train. The skyline of KL and its shopping center, the fancy cars, and the elegantly dressed people would suggest you were in the most advanced city in the world. But when you continued your journey on a rickety bus to a rural village, you'd find bad roads, dilapidated buildings, risky-looking street food, and many people living without reliable electricity, plumbing, or sanitation—conditions that might be more consistent with your ideas about life in a "Third World" country. Where would Malaysia fit?

This brief consideration of Malaysia suggests that no taxonomy is fully satisfactory, given the complexity of countries. The most common approach for classifying all the world's countries distinguishes between "developed countries" and "developing countries," often based on a single measure of economic development such as GDP per capita. If there is a second dimension, it is often region. For example, the World Bank utilizes four economic categories (high income, high middle income, low middle income, and low income) as its main taxonomy and sometimes adds a regional dimension.

This chapter proposes a taxonomy of countries with only three categories, but it is based on a more nuanced measurement of a country's level of development. This alternative taxonomy begins with a measure of *economic development*. It then adds a second, *social development* dimension, guided by the broader conception of the dimensions of development suggested earlier in this chapter.

- **Economic development.** Like many classificatory schemes, the taxonomy created here uses a standard measure of the total value of goods produced in a country divided by the population of the country: GDP per capita, correcting for purchasing power parity (PPP). As noted in Chapter 8, PPP seems useful for comparing the relative levels of economic development in a manner that reflects domestic purchasing power in each country.

- **Social development.** To enrich the classification, this book employs a second dimension, grounded in the types of organizational, technological, and attitudinal development discussed above. Like Malaysia, each country is a unique mix, in terms of the complexity of its organizations, the pervasiveness of high technology, and the blend of traditional and modern attitudes. To measure this mix, an index has been calculated for each country to reflect the levels of

  - knowledge (measured as the adult literacy rate);
  - urban lifestyle (measured as percent of population in urban areas);
  - health (measured as longevity and mortality rates to age five); and
  - communication capabilities (measured as cell phones per capita and computers per capita).

Each country's values on these four components are weighted equally (on 10-point scales) to generate a social development index score from 0 to 40. As you assess this social development index, consider whether these four dimensions seem appropriate, whether the operational indicators used to measure each one seem valid, and whether equally weighting the four dimensions seems defensible.

Figure 10.1 displays a selection of countries plotted on the economic development and social development dimensions. The figure also suggests a taxonomy for our analyses, by highlighting three clusters of countries. Examine these clusters to see if they seem a reasonable way to classify countries. We offer names for each of the three clusters: the developed countries of the Global North; the developing countries of the Global South; and the transitional developed countries. The following paragraphs briefly characterize the countries in each category. Each cluster will be the focus of a later chapter (Chapters 13–15), which will offer generalizations about the quest for prosperity, stability, and security by the states in that group.

Figure 10.1 Classification of Selected Countries Based on Economic and Social Development

SOURCES: World Bank 2013; UNDP 2013.

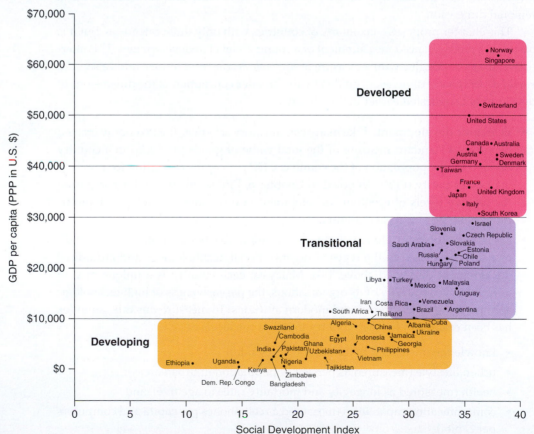

The Developed Countries of the Global North

The countries in the upper-right corner of Figure 10.1 are mainly in Western Europe, plus Canada, Japan, the United States. But the cluster also includes a few others, such as Australia, Singapore, South Korea, and Taiwan. Most of these countries are usually referred to as the *developed countries* or the *Global North*, and occasionally most are still called the "First World." This group includes most of the countries with the world's highest levels of GDP per capita, but these states also rank very high on the social dimensions of development. Their populations generally enjoy relatively high levels of literacy, health, and welfare; their technological infrastructure is advanced; and most have a high material standard of living. Do any countries that are in this group or their relative location in Figure 10.1 surprise you? Chapter 13 provides a more in-depth look at the strategies and obstacles to development for the countries in the Global North.

The Developing Countries of the Global South

You will notice that the lower cluster in Figure 10.1 includes a diverse set of countries in terms of size, region, culture, geopolitical significance, and so on. As you would expect, these countries have lower levels of economic development and are also less developed on the technological, organizational, and attitudinal dimensions than the developed countries. They tend to spread more broadly across the social development index because some of them are more advanced than others in areas such as literacy, urbanization, and longevity. Are you surprised by any countries that are or are not in this group?

Social scientists, political actors, and the media often refer to most of this group of about 140 countries as the *developing countries*. Since the 1950s, many developing countries were also called the "Third World." Initially, this term was applied in the context of the Cold War to those states that claimed they were "nonaligned": not in the camp of either the United States and its allies (the First World) or the Soviet Union and its allies (the Second World). Soon, the term was used to refer to almost all developing countries. In the post–Cold War era, the concept of a Third World is used less frequently, and another term has emerged: the *Global South*. Nearly all of the developing countries are located geographically south of the developed countries (the *Global North*). This large and diverse cluster of developing countries of the Global South will be explored in Chapter 14.

The Transitional Developed Countries

The developed countries and the developing countries are standard categories in analyses by governmental agencies and social scientists. But there are countries in Figure 10.1, like Malaysia, that seem especially difficult to classify. Currently, the levels of economic and/or social development in these countries put them "in the middle." In Figure 10.1, these countries are called *transitional developed countries* to reflect their middle range on one or both dimensions of development and, in some cases, their high rate of change.

Although all the countries in the world are always in transition, Chapter 15 will distinguish and examine three subsets of transitional countries. Each of these subsets is made up of countries with some important commonalities in their economic situation or political culture. These countries also face particularly interesting development challenges, and their approaches to achieving their goals are worth studying. One subset of countries that emerged from the breakup of the Soviet Union and its former Eastern and Central European allies, such as Hungary and Poland, is termed the *postcommunist developed countries*. A second subset is called the **Latin American Transitionals**, and it includes such countries as Argentina, Chile, and Mexico. The third group, which is not a cluster in Figure 10.1 but has been widely cited as a group of key countries with growing importance for the global economy, is the **BRICS** (composed of Brazil, Russia, India, China, and South Africa). Chapter 15 will provide details about each of these three groups.

Like any taxonomy (see the Appendix), Figure 10.1 is an attempt to create groups that can be distinguished analytically, are based on some specifiable criteria, and seem to make sense. However, not every country fits neatly into a category. Examples of this in the framework in Figure 10.1 include some resource-rich (oil) states in the Middle East and Africa (e.g., Libya) and some postcommunist countries that have high social development but have not prospered economically (e.g., Ukraine). The categories proposed from the analysis in Figure 10.1 are acceptable if their use provides clarification and insight and, ideally, if they facilitate the development of generalizations and theory. As a political analyst, *you* should assess the utility of this taxonomy relative to alternative ways of grouping countries for analysis. The remainder of this chapter focuses broadly on the dynamics and challenges of economic and political development facing all countries.

The Dynamics of Economic Development

GENERAL STRATEGIES The actual economic development of a country is the product of a complex set of actions by both major players (e.g., the government, large corporations, and international banks) and small players (e.g., small businesses and individuals as consumers and workers) that is staggering in scale and almost incomprehensible in nature.

In the abstract, the discussion of political economy in Chapter 8 (look again at Figure 8.3) provides the key to understanding what is happening. Economic development occurs as more and more households and firms are engaged in ever-higher levels of production and consumption. More goods (and, ideally, more diverse and complex goods) are produced, more income and expenditures are exchanged, and thus the GDP gets larger relative to the number of people sharing in the carnival of production and consumption. And a political economy is normally healthier if it is not only growing but also bringing more income into the country by selling exports than it sends out of the country to pay for imports.

Chapter 8 explored some of the general challenges facing every political economy in the quest for economic development. From a public policy perspective, the underlying puzzle is: How can the state facilitate economic development? Recall from Chapter 8 that in recent decades, three competing visions have guided the answer to this question in most political economies: statism, state capitalism, and neoliberalism.

As Chapter 8 indicated, both statism and state capitalism are characterized by very intensive state intervention in the political economy. **Statism** is a political economy in which the *state, to serve the primary goal of national economic growth and development, actively manages the system of production and distribution of goods, including ownership of major assets.* **State capitalism** is a political economy in which the *leaders of the political system own and manage many major assets or assert extensive control over who is allowed to control key sectors of the economy, and the primary goal of the economy is to increase the leaders' resources.* Thus statism is oriented more toward enhancing the country's power and serving the national interest through maximizing development, and it is less concerned than state capitalism about increasing the political and economic power of the elite (Bremmer 2010). Many developing countries of the Global South and transitional developed countries have been strongly oriented to one of these two approaches for part or all of the last 60 years.

Neoliberalism is grounded in the market political economy model (see Chapter 8), and its guiding principle is to *maximize the economic freedom of firms, households, and individuals.* The state's interventions in the economy must be severely limited because they undermine and distort the efficiency of the free market. Public expenditure is minimal, there is limited government regulation of the economy, and direct foreign investment and free trade across state boundaries are encouraged. The state is mainly concerned with maintaining fiscal and monetary discipline (not taxing or spending much, keeping the currency stable) and facilitating the activities of firms in the national and global marketplaces. This approach has generally been dominant among countries in the Global North, particularly the market economies described in Chapter 13. And since the mid-1970s, many other countries have adopted versions of the neoliberal approach, especially due to two factors: the disappointing levels of economic growth achieved with the statist and state capitalist approaches and strong pressures from the international financial community and the global economy to embrace neoliberalism (Rodrik 2003; Linz and Stepan 1996).

Of course, like many aspects of politics, these strict categories do not tell the whole story. Most countries blend elements of all three approaches, and some states created a hybrid approach that attempts to combine the strengths of the statist and neoliberal approaches. The ***developmental state*** hybrid *blends an emphasis on a private, market-based system of firms with a state that actively intervenes to promote and protect the country's firms in the global economy.* Generally, as in neoliberalism, aggressive capitalism is favored and there are minimal governmental constraints on firms. However, as in statism, the state is very interventionist in enacting taxing, spending, and regulatory policies that promote the export of goods, encourage savings and investment, discourage high levels of domestic consumption, and provide a productive, docile labor force. The state also works cooperatively with firms to identify and then produce particular goods that can be successfully sold in the international marketplace. Government subsidies enable firms to sell goods at low or no profit while the firm captures a share of the market and gains consumer support. The state's policies (e.g., tariffs) also protect firms against imported goods. Japan is an early innovator shaping the developmental state approach, which has been copied with varying success by other countries.

Chapter 14, on the Global South, and Chapter 15, on the transitional developed countries, will explain in more detail the policies and challenges associated with these countries' quest for economic development and prosperity. In general, countries have tried variations of all of the approaches described above. Overall, no approach has proven successful for all countries that have implemented it. Many Global South countries, such as those near the bottom of Figure 10.1, have languished regardless of approach. The developmental state approach has arguably been the most successful because it has enabled some countries to grow their economies substantially over multiple years. It has been particularly effective in some countries in Asia, such as Singapore, South Korea, and Taiwan, but far less successful in other regions (Simone 2001; Woo-Cumings 1999).

Many countries have embraced statism or state capitalism for periods of time, assuming that strong management by the state is necessary to achieve growth in the complex global economy and/or to maintain the existing power elite. Most of these attempts have been sporadically successful, at best, in countries like Brazil, Russia, and South Africa. China, and more recently Vietnam, are among the few examples in which state capitalism has generated sustained high growth. State capitalism as an economic development strategy has not fared well in many countries in Africa, Asia, and Latin America where it was implemented.

As noted above, neoliberalism has been adopted in many Global South and transitional developed countries, at least in part due to pressure from the Global North. Solid growth for multiple years has been the result in certain countries, such as Chile and Peru in Latin America, Estonia and Poland among the former Soviet allies in Europe, and India. Others, such as Brazil, Mexico, and Hungary, have had periods of high growth followed by low or negative growth. Some analysts credit neoliberalism with the economic "rise of the South" since 2000 (see Chapter 14), but critics counter that overall economic growth associated with neoliberalism has been coupled with increased poverty and inequality (Acemoglu and Robinson 2012; Huber and Solt 2004; Rodrik 2003).

The globalized economy has increased the complexity and pressures of achieving economic growth in every country attempting to sustain it. In the late 1990s and since 2008, in particular, economic difficulties in some economies have quickly spread to many other countries, given the increasingly global economic interdependency. In every country, the debate continues about the best strategy for broad and stable economic development (Scherer, Palazzo, and Seidl 2013; Stein 2006).

DEPENDENCY WITHIN THE INTERNATIONAL POLITICAL ECONOMY Why have so many developing countries been unable to achieve high, sustained economic growth during the postcolonial period (since about 1960)? Some analysts offer a perspective known generally as the **dependency approach**, which argues that *the "late developers" face specific challenges because of their subordination to and dependence on the more developed countries and the transnational institutions they control in the current world.*

According to the *ideological* framing of the dependency approach, the key problem for current developers is a long history of exploitation by the more developed capitalist/imperialist states. The developed countries have manipulated and controlled the political economies of the developing countries for decades or even centuries by means of their economic, military, and political domination of the world system. Indeed, a major reason the developed countries have sustained their prosperity since the mid-twentieth century is that they still exploit and reap benefits from the developing countries, especially through their broad control of capital, markets and prices, and multinational corporations. In this view, the activities of the developed countries have not merely inhibited the progress of the late developers—they have actually deformed (distorted and ruined) the efforts of the developing countries.

The *descriptive* version of the dependency approach provides a similar analysis but without heaping blame exclusively on the advanced states. It posits an economic hierarchy in which economic actors at every level take advantage of those below them in the global economic system. At the top of the heap is a *core*, composed of the powerful states, large firms (especially multinational corporations such as JPMorganChase, General Electric, and Exxon Mobil), and financial institutions controlled by the most developed countries. At the bottom of the heap on the *periphery* are the villages of the developing countries (Isbister 2006; Wallerstein, Lemert, and Rojas 2013; Wiarda 2003). In this version, many actors engage in exploitation. The resources of villages and the urban poor (raw materials, cheap labor) are exploited by local and regional economic actors, who are in turn exploited by national economic actors, who are exploited by the powerful core actors in the global economy.

CONTINUING DEPENDENCY? It is clear that the process of development is intertwined with the global economy. However, three arguments are offered by analysts who dispute the validity of the dependency approach. First, serious internal problems in many developing countries, especially extensive corruption and conflicts among nationality groups, are major limitations on development (Calderisi 2007; Isbister 2006; Johnston 2006). Second, the economic success of some Asian developing countries, relative to those in Africa and Latin America, suggests that cultural and institutional factors are more crucial to development than is the level of dependence on foreign capital or foreign companies (Fallows 1995; Fallows 1995; Stevens and Cooper 2010). Third, the low- and middle-income countries of the Global South, measured either as a group or by region, have actually achieved higher average annual rates of economic (GDP) growth since the early 1990s than the developed countries (World Bank 2013). In response, dependency theorists note that when income inequality continues to rise worldwide—the disparity between the top and bottom 20 percent has nearly doubled in the last three decades to a ratio of 50:1—the systematic subordination of those on the periphery cannot be dismissed (UNDP 2006).

Political Development

10.4   **Outline the characteristics and stages of political development.**

To this point, this chapter has broadly considered development in all spheres of human activity, particularly in the economic and attitudinal spheres. Let us now turn to the specifically *political* aspects of development. **Political development** refers to *the emergence of more extensive capabilities in the political system*, especially in the sense that political structures and processes become more specialized and more effective in managing internal operations and in responding to the environment.

Characteristics of Political Development

Political development is typically measured by the extent to which a political system exhibits relatively high levels on the following four dimensions:

1. **Concentration of power in the state.** Most power and authority are centralized in a single state-level governmental system, and traditional sources of political authority weaken. The citizens agree that the state has the right to make and enforce public policies, and they accept those decisions as authoritative. The formal–legal aspects of government (e.g., constitutions and laws) are well established.
2. **Specialized political structures.** Most key political functions are fulfilled by complex, organized political institutions such as legislatures, executives, political parties, and political interest groups. The actions of these institutions are generally guided by bureaucratic principles such as rationality and efficiency (recall Chapters 6 and 7).
3. **Political institutionalization.** The citizens value and support the political structures and processes, which become more stable, and the citizens fulfill their roles of conventional political participation as voters, foot soldiers, and so on (recall Chapter 3).
4. **Extensive capabilities of the state.** The political system becomes better able to generate support, to respond to demands from its population, and to control the environment. Overall, its organization is more stable and coherent, its structures are more efficient, and its actions more effectively serve its goals and objectives. In a capabilities analysis, a political system achieves a higher level of political development when it improves its effectiveness on any of five key capabilities (Powell, Strom, and Dalton 2012):

   Extractive: using human and material resources from the environment

   Regulative: controlling individual and group actions

   Distributive: allocating values through institutionalized structures and procedures

   Responsive: making decisions and policies that react to demands for value allocations

   Symbolic: manipulating images and meanings and distributing nonmaterial rewards and values

The Process of Political Development

Figure 10.2 presents one model of the process through which political development occurs. From this perspective, the elements of modernization (in the figure) provide the material and human resources that lead to the emergence of a developed political

Figure 10.2 Model of Development I

system. Greater economic capability produces goods that the political system can distribute. An urban population with increasingly modern beliefs is more willing to accept the authority of government and to participate meaningfully in politics. In essence, the political system develops more complex and specialized structures as a response to changes that are occurring in the society and the economy.

Conceptualizing political development as primarily a response to economic and social change is based on the historical analyses of political systems that developed in the eighteenth and nineteenth centuries. However, the power and impact of the political system itself, as a causal force for change, are more evident when one analyzes the societies that have undergone substantial development during the last 50 years (Acemoglu and Robinson 2012; Wiarda 2003).

This leads to a second perspective in which the political system is the crucial force that causes development of the social and economic systems. Thus, Figure 10.3 emphasizes the central importance of the political system as an agent of change in relation to other societal characteristics. As Kwame Nkrumah (1909–1972), the first president of Ghana, observed: "Seek ye first the political kingdom, and all else shall be added unto you." This nearly religious invocation asserts that if the political system is developed first, it can then serve as the instrument through which social and economic development is achieved. Of course, if wrong choices are made about the political system, it can inhibit change and development. Public policy decisions by an assertive political leadership can establish specialized political structures, expand the capabilities of the political system, and mobilize certain groups into the political process. The political leadership can then deploy these more developed political structures to enact public policies that empower governmental officials to perform new functions, assert state

Figure 10.3 Model of Development II

control over key human and natural resources, and allocate those resources in ways that result in social and economic development in domains such as the political economy, the educational system, the culture, national identity, the media, and religious practices (Acemoglu and Robinson 2012).

Obviously, change and development in the political, social, economic, and other domains are interdependent; that is, they affect one another. But Figure 10.3 emphasizes the central role of politics and political choice as drivers of development. In this conception, overall development is shaped by the ideology, will, and actions of political actors rather than being driven primarily by economic growth. This was the case for China under Mao Zedong, the example that opened this chapter. Another compelling example of a leader's explicit use of the political system as a powerful instrument to change many aspects of the society is Kemal Atatürk's efforts to modernize Turkey, described in Focus in 10.

Focus in 10

Political Development and Modernization in Turkey

The modernization effort in Turkey is an example of "seeking the political kingdom first." Historically, the area of the Turkish nation was part of the large Ottoman Empire ruled by a sultan. After World War I, an army commander named Mustafa Kemal led a fierce military struggle for national independence. Victory resulted in the creation of the sovereign state of Turkey in 1922. Mustafa Kemal, who seized political power in the new republic, was committed to rapid modernization. At the time, Turkey had very traditional political, economic, and social systems, with Islamic law dominating the actions of the 98 percent Muslim population. The new leader decided that the key to modernization was to lessen the hold of Islam on the people.

In a stroke of symbolic politics, Kemal began his modernization drive at the personal level. He changed his name to Mustafa Kemal Atatürk, the addition meaning "father of the Turks." (Kemal was also a fortunate name because it means "perfect one.") Atatürk initially focused on political development, establishing a new state based on the principles of independence and democracy. A constitution was approved in 1924, executive power was granted to a president, the sultan was exiled, a legislature was elected, and a single political party

was established. Atatürk thus created a political system with modern structures of governance and modern forms of political participation. This political system then became the instrument for Atatürk's broader efforts to reform Turkey.

From 1925 until his death in 1938, Atatürk employed his great political power to implement three major sets of public policies that were meant to modernize Turkey and to separate it from the traditional Muslim world. First, he enacted laws that prohibited the wearing of religious garments in everyday life, abolished religious schools, and closed religious tombs as places of worship. Second, he encouraged the emergence and empowerment of a nationalist elite by steps such as creating a new Turkish language and banning the public use of other languages (recall his suppression of the Kurds described in Chapter 5); replacing the Ottoman script with the Latin alphabet; and establishing Turkish literacy programs, especially in urban areas. Third, he established a new civil code (copied from Switzerland) to govern the legal relations between individuals and collectivities, relegating sharia law and the Koran to peripheral status in guiding public life. For example, he tried to eliminate the subordinate role of women, encouraging them to work, providing them with rights of divorce and inheritance, allowing them to vote and hold public office, and banning polygamy.

The effects of Atatürk's changes are evident in contemporary Turkey, whose 81 million people are 99.8 percent Muslim. While 70 percent of the population lived in villages in 1964, Turkey is now 72 percent urban. The economy, 75 percent agrarian in 1978, is 91 percent industrial and service-based (CIA 2013). Turkey now has the most educated and modern women in the Muslim world, and Tansu Çiller was Turkey's first female prime minister (1993–1996). A 2004 constitutional amendment says: "women and men have equal rights," and about one-fourth of Turkish professionals are women; yet substantial gender inequality remains due to a continuing gap between legal standing and social realities.

Politically, the attempt to create an effective multiparty democracy in Turkey remains unfinished. There have been periods of serious social instability and governmental corruption and three periods of military rule since 1960, although the military returned the reins of government to civilians in each case after order was restored. For the first time since Atatürk, an Islamist party (the Welfare Party) came to power in 1996. When the government began to promote numerous policy changes based on Islamic principles and practices, the military responded with warnings and then forced the party from office in a "soft coup" that revealed the continuing power of the military in what is perhaps best characterized as an illiberal democracy (see Chapter 7).

A reformulated Islamist party (the Justice and Development [AK] Party) has dominated the last four elections (2002 to 2014). Recep Erdogan, AK's three-time prime minister and Turkey's first ever popularly elected president (in 2014), has attempted to reassure the military of his support for Atatürk's secular society. However, he now very actively implements public policies that protect and expand the role of Islam in the public realm. This combination of political power and religious orientation has heightened the uneasiness within Turkey's military and secular elements, increasing tensions over the drift away from secularism.

Students carrying a portrait of Atatürk, founder of modern Turkey, chant slogans to protest the attempts by the government to reduce the secular orientation of education policies.

Thus, Atatürk's strong policies have not totally transformed Turkey. However, his legacy is an illuminating example of how a committed political leader can reform the political system and then use political power to achieve considerable social and economic development within a society, consistent with Figure 10.3.

Further Focus

1. Which of Atatürk's policies do you think was the most important for overall development in Turkey?

2. As the leader of a developing country, if you had to emphasize economic development or political development, which would you choose?

Political Development as Democratization

In contrast to the capabilities analysis described above, some scholars (e.g., Cutright 1963) define political development as the establishment of the rule of law, legitimate elections, and representative institutions. Others object that this conception of a developed political system is extremely biased. Can you see why? What concept do such characteristics seem to measure?

You might answer that the preceding paragraph describes a *democratic* political system (recall Chapter 7). If you agree that the essence of political development is the capability of the political system to handle basic functions, it is possible to have a political system that is quite developed but nondemocratic (e.g., China, Cuba, Swaziland, and Saudi Arabia). However, it is certainly valid to conclude that one highly desirable outcome of political development is a system that is democratic. **Democratization** can be understood as those *changes that deepen and consolidate democratic processes* (Diamond 2008; Schneider 2011). Democratization was proposed as one of the pillars of the stability goal of states in Figure 5.1, although not every political system aspires to this goal.

Samuel Huntington (1991) suggests that there have been three long waves of democratization among modern states. The first occurred between the 1820s and 1926, when about 30 countries established liberal democracies. Some of these then "reversed" (democracy was abandoned), until a second wave produced 36 democratic governments between 1945 and 1962. After another period of reversal, the third wave began in 1974. In the early 1990s, the push toward democratization was strong in some of the postcommunist states that emerged from the former Soviet Union, in Central and Eastern Europe, and in some former military regimes in Latin America, Asia, and Africa (e.g., Chile, Ghana, Panama, South Korea, Taiwan, and Uruguay). Then the Arab Spring of 2011 appeared to move some countries in the Middle East (e.g., Egypt and Tunisia) toward democratic practices. While there are currently 118 electoral democracies, Freedom House notes "a decline in global freedom" for eight consecutive years (Freedom House 2014). It is unclear at this point whether the third wave of democratization will be sustained by more popular uprisings or is now in reversal.

What might account for the broad expansion of democracies since the 1970s? Consider the following six explanations.

First, the level of *economic development* has long been presented as a crucial factor. As suggested by Figure 10.2, economic development can cause changes in the social system that facilitate democratization. Greater wealth and a credible commitment to distribute it with reasonable fairness reassures both citizens and leaders that the increased participation and demands associated with democratization can be handled with less risk of instability (Acemoglu and Robinson 2012; Huntington 1991; Stevens and Cooper 2010). Notice that some might turn the argument on its head and claim that greater democracy generates the conditions of freedom and opportunity that result in a more robust and productive economic system. The empirical data seem to support the claim that there is at least a correlation between economic development and democracy. This relationship is evident in Figure 10.4, which examines the EIU Democracy Index scores (2013) and GDP per capita (PPP) for selected countries. There is a visible correlation between higher and lower scores on these two measures. The correlation statistic is quite high: +.688. However, remember that correlation does not in itself demonstrate directionality: Either of these variables could influence the level of the other, and over time, they could influence each other's value. More fundamentally, correlation does not prove that there is a causal relationship between the two variables, since both could be associated with another variable (see the discussion in the Appendix). The Debate in 10 takes the analysis to a more challenging level, exploring whether economic development is a *necessary* prerequisite for democracy. And there are other ways for you to assess Figure 10.4. For example: Do you see any clusters of countries in Figure 10.4 that might suggest an alternative taxonomy to the one in Figure 10.1? Do the outliers suggest any qualifications in the relationship between economic development and democracy?

Second, *external actors* have been an important force in the shift toward democracy. Global actors, such as the World Bank, the EU, and the United Nations, among others, have insisted that countries introduce democratic reforms as a condition for economic assistance. Countries have sometimes withdrawn their support for authoritarian leadership, as the Soviet Union did in Central and Eastern Europe during the late 1980s. And external actors sometimes intervene directly in another country with the stated purpose of promoting democracy, as the United States and its allies did in Iraq and Afghanistan (Pickering and Peceny 2006; Robinson 1998).

Third, the *breakdown of authoritarian and totalitarian regimes* has provided a window of opportunity for democratization. In such cases, nondemocratic political systems have lost their capabilities to suppress the pressure for change. This seems to have been a particularly important factor in the states of the former Soviet Union and Central and

Figure 10.4 Association of Economic Development and Level of Democracy

SOURCES: World Bank 2013; Economist Intelligence Unit 2013

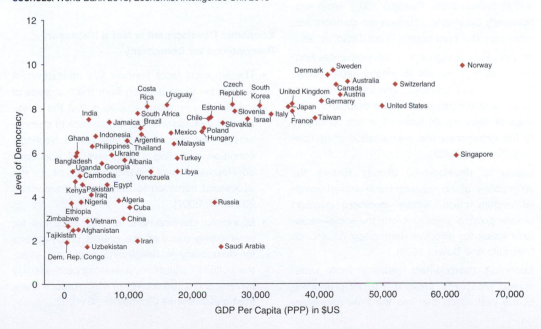

Debate in 10

Is Economic Development a Necessary Prerequisite for Democracy?

Currently, few research questions in political science attract more interest than the attempt to identify the conditions that are most conducive to establishing democracy. Over 50 years ago, the distinguished social scientist Seymour Martin Lipset (1959) argued that economic development is the crucial prerequisite for democracy. Supported by the fact that all the most developed countries at the time were democracies, Lipset's thesis became conventional wisdom. However, as a much more diverse set of countries has attempted to introduce democracy during the third wave of democratization, there has been considerable debate about whether economic development really is a *necessary* precondition for establishing and maintaining a democratic regime.

Economic Development Is a Necessary Prerequisite for Democracy

- The empirical facts support this linkage. Numerous comparative analyses, such as Figure 10.4, indicate that there is a strong correlation between a higher level of economic development and stronger democracy (Acemoglu and Robinson 2009; Richards 2007). Most economically developed countries are democracies, while very few poor countries are democracies.

- As indicated in Figure 10.2, economic development typically results in greater urbanization, higher levels of education, and the development of a political culture with more trust and tolerance of diversity, all factors that are conducive to the emergence and maintenance of democracy (Spagnoli 2003).

- Economic development directly fosters the emergence of an educated and entrepreneurial middle class, whose members demand greater political voice and form the social–structural basis for effective democracy (Bueno de Mesquita and Downs 2005).

- Economic development results in more widespread prosperity, creating a larger proportion of the population that has the time necessary

for active democratic participation. Conversely, in a society that lacks economic development, a substantial proportion of the population is so concerned with survival and economic advancement that people have little time or motivation to participate extensively in democratic life (Spagnoli 2003).

- The effects of economic development in raising education levels also promote greater political knowledge and awareness among the population, encouraging more extensive political participation and greater political tolerance.

- No democratic country with a GDP per capita of greater than $6,000 has ever abandoned democracy (Przeworski 2004). Thus, the prosperity that results from economic development is a crucial element in sustaining democracy.

- Economic development leads to greater access to a broader range of political information and more openness to global society. Such inputs reduce a nondemocratic government's ability to limit its citizens' exposure to ideas that promote the concept of democracy and undermine authoritarian control.

Economic Development Is Not a Necessary Precondition for Democracy

- The empirical facts support this conclusion. A reasonable generalization from the hundreds of comparative empirical studies is that the conditions associated with the emergence of democracy are complex, multiple, and varied. No single condition, including a high level of economic development, must always be present for the successful transition to democracy (Przeworski 2010; Tilly 2007).

- Economic development is not essential for establishing many of the critical preconditions for democracy in developing countries: effective political institutions, a working political party system, and a civil society in which groups share trust and tolerance (Schneider 2011).

- Many countries with high economic growth remain authoritarian regimes and have been very effective at resisting the demands for democracy, as cases such as China and Singapore clearly demonstrate. Indeed, high-income countries that are nondemocracies are *less* likely to transition to democracy than middle-income countries that are nondemocracies (Bueno de Mesquita and Downs 2005).

- Many relatively poor countries have successfully implemented democracy. In fact, the proportion of countries that are democracies is substantially higher than the proportion that is at high levels of economic development (Freedom House 2013).

- The spread of information and communications technologies (ICTs) and the Internet has reduced the significance of economic development in facilitating key preconditions of democracy such as mechanisms for interest aggregation, shared cultural identity, and a community of communication (Papacharrisi 2010).

- Some of the most durable democracies in the developing world maintained their high levels of political rights and civil liberties during long periods of limited economic development and negligible economic growth. Examples include Botswana, Costa Rica, and India.

More questions...

1. Which argument (bullet point) on each side of the debate is least persuasive? Why?

2. What is your evaluation of the argument that every wealthy country will eventually become a democracy?

Eastern Europe, as well as in countries such as Argentina, Egypt, and Tunisia (Linz and Stepan 1996).

Fourth, *changing norms favoring democracy* is often a factor. As citizens perceive that democracy is a positive value and that other countries are making the transition to democracy, they become more insistent that their leaders implement democratic reforms (Diamond 2008).

Fifth, nonviolent *"people power" movements* have become a crucial force for change in almost three-fourths of the countries that have democratized. There is a clear relationship between the strength of such movements and the level of democratic freedom that is achieved and maintained (Karatnycky and Ackerman 2006). Recently, such movements have been significantly facilitated by the Internet and social media, as in the Arab Spring of 2011 (Farrell 2012; Ritter and Trechsel 2011).

Sixth, the presence of *political leadership* committed to democracy can be important. In many countries, new leaders attained power based on their promise to pursue democratization as a central goal (as with Vicente Fox in Mexico, South Africa's Nelson Mandela, and Ukraine's Viktor Yushchenko). Indeed, most current leaders declare allegiance to democratization, if only to maintain domestic and international support (Sorensen 2008).

World of Changes

10.5 **Analyze how political systems respond to environmental challenges through political institutionalization and system transformation.**

Easton's model in Chapter 5 emphasized that the political system must attempt to respond to constant changes in its internal and external environments. Thus, Easton

(1965) asked: How can a political system persist in a world of changes? His answer is that the political system must produce decisions and actions that increase the support for the political institutions and the authorities and that manage the complex demands and challenges from the environment.

Thus political systems, like the global environment in which they function, are constantly engaged in both system maintenance and adaptive change. Most political change is modest, resulting from the effects of (1) new policy decisions, (2) alterations in the way existing policy is implemented, or (3) variations in the inputs from the internal or external environments. We could probably identify thousands of small changes in a single week. Although political change usually results from the gradual accumulation of minor adjustments, it is more noticeable when there is a substantial shift. For example, there could be a major change from a dominant party to a multiparty system, from authoritarianism to electoral democracy, from social order to widespread rioting, from a statist political economy to a neoliberal one, from male-only to gender-neutral political rights, or from an elected leader to a military dictatorship.

Even more *fundamental change in the nature of the political system or the political economy* can be called a **system transformation**. The emergence of a secular regime in Turkey under Atatürk, the destruction of the Saddam Hussein regime in Iraq, the abandonment of state socialism in Russia (see Compare in 15), and the dramatic alterations in Cambodia's political system that are the subject of the Compare in 10 are examples of system transformation. One striking feature of the political world in the last several decades has been the substantial number of such transformations. Chapter 15 will focus on systems in which political and economic transformations have been particularly extensive in the past several decades: two groups of transitional developed countries from within the middle cluster in Figure 10.1 and the BRICS (Brazil, Russia, India, China, and South Africa). In addition, coming chapters explore major transformations that seem to be occurring at the international level and are generally associated with *globalization.* System transformation is rare. Incremental change is the norm.

Change, when incremental and certainly when more dramatic, can generate both optimism and concern in any society. It might seem that key actors in most political systems would value political development as one desirable mode of change. This is probably the case if such development is understood as an increase in **political institutionalization**—*the depth of capabilities, stability, and citizen support for the existing political system.* And greater economic growth and development—the increased capacity to produce and distribute a broad array of goods—is a second change goal valued in almost all countries (Chapter 8).

However, change can be destabilizing. Thus there is more caution about what, if any, political and economic development will be encouraged in countries where the existing elites fear a loss of their advantaged position. For example, there are nondemocracies, such as Belarus, China, Oman, and Vietnam, in which leaders aim to increase the capabilities of the economic system and the political system without substantially expanding the processes and institutions of democracy. And there are some countries, such as Iran, Sudan, and Saudi Arabia, in which the current leaders have a very specific vision of what forms of political and economic development they will facilitate,

Compare in 10

Six Political Systems in Cambodia?

The case of Cambodia illuminates a political system that has undergone six major changes in the span of less than 50 years.

Cambodia I. The Cambodia of 1962 was a small, beautiful state in Indochina that had been granted its independence by France in 1953. It has been said that the most important activities in the lives of Cambodians were to dance, make love, and watch the grass grow. They were ruled under an authoritarian political system by Prince Norodom Sihanouk, a hereditary leader who attempted to balance the forces of the left and the right within Cambodia and to keep Cambodia on a neutral course. However, in the late 1960s, Sihanouk was unable to prevent Cambodia from being drawn into the increasingly widespread and intense war in neighboring Vietnam. Some Vietcong (the leftist guerrillas attempting to overthrow the South Vietnamese state) took sanctuary in Cambodia, but Sihanouk insisted that Cambodian sovereignty prevented the U.S. and South Vietnamese armies from invading Cambodia to attack these Vietcong. Sihanouk also attempted to direct international attention to the secret bombing raids in Cambodia conducted by the U.S. military but denied by the political leadership in the United States.

Cambodia II. Because of Sihanouk's resistance to their military objectives, the U.S. leaders supported (and perhaps directed) a March 1970 coup in which Cambodian army leaders overthrew Sihanouk and replaced him with General Lon Nol, a rightist dictator who was generally viewed as a puppet of the United States. There were dramatic changes in Cambodia's political structure and foreign policy under the new Lon Nol government (1970–1975), which was kept in power by the United States. In turn, the Cambodian government and military assisted the U.S. military in fighting the Vietcong and battling an expanding internal civil war led by the Khmer Rouge, Cambodian communists who opposed Lon Nol and his U.S. allies.

Cambodia III. With the collapse of the U.S. military effort in Southeast Asia, Lon Nol's government was among the casualties. Thus, the Khmer Rouge came to power in April 1975 and created yet another political system, renaming the country Kampuchea. Under the communist regime of Pol Pot, Kampuchea experienced one of the most dramatic transformations in a political system during the twentieth century. The new government immediately relocated everyone from urban areas to the countryside, organized the entire population into collective farms that were really forced labor camps, and implemented a massive reeducation (indoctrination) program. In a brutal reign of terror, about one-third of Cambodia's population of 7 million was either killed or died during a total restructuring of the society.

Cambodia IV. The Vietnamese exploited this time of disruption by invading and conquering the Cambodians, their centuries-old enemies. In January 1979, the Vietnamese army installed a puppet Cambodian government under Prime Minister Hun Sen (a dissident member of the Khmer Rouge). Thus, Pol Pot's barbaric regime was replaced with a new political system that operated as a satellite of Vietnam's communist government.

Cambodia V. After 13 years of guerrilla warfare against Hun Sen's government by groups loyal to the Khmer Rouge and Sihanouk, a treaty in Paris led to United Nations–supervised elections for a national legislature in 1993. The election and subsequent constitution created a fifth political system, an odd combination bringing together many of the old adversaries. Sihanouk became king, a constitutional monarch with mainly symbolic power. His anticommunist son, Prince Ranariddh, as "first" prime minister, shared political power with communist Hun Sen, the "second" prime minister. The Khmer Rouge, which refused to participate in the election, continued a punishing guerrilla war and controlled large parts of the countryside.

Cambodia VI. After another civil war, Hun Sen's forces were victorious in a 1997 coup that deposed Prince Ranariddh, who was exiled. Key supporters of the prince's political party either fled the country or were executed. Meanwhile, rival forces within the Khmer Rouge captured Pol Pot, who was imprisoned and soon died. In four subsequent national elections, most recently in 2013, Hun Sen has continued as prime minister and his party controls 55 percent of the seats in the lower house. Another son of Sihanouk (Sihamoni) is now king, but his duties are mainly ceremonial. Despite a multiparty system with open elections and some freedom of opposition, Cambodia is not an electoral democracy according to Freedom House. Corruption, abuse of power, and political violence are still so severe that the World Bank terms Cambodia a "fragile state."

A phrase in the Cambodian national anthem aptly describes the country's recent history: "The bright red blood…spilled over the towns and over the plain." It is unusual for a political system to undergo six dramatic changes in about 50 years, several of which were system transformations. Has the fragile state of Cambodia, and its 15 million people, now stabilized sufficiently for the existing political system to persist, at least for a while?

Further Questions

1. If you were to do a detailed comparative analysis of two of the six political systems in Cambodia, which two would you compare? Why?

2. How might a small country like Cambodia avoid being drawn into an intense conflict among major powers that spills over into its territory?

Skulls of the victims of the brutal Khmer Rouge reign of terror (1975–1979) are on display in many villages around Cambodia as memorials to honor the dead and strengthen Cambodians' resolve to prevent a reoccurrence of such state violence against its own people.

since any change must serve religious and social values that might be undermined by the type of twenty-first-century development described above.

Regardless of the form of development envisioned by the political leadership, the elites in most countries recognize that it is very difficult to control the *directions* of change with precision. The recent economic turmoil in many countries is an ominous indicator of the extent to which economic systems are vulnerable to decline and disarray. Their extraordinary complexity, both internally and as part of the global economy, makes it increasingly difficult to understand how they are changing and how to control them.

Political systems are arguably even more vulnerable to decline and disarray. Samuel Huntington (1968) has described how some political systems that appear to have achieved a reasonable level of political development then experience a substantial deterioration of political structures, processes, and roles. He calls this situation **political decay**—*a significant decline in the capabilities of the political system and its level of political institutionalization, especially in its capacity to maintain order.* Political decay is evident in high levels of civil disorder—strikes, violent crime, riots, nation-based conflict, and rebellion.

Political decay can have multiple causes, many of which are associated with the change processes discussed in this chapter. The development process is inherently destabilizing. Economic growth produces new resources over which to compete; urbanization concentrates heterogeneous groups into large, densely packed, and volatile masses; expanded, globalized communications make the people aware of the many resources and values that they do not currently enjoy. Most people expect their political system to provide stability, prosperity, and security. If the political system does not adequately meet these expectations and if it lacks solid political institutionalization, citizen support and social order can decline. In response to political decay, several scenarios can evolve:

- The political system cracks down on disorder, limiting the rights of protest groups, opposition parties, the free press, and so on and deploying its security forces (e.g., the police, the military) to suppress any antiregime activities.
- A charismatic leader emerges. The leader gains the support and obedience of the people but only by personalizing power and thus weakening the overall processes through which power and political structures are institutionalized.
- The military—the one organization in most societies that *is* institutionalized— forcibly takes over political power under the justification of restoring order.
- A popular uprising, typically supported by external actors, drives out the old leadership; but if the active groups are fragmented and do not rapidly provide a coherent governing alternative, extensive, widespread disorder is likely.

In each of the first three scenarios, there is usually a shift toward greater authoritarianism. If the country had been deepening its democratic practices, these scenarios of political decay can lead to democratic breakdown and illiberal democracy. Such trends are evident in most regions in recent years (Freedom House 2014; Schedler 2013; Wiarda 2004; Zakaria 2007). If the situation approaches the fourth scenario of widespread disorder, even the fundamental goal of state survival is under threat.

Almost 60 countries are currently under such severe pressures, relative to their level of political institutionalization, that they are classified as at least "seriously fragile states" (Marshall and Cole 2011). When *a political system completely loses its capacity to maintain basic order*, it can be characterized as a *failed state*. Recent examples include Afghanistan, Congo (DR), Haiti, Somalia, Sudan, and Zimbabwe (Fund for Peace 2013; Rotberg 2003). Such widespread disorder can be almost akin to Hobbes's notion of the "state of nature." Life for most citizens truly is nasty, violent, and short, and many people engage in behaviors that are brutish. A failed state also creates dangers for other states in its region, due to disruptions caused by displaced populations and economic hardships. And in some cases, a state actually does cease to exist, as occurred several times in the recent history of Cambodia described in Compare in 10.

Concluding Observations

Ultimately, all political systems aim to increase their capabilities and thus achieve greater political and economic development. In general, most people assume that development in other countries should result in political systems and political economies that resemble those in their own country. It is debatable, however, whether all states should or even can follow the same developmental path. Some, perhaps most, developing countries might have characteristics that are not compatible with the patterns of development or the political structures and processes that worked in other countries, especially those that developed in earlier eras.

The leaders in most countries try to assess whether the prior experiences and strategies of some other state provide a model for their own change and development. Even if leaders do select and properly implement a model that seems compatible with the goals and unique characteristics of their countries, achieving political development and political institutionalization as well as sustaining economic growth are extremely difficult for many countries in the contemporary world. The remainder of this book will continue to illustrate the extent to which the choices and actions of states are influenced and sometimes controlled by other actors in the global system and by limits on their own resources. This is a particular problem for states with low capabilities and minimal stability—that is, states that lack political institutionalization. You will see these states in the lower-left sector of Figure 10.4.

Huntington is certainly correct that the challenges to political development are great. There have been periods of major political instability even in some European and Latin American countries—and these countries had the advantage of a long period in which the structures of a modern state could evolve into more complex and effective forms and in which the citizens could come to accept and value their political system. In contrast to those countries, most other states began creating their own modern political systems in the last 60 years. While these systems have the appearance of modernity—specialized political structures, widespread political participation, and so on—many lack the stability and value that come with a long evolutionary development.

The political elites in these states face many fundamental dilemmas in a world of changes. How much political participation and opposition should be allowed? Into what aspects of people's lives should *res publica* be extended? In what ways should the state intervene in the political economy? What benefits and what burdens should the state allocate to particular groups? What should government do to nurture civil society and social order? In essence, can the political system shape political, economic, and social change? All states continually deal with these challenging issues, which will be recurrent themes in the remainder of this book.

Key Concepts

BRICS, p. 268
change, p. 259
civil society, p. 263
democratization, p. 276
dependency approach, p. 270
developing countries, p. 267
developed countries, p. 267
development, p. 261
developmental state, p. 269
economic development,
   p. 261

failed state, p. 283
Global North, p. 267
Global South, p. 267
Latin American Transitionals,
   p. 268
modernization, p. 260
neoliberalism, p. 269
political decay, p. 283
political development, p. 271
political institutionalization,
   p. 280

postcommunist developed
   countries, p. 268
social development, p. 265
statism, p. 269
state capitalism, p. 269
system transformation,
   p. 280
transitional developed
   countries, p. 267
Westernization, p. 261

For Further Consideration

1. Most people in Western societies have been socialized to believe that change is associated with progress and is generally a good thing. However, the ideology of conservatism (as outlined in Chapter 2) does not make this assumption. What are the conservative's views about change? More broadly, can you specify types of change that would not necessarily be positive for a given political system?

2. The success or failure of the developmental state strategy in certain developing countries is sometimes attributed to elements of culture. How important do you think a society's culture might be in shaping development? Why? What factors other than culture might affect a country's capacity for rapid development?

3. Many countries have recently established democratic political processes. Is political decay inevitable in most of these countries? Why or why not? What strategies, general and specific, seem most promising in the attempt to avoid serious political decay?

4. Write a dialogue between two analysts: One contends that the dependency approach offers the best explanation for the failure of many countries to achieve development, while the second argues that other factors best explain why some countries have limited development.

For Further Reading

Acemoglu, Daron, and James A. Robinson. (2012). *Why Nations Fail: The Origins of Power, Prosperity, and Poverty.* **New York: Random House.** A fascinating read and a compelling, sweeping (and controversial) analysis across the centuries (with emphasis on the most recent period) exploring the reasons, grounded in political choices, why some countries develop economically and others do not. See also the more technically grounded analysis by these two economists, *Economic Origins of Dictatorship and Democracy* (New York: Cambridge University Press, 2009).

Achebe, Chinua. (1959). *Things Fall Apart.* **New York: Doubleday.** In this highly acclaimed and moving novel, Achebe describes how the beliefs and lives of a virtuous leader and others in his Nigerian village are undermined by missionaries and the colonial administration, as modernization results in the disintegration of their cultural traditions.

Becker, Elizabeth. (1986). *When the War Was Over: The Voices of Cambodia's Revolution and Its People.* New York: Simon and Schuster. A gut-wrenching description of Cambodia under the Pol Pot regime (Compare in 10).

Collier, Paul. (2008). *The Bottom Billion: Why the Poorest Countries Are Failing and What Can Be Done about It.* New York: Oxford University Press. The author elaborates on four key reasons for the development failures of the world's poorest countries: civil wars, abundant resources that others covet, poor geography, and bad governance.

Cornwall, Andrea, Elizabeth Harrison, and Ann Whitehead, eds. (2007). *Feminisms in Development: Contradictions, Contestations, and Challenges.* London: ZedBooks. Case studies and broader analyses examine development theory from a feminist perspective and provide strong examples regarding both the crucial roles and the marginalization of women in development.

Diamond, Larry. (2008). *The Spirit of Democracy: The Struggle to Build Free Societies throughout the World.* New York: Holt. A leading scholar of democratization offers an analysis of how countries can deepen their democracies, how other countries can help, and the strategies necessary to avoid the "democracy recessions" recently evident in a number of countries.

Dubash, Navroz K., and Bronwen Morgan. (2013). *The Rise of the Regulatory State of the South: Infrastucture and Development in Emerging Economies.* Oxford: Oxford University Press. This interdisciplinary book considers how development choices and approaches to institutional design have long-range political, economic, and social consequences.

Elliott, Jennifer. (2012). *An Introduction to Sustainable Development.* 4th ed. New York: Routledge. A solid textbook exploring the various meanings of "sustainable development," including an examination of the contested nature of its realization and the key actors involved.

Huntington, Samuel P. (1991). *The Third Wave: Democratization in the Late Twentieth Century.* Norman, OK: University of Oklahoma Press. A wide-ranging assessment of transitions to democracy by one of the major scholars of comparative development. The general argument about political institutionalization and political decay discussed in this chapter is fully elaborated in his earlier sweeping study *Political Order in Changing Societies* (New Haven, CT: Yale University Press, 1968).

Johnson, Chalmers. (1996). *Japan: Who Governs? The Rise of the Developmental State.* New York: W. W. Norton. This book provides a broad framework characterizing the government–industry cooperation that produced the "Japanese miracle" and became the basis of the development approach taken by other countries, especially in Asia.

Lipset, Seymour Martin. (1988). *Revolution and Counterrevolution: Change and Persistence in Social Structures.* Rev. ed. Rutgers, NJ: Transaction Books. Provocative essays on the processes of change and development, with a particular emphasis on the effects of culture.

Rotberg, Robert I., ed. (2003). *When States Fail: Causes and Consequences.* Princeton, NJ: Princeton University Press. The first part of the book is a series of essays examining the conditions under which states deteriorate to the point of collapse; the second part offers analyses of what can be done to prevent failed states and how to rebuild such states.

Schneider, Carsten. (2009). *The Consolidation of Democracy: Comparing Europe and Latin America.* London: Routledge. A careful analysis of the conditions under which democratic consolidation (institutionalization) is more likely, placing particular importance on the fit between the political institutional arrangements and the dispersion of power in the society.

Sorensen, Georg. (2007). *Democracy and Democratization: Processes and Prospects in a Changing World.* **3rd ed. Boulder, CO: Westview.** A wide-ranging discussion of the spread of democratic processes in many countries, defining the patterns and conditions under which democracy is viable and the likely evolution of various democratic systems.

Wiarda, Howard J. (2004). *Political Development in Emerging Countries.* **Belmont, CA: Wadsworth.** A sensible description of the major theories of development in the developing countries (see Chapter 14). It indicates how frameworks such as dependency theory, neoliberalism, globalization, and the developmental state approach apply to the situation in such countries.

On the Web

http://hdr.undp.org/en/reports
This is the site for the United Nations Development Programme office, the source of the yearly Human Development Report, which provides an exceptionally comprehensive set of social and economic data about every country as well as detailed thematic explorations of topics regarding environment, health, human rights, economic development, and so on.

http://worldbank.org
At the official site of the World Bank, an international consortium of banks and other major financial institutions, extensive economic data are available, including selections from the annual World Development Report and information on issues of development and trade.

http://www.iisd.ca
The Web site of the International Institute for Sustainable Development offers information and essays on this topic, ranging from policy statements and economic data to book-length studies.

http://www.acdi-cida.gc.ca/home
This site from the Canadian International Development Agency provides links to many sources of information about development issues, such as aid, economic growth, environmental impacts, and human rights.

http://www.sustainabledevelopment.un.org
The home page of the United Nations Division for Sustainable Development, this site provides access to a wide variety of relevant UN resolutions and publications.

http://www.ulb.ac.be/ceese/meta/sustvl.html
This section of the very comprehensive World Wide Web Virtual Library (http://vlib.org/) contains an extensive listing of Internet resources related to sustainable development and political change.

http://www.foreignpolicy.com/articles/2009/06/22/the_2009_failed_states_index
The Fund for Peace, an independent research organization, and the journal *Foreign Policy* use 12 indicators of state cohesion and performance to compute an annual Failed State Index for all countries and provide details of the challenges facing the 60 countries most at risk of failure.

http://www.crisisgroup.org
This is the International Crisis Group's "Crisis Web," which details the current crises within countries with serious levels of political decay and offers policy suggestions for conflict management and a return to political order.

Chapter 11
Politics Across Borders

 ## Learning Objectives

11.1 Compare realist, liberal, and constructivist perspectives of the state.

11.2 Classify the main actors in the global system and characterize the mechanisms of cooperation between states.

11.3 Analyze the types of power politics between actors in the international system and evaluate the impact of globalization.

After being ravaged by the two bloodiest and most costly wars in modern history (World War I and World War II), bitter rivals France, Germany, and Italy, along with Belgium, Luxembourg, and the Netherlands, decided to create political and economic ties that would ensure their countries would cooperate rather than fight. In 1952, the six countries established an economic union and then, with the Treaty of Rome (1957), created the European Economic Community (the "Common Market"). Countries that had periodically fought began an era of cooperation. Cultures that had clashed attempted to blend and share common goals.

In 60 years, this competitive group of states has evolved into the European Union (EU) and grown to 28 member states and 504 million citizens, operating with 24 official languages. Greater economic integration has led to an efficient sharing of markets and labor across borders and the elimination of most tariff fights. The economy of the EU is currently the world's largest, characterized by diversity, growth, and prosperity.

The EU is governed by effective legislative, executive, administrative, and judicial branches, which operate on democratic principles and exhibit strong political institutionalization. The Lisbon Treaty of 2009, approved by all members, increased coherence in collective policymaking by implementing a more integrated, majority-based political framework under a strong president. The EU has established a collective security pact that not only prevents these states from going to war against each other but also makes the EU a formidable military power, such that no country in the world is likely to challenge one of its members.

Yes to the EU!: Tens of thousands of Ukrainian demonstrators march through central Kiev in November 2013, demanding that their government reverse its position and sign a major agreement with the European Union, whose flag is displayed. The government was overthrown within weeks of its refusal to sign the agreement.

However, all is not perfect in the EU (Webber 2013). While several countries, especially France and Germany, advocate increased integration and seek to create "pooled sovereignty" by establishing a federation, the EU is still a rather loosely connected confederation. Long-held cultural and national identities remain a major obstacle to complete integration. The broad voting consensus required for EU policymaking can be difficult to achieve when some of the 28 countries disagree or act on their own national interests. There are substantial challenges in sustaining a single economic policy; for example, while 17 countries in the EU have joined the eurozone, other countries like the United Kingdom and Sweden continue to use their own national currencies (Moravcsik 2012). And weaknesses, just like strengths, become a shared problem for all member states, as the eurozone crises in Greece, Ireland, and Portugal during the recent global recession have revealed. The fiscally sound countries have been obliged to bail out the countries running high deficits, fostering distrust and resentment.

Critics argue that the EU does not have a coherent military policy or even a standing military. Some members have refused to provide military forces to support EU security initiatives outside the EU countries. Moreover, the EU's open borders allow unrestricted movement of people across all EU countries, including individuals who have entered any EU country illegally from elsewhere in the world. Thus, the native population of every EU country is attempting to adapt to the influx of many new cultures. This has generated considerable tension and a rise in popularity of nationalistic (and increasingly anti-EU) political parties and social movements. Some countries are now considering a return to controlled borders—a serious retreat from the vision of an integrated Europe.

Clearly, the European Union has a long way to go in terms of integrating and establishing a unified Europe, but the countries that make up the EU generally are more successful working together than they ever were as competing, independent states. The EU is one of the most remarkable recent efforts by states to establish institutions that overcome historical conflict and facilitate cooperation (McCormick and Olsen 2013).

The states in the EU are among the millions of political actors whose interests and actions cross national borders. Many of the most important aspects of contemporary politics occur across borders. Mexico and the United States attempt to cooperate to reduce the flow of guns, drugs, and people across their shared border. India and Pakistan argue about who should control Jammu and Kashmir. UN peacekeeping forces are active in the Central African Republic to provide humanitarian assistance and promote security in the region. Multinational corporations such as Toyota work with and around government regulations to produce goods in many countries and then sell them in other countries. More than 100 countries discuss how to reduce carbon emissions in response to climate change. One billion people live in countries in which they are not citizens. Almost everyone now recognizes that no country can function within its own borders without extensive engagement with actors beyond those borders.

Understanding how these kinds of political behaviors and institutions function across borders is the focus of this chapter. Some of the many important nonstate actors are highlighted in the discussions, although states are central to most of the topics because they are still crucial actors in the politics across borders. Globalization (discussed later in this chapter) is dramatically increasing the extent to which outside forces influence states, and many states expend much—and, in some cases most—of their political energy on their relations with other states and with transborder actors. *One state's decisions and actions in its relations with all actors operating outside the state's borders* are called **foreign policy**. The *politically relevant interactions among two or more actors from different states* are called **international relations**. Initially, this chapter details key perspectives and certain constraints that might guide states as they pursue their goals in the politics that occurs across borders. Second, it discusses the means by which states and transborder actors attempt to facilitate cooperation and resolve conflict. Third, it examines key forms of power politics across borders, such as balance of power and colonial domination. The causes and use of force and violence across state borders will be considered in Chapter 12.

Perspectives on States' Behavior

11.1 Compare realist, liberal, and constructivist perspectives of the state.

States' Motives from Alternative Perspectives: Realism, Liberalism, and Constructivism

Chapter 5 identified three core goals that all states pursue—prosperity, stability, and security—as well as an array of key subgoals. All of these goals, but especially security, can be influenced powerfully by the politics that occurs across states' borders—politics in which states remain critical actors. While a state has sovereign rights to control what occurs within its territorial borders, every state faces a **security dilemma** in the global system because the politics between and among states occurs in an international system that is generally assumed to be *anarchic*. This does not mean that the system is chaotic; rather, it means that *a state's security is always at risk because there is no overarching authority that can consistently impose order and "good behavior" on all the states* in their relations with one another and with other actors in the global system.

Scholars attempt to explain how and why states behave in certain ways, given the absence of such an authority. This raises questions about a state's primary motives, its key values, and the context within which it acts. Three perspectives have especially influenced international relations theory on these issues: realism, liberalism, and constructivism. While there are variations and overlaps, distinctions among the three perspectives can be drawn.

Realism assumes that *states, like people, are naturally disposed to base their behavior on self-interest, and the core of this interest is survival.* Realism focuses on the security dilemma: There is no supreme authority, no transborder institution, and no international rules that will necessarily protect the state from predatory behavior by other actors in the international system. Thus, to ensure its own security and survival, the key motivation of a state is to maximize its military (coercive) power in order to protect itself. A broader version of realism, *neorealism*, adds the idea that a state's capacity to survive and prevail can also be based on other forms of power, such as economic power, knowledge power, and diplomatic power. Neorealism also attaches significance to the structure of the international system, such as how many other powerful states exist. According to neorealists, the state makes calculated decisions based on its power capacities, its internal and external environments, and its assessments of its best chances at security. From the realist perspective, states are in constant competition for power, especially because power is a zero-sum commodity—an increase in power for one actor results in an equivalent decrease for others. There is no expectation that another state can be trusted, will avoid violence, or will act ethically. A state makes treaties or breaks them, makes war, or cooperates with other countries for only one reason: to maximize its security goals and serve its national interest (Mearshimer 2001; Walt 2006).

In contrast, the crucial assumption of **liberalism** is that *each state will make decisions and act in the international system based on its own mix of principles, and these might encourage cooperation.* From the perspective of liberalism, and its variations termed *neoliberalism*, states can have multiple goals, and aggressive, power-maximizing behavior is not inevitable. While every state wants to survive, states might also take actions in the politics across borders that support other values such as economic prosperity, political stability, peace, or the spread of democracy. Liberalism also diverges from realism in emphasizing that key groups within the state can influence the array of preferences that lead to action in the international system. Neoliberalism further holds that it is possible to establish well-designed transnational institutions that can harmonize the mixed motives of multiple states, facilitate cooperative behavior among states, establish rules of behavior that are somewhat stable, and create situations that are positive sum—some gain, no one loses (Glanville 2013; Ikenberry 2011; Keohane and Nye 2011).

Constructivism, a third perspective, assumes that *analysis of the politics across borders must recognize that each state and the key actors who influence the state's actions develop unique understandings of the relevant events and institutions based on their particular knowledge, experiences, norms, and habits* (Weber 2013). From the constructivist perspective, neither realism nor liberalism is adequately sensitive to the "socially constructed" nature of the identities and norms that shape beliefs and guide actions taken by individuals, groups, and states in the international system. A condition (e.g., anarchy in the international system) or an institution (e.g., the United Nations) can have very different meanings for different actors, and these meanings determine its influence on actions by a state. Nonstate actors, both domestic and transnational, can have a significant role in influencing the value preferences that result in a state's actions. For example, key actors in Canada, Cuba, and the global system would have very different interpretations of a substantial increase in military spending by the United States. Thus any adequate analysis of the reactions of Canada and Cuba to the U.S. military buildup must include the effects on each state of the viewpoints of some of these other actors (Barnett and Finnemore 2004; O'Farcheallaigh 2013; Wendt 1995, 1999).

While variations of realism, liberalism, and constructivism are prominent in the current theories of international relations scholars, among the interesting alternatives is feminist IR. As you might expect, *feminist IR analyzes topics from the frames of reference and assumptions of feminist theory and gender studies*. Feminist IR critiques theories that focus on the anarchy of the international system or simply on the behavior of current state and transnational institutions. Rather, it posits that, in general, IR theory has neglected to consider the role in international relations of half the population or the effects on state behavior of predominantly male leadership. Whether due to socialization, social construction, biology, or gender roles, women and men might engage politics and problem solving in different ways. Some suggest that women are more inclined toward cooperative interactions and nonviolent solutions and that if more such women were in positions of power, states would interact somewhat less aggressively (Basu 2013; Enloe 2001; Steans 2013; Tickner 2001).

As you read the discussion of politics across borders in this chapter, consider how the different assumptions of realism, liberalism, constructivism, or feminism can alter one's interpretations of the topics and also one's prescriptive ideas of how actors should behave in the international system. Your understanding of the political world will be influenced by the extent to which you share elements of each of these perspectives. Does any one of these four seem most compelling to you?

A Geopolitical Perspective

As we begin an empirical analysis of how states behave in the global system, it is worth noting that a state's pursuit of its goals is always constrained by many factors, both within and outside its borders. The political system model outlined in Chapter 5 reminds us that a state's actions can be influenced substantially by many aspects of the extrasocietal environment, including the actions of other state and nonstate actors. There are also influential factors within a state's intrasocietal environment, such as its history and political culture, the style of its major political leaders, and the nature of its political structures.

Geopolitical analysis emphasizes one set of critical factors that might constrain a state's behavior, especially in its relations with other actors in the international system. **Geopolitics** assumes that *the geography of a state—that is, its physical characteristics (e.g., strategic location, topography) and its natural and human resources (e.g., population size, fossil fuel resources, arable land, water)—might significantly affect both the internal and external politics of the state* (Cohen 2008). Few argue that geography is destiny. However, it is reasonable to assume that a state's geography can be a significant source of both opportunities for and constraints on its political actions in the international system (Dalby 2008; Dwyer 2013; Kaplan 2009; Montgomery 2013). Compare in 11 proposes how a geopolitical analysis might offer insights into the foreign policies of two states.

Compare in 11

Geopolitics in Two Countries

Imagine two island countries, Sigma and Theta. Each lies just off a (different) large landmass that is dominated by one of the world's most powerful countries. Unfortunately, this powerful neighbor is a major enemy and a threat. Each island nation has a well-educated, mainly urban population. Each has a fickle, tropical climate, and one-fourth of the land is arable. Sigma has relatively abundant natural resources while Theta has far fewer such resources, but both need to import sources of energy.

If you knew nothing more about either country, could you make any educated guesses about how these countries might pursue key political and economic goals and about the relations these countries might develop with other actors in the international system? This is the core of geopolitical analysis. For example, to enhance their security, each might look for an alliance with another country that is a powerful enemy of their neighbor. Each would probably establish a strong military. So that the hostile neighbor does not sense instability and weakness, the political system might be somewhat authoritarian to control its population and minimize internal conflict. Sigma might be able to rely on its fertile land and natural resources as a solid basis for exports. Theta might need to rely more heavily on its workforce to produce more sophisticated value-added goods and services to gain trading partners. Both would need to secure energy resources.

Sigma could be Cuba. Cuba achieved independence from its colonial master, Spain, in 1902. After nearly 50 years of corrupt, authoritarian regimes that left most of the population minimally educated and economically exploited, a successful guerrilla war led by Fidel Castro installed a communist regime in 1959. This antagonized Cuba's powerful neighbor and former best friend, the United States. As Cuba perceived numerous attempts by the United States to undermine its regime (some real, some imagined), its leadership increased Cuba's military readiness, with universal military service and constant political socialization regarding the threat from the United States (recall the Cuban math problem at the beginning of Chapter 4).

Castro and the Communist Party became increasingly authoritarian politically, suppressing almost all opposition voices. While its command political economy resulted in low productivity, the system did manage to provide good health care, universal literacy, greater social and economic equality, and social security for all citizens. Cuba forged a strong alliance with the major Cold War enemy of the United States, the Soviet Union, which served as Cuba's military protector and which provided it with $4 to $6 billion in subsidies each year, including energy resources. After the Soviets unsuccessfully tried to install missiles on Cuba pointing at the United States (the Cuban missile crisis in 1961), the United States intensified its pressure for an extensive trade embargo that has undermined the Cuban economy.

Since the collapse of the Soviet Union (1989) and the loss of Soviet subsidies, Cuba has struggled even more because only limited trade bypasses the embargo. More recently, Cuba developed strong ties with Venezuela's late Hugo Chavez, who exported energy resources to Cuba in exchange for skilled Cuban professionals who work in Venezuela, especially in health care and education.

Theta could be Taiwan. An island extension of China, it was conquered by Japan in 1895 and subjected to harsh colonization until Japan's defeat in World War II. When the Nationalists under Chiang Kai-shek lost to Mao Zedong in the civil war on mainland China in 1949, the Nationalists fled to Taiwan and took control of its political and economic systems. The Nationalists were in fundamental opposition to Mao Zedong's government, insisting that they were the rightful rulers of China and would one day regain control of the mainland. In response, Mao's government insisted that Taiwan was a "renegade province" that would ultimately be reunited with China. The United States, deeply threatened by China's communist government, stepped in to become Taiwan's protector.

Taiwan took advantage of extensive military and economic support from the United States. It established a strong military presence, backed by U.S. arms. And it developed an aggressively capitalist political economy, following the developmental state approach described in Chapter 10. Because it had limited natural resources, Taiwan became a manufacturing economy, importing materials and moving from the production of toys, textiles, and other less sophisticated goods to the export of goods such as electronics components, armaments, chemicals, iron, and steel. It relied on the United States as its main target for exports and imports, including energy.

In 1971, the United Nations voted to deny Taiwan recognition as an independent sovereign state. Given concerns that instability in Taiwan would encourage China to intervene or invade, Taiwan's government was highly authoritarian, with strict limits on political opposition, and full democratization has emerged only since 2000. Over time, Taiwan has managed its human resources very effectively and created a strong economy within the global system. Because Japan and China are such juggernaut regional economies, Taiwan has slowly built trade relations with these historical enemies, and they are now its main trading partners. Tensions with China remain high, however, with China continuing to claim sovereignty over Taiwan and Taiwan relying on its substantial military and the ongoing protection from the United States to retain its independence (CIA 2014).

While geography is not destiny, it is evident that the domestic and foreign policies of both Cuba and Taiwan have been influenced significantly by their geopolitical circumstances.

Further Questions

1. How might Cuba and Taiwan have acted differently if their powerful neighbor was a strong ally instead of an intransigent enemy?

2. What are other countries for which a geopolitical analysis might be especially insightful?

Compare in 11 also reveals how politics across state borders is usually characterized by a mix of cooperation and competition. For example, Taiwan interacts with the United States as a cooperative partner on security issues, and it both cooperates and competes with the United States regarding imports and exports. Taiwan strongly resists China's goal of reunification, yet China has become Taiwan's main investor and trading partner. The rest of this chapter explores cooperation and competition as the two dominant patterns in international relations. In most instances, a state realizes more benefits and fewer costs if it pursues its goals by strategies of cooperation with other states and with transborder actors. However, competition is always a possibility as states come into conflict with other actors as they pursue their goals. The final section in Chapter 12 will examine those crucial situations in which conflict resolution fails and the competition escalates into violence across borders and even into war.

Mechanisms of Political Cooperation Across Borders

11.2 **Classify the main actors in the global system and characterize the mechanisms of cooperation between states.**

Do you agree with the proposition that, under most circumstances, a state is likely to accomplish more of its goals at lower costs if it can develop mutually advantageous cooperative arrangements with other states? This section will consider the various ways in which states can cooperate. From the neoliberal (contemporary idealist) perspective, a state has an inherent preference to establish arrangements through which such cooperation can be nurtured. Realists are likely to be more cynical about such cooperation, viewing such arrangements as strategic actions to be made or broken as they serve the state's national interest.

Even in the absence of any formalized mechanisms of cooperation, a state might adopt several patterns of behavior that are noteworthy for their nonconflictual approach:

1. **Altruism:** A state acts in accordance with moral principles, not its national interest. Thus, the state might provide humanitarian aid to the population of another country with no expectation of direct benefits, or it might make a unilateral decision to reduce its military capabilities or its carbon emissions to improve the global environment.

2. **Accommodation:** A state willingly makes concessions on one or more values of importance in order to promote an acceptable outcome or a nonviolent resolution of a dispute with another actor. This might involve a compromise in which several states find common ground, or one state might make a disproportionate level of concessions in an attempt to improve its relations or avoid conflict with another actor (e.g., a state, a multinational financial institution, or an international judicial body).

3. **Neutrality:** A state claims its right to be impartial among competing states and to refrain from supporting any states in a conflict. A key goal of a neutral state is to avoid being drawn into a dispute among other states. In recent decades, countries such as Austria, Finland, Sweden, and Switzerland have defined themselves as neutral states.

Diplomacy and Interstate Agreements

One of the most widely used mechanisms through which states communicate to enhance cooperation is *diplomacy*. Diplomatic practices enable a state's skilled representatives to engage in regular discussions and negotiations with the representatives of other states. Thus, most states maintain an array of actors (e.g., ambassadors, cultural attachés) and institutions (e.g., embassies, trade delegations) that attempt to further their state's interests and resolve potential problems with other states by means of "normal diplomatic channels" and informal communications. The essence of traditional diplomacy is strategic, face-to-face discussions between diplomats on behalf of their countries. However, modern communications technologies (e.g., video-conferencing) have provided new ways for leaders and diplomats to interact, allowing them to deal with one another directly, even if not in person. In the world of 24/7 news media, political officials are aware that every public utterance is being recorded and is accessible around the world to other political actors via some medium, ranging from Al-Jazeera to YouTube.

A special form of diplomacy is when the top leaders of countries meet to share views and seek common policy ground. In any given week, there are one-on-one meetings, such as when chief executives or foreign ministers travel to meet their counterparts. During a single week in September 2013, for example, U.S. president Barack Obama held private meetings with Brazil's president Dilma Rousseff, China's president Xi Jinping, Germany's chancellor Angela Merkel, and India's prime minister Manmohan Singh, among others.

So many private meetings in such a short time were possible because the leaders of major countries (the G20) were holding a summit meeting in St. Petersburg, Russia. The G20 is a global group of key industrial and emerging-market countries (plus a representative from the European Union) that focuses on financial issues. The leaders of an even more elite group of powerful industrialized countries, the G8, also meet periodically to discuss shared policy concerns. Table 11.1 lists the members of these two groups. There are numerous other regional groups that hold recurrent meetings

Table 11.1 Major Diplomatic Groupings of States

G8	G20 (adds to G8)	
Canada	Argentina	Mexico
France	Australia	Saudi Arabia
Germany	Brazil	South Africa
Italy	China	South Korea
Japan	India	Turkey
Russia*	Indonesia	European Union
United Kingdom		
United States		

*Russia was suspended from the G8 in 2014 due to its actions in Ukraine.

in an attempt to cooperate on policy (e.g., Association of Southeast Asian Nations [ASEAN] in South Asia, MERCOSUR in Latin America, the Organization of African States [OAS]).

More explicit cooperation among states is usually established by bilateral (between two states) or multilateral (among three or more states) agreements. The two most prominent forms of these agreements are treaties and regimes. **Treaties** are *formal agreements between states that they will cooperate or assist one another,* usually in the domains of military, economic, or political interactions. A treaty is a contract between states (or with an international organization), and there is an expectation that the agreement is binding on all signatories. Most treaties involve a limited set of countries. For example, the North American Free Trade Agreement (NAFTA) is a treaty among three states (Canada, Mexico, and the United States) to cooperate on a complex set of trade arrangements. The Strategic Arms Reduction Treaties (e.g., START II, 1993) are weapons-limitation pacts between the United States and Russia. The European Union (EU), described at the beginning of this chapter, is an example of a major multistate, multipurpose confederation based on treaties for economic, political, cultural, and military cooperation among its 28 member countries.

Some multistate agreements are called **international regimes** to signify *a set of norms, rules, and procedures accepted by many countries that guide their behavior regarding a particular issue area.* There are only a limited number of international regimes. They are like treaties, but typically have a very large number of signatories, and compliance is less rigorously enforced. Current examples are in the area of arms control (e.g., the Nuclear Nonproliferation Treaty [1968], now including 189 countries) and environmental protection (e.g., the 1997 Kyoto Protocol on climate change and greenhouse gas emissions, accepted by 191 countries and the EU). Many international regimes establish a permanent organization through which the member states can enact, modify, and implement the agreements and facilitate crossnational cooperation (Drezner 2008; Keohane 2005).

The World Trade Organization (WTO) is one of the most powerful and controversial international regimes. Established in 1995, the WTO emerged from an international trading regime that had evolved over the prior 50 years. The WTO, which currently has 159 member countries, states that its main goal is "to enable trade, to the extent possible, to flow freely in a predictable and smooth manner" among all countries. It works with member countries to establish and enforce policies that eliminate all barriers to global free trade (e.g., tariffs on imports, subsidies to producers, "dumping" strategies [selling goods abroad at below cost to cripple competitors]). Hence, the WTO claims that the primary result of its actions is "a world economy which is more prosperous, has less conflict, and is more transparent" (WTO 2013).

However, critics assert that, as elite theory posits (recall Chapter 9), WTO rules and agreements primarily benefit the financial elites and multinational corporations that dominate global trade (Meckled-Garcia 2013). They claim that the free trade agreements implemented by the WTO increase the profits of multinational corporations (MNCs) but reduce the power of workers, are indifferent to violations of human rights, fail to protect the environment, and undermine the sovereignty of national governments, which must accept WTO regulations. To its detractors, the WTO is "one of the most powerful, secretive and antidemocratic bodies on Earth," and the main results of its actions are to "preside over the greatest transfer in history, of real economic and political power away from nation-states to global corporations" and to "run roughshod over the rights of people and nations, causing all manner of environmental and social harms" (Global Exchange 2009; Mander 1999).

The direct, day-to-day interactions among most states are substantially governed by a variety of formal and informal agreements, of which treaties and regimes are among the most important. Like other forms of international cooperation, such agreements are binding only as long as the participating states are willing to abide by the conditions of the agreement or are willing to submit disputes to some form of resolution. But such agreements can collapse for various reasons:

- Some participants might find that their national goals are not well served, so they ignore or violate the agreement. For example, countries sometimes conclude that their own national economic needs justify subsidies to their producers (e.g., farmers, steel producers), even if other countries object that such subsidies violate WTO agreements.

- Participants might have different interpretations of what actions are deemed acceptable under the agreement. For example, Iran is among the 190 countries that have signed the Nuclear Nonproliferation Treaty, but there is considerable dispute over whether Iran's ongoing uranium enrichment programs are in violation of the treaty. Iran insists its actions are within its rights to develop nuclear energy for peaceful purposes. As agencies of the UN continue to investigate, some countries such as the United States argue for stronger sanctions against Iran, while others such as China and India have opposed additional sanctions.

- Fulfillment of the key objectives in an agreement might be impossible. For example, the Treaty of Locarno (1925) between Britain and Italy failed to deter Germany from violating the borders of France and Belgium because Britain and Italy were not strong enough to counteract Germany's military power and Italy's government eventually concluded that Italy's national interests were better served by becoming more pro-German.

International Law

The *broadest attempt to formalize and constrain the interactions among states* is **international law**. In 1625, Hugo Grotius, the "father of international law," published *De jure belli et pacis* (*On the Laws of War and Peace*) (Grotius 1625/1957). This document emphasized that **natural law**—*universal principles of behavior that are recognizable through human reason and human nature and that direct us to act with goodness*—should guide the relations among states and restrain hostile or destructive interactions. Unfortunately, states often define reasonable behavior according to their own political interests rather than shared abstract moral rules. Thus, by the nineteenth century, natural law had been supplanted by **positivist law**—*explicit written agreements that define both appropriate and unacceptable behaviors among states*, in the form of international treaties or conventions. Positivist laws have attempted to adjudicate geographic boundaries (e.g., the 12-mile limit on the territorial waters of states), to regulate states' use of environmental resources (e.g., laws limiting whale hunting in international waters), and to establish states' rights and limits over non-national resources (e.g., the law of outer space).

The treaties and conventions of positivist law even attempt to distinguish acceptable from unacceptable behavior during conflicts among states. For example, the Helsinki Agreement binds combatants to use no glass-filled projectiles or other forms of violence that produce "unnecessary suffering." The Geneva Convention on "fair" war prohibits the use of poison gases and insists that captured soldiers be treated with dignity, although it does not preclude most of the terrible forms of suffering or death that a soldier can experience *before* he becomes a prisoner.

While positivist law has the great advantage of being formulated in explicit written agreements, the effectiveness of such agreements ultimately depends on the willingness of states to comply with them. Even if states sign a particular agreement, they sometimes openly violate the agreement and later deny accusations of such a violation. The International Court of Justice (also known as the ICJ or the World Court) at The Hague was established in 1946 to adjudicate violations of positivist international law and to offer advisory opinions on issues of international law.

Part of the United Nations, the International Court of Justice has occasionally served as a valuable mechanism for conflict resolution between states. However, the court has jurisdiction and binding authority only if both parties to the dispute accept its ruling. Less than one-third of the member states of the United Nations have agreed to accept automatically the ICJ's jurisdiction in matters affecting them. When the political or economic stakes are high or even when emotional elements of the disagreement are intense, states have often refused to accept the court's jurisdiction or to be bound by its judgments. The United States has taken cases to the court, but it is among the majority of states that rejects the court's automatic jurisdiction, as it did in a 1984 case brought by the Nicaraguan government that objected to covert U.S. actions against it (such as mining Nicaraguan harbors).

Prior to the 1990s, the ICJ was not particularly active. Between 1946 and 1991, it considered only 64 cases, gave advisory opinions in 19 cases, and handled very few cases that actually concerned violent conflicts between states. However, the ICJ has averaged 14 cases per year since the mid-1990s, is dealing with more disputes involving political violence, and is now issuing numerous advisory opinions each year (http://www.icj-cij.org). Another important recent development is the expanded use of international law to arrest and prosecute political leaders and other individuals accused of extensive human rights violations. Such trials can be handled by the relevant country, like the trial of Saddam Hussein in Iraq. Since 2002, a permanent International Criminal Court (ICC) at The Hague is a "court of last resort" that can take up cases of genocide, crimes against humanity, and war crimes if any of the 122 countries that support the court is not prepared to handle such a case in its national court system. The role of the ICC in international affairs is still evolving (Shniderman and Smith 2014). In its early years, the ICC has tried cases of human rights violations involving top government leaders from Ivory Coast (Laurent Gbagbo) and rebel leaders from the Democratic Republic of Congo and Uganda. It has also pursued international criminal justice in other ways, such as the indictment of a sitting leader, Omar Bashir of the Sudan (Smith and Gonzalez 2013).

The increased activities of these international courts reflect a growing interest in using international law more aggressively, not only to adjudicate disputes between states but also to hold individuals accountable for the ultraviolence perpetrated by their states. Do you think political leaders should be legally responsible before an international court system for the actions of their soldiers? More broadly, is it acceptable for a state to refuse the court's jurisdiction? What do you think would happen to international politics if all states automatically accepted the jurisdiction of the International Court of Justice and the ICC?

International Organizations

INTERNATIONAL ORGANIZATIONS is a broad term for many of the transnational institutions whose core objectives include actions to influence the behavior and policies of states and other transborder actors. (**Transnationalism** describes *institutions or actors who engage in a significant array of activities that cross state borders*.) A few international organizations attempt to prevent or resolve conflict among states. Most such organizations focus on specific issue areas that are of global significance in the economic, social, environmental, cultural, or political domain and, in their actions, tend to facilitate cooperation across borders. There are three major types of international organizations: intergovernmental organizations (IGOs); international nongovernmental organizations (NGOs); and multinational corporations (MNCs).

IGOS Intergovernmental organizations (IGOs) are political institutions whose members are states, not private groups or individuals. Although there are currently fewer than 300 permanent IGOs, they have vast potential to shape the politics across borders. States jointly establish IGOs for a variety of different purposes: to provide a forum for communication among states; to implement policies that respond to political, social, or economic problems transcending national boundaries; to enact international laws and treaties; and to intervene in disputes between states. Most IGOs are regional, such as the EU, the North Atlantic Treaty Organization (NATO), the Association of Southeast Asian Nations (ASEAN), and the Arab League. Others have a global membership and focus, such as the World Trade Organization (WTO), the International Monetary Fund (IMF), and the World Health Organization (WHO).

The most powerful and wide-ranging IGOs in the twentieth century were two major international organizations: the League of Nations and the United Nations. The League of Nations was formed in 1921 (after World War I) as a mechanism for collective security against aggression. But Italian aggression in Ethiopia and Japanese aggression in Manchuria in the 1930s revealed that the League lacked the diplomatic, political, or military power to achieve its goal.

The United Nations (UN) was created in 1945 (after World War II) as an international organization dedicated to managing international security. In pursuit of this objective, the UN has five principal organs with specific functions:

1. The *Security Council* is the body within the UN that has the authority to directly manage international conflicts because it can pass binding resolutions that authorize the use of force, peacekeeping missions, and sanctions. Its membership includes 5 permanent members with veto power (China, France, Russia, the United Kingdom, and the United States) and 10 rotating members.

2. The General Assembly has representatives from all 193 member states of the UN and serves as a forum for discussion of global issues. Although the General Assembly lacks the legal authority to pass binding resolutions, it oversees the entire UN budget as well as many specialized bodies.

3. The Economic and Social Council (ECOSOC) promotes economic and social cooperation and development. To achieve this goal, ECOSOC works with the General Assembly to coordinate and oversee most UN committees.

4. The Secretariat is the central bureaucracy, responsible for the UN's day-to-day operations. It is headed by the UN's most visible representative, the secretary-general (currently, Ban Ki-moon).

5. The *International Court of Justice* is the UN's primary judicial body. It is responsible for interpreting international law (described in the previous section).

Figure 11.1 shows a number of the special units that function within the principal divisions of the UN.

While the United Nations has a mixed record of success and failure in its central objective of maintaining global peace, it has improved the international political climate. At the least, the United Nations has been a highly effective setting within which rivals can engage in continuing diplomacy. Particularly within the Security Council and the General Assembly, UN officials and representatives from various countries can attempt to mediate conflicts and prevent escalation to war. The UN can also pass resolutions that might constrain certain countries from acting in opposition to the moral force of international public opinion (Kennedy 2006; Weiss and Daws 2009).

Most directly, a UN *peacekeeping operation* can intervene between combatants. This is an impartial, multinational military and civilian force authorized by the UN Security Council with the consent of the disputing parties. The peacekeeping force literally stands between the combatants in an attempt to ease tensions, and it uses force only in defense. The United States and the Soviet Union used their veto power in the Security Council to block many potential peacekeeping initiatives during the Cold War. In the post–Cold War period (beginning in the late 1980s), the use of UN peacekeeping forces has expanded. Thus, 50 UN peacekeeping operations have been deployed since 1990, compared with only 18 in the preceding 42 years (United Nations Peacekeeping Operations 2013). By its various actions, the UN has contributed to what former UN Secretary-General Dag Hammarskjold (1953–1961) called "preventive diplomacy"—limiting the extensive political and military involvement of major

Figure 11.1 United Nations Organization: Principal Organs and Selected Units

powers during conflicts between other countries. In 1988, the UN peacekeeping operations were awarded the Nobel Peace Prize.

Significantly, most of the post–Cold War operations differ from earlier operations in that their central objective is to establish internal peace among factions *within* a country. Of 15 peacekeeping missions active in 2013, for example, the primary objective in 13 (including the Democratic Republic of Congo, Haiti, Ivory Coast, Kosovo,

and Lebanon) was to prevent political violence among groups within
the country. It has been difficult
for UN forces to end the violence
in these internal conflicts in which
both the borders and the identity of combatants are ambiguous.
However, a study of 124 UN peacekeeping actions in internal conflicts
concludes that they generally have
been successful in ending the violence and increasing the likelihood
of greater democratization (Doyle
and Sambanis 2000). Recent concern
has focused on the unintended consequences of UN intervention, such
as an increase in human trafficking
associated with the peacekeeping
efforts (Smith and Smith 2011; Smith
and Miller-de la Cuesta 2011).

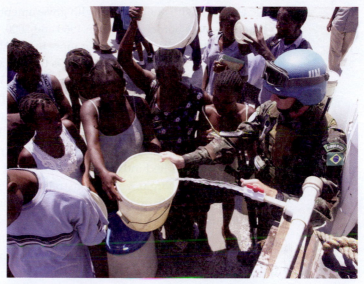

Haitians line up to receive water from soldiers in a UN operation in the
Cite Soliel slum of Port-Au-Prince as part of the UN's humanitarian aid
function.

The UN's other main goals concern improving the relations among states and helping
countries improve the health, welfare, and human rights of their people. Coordinated by
both the General Assembly and the Economic and Social Council, committees, agencies,
and commissions, such as the World Health Organization (WHO), the United Nations
Educational, Scientific, and Cultural Organization (UNESCO), and the United Nations
Conference on Trade and Development (UNCTAD), attempt to mitigate global problems
and enhance the quality of human life in areas such as human rights, agricultural development, environmental protection, refugees, children's health, and disaster relief.

The continuing level of political violence in the international system underscores
the fact that the United Nations lacks the power to prevent all interstate conflict. Many
states threaten to withdraw their support (financial and political) when UN actions are
at variance with the states' perceptions of their national interest. However, through
its agencies, its debates and resolutions, its continuous open forum for formal and
informal communications among states, and its peacekeeping operations, the UN
does contribute to greater cooperation, reduced human suffering, and reduced conflict
among states. For such contributions, Nobel Peace Prizes have been awarded to the
UN six times, including the UN and then Secretary-General Kofi Annan in 2001, the
UN International Atomic Energy Agency and its then head Mohammed Elbaradei in
2005, and the UN Organization for the Prohibition of Chemical Weapons in 2013.

NGOS The second type of international organization is **nongovernmental organizations**. NGOs are composed of *nonstate actors (private individuals and groups) who work
actively in a particular issue area* to provide information, promote public policies, and
even provide services that might otherwise be provided by governments. *International*

NGOs work with one another, with governments, and with IGOs to address problems that cross state borders. Between 1960 and 2000, the number of NGOs active in at least three countries rose from 1,000 to more than 30,000 and currently is more than 50,000. This includes about 5,000 major NGOs that are very active in a large number of countries (Union of International Associations 2011; Weiss 1996).

International NGOs are committed to furthering political and social issues with transnational dimensions. Although their issues tend to be regional or global, the actions and effectiveness of these NGOs can be analyzed in the same framework applied to the analysis of national interest groups (see Chapter 3). These groups encourage concerned individuals, groups, and even the governments of other states to write letters, organize demonstrations or boycotts, or engage in other political actions to pressure a government or transnational actor to change its practices (Smith 2007).

For example, you might be aware—from media, mailings, or other information sources—of the environmental protection actions of Greenpeace, the animal preservation goals of the World Wildlife Federation, or the lobbying by the Union of Concerned Scientists to limit destructive technologies. Amnesty International, another well-known NGO, is concerned with protecting human rights and is engaged in campaigns to focus attention and pressure on governments that are violating the rights of their citizens. It is one of the leading NGOs among an expanding group of transborder organizations that promote the protection of human rights. Often, local movements of human rights activists coalesce with others outside their state's boundaries to promote this issue.

The actions of some NGOs extend far beyond lobbying because they generate resources and actually deliver goods and services, such as the humanitarian medical services provided by Médecins sans Frontières, winner of the 1999 Nobel Peace Prize. With the globalization of communications and greater mobility, many other groups, advocacy networks, and social movements are able to engage in a mix of persuasion and action, although most operate in a limited set of countries. Overall, transnational NGOs enjoy higher public trust than either governments or business, and they have a growing economic base (more than $1 trillion). They are "increasingly important in shaping national and international politics, governance processes and markets" and are "amongst the most influential institutions of the twenty-first century" (Elkington and Beloe 2003).

MNCS It is also clear that the actions of many *multinational corporations* (MNCs, also referred to as TNCs—transnational corporations) have significant impacts on the politics within and between states. From a political economy perspective, MNCs are powerful firms that produce and sell a diversity of goods in many countries in pursuit of private profit (e.g., Exxon, British Petroleum, Samsung, CITIC Group-China, Sumitomo). The global impacts of major MNCs are based on their sheer economic weight as some of the richest institutions in the world. In terms of comparative economic power (measured as gross economic product), only 63 (42 percent) of the top 150 economic units in the world are countries and 87 (58 percent) are multinational corporations (White 2012).

Three other crucial features of MNCs add to their importance in the global system. These features enhance an MNC's flexibility and bargaining power in dealing with the governmental institutions and the political economy in any state. First, a major MNC functions as a globalized network. Because its operations are spread across many countries, an MNC can rapidly move its activities to exploit opportunities and avoid problems in any host country and even in its home country. This enables the MNC to pressure governments into competing for a share of its operations by providing the MNC with large financial inducements (e.g., tax breaks, enhanced government services, bribes) and by minimizing the state's regulatory constraints on the MNC's undesirable activities (e.g., negative environmental impacts, labor practices, product safety). Second, the MNC's capacity for product diversification enables it to shift its balance of production among a variety of different goods, further reducing its dependence on any single country or any particular source of land, labor, or capital. And third, an MNC can transform itself, breaking off units into independent companies, engaging in mergers, launching completely new areas of activity, or even shutting down entire divisions. These three strategic elements increase the MNC's autonomy, influence, and profitability at the expense of the host country's political economy and its government, which must continue to make costly concessions to compete for a share of the MNC's operation and are constantly vulnerable to the MNC's decisions.

Moreover, those MNCs that engage in financial services can shift assets in nanoseconds, since they operate primarily in the virtual world. When globalized financial institutions suddenly move in similar directions, such as speculating in a country's currency or dumping its bonds, the country's overall financial stability and strength can be altered quickly. Such actions by financial MNCs can result in a rapid credit crunch or a run on the currency. With all of this leverage, these financial MNCs are able to exert tremendous influence on government policy in ways that serve the goals of the MNC.

For all these reasons, some critics claim that MNCs challenge the very sovereignty and autonomy of the state because they can avoid most of the laws and taxes of any state and can pressure the state to enact favorable policies. Critics also argue that MNCs monopolize the production and distribution of important goods in the world marketplace, squeeze out many small firms, and widen the economic gap between the rich and poor countries (Keohane and Nye 2011; Russett, Starr, and Kinsella 2009). Hence, "the MNC remains one of the most controversial actors in the international political economy" (Jenkins 1993: 606).

Power Politics Across Borders

11.3 **Analyze the types of power politics between actors in the international system and evaluate the impact of globalization.**

Actors operating across state borders often attempt to engage in mutually beneficial interactions. But when the divergent interests of states and other transborder actors are stronger than their mutual interests, competitive or conflictual behavior is more likely than cooperation. From the realist perspective in particular, such power politics and conflict are a central feature of interactions in the international system.

In politics across borders, there are frequent examples of *power politics*. Recall that power is exercised when one actor (A) uses its actions or resources to cause another actor (B) to do something that B otherwise would not do (see Compare in 5). In most of the examples in this section, both A and B will be states. However, in current global society, many instances of power politics across state borders now involve nonstate actors in the role of A, B, or both A and B. As described earlier in this chapter, these non-state actors are often IGOs, NGOs, or MNCs. In some situations, power politics results in the resort to violence. Chapter 12 will examine the uses of violence across borders.

When cooperative approaches do not succeed, a state or other transborder actor can attempt to persuade the other actor to behave in a manner that the other actor does not view as in its best interests. The argument might be that such behavior does serve the actor's goals in ways it does not realize or that the behavior is morally or ethically the right thing to do, as neoliberal theory might suggest. Usually, however, it takes more than persuasion to cause a state or other transborder actor to behave against what it perceives to be its self-interest. This is when power politics is a likely strategy.

Some analysts suggest that states can successfully use "**soft power**" (Fraser 2005; Nye 2009, 2011). This is a variation on the power/influence theme, positing that one state so admires another state's values, its policies, or even its culture that the first state agrees to go along with the demands of the admired state. For example, it is argued that the soft power of the United States (e.g., its political institutions, music, values, Barack Obama) has penetrated some other countries so deeply that it gives the United States leverage in interstate dealings with those countries. The concept has been applied to other countries like China (Ikeda and Tago 2014; Shambaugh 2013), although not all scholars are persuaded about the strength of soft power (Berenskoetter and Williams 2007).

Compare in 5 also described "exchange power." This means a state (or nonstate actor) can offer something of value to another state to cause the other state to do something it would not otherwise do. Or the state can threaten or actually act to withhold something of considerable value to another state in an attempt to induce compliance. States use such exchange power in many ways. If another state needs a good (a few of the thousands of examples are oil, military protection, a trade agreement, a UN vote, a useful technology, a loan, sensitive information), the power-exercising state might be in a position to provide this good, thus forcing the needy state to comply with its wishes.

When a group of states combine to withhold a desired good to pressure a state, the strategy can be called *sanctions*. To avoid using violence, states or an IGO such as the United Nations apply sanctions to a country whose behavior they want to alter. They might withhold food, loans, replacement parts, or any other good. Recently, there have been more attempts to apply comprehensive sanctions, in which many important restrictions are placed on a state's acquisition or sale of goods. Sanctions, or even the threat of sanctions, can be an effective mechanism of coercion (Whang et al. 2013). During the 1990s, for example, there were 20 cases in which the United Nations successfully applied comprehensive sanctions to drive a country's leader from power or to force regime change (Cortright and Lopez 2002).

Transnational Systems of Power

If soft power and exchange power approaches do not resolve the differences, a transnational system of power politics might still prevent major, direct conflict between competing states. One important system is a **balance of power**. This occurs when there is *a rough equality in the power resources (political, economic, and especially military) that can be exercised by sets of competing states.* An actor is prevented from taking advantage of others because of the power of other actors to retaliate. The term balance of power is widely used and has many meanings. In the broadest sense, it implies that there is a rough equilibrium of power between competing states, and this discourages any state from taking aggressive action against rivals because the state fears effective retaliation. This concept often refers to a regional or global balance of power that involves a number of states. Six key elements in this classic notion of balance of power, listed below, are especially associated with the political realist perspective (Morgenthau 2005; Little 2007).

1. It is an attempt to maintain a general stability in the relations among states and to preserve the status quo.
2. It assumes that peace can be maintained if potential aggressor states are deterred by overwhelming opposing power.
3. There are typically a few (usually four to six) major power states that are decisive in ensuring that the balance is sustained.
4. These states, and others, create shifting alliances based only on self-interest and system equilibrium, not on friendship or ideology.
5. One or more power states must intervene if the behavior of other actors threatens the overall balance of the system.
6. There will be periodic political violence and war because states must use force to preserve themselves and because the system is not always in such good balance that all conflict between states is deterred.

A relatively effective balance of power system functioned in Europe for about 250 years, until World War I in 1914. In describing Britain's role in this system, Winston Churchill (1948) observed, "For 400 years the foreign policy of England has been to oppose the strongest, most aggressive, most dominating power on the continent, in joining the weaker states." However, the growing importance of both ideology and nationalism and the permanent hostility among certain major powers undermined the logic of the balance of power approach after 1914.

After World War II, the classic balance-of-power system was replaced by a *bipolar* balance-of-power system, in which the United States and its allies were generally balanced against the Soviet Union and its allies. The groups associated with each superpower were rigid in their ideological antipathy to the other bloc and were inflexible in their alliance formation. Each bloc attempted to achieve **hegemony**—*sustained domination of the international system.* However, the formidable military power on each side deterred them from fighting each other directly during a 40-year "cold" war (see page 370 in Chapter 13).

From the early 1970s until the breakup of the Soviet Union in 1991, the international system of power became increasingly *multipolar.* The coherence of the U.S. bloc and the

Soviet bloc declined, as powerful actors such as China, Japan, Western Europe, and groupings of nonaligned states began to act with greater independence. At the same time, the United States and the Soviet Union continued to be the preeminent global powers and to engage in a massive buildup of military capability and nuclear weapons. Each side attempted to gain an advantage in weaponry and feared that its rival would gain some form of technological superiority. The result was an arms race that produced nuclear arsenals capable of massive, even total, annihilation of humankind. At the highest point, there were more than 60,000 operational nuclear weapons in the world. Even now, there are more than 17,000 such weapons (Federation of American Scientists 2013). In this situation of *mutually assured destruction (MAD)*, a form of balance-of-power politics evolved that was, and still is, a dangerous and possibly irrational mechanism for regulating the relations among powerful states in the nuclear age.

In the post–Cold War era (since the early 1990s), the state system continues to have multipolar elements, especially through the United Nations. However, the military and economic dominance of the United States has provided some characteristics of a *unipolar* period, in which the international system is generally controlled by a single hegemon. The United States has often taken the lead in spearheading collective military action through the United Nations (e.g., the 1991 Persian Gulf War) or through NATO (e.g., the 1999 actions against the Serbs in Kosovo; the opposition to Gaddafi's forces in Libya in 2011). In some cases, the United States has operated somewhat unilaterally (e.g., the military campaign against Afghanistan beginning in late 2001) or dominated a military "coalition of the willing" (the war against Iraq in 2003).

Domination and Dependence

While all states enjoy sovereign equality, it is obvious that some states are far more powerful than others. Students of the contemporary, and increasingly globalized, political world must understand how and in what situations one state exercises substantial power over another. The capacity of one state to alter the actions of another state can be based on different forms of leverage; the primary three are:

1. **Economic** leverage, based on the advantageous trade relations, financial interactions, or economic aid that the state can provide to (or withhold from) another state.
2. **Military** leverage, which can be applied either negatively, via the use or threat of military action against a state, or positively, via military assistance in the form of protection, provision of military resources, or training.
3. **Political** leverage, derived from the ability of a state to affect the actions of another state through the use of its political resources, such as its negotiating skills, its effective political institutions, or its influence in interstate relations.

COLONIALISM During the twentieth century, particular attention focused on **colonialism**, which is characterized by *one state having extensive dominance over another state, including manipulation or control of key economic and military structures for the benefit of the dominant state*. A state might have a variety of reasons for attaining mastery over another state. First, the subordinate state can provide resources, both human and physical, for the dominant state. Second, the subordinate state can be a controlled market for the products of the dominant state. Third, the subordinate state can serve important strategic functions, either as a buffer between the dominant state and its rivals or as a staging area for the dominant state's political or military objectives. Fourth, a state with a missionary zeal might dominate another state to ensure that its values (usually political or religious) guide the subordinate state. Fifth, a state might want to dominate another state to gain international prestige.

While all forms of colonial domination entail a mix of economic, military, and political control, dominant states have employed three different styles:

1. In the *segregationist* style of colonialism, the interaction is pure exploitation. The dominant state makes little or no attempt to improve the economic, political, or social systems in the subordinate state. This style generally characterized the relations of Belgium, Germany, and Portugal with their African and Asian colonial territories.

2. In the *assimilationist* style, the dominant state makes some attempt to transform the subordinate state into an external extension of itself. While the subordinate state is still being exploited, the institutions, knowledge, and culture of the dominant state are introduced to the elite of the subordinate state and become a basis for political, economic, and cultural development. This style is particularly associated with French colonialism in Africa and Asia and the extensive colonialism of the former Soviet Union.

3. In the style of *indirect rule*, the dominant state works with the traditional leaders and institutions of governance and culture in the subordinate state as intermediaries in its control, but it also introduces the modern forms of the dominant state that will eventually supplant traditional forms. The British approach to its vast empire is the classic example of indirect rule, and this mode of colonialism also characterizes the style of the United States in some Latin American and Pacific Rim states.

NEOCOLONIALISM In the decades after World War II, most states willingly or reluctantly granted independence to their colonial holdings. But political independence does not necessarily end a state's subordination to a strong state. The label **neocolonialism** is given to *new, more indirect forms of domination and dependence that are nearly as powerful as those under colonialism*. Although the dominant state may officially withdraw its direct political and military presence, it can maintain domination, primarily by economic leverage. Through foreign aid, loans, technology transfer, military support, and economic intervention, the dominant state can continue to control many actions of a supposedly independent state. The dominant state's manipulations become relatively invisible, and its interests are served by a subtle alliance among a small elite within the subordinate country, MNCs, and other transnational actors (such as the IMF) (Maxfield 1997). These new forms of domination were described in the discussion in Chapter 10 of the dependency approach, which posits that the patterns established under colonialism have evolved into a *world system* of dominance and dependence that is global and systemic (Wallerstein, Lemert, and Rojas 2013). The recent history of the Democratic Republic of Congo, described in Focus in 11, exemplifies how colonialism and neocolonialism can contribute to the plight of vulnerable states on the periphery.

Focus in 11

The Faces of Colonialism: Congo

The Democratic Republic of Congo is a large, resource-rich state (one-fourth the size of the United States) located in the center of the African continent. It encompasses 75 million people and 250 ethnic groups. King Leopold of Belgium claimed the area as his own private kingdom in 1879 and placed it under Belgian colonial administration in 1908. As they extracted the Congo's natural resources with ruthless efficiency, King Leopold's companies and Belgian-led military forces treated the local people with brutality, forcing the men into virtual slavery as workers in the mines and on the plantations. The colonial regime provided only minimal education to the people and encouraged Catholic missionaries to teach the great virtue of obedience to authority.

The Belgians exploited the resources of the Congo until internal resistance and the widespread liberation of African colonies made it clear that continued colonial rule was not acceptable. The Congo was granted its independence on June 30, 1960, and Belgium rapidly withdrew its military and administrative personnel and most of its financial and technical support.

Unprepared for self-rule, the Congolese elite broke into competing factions, and the country collapsed into political decay and civil war. A faction under soldier Joseph Mobutu and assisted by Western countries (and the U.S. Central Intelligence Agency) was victorious in the civil war and then assassinated the pro-Soviet prime minister.

In 1965, Mobutu, now army chief of staff, led a coup that overthrew the civilian government. Mobutu installed himself as the leader of a one-party, authoritarian regime. He "Africanized" his society, changing the country's name to Zaire and his own name to Mobutu Sese Seko ("all powerful one"). Despite Mobutu's repressive rule, several civil wars, the persistent failure of the economy, widespread corruption, and the massive diversion of funds to Mobutu and his cronies from state-owned mines, he remained in power for more than three decades.

Mobuto's long tenure in office was completely dependent on neocolonialism—the foreign aid, loans, technology transfer, and military support he received from Western countries, especially the United States (which appreciated his staunch anticommunism). Zaire relied heavily on foreign corporations to build and maintain its mines, factories, and infrastructure. The IMF (the consortium of Western banking institutions) loaned Zaire enormous amounts and repeatedly restructured Zaire's debt (the largest in Africa). In return, the IMF demanded conditionality—that Zaire implement strong economic policies, including devaluing the currency, lowering real wages, and drastically reducing social welfare programs. There were extended periods during which the IMF sent in European citizens to directly manage Zaire's national banking system.

The combination of internal corruption, exploitation by foreign corporations, and IMF's conditionality left few resources for the people of Zaire. The level of education declined, the country could no longer feed itself, and the infrastructure (e.g., roads, water supply, telecommunications) was in shambles. The real wages of urban workers fell to less than one-tenth of what they were at independence. Surrounded by the appalling poverty of most of the population, Mobutu was rumored to be the wealthiest person in sub-Saharan Africa, with holdings of more than $10 billion.

When the Cold War ended, the United States found Mobutu to be an embarrassment and tried to pressure him to make democratic reforms. Mobutu finally allowed elections in 1993, but when his own candidate for prime minister was defeated, he ordered the armed forces to prevent the winning candidate from taking office and installed a puppet government. Multinational corporations continued to exploit Zaire's resources.

After years of political decay, Mobutu's demise came suddenly in 1997. After a Zairean guerrilla group (composed mainly of Tutsis) expelled 1.2 million Hutu refugees who had escaped the ethnic chaos in Burundi and Rwanda, they turned on Mobuto. When Mobuto's army deserted him, he fled. The guerrilla army's leader, Laurent Kabila, declared himself president and renamed the country the Democratic Republic of Congo. Not all Congolese accepted Kabila's rule, and there was a destructive civil war. When Kabila was assassinated in 2001, his son, Joseph Kabila, took power.

From 1998 to 2003, military groups from eight countries engaged in vicious fighting in Congo in what became known as Africa's World War. This complex mix of civil war, ethnic conflicts, refugee issues, and exploitation of Congo's resources by all groups was the bloodiest conflict since World War II, with at least 4 million deaths and millions of refugees. Joseph Kabila has manipulated the electoral system to win elections in 2006 and 2011; but there have been coup attempts in 2003, 2004, and 2011, and turmoil continues (Turner 2011). Congo ranks second highest among "failed states" worldwide and has the world's lowest score on the Human Development Index.

After 90 years under a brutal and exploitative colonial system, 55 years of "independence" have brought no blossoming of democratic politics, no sharing of the Congo's abundant resources among its people, and no economic development. Rather, contemporary Congo is a tragic product of colonialism and neocolonialism, as well as its own internal failings—a state characterized by poverty, corruption, oppression, economic chaos, political decay, and continuing dependence on foreign states and foreign economic actors.

Further Focus

1. Which of the specific foreign interventions in the Congo described above might have done the greatest long-term damage?

2. Are there any benefits that a developing country might gain from a lengthy period under colonialism or neocolonialism?

Globalization?

According to Thomas Friedman, "[a] new international system has now clearly replaced the Cold War: globalization. That's right, globalization—the integration of markets, finance and technologies in a way that is shrinking the world from a size medium to a size small and enabling each of us to reach around the world farther, faster and cheaper than ever" (Friedman 1999: 110). The new conventional wisdom is that the forces of globalization are reshaping everything, from international politics to national economies to our individual values.

What is globalization? As a working definition, **globalization** can be viewed as *the increasing integration of diverse economic, social, cultural, military, and environmental phenomena by means of dense networks of action and information that rapidly span vast distances around the world*. This definition is guided by the suggestion of Keohane and Nye (2000: 105) that we first define *globalism* as "a state of the world involving networks of interdependence at multicontinental distances." Two defining characteristics of such networks affect globalism: (1) The networks are increasingly dense and (2) they involve extremely rapid transmission of phenomena across substantial distances. These networks allow the movement of people, goods, ideas, information, financial capital, and even biological substances. *Globalization* refers to an increase in the level of globalism (Keohane and Nye 2000).

What aspects of human existence are affected by globalization? It is particularly associated with economic factors: a worldwide market political economy with private economic actors minimally constrained by states or borders, open capital markets, vigorous competition, and a reduction of state control over the economy (Starrs

2013). However, the linkages associated with globalization can affect many important aspects of our world. Thus, Keohane and Nye (2000) suggest four major domains of globalism: (1) *economic globalism*: the long-distance flows of goods, services, capital, and information that shape market exchanges (e.g., less costly imports, instantaneous transfers of financial capital); (2) *social and cultural globalism*: the movement of people, ideas, information, and images, which then influence the individuals, societies, and cultures into which they flow (e.g., MTV, international tourism); (3) *military globalism*: the long-distance networks of interdependence, in which the threat or exercise of force is employed (e.g., mutually assured destruction, international terrorist networks); and (4) *environmental globalism*: the long-distance transport of materials and biological substances via natural movement (e.g., ozone depletion, bird flu) or via human agency (e.g., HIV-AIDS, Ebola).

There is heated debate about the overall impacts of globalization on individuals, countries, and the international system. The Debate in 11 summarizes a few of the central claims. As is often the case, there is considerable truth as well as substantial hyperbole associated with the assertions of both the advocates and the foes of globalization. It is clear that the extraordinary increases in the speed, distance, and density of networking have altered the global economic and sociocultural systems, facilitating capitalism and markets and richly connecting some peoples and groups. Yet most of the world's population continues to live, work, and experience life on the margins of those systems. There are powerful and contradictory forces at work. Some forces create enhanced interactions and shared identities across vast spatial and political boundaries, while other forces, reacting against globalization, intensify the importance of local activities and particularistic identities.

Even as states are increasingly penetrated by outside forces, the states remain formidable actors in the international system. Thus, it is possible that globalization could be substantially limited by the policy actions of the most powerful states. This might occur if such states conclude that their national interest (especially their prosperity and stability) is being undermined by globalization or if states enact policies that support resistance by powerful, well-organized domestic actors harmed by globalization. Alternatively, states might cooperate with one another to coordinate their national policies in ways that limit the most negative effects of globalization. In this case, the calculus of the states would be, as in other forms of interstate cooperation, that collaborative approaches are the best means to serve their goals.

Protesters in Manila, unhappy with the impacts of globalization, demand the Philippines withdraw from the WTO.

The Debate in 11

Is Globalization a Positive Development?

Human society has evolved from small groups of self-sufficient hunter-gatherers to huge urban populations that rely on others for almost every aspect of existence. Many observers suggest that globalization—with its powerful forces that integrate economies, spread knowledge, and mix cultures—is shifting us to a new stage of human development. The global availability of more diverse goods and services, the vast worldwide communications network, and the widespread sharing of technological capabilities are presented as evidence that globalization is a positive force enhancing the quality of life for nearly all countries and peoples. However, others argue that the current forms of global integration have had extensive negative impacts on many countries and individuals. On balance, is globalization a positive development?

Globalization Benefits Most Societies and Individuals

- A unified global market and free trade create a more efficient system for the production and distribution of goods that results in lower prices and improved product quality. Financial capital flows quickly to the places where it will produce the highest, most effective return on investment (Malloch-Brown 2012).

- Greater integration increases the transfer of technology and expertise across borders, resulting in the diffusion of best practices, more extensive innovation, and increased global productivity (Friedman and Friedman 2013).

- Higher productivity, higher-quality goods, and lower prices will generally "raise all boats." That is, these improvements will raise the level of material living standards and the prosperity enjoyed by large numbers of people in many countries (Baghwati 2007; Wolf 2004).

- Globalization results in greater sharing and homogenization of culture and values across borders, creating a world with more shared understandings. This leads to a reduction in the kinds of nation-based differences that cause conflict (Fukuyama 1999).

- Global communication enables individuals who share political interests but are dispersed geographically to engage in effective cooperation and mobilization, thus enhancing their political power (Shirky 2011).

- As trade and economic interdependency increase in a global system, powerful economic and political actors view war and major armed conflict as disruptive and undesirable, and thus they will act to prevent them. Even more positively, these powerful actors have strong incentives for crossnational cooperation (Mandelbaum 2004; Dafoe et al. 2013).

Globalization Results in Many Negative Effects on Societies and Individuals

- Globalization encourages production, capital, and jobs to move wherever costs are lowest and profits are highest, resulting in considerable economic instability from country to country and hardship for many workers whose jobs are outsourced (Smick 2008).

- Similarly, as production shifts to countries with the fewest regulations on labor and the least restrictive environmental standards, the results include a "race to the bottom" characterized by hazardous working conditions, dangerous products, and environmental degradation.

- A large share of the benefits of globalization are captured by the most powerful economic actors in the world (Stiglitz 2006), and thus the system is best understood as the newest form of neocolonialism.

- With globalization, the distribution of wealth grows even more unequal between core countries in the Global North and most countries in the Global South that are at the periphery of the international system (Klein 2008) (recall dependency theory in Chapter 10).

- As globalization produces more interdependency and mobility of goods, local problems spread quickly and can have global consequences, whether they are economic problems (e.g., the global economic crisis that spread from East Asia to many countries in the late 1990s) or dangerous pathogens (e.g., the H1N1 virus).

- In response to the destruction of their culture and their economic stability from globalization, many groups (e.g., nation-based, religious) become mobilized, resulting in political disorder and violence as groups attempt to protect their identities and economic interests. Thus, there is greater local and global instability.

- As national governments lose control of MNCs and economic activities, they will be weakened and less able to respond effectively to the growing negative impacts on their people and their economy. This will expose each country to more social turbulence and increase hostilities and conflicts between states (Rodrik 2011).

More questions…

1. On balance, is globalization a positive development for you personally? For your country? For most people in the world?

2. If globalization is the current general stage in human development, is it the final stage? If not, what might be the next stage after globalization?

Most analysts conclude that state policies will not stop current globalizing trends. They emphasize that states have less and less capacity to control their participation in or insulation from the globalizing international system as borders become more permeable to goods, people, capital, and ideas. There is also considerable skepticism that states can sustain sufficient cooperation with other states in the brutally competitive system. Indeed, almost all analysts assume that the forces of globalization are transforming the international system in ways that are probably not controllable and are certainly not understood (Baghwati 2007; Bremmer 2013; Friedman 2007; Rodrik 2011; Stiglitz 2003, 2006).

Competition in the Globalizing World

The disintegration of the Soviet Union in 1991 is regarded as the crucial event ending the bipolar, Cold War era. The nature of the current era is subject to debate (Betts 2010). One conception is that the United States will continue to dominate as a hegemon in a generally unipolar international system (Posen 2003). Another conception anticipates that the rising power of China or perhaps of all the BRICS (Brazil, Russia, India, China, South Africa; see Chapter 15) countries as well as the EU will generate a multipolar system (Ikenberry 2011). A third scenario anticipates that the United States has punched itself out by overextending its global military activities and that the emerging system will have features of international anarchy that have always been a core assumption of the realists (Szabo 2011). Or perhaps a variety of global actors will create effective transnational institutions that will fulfill the idealists' conception of a world in which cooperation is the dominant style. Or…??? Three major trends are likely to be particularly important in shaping the near-term evolution of politics across borders in the globalizing world.

First, *military power* remains a significant factor in the relations among states. The lessening of Cold War tensions has been balanced by the rise of new forms of militarism in every region and continuing militarism by Russia and the United States. Military spending is now more than $1.74 trillion per year worldwide, an increase of 35 percent in just the last decade (SIPRI 2014). Despite the presence of multilateral military forces and multistate alliances, most military power remains under the control of individual states. If powerful and politically effective groups are increasingly threatened by globalization, it is possible that they will pressure their governments to be more active in protecting their citizens, their economies, and even their cultures. And leaders might become more assertive in response to the breakdown of borders and challenges to state sovereignty.

This might produce protectionist and isolationist policies toward other states and the use of the state's military to protect and project the state's interests. It is likely that conflicts will be more frequent if globalization and ethnonationalism are rampant. Empirical research suggests that in the twentieth century, unlike the nineteenth century, aggressive competition and military conflict became more likely as the international system became highly diffuse and multipolar—rather like the system that seems to be emerging (Brecher and Wilkenfeld 2000; Mearsheimer 2001; Russett, Starr, and Kinsella 2009). As was discussed earlier in the chapter, it is not obvious that the United Nations or any other actors have the will and capacity to prevent such conflicts.

Second, intense *economic competition* could split the countries that were allies during the Cold War. In fact, competition among the major powers will pivot more on economic issues than on military or ideological issues (Rodrik 2011). In the global economy, regional groupings have formed as states coordinate their policies with similar states ("harmonization") to protect their group of states from outside pressures. The EU might become this type of coordinating mechanism for its member states. The major economic competition might be among three groups: North America under leadership from the United States, the European Union, and an East Asian group under Chinese leadership. Other regional economic groups have formed around Russia, in South America, and among the Muslim states of Central Asia. As the competition for increasingly scarce goods like energy resources, minerals, water, and food becomes ever more intense, how will states organize to gain more than their fair share?

Third, the state-centered system is evolving toward one in which *transnational entities* are extremely important. The dynamics of globalization seem to be generally beyond state control, as does the extensive and growing power of the MNCs, described above. States might actually be willing accomplices of these transborder actors because the most powerful elites controlling these states could reap substantial benefits from a globalized international order structured by the MNCs. IGOs such as the WTO and the IMF could facilitate further globalization (Sassen 1996).

Alternatively, states might continue to lose power to transborder, global actors and, as a consequence, lose their central role in structuring the international system. State borders have little significance for transnational actors. IGOs and NGOs pursue international agendas that are not shaped by the goals of individual states or negated by state sovereignty. MNCs can shift their resources and their operations from country to country in single-minded pursuit of profit maximization within the global economy.

Although located in a home country, MNCs have operations in other host countries as well. The MNC's loyalty to the prosperity and security goals of its home country can become limited or nonexistent.

Thus it might be that the emerging international order will soon be dominated by "imperial corporations," whose globalized systems of production and distribution of goods, finance, technologies, and communications enable them to transcend sovereign states and shape the global system (Barnet and Cavanagh 1994). For these reasons, some predict that a key conflict in the early twenty-first century will be among the MNCs or between MNCs and states (Heilbroner 1993). Do you think it would be desirable to have an international system dominated by transnational actors rather than by states? Would the relentless pursuit of profit produce a more peaceful or a more just world than the relentless pursuit of national interest and state power? Will there be a decrease or an increase in international political violence? This last question is among those that are addressed in Chapter 12.

Key Concepts

balance of power, p. 307
colonialism, p. 308
constructivism, p. 292
diplomacy, p. 296
feminist IR theory, p. 292
foreign policy, p. 290
geopolitics, p. 293
globalization, p. 311
hegemony, p. 307
intergovernmental
    organizations (IGOs), p. 300
international law, p. 298
international organizations, p. 300

international regime, p. 297
international relations, p. 290
liberalism, p. 291
multinational corporations
    (MNCs), p. 304
mutually assured destruction
    (MAD), p. 308
natural law, p. 298
neocolonialism, p. 309
neoliberalism, p. 291
neorealism, p. 291
nongovernmental organizations
    (NGOs), p. 303

peacekeeping operation,
    p. 301
positivist law, p. 298
power politics, p. 306
realism, p. 291
sanctions, p. 306
security dilemma, p. 291
soft power, p. 306
transnationalism, p. 300
treaties, p. 297
world system, p. 309

For Further Consideration

1. The chapter suggests that a new pattern will emerge to structure politics across borders. What is the most desirable pattern for the international system in the early decades of the twenty-first century? What is the least desirable? What seems most likely?

2. Can the United Nations, or *any* multinational body, be so effective in imposing an international order that major

conflict between states becomes highly unlikely?

3. What is the most effective strategy to produce increased cooperation among key actors in the international system?

4. Is globalization likely to change the distribution of power among states and other transnational actors in significant ways? Who is likely to benefit most from globalization?

For Further Reading

Baghwati, Jagdish. (2007). *In Defense of Globalization.* **New York: Oxford University Press.** An elegant argument for the benefits of globalization, in developing countries as well as developed countries, and thoughtful rebuttals of the main critiques.

Barnet, Richard J., and John Cavanagh. (1995). *Global Dreams: Imperial Corporations and the New World Order.* **New York: Simon and Schuster.** A rich, insightful, and often scathing analysis of the enormous power and impacts of major multinational corporations on the international system and the lives of citizens in many countries.

Bremmer, Ian. (2013). *Every Nation for Itself: What Happens When No One Leads the World.* **New York: Portfolio Penguin.** An interesting argument that there is an emerging new world order in which no country or group of countries (such as the UN or the G20) can control the global system. In the absence of strong leadership, there will be incapacity to deal with global disarray, including the many "problems without borders."

Cohen, Saul Bernard. (2008). *Geopolitics: The Geography of International Relations.* **2nd ed. Washington, DC: Rowman & Littlefield.** A thorough explanation of the geopolitical perspective on analysis (the subject of the Compare in 11), grounded in numerous examples of all regions in the current globalized world.

Drezner, Daniel. (2008). *All Politics Is Global: Explaining International Regulatory Regimes.* **Princeton, NJ: Princeton University Press.** A persuasive argument that strong states remain the most powerful actors in the international system, despite globalization, through their leadership in international regulatory regimes.

Friedman, Thomas. (2007). *The World Is Flat: A Brief History of the Twenty-First Century: Release 3.0.* **2nd revised ed. New York: Farrar,** Straus and Giroux. The author offers his second engaging exposition of globalization (following *The Lexus and the Olive Tree*, published in 1999). He argues that new technologies, especially information and communications technologies (e.g., the Internet, wireless mobile communication, integration software), are reducing both global productive inequalities and the obstacles to transborder activities in ways that are transforming the global political economy as well as political, social, and individual power.

Fukuyama, Francis. (2004). *State-Building: Governance and World Order in the 21st Century.* **Ithaca, NY: Cornell University Press.** The scholar famous for predicting "the end of history" due to the triumph of global capitalism revises his views to focus on how it is legitimate for the international community to intervene in an attempt to establish viable political institutions in weak and failed states where the emergence of liberal democracy is not occurring naturally.

Goldstein, Joshua, and Jon Pevehouse. (2013). *International Relations.* **10th ed. New York: Pearson.** A readable and comprehensible explanation and assessment of the major theories of international relations; of key topics such as conflict, international organization and violence; and of international political economy.

Gruber, Lloyd. (2000). *Ruling the World: Power Politics and the Rise of Supranational Institutions.* **Princeton, NJ: Princeton University Press.** The author argues that, although countries voluntarily decide to transfer power to supranational institutions such as the EU and NAFTA, many of the countries, and perhaps the international system itself, do not benefit from the increasing power of these supranationals.

Ikenberry, G. John. (2012). *Liberal Leviathan: The Origins, Crisis, and Transformation of the American World Order.* **Princeton, NJ: Princeton University Press.** An argument that the international system will continue to build on the rules, norms, and power relations in the current liberal regime led by the United States, even as new powers emerge.

Joseph, Sarah. (2011). *Blame It on the WTO? A Human Rights Critique.* Oxford: Oxford University Press. A thorough vetting of the negative consequences for human rights that arise from adherence to WTO rules.

Kelemen, Daniel R. (2011). *Eurolegalism: The Transformation of Law and Regulation in the European Union.* Cambridge, MA: Harvard University Press. Economic and judicial integration in the EU has transformed the relations among the member states, as both public and private litigation are increasingly the mode of state interaction.

Malloch-Brown, Mark. (2012). *The Unfinished Global Revolution: The Road to International Cooperation.* New York: Penguin. The former Deputy Secretary General of the United Nations offers a fascinating rendering of his experiences promoting international development and his arguments about why international cooperation must trump nationalistic obstacles in the era of globalization.

McCormick, John, and Jonathan Olsen. (2013). *The European Union: Politics and Policies.* 5th ed. Boulder, CO: Westview Press. A thorough description of the most significant regional alliance in the global system.

Pastor, Robert A., ed. (2000). *A Century's Journey: How the Great Powers Shape the World.* New York: Basic Books. Noted scholars explore the twentieth-century foreign policy behavior and resulting international impacts of each of seven major powers—China, France, Germany, Great Britain, Japan, Russia, and the United States. The authors illuminate the pervasive influence of these powers on the relations among states, the international political economy, and the international system.

Rodrik, Dani. (2011). *The Globalization Paradox: Democracy and the Future of the World Economy.* New York: W. W. Norton. An economist's readable argument that democracy cannot be sustained in a world of "hyperglobalization," particularly given its reshaping of financial institutions, plus suggestions of policy remedies.

Steans, Jill. (2013). *Gender and International Relations.* 3rd ed. Malden, MA: Polity Press. A comprehensible and thoughtful explanation of feminist perspectives on international relations theory, an important approach that particularly challenges the key assumptions and interpretations of realist theory on core topics such as war and peace, international political economy, development, and human rights.

On the Web

http://www.unsceb.org

The official Web site for the United Nations, including detailed information about many of its major agencies and programs.

http://www.smartbrief.com/un_wire

The UN Wire, an independent news service partnered by the United Nations focusing on issues of global political concern.

http://europa.eu/index_en.htm

The official Web site of the European Union, with extensive information about the workings of the EU and its major institutional elements.

http://www.icj-cij.org/homepage/index.php?lang=en

The official Web site of the International Court of Justice provides details of current cases as well as a history of the court.

http://www.people.virginia.edu/~rjb3v/rjb.html

This wide-ranging Foreign Affairs Online Web site provides many links regarding matters of international relations, international law, and foreign policy.

http://www.aseansec.org/index.asp

The official Web site of the Association of Southeast Asian Nations includes information and documents relevant to ASEAN and news about countries in the region as well as somewhat self-serving Web pages constructed by each member state.

http://www.nato.int/

This Web site focuses on military, strategic, and policy issues of importance to the North Atlantic Treaty Organization, a collective security association of 28 partner countries dominated by the United States and West European powers.

http://www.theglobalist.com

The Globalist, a "daily online magazine on the global economy, politics, and culture," offers a strong set of links to think pieces by many interesting commentators as well as relevant articles on issues in the global society.

http://www.globalissues.org

This site explores a variety of global issues, including globalization, environmental issues, international law, and population.

http://www.globalpolicy.org

Global Policy Forum is an independent policy watchdog that monitors the work of the United Nations and scrutinizes global policymaking, especially in such areas as the UN Security Council, the food and hunger crisis, and the global economy.

http://www.g7.utoronto.ca

The G8 Information Centre, developed by the University of Toronto, provides a wealth of information on the G8 (a cooperative institution with representatives from the major developed countries—the G7 plus Russia = G8), ranging from academic journal articles to recent summit information.

http://osce.org

The official Web site of the Organization for Security and Cooperation in Europe (OSCE), the largest regional security organization in the world, with 55 participating states from Europe, Central Asia, and North America active in conflict prevention, crisis management, and postconflict rehabilitation.

http://www.apecsec.org

The electronic home of Asia-Pacific Economic Cooperation (APEC), an organization focusing on economic growth, cooperation, trade, and investment among 21 governments in the Asia-Pacific region, including Canada, China, Japan, Russia, and the United States.

http://www.oas.org/en

The home page of the Organization of American States provides a comprehensive database of information regarding the group's activities and policies.

http://www.coha.org

The Council on Hemispheric Affairs is a progressive NGO that monitors and provides analyses of events in the Western Hemisphere.

http://www.unhcr.org/cgi-bin/texis/vtx/home

The United Nations High Commissioner for Refugees is the agency that attempts to document the scale and details of the movement of populations across borders and to suggest appropriate policy responses to deal with the challenges of coping with the large numbers of dislocated people.

Chapter 12
Political Violence

 Learning Objectives

12.1 Define political violence.

12.2 Relate the use of violence to the formation and maintenance of political society.

12.3 Classify the major types of political and nonpolitical violence.

12.4 Analyze the nature and causes of war.

12.5 Evaluate the normative implications of political violence.

The Balkans is a small area in Central Europe. The troubled history of the area has resulted in the terms *balkanization* and to *balkanize,* which describe an area that has broken down into small units, often associated with violence.

Given its geopolitical location at the crossroads of Western and Eastern Europe, the Balkans have historically been a site of conflict, and its peoples had been conquered by imperial powers such as the Romans, the Austrian Hapsburgs, and the Ottoman Turks. When not engaged in resistance to the imperial invaders, the multiple ethnic groups lived in uneasy tension and occasional fighting with one another. Even during World War II, when the Germans invaded, more members of these ethnic groups were killed by one another than by the Nazis. A powerful communist leader, Josip Broz Tito, held these groups together as a single country (Yugoslavia) between the end of World War II and the late 1980s.

However, the breakup of the Soviet empire in Central and Eastern Europe after Tito's death reopened old nation-based animosities as emerging states each attempted to maximize their borders and eliminate all those with a different ethnic identity. During the 1990s, the Balkans was again the site of brutal violence among its major ethnic groups. More than 250,000 were killed, often in house-to-house fighting and in cold-blooded executions of men, women, and children, and more than 700,000 were displaced from their homes. The key protagonists were military and paramilitary forces drawn from the 9 million Serbs (generally Greek Orthodox, procommunist), 600,000 Montenegrans (Greek Orthodox, pro-Serbian), 4.5 million Croats (Catholic,

Balkan violence: Serbian paramilitary gunmen shoot three Bosnian Muslims (a man and two women) and then kick one of the women in the head as she lays dying.

noncommunist), 4.5 million Bosnians (Muslim), and 2 million Slovenes (Catholic, noncommunist).

When the Croats declared independence in the early 1990s, the dominant Serbs resisted the breakup of Yugoslavia and the Serbian military engaged in a bloody, if sporadic, conflict with Croatian forces until 1995, despite international recognition of Croatia and a United Nations–arranged cease-fire. Bosnia also declared independence but did not gain immediate recognition. Serbs, about one-third of the population within Bosnia, launched a civil war to secure as much of the region of Bosnia-Herzegovina as possible for Serbia. In devastating town-to-town fighting, Serbian and Bosnian para-military groups murdered and brutalized civilians as well as one another. Eventually, the United Nations and the European Union (EU) imposed a settlement in Bosnia, based on a complex federation representing all key ethnic groups.

The next explosion of violence was in Kosovo, an impoverished southern province in Serbia. About 90 percent of the Kosovo population is ethnic Albanians, whose desire for autonomy resulted in a separatist guerrilla war in the late 1990s. While the United Nations attempted to intervene, Serbian president Slobodan Milosevic encouraged the local Serbs to engage in ethnic cleansing. Within months, the Serbs had either killed or exiled the majority of ethnic Albanians. In response, massive North Atlantic Treaty Organization (NATO) airstrikes against Serbian forces enabled the ethnic Albanians to return to their homes in Kosovo. The Kosovars than executed many local Serbs and drove most of them from their homes and communities. In 2010, two years after Kosovo declared its independence, the International Court of Justice ruled its declaration was legal, although Serbia and Russia are among about eighty countries that still do not recognize Kosovo's sovereignty.

The recent history of the Balkans is an example of the complex forms of political violence that occur in the contemporary political world. The people have experienced extensive and brutal civil war, nation-based violence, terrorism, war, foreign military intervention, systematic rape, arson, and their own government's violence against them. Our awareness of such violence is usually high. On a given day, the media are likely to report on the few regions that experience armed conflict, riots, assassinations, terrorist incidents, and so on rather than on the great majority of regions worldwide that do not experience such violence.

In part, this selective reporting reflects our general fascination with the horror of violence. It also indicates our underlying sense that such political violence is extraordinary—an aberration from politics as usual. Unfortunately, there is considerably more political violence in the world than most of us recognize, violence that occurs below the few headlines that grab our attention.

Violence is excluded from some definitions of politics, such as the pluralist approach, because violence is viewed as a breakdown of politics, which is understood in terms of consensus building, compromise, and conflict resolution. However, other definitions treat conflict and violence as one possible, and perhaps inevitable, form of politics or as the politics of last resort. Indeed, in some approaches, including the class approach, some political violence is portrayed as a positive force, producing necessary change and constructive outcomes. Given its omnipresence, description and analysis of the nature and dynamics of political violence will help us gain a better understanding of the political world.

Violence

12.1   Define political violence.

Initially, we need to consider the concept of violence itself. The most common notion is that *violence* entails *the use of physical force, usually with the purpose of injuring or damaging the target of the violence.* In the political world, the tools of such violence can range from flying fists and bullets to weapons of mass destruction.

But some analysts take a much broader view of violence. First, the *threat* of violence might be understood as a form of violence, even if the violent act is not committed. If someone points a gun in your face and you hand over your money, you will probably view this interaction as a violent one, even if the person does not fire the gun. Similarly, if a state points nuclear missiles at the state across its border but does not launch any, would you classify this as an act of violence? Is it a violent act if a group threatens to blow up a public building unless its demands are met? Is it a violent act if a group shouts down a speaker at a public rally? Do you think that such acts of intimidation and threat of force have a violent element, even if there is no actual physical injury or damage?

Second, an even broader view of violence includes various forms of subjugation and manipulation that do not involve even the threat of direct physical harm. For example, consider a group that is an underclass within a society. The group is subjected to discrimination in education, in health care, in jobs, and in housing. This intentional pattern of *systematic deprivation* continues over time. The group is not targeted for any specific physical violence, but the economic and cultural systems provide the group with minimal opportunities to gain a significant share of the values in the society. Some would classify such oppression as a form of violence by the dominant group(s) against the fundamental rights of the deprived group to life, liberty, and the pursuit of happiness.

This chapter defines **political violence** as *the use of actual physical violence or very serious threats of such violence to achieve political goals*. As you assess the role of violence in politics, however, consider the other ways in which the world of politics generates actions and impacts that "do violence" to many people. Although the use of physical force is evident in politics, the more subtle forms of coercion and manipulation are more extensive, if less visible.

Political Society

12.2 **Relate the use of violence to the formation and maintenance of political society.**

Chapter 2 described the claim by Thomas Hobbes (1588–1679) that the formation of political society is an attempt to overcome the frequent reliance on force and violence in human interactions. As individuals use whatever means necessary to pursue their self-serving interests, interpersonal violence is inevitable. To overcome such violence, Hobbes observes, individuals accept the *social contract* in an attempt to submit force to reason—to ensure that force becomes the *ultima ratio* (final resort), not the *prima ratio* (first resort). In **political society**, *individuals accept the authority of the state and cede to the state a monopoly over the legitimate use of violence*, sacrificing their own right to use violence in exchange for a similar sacrifice from others (recall Chapter 5).

Even if most people accept the social contract, some individuals and groups do not, arguing that the existing political society and its social contract have no authority over their actions. They may claim a right to engage in justifiable violence based on motives such as self-defense, the restoration of order, the promotion of fundamental values, or retribution. They might claim they have never accepted the authority of the current government or that the political system is illegitimate (because it lacks a democratic mandate or because it has failed to deliver security, stability, and prosperity). International law, as embodied in the United Nations Charter, recognizes a people's right to self-determination but also recognizes the state's sovereignty and right to territorial integrity. Much of the political violence we see today is the result of tension between these principles, particularly when actors do not recognize a state's authority.

Types of Political Violence

12.3 **Classify the major types of political and nonpolitical violence.**

A simple taxonomy of political violence can be based on specifying the *source* of the violence and the *target* of that violence. Either actor may be a state or an individual/group. Figure 12.1 distinguishes four categories of political violence. Although these categories help organize and clarify our discussion, this taxonomy is imperfect and the boundaries between categories are imprecise (hence the dashed lines) because the states, groups, or individuals who engage in political violence are usually motivated by multiple objectives, can operate in fluid groupings, employ complex strategies, and focus on multiple targets.

State Violence against Individuals or Groups

Given the state's monopoly of the legitimate use of violence, there are many instances in which the state's application of political violence seems justifiable. The state typically characterizes its own use of violence as an *order-maintenance* activity. The state's agents act as security forces, judges, and executors of punishment when individuals or groups seem to have violated the society's legal system. Thus, the state might arrest, try, and punish an actor who breaks a criminal law, as in actions such as robbery, or a civil law, as in actions such as tax fraud. In such matters, most citizens are likely to support the state's efforts to create and maintain public order.

But some state uses of violence are more problematic. V. I. Lenin (1870–1924) defined the state as "a body of armed men, weapons, and prisons." Because the state has the capacity to define the nature, severity, and punishment of all crimes, it is possible for the state to be highly repressive and discriminatory in its use of violence. *The state's excessive reliance on force and oppressive laws* can be called **establishment violence** and can be contrasted with the state's legitimate use of violence to maintain public order.

The boundary between a crime against society and a crime against the existing political order can blur. In some countries, political actions that oppose the current political leadership are treated as crimes. Thus, political opponents become "enemies

Figure 12.1 Types of Political Violence

Source	Target	
	Individual/Group	**State**
Individual/ Group	Crime Terrorism Nation-based conflict Class conflict	Riots/Rebellion Separatist violence Coup Revolution
State	Order maintenance Establishment violence	War

of the people" and are subject to constraints on their behavior, deprivation of resources, imprisonment, and death. The state can also institute systematic policies of violence against certain groups that are not overt opponents of the regime but are blamed for problems faced by the state and thus are made scapegoats.

A key instrument of a state's power against its enemies is its security forces. These include official groups like the regular military and police (e.g., those recently using violence against antigovernment demonstrators in Egypt, Syria, and Russia) as well as unofficial armed groups (e.g., Colombian paramilitary forces). Judicial systems and prison systems are another form of state power that can be used to punish those whose behaviors displease the state. According to Amnesty International (2014), a nongovernmental organization (NGO) that monitors violations of individual civil rights by agents of the state, political opponents are subjected to establishment violence in two-thirds of all countries. In addition, the state can cause great suffering or even death to individuals through its power to withhold access to rewards such as good jobs, shelter, and welfare services.

In the contemporary world, extensive attention is paid to certain forms of political violence, especially violence between states (war) and individual/group violence (such as terrorism). This attention is understandable because such violence is dramatic and terrifying. Yet an extensive analysis by political scientist R. J. Rummel (2014) of democide—"murder by government"—concludes that the death toll from establishment violence far outweighs the deaths from war during the twentieth century. These data are summarized in Table 12.1.

According to Rummel, the deaths of more than 300 million people in the twentieth century are directly attributable to government violence and war. The most staggering aspect of these data is that fully 86 percent of those deaths are the result of establishment violence. While about 41 million people were killed in wars, it is estimated that governments killed more than 260 million of their own citizens (including their colonial subjects)—the people they are supposed to serve. Rummel includes any murder committed by agents of the government, including genocides, politically motivated

Table 12.1 Death by Government and War in the Twentieth Century

	Total Deaths (millions)			
	Domestic	**Foreign**	**All**	**Percentage of Total Deaths**
Establishment violence	*173*	*90*	*262*	*86%*
By communist governments	145	8	153	50
By other totalitarian governments	1	26	28	9
By authoritarian governments	26	53	79	26
By democratic governments	0.2	2	2	1
War	*10*	*31*	*41*	*14*
TOTAL	182	120	303	100.0%

Note: The totals are rounded to the nearest million.

SOURCE: Adapted from Rummel (2014), 20th Century Mortacracies Table.

executions, massacres, and intentional famines. Most deaths through establishment violence have been the work of nondemocratic governments. Half of the deaths (50 percent) are attributable to communist regimes, about 9 percent are the responsibility of other totalitarian governments, and 26 percent are by authoritarian governments (Rummel 2014: 20th Century Mortacracies Table).

Rummel particularly emphasizes the massive death totals attributable to the twentieth century's bloodiest dictators: Mao Zedong's regime in China killed 76.7 million between 1923 and 1976; Joseph Stalin's Soviet regime killed 42.6 million between 1929 and 1953; more than 20.9 million were eliminated by Hitler and the German Nazi regime (1933–1945); 10 million were killed by King Leopold in his colony of Congo (Focus in 11); and 2.4 million Cambodians died by execution and starvation under Pol Pot's regime (Compare in 10). If you need evidence of the fundamental importance of the state in determining the quality of citizens' lives, the 262 million deaths attributable to the citizens' own governments should be compelling.

Individual Violence against an Individual

When an individual is the source of violence and another individual is the target, the violence is usually not explicitly political. Most such violence (e.g., murder, robbery, rape, assault, and certain crimes against property, such as burglary and arson) is best characterized as *ordinary crime*. Because only the state (and its agents) has a legitimate right to use violence (this is one definition of the state in Chapter 5 as well as in Hobbes's social contract notion), an individual who does violence without the approval of the state is normally in violation of the law. Even these ordinary crimes have a political element in the sense that the state is usually involved in determining what behaviors are criminal and then in apprehending violators, judging them, and punishing them on behalf of "the people." Notice also that in most societies, members of deprived or subordinate groups tend to engage in violent crimes far more frequently than members of the more advantaged classes. Do you think this pattern might suggest that the commission of some violent crimes and even the nature of the punishment have, in part, a subtle political element?

There are instances in which one individual engages in an act of political violence against another individual. For example, U.S. presidents James A. Garfield in 1881 and William McKinley in 1901 were assassinated by individuals who seemed to be acting alone, primarily on political motives. Occasionally, a person's motivation for violence against a political actor is more personal than political. In a famous example from 1804, U.S. Vice President Aaron Burr shot and killed distinguished Founding Father Alexander Hamilton in a duel. The two were bitter political enemies from rival political parties, but Burr was also offended by disparaging personal comments that he thought Hamilton had made about him. Burr challenged Hamilton to a duel, and after Hamilton shot in the air as gentlemen normally did, Burr mortally wounded Hamilton. In 2001, the king and queen of Nepal and six other members of the royal family were shot to death by the king's son, the crown prince, who had quarreled with his mother over his choice of a bride.

Group Violence against an Individual

Most violence in which a person is targeted for political reasons, including assassinations, is committed on behalf of a group, even if the act is performed by an individual. Focus in 5 noted the assassinations of two Indian prime ministers, Indira Gandhi and her son Rajiv Gandhi seven years later. Although Indira Gandhi was killed by two guards and Rajiv Gandhi by one woman, in each case the assassins believed they were acting to further the political interests of their nationality group (the Sikhs and the Sri Lankan Tamils, respectively). U.S. president Abraham Lincoln was assassinated in 1865 by one man who was part of a broader group attack on the American political leadership, and some believe that President John F. Kennedy's assassination in 1963 can be attributed to more than one person. And the murders of former Lebanese prime minister Rafik Hariri (in 2005) and former Pakistani prime minister Benazir Bhutto (in 2007) were each the work of a suicide bomber, although organized groups or perhaps even governments were behind the attacks. It could also be argued that Libya's Muammar Gaddafi was assassinated by the rebels who captured him (2011).

TERRORISM An act is usually called **terrorism** when there is *premeditated, politically motivated violence perpetrated against noncombatant targets by subnational groups or clandestine agents* (U.S. State Department 2014). In other words, terrorism is a violent criminal act with a political motive. Note that terrorism now takes many forms and is arguably the most difficult form of violence to classify in Figure 12.1. Both the source and the target could be individuals, groups, or the state. Bombs can be planted in public places such as markets or airplanes; civilians can be kidnapped or murdered; harmful chemicals can be placed in food, water, or air; a country's embassy can be attacked. In 2013, there were more than 9,700 terrorist attacks, more than 17,000 deaths, and 32,500 serious injuries. The number and severity of terrorist acts in each country changes over time. In the recent past, terrorism has tended to occur more frequently in countries with modest levels of political freedom, in comparison to countries with substantial freedom or minimal freedom (Abadie 2004).

Figure 12.2 reports on the 9 countries with the most terrorist attacks in 2013. Terrorist attacks were documented in 93 different countries, although the incidence was very high in just a few countries. Over half of the fatalities (57 percent) and most injuries (73 percent) occurred in only three countries: Iraq, Pakistan, and Afghanistan. In addition to these three, only two other countries, Nigeria and Syria, had more than 1,000 deaths. In recent years, about two-thirds of the terrorist acts were bombings and one-fourth were armed assaults (U.S. State Department 2014).

Some peoples, such as the Pakistanis, Iraqis, and Afghanis, despair of the recurrent terrorist attacks that make their lives feel like Hobbes' state of nature. In other countries, people are scarred by a particularly traumatic terrorist act. For Norwegians, it is the massacre of 77 people, mostly teenagers, at a political camp in 2011. For Indonesians, it is the death of 202 people, mostly foreign tourists, in the 2002 bombings of two nightclubs in Bali by Indonesian militants. In Spain, it is the coordinated backpack bombings of Madrid commuter trains in 2004, killing 191 and wounding more than 2,000. And in the United States, it is the most massive terrorist

Figure 12.2 Terrorist Attacks and Victims, by Country, 2013

SOURCE: U.S. State Department 2014.

attack in modern history on September 11, 2001. A well-organized group, composed mainly of Saudi Arabians, hijacked four transcontinental passenger airplanes. Two of the planes were flown into the towers of the World Trade Center in New York, one crashed into the Pentagon near Washington, DC, and the fourth crashed in a field in Pennsylvania after passengers struggled with the hijackers. The carnage was staggering, with almost 3,000 deaths, and the costs of the attack have been estimated at more than $600 billion.

For some, the central question regarding those who engage in terrorism is: Why use violence to harm noncombatants? The motives of political terrorists vary, but some combination of five rationales guide most such acts. First, the terrorists can attempt to punish an existing state (their own or another) for perceived grievances, even when noncombatants are the victims of their actions. From the terrorists' perspective, no citizens of the targeted state are innocent of their state's misdeeds. (Recall the views of Osama bin Laden in Compare in 4.) Second, terrorists can attack a domestic group that they wish to subordinate or retaliate against for previous offenses. This characterizes much of the recent violence in Iraq between Shia and Sunnis as well as Sunni attacks on police recruits. Third, the terrorist act can be a means to gain international publicity for the group's claims and grievances. Unlike those committing ordinary crimes, terrorists often take credit for their violent actions and hope for extensive media coverage. Fourth, terrorists may seek to secure financial resources for the group's political activities or may demand the release of imprisoned members. Many acts of violence that involve hostages and ransom demands are of this type. And fifth, an objective of terrorist violence may be to promote revolution—a strategy discussed later in this chapter.

Different approaches are used to study terrorism. Some studies search for patterns and correlations in the nature of terrorist acts (U.S. State Department 2014). Some explore the psychology of the terrorists in terms of their personal and social traits (Bongar et al. 2006). Some apply rational choice theory to explain the calculations terrorists make regarding such decisions as which target to attack (a weakly defended site), when to allocate the scarce resources that they hold, how to alter strategies in response to the various counterterrorist mechanisms in place, and how to utilize traditional and new technologies (Enders and Sandler 2012).

The research suggests that terrorism is undergoing at least three ominous changes in the early twenty-first century. First and most important, terrorists have an increased capacity to inflict massive damage and disruption. The terrorists' ability to move people, information, and weapons is enhanced by globalization, with its permeable national borders, extensive cross-border travel, and growing immigrant populations. Terrorists also benefit from the rapid expansion of technologies that provide them with far greater destructive capabilities, ranging from digital networks (cyberterrorism), to chemical and biological weapons (bioterrorism), to weapons of mass destruction (WMDs).

A second change is that many terrorists are now operating in very small cells (3 to 10 people) that are only loosely connected with one another, making penetration and destruction of terrorist networks almost impossible. While there is some broad collaboration in training and provision of materials, most terrorist acts are carried out by small, isolated cells (Sageman 2008; recall the discussion in Chapter 4). However, the rich environment of global information enables the groups to learn from the successes and failures of other terrorist groups and refine their decisions regarding tactics, venues, and targets (Enders and Sandler 2012).

A third change is that some groups, especially religiously motivated terrorists, now seem less constrained regarding the scale of death and destruction they are willing to inflict, even on those who are noncombatants. And an increasing proportion of terrorist acts are committed by individuals who are not only willing to die for the cause but also intend to die in a suicide act (Council on Foreign Relations 2005; Smelser 2007).

There are ambiguities in the assessment of terrorism. One issue is defining "noncombatants." One attempt to identify combatants states that they are "personnel in the military, paramilitary, militia,

People flee from the collapsing towers of the World Trade Center in New York shortly after the shocking terrorist attack on September 11, 2001, that killed almost 3,000 people.

and police under military command and control who are [on duty] in…areas…where war zones or war-like conditions exist" (NCTC 2011). Even some who are not terrorists argue that this definition of combatants is too narrow. Are military personnel who are not on duty at the moment really noncombatants? What about attacks on other potentially "repressive agents" of the state, such as police, security guards, judges, or civilians working for the military? While there is agreement about the sheer terror associated with acts of political violence, it is not always clear whether such acts are best understood as terrorism or just brutal violence against "the enemy" in the service of some political goal.

With the proliferation of groups employing terrorist tactics, it is wryly observed that "one person's terrorist is another person's freedom fighter." The root problem with using terrorism as an analytic concept is that it has become a powerful and negative label in the manipulative language of politics. It is sometimes used regardless of the innocence of the victim, the identity of the actual sponsor of the violence, the justifiability of the goal, or the validity of the grievances. The label communicates a disgust for extreme political violence against innocent individuals, but it can also be used to discredit any group that uses violent means to achieve its political ends or to condemn a group whose political ends, as much as its means, are unacceptable. Ultimately, the issue centers on moral and political values: Are there *any* circumstances in which group political violence against any individuals is justifiable? If so, when is violence acceptable, and what are the limits on violence? The Debate in 12 considers whether terrorism is ever justifiable.

Group Violence against a Group

NATION-BASED VIOLENCE Nationality groups are increasingly mobilized to demand political autonomy, a process grounded in a deep attachment to the group's identity, described in Chapter 5 as nationalism or ethnonationalism. When these groups clash directly, *the use of force between identity groups* is termed **nation-based violence**. Many of the major armed conflicts during the last several decades have been between nation-based groups within countries, not between countries (Laitin 2007; SIPRI 2014; Taras and Ganguly 2010).

In some cases, groups attempt to establish their own sovereign state based on national identity, a situation discussed later in the chapter as separatist violence. In many instances, however, the nation-based groups are struggling against each other for political, cultural, or economic domination or autonomy rather than for separation. The continuing violence between Hindus and Muslims in India (recall the Focus in 5) demonstrates how the antipathy between nationality groups can poison their relations as they attempt to share a country or even a remote village. In the southern African country of Angola, more than 1.5 million people died in the prolonged civil war (1975–2002) among three rival groups, each representing a different linguistic/ethnic region, that struggled for control of the entire country. Less than two months after violence began in early 2014, more than 10,000 were killed among the Dinka and Nuer tribal nations in South Sudan. And the ongoing violence in Iraq reveals the deep antagonisms among groups within the Shia, Sunni, and Kurdish nations.

The Debate in 12

Is Terrorism Ever a Justifiable Form of Political Violence?

Throughout history, some individuals and groups have engaged in political violence to achieve their goals. Few would argue that political violence is *never* justified. Most political theorists specify conditions under which people can legitimately engage in political violence to achieve justice and define what constitutes a "just war" (Walzer 2006). However, there are also circumstances in which either the ends to which violence has been used or the means that are employed are unacceptable. In the contemporary world, some of the most serious concerns about political violence relate to attacks labeled "terrorism" because they victimize people who some claim are innocent non-combatants. Is such terrorism ever justified?

Some Terrorism is Justified

- Individuals who engage in terrorist acts believe they are acting to defend many people, almost all of whom are "innocents" and "noncombatants." These innocents are themselves a violated group that has been the victim of establishment violence or has experienced severe and prolonged oppression, which is also understood to be a form of violence.

- Terrorist tactics are employed as a last resort, but such actions are necessary because the oppressed group is prevented, by establishment violence or by its exclusion from resources, from using nonviolent political means to displace the oppressors. John Locke, in his *Second Treatise of Government* (1690), is among the many theorists who vigorously defend the right of an oppressed people to use violence against unjust governance.

- Innocent people might be harmed by terrorist acts in some instances, but they are the unlucky people who are in the wrong place at the wrong time. They are no different from the individuals that those with power call "collateral damage" when they are killed during state-sponsored violence.

- Many of the targets of terrorism are individuals who sustain and actively support the domination and violence of the oppressors, even if they do not wear the uniforms of combatants. They are certainly not "innocents."

- Ultimately, there are no true innocents: Those who acquiesce to and enjoy benefits from the policies of the oppressors are also responsible for the harm caused to those who suffer. Those who gain life's advantages while accepting injustice and violence directed against the less advantaged cannot also claim immunity from responsibility and harm.

All Terrorism Is Indefensible

- The destruction of innocent lives for political gain is morally unacceptable, without exception.

- Only the state has the right to use violence under the conditions of the social contract. Thus, any act of extreme political violence that is not committed by the representatives of the state is illegitimate, regardless of the targeted victim or motivation.

- Terrorism is tactically unwise because it pushes the existing regime to become even more aggressive and less willing to engage in dialogue and compromise (e.g., consider the response of the Israeli government to Hamas in Gaza, which is described in Focus in 12).

- From a pragmatic perspective, terrorism is also tactically unwise because its ultraviolence alienates potential supporters, both within and outside the country. Eventually the terrorist group is isolated and without allies.

- There are considerably more cases in which relatively powerless groups were able to replace an oppressive regime with persistent political mobilization than with terrorism.

- If the goal is to achieve social justice, there are effective nonviolent alternatives to terrorism, even for those who lack extensive political resources (e.g., nonviolent resistance to colonialism by India's Mohandas Gandhi; the use of the electoral process, as in many post-communist countries).

- History reveals that terrorism rarely succeeds in achieving the goals desired by the terrorists. Those who do gain power by such brutal violence typically become as oppressive as those they have overthrown. Moreover, they are usually driven from power by further violence before they attain any idealistic outcomes they sought.

- The use of unrestrained violence for political ends becomes an ethical slippery slope into chaos. It establishes the right of every unhappy group to use any means necessary in an attempt to achieve its political ends.

More questions ...

1. Are those noncombatants who gain considerable benefits from an unfair political regime truly innocents who should not suffer from the consequences of political violence directed against the regime?

2. Do the conditions, motivation, and political goals of the terrorists have any relevance in determining the acceptability of the action, or is terrorism *always* wrong, regardless of conditions, motivation, and goals?

3. Is it possible to make a precise distinction between terrorists and those who fight for freedom and justice?

When *group political violence results in the murder of many members of one ethnic group by its rival*, it can be called **genocide** (Weitz 2005). The political system is often a partner in such situations when its machinery of violence is employed by the dominant group. When the state organizes the campaign against an ethnic group, such genocide can also be classified as *establishment violence* (see Figure 12.1). Examples of genocide in the twentieth century include the killing of Armenians by the Turks (in 1915), six million Jews in Hitler's Germany (1933–1945), the Tutsis by the Hutus in Rwanda (1963–1964), and the Hutus by the Tutsis in neighboring Burundi (1972). Since 1990, the killing of nearly one million Tutsis in Rwanda; the Serbs' "ethnic cleansing" of civilian populations, including Bosnians and ethnic Albanians (in Kosovo); and the systematic violence against ethnic groups in Myanmar and Sudan have renewed international concern about preventing genocide and punishing those who are responsible for it.

Many recent conflicts grounded in nation-based hostility can also be a blur of class conflict, separatist violence, revolutionary struggle, and conflict between states, topics addressed below. What is clear is the massive toll that these conflicts levy on their populations. Table 12.2 provides data on just a few conflicts and some of the most visible indicators of human devastation. It lists the number of deaths attributable to political violence. In addition, the toll in disrupted lives is revealed by the number of people who have been forced by the violence to leave their homes and communities—there are currently 26.4 million internally displaced persons worldwide. An additional 15.2 million people have actually fled their country, crossing the border in an attempt to escape the violence. The large majority of these 42.7 million people, more than 70 percent of whom are women and children, live in squalor and unremitting hardship; they are homeless or are surviving in miserable refugee camps (UNHCR 2013).

Table 12.2 Human Devastation from Recent Internal Violence and Ethnic Conflict

Country	Deaths [a]	Refugees [b]	Internally Displaced Persons[c]
Congo, D. R.	3,956,941	509,200	2,669,000
Sudan	3,037,015	569,000	1,873,000
Afghanistan	1,777,964	2,585,600	486,000
Rwanda	846,800	97,500	na
Iraq	567,321	746,400	1,132,000
Myanmar	268,916	415,000	430,000
Syria	115,000	1,900,000	6,500,000
Burundi	108,068	73,600	79,000
Colombia	67,271	394,100	3,943,500
Uganda	32,850	5,580	30,000[d]
Nigeria	na	18,000	1,210,000[d]
Serbia (and Kosovo)	na	158,000	228,000

[a] Deaths attributable to political violence (recent period).
[b] Refugees and asylum seekers who have left their country of origin (as of January 1, 2013).
[c] People driven from their home location due to persecution, armed conflict, or widespread violence (as of January 1, 2013).
[d] End of 2011 data.

DATA SOURCES: Deaths: http://siteresources.worldbank.org; Refugees: UNHCR (2013); Internally Displaced Persons: IDMC (2013).

CLASS CONFLICT In some cases, intergroup violence might be attributable to an underlying *class conflict* (see Chapter 9), which is often linked to an ethnic or religious cleavage. In recent conflicts in Rwanda, Sudan, and Sri Lanka, for example, one of the groups in the conflict has dominant social, economic, and political power over the others. Thus, class theorists argue that the conflict in many settings is not actually due to religion, language, or ethnicity; rather, it is a result of the inevitable class struggle that emerges from stratification and inequality. Of course, class conflict can occur between any strata, such as the peasant class against the landlord class or the capitalist class against the worker class, independent of any nation-based cleavage that might reinforce the class distinctions. The group-based political violence in some Latin American countries, such as Colombia and Guatemala, seems best interpreted as a struggle between deeply unequal classes.

Individual or Group Violence against the State

Individual or group political violence directed against the political system can have several causes. The motivation underlying many acts of terrorism is actually to direct violence against a state, even if the immediate targets are noncombatants. In this section, we examine other forms of violence in which the state is the target. At one extreme, such violence might be a person's or a group's spontaneous outburst of frustration with life conditions. At the other extreme, the individual or group might have such deep-seated hostility toward the existing political system that it undertakes a lengthy series of violent actions to overthrow the system.

COUP A **coup** occurs when *the top leader or part of the leadership group is replaced by violent means or the explicit threat of violence.* Those carrying out the coup have no intention of overthrowing the entire political-economic order, although their opposition to the existing leadership can be based on differences in policy as well as on personal rivalry. Coups are most common in political systems that have no institutionalized procedures for leadership succession. Political violence against the top leadership group is typically organized by other members of the political leadership, by a rival political group, or by the military. An extreme example is Bolivia, where 190 coups occurred over a 156-year period ending in the 1980s. Bangladesh had 21 coups or attempted coups in its first 36 years of existence.

Most coup attempts fail, and the number of successful coups per year has dropped from about 12 to 6 in the last two decades. The coup is typically followed by a period of extremely autocratic rule, but the period until there is a turnover to competitive elections has shortened, particularly due to international pressure for democratic processes (Marinov and Goemans 2008). In Egypt, the military led a coup in June 2013, arresting the country's first democratically elected president, Mohammed Morsi. The new constitution was suspended, Morsi's government was temporarily replaced by leaders supported by the military, and a former military leader was elected president with no serious opposition in May 2014. Among other states in which coups have recently ousted leaders are the Central African Republic, Fiji, Guinea, Haiti, Honduras, Madagascar, Mauritania, and Thailand.

RIOTS AND REBELLION When people find their political, social, or economic conditions intolerable, their frustration can escalate from demonstrations and civil disobedience to riots. *Riots* historically have been *spontaneous and relatively disorganized group violence* against property, agents of the political system, perceived opponents in the society, or random targets. Riots are often triggered by a specific incident, such as a police shooting or an economic problem such as a sudden large increase in the price of basic foodstuffs. The emergence of social networking technologies, like Facebook and Twitter, has allowed individuals to communicate *en masse* to many people at once. These technologies have lowered the barriers to organization—riots can now be planned. Once riots start, they can spread or become more organized into violent demonstrations as others are motivated to express their dissatisfaction with the political system or social conditions. And new communications technologies make it far more likely that others within the country and around the world will be aware of both the political action and the often brutal response by the state.

Riots are expressions of frustration in which there is an implicit or explicit demand for redress of grievances. The basic grievances might involve opposition to or support for certain public policies or political leaders. Black South Africans engaged in many riots in their ultimately successful opposition to apartheid during the 1980s. Mass protests and riots have forced many unpopular leaders from power in recent years (e.g., in Bolivia, Egypt, Haiti, Indonesia, Lebanon, Tunisia, and Ukraine).

Such political violence turns into *rebellion* when there is *more frequent, premeditated, and widespread violence involving more people.* At this point, many of those engaged in violence no longer believe the system will respond to their problems. This deterioration of citizen support and escalation of political action to more intense political violence are at the heart of Samuel Huntington's description of political decay (in Chapter 10).

The violence during some of the Arab Spring uprisings directed against their country's leaders since 2010 provides examples of rebellions. Inspired by a Tunisian fruit vendor who burned himself to death in protest against his government, protests and riots expanded to rebellion in Tunisia, then in Libya, and twice in Egypt, resulting in the overthrow of the leaders. In Libya, groups of citizens engaged in peaceful protests calling for Muammar Gaddafi to step down after 42 years of repressive rule. These protests were met with violent response from the regime's security forces. As arrests and deaths escalated among the protestors, they begin to increase the violence of their opposition. Groups of rebels took control of some regions, especially in Eastern Libya. The rebellion escalated into a full-scale conflict between forces loyal to Gaddafi and those committed to ending his rule, which resulted in extensive casualties. The situation was further complicated as other countries, primarily from NATO, entered into an air war against Gaddafi's forces under the rationale of humanitarian intervention (recall the Debate in 5) to protect rebellious Libyans (and to force Gaddafi out of power). By Gaddafi's overthrow and death, between 25,000 and 35,000 had been killed.

SEPARATIST VIOLENCE At the heart of some nation-based violence is the nationality group's struggle for autonomy—for the right to control its own political, economic, and cultural destiny. Some groups engage in *separatist violence to achieve substantial or total political autonomy* from the existing political system. If the separatist group is small and lacks political resources, it usually turns to acts of terrorism or attacks against specific individuals within the political system. This characterized the actions of the Irish Republican Army (IRA) throughout much of the twentieth century as it attempted to separate Northern Ireland from the United Kingdom and merge it with the Republic of Ireland. Targets of the IRA's bombs and murders were usually the British "occupying army" and members of the Protestant paramilitary groups in Northern Ireland. Separatist violence characterizes recent activities by the Kurds against Turkey, South Ossetians against Georgia, Kashmiris against India, and pro-Russian groups against Ukraine.

Violent uprisings against colonial power were often one element in native people's political struggle for independence. Sometimes separatist violence is weak or poorly organized, but other times separatist violence has been coordinated by an organized group, such as the Mau Mau versus the British in Kenya (1950s) and the Vietminh/Vietcong versus the French and then the Americans in Vietnam (1940s–1970s). The violent resistance (after 2003) to the U.S. military and its allies in postwar Iraq is also characterized by some as native opposition to foreign occupation. Moreover, group cleavages within Iraq mean that the violent resistance to the U.S. military simultaneously occurs with violent opposition to the central government. Accordingly, for Iraq, group political violence against the state occurs for more than one reason.

A **civil war** results when *a significant proportion of the population in a region actively supports a separatist movement and political violence emerges on a large scale.* In the early 1860s, the political leaders of the slaveholding southern states decided that they no longer wished to be part of the United States federation, and they announced that their states were seceding (withdrawing formal membership). The central government rejected their request to secede, forcing 11 southern states to declare their independence, create a confederation, and initiate a military struggle against the central government. In the bloody U.S. Civil War (1861–1865), the Union forces of the central government ultimately defeated the army of the Confederacy and forced the southern states to remain in the federation.

A similar civil war occurred in Nigeria in 1967–1970. The Igbo tribe, which differed from other major tribes in religion, language, and political traditions, attempted to secede from the Nigerian federation and create a separate state called Biafra. After four years of civil war and nearly a million deaths, the central government's army was victorious, and Biafra was never established as a state. In contrast, the Bengalis were successful in their separatist civil war against the central government of Pakistan (recall the Focus in 4), and the new state of Bangladesh was created in 1971.

The opening of this chapter described an example of the complex nature of contemporary political violence. It centered on separatist violence—the devastating struggle among the Serbs, Bosnians, Croatians, Kosovars, and other nationality groups after the breakup of Yugoslavia in 1991. It also included extensive interpersonal violence, terrorism, civil war, and genocide. These groups' differences in ethnicity, history, language, and religion all reinforced their separate national identities. Widespread separatist violence resulted from the groups' antipathy toward one another and their efforts to determine precisely what states would emerge and where the borders between the states would be. The conflict in Syria can also be classified as both a rebellion and a civil war. There is widespread resistance to the authoritarian rule of Bashar al-Assad. In addition, he and the ruling class are from the Alawite religious minority, which is in violent conflict with the Sunni majority. However, the numerous nation-based internal divisions among those opposing al-Assad have also contributed to a death toll of more than 115,000 Syrians, 6.5 million internally displaced people, and 1.9 million refugees since 2011 (Table 12.2).

REVOLUTION A **revolution** is *a rapid and fundamental transformation of the state organization and the class structure* (Skocpol 1979). In contrast to the other forms of political violence against the state, the explicit objective of a revolution is to destroy the existing political system and establish a new one with a fundamentally different distribution of power and value allocations. After a revolution, new leadership takes power, claiming that it will reorganize the state, serve a new ideology, and allocate power and resources to different groups.

Although some of the most famous revolutions had occurred earlier (e.g., the American Revolution in 1776, the French Revolution in 1789, the Russian Revolution in 1917), there were many revolutionary movements and revolutions in the period when many colonial territories transitioned to independent countries (especially from about 1950 to 1980). When Fidel Castro and his forces drove out the Batista government in Cuba in 1959, he launched a complete restructuring of the state, society, and economy. In Libya, Colonel Muammar Gaddafi overthrew a hereditary king and created a revolutionary "state of the masses" built on egalitarianism (1969). Similarly, when Shah Reza Pahlavi and his "White Revolution" were overthrown and replaced by an Islamic theocracy (in 1979), there was a fundamental transformation in Iran's politics and society.

However, it can be difficult to specify the precise extent of system transformation that must occur to achieve "revolutionary" changes in the state organization, class structure, or distribution of values (recall the discussion in Chapter 10). In many instances, it is not clear whether the essential features of the political system have dramatically changed. This situation can occur either because the attempt to transform the political system is a charade or because it falls far short of its objectives. For example, since Gaddafi's regime was destroyed in 2011, his system of governance and political economy has been eliminated, but there is now widespread violence and substantial disorder in the attempt to transform the government and society. In Egypt, the Morsi government appeared to be introducing revolutionary changes, but the current regime under the control of the military has much in common with the period under Mubarak.

Can you currently determine whether any of the recent violent replacement of governments in the Arab Spring that began in 2011 (e.g., in Tunisia, Yemen, Egypt, and Libya) should be characterized as revolutions?

STRATEGIES FOR REVOLUTION Four broad strategies can be employed to achieve a revolution.

Strategy 1: Terrorism. As a revolutionary strategy, *terrorism* involves selective acts of violence, usually by small, organized cells of political activists that lack sufficient membership and resources to sustain a direct struggle against the existing state. Violence is used to disrupt public life and to provoke repressive responses from the state, and thus to foster political decay and undermine support for the state. The anticolonial resistance in Algeria is a clear example of the successful use of terrorism. A mixture of random public bombings, disruptions of infrastructure services, and violence against the agents of the colonial French led to a dramatic decline in the quality of life and provoked repressive responses from the French political and military authorities. As conditions deteriorated, France decided to abandon the ungovernable country, and the anticolonial/terrorist leadership, under Ben Bella, formed a new political system in 1962. (Gillo Pontecorvo's powerful film *The Battle of Algiers documents this period.*)

Obviously, terrorism, like other revolutionary strategies, does not always produce the expected results. Sometimes the terrorists are crushed without achieving any of their objectives, like the terrorist groups in the United States in the 1960s. And sometimes the repression evoked by terrorism merely makes things worse. In Iran, leftist terrorists were successful in destabilizing Shah Reza Pahlavi's regime, but it was the conservative Islamic fundamentalists supporting the Ayatollah Khomeini who

Militarization, extensive violence, death and destruction are recurring conditions for those in many countries, as for these commandos during the regionalized civil war in the Democratic Republic of Congo.

succeeded in grasping political power (1979) and forming a new political system even more unappealing to the leftists than the shah's. Nonetheless, terrorism continues to be the preferred strategy for certain revolutionary groups that lack popular support or significant resources, such as Abu Sayyaf in the Philippines.

Strategy 2: Revolution from above. In a revolution from above (Johnson 1983), violent resistance to the regime occurs primarily in the urban centers, especially the capital city. Usually, the rural areas have minimal involvement in the revolutionary struggle. At least some parts of the political elite and the military are sympathetic to or even supportive of the goals of the revolution. Typically, the final collapse of the old regime is rapid because its leaders are killed or flee. The new political system then penetrates the countryside in an attempt to control the entire country. Examples of revolution from above in the twentieth century include Gamal Abdel Nasser's replacement of King Farouk in Egypt (1952), Muammar Gaddafi's victory over King Idris in Libya (1969) and then his violent overthrow (2011), the execution of communist Premier Nicholae Ceauçescu in Romania (1989), and the flight of socialist leaders Mengistu Mariam from Ethiopia and Said Barre from Somalia (1991).

Strategy 3: Guerrilla war. The essence of **guerrilla war** is *a long, protracted campaign of political violence against the state from rural bases*, although the fighting can be in both rural and urban areas. It is a direct struggle against the military because the guerrilla forces persistently harass the regime's military and authorities by fighting in a hit-and-run style, suddenly attacking an exposed point and then disappearing into the population and the countryside. There is an effort to win the loyalty of the rural population by mixing intimidation and promises of reform. Eventually, the guerrillas gain control of the countryside and then march into the collapsing capital city.

The Chinese revolution, culminating in victory in 1949, is the classic example. Mao Zedong observed that success in the revolution depended on the support of the rural peasants, for "without the poor peasants, there can be no revolution." Many of the successful Third World revolutions after 1950 employed guerrilla warfare, including Cuba under Fidel Castro (1959), Vietnam under Ho Chi Minh (1975), and Zimbabwe (formerly Rhodesia) under Robert Mugabe (1980). This strategy is evident in recent struggles in Afghanistan by the Taliban, Algeria, Colombia, and Congo.

Strategy 4: Democratic revolution. **Democratic revolution** occurs when *legal, generally nonviolent political action is effectively mounted to achieve a fundamental transformation of the political system.* In one form, the population uses the democratic electoral process to select a new leadership elite, which then dismantles the existing political system and creates a new one. Examples of this form are the rise of Hitler and establishment of the Third Reich in Germany (1933) and the election of the anti-Sandinista coalition in Nicaragua (1990).

In a second form, widespread but generally nonviolent citizen resistance to a regime forces the elite to resign (Sharp 2010; Thompson 2003). The new leadership, though not initially elected, implements fundamental transformations in the political system. This occurred in the negotiated "Velvet Revolutions" in Soviet bloc states such as Czechoslovakia, East Germany, and Poland in the late 1980s. More recently, there have been numerous instances of a third form that falls short of revolution but does involve extensive, generally peaceful demonstrations against a leader that result in the leader's resignation and the rapid installation of a significantly different political regime. Among the many examples are the Philippines (2001), Georgia's "Rose Revolution" (2003), Ukraine's "Orange Revolution" (2004), and Kyrgyzstan's "Tulip Revolution" (2005). As noted above, the recent "revolutions" in Egypt and Tunisia drove out the old regime leadership through predominantly nonviolent action in the hope of political transformation, but it is not yet clear whether fundamental change will be established.

CONDITIONS FOR REVOLUTION The conditions under which political revolution occurs is an issue that has fascinated many people, especially those who want to analyze revolution and those who want to lead a successful revolution. The most widely cited studies of major historical revolutions include those by Hannah Arendt (1963), Crane Brinton (1957), Chalmers Johnson (1983), Barrington Moore (1966), and Theda Skocpol (1979).

One long-standing explanation of revolution is substantial inequality, a factor emphasized in analyses from Aristotle to Karl Marx to contemporary theorists. A second general approach is the theory of rising expectations, associated with Alexis de Tocqueville (1835/1945), James Davies (1971), and others. In this view, the key cause of revolution is a sudden increase in the disparity between the values the population expects to enjoy from the government and the actual value distribution the population receives. It is also called the *J-curve theory* because, as indicated in Figure 12.3, the *disparity resembles an inverted J,* and revolutionary violence occurs when the disparity becomes substantial.

Empirical analyses have defined certain conditions that are associated with countries in which revolutions occur: (1) conflicting elites; (2) deep ethnic divisions; (3) rapid economic growth, especially when it is followed by a sharp decline in prosperity; (4) a relatively short history as an autonomous state; (5) divisive interventions by actors in the international system; (6) rapid population growth, especially a high proportion of younger people; and (7) social mobilization. None of these is a necessary condition for revolution, and unique events are critical, but the probability of revolution increases as more of these conditions are present.

Figure 12.3 J-curve Description of Revolution

SOURCE: Derived from Davies 1971.

Use of Force Between States

12.4 **Analyze the nature and causes of war.**

The final box in Figure 12.1 includes those cases in which both the source and target of violence are states. While this form is primarily referred to as a war, there are some situations in which the use of violence between states is more limited (Gochman and Maoz 1984):

- In a *blockade*, the military (e.g., ships, troops, munitions) of one state is used to seal off territory (e.g., border crossings, harbors), preventing entry or exit by the rival state.

- In *state-sponsored terrorism*, the state provides financial or material support to groups committing occasional acts of political violence within the rival state.

- A state can engage in a brief, *single use of force*, such as a bombing raid, firing munitions into the enemy state, or rapid invasion for a specific purpose (e.g., the sabotage of a facility).

- In a *clash*, there is a brief engagement between the armed forces of two states, as in a border skirmish.

- In a **low-intensity conflict (LIC)**, *contending groups engage in armed struggle that is usually sporadic and prolonged but does not involve full-scale military conflict*, with the goal of inflicting maximum harm while suffering few or no casualties.

War

War is *interstate violence that is sustained and organized and (usually) involves hostilities between the regular military forces of the states*. Such violence is the ultimate mechanism for resolving conflict between states. For those who define politics as conflict resolution, war represents the utter failure of politics. But many probably agree with Karl von Clausewitz's famous dictum: "War is regarded as nothing but a continuation of political activity by other means" (Clausewitz 1833/1967: 87). Thus, war is the use of violence by one state to achieve its political goals at the expense of another state.

Robert Ardrey (1966: 27), a well-known ethologist (a person who studies animal behavior to better understand human behavior), wryly observed that "human war has been the most successful of all our cultural traditions." Indeed, the study of world history is usually dominated by wars and recurrent episodes of organized violence among states.

The elimination of war is not among the accomplishments of the modern world. The comprehensive analysis of major interstate wars between 1816 and 1980 found some good news: Wars are less frequent, are considerably shorter, and involve fewer states. But the bad news is that the number of wars in progress at any given time has increased substantially since 1900, and the total number of deaths from war has risen astronomically (Sivard 1996). The post–Cold War context has possibly reduced the number of interstate wars (Russett 2010). Yet since 1990, nearly half of the world's countries have suffered the enormous costs of a major armed conflict (SIPRI 2014).

Few of the recent major conflicts are *conventional wars*—that is, wars that entail the direct, sustained confrontation of the military forces of two or more states within a defined space on the soil of one of the combatants. Conflicts that do fit the definition of a conventional war include the Argentina–United Kingdom War (Falklands War, 1982), the Iran–Iraq War (1980–1988), the Iraq–Kuwait War (Persian Gulf War, 1990), the Ecuador–Peru War (1995), the Ethiopia–Eritrea War (1998–2000), the Iraq–U.S.-led-coalition War (2003), and the brief Georgia–Russia War (2008).

Many contemporary conflicts are complicated mixes of internal, regional, and transborder combatants. While most are not classic wars, analysts combine them with war into a broader category: *major armed conflicts*. Major armed conflicts have three defining characteristics: (1) the use of armed force between two or more governments or one government and at least one organized, armed group; (2) at least 1,000 battle-related deaths in a year; and (3) conflict over control of the government or territory. In the last two decades, between 10 and 30 major armed conflicts were being waged per year. All 10 such conflicts in 2012 (e.g., in Afghanistan and Colombia) were intrastate—that is, sustained violence within the borders of a country (although combatants from other countries might be participants). And there were about 100 instances of "organized violence" with at least 25 deaths in 2012 (Uppsala 2013).

Africa's "world war" in Congo (1998–2003, but the fighting continues; recall the Focus in 11) seems a prototype of the contemporary unconventional war. At one level, it is an internal civil war between the military forces loyal to President Kabila and several large paramilitary groups that rejected his authority to rule. Some of the cleavages underlying the conflict are regional, some are nation-based, and some are based on merely personal animosity and ambition. Other motivations include greed to capture Congo's valuable resources. At its height, the war involved militaries and paramilitaries from eight countries and UN peacekeeping forces, and as many as 5.4 million deaths are attributable to the war (Prunier 2008). Another striking example of this type of complex "war" is the bloody conflict in Israel and Palestine, where all forms of political violence collide, as discussed in the Focus in 12.

The changing nature of many contemporary wars is evident in the enormous increase in the proportion of civilian deaths. Whereas in World War I there was only one civilian death for every eight military deaths, in World War II there were two civilian deaths for every military death. In the 1990s, 9 out of every 10 war deaths were *civilians*, and the major armed conflicts going on since 1990 have been killing more than half a million civilians each year. And the remarkable and efficient technologies of modern war are dramatically increasing the casualties. In the twentieth century, there were six times as many deaths per war as in the nineteenth century and four more times as many war deaths as in the preceding 400 years (Sivard 1996: 7, 17).

Worldwide, the nearly $2 *trillion* per year that states spend directly on the military to support their security goals could, if reallocated to their prosperity goals, greatly enhance their citizens' quality of life. Total world military spending has increased by 50 percent between 2000 and 2013 (SIPRI 2014). The problem is that many policymakers believe that security goals have the highest priority and that without security, no other goals can be achieved. Yet in an era of high-tech warfare, almost no one feels truly secure. This insecurity leads every state to push itself and its rivals into an accelerating, unending, and potentially devastating expansion of the capacity for massive political violence.

Do you think some states are more warlike than others? That is, do some states have a much more extensive history of interstate conflict than others? This issue is explored in Compare in 12.

What Causes War?

Can we explain why states go to war? As a partial answer, scholars have attempted to determine whether some states or their populations have particular attributes that result in a greater propensity to engage in war. The findings are inconclusive, since there are always unique contingencies associated with particular wars. However,

Focus in 12

Ultraviolence among the Children of Abraham: Israelis and Palestinians

Israelis and Palestinians share a common understanding of their beginnings, yet they split into two nations whose recent history is marked by ultraviolence. Perhaps more than anywhere else in the world, almost every type of political violence in Figure 12.1 occurs with depressing regularity in this region. Helicopter gunships fire missiles at cars to assassinate leaders, suicide bombers kill and maim scores of innocents, bulldozers destroy residential neighborhoods, and bloody wars wreak havoc in several countries. How did things get so bad?

According to legend, the patriarch Abraham settled in and was eventually buried in the land of Canaan, near what is now Hebron, Israel, in about 2000 B.C.E. Abraham developed the foundational principles of a new religion, Judaism. The offspring of one of his two wives (son Isaac and grandson Israel) followed this new religion. The line descending from Abraham's other wife continued to live in the area and did not embrace Judaism. Most family members in this second line were later attracted to the teachings of Mohammed (born in Mecca in 570 C.E.) and another new religion, Islam. Arab military conquests in the seventh to tenth centuries added to the near-total religious domination of Islam in the region.

"The children of Israel" (the Jews) lived in the Canaan area from about 1300 to 700 B.C.E. but ultimately migrated to many countries. Almost everywhere they went, the Jews felt themselves to be a target of discrimination and described themselves as part of a dispersed (diaspora) nation with no homeland. Thus, in 1897, European Jewish leaders founded the World Zionist Movement, the central goal of which was to establish a Jewish homeland and a sanctuary from anti-Semitism. After a debate in which locations in Europe, Africa, Latin America, and the Near East were considered, the Zionists concluded that their homeland should be the "Promised Land" of Abraham's birth, Palestine. They began purchasing land and establishing colonies of Jewish settlers in Palestine. By the outbreak of World War I (1914), they owned 100,000 acres, and 70,000 Jews had migrated to Palestine, living alongside more than 800,000 Arab Muslims (see Figure 12.4).

After the war, the British government, which had a mandate to govern Palestine, agreed under pressure from European Jews that it would assist in establishing a Jewish "home" in Palestine. As discrimination against the Jews in Europe reached horrendous levels with the rise of Nazism, the flow of Jewish immigrants to Palestine became a flood. By the outbreak of World War II, the number of Jews in Palestine had increased sixfold.

The Muslim Arabs in the Palestine area were increasingly distressed by this massive invasion of Jewish "foreigners." There was violence and guerrilla war between extreme groups of Arabs and Jews. The recently founded United Nations proposed a plan to split Palestine into two states, maintaining Jerusalem as a shared city under UN trusteeship. The Jews accepted this plan in 1947, but the Arabs rejected it, angry that the Jews, who constituted only one-third of the population, would receive the majority (55 percent) of the land. Two hours before the British mandate in Palestine ended in 1947, the Jewish leaders declared a new sovereign state, Israel. The next day, the armies of the surrounding Arab states (Egypt, Lebanon, Syria, and Transjordan) declared war on Israel. The defeat of these armies by the Israeli army resulted in 800,000 homeless Palestinians, many of whom fled to neighboring lands.

Full-scale war erupted three more times between Israel and its Arab neighbors (in 1956, 1967, and 1973). Each time, Israel defeated the Arab armies and conquered more land, the Occupied Territories (especially the West Bank and Gaza). By the late 1960s, these territories were inhabited by 1.2 million Palestinians, who were now an unwelcome nation subjugated within the Israeli state. More than 1 million additional Palestinians were exiles living in Jordan and other Arab states. Jewish settlements continued to expand in the Occupied Territories, establishing new outposts of Jewish control on the best land.

Frustrated Palestinians formed active resistance groups, most notably the Palestine Liberation Organization (1964) and Hamas (1987). These groups were convinced that only political violence and the destruction of the state of Israel would enable them to regain control of their lands. The

Figure 12.4 Population in Palestine/Israel at Key Dates

combination of civil disobedience, armed resistance, and terrorist acts by Palestinian groups, on the one hand, and the strong and often brutal responses by the Israeli military and Jewish militant groups, on the other hand, has resulted in an endless cycle of violence and retaliation. The more militant groups on each side are willing to engage in "whatever means necessary" to protect their land.

The United Nations, the United States, and others have promoted a two-state solution based broadly on the pre-1967 borders to achieve stability and peace in the region, but all agreements have collapsed. Some Palestinian groups have renounced terrorism and accepted the continued existence of Israel, and some Israelis agree that there should be a Palestinian state. But since the 2006 election of Hamas as the dominant party in Gaza, there have been new rounds of devastating violence between the Israelis and Palestinians.

Beneath this basic story line there are extraordinarily complex subplots: factional struggles among the Jews and among the Palestinians, disagreements about the legitimacy of violence by each group, and the complicated agendas of external actors (e.g., other Arab states, the United States, MNCs) regarding Islam, oil, terrorism, and so on. The land of Abraham is the cauldron in which this volatile stew of violence boils furiously.

Further Focus

1. Should the UN have proposed a land split in 1947 that closely reflected the size of the two populations?
2. If one accepts the idea that "to the victor go the spoils" after a war, do both the Israelis and the Arab states have a good reason to reject a compromise settlement at this point?

empirical research does suggest seven state characteristics that are generally correlated with the likelihood of war (Kegley and Wittkopf 2004: 411–418):

1. Newer nations are more likely to initiate war than are mature states.
2. War is more likely in states that have effectively *socialized their citizens to accept the government's actions* on national security.
3. The most warlike states have *rising prosperity* but are *relatively poor*, though they are not the very poorest states.
4. Countries with *desirable geopolitical features* (i.e., resources and location—recall Chapter 11) have a higher probability of warfare.
5. Countries *not well linked to the global economy* are more likely to engage in war.
6. States that are most *highly militarized,* and especially those that are rapidly expanding their military power, are more warlike.
7. Countries whose political culture reflects a high degree of *nationalism* are more warlike.

The contemporary global system has conditions that make many analysts (particularly those with the political idealist perspective described in Chapter 11) optimistic that war is declining. Several forces seem to encourage this optimism. First, democracy has spread to many major countries, and *established democracies rarely fight one another* (the so-called **democratic peace**). In particular, there is a growing "security community" of countries, mainly among the Global North countries in the EU and NATO, among whom an interstate war seems inconceivable. Second, globalization has substantially increased countries' *economic interdependence*. And third, *transnational organizations*, ranging from the UN to NGOS to MNCs, have become more significant

Compare in 12

Levels of War and Peace

How can we compare the extent to which particular countries are more war-prone or more peaceful? One comprehensive study determined the frequency with which more than 100 countries engaged in interstate conflict between 1816 and 1976. The analysis focused on empirical data measuring 14 types of militarized interstate disputes, including major displays of force and uses of force. A state is considered to be in a dispute whether it is the initiator or the target of the conflict. Because some countries have considerably longer histories as states, the analysis measured disputes per year of the state's existence. The study concluded that less than one-third of the states, primarily major powers, initiated more than 70 percent of all disputes, were the primary targets of more than 60 percent of the disputes, and were also most likely to enter disputes in which other countries were already engaged. Table 12.3 lists the 10 most dispute-prone states in the analysis. Notice that the list of most conflict-prone states is topped by Israel, the United Kingdom, India, the United States, and Pakistan, all

of which averaged more than one dispute per year (Gochman and Maoz 1984).

A recent empirical study takes a different approach. It calculates a yearly Global Peace Index for 162 countries, using 22 indicators such as external and internal conflicts, military expenditures, and relations with neighboring countries (Institute for Economics and Peace 2014). In contrast to the earlier study, this index attempts to measure and compare countries' level of peacefulness and nonviolence, although most of the measures in the index do relate to the level of preparation for and engagement in violent activities, both domestic and international. Table 12.3 lists the 10 most peaceful countries, led by Iceland and Denmark. Other rankings in the top half of all countries on peacefulness include Germany (17), Singapore (25), Spain (26), Vietnam (45), the United Kingdom (47), and Ghana (61). The index can also be examined from the bottom up to identify the *least* peaceful countries in the contemporary world. Table 12.3 indicates that the three least peaceful countries are Syria, Afghanistan,

Table 12.3 Most Dispute-Prone and Most Peaceful Countries

A. Most Dispute-Prone (1816–1976)*	B. Least Peaceful (Current)	C. Most Peaceful (Current)
Israel	Syria	Iceland
United Kingdom	Afghanistan	Denmark
India	South Sudan	Austria
United States	Iraq	New Zealand
Pakistan	Somalia	Switzerland
Germany	Sudan	Finland
Russia/Soviet Union	Central African Republic	Canada
France	Democratic Republic of Congo	Japan
China	Pakistan	Belgium
Italy	North Korea	Norway

*Other highly dispute-prone countries are Zambia, Rhodesia/Zimbabwe, North Vietnam, and Uganda; but these states were independent for only a short amount of the analysis period, thus causing potential measurement error.

SOURCES: A = Gochman and Maoz 1984: Table 8; B and C = Institute for Economics and Peace 2014.

and South Sudan (160–162). Other countries ranking in the lower half on peacefulness include the United States (101), China (108), Egypt (143), South Africa (122), Mexico (138), and India (143).

Further Questions

1. If you were creating a comparative index of how peaceful various countries are, what are the three or four most important variables you would include in your index?

2. Is it reasonable that the comparative index for dispute-prone countries makes no distinction among the following three situations: whether a country started a dispute, whether it responded to a violent challenge, or whether it joined a dispute in progress?

---

and more powerful. Both the second and third factors force countries to recognize their shared interests, create strong inducements for cooperation, and provide institutional support for conflict resolution. Thus, the optimists point to a decrease in the number of interstate wars in recent years and the growing sense that major powers will not fight one another (Goldstein 2012; Rasler and Thompson 2005; Russett 2010).

However, others, especially the realists, see the glass as half empty. First, if one considers the broader definition of political violence, the Global Peace Index study concludes that 110 *countries are more conflictual and more militarized* than in 2008 and only 48 countries have become more peaceful (Institute for Economics and Peace 2013). And while there are fewer major armed conflicts, there has been an *increase in the number of intrastate conflicts that are internationalized*—conflicts in which another state supports one side or the other and the danger of escalation is greater (SIPRI 2014). And democracies are as likely as nondemocracies to be involved in these conflicts. Even if the democracies rarely fight one another, there are plenty of potential opponents. Second, globalization and development have dramatically intensified the competition for resources, which will provoke more conflict and *resource wars*. And third, global wars are most likely when a dominant power (a *hegemon*) weakens and new challengers rise, and the current hegemon (the United States) seems to be in decline. Even before that occurs, the emerging *multipolar system* is more conflict prone than either the unipolar system or bipolar system that preceded it (Gowa 2000; Klare 2002, 2012; Mearsheimer 2001; Nye 2011; Organski 1968).

At the highest level of abstraction, there are three broad alternative explanations for the causes of war:

1. War can be attributed to scarcity in nature. Because the consumption goals of states are greater than the natural resources available, states undertake war to protect or capture resources from other states. Thus, states struggle with one another for the control of resources such as energy, food, minerals, and strategic locations (CNA 2007; Klare 2012).

2. War can be attributed to the inadequacy of institutions. In this view, neither the existing sociopolitical structure nor the rules governing the conduct among states are adequate to prevent states from using force to achieve their objectives. Thus, states are guided by self-interest, and there are no conflict-resolution mechanisms that prevent the occasional eruption of large-scale interstate violence.

3. War can be explained by human nature. From this perspective, humans are innately aggressive as a biological species. Humans are nearly the only species

that engages in widespread killing of its own kind. And humans, it is claimed, are acquisitive, competitive, and selfish by nature rather than by nurture. Thus, war becomes a predictable group-level manifestation of these inherent qualities. A variation on this explanation emphasizes the importance of an aggressive leader who draws her country into war (Stoessinger 2010). The gender reference in the previous sentence, while consistent with the alternate chapters referencing in this book, prompts a reminder of the discussion in Chapter 11 of the subfield of international relations theory that asserts female leaders are far less likely than males to resort to violence in interstate disputes (Steans 2013).

Each of the preceding "ultimate" explanations of war also suggests possible solutions that might eliminate war:

1. If the problem is scarcity of natural resources, one might look to technological solutions as states develop new techniques to use natural resources more efficiently and to develop abundant substitutes for scarce resources.
2. If the problem is inadequate institutions, the need is for social engineering—the creation of organizational arrangements that more effectively structure the relations among individuals and states. In the political domain, this might ultimately entail the creation of a viable world government.
3. If the problem is human nature, the solution is found in human engineering by means of comprehensive political socialization or perhaps even genetic manipulation to create a population with nonaggressive, "peace-loving" qualities.

There is some evidence to support each of these three general explanations of the causes of war. But there is also sufficient counterevidence so that none of the three positions is compelling as a complete explanation. Neither an abundance of natural resources nor an advanced technology has stopped intergroup violence. And while there are societies whose members have not been driven by human nature into warlike behavior against their neighbors, no set of human institutions or patterns of human learning have been shown inevitably to generate war or perpetuate peace among states.

While the complete elimination of war might be impossible, it does seem that a combination of material abundance, effective institutions, and thorough socialization might reduce the incidence of war. This leads to more questions: Can an effective combination be identified and implemented by political actors? Might the solution produce human conditions nearly as unpalatable as occasional wars?

Evaluating Political Violence: Means and Ends

12.5 **Evaluate the normative implications of political violence.**

Political violence can be understood as a failure of institutionalized political action. A strong and persuasive normative perspective contends that political violence, especially within a country, is unacceptable, deviant behavior. Conservative ideology provides the most explicit condemnation of such violence, concluding that the only legacy of violence is to undermine order in the society. The resort to violence is part of an erroneous belief that radical social change can lead to lasting improvements. As Englishman Edmund Burke (1729–1797) observed: "Time is required to produce that union of minds which alone can produce all the good we aim at. Our patience will achieve more than our force" (Burke 1790/1955: 197).

A contrary perspective argues that political violence is often the best or even the only mechanism for liberation from oppression and tyranny. This view contends that many societies are controlled by dominant elites who manipulate the state to serve their interests, not the collective good. If a government and its leaders refuse to be constrained by a limited mandate and are not responsive to the legitimate rights of citizens, then the people have the right to overthrow them by any available means. Although this perspective is mainly associated with class theorists and Marxist ideology, the counterpoint to Burke is provided by another English political thinker, classical liberal John Locke (1632–1704), who argued that citizens create government to protect their rights to life, liberty, and property. If the existing government does not serve these purposes well, argued Locke, the people can and must revolt to replace tyranny and create a new and better government (Locke 1690/1963: 466).

Political violence can be a source of either desirable progress or nearly universal suffering and chaos. Clearly, fundamental issues about means and ends are tied up with any assessment of political violence. On the one hand, if the maintenance of public order and political institutionalization are valued goals, you must consider whether resorting to political violence undermines long-term prospects for peaceful, orderly governance. Many cynics would share Italian novelist Ignazio Silone's (1937) assessment: "Every revolution begins as a movement of liberation but ends as tyranny." On the other hand, if you value social and political justice, it is important to consider whether the processes of political violence can be a legitimate means of last resort to ensure such justice. Those who justify some forms of political violence might sympathize with African American Eldridge Cleaver's claim that "a slave who dies of natural causes will not balance two dead flies on the scale of eternity."

There are no tidy answers to the question of whether or when political violence is justifiable. Perhaps one way to organize your own assessment of political violence is to reflect on three basic questions:

1. Is political violence unacceptable under *every* possible circumstance?
2. If you answered no to question 1, could an outcome emerge from the use of political violence that is so preferable to the existing situation that establishing the precedent of using political violence is justifiable?
3. If you answered yes to question 2, what specific circumstances would be necessary to justify the resort to political violence?

These issues about the conditions under which political violence might be legitimate are germane on an even larger scale regarding the justification of war. Despite the massive human and financial costs of war, few would support the proposition that there are absolutely no conditions under which war is justified. But what are the circumstances that justify war?

A classic justification is the doctrine of *self-defense*, a position associated with Augustine (354–430 C.E.). A victim of an unprovoked attack has the right to use violence as a means of protection. Apart from total pacifists, few would reject the principle of self-defense as a legitimate rationale for violence. But the application of this principle, whether group versus group or state versus state, might be a subject of considerable disagreement. Here are some examples in the relations between states: Might state A engage in nonviolent actions that are so provocative that state B is justified in responding with violence? What if the initial violence against state B is by an actor from state A who does not have the explicit support of state A? What if the violence by state A was unintentional? What if the initial violence is within the territory of state A but is perceived as directly harmful to citizens or interests of state B? What if state B uses violence to prevent state A from the (expected) use of far more substantial violence? What if the violent response of state B is of far greater magnitude than the violence by state A? Wars sometimes develop because of such patterns of misperception, accident, preemption, and incremental escalation (Schelling 1960).

Frequently, however, violence and war are justified on a more ambiguous rationale associated with Ambrose (339–397 C.E.), the *defense of universal principles*. In this view, "man has a moral duty to employ force to resist active wickedness, for to refrain from hindering evil when possible is tantamount to promoting it." In accepting the 2009 Nobel Peace Prize, U.S. president Obama cited "just war" principles. Yet the interpretations of "active wickedness" and "evil" are not shared across all cultures. For example, many citizens in most countries believed that Iraq's Saddam Hussein was an evil ruler. However, most did not find this an adequate justification for U.S. president George W. Bush's insistence on a "preemptive war," especially in the absence of compelling evidence that Iraq endangered other countries with weapons of mass destruction that could not be eliminated except by war. Similarly, what level of evil by a ruling group justifies the resort to violence against that group?

In most cases of political violence, a justification based on universal principles is invoked. Violence is used against others in the name of principles such as freedom, social justice, human rights, self-determination, territorial integrity, egalitarianism, religious freedom, religious orthodoxy, anticommunism, communism, and so on. But all political actors do not accept a single vision of natural law that provides universal principles to govern the relations among states and groups.

When the major actors are states, a core problem is that the international system has not implemented powerful and effective institutional mechanisms that eliminate conflict. Thus, occasional outbreaks of interstate conflict and war are inevitable. The context of international politics is essentially *amoral*. Recognizing this fact is the key to understanding most politics across borders, whether diplomatic activities, alliances, or war. In some instances, a state's actions in the international environment are constrained by the state's views of morality and universal principles. But in other instances, a state's decision makers might conclude that almost any action is acceptable if the action seems to further the state's security, stability, and prosperity goals. What are the chances that contemporary states will ever meet the requirement of the UN Charter to "settle their international disputes by peaceful means in such a manner that international peace and security, and justice, are not endangered"?

In the current technological era, the mechanisms for committing violence are more efficient, powerful, and horrifying than at any other time in human history. The implications of this fact are especially evident in the relations among states. But even subnational political groups can now inflict massive and destructive political violence. Thus, in understanding the political world, questions about the use of force and the balance between liberation and destruction are more pressing now than at any other time in human history.

Key Concepts

civil war, p. 336	guerrilla war, p. 338	revolution, p. 336
class conflict, p. 333	J-curve theory, p. 339	riot, p. 334
coup, p. 334	low-intensity conflict, p. 340	separatist violence,
democratic peace, p. 344	nation-based violence, p. 330	p. 335
democratic revolution, p. 339	political society, p. 323	terrorism, p. 327
establishment violence, p. 324	political violence, p. 323	violence, p. 322
genocide, p. 332	rebellion, p. 334	war, p. 340

For Further Consideration

1. Is the state more to be feared than its enemies? Assess the implications of the prevalence during the twentieth century of "murder by government," in which the state is the actor committing violence and the state's citizens are its target.

2. Summarize the key elements of a three-way debate among an absolute pacifist, a committed revolutionary, and yourself regarding the conditions under which political violence is justifiable.

3. It is suggested that much contemporary political violence is nation-based. Analyze the nation-based conflicts of which you are aware. Is most of the violence caused by fundamental antipathy between two nationality groups due to differences in ethnicity, religion, language, and so on? Which one seems most prominent? Or is the violence primarily motivated by other issues, such as inequality and class conflict, quest for power, geopolitics, or some other cause?

4. Must every revolution end in tyranny (as suggested by Ignazio Silone)? Can you identify a modern revolution that, by the criteria you establish, can be viewed as a success?

5. Which of the characteristics of warlike states on pages 338–339 is most surprising to you? Why? What characteristic did you expect that is not among those listed?

For Further Reading

Brecher, Michael, and Jonathan Wilkenfeld. (1997). *A Study of Crisis.* **Ann Arbor: University of Michigan Press.** A comprehensive, usable database from the International Crisis Behavior project that provides valuable information on 412 crises between 1929 and 1992, following the authors' thoughtful analyses of and generalizations about the patterns of interstate crises.

Brownlee, Nathan, Tarek Masoud, and Andrew Reynolds (2013). *"Tracking the 'Arab Spring': Why The Modest Harvest?" Journal of Democracy* **Vol. 24/4.** A clear assessment of the limited success in achieving positive change from the Arab Spring, three years after its beginnings.

Cimbala, Stephen J. (2012). *Nuclear Weapons in the Information Age.* **New York: Continuum International Publishing Group.** The author analyses how nuclear weapons, combined with advanced conventional weapons and new information-age weaponry, have created an extremely dangerous mix and new forms of global risk and instability that must be addressed.

Cinema of War. Film, in addition to literature, has often been a compelling visual and visceral medium for evoking the heroism and absurdity of war. Among the films that are especially effective are *The Hurt Locker* (Kathryn Bigelow, 2008), *Apocalypse Now* (Francis Ford Coppola, 1979, 2001); *The Sands of Iwo Jima* (Allan Dwan, 1949); *The Big Red One* (Samuel Fuller, 1980); *Full Metal Jacket* (Stanley Kubrick, 1987); *In Which We Serve* (David Lean, 1942); *All Quiet on the Western Front* and *Pork Chop Hill* (Lewis Milestone, 1930, 1959); *The Grand Illusion* (Jean Renoir, 1937); *Saving Private Ryan* (Steven Spielberg, 1998); and *Platoon* (Oliver Stone, 1986).

Downes, Alexander B. (2008). *Targeting Civilians in War.* **Ithaca, NY: Cornell University Press.** A blend of case studies and quantitative data are combined to make the controversial argument that democracies are as likely as other forms of government to target noncombatants in interstate conflicts.

Dworkin, Anthony, Roy Gutman, and David Rieff, eds. (2007). *Crimes of War 2.0: What the Public Should Know.* **Rev. ed. New York: W. W. Norton.** Diverse and enlightening discussions on the legal and ethical issues regarding war crimes and international humanitarian law, with powerful commentaries on cases such as Afghanistan, Cambodia, Chechnya, and Rwanda, and dramatic illustrations by photojournalists.

Enders, Walter, and Todd Sandler. (2012). *The Political Economy of Terrorism.* **2nd ed. New York: Cambridge University Press.** A comprehensive database on terrorism is analyzed using the methods of the rational choice approach (see Chapter 4 and the Appendix) to illuminate the choices terrorists make, such as shifting to weak link targets, allocating their scarce resources to the best available target, shifting attack modes, and utilizing the new ICTs.

Freedman, Lawrence, ed. (1994). *War.* **New York: Oxford University Press.** A splendid collection of readings, ranging from the greatest classical treatments of the reasons for and the nature of war to significant recent (but slightly dated) analyses.

Goldstein, Joshua S. (2003). *War and Gender: How Gender Shapes the War System and Vice Versa.* **Cambridge, England: Cambridge University Press.** This book explores why warfare is dominated by men and concludes that it is primarily due to culturally constructed male domination and "militarized masculine stereotypes" rather than genetic differences.

Goldstein, Joshua S. (2012). *Winning the War on War: The Decline of Armed Conflict Worldwide.* **New York: Dutton.** A detailed account of how the recent reduction in major armed conflicts in the Global South can be explained by the interventions of international actors, especially UN peacekeepers and a variety of IGOs.

Goldstone, Jack A., ed. (2003). *Revolutions: Theoretical, Comparative, and Historical Studies.* **3rd ed. Florence, KY: Wadsworth Cengage.** A readable set of articles that includes both detailed case studies of revolutions and more analytic work that attempts to develop generalizations about revolutionary violence. See also Goldstone's 2014 *Revolutions: A Very Short Introduction.*

Gourevitch, Philip. (1999). *We Wish to Inform You That Tomorrow We Will Be Killed with Our Families: Stories from Rwanda.* **New York: Farrar, Straus and Giroux.** A powerful account of the ways in which ethnonationalist rhetoric was used to mobilize the Hutu people to massacre almost one million Tutsis and Hutu moderates in Rwanda in the mid-1990s, while the international community was unwilling to intervene to prevent the genocide.

Gurr, Ted Robert. (2000). *Peoples Versus States: Minorities at Risk in the New Century.* **Washington, DC: United States Institute of Peace Press.** Based on the valuable Minorities at Risk Project database, the book is an exceptionally rich blend of data-based analyses and case studies of nation-based conflict.

Hoffman, Bruce. (2006). *Inside Terrorism.* **Revised and expanded ed. New York: Columbia University Press.** A broad-ranging and troubling exploration of terrorism, with particular attention to the recent evolution of strategies and goals of terrorists.

Jenkins, Philip. (2003). *Images of Terror: What We Can and Can't Know About Terrorism.* **New York: Aldine de Gruyter.** A fascinating array of examples is provided to examine how stories about terrorism are transformed in public discussion, especially by the media.

Klare, Michael. (2008). *Rising Powers, Shrinking Planet: The New Geopolitics of Energy.* **New York: Henry Holt.** This is among Klare's persuasive books (see also *The Race for What's Left*, 2012; and *Resource Wars*, 2002) about the "new geography of conflict," driven by competition for scarce resources, among states in the early twenty-first century.

Moghadam, Assaf. (2008). *The Globalization of Martyrdom.* **Baltimore: Johns Hopkins University Press.** The role of al Qaeda and the ideology of Salafi Jihad in almost 1,300 suicide attacks during the past 30 years are analyzed, and suggestions for combating such attacks are offered.

O'Brien, Tim. (1990). *The Things They Carried.* **New York: Doubleday Broadway Books.** In 22 fictional short stories about a U.S. military platoon in the Vietnam War, the author powerfully conveys universal themes regarding the horror of war from the perspective of the individual soldier.

Parker, Geoffrey, ed. (2005). *The Cambridge History of Warfare.* **2nd ed. London: Cambridge University Press.** An ambitious series of essays examining many aspects of war in the Western world, from ancient Greece through recent wars in the Middle East. A key theme is that Western technology and prosperity produced a dominant military that ensured Western global supremacy.

Pinker, Steven. (2011). *The Better Angels of Our Nature: Why Violence Has Declined.* **New York: Viking.** A readable, widely discussed book by a neuroscientist who claims that violence, including political violence, has declined because humans have evolved over many centuries into a less violent species, in part due to the role of the state and of education.

Prunier, Gerard. (2008). *Darfur: A 21st Century Genocide.* **3rd ed. Ithaca, NY: Cornell University Press.** A gripping exploration of the causes and nature of the brutal conflict in Sudan, including a critique of the failure of the international community to prevent the genocide. Equally powerful is his 2008 *Africa's World War: Congo, the Rwandan Genocide, and* *the Making of a Continental Disaster* (New York: Oxford University Press).

Rasler, Karen, and William R. Thompson. (2005). *Puzzles of the Democratic Peace: Theory, Geopolitics, and the Transformation of World Politics.* **New York: Palgrave Macmillan.** A thorough examination of the theories and data regarding the "democratic peace" debate, refining and supporting the concept.

Sassoon, Siegfried. (1968). *Collected Poems: 1908–1956.* **London: Faber and Faber.** The deeply moving poems about war by a young British intellectual who suffered the horrific experiences of European trench warfare during World War I.

Sharp, Gene. (2011). *From Dictatorship to Democracy: A Conceptual Framework for Liberation.* **London: Serpent's Tail.** http://www.aeinstein.org/organizations/org/FDTD.pdf. First written to help the democracy movement in Myanmar, this remarkable little book provides guidelines for overthrowing a dictatorial regime. Leaders of recent people's revolutions indicate they found it very helpful.

Stoessinger, John G. (2010). *Why Nations Go to War.* **11th ed. Boston: Bedford.** A readable set of descriptive case studies of modern wars, emphasizing individual behavior and motives, including World War I, Korea, Vietnam, India–Pakistan, Israel–Arabs, Iran–Iraq, the Balkans, and the U.S. wars in the Middle East.

Walter, Barbara F., and Jack Snyder, eds. (1999). *Civil Wars, Insecurity, and Intervention.* **New York: Columbia University Press.** Centering on thoughtful case studies of the civil wars in Bosnia, Cambodia, Somalia, and Rwanda, important scholars analyze why the international community has not been particularly effective in either preventing the outbreak of or resolving civil wars.

Walzer, Michael. (2006). *Just and Unjust War.* **4th ed. New York: Basic Books.** A political philosopher presents a careful argument about the morality of war, grounded in the context of numerous actual wars.

Weiss, Peter. (1965). *Marat/Sade: The Persecution and Assassination of Jean-Paul Marat as Performed by the Inmates of the Asylum at Charenton Under the Direction of the Marquis de Sade.* **New York: Atheneum.** A brilliant play (and a dazzling film with the same title directed by Peter Brooks) that offers a debate about a revolution between Jean-Paul Marat, a leader of the French Revolution who attempts to retain his idealism about revolutionary change despite having become a victim of extremists, and the Marquis de Sade, the ultimate cynic.

Weitz, Eric D. (2005). *A Century of Genocide: Utopias of Race and Nation.* **Princeton, NJ: Princeton University Press.** A historian offers a compelling and readable comparison of the way in which four major genocides in the twentieth century (under Stalin, Hitler, and Pol Pot and in the former Yugoslavia) drew popular support through the strategic mixture of nationalism and racial identity.

On the Web

http://www.amnesty.org
Amnesty International is the world's leading NGO monitoring establishment violence and human rights abuses and attempting to mobilize citizen support to pressure governments to end such actions.

http://wps.cfc.forces.gc.ca/en/index.php
The Information Resource Centre of the Canadian Forces College provides links to numerous sites detailing current major international conflicts.

http://www.sipri.org

The site of the Stockholm International Peace Research Institute, which conducts research on questions of conflict and cooperation relevant to international peace and security, includes rich databases and significant articles on topics of peace and violence.

http://www.hawaii.edu/powerkills/welcome.html

This site, managed by Professor Rudolf Rummel, an avowed "freedomist," is an exceptionally rich resource of information and links regarding themes of war and peace.

http://www.usip.org

This site for the U.S. Institute of Peace was established and is funded by the U.S. Congress with the goal of preventing conflict, ending current conflicts, and aiding in reconstruction after the hostilities.

http://www.nctc.gov

The National Counterterrorism Center has become the major source of information and data from the U.S. government regarding global terrorism.

http://www.un.org/terrorism

On the official site of the United Nations, one can access information on terrorism and both Security Council and General Assembly resolutions related to political violence.

http://www.ccc.nps.navy.mil/si

The Center for Contemporary Conflict is hosted by the Naval Postgraduate School in California. The site provides information, including many position papers and briefings, regarding current and emerging security concerns in all regions of the world.

http://www.pvtr.org

Centered in Singapore, the International Center for Political Violence and Terrorism offer details and commentaries on current situations of political violence.

http://www.visionofhumanity.org

The Institute for Economics and Peace's Global Peace Index details the components of its yearly rating of the peacefulness of every country.

http://www.hrw.org

The electronic home of Human Rights Watch provides access to an extensive database regarding human rights violations taking place throughout the international community.

http://www.sfcg.org

The site of Search for Common Ground, the world's largest NGO working on conflict resolution, is an excellent source for material on this topic.

http://www.historyguy.com

The electronic home of the "History Guy" provides a number of links to detailed information, articles, and news reports related to political conflicts.

http://www.pcr.uu.se

The Conflict Data Project at Uppsala University (Sweden) maintains a rich and current database on armed conflicts in the world.

Chapter 13
The Developed Countries of the Global North

Learning Objectives

13.1 Characterize the types of markets in the Global North and assess their challenges and achievements regarding the goal of prosperity.

13.2 Identify the obstacles to the political stability of the Global North.

13.3 Trace the development of security challenges to the Global North.

"O, Canada! Our home and native land! True patriot love in all thy sons command …" Voices fill Toronto's Maple Leaf Gardens as the singing of the national anthem precedes the Maple Leaf hockey game. But then as the vocalist intones, "O Canada! Terre de nos aieux, ton front est ceint de fleurons glorieux!" there are boos and catcalls. The Canadian national anthem continues to glorify the same native land of brave forefathers and heroic exploits. What has happened?

The lyrics are now a symbol of the conflict and disagreement within Canada. Canada is a single territorial space with one government that is attempting to rule a population in which "all thy sons" (and daughters) are split into two groups that share neither culture nor identity. The English-speaking Canadians and the French-speaking Canadians struggle to establish harmonious coexistence within the same state. A referendum in 1995 narrowly defeated independence for Quebec, and in 2006, the Quebecois became an official "nation" within Canada. Although the majority of Canadians prefer a single country, some continue to argue vehemently that the only solution to the conflict is the separation of Canada into two countries. The Quebec separatist party, Parti Quebecois, won the most seats in the 2012 election and, for the first time, claimed the office of Premier of Quebec.

Canada is a complicated place. Although it is the second largest country in the world, it has a population of only 35 million. It has a skilled labor force and the twelfth highest GDP (PPP) in the world; yet its economy is dwarfed by its NAFTA partner and number one export market, the United States, and more than half its assets are foreign owned. Its annual GDP per capita growth has been a modest 1.9 percent from 2000 to 2012, but it remains extraordinarily rich in natural resources and contains the world's third highest level of untapped energy resources.

Canada's bicameral, parliamentary system has earned the world's eighth highest score on the EIU's Democracy Index as well as top scores on press freedom and religious freedom. However, there has been significant political instability in the recent period. The multiparty system experienced a government overthrown by a contempt (no confidence) vote in 2011. There have been several highly controversial episodes of "prorogation," a procedure in which the prime minister dismisses the House of Commons for a fixed period to prevent the opposition from taking an action viewed as detrimental to government functioning. Despite a plurality electoral system, there are multiple parties. In the last two decades, electoral support for some parties has risen and fallen dramatically and there have been several minority governments.

On balance, Canadians have much to celebrate. Canada is among the "Top Ten" countries in the world on many measures of quality of life: fourth highest on average years of schooling, seventh on the Global Peace Index, fifth on economic freedom,

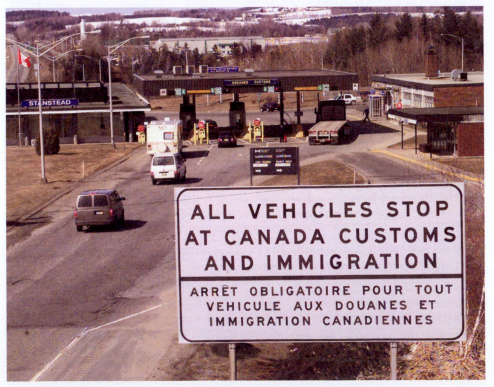

O, Canada! Canada attempts to sustain its national identity, despite the internal split between Anglophones and Francophones and its long border with the world's superpower.

seventh on the Social Progress Index, eighth on average life expectancy, fifth on clean energy investment, and among the ten lowest on corruption. Canada has one of the world's most equal income distributions and a relatively low rate of absolute poverty.

Like Canadians, most citizens of Global North countries live somewhat in the shadows of the big three: the United States, Germany in Europe, and Japan in Asia. In these other Global North countries, the average citizen has a high standard of material well-being, access to a vast array of high technologies, and full integration into global society. This Global North citizen enjoys levels of prosperity, stability, and security that are the envy (and the goal) of most of the people in the rest of the world. How the countries of the Global North attempt to meet challenges to their continued high levels on these elements is the focus of this chapter (CIA 2014; EIU 2013; Freedom House 2014; Transparency International 2013; World Bank 2013).

The Developed Countries of the Global North

In the classificatory scheme presented in Chapter 10 (Figure 10.1), the countries in the upper-right corner were identified as the developed countries of the *Global North*. These countries are also sometimes referred to as *postindustrial societies* because of the growing dominance of the knowledge-based and service-based sectors of their economies. Figure 10.1 indicates that this group of countries includes Canada, all the countries of Scandinavia and Western Europe, Australia, Japan, New Zealand, Singapore, South Korea, Singapore, and the United States, among others. The countries in this group not only have the highest levels of average wealth in the world, as measured by GDP per capita (PPP), but also have the world's highest levels of overall social development, as measured by the index created for Figure 10.1. Thus these countries are generally urbanized and secularized, with highly specialized and institutionalized organizational systems. Their populations are generally characterized by very high rates of adult literacy, extensive use of information and communications technologies, the world's highest-quality health care, and a relatively high standard of material living.

Chapter 13 examines these developed countries of the Global North, and Chapters 14 and 15 focus on the developing countries of the *Global South* and the transitional developed countries, as defined in Chapter 10. Each chapter describes critical issues for countries in the group. The country clusters are meant to allow for broad generalizations about their quest for the key goals of prosperity, stability, and security. General patterns and similarities within each group are emphasized, but you should keep the following points in mind:

- There are substantial differences among states within each group, especially among the large number of states lumped together as the developing countries of the Global South.

- Each state has unique features that are lost in such generalized discussion.

- In some instances, a trait is more similar among certain states across groups than among all the states within one group.

As these qualifications suggest, this method of grouping countries for analysis and generalizations is not perfect. Chapter 10 noted that a taxonomy is valuable to the extent it facilitates comparative thinking and greater understanding of the topics of interest. You must decide whether the analyses of the country clusters in these three chapters achieve those objectives. The remainder of this chapter focuses explicitly on the developed countries of the Global North and their pursuit of prosperity, stability, and security within the context of the global system.

Goal: Prosperity

13.1 **Characterize the types of markets in the Global North and assess their challenges and achievements regarding the goal of prosperity.**

The Global North countries pursue the goal of prosperity (and its components of economic development, economic growth, and welfare distribution) with great energy. Based on our classification, these are already the most economically developed countries in the world. Thus, the emphasis in these countries is on sustaining a high level of economic growth under the assumption that this will generate an expanding economic base that provides more material benefits to the population and also enables government to distribute greater welfare to the citizens.

Mixed Economy

To achieve prosperity, these countries have relied on a **mixed political economy**, which includes considerable private ownership and control of productive resources (land, labor, and capital). Private actors (firms and households) are encouraged to use their resources aggressively to acquire desired goods, to produce goods, and to maximize their profit. Chapter 8 characterized the state's key roles in the mixed political economy: regulating the free market, providing guidance and incentives for production decisions, and redistributing some money and goods, mainly to less-advantaged individuals in the society.

A central policy debate in most of the Global North countries is the appropriate level of state activity in the political economy. Should the state reduce the taxes and regulations imposed on private actors under the assumption that the market economy is more likely to stimulate greater production and higher economic growth, thus benefiting all? Or should the state capture more resources and redistribute them as welfare to its citizens? This debate is sometimes characterized as "growth versus welfare."

The countries vary considerably in the extent to which the free market dominates in the political economy. Each country's political economy is slowly adjusted as the balance of political power among key policymakers shifts between those supporting greater economic freedom and limited government, consistent with classical liberal ideology, and those supporting a more active state committed to redistributive and regulatory public policies, consistent with the ideology of democratic socialism. One broad comparative measure of the public–private mix is the percentage of productive capacity (measured as GDP) that is in the public sector. Figure 13.1 indicates that this varies substantially, from more than 50 percent in Denmark, France, Finland, and

Figure 13.1 General Government Expenditures as a Proportion of GDP

SOURCE: OECD (2013): Table 25.

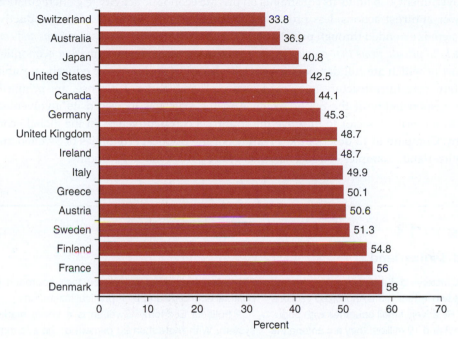

Sweden to less than 40 percent in Switzerland and Australia. While all of the developed countries have mixed political economies, the break between a more capitalist system and a more democratic-socialist system might be defined loosely as about 45 percent of total GDP.

The more democratic-socialist regimes are usually evident in the Scandinavian countries as well as Austria, Belgium, France, Italy, and the Netherlands. These Global North countries with mixed economies are called **social market systems** because *the state encourages an extensive free market economy but is also committed to social welfare distribution and economic regulation*. They are more commonly termed **social democracies** because the social market system operates within a highly democratic political society. Compared with the more free market–oriented countries discussed below, taxation is higher in these systems and more revenue is reallocated either as transfer payments or as subsidized goods and services (e.g., health care, housing, educational and cultural opportunities, public transportation) to the citizens. The state is also more active in regulatory policy, protecting individuals and society from the undesirable actions of firms (e.g., price fixing, unsafe working conditions, environmental degradation). In some of these social market systems, the public sector retains control or ownership of some major productive resources (e.g., energy, transportation) that have strategic importance for the country.

The *developed countries in which most economic activity is in the private sector and the government has a limited role in regulatory and redistributive policies*, designated as **market economies**, currently include Australia, Canada, Japan, Switzerland, and the

United States. Social welfare services are limited toward a basic "safety net" with which the state protects individuals from only the harshest consequences of poverty. Government also limits its constraints on private economic activity (e.g., deregulation, fewer antitrust actions, less protection of unions). Private control of the productive system is extended through **privatization** (i.e., *the selling off of state-owned firms and contracts to private firms that provide public goods and services*). Even in market economies, most of which are full democracies, certain domains, such as basic education, public safety, core infrastructure (e.g., roads, sewers), and national defense, are primarily the responsibility of the public sector. And the state has increased its involvement with the private sector to improve the country's competitiveness in the global economy. Compare in 13 describes key features of the political economies of Sweden and Switzerland, examples of a social market system and a market economy.

Compare in 13

Sweden and Switzerland

Sweden and Switzerland have a lot in common besides the first two letters in the Anglicized versions of their names. Relatively small countries with populations between 8 and 10 million, they are among the world's most developed countries on almost every measure. Both are very prosperous, with among the world's best Human Development Index scores (ranking seventh and ninth, respectively) and very high levels of GDP per capita (PPP). Both are export-oriented economies, with about 70 percent of the workforce engaged in services and about 30 percent in industry jobs. Most citizens in each country enjoy a long life (averaging 82 years) filled with high-quality material possessions, and the countries rank sixth and second globally on the Social Progress Index reflecting quality of life and ecosystem sustainability (CIA 2014; Social Progress Imperative 2014).

Public services and the infrastructure of roads and telecommunications are excellent. Nearly the entire adult population is literate and multilingual. The incidence of violent crime is very low. Each political system is a stable, highly institutionalized multi-party democracy with an efficient administration and independent judiciary. They have a long history of neutrality in international affairs, spend among the world's lowest amounts on the military (as a percentage of GDP), and rank in the top 7 on the Global Peace Index (Institute for Economics and Peace

2014). Yet they differ notably on their approach to political economy and their political institutions.

Political Economy. Sweden is a social market system. With more than 90 percent of the economy in private hands, the Swedish state is committed to market capitalism. Sweden is ranked sixth in the world on economic competitiveness (World Economic Forum 2013); yet Sweden has one of the most expansive welfare states in the world. About one-third of the national economic output is spent on social programs. Among the benefits available to all citizens at little or no direct cost are comprehensive health care, higher education, child care, maternity/paternity leave, job training, and public transportation. Those suffering economic hardship receive substantial income supplements and support for amenities such as housing. Sweden has the world's most equal distribution of wealth and income (ranking first on the Gini index). It also has one of the world's highest scores on gender equality, with many women in positions of power and authority in both the public and private sectors (ranking fourth in the world, for example, on the percentage [45 percent] of women in the national legislature).

Systems like Sweden's are sometimes termed "cradle to grave" socialism. As one example, the state provides complete nursing home care to any elderly citizen for less than 5 percent of the actual costs. The regulatory policies of the state are also extensive in both economic life (e.g., environmental protection, working conditions, product safety) and social life (e.g., the state has even banned parental spanking to protect children against physical abuse). This extensive social welfare is financed by high taxes. Total taxes paid by citizens and firms are about 57 percent of GDP. While this tax burden reduces Swedes' disposable income, most citizens are supportive and proud of their social market system.

In Switzerland, the state follows a model of limited government with regard to the political economy. The state exercises very little regulatory control over its free market economy, which is one of only six countries providing full economic freedom according to the Heritage Foundation (2014), and the country is ranked as the most competitive economy in the world (World Economic Forum 2013). The constitution explicitly emphasizes the role of the private sector in setting economic policy. Switzerland has one of the lowest rates of taxation and the lowest proportion of overall government spending (about 34.7 percent

of GDP) among all the developed countries. The Swiss state generally expects citizens to take care of themselves through the private market, with minimal provision of most public services, except education. Recently, there has been considerable opposition among the citizens to increases in the modest level of welfare support that government provides to the least advantaged Swiss.

Political Institutions. Sweden is a constitutional monarchy with a king. A unitary state, all power emanates from the central government. It is a classic multiparty parliamentary system, with political power centering on the prime minister and cabinet, who control a unicameral legislature elected by proportional representation. It is ranked number two in the world on the EIU Democracy Index and is the world's third least corrupt country. The progressive Social Democratic Party has held a majority or led a majority coalition for more than 80 percent of the period since 1932. Sweden joined the European Union in 1995, but rejected participation in the euro (currency) zone.

Team Switzerland. The unique Federal Council, a collective executive of seven equal members, poses with Federal Chancellor Corina Casanova (front row, far right). Each councillor is responsible for one major department.

Switzerland's political institutions are unique. The executive (Federal Council) is a collective group of seven equal members who each run one major department and cannot veto legislation, with the president of the executive changing yearly. The national legislature has two houses, one elected by proportional representation (PR) and the second by majority vote. There is no judicial review of the laws. Another aspect of Switzerland's limited government is the substantial use of popular voting on policies, based on the view that the people should hold ultimate power. Thus, citizens can use the referendum process to hold a national vote on any piece of legislation passed by the legislature. Switzerland is a confederation composed of 26 cantons (states) with substantial local power and autonomy. This reflects a country with complex nation-based distinctions, including four official languages (German, French, Italian, and Romansch). Switzerland ranks seventh globally on both the Democracy Index and the (least) Corruption Perceptions Index. Given its long-standing desire for neutrality, Switzerland delayed joining the United Nations until 2002 and does not belong to the European Union.

Further Questions

1. Which of Switzerland's rather unique political institutions do you find most appealing?

2. Is it surprising that two countries with such different political and economic systems could be so similar in prosperity and quality of life?

Performance

The developed countries assess their prosperity primarily in terms of economic activity, usually measured as GDP per capita. Figure 13.2 provides comparative data on GDP per capita (adjusted for PPP) for many developed countries. Measured on this indicator, all of the countries in the Global North enjoy considerable prosperity. Only a few oil-rich ministates (e.g., Qatar, Kuwait) have higher GDP per capita than most of the developed countries. Most of these countries have been very concerned about their low rates of growth in GDP per capita, especially in the recent period of global recession, because there is an assumption that economic growth is critical to the vitality of the society. Some critics accuse the developed countries of "growthmania" and suggest that quality of life and citizen satisfaction are better measures of performance than an increasing GDP and should be the focus of public policy (Luke 2013).

The *Human Development Index (HDI)*, the second measure in Figure 13.2, is computed by the UN Development Programme (2013) to reflect the quality of life enjoyed by citizens in a country. It is a composite index that gives equal weight to three indicators: "a long and healthy life, as measured by life expectancy at birth; knowledge, as measured by the adult literacy rate and ... [school] enrollment levels; and a decent standard of living, as measured by GDP per capita (PPP)" (UNDP 2008: 394). HDI scores range from 1.00 to 0.0. A score of 1.00 would indicate that all the country's citizens have attained the most desirable levels of health, education, and living standards. Broadly, a score of .800 or above currently represents a "very high" level of human development (47 countries), scores in the .799–.711 range are "high" levels (47 countries), .710–.535 constitutes a "medium" level of human development (46 countries), and a score below .535 indicates a "low" level (45 countries) (UNDP 2013).

Every developed country achieves an HDI score in the "very high" range. Norway currently has the highest HDI score in the world (.955), followed closely by Australia.

Figure 13.2 Prosperity Measures for Selected Developed Countries

SOURCE: World Bank 2013; UNDP 2013.

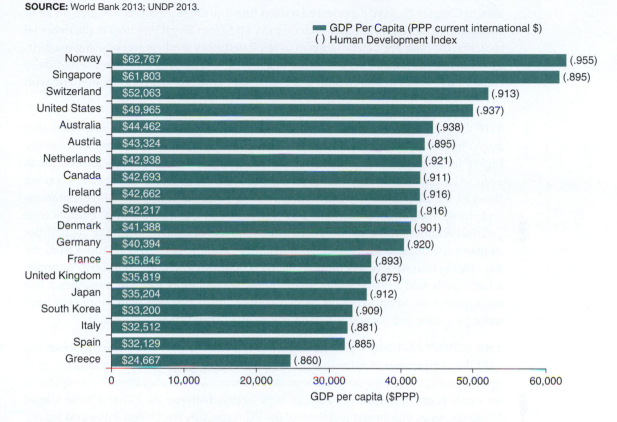

■ GDP Per Capita (PPP current international $)
( ) Human Development Index

Country	GDP Per Capita	HDI
Norway	$62,767	(.955)
Singapore	$61,803	(.895)
Switzerland	$52,063	(.913)
United States	$49,965	(.937)
Australia	$44,462	(.938)
Austria	$43,324	(.895)
Netherlands	$42,938	(.921)
Canada	$42,693	(.911)
Ireland	$42,662	(.916)
Sweden	$42,217	(.916)
Denmark	$41,388	(.901)
Germany	$40,394	(.920)
France	$35,845	(.893)
United Kingdom	$35,819	(.875)
Japan	$35,204	(.912)
South Korea	$33,200	(.909)
Italy	$32,512	(.881)
Spain	$32,129	(.885)
Greece	$24,667	(.860)

GDP per capita ($PPP)

Thus, on both a basic measure of economic production and a quality-of-life index that adds measures of literacy and health, the developed countries seem relatively successful in achieving their overall prosperity goals. A more comprehensive quality-of-life index might include many other indicators in addition to the three employed by the United Nations. If you were attempting to create a comparative measure of the quality of life across many countries, what indicators would *you* include?

Challenges to Prosperity

ERRATIC ECONOMIC GROWTH Most Global North countries have periods of solid economic growth (about 4 percent or higher per year). However, there are also extended periods, such as in the early years of the decades of the 1980s, 1990s, 2000s, and 2010s, when many have not sustained the high levels of economic growth that are the basis of their own definition of prosperity. These countries averaged only 1.7 percent annual GDP growth from 2000 to 2012 (World Bank 2013). And, more seriously, there are periods of recession (a negative change in a key economic growth measure). The worldwide economic decline that began in 2008 has been the most significant period of low or negative growth that developed countries have suffered in more than 70 years. Almost every developed country has struggled with weak economic growth in the period since 2008, and some, such as Portugal, Spain, Ireland, and Greece (recall the opening discussion in Chapter 8), have experienced a deep financial crisis. Analysts disagree on all of the causes of this crisis, but they include risky and often illegal practices in the financial industry, the dramatic deterioration of overinflated stock markets and housing markets, government debt, shrinking consumer demand, and high unemployment. All of these caused huge losses in asset wealth and interacted negatively with one another and with poor economic growth.

THE COMPETITIVE GLOBALIZED ECONOMIC SYSTEM The economic crisis that began in 2008 is a powerful example of the vulnerability that all economies face in the highly interdependent global system. Serious problems in only a few Global North economies can quickly infect the economies of many other countries, especially among those in the EU. Moreover, with the increasing power of multinational corporations and the spread of global markets, a government has less direct control over its own political economy (Chapter 11). As globalization increases the productive capabilities of many countries, every Global North country faces increasing competition from the developing countries, newly industrializing economies, and postcommunist countries, all of which tend to have lower production costs. As more jobs are outsourced and more goods are imported, a developed country must struggle with more structural unemployment and declining economic vitality (Zakaria 2009).

THE EUROPEAN UNION (EU) AND THE OTHERS The developed countries face not only the complexities of international competition and globalization but also the multiple challenges of sorting out their economic relations with one another. The competition for markets and resources has become very intense between the EU and those Global North countries that are not members of the EU (especially the United States and Japan). While the 28 member states within the European Union enjoy substantial economic advantages, some members have resisted its uniform policies (e.g., on agriculture, on government debt, on contributions) and have continued to protect their national economic prerogatives. Moreover, the less prosperous EU members (many of which are not yet Global North countries in Figure 10.1) drain resources from the wealthier members. And the fragile interdependencies among the stronger and weaker member states in the eurozone have been highlighted by the economic crises in countries such as Greece and Ireland, which required major bailouts to protect the value of the euro (McCormick 2006).

THE DISTRIBUTION OF PROSPERITY The governments of the developed countries have a substantial list of goods and services that they want to distribute to their citizens. However, extensive public spending combined with low economic growth results in serious fiscal challenges. An increasing proportion of the population does not work due to unemployment or aging. Despite the high GDP per capita, the proportion of people in poverty is between 10 and 20 percent in the majority of these countries and inequality in the distribution of prosperity among the citizens is growing (CIA 2013). In the market economies, persistent poverty and inequality are especially problematic issues because the state is not very generous in alleviating these hardships. This situation can produce an *"underclass"* of citizens who are permanently disadvantaged in education, job skills, housing, health care, and most broadly, quality of life (Wilson 1997). The current situation is also a problem for the social democracies, given their commitment to an extensive role for government in the redistribution of prosperity to all their citizens (Castles 2004; Castles et al. 2010).

Twelve of these countries, mostly the social democracies, are still among the 20 major countries with the world's most equal income distributions (the others are postcommunist developed countries discussed in Chapter 15). As the costs of government continue to rise, there are larger budget deficits and growing resistance to higher taxes. The Debate in 13 considers whether the costly commitments of the social democratic model can be sustained. In the brutally competitive global economy, no developed country has resolved the public policy issues related to sustaining economic growth and distributing prosperity, and the debate over these issues is intense. Nevertheless, the current bottom line is that the developed countries of the Global North have a better overall record than any other set of countries in the world in delivering higher absolute levels of prosperity to most citizens.

The Debate in 13

Are the Social Democracies Dying?

Surveys often identify most of Europe's social democracies as among the happiest places on Earth, where citizens enjoy a high level of services provided by the state (Levy 2010). These services include deeply subsidized or free health care, education, and public transportation, as well as unemployment protection, care for the elderly, and many other publicly provided benefits (an example of a social democracy is Sweden, described in the Compare in 13). However, critics suggest that these social welfare states are unsustainable because this vast array of government services is too expensive for the public sector to afford. Particularly during the global recession, an animated policy debate in the countries in Scandinavia and Western Europe is: Are the social democracies dying?

The Social Democracies Are Dying

- The governments of most European social democracies (e.g., Greece, Spain) are running very large deficits as they attempt to provide extensive welfare services. Social welfare goods substantially drain government resources relative to the revenue they generate. This overspending undermines the country's credit rating, currency strength, and overall fiscal health (Laquer 2009).

- The social democratic model puts an enormous burden on economic growth by aggressively taxing wages and profits. Those funds should be left in the hands of wage earners and entrepreneurs where they will stimulate innovation, encourage investment, and create more incentives for people to work hard.

- The citizens' votes tell the story: There has been a significant decline in voter support for parties (e.g., the Social Democrats in Denmark, Germany, and Sweden; Spain's Socialist Workers Party; and Britain's Labour Party) that are associated with higher taxes and extensive public spending on social welfare. And the anti–social welfare, anti-tax parties and movements have gained substantial strength in the social democracies (Castles et al. 2010).

- Many citizens agree that generous provision of welfare services produces a significant number of people who become dependent on government support and who lose the initiative to work and take responsibility for themselves (Murray 1984).

- The government can no longer afford the excessive salaries and generous pension plans that have historically supported the large and overstaffed public employee unions that provide most of the state's social welfare services.

The Social Democracies Are Alive and Well

- Citizens of most social democracies enjoy a combination of the world's highest standard of living, greatest prosperity, greatest income equality, and strong democracy. The social democratic model is sustainable because its citizens recognize that that they are generally more satisfied with their lives than the citizens in any other system in the world (Brandal, Bratberg, and Thorsen 2013; Levy 2010).
- The current revenue and deficit problems affect the governments of all developed countries, not just the social democracies. It is the global recession and financial crisis, not social welfare programs, that are the root cause of current fiscal problems in the Global North (Rajan 2010).
- The majority of citizens in social democracies do not support severe and permanent cuts in their governments' policies that provide social welfare services. Even if social democracies reduce some programs to balance budgets during the recession, reinstatement of those program levels will be

in demand when the economy improves and revenues increase (Cronin, Ross, and Shoch 2011).

- The political and social costs of severe reductions in social welfare programs, such as health care or poverty assistance, would be dramatic. Even citizens who support long-term cuts in social welfare services will reconsider their views when they see the actual impacts of such reductions, resulting in a substantial decline in the support for extreme fiscal restraint and anti-tax movements (Castles et al. 2010).
- The political parties most closely aligned with the social democratic ideology have been extremely successful in elections during the past three decades, reflecting broad, long-term citizen support for their policies. As economic conditions improve, a resurgence of support for these parties will occur (Hill 2010).

More questions ...

1. Will the strong, sometimes violent, resistance to reductions in social welfare programs (e.g., in Greece, Spain, and others) enhance or reduce the overall support for social democracy?
2. What reductions in the social welfare programs do you think are most defensible? Which are least desirable?

Goal: Stability

13.2 **Identify the obstacles to the political stability of the Global North.**

The developed countries of the Global North have been generally successful in achieving their stability goals of democratization, political institutionalization, and order maintenance.

Liberal Democracies

All the Global North countries are constitutional democracies, and thus leaders and policies are constrained by the rule of law. Extensive political rights and civil liberties are enjoyed by the citizens, as reflected in the world's highest scores from Freedom House (2014), except for Singapore, which is only "partly free." Individuals and groups have substantial freedom to criticize and oppose the government and to engage in a wide variety of nonviolent political actions to change leaders and policies. Leaders operate with a limited mandate, leadership succession is regularized, and the selection of many public officials is based on citizen elections with genuine alternatives. Chapter 3 indicated that most Global North countries have moderately high political involvement, at least with regard to elections and interest in politics.

Chapters 6 and 7 described the variation in the political structures and institutions of these liberal democracies. Most are stable parliamentary governments, with multiparty systems based on coalitions (e.g., Denmark, Germany, Sweden). A few experience instability due to the fragmented nature of the party system (Italy). Many countries have dual executives, often with a constitutional monarch (e.g., the United Kingdom, Japan, Sweden). There are a few hybrids with an elected president in addition to the cabinet and prime minister (e.g., Austria, France [recall Focus in 7]). The United States is an exception as a presidential government with a two-party system, and Switzerland is an exception as a council system.

Political power is distributed rather than concentrated in a single governmental structure. Most are unitary states, although there are several federations (e.g., Canada, Germany, the United States). Even in the unitary states, policy implementation for many human and welfare services is decentralized to local governments. The national legislatures are important actors in the policy process, with about half being unicameral. These countries generally have the world's lowest levels of corruption, and their governments operate with large, efficient bureaucracies and relatively independent judiciaries.

Political Institutionalization

The developed countries have high levels of **political institutionalization**; that is, *substantial capabilities, value, and stability support political structures and processes.* Some developed countries have restructured their political system in the last 70 years. Many created new constitutional systems after World War II had undermined the legitimacy of their previous political regimes, as in Austria, France, Italy, Japan, and Germany. One goal of the restructuring was to distribute power more broadly within the political system and to increase the participation and influence of the citizens. Democratic political processes are now firmly established throughout the Global North.

The governments in many of the developed countries evolved over centuries by means of gradual and generally nonviolent mechanisms of political change. This pattern applies to states such as Belgium, Canada, Denmark, Sweden, Switzerland, the United Kingdom, and the United States. The distribution and uses of political power have changed as new groups gain admission to and influence in the political system, extending participation steadily until mass representative democracy is created. This "politics of inclusion" has drawn important groups into the political process and built their support for the political system, reducing their need to use mechanisms such as violence to achieve their political goals.

In the United Kingdom, for example, evolving political inclusion for more than 800 years has ensured the stability of the regime. The basic story line is that the political system has slowly drawn new groups into the political process, penetrating downward from the most powerful to the least powerful citizens. Starting in 1215, the substantial political powers of the hereditary monarch were limited and the power of the national legislature was increased. Equally significant, the British electorate expanded steadily, as new classes of the population were granted political rights by lowering barriers based on wealth, gender, and age. Political inclusion also affected the political party system, which adapted to the social and economic composition of the citizenry. For example, at the beginning of the twentieth century, a new Labour Party was formed to represent the British working class. In 1945, the Labour Party gained enough seats in the House of Commons to form a government majority and enact significant new public policies that established "the welfare state" and greatly benefited the working class and the poor. Further adaptations in the party system have accommodated the growing national identity in Northern Ireland, Wales, and especially Scotland. While there are occasional outbreaks of political instability in Britain, the politics of inclusion have been effective in incorporating new political forces into the institutionalized political regime and sustaining a highly stable political system.

Order Maintenance

The developed countries have had varying levels of success in meeting the stability goal of order maintenance. This goal can be interpreted as the *absence of disorder* in the political, social, and personal domains. Disorder includes political violence (e.g., illegal demonstrations, riots, rebellions, coups, and revolutions), social disorders (e.g., murder, rape, robbery, white-collar crime, and organized crime), and personal disorders (e.g., suicide and substance abuse). While a few Global North countries have exceptionally high levels of order maintenance, such as Switzerland and Singapore (see Focus in 13), most are neither the most orderly nor the most disorderly in the political world.

Focus in 13

Welcome to the Brave New World: Singapore

Singapore has used government policy more expansively to achieve order maintenance than any other developed country. A small island of 5.5 million people located off Malaysia, Singapore gained independence from Britain in 1963 and became a republic in 1965. Prime Minister Lee Kuan Yew exercised singular power for 31 years (until 1990) and guided the country to remarkable economic success. Lee still plays a powerful role, with his son as prime minister. Its annual economic growth rate has averaged more than 7 percent since 1965. Its GDP per capita (PPP) has risen dramatically, placing it fourth in the world in terms of its overall prosperity.

Singapore is also notable for the remarkable social control policies first instituted by Prime Minister Lee and the parliament he dominated for three

decades. For example, to deal with traffic congestion, the government maintains a strict quota on the number of cars imported. An individual who purchases a new car must pay import duties and registration taxes that triple the car's market price. To reduce the massive yearly automobile registration fee, the driver can save $10,000 per year by purchasing a special red license that allows only nighttime and weekend driving. The high toll road charges and other auto fees are used to subsidize an efficient mass transit system.

To promote financial responsibility and personal savings by its citizens, the government places 34 percent of each worker's wages in a special fund. The worker can use these forced savings only to buy government stocks, to purchase a house, or for retirement.

The state uses the media and the schools to support extensive campaigns to discourage certain behaviors, such as spitting in public, long hair on men, and littering. The stiff penalties imposed to enforce its social control policies received worldwide attention in 1994 with the caning of visiting U.S. teenager Michael Faye for painting graffiti on automobiles. For many offenses, there are heavy on-the-spot fines: in U.S. dollar equivalents, $400 for jaywalking, $800 for littering, $400 for eating on public transit, $800 for smoking in a public place, $800 for dropping chewing gum, and $400 for feeding birds in the park. To prevent speeding, all taxicabs are equipped with a bell that begins to ring loudly as soon as the taxi exceeds the legal speed limit, and there is a yellow light on top of trucks that flashes when the driver goes too fast. Technological surveillance includes computerized camera systems that record the license plates of cars that violate traffic laws and odor-activated video cameras in elevators that record anyone who urinates in the elevator (the person is also locked in). There is even a law against failing to flush after using a public urinal.

Singapore also instituted a set of unsubtle eugenics/population control policies. Women with less than a high school education are given a government-subsidized home mortgage, but they lose the subsidy if they have a third child. To increase the low childbearing rate among college graduates, the government's Social Development Unit offers a computer-matching service for educated singles. One program, eventually discontinued, offered these smart singles a government-funded vacation at a romantic seaside holiday camp.

Because of such extensive policies of social control, Singapore has been subjected to jokes and serious criticism about its limitations on civil liberties. But no one denies that the country is exceptionally orderly, clean, and efficient.

Further Focus

1. Would you accept Singapore's substantial restrictions on personal freedom in exchange for an exceptionally high level of order, cleanliness, and efficiency in your society?

2. Does Singapore demonstrate that a country with minimal democracy (recall Chapter 7) can sustain high prosperity (a GDP per capita [PPP] greater than every major developed country except Norway)?

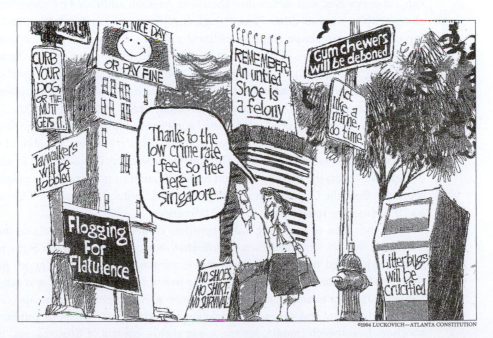

SOURCE: By permission of Mike Luckovich and Creators Syndicate, Inc.

The politics of these states is characterized by pluralism (see Chapter 9), with multiple competing elites and groups. The vigorous group politics and the broad opportunities for political action allow for some political turbulence, which does occur, especially during periods of citizen dissatisfaction with economic or social conditions. Although there are occasional outbursts of significant political violence, these states enjoy relatively high levels of political order.

The level and nature of social and personal disorder varies considerably among the states and among different populations within states, and thus it is difficult to generalize. The Netherlands, Norway, and Japan, for example, have relatively low levels of social disorder such as violent crime. Yet Japan has one of the highest suicide rates in the world, alcohol abuse is high in Norway, and drug abuse is high in the Netherlands. France, Italy, and the United States, in contrast, are relatively high on most measures of social and personal disorder and are among the increasing number of developed countries with substantial problems related to substance abuse and drug-related crime, especially among the lower classes. What explanations do you think best account for the fact that some of the developed countries seem to have such high levels of social and personal disorder?

Challenges to Stability

VALUE CONFLICTS AND DISPUTES Because the Global North countries allow open group politics, the active disagreements about specific policies and even about fundamental values can produce instability. The political ideologies of classical liberalism, conservatism, and democratic socialism are each embraced by some citizens and, along with numerous other "isms" (e.g., feminism, environmentalism, and religious fundamentalism), shape complex political cultures. There is strong support for the fundamental principles of democracy. However, during the last several decades, most developed countries have experienced a substantial decline in citizens' trust and confidence in political leaders and in key political institutions, including legislatures, political parties, and bureaucracies (Dalton 2013; Pharr and Putnam 2000).

There are ongoing political debates, sometimes intense, regarding the degree to which the state should have an active role in the *political economy* and should distribute generous welfare benefits to various groups in the society. This is related to other policy disagreements on the level of taxation and the extent of government regulation of the economy. Both the Compare in 13 on Sweden and Switzerland and the Debate in 13 on social democracy reflect some of these differences.

Another area of enduring value conflicts centers on disputes about the circumstances in which *state regulation of individual behavior* is legitimate. Such regulation might be justified to preserve social peace, promote the collective good, protect the rights and freedom of others, or protect the individual from himself and others. In the United States, for example, state constraints on private behavior generate controversy, political disorder, and occasional violence regarding such areas of public policy as abortion, free speech (media, Internet), gay rights, control of firearms, and marijuana legalization.

MULTICULTURALISM AND IMMIGRATION Most developed countries are struggling with issues arising from their cultural diversity. The desire for regional autonomy has been a source of occasional instability in some countries with a long history of multiple nationalities (e.g., the Quebecois in Canada, the Basques and Catalans in Spain, the Walloons and Flemish in Belgium). And some of the instability is due to clashes between the majority ethnic group and native-born minorities, especially people of Afro-Caribbean or Arabic descent. For example, the concern about "home-grown terrorists" in England has soured relations between the Anglo majority and Britain's Muslims (Leiken 2009). However, the main source of recent instability is due to intensifying conflicts related to *immigration*. Legal immigration within the EU, for example, has resulted in large enclaves of "foreigners" from Southern and Eastern Europe whose languages and customs grate on some in the ethnic majority in Western and Northern European countries. And *illegal* immigration is an even more disruptive issue in some Global North countries such as the United States, where the treatment of nearly 12 million individuals who have entered the country without permission is a major public policy puzzle.

Every country faces policy debates about cultural diversity: The French banned full-face-hiding veils in public and the wearing of head scarves and other "religious symbols" in schools; the Danes reversed their open-door policy and place stringent restrictions on immigration; Italy called for revision of the EU's open internal borders policy. These kinds of responses have generated counterdemands for policies supporting multiculturalism and protecting minority rights (e.g., bilingualism in Canada, a citizenship process for illegal immigrants in the United States). At this point, the conflicts associated with diverse cultures and nonnative populations are an issue in almost every developed country.

POLITICAL POLARIZATION The political elites and governments are committed to working within the framework of representative democracy and group politics as they attempt to resolve value conflicts. They are generally successful in establishing compromises on issues that might become highly politicized. However, pluralism is not well suited to situations in which there is substantial *political polarization* as *politics becomes a battleground between large, mobilized groups with conflicting and deeply held values* and centrist policies and center parties are only weakly supported by the citizens. In such situations of "hyperpluralism," it is extremely difficult for policymakers to make decisions and resolve conflicts because it is often impossible to satisfy the opposing viewpoints. If key groups become dissatisfied with government paralysis and unresponsiveness, they can make increasingly strident political demands, engage in aggressive political actions in support of their policy preferences, and produce high levels of political instability. Some states, such as the Netherlands, Norway, and Switzerland, have limited these problems by nurturing a cultural style of social tolerance or by developing political institutions that accommodate competing groups (Lijphart 2007). However, the governments of most Global North countries currently are challenged by increasing polarization and intolerance among political groups.

DOMINATION AND CONTROL? Some analysts offer a far more critical description of how many of the developed countries maintain order. They describe societies in which the state controls its citizens by coercion rather than consensus, combining limited welfare distribution, extensive political socialization, and effective restraints on public life by the state's agents (e.g., the police, the bureaucracy, the judicial system). Some class and elite theorists also argue that most developed countries are controlled by a "hegemonic elite"—a network of extraordinarily powerful, overlapping groups that sustain their domination over a long period of time (Domhoff 2005, 2013; Esping-Andersen 1990; Poulantzas 1973). These theorists insist that politics in the Global North countries is not a fair competition among groups, that the state is not a neutral referee, and that most public policies enable certain groups to maintain their advantaged position in society. Thus, privileged groups reap huge benefits from public policy, and most citizens derive minimal gains in the quality of their lives (Chapter 9).

It is clear that the developed countries do have powerful and effective institutions that can shape the political process, control groups, and contain instability. Even the pluralist explanation acknowledges that there are huge inequalities in the political resources available to different groups (Dahl 1961; Lundberg 2013). There is no doubt that certain institutions and individuals have extraordinary powers to shape political life in Global North countries (Johnson 2009). Yet most analysts and most citizens see no compelling evidence that these political systems are dominated by self-serving, nondemocratic elites. In response, radical (Marxist) theorists interpret such citizen views as evidence that the state *can* fool most of the people all of the time. One of the great (and perhaps impossible) challenges for political scientists is to develop an indisputable empirical analysis of how political power is exercised, how values are allocated, and how order is maintained in the developed countries.

Goal: Security

13.3   Trace the development of security challenges to the Global North.

The first half of the twentieth century was a period with substantial insecurity, marked by two massive multistate wars among Global North countries. The borders of most of the states survived intact (there are notable exceptions, including Austria-Hungary after World War I and Germany after World War II), but many states were devastated in human, material, and political terms by these wars. Since the end of World War II in 1945, the developed countries have generally enjoyed success in the pursuit of their basic security goals, especially survival and freedom. Arguably, the greatest security victory during the recent period is the collapse in 1990 of the communist state in the Soviet Union, which had been a significant threat to the countries of the Global North. Global North countries are still establishing new arrangements for security in the post–Cold War global system.

The Era of Colonialism

Some Global North countries have been extremely successful at extending their influence or control over other states to enhance their own security goals. Belgium, France, Germany, Japan, Portugal, Spain, and the United States dominated substantial colonial territories until the mid-twentieth century. In 1945, Great Britain was the leading colonial power, controlling more than one-fourth of the world's population in its worldwide empire. Colonialism was a means by which many of these countries furthered their security goals. Although their colonial holdings are now independent states, some developed countries continue to exert their power through neocolonialism, as described in Chapter 11.

The Cold War Period

From World War II until the late 1980s, the security-oriented actions of most developed countries were powerfully influenced by *the international struggle between the United States and the Soviet Union*, generally called *the Cold War*. During the Cold War period, both U.S. and Soviet policies were based on the assumption that the main threat to the security of the world was the other superpower. Each country maintained an extensive military, including a large nuclear arsenal, and a collective security group in an attempt to protect its own territory and allies. Each also applied considerable military, economic, and political power in competitive and costly efforts to influence or control the actions of many developing countries and deter its rival from gaining advantage in those countries.

Not all political elites in the Global North countries shared the perception of a bipolar struggle between the forces of good and evil. Some states (e.g., Austria, Finland, Switzerland) maintained a position of neutrality during the Cold War. Others (e.g., Denmark, France, Greece, Italy, New Zealand, Sweden) emphasized a more conciliatory policy of *détente* (relaxation of tensions) between the United States and Soviet Bloc, based on the view that both blocs had common interests in maintaining their superior position internationally and preventing a global nuclear war. This latter view became more widespread by the late 1980s due to the conflict-reducing initiatives of Soviet leader Mikhail Gorbachev.

The Post–Cold War Period

By 1990, with a speed that stunned the world, the Soviet Bloc countries and even the Soviet Union were transformed (see Chapter 15). These countries moved away from communism and toward democratic politics and market economies. They sought economic cooperation rather than military conflict with the United States and Western Europe. The Cold War seemed to end with the unification of East and West Germany (1990) and even more with the breakup of the Soviet Union (1991) into 15 countries.

Currently, 8 of the world's 13 highest spenders on military are Global North countries, whose combined military spending is more than $970 billion per year. The United States alone accounts for 37 percent of this total (SIPRI 2014). The global military power of the United States is unmatched, and it projects this power extensively in some cases, as in Iraq and Afghanistan. However, the developed countries now generally emphasize collective security arrangements through the United Nations and NATO (Walt 2006). Most are not conflict oriented. For example, 16 of the Global North countries are among the 18 countries with the highest scores on the Global Peace Index (IEP 2013). While there is a general assumption that a major military conflict among any Global North countries is inconceivable, the evolving international system does pose at least four major security challenges, which are described next.

Challenges to Security

DISORDER IN THE REST OF THE WORLD Most major political violence occurs in the Global South, as it did during the Cold War period. In Afghanistan, Colombia, Congo, Iraq, Syria, Somalia, and Tibet, among others, complex patterns of disorder persist, despite various strategies of intervention by the developed countries and international organizations. In each situation, governments of the Global North must weigh the security benefits from stabilizing a distant part of the international system against the substantial costs of intervening and the difficulty (impossibility?) of maintaining stability in many of those countries (Brzezinski 2004). And Russia has recommitted itself to a strong military presence and a sphere of influence along its very long borders, which can result in disorder and conflict affecting the Global North, as in the recent turmoil related to Ukraine.

GLOBALIZATION OF TERRORISM The individuals perceived to represent Global North institutions in the rest of the world are attractive targets for terrorist violence. As recent beheadings by Islamic State reveal, protecting them is difficult. And while the great majority of terrorist acts are committed in developing countries, globalization has facilitated the extensive movement of people and information that has placed cells of terrorists in every country in the Global North. The Global North countries have never been more vulnerable to terrorist attacks by "home-grown terrorists" and individuals from the Global South. Such groups committed the deadly attacks on the U.S. World Trade Center and the Pentagon in September 2001 and on the mass transit systems in Madrid (2004) and London (2005).

PROLIFERATION OF WEAPONS The heavy armaments of Russia and the United States have been significantly reduced by agreements during the post–Cold War period (e.g., START II). However, this period is also characterized by the expansion of military power in many states, the ease with which chemical and biological weapons can be acquired, and the spread of nuclear capabilities. Equally serious is the widespread distribution of light weapons (e.g., guns, shoulder-fired missiles, land mines) to irregular forces in countries everywhere, because such weapons cause most of the casualties from political violence (Klare 1997). The developed countries, which lead the world in the production and sales of military hardware, have failed to implement effective strategies to prevent the further proliferation of weapons. Indeed, more than half of the weapons sold in the global market are supplied by Global North countries, led by the United States, Germany, and France (SIPRI 2014).

COMPETITION FOR MARKETS AND RESOURCES Earlier discussion emphasized that the global economic competition for markets and resources has become a source of increasing conflict (Chapter 11). The countries of the Global North compete not only with one another but also with an increasing number of other countries. China has led the way among many Global South countries and transitional economies whose lower labor costs and increasing ability to purchase worldwide resources have been a net negative for economic health of the most developed countries. Global North countries can no longer dictate to their advantage where the desirable jobs are, who gets scarce resources (e.g., energy, food), and who garners the maximum benefits and profits in the global marketplace. Fierce economic competition among states, regions, and multinational corporations could be the greatest source of insecurity for the developed countries in the era of globalization (Zakaria 2009).

The Developed Countries of the Global North Overall

In terms of pursuing the broad goals of prosperity, stability, and security, the developed countries of the Global North generally have the highest levels of success in the world. These states have the most advanced systems of economic production, with evolved political economies based on a mix of capitalism and democratic socialism. The majority of productive resources remain under private control, and most states have established a substantial program of welfare distribution to the citizenry. Most of their citizens enjoy a higher standard of living than is available to the majority of people in any other part of the world.

By exercising their considerable economic, military, and political power in the global system, the developed countries have also met their security goals. They have a strong record of survival, influence, and some domination of countries outside the Global North. In their pursuit of security goals, they achieved "victory" in the Cold War against the Soviet Union. The leading developed countries still exercise their power energetically to maintain their advantages in the international system.

The developed countries, perhaps because of their prosperity and security, have been able to maintain relatively open, fair, and stable politics. There are tensions between the commitment to individual freedom and limited government, on the one hand, and state intervention to increase equality of outcomes, on the other. Although pluralism is occasionally strained, a wide range of political beliefs and actions is tolerated. Many individuals and groups are able to mobilize their political resources to influence the processes of government and decision making, and citizens have the right to select among leadership elites at regular intervals. In comparison with other countries during the past 60 years, the developed countries of the Global North receive high marks for maintaining constitutional, participatory politics.

The success of the Global North countries in achieving prosperity, stability, and security is not unqualified. Some of their citizens live in relative poverty and despair, and increasing inequalities in wealth and income might be the Achilles' heel of their prosperity. The recent economic turbulence has resulted in reduced economic vitality, cuts in the distribution of welfare, and lowered confidence that there is greater prosperity in the future. Also, critics, especially in developing countries, argue that the developed countries have maintained their prosperity by exploitation—of the poor within their own societies and of the populations and resources of other states by means of neocolonialism and military intervention. The countries of the Global North have not reached the top by being passive or generous, but globalization and the emergence of new economic powers might undermine some of their advantages in access to resources and markets. Chapters 14 and 15 identify some of the emerging issues that the Global North will face from the Global South and the transitional developed countries.

Security issues have become more complex as the Soviet threat, which encouraged cooperation among the developed countries, has been replaced by more diverse and complex threats. These include increasingly violent regional instabilities in the Global South; the insecurities associated with the current forms of terrorism; the intensifying competition for diminishing resources; and the complex destabilizing impacts of globalization on relations with allies, competitors, and adversaries. All of these pressures present important challenges to Global North countries in their effort to remain dominant in the global system.

Key Concepts

Cold War, p. 373
Global North, p. 357
Global South, p. 357
mixed political economy, p. 358

Human Development Index (HDI), p. 362
political institutionalization, p. 367
political polarization, p. 371

postindustrial societies, p. 357
privatization, p. 360
social democracies, p. 359
social market system, p. 359
underclass, p. 365

For Further Consideration

1. How would you further classify the countries of the Global North into two or more subsets? What criteria would you use?

2. In the current period, what is the greatest threat to the stability of the Global North? What is the most appropriate strategy to reduce that threat?

3. How should the desirable level of distribution of prosperity among citizens in a society be determined? Should the state do anything to ensure that prosperity is distributed more equally among its citizens? What actions

by the state are appropriate and might be effective?

4. Write a script or role-play (with others) a situation in which a classical liberal, a conservative, and a democratic socialist discuss the virtues and failings of a particular developed country.

5. If you were to create a quality of life index, what measures would you include? Rank the importance you would attach to the various measures and explain why you have given those rankings.

For Further Reading

Burgess, Anthony. (1970). *A Clockwork Orange.* **Harmondsworth, UK: Penguin.** A dystopian novel describing a near-future Britain in which youth gangs rule the mean streets of a divided and amoral society. Stanley Kubrick's chilling film of the same title was based on this book.

Castles, Francis G., Stephan Leibfried, Jane Lewis, Herbert Obinger, and Christopher Pierson, eds. (2010). *The Oxford Handbook of the Welfare State.* **New York: Oxford University Press.** A comprehensive set of more than 50 essays exploring many topics regarding the philosophy, implementation, challenges, and future of the modern welfare state.

Cini, Michelle, and Nieves Pereze-Slorzano Borragan, eds. (2013). *European Union Politics.* **4th ed. Oxford: Oxford University Press.** A comprehensive overview of the theories, policies, institutions, and issues that make up the politics of the EU in a data-rich and current volume.

Hill, Stephen. (2010). *Europe's Promise: Why the European Way Is the Best Hope for an Insecure Age.* **Berkeley: University of California Press.** A detailed argument that the social democracies of Western Europe provide the most desirable future course, based on such virtues as their approaches to health care, environmental sustainability, pluralist democracy, trade network, and social market economies

Hubbard, Glenn, and Tim Kane. (2013). *Balance: The Economics of Great Powers from Ancient Rome to Modern America.* **New York: Simon and Schuster.** Written by two economists, this book demonstrates how economic imbalances within a state can lead to civil collapse.

Kennedy, Paul. (1989). *The Rise and Fall of the Great Powers.* **New York: Random House.** A sweeping analysis of how countries such as the United Kingdom and the United States become the strongest in the world and then decline.

Laquer, Walter. (2009). *The Last Days of Europe: Epitaph for an Old Continent.* **New York: St. Martin's Griffin.** A strong critique of the current directions of European social democracies, especially due to the problems with sustaining the welfare state, difficulties within the EU framework, and the challenges of immigration.

Marmor, Theodore, Richard Freeman, and Kieke Okma, eds. (2009). *Comparative Studies and the Politics of Modern Medical Care.* **New Haven, CT: Yale University Press.** A series of thoughtful essays by experts on the key policy issues facing health care reform in the developed countries, including Canada, Germany, the United Kingdom, and the United States.

Nye, Joseph S. (2011). *The Future of Power.* **New York: PublicAffairs.** Nye extends his ideas about military, economic, and soft power through a rich analysis of how the United States can combine these with "smart power" to limit its decline as the dominant power in the world.

Pharr, Susan J., and Robert D. Putnam, eds. (2000). *Disaffected Democracies: What's Troubling the Trilateral Countries?* **Princeton, NJ: Princeton University Press.** A strong and diverse set of essays exploring the extent to which citizens in the advanced democracies have lost confidence and trust in their political leaders and political institutions, and even in democratic processes.

Powell, G. Bingham, Kaare Strom, and Russell J. Dalton, eds. (2012). *Comparative Politics Today: A World View.* **10th ed. New York: Longman.** Solid case-by-case studies of selected developed countries (England, France, Germany, Japan, and the United States) as well as Brazil, China, Egypt, India, Mexico, Nigeria, and Russia, employing structural-functional concepts (recall Chapter 5).

Rawnsley, Andrew. (2010). *The End of the Party: The Rise and Fall of New Labour.* **London:**

Penguin. A spellbinding account of the political machinations among the leaders of the British Labour Party (especially Tony Blair and Gordon Brown) from 2001 to 2010 by an acclaimed journalist. For a hilarious, rude satire of British politicians in the same era, see the film *In the Loop* (2009).

Tsoukalis, Loukas, and Janis Emmanouilidis, eds. (2011). *The Delphic Oracle on Europe: Is There a Future for the European Union?* **New York: Oxford University Press.** The current debates over the challenges facing the EU during a period of internal disagreements, evolving institutions, and global complexity are explored by scholars and policymakers.

Wilensky, Harold. (2002). *Rich Democracies.* **Berkeley: University of California Press.** Using case studies, interviews, and quantitative data, a distinguished political scientist offers a comprehensive (at 900+ pages) and compelling perspective on how the 19 "rich democracies" have evolved over the last half-century, with particular attention to social policy and a focus on the interplay among the form of political economy, political institutions, and key political actors.

Zakaria, Fareed. (2009). *The Post-American World.* **New York: Basic Books.** This provides a readable exploration of the likely reduction in dominance, but also the continuing strengths, of the United States in the emerging global system characterized by "the rise of rest" and especially countries like China, India, and Russia.

On the Web

http://europa.eu/index_en.htm
The official Web site of the European Union provides detailed information about each EU member state.

http://www.oecd.org
The Organization for Economic Cooperation and Development is a cooperative association of 30 member countries, primarily the developed countries plus a few of the most economically advanced countries in Eastern Europe and Asia. The OECD site provides information about its activities as well as data on member states.

http://www.coldwar.org
The home page of the Cold War Museum contains a number of fascinating online exhibits and an online discussion forum regarding this important period.

http://www.osce.org
The electronic home of the Organization for Security and Cooperation in Europe, the world's largest regional security organization, which is centered in Europe but now includes 56 member states, provides extensive information regarding issues related to the goal of security.

http://www.usa.gov
The official Web portal for the U.S. government, the site offers many links to the agencies and information associated with the various governmental institutions in the United States.

http://www.canada.gc.ca
The official Web site of the Canadian government, with links to the agencies of the central and provincial governments.

http://gov.uk
The Web site for the government of the United Kingdom, with multiple links to government agencies, services, and information.

Chapter 14
The Developing Countries of the Global South

Learning Objectives

14.1 Group the Global South into distinct geographical and political regions.

14.2 Identify the main obstacles to development faced by those in the Global South.

14.3 Outline the strategies the Global South has used to achieve economic development.

14.4 Assess the level of interstate violence and economic security within the Global South.

14.5 Identify factors that lead to political stability in the Global South.

14.6 Evaluate the reported "rise of the South."

In ancient times, the Gold Coast of West Africa was home to several flourishing kingdoms and many linguistic groups. The area had sufficient food, rich resources, and land for all. From about the sixteenth century, the peoples of the Gold Coast developed trade with several European powers, exporting commodities, especially gold and cocoa, and serving as a key location in the extensive slave trade in West Africa. The British conquered the area in the 1870s and ruled it as a colony for 90 years. Then, in 1957, the Gold Coast became the first colonial territory in sub-Saharan Africa to gain its independence, as a country called Ghana.

At independence, there was widespread optimism that Ghana would be the model of political and economic development for many countries emerging from colonialism. Its leader, Dr. Kwame Nkrumah (in photo on page 380), became an effective spokesperson for African freedom and development in the postcolonial era. Ghana's first fair

Giants of the postcolonial era: President Kwame Nkrumah of Ghana greets President Sukarno of Indonesia (right) and Prime Minister Jawaharlal Nehru (center) of India at the United Nations in 1960. All three were leaders in their countries' independence movements and then the first elected political leader, for 14, 22, and 17 years, respectively.

and contested election was an active multiparty competition won by Nkrumah and his Convention Peoples Party (CPP). GDP per capita was about $1,200 in a predominantly agricultural economy that was also successful in exporting major raw materials, and most Ghanaians had a decent material life.

However, significant problems emerged soon after the election, including economic shortfalls associated with a decline in world cocoa prices and widespread corruption and inefficiency within the CPP and the government administration. Opposition groups vehemently criticized both the failures of the CPP, calling it "a party of incompetents," and the extensive powers exercised by Nkrumah, whom they labeled a dictator. Angered by these criticisms, Nkrumah and the CPP passed laws restricting opposition activities. When these restrictions caused opponents to protest verbally and then violently, the government responded with even more repressive measures.

The government became increasingly autocratic. An election in 1960 and a referendum of support for the government in 1964 were rigged by the CPP. By the 1965 election, legal opposition was nearly eliminated and all CPP candidates were declared elected. With the economy and the social order collapsing, an army-led coup in 1966 overthrew Nkrumah and installed a "temporary" military junta. From 1966 to 1981, Ghana alternated between civilian governments and military regimes that seized control by further coups in 1972, 1978, 1979, and 1981, with each successive coup of civilian governance justified on the grounds of incompetence and corruption. A young air force officer, Jerry Rawlings, led the last two coups. By 1981, Rawlings concluded that he was Ghana's best hope and that he should lead the government. Despite several assassination and coup attempts, Rawlings ruled continuously from 1981 until 2000.

Nkrumah had attempted to install a command economy with strong state ownership and control, but there had been minimal economic growth, a declining standard of living for most people, and increasing reliance on neocolonial assistance. Rawlings used his consolidated political power to shift Ghana to a market economy. He collaborated with the International Monetary Fund (IMF) to secure loans, privatized most public enterprises, and radically cut public services. After GDP per capita growth of only about 2 percent per year during the 1990s, Ghana's growth rate has improved to 7.9 percent in 2012, and inflation has been held under 10 percent in recent years (World Bank 2013).

Under international pressure, Rawlings allowed an open and fair election for the presidency and parliament in 2000, the first peaceful, democratic transition of power in Ghana's history. Since then, candidates from opposing political parties have alternated in power in a series of close, contested elections. Even in 2012, when the sitting president died only a few months before his expected reelection, there was a vigorous but peaceful campaign and broad acceptance of John Mahama's narrow victory. Freedom House classifies Ghana as a "free" electoral democracy. However, with GDP per capita (PPP) of only $1,684, life expectancy at 64 years, and almost 30 percent of the population living beneath the national poverty line, the overall level of development for such a promising, resource-rich country remains disappointing (World Bank 2013; CIA 2014; UNDP 2013).

The history of Ghana reveals some of the patterns of political, economic, and social development relevant for many of the countries in the Global South. After exploitation during colonial domination, an independent state formed with high hopes of economic and political progress. However, the country has struggled with long periods of low or negative economic growth, political authoritarianism, social disorder, and violence, and it still has a low overall standard of living and economic dependence on developed countries and multinational corporations. Given the improvements in the political system, will the optimism about Ghana's development trajectory finally be realized?

This chapter will explore more fully how the countries of the developing world have attempted to make progress in the pursuit of prosperity, security, and stability, given such challenges. These challenges can be huge. As the United Nations (UNDP 2007: 68) observed:

> Many people are poor because they live in countries that are poor. Because they are poor, these countries do not have the resources—finance, technology, and skills—they need to extricate themselves from their predicament. This vicious circle has become more pronounced with globalization. Because they lack the human, financial, physical, and institutional resources required to take advantage of globalization, these countries are unable to reap its benefits and are becoming marginalized in the world economy. Like certain individuals or regions within a country, the countries themselves are, in a sense, caught in a "poverty trap." They therefore require special help to change the conditions in which they find themselves.

Grouping Countries in the Developing World

14.1 **Group the Global South into distinct geographical and political regions.**

Understanding the developing countries of the Global South is challenging because of their diversity. Developing countries contain dusty villages where poor and uneducated people scrape out a subsistence diet from their small farms and large cities where some people are exceptionally rich. Some live and work in modern, technologically advanced settings; yet many others live in poverty and squalor. Some developing countries are huge states with a billion people, while others are small islands with a population of fewer than 50,000. Some developing countries are successfully adopting European political forms of representative democracy, popular participation, and freedom of opposition. Others are run by small governing cliques that ruthlessly eliminate all opposition, and changes in leadership occur through brute force.

Developmental Classification

All of these characteristics fit some of the 140+ developing countries that can be considered part of the Global South, with their combined population of more than 5.2 billion people. While there are a variety of ways in which particular countries can be classified as "developing," this book uses the classificatory scheme described in Chapter 10 and illustrated in Figure 10.1. Rather than just using a gross national income (GNI) per capita figure as the World Bank does (where any country below $12,616 per capita is a developing country), Figure 10.1 adjusts the income figure for purchasing power parity and then utilizes a second multifaceted dimension measuring the country's overall level of social development, based on key indicators of literacy, urbanization, health, and communications.

Developing countries, *Global South*, Third World, low-income countries, least developed countries, and similar labels are a useful shorthand for a set of traits attributed to states that, relative to the developed countries (and even to most of the transitional countries discussed in Chapter 15), *are generally less advanced economically, have lower levels of competitive and representative politics, have a lower proportion in the middle class, and have a lower overall standard of living*. Most also have high birthrates (sometimes higher than their economic growth rates) and youthful populations (in more than 40 developing countries, at least 45 percent of the population is below age 15). For some of these countries, it is not clear when, if ever, they will reach the levels of political, economic, and social development currently enjoyed by the developed countries of the Global North. However, some developing countries will certainly achieve these levels.

This chapter helps you identify dominant patterns and general trends among the developing countries, although generalizations oversimplify political reality and are subject to qualifications. The countries of the Global South encompass many different histories, traditions, religions, and political ideologies, and they do not share a single political culture. They also have different approaches to politics and strategies of development.

As you read this chapter, and especially as you formulate your own understanding about the developing countries, be sensitive to the variation *across* these states and, in many cases, *within* each state. Just as the most developed countries have some people living in abject poverty and primitive conditions, even the poorest developing countries have advanced technology, and some citizens enjoy enormous wealth and an exceptionally high standard of living. The discussion will be broad, and it will offer examples from many countries that can be considered part of the Global South.

Regional Classification

Although this chapter generalizes across all developing countries in the Global South, it sometimes uses region as a second element of classification. Before this chapter presents generalizations regarding the pursuit of prosperity, security, and stability, it is illuminating to note some broad regional differences.

EAST ASIA AND THE PACIFIC One regional group includes East Asian developing countries as well as the few Pacific island states with a population of at least 300,000. Most of these countries have been traditional, village-based agrarian societies until recently, and most cope with the challenges of multiple ethnicities. China dominates this group in human and historical-cultural terms, given its huge size (1.3 billion people), the dispersion of ethnic Chinese to many of the other countries, the diffusion of Confucian culture, and China's attempts to dominate many of its neighbors. As discussed in Chapter 15, China is now the second largest economy in the world. Most of these countries had a late experience with colonialism, which never penetrated too deeply into the societies. China and some of the other East Asian countries (e.g., Cambodia, North Korea, Vietnam) have a recent history of communist political regimes that have been brutal and repressive. This region is also the site of some of the developing world's most successful emerging economies, including several "Asian Tigers" that have advanced to developed-country status in recent decades (e.g., Singapore, South Korea, Taiwan) and newly industrialized countries such as the "Little Dragons" (e.g., Malaysia and Thailand).

SOUTH ASIA AND CENTRAL ASIA The Central Asian group is primarily composed of the "Stans"—countries with nomadic, kin- and clan-based social organization, localized power bases and weak central authority, and cultures that have been dominated by Islam for hundreds of years. The primary colonial experience for most of the "Stans" (with the exception of Pakistan) occurred late, when they were annexed by the Soviet Union in the early twentieth century and were socialized in its totalitarian social order, if not its command economy model. The South Asian group, composed mainly of the multistate, multiethnic Indian subcontinent (recall Focus in 5), did have considerable colonial penetration from the late seventeenth century as part of the British Empire. India, Bhutan, and Sri Lanka differ from most other developing countries in the region because of their Hindu culture. While similar to the Islamic societies in reinforcing a rigid, traditional, male-dominated social order, these Hindu cultures are also highly stratified on the basis of caste. Huge India (over 1.2 billion people) is arguably the only institutionalized democracy in the region. While India's villages remain traditional, some of its urban areas have evolved into sites of substantial economic growth and development, driven by its large sector of well-educated, technology-savvy, English-speaking men and women.

MIDDLE EAST AND NORTH AFRICA This region, sometimes referred to as MENA, includes the dozen states and ministates of Southwest Asia (e.g., Iraq, Iran, Saudi Arabia) as well as the five North African states that are on the Mediterranean Sea and are dominated by the Sahara Desert (Algeria, Egypt, Libya, Morocco, Tunisia). Most of the peoples of North Africa and the Middle East are Islamic in religion and culture and mainly Arabic in ethnicity and language (Persian Iran is an exception). The area has major geopolitical importance because of its petroleum resources as well as its strategic location for petroleum supply lines and proximity to oceanic shipping lanes. Much of the region was controlled by the Ottoman Empire between 1453 and 1918. In the nineteenth and twentieth centuries, Europe exercised colonial power mainly through indirect economic and military involvement, but European values and structures did not penetrate deeply into most of these states. Many remain socially conservative and somewhat tribal-feudal, and it is a region currently experiencing considerable political turmoil. Economically, most of these countries are in the middle-income group, although several of the small oil-rich states are very wealthy (e.g., Bahrain, Qatar, United Arab Emirates).

SUB-SAHARAN AFRICA Despite its substantial natural resources, sub-Saharan Africa (the African continent excluding the states of North Africa listed above) is the poorest and least economically developed region in the world. About two-thirds of the world's poorest countries (as measured by GDP per capita) are in this region. After the abolition of the slave trade, the experiences with colonialism in most of these states were late, occurring between the 1880s and the 1950s, and were extremely intensive and exploitative. Many of these countries are still characterized by aspects of neocolonialism, with limited control over their own resources and a dependency on foreign financial and technological assistance. A strong sense of national unity is rare because colonial powers created states that arbitrarily merged many nationality groups that had no historical commonality. More than two-thirds of the population in these countries is rural, although increasing numbers of people are migrating to cities. In many countries, political and social stability are problematic and political structures still lack institutionalization.

LATIN AMERICA There are two subsets of countries in Latin America. One subset includes countries that tend to be relatively advanced in both economic and social development, with a substantial technological sector. This relatively developed group (most will be discussed as transitional developed countries in Chapter 15) includes Argentina, Brazil, Chile, Costa Rica, Mexico, and Uruguay. After long periods of colonial control, most of these states were granted independence before the mid-nineteenth century. In most, there is a strong national identity corresponding to the country's geographic boundaries, and the state has considerable political institutionalization. Most of these states are highly urbanized with more than 80 percent of the population throughout Latin America now living in cities.

A second subset of Latin American countries is composed primarily of the small states of Central America and the Caribbean. These small states (e.g., Honduras, Nicaragua) and hundreds of Caribbean islands (e.g., Jamaica, Haiti) are extremely diverse in culture and geography. Compared with the rest of the region, these states tend to have longer colonial legacies and to be less developed and less urban. Their political systems have less stability, and democratic practices are not deeply institutionalized. The Caribbean states have an ethnic-cultural heritage that is African and Asian (and, secondarily, English and French) more than Indian and Hispanic (the heritages that predominate in the rest of Latin America).

Achieving Development in the Global South: Some Obstacles

14.2 Identify the main obstacles to development faced by those in the Global South.

All developing countries strive for the benefits of prosperity, security, and stability. Each country has its own unique bundle of reasons why it has not yet achieved a high level of economic, political, and social development. These include its history, geopolitical situation, leadership, culture, and many other factors. When analysts attempt to generalize about some of the most common obstacles to development in the

Global South, there are several that seem to be identified most frequently. It is helpful to briefly consider some of these obstacles.

OVERPOPULATION On average, each woman in the Global South has more than three children, ranging from an average of about five children in Africa to about two children in Latin America (Population Reference Bureau 2012). In comparison, the average range is one to two children in the Global North. The population of the developing countries more than doubled from 1950 to 2005 and is estimated to grow from 5 billion to about 9 billion by the mid-twenty-first century. Today, 97 out of every 100 births are in countries that cannot meet the needs of their existing population. More people results in even greater demands on existing resources, such as land, fuel, and water, and the poorest countries do not fare well in global competition for these finite resources. The additional people will require 2 billion new jobs, hundreds of millions of new schools and houses, and a significant expansion in health care just to maintain the current low standard of living (UNDP 2012). A high birth rate also means a high proportion of young people who, especially if they are frustrated with their conditions, increase the potential volatility of social order. Development can only occur when resources expand faster than the people to whom they are distributed.

CORRUPTION AND INEFFICIENCY Many countries in the Global South are characterized by high levels of corruption, inefficiency, or both (Bates 2008; Isbister 2006). Inefficiency has many sources, including poor management, the ineffective use of modern technologies, and the absence of Weberian bureaucracies (as defined

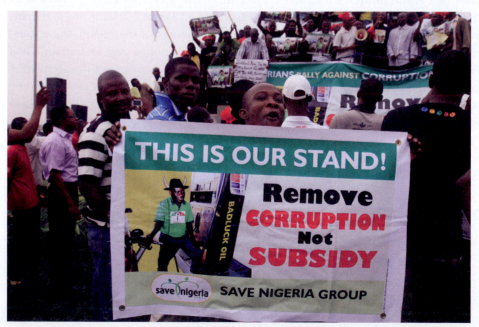

Pervasive corruption undermines the processes of development. Nigerians protest the removal of oil subsidies in their oil-rich country and criticize President Goodluck's "Badluck Oil" policies.

in Chapter 6), in which organizational actors behave in predictable, rule-following ways. And corruption is an even more serious obstacle—in the Middle East and South Asia the terms *baksheesh* ("something given") or *chai* ("tea") and in Mexico the term *mordida* ("the bite") describe the private payoffs that organizational personnel (from high-ranking leaders to low-level functionaries) expect to receive before they will assist citizens. Widespread corruption demoralizes the population and drains productive energy from the political economy. Corruption exists in every society, yet it seems especially pervasive in public and private organizations in the Global South. According to Transparency International (2013), a nongovernmental organization that measures levels of corruption in 177 countries, 57 of the 60 most corrupt countries are in the Global South. Among the world's 25 *least* corrupt countries, not one is a Global South country, although the list does include two middle-income transitional developed countries (Chile and Uruguay).

GEOPOLITICAL VULNERABILITY A developing country's resource base and its strategic location can substantially influence its development trajectory (recall Compare in 11 on geopolitics). Each country's geopolitical situation is different. Some countries are heavily reliant on only one or a few primary commodities (e.g., copper, bananas), and their economic health can be closely tied to how much wealth those commodities generate in the global economy. At least 50 percent of exports are still from primary commodities in two-thirds of all developing countries, especially the least developed countries, where 80 percent of exports are primary commodities (UNCTAD 2013). Some countries are located at strategically important nodes or have such desirable resources (e.g., oil, diamonds) that both internal actors and external actors are motivated to engage in behaviors that are very damaging to the country, such as political corruption or violence, to secure control of the benefits. And some developing countries are so impoverished of basic resources that they struggle to provide their own population with food or water, have few resources to trade in the international marketplace, and have so little strategic importance that they tend to be ignored by the rest of the world, even if their circumstances are dire (Collier 2010; Klare 2012).

INTERNAL DISORDER Many countries in the Global South struggle with various forms of internal disorder, especially due to political violence and insufficient political institutionalization. All of the bottom 40 countries on the Failed State Index are developing countries that are wracked by some combination of civil war, nation-based conflict, terrorism, and high crime rates (Fund for Peace 2014). Many countries in the Global South suffer from limited citizen support for their government institutions, including the absence of any mechanism for the legitimate transfer of government authority. Development is hampered by the absence of a governmental system that functions effectively and has solid capabilities (recall Chapter 5). Moreover, extensive violations of human rights are common in Global South countries where governments either fail to protect those rights or actually violate them. An associated effect of such internal disorder is a substantial increase in IDPs (internally displaced people who have been forced to flee their communities but remain inside their own country) and refugees who have fled their country. The refugees often add burdens and disorder in the neighboring Global South countries to which they flee. As noted in Chapter 12, there were nearly 27 million IDPs and more than 15 million refugees at the beginning of 2013 (UNHCR 2013).

NEOCOLONIALISM The discussions of the dependency approach in Chapter 10 and of colonialism and neocolonialism in Chapter 11 (including Focus in 11, on Congo) reveal that a developing country's official independence does not necessarily end its subordination to the developed countries and global institutions. The developed countries, international financial institutions, and multinational corporations are the major sources of the financial capital, advanced technologies, and even the security that many actors in developing countries need to survive in the global system. With this can come **neocolonialism**—*informal and indirect, but still significant, control of the resources, the economic system, and even the political system of a developing country by powerful external actors* (Wallerstein 2004; Weatherby 2011).

The Compare in 14 briefly considers how some of these obstacles have affected development in two countries. However, before you read the Compare, consider the "acid test" types of indicators in Table 14.1. Which country would you prefer to have been born into 20 years ago, knowing nothing of your personal circumstances? (Recall Compare in 1.) You will probably think this choice is clear.

Table 14.1 Select indicators for Nigeria and the Philippines

	Nigeria	Philippines
Population	177 m	108 m
Democracy index (148 countries)	120th	69th
Political rights (1–7, 1 = best)	4	3
Civil liberties (1–7, 1 = best))	4	3
GDP/capita (PPP)	$2,800	$4,700
Human Development Index	.471	.654
Average annual GDP growth, 2000–2012	6.8%	4.9%
Literacy rate	61%	95%
Economic freedom index (177 countries)	128th	88th
% in poverty	70%	27%
Life expectancy (years)	52.6	72.5
Population growth rate (annual)	2.5%	1.7%
Corruption (175 countries) (1st = least corrupt)	144th	94th
Internet users/100	24.5	7.8
Failed State Index (178 countries) (1st = most failed)	17th	52nd
Global Peace Index (161 countries) (1st = most peaceful)	148th	129th
Income inequality (136 countries) (1st = most unequal)	47th	42nd
Gender inequality index (186 countries) (1st = most equal)	142nd	77th

Compare In 14

Obstacles to Development: Nigeria and the Philippines

When you examine the indicators for Nigeria and the Philippines in Table 14.1, it is evident that each of these countries has achieved only a modest level of development. These indicators, as well as Figure 10.1, place both countries in the Global South. Each country has a long and rich history, and each was viewed as having great potential for successful development at the time of independence. Yet many decades later, each still has a relatively low GDP per capita, a medium or low score on the Human Development Index, limited political rights and civil liberties, substantial poverty, and so on. Among the many factors that might offer partial explanations for their development trajectories, let's briefly consider the five obstacles to development listed in the previous section. The differences in the scale of some of these obstacles might also help account for the high probability that you selected the Philippines in the acid test.

Population growth has placed significant strains on both countries. In each country, the population has quadrupled since 1950. Just since 1990, the populations have increased by 57 percent in the Philippines (adding 46 million) and by 56 percent in Nigeria (adding 77.5 million). And it is estimated that by 2050, the Philippines will add 40 million and Nigeria will add more than 180 million (UNDP 2011; UNDP 2013). The many extra people and increasingly youthful population in each country during recent decades has created the need for extensive new infrastructure, generated more social disorder, and caused any increases in economic resources to be distributed among far more people.

Corruption is a serious problem in both countries. In Nigeria, much of the considerable wealth generated by oil revenues that does not leak out to the MNCs seems to remain in the pockets of the power elite and does not benefit the general population or facilitate economic growth. Nigeria has an entrenched culture of corruption in which those with control over almost any action expect a payoff to do their job, whether it is providing a license, recording a document, dealing with a legal infraction, and so on. The Philippines is "the Asian country that has been most hurt by corruption" in a region known for

corruption (PERC 2011). The corruption of top government officials in the Philippines became legendary during the rule of President Ferdinand Marcos, from 1965 to 1986. He, his infamous wife Imelda, and his political cronies drained the country of an estimated $10 billion. Subsequent President Joseph Estrada was convicted of corruption valued at more than $85 million. Estrada was pardoned by his successor, Gloria Arroyo, who is now under investigation for corruption. Arroyo's replacement in 2010, Ninoy Aquino, ran on the slogan: "If there is no corruption, there is no poverty" and made the usual promise: "I will not only not steal, but I'll have the corrupt arrested."

Dependence on primary commodities is a key *geopolitical* problem for Nigeria, which gets 95 percent of its foreign exchange capital and 80 percent of its federal government revenue from oil. The heavy reliance on oil has benefitted Nigeria when oil prices are high but leaves the economy vulnerable to price changes. The huge wealth associated with the oil resources provokes unscrupulous behavior among many who want to capture a piece of the action. Although 70 percent of the labor force is still in agriculture, Nigeria suffers periodic food shortages due to inefficiencies and drought. The Philippines benefits from a more favorable geopolitical situation. The country is a successful producer of foods for domestic consumption and export. As an island with strategic importance in its region, the Philippines receives benefits from the United States, which has located military operations there. These conditions have helped the country diversify its economy, with the service sector generating 57 percent of GDP and the industrial sector adding nearly one-third.

In the 50 years since independence, Nigeria has experienced persistent political *disorder*, due to deep nation-based divisions among regional groups. The struggle to control oil resources and the reins of government are at the base of most of these conflicts. There have been at least six successful coups by military officers who then led oppressive regimes that target opponents with establishment violence. Among the recurrent episodes of violence, the bloodiest (with at least 300,000 deaths) was a civil war from 1966 to 1970, in which the Igbos failed in the attempt to create an independent state (Biafra). In the Philippines, President Marcos used increasingly repressive tactics to retain power during his 20-year rule. He declared martial law in 1972, and his security forces ruthlessly punished opponents. When Marcos attempted to steal another election in 1986, the citizens had enough of his corrupt and autocratic rule, and through a "people power" mass movement, they forced him to flee the country. His successor as president, Cory Aquino, survived at least nine coup attempts. Aquino's successor, Joseph Estrada, was driven from power in 2001 by another populist movement that was orchestrated by the country's power elite. Continuing political violence by communists and political Islamists in the populous south undermines order maintenance (CIA 2014).

Neocolonialism is more evident in Nigeria. After independence from Britain in 1960, Nigerian governments asserted increasing control over oil resources. However, the elite collaborates with multinational companies similar to those that exploited Nigeria's oil during colonialism. Nigeria remains very dependent on financial aid, technological support, and business capabilities from the Global North. The Philippines had a considerably longer experience under Spanish (1521–1892) and U.S. (1892–1946) colonial control. But in recent decades, it has established substantially more autonomy over its economy and is more capable of pursuing its own goals in the global system.

Further Questions

1. Which obstacle to development is likely to be the most difficult to overcome in each country?

2. If you were the top leader in Nigeria or the Philippines, what one policy might you push hardest to improve the country's overall development trajectory?

Goal: Prosperity

14.3 **Outline the strategies the Global South has used to achieve economic development.**

All developing countries in the Global South strive for the benefits of prosperity associated with economic growth and development and welfare distribution. While these countries often employ the same economic strategies as the more developed countries, many of them have had only limited success in achieving prosperity. Indeed, a low level of overall economic performance is the most conventional indicator of a developing country. These countries range from the lowest current GDP per capita (PPP) average of only $415 *per year* (Democratic Republic of Congo) to the upper limit defined in Figure 10.1 at about $10,000 (countries such as Cuba and Tunisia). The average income per person for all 40 low-income countries is only $1,387 per year; and even those in the 103 middle-income countries average only $7,194 per year, in comparison to $36,868 for the high-income, developed countries (World Bank 2013).

A very low level of income per capita suggests limited resources within the society, but it does not reveal the additional fact that these resources are often very unequally distributed and that even the most basic goods are minimally available to many people. More than 1.2 billion people in the Global South live on less than $1 per day, and 2.8 billion, almost half the world's population, live on less than $2 per day, under conditions of severe poverty. Nearly 1 billion adults are illiterate, more than 1 billion have no access to clean water, and about one-third of children under five years old suffer from malnutrition (UNDP 2013). At a minimum, developing countries need to feed their own populations. Over 827 million people in the Global South do not have daily access to enough food (UNWFP 2013). Consider that every year, more people die from hunger than from AIDS, malaria, and tuberculosis combined (UNWFP 2013).

These stark statistics might be hard to grasp, but they are graphic illustrations of the difficult life conditions that are the daily reality of millions in the Global South. What can be done to improve the conditions of all these people? It is clear that political choices (such as decisions regarding the organization of the political economy, the distribution of prosperity, the education of women, and the form of government) *can* have a powerful impact on the quality of citizens' lives. Let's explore some of the choices that governments must make in the quest for prosperity.

The Quest for Prosperity: Strategic Choices

Each developing country must make choices in at least five key strategic areas in its broad approach to economic development, given the obstacles to prosperity described above, its conditions, and its vulnerability to the many stronger actors in the global system: (1) the balance between state control and the market; (2) the balance between import substitution and export promotion; (3) the mix of manufacturing, services, and commodities; (4) the role of agriculture; and (5) the extent of collaboration with foreign capital.

STATISM VERSUS NEOLIBERALISM A basic policy decision for a developing country is whether to foster economic growth by means of greater state control of the political economy or a more market-oriented approach (see Chapter 8). After independence, many developing countries opted for **statism**—*extensive state control of the political economy*, as described in Chapter 10. Leaders assumed that economic dependency and underdevelopment could best be overcome by a strong centralized effort to plan and control the production and distribution of goods in the society. In this approach, the state's role is expansive—it owns major industries and natural resources (via nationalization), controls production decisions, regulates prices and wages, protects domestic producers from foreign competition, and encourages import substitution. In some Global South countries, especially many of the more authoritarian regimes, the political economy more resembled **state capitalism**, with those in political power controlling the economy to add to their wealth and the wealth of their friends and to retain political power.

By the late 1980s, many Global South countries had rejected statism and state capitalism because of the disappointing results and the emerging realities of the globalized economy. The states shifted in varying degrees to a strategy of **neoliberalism** (the *market-oriented approach* described in Chapters 8 and 10). With neoliberalism, the state plays a very limited role in owning, controlling, or regulating economic resources; it supports globalized free trade; it facilitates foreign direct investment; and it holds down taxes and public spending to keep more money in the hands of private entrepreneurs. Some Global South countries have fully embraced neoliberal principles.

However, numerous countries that abandoned the more extreme forms of state control of the economy still exercise substantial control over which firms are allowed to prosper in the marketplace. That is, some states still select and nurture certain firms and certain entrepreneurs who are given greater financial support from the state (e.g., subsidies, lower taxes) and experience less negative interference from state actors. These countries, often characterized by a highly authoritarian political system, continue to function with political economies that most closely resemble either state capitalism or statism.

PRODUCING FOR DOMESTIC CONSUMPTION OR EXPORT Every political economy produces some goods and services for its own population and some for export to other countries. And some products are imported from other countries because of cost and quality considerations. Ideally, a developing country will export goods with greater value than the goods it imports to avoid a "balance of payments" deficit and increased borrowing and debt.

A developing country can use public policy to influence its mix of imports and exports. One policy option is *import substitution—a country decreases the share of goods that are imported by producing more of those goods domestically*. The government can exhort its citizens to buy domestically produced goods (e.g., "Buy Nigerian!"), or it can provide subsidies to its firms or consumers to lower the prices of those goods. A common tactic is trade protectionism—the use of tariffs and other procedures to discourage imports or make imports more expensive than goods produced in the country. In the current globalized economic system, powerful economic actors (e.g., the World Trade Organization, the International Monetary Fund) apply considerable pressure on developing countries to eliminate such protectionism and allow free trade.

A second policy option is *export promotion—firms are encouraged to produce goods and services that can be exported and sold at a profit in the global economy*. The government can implement policies that provide its domestic firms with an advantage over global competitors. The effect of such policies could be lower taxes on domestic firms, a well-trained labor force, less restrictive environmental policies, subsidized materials, less costly regulations on business practices, and so on. In recent decades, almost all developing countries have enacted policies intended to facilitate export promotion. This strategy has been used very effectively by many countries in Asia and Latin America but less successfully across sub-Saharan Africa.

THE ROLE OF AGRICULTURE Food is a crucial good in all economies. Globally, 30 percent of all workers are still engaged in agriculture, and the percentage is considerably higher in most developing countries. More than 70 percent of the world's poor live in rural areas, where most small farms produce little more than is necessary for family subsistence (World Bank 2013). Some political regimes attempted to achieve food surpluses through statist control over agriculture. The state organized most arable land into large farms and developed a plan for production based on shared labor and technology. This approach was most fully implemented in command economies, such as Cambodia, China, Cuba, and Tanzania. State-controlled agriculture was

The shift from subsistence farming to cash crops for the domestic market and for export is one key to rural development, as in this field of broccoli in Ecuador.

not successful because most rural people resisted social restructuring and were not motivated to work as hard for the general welfare as for their own profit.

Consequently, nearly all Global South countries now encourage market-based production of cash crops by private farmers or local collectives (Isbister 2006). In general, the vision is to implement public policies that facilitate: (1) stable and attractive prices within a reliable market, (2) an efficient system of distribution, and (3) increased crop yields. One key strategy is to transition from subsistence farming to *commercial agriculture*, a system in which people produce a surplus of food that can be sold in a market. This generates cash for rural people, food to support a growing urban population, and financial capital from food exports. This strategy is especially effective on large farms. However, small farms still produce half of the food grown in developing countries and are especially vulnerable to the complex global food market. Ironically, some of the most successful small farmers are those producing lucrative but illegal cash crops such as coca and opium rather than legal crops, which are less profitable. Governments have encouraged some agricultural self-help programs through the use of natural farming techniques, have provided loans to small farmers for irrigation projects and soil protection, and have attempted to stabilize market prices, at least in the domestic food market.

Government policies have also facilitated the ***green revolution***, which employs *new farming technologies, including hybrid grains, chemical fertilizers, and pesticides.*

These technologies doubled average yields for rice, corn, and wheat in the Global South between 1960 and 1996. However, the costs of purchasing fertilizers and pesticides have risen dramatically, making profitability more challenging. And unanticipated negative consequences from high-tech farming sometimes emerged. In Indonesia, for example, the green revolution initially increased rice yields dramatically. But yields soon dropped because pesticides were killing off many good insects and the new hybrid rice breeds were less resistant to the bad insects. So the government implemented policies by the mid-1980s that limited pesticide use and required farmers to return to traditional crop rotation techniques and natural fertilizers.

Despite advances in agriculture, the pressures to provide food and fuel remain intense in many of the least developed countries, especially due to the growing population, social disorder, and impacts of climate change (Klare 2009; von Braun 2008). Many rural people engage in extensive deforestation, overgrazing, and aggressive farming techniques that exhaust the soil, destroy forests, and harm ecologically sensitive areas. Since 1960, for example, mainly in the Global South, one-third of all the world's arable land has been lost, more than the total amount of land currently producing food. And 29 million acres of land are lost each year to desertification. As a result, Global South countries are destroying an additional 300 million acres of forest and natural habitat to grow crops (World Wildlife Federation 2013).

An additional challenge is that governments of the Global North pay their own farmers agricultural subsidies (on key crops such as sugar, rice, and cotton) that enable their farmers to make a profit even when selling (below cost) at prices lower than the prices of crops imported from the Global South. The Global North's protectionist trade policies and $360 billion per year spent subsidizing farmers in the Global North distort the world markets for food and lead to many billions of dollars per year in lost revenue for the countries in the Global South (International Food Policy Research Institute 2013).

THE MIX OF MANUFACTURED GOODS, SERVICES, AND COMMODITIES A political economy is developed most effectively by diversifying its goods. This entails producing and profitably marketing a balanced mix of commodities, manufactured goods, and services. Industrialization is a classic strategy for increasing economic development and hence prosperity via *manufacturing*. The aim is to use labor and capital to transform commodities into intermediate goods (e.g., cotton to cloth, trees to lumber, ore to steel, water to electricity) and then into more refined and valuable goods (e.g., clothing, furniture, televisions, trucks). For example, Bangladesh and Indonesia produce an increasing share of the shoes and clothing that are exported. More electronic equipment, furniture, cars, and other relatively sophisticated goods in the global marketplace are now being manufactured in countries such as China, Brazil, and the Philippines.

And in the postindustrial period, there is increasing emphasis on producing *services* (e.g., data entry, tourism) and knowledge-based goods (e.g., banking services, computer software) instead of manufactured goods. For example, India's large population of well-educated, English-speaking technical workers has made it an international center for activities such as writing computer software and staffing call centers. While greater prosperity is a key driver of more service jobs, a government can also stimulate its service sector by improving its educational system and its technological infrastructure.

Diversification can be most difficult for those countries that are particularly rich in primary *commodities* such as energy resources (e.g., oil), foods (e.g., coffee), or minerals (e.g., cobalt, copper). Under colonialism and neocolonialism, much of the profit from such commodities was exported to other countries or multinational corporations. Governments can take control of their commodities through nationalization or by awarding contracts to domestic entrepreneurs. But it can be difficult to ensure that the profits are captured by the state and then invested in national development, rather than being accumulated by a small elite. Some analysts conclude that developing countries with rich commodities are particularly vulnerable to instability because external and domestic actors attempt to exploit those resources, as in Bolivia (mining) and Nigeria (petroleum) (Collier and Venables 2010).

COLLABORATION WITH FOREIGN CAPITAL Economic growth in any country requires a stable political and economic environment, a trained and disciplined workforce, effective use of technologies, an efficient infrastructure for distributing goods, and the infusion of financial capital. Most developing countries are challenged on all these dimensions and especially suffer from the absence of sufficient capital to invest in the production system, to purchase imports, and to distribute welfare benefits to a needy population. Because their internal financial resources are often too limited to serve all these needs, many developing countries look to the Global North and its major national and multinational corporations and financial institutions for three types of financial capital: foreign aid, foreign direct investment, and loans.

Foreign aid. Most aid from the Global North has been in the forms of shared technology, grants and loans (with no expectation of repayment), and debt forgiveness on existing loans. Many developing countries argue that the Global North owes them such aid as compensation for decades or even centuries of colonial and neocolonial exploitation that left the developing countries with depleted resources and severe underdevelopment. While the provision of aid is sometimes altruistic, Global North countries usually offer such aid with strings attached that serve their own self-interest: economic (to obtain resources, to open markets for their own goods and services); political (to establish alliances or a political sphere of influence, to exclude ideological rivals); or military (to deploy strategic military power in Global South territory).

Foreign direct investment. Consistent with the ideology of neoliberalism described above, most Global North countries, MNCs, and financial institutions offer **foreign direct investment (FDI)**, not aid. That is, they *invest in the developing country's firms or set up their own firms within the country.* Such investment is provided by those who expect substantial profits due to the rich resources, cheap labor, tax advantages, and minimal regulation in the developing country. Many developing countries accept such foreign involvement in their economy on the assumption that capital, jobs, and other economic benefits will "trickle down" to their population.

Loans. The simplest approach to acquiring financial resources is to borrow funds from the international financial community, composed primarily of major banks and coordinated by the International Monetary Fund and the World Bank. Loans offer an enticing short-term solution for securing funds to finance economic growth and distribute welfare benefits to the population. Eventually, however, resources must be found to repay both the loans and the interest on those loans and many Global South countries are burdened with huge debt service costs.

Microcredit. One reaction to the reliance on foreign capital is an innovative approach to investment that has emerged in the Global South. This strategy recognizes that effective entrepreneurial activities often begin with small, local firms. However, billions of people in developing countries have no capital with which to start their own small enterprises. Therefore, energetic but poor individuals are provided with *microcredit— tiny loans* to enable them to launch such ventures. Women, who perform a substantial portion of all work in the developing countries, have been the recipients of 83 percent of this financial assistance. Microcredit approaches are now utilized in more than half of all developing countries, and loans have been extended to more than 195 million clients, including 125 million of the world's very poorest (Microcredit Summit Campaign 2013). Focus in 14 describes how this program emerged and has evolved in Bangladesh. Many governments and NGOs are actively expanding their efforts to provide such small-scale, local financial support due to the success of this strategy. However, some analysts present considerable data that microfinance does not enable many to escape poverty (Roodman 2012). And, of course, this modest level of internal capital is not a substitute for a large-scale infusion of capital from the international community.

Focus in 14

Poor Women and Development: Microcredit in Bangladesh

Each economic development project requires financial capital. Such funds are typically provided by national or global banking institutions to companies and other major economic actors who have a record of business success. However, a very different approach was crafted by some innovative thinkers in the Third World. Professor Muhammad Yunus in Bangladesh began with a bold and visionary assumption: that "millions of small people with their millions of small pursuits can add up to create the biggest development wonder." Yunus built on the novel concept of microcredit. That is, he assumed that if motivated individuals in humble circumstances were given access to a small amount of financial capital, they would use their creativity and energy to establish successful small firms.

In 1976, Yunus and his associates established the Grameen Bank to test their faith in the untapped entrepreneurial abilities of ordinary women and men. The bank makes small loans to those Bangladeshis who present promising ideas and show willingness to work hard to implement them. These small loans, averaging $160, are extended to people without land or assets— people too poor to qualify for traditional bank loans. Before microcredit, most of these people had no option for borrowing except from intermediaries who charged extremely high interest rates, thus worsening their economic situation. In contrast, the Grameen Bank offers these small loans at a reasonable interest rate and allows an extended time for repayment.

A notable feature of the Grameen Bank's microcredit program is that 96 percent of the 8.5 million borrowers are women. Prior to receiving a loan from the bank, the typical female borrower had never controlled much money. Most of the women have used these loans effectively, establishing diverse small businesses in their communities: enterprises such as paddy husking and lime making; services such as storage, marketing, and transport; and manufacturing activities such as pottery making, weaving, and garment sewing.

Overall, the women have been reliable borrowers and prudent entrepreneurs. Kept on track by peer pressure and peer support, the women repay their loans in tiny weekly payments and use their businesses to move themselves and their families out of poverty. Surprising many in the global financial community, more than 98 percent of the borrowers fully repay their loans from the Grameen Bank. Eventually, many of the women reapply for larger loans as they expand their business enterprises. These loans have provided a rich base of small businesses and economic growth for the country. The program has extended into such areas as loans for higher education and the provision of mobile phones. According to the bank, microcredit has "enabled women to raise their status, lessen their dependency on their husbands, and improve their homes and the nutritional standards of their children."

Microcredit has now spread to nearly all of the villages in Bangladesh. More than $14.3 billion has been lent, and more than 10 percent of the Bangladeshi population has benefited directly from microcredit. About 70 other developing countries (and even some developed countries) have replicated the methods of the Grameen Bank, and these microloans have assisted more than 195 million clients and more than 500 million family members worldwide. The Grameen Bank remains a remarkable and inspiring model of the capacity of poor women and microcredit to be a powerful source of economic development. In recognition, Yunus and the Grameen Bank were awarded the Nobel Peace Prize in 2006. (This discussion is based on Grameen Bank 2013.)

Further Focus

1. What is your assessment of the granting of microcredit almost exclusively to women?

2. Are there limits to extending microcredit to *billions* of poor people in developing countries?

Current Outcomes

Figure 14.1 presents two prosperity measures for selected developing countries. Although GDP per capita (PPP) is not a perfect measure of prosperity (recall Chapter 8), it is one reasonable indicator for comparative purposes. A striking aspect of Figure 14.1 (as well as Figure 10.1) is the low yearly GDP per capita in many countries, especially in comparison with the developed countries. Many Global South countries average less than $5,000 per year (in PPP), and some of the poorest are less than $700 per year.

The limited prosperity is also evident in the low Human Development Index (HDI) scores of many Global South countries (Figure 14.1), with the very lowest scores predominantly in Africa. Niger and the Democratic Republic of Congo have the lowest HDI score among these countries, at only .304, and Cuba is the highest at .780. There is a broad correlation between GDP per capita (in PPP) and quality of life scores, but the relationship is far from perfect. In a striking example, Vietnam and South Africa have similar HDI scores, but Vietnam's GNI per capita is less than one-fifth of South Africa's. The variation between the two measures reinforces the point that quality of life can be based on more than the average current economic product of the country and that the policies of government do matter. As the United Nations notes, in

Figure 14.1 Prosperity Measures for Selected Developing Countries of the Global South

SOURCES: World Bank 2013; UNDP 2013: *Table 1*

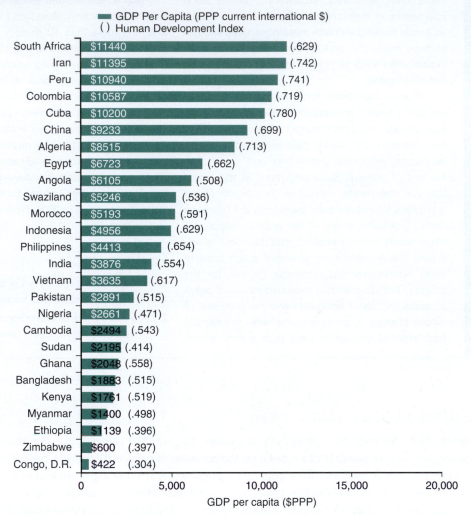

considering such differences: "So, with the right policies, countries can advance faster in human development than in economic growth. And if they ensure that growth favors the poor, they can do much more with that growth to promote human development" (UNDP 2001: 13).

Figure 14.2 offers another way to think about countries' varied success in achieving prosperity by comparing the rate of recent economic growth (2000–2012) with the proportion of the population that survives on less that $2 per day. Most of the countries in the figure achieved good average rates of economic growth, with the majority in the 4–8 percent per year range. However, most also have a large proportion of very poor people, with the majority of these countries having more than 40 percent

Figure 14.2 GDP Growth Rate and Severe Poverty Rate (Less that $2 per day)
for Selected Developing and Transitional Developed Countries

SOURCE: World Bank (2013)

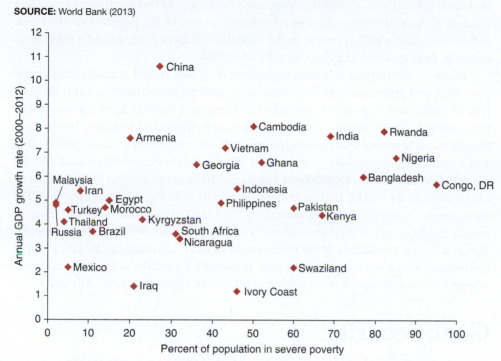

of their population in severe poverty. Notice the extremes from China, which has very
high growth and relatively high poverty; to Ivory Coast, which has very low growth
and substantial poverty; to Rwanda, which has high growth but a very high incidence
of poverty. Most of the transitional developed countries to be explored more fully in
Chapter 15 have achieved moderate growth with low levels of severe poverty.

Regional data provide a different perspective on varying rates of growth. The average annual GDP growth rate between 2000 and 2012 is highest in East Asia (9.3 percent),
led by China. The annual growth in South Asia is 7.2 percent, followed by sub-Saharan
Africa (5.0 percent), Eurasia (4.7 percent), the Middle East and North Africa (4.5 percent),
and Latin America and the Caribbean (3.5 percent) (World Bank 2013).

The differences among countries and regions are one aspect of "uneven development." The distribution of prosperity at the *individual* level is also uneven. Most of the
countries with huge inequalities in the distribution of prosperity, as measured by the Gini
index, are in the Global South (recall Compare in 8). Of the 20 countries with the world's
most unequal distributions of income, 18 are in the Global South. These countries have
extremely high Gini index scores, ranging from 63.2 in Lesotho to 50.2 in The Gambia.
Nineteen of twenty are in either sub-Saharan Africa (9) or Latin America and the Caribbean
(10). Less than one in five of the quartile of the world's countries with the most *equal* distributions of wealth are in the Global South (e.g., Armenia, Ethiopia, and Pakistan).

In many developing countries, both the decisions of the political system and the actions of the international financial community have resulted in an array of policies that have generally increased the economic advantages of the wealthier groups and reduced welfare benefits to the less advantaged sectors of the population. The result is that more than a billion people in the Global South have experienced a substantial *decline* in their standard of living since the late 1980s.

As many developing countries experience decreases in real wages, rising unemployment, and greater income inequality, some leaders, particularly in Latin America (e.g., the late Hugo Chavez in Venezuela, Evo Morales in Bolivia), have reacted against neoliberalism. Their strategy allows participation in the global economy but shelters the country's economy from global free trade. It also emphasizes public policies that aim to provide substantially more welfare distribution, social services, and jobs for the poor. President Morales (2006) of Bolivia, with the seventh most unequal income distribution in the world, is clear in his condemnation of the neoliberal model: "The worst enemy of humanity is U.S. capitalism. That is what provokes uprisings like our own, a rebellion against a system, against a neoliberal model, which is the representation of a savage capitalism. If the entire world doesn't acknowledge this reality, that the national states are not providing even minimally for health, education and nourishment, then each day the most fundamental human rights are being violated."

Goal: Security

14.4   **Assess the level of interstate violence and economic security within the Global South.**

The developing countries search for security in the face of pervasive insecurity. Their problems are grounded in low levels of political and economic development, which reduce their capacity to control their own population and resources and make them vulnerable to intervention by other states. Paradoxically, this relative weakness can also lead a state to be more aggressive in its interstate relations, both as a defensive reaction against perceived threats and as a means to divert its citizens' attention from internal problems. Only 2 of the top 25 countries on the Global Peace Index are Global South countries (Bhutan and Mauritius). However, all 10 (Table 12.3) and 22 of 25 states with the lowest scores on the Global Peace Index are developing countries (Institute for Economics and Peace 2014).

Interstate Violence

At any given time, most developing countries are *not* involved in violent interstate disputes. However, most wars since 1950 and most major armed conflicts occur in the Global South, often between neighboring states (SIPRI 2013). The following list offers five reasons for the frequent interstate violence between *adjacent* developing countries:

- The *geographic boundaries* between some states do not correspond to the boundaries of historically established nations, so conflict develops in an attempt to realign states with nations.

- Differences in the *cultures* of two states, especially differences grounded in nationality, political ideology, or religious belief, can produce animosities so strong that violence erupts.
- States look covetously at valuable *resources* in neighboring states and sometimes attempt to gain control of those resources by force.
- States with severe *internal problems* can use neighboring states as scapegoats, redirecting internal frustration into violence against those states.
- Conflict between states can be encouraged by the *actions of other states* that are attempting to serve their own national interests.

Most interstate conflicts between adjacent developing countries happen for a combination of reasons. For example, the Iran–Iraq War (1980–1988, with an estimated one million dead) is an example of a conflict resulting from the complex, interrelated impacts of nationality (Persian versus Arab), competition for resources (especially oil in Kurdish areas), religious ideology (Shia versus Sunni), personal animosity between leaders (Saddam Hussein versus Ayatollah Khomeini), internal problems in each country, and external influences from global superpowers with interests in the region. As noted in Chapter 12, interstate conflicts in the Global South only occasionally expand into a war (e.g., Cambodia–Vietnam, China–India, Eritrea–Ethiopia, India–Pakistan). It is more common for the conflict to take the form of a more limited "militarized dispute" short of war (e.g., Cambodia–Thailand, Colombia–Ecuador, India–Pakistan).

Occasionally, there are interstate conflicts between a developing country and a more developed country *on its border*. Most notable have been the five wars and many militarized disputes since 1948 between Israel and the neighboring Arab states, especially Syria, Egypt, and Jordan. In another example, the Soviet Union was concerned about the political decay in neighboring Afghanistan. It dispatched more than 115,000 troops to set up and defend Afghanistan's Marxist government, but it became entrenched in a long guerrilla war (1979–1987) in which one million Afghans died and the Soviets retreated in defeat.

When a developing country has been involved in interstate conflict with a *non-adjoining* state during the postcolonial period, the other combatant is usually a country from the Global North that uses force to serve its strategic, economic, or ideological interests. This can involve intervention in an internal war within the developing country (e.g., the United States in Vietnam in the 1960s, France in the Central African Republic in 1996, the NATO-led coalition in Afghanistan since 2001) or a somewhat more conventional war (e.g., between the United Kingdom and Argentina in 1982 and between the U.S.-led coalition and Iraq in 2003).

Some argue that the entire period of colonialism and neocolonialism should be understood as the sustained use of military, economic, and psychological violence by the developed countries against the developing countries. Certain actors in the Global South use this claim to justify their use of political violence against those representing the Global North or its allies in the Global South—as exemplified by the sponsorship of terrorist activities by actors from the Global South (e.g., al-Qaeda, Islamic State).

The search for security can be extremely costly. Although some Global North countries have slightly reduced their overall military spending in the last several years, many countries in the Global South continue to increase their spending levels (SIPRI 2013). Obviously, these huge military expenditures can enhance security and stability. But empirical analyses suggest that greater military might is actually associated with a *higher* probability that a state will be involved in interstate conflict (Bremer 1980; Collier and Hoeffler 2007). And expenditures on the military are resources that are not available for economic development, education, health care, and other forms of welfare distribution.

Economic Security

The fact that many developing countries have such fragile economic systems is also a crucial element in their quest for security because a state's goal of *autonomy*—controlling its own destiny—depends in part on its *capacity to resist external manipulation of its political economy*. When the developed countries and multinational corporations provide economic and technological assistance, they expect to exert substantial influence and to receive generous benefits such as favorable regulations and advantageous trade relations. And because Global South countries owe more than $2 trillion to the financial institutions of the Global North, those institutions expect some control over each country's internal affairs.

This economic intervention has come most explicitly from the **International Monetary Fund (IMF)**, a consortium of financial institutions that sets economic policy and monitors the behavior of global lenders and debtors. To grant additional loans or to reschedule payments on existing loans, the IMF requires "conditionalities"—the debtor state must fulfill specific conditions that the IMF sets. The IMF's conditions (sometimes called "the Washington Consensus") often include requirements that the state implement a *structural adjustment program (SAP)*, which increases the debtor state's openness to the global economy by facilitating free trade and foreign direct investment. Often, the SAPs also require the state to reduce public spending, with particularly severe reductions in the distribution of welfare services to its population, tax cuts, and privatization of state-owned firms (Petrik 2009).

Leaders in some of the major developing countries have recently become more vocal in their opposition to this external manipulation of their internal affairs, especially to the economic and trade policies associated with conditionality. Some developing countries have organized their own regional free-trade zones to increase their autonomy from the developed countries. For example, Mercosur is comprised of Argentina, Brazil, Paraguay, Uruguay, and Venezuela, representing more than half of Latin America's population (plus five associate members), and there is a trade group of Islamic states with 300 million people, including Iran, Kazakhstan, Pakistan, and Turkey.

However, the political and financial elites in nearly all developing countries seem to believe that their interests are currently best served by cooperation with the developed countries and the international financial community and that loss of some control over their political economy and even over their policy processes is an acceptable cost. This continuing need for support is captured in a paradoxical comment by Kenya's former president Daniel arap Moi: "No country can maintain its independence without assistance from outside." In the contemporary political world, no state can survive as an independent entity. But the developing countries are particularly dependent on outside assistance in many forms, especially economic and technological. This dependency makes them susceptible to influence, manipulation, or even control by other states. Thus, few of them can escape this economic component of their insecurity.

Goal: Stability

14.5 **Identify factors that lead to political stability in the Global South.**

Many countries in the Global South find that achieving stability is as elusive as achieving prosperity and security. They have not been able to establish and institutionalize structures that maintain social order and ensure effective functioning of the political system through time. This reduces their capacity to govern, raises the probability of political decay, and increases their vulnerability to outside actors.

Inadequate Political Development

Recall from Chapter 10 Kwame Nkrumah's credo: "Seek ye first the political kingdom and all else shall be added unto you." This perspective identifies the political system as the crucial instrument for achieving the developing country's major goals. Often, the people who staff the various positions within governmental institutions have good intentions and attempt to perform their responsibilities in a manner that serves the public interest. However, in many developing countries, the political system is a flawed instrument for achieving those goals. And good intentions can be swamped by harsh political realities.

Political development is one of the three pillars in the stability goal of states (recall Figure 5.1). In its essence, this is achieved as the government's capabilities increase and it has greater political institutionalization (Chapter 10). Modern political institutions in many developing countries (South American states are the general exception) have existed for fewer than 60 years. The governments in most countries have increased their political capabilities in that period; but the effective functioning of the various political institutions described in Chapters 6, 7, and 8 such as political parties, judiciaries, center–periphery relations, and so on is still a work in progress. Indeed, many countries have already significantly altered their institutional arrangements and even their constitutions one or more times, making political institutionalization more challenging.

Capabilities analysis emphasizes the state's control of the environment, but from climate change to global economic recessions to the price of oil, there is so much that the government in these countries simply cannot control, especially in the external environment. Globalization has made the difficulties in dealing with the world outside the country's borders even more complex. And within their border, these political institutions are faced with strong and often competing demands from citizens. There are conflicting values and agendas among different groups, based on differences in economic well-being, nation-based identity, region, and many other cleavages. Their political economies do not provide an adequate level of material well-being for many within their population, and marked inequality in the distribution of the existing resources can make the situation even more volatile (Collier 2008). Given all these circumstances, it is unsurprising that many citizens have not yet invested the confidence and trust in their political institutions that are among the key elements of political development. Thus these political institutions, when subjected to the (inevitable) internal and external pressures, function ineffectively or break down in political decay (Bratton and van de Walle 1997; Sorensen 2008).

The Decline of Order

POLITICAL DECAY Order maintenance is another pillar of the stability goal in Figure 5.1. Samuel Huntington's (1968) model of political decay, described in detail in Chapter 10, is based on the problems of achieving political order in developing countries. The postcolonial history of Ghana that opened this chapter, like the case studies of Cambodia, Congo, and India examined in other sections in this book, includes episodes of serious political decay. As the citizens' dissatisfaction with the political system rises, in the absence of political institutionalization, the result is usually an increase in political decay—noncompliance with political authority, protests, strikes, riots, terrorism, and nation-based violence. In some cases, authoritarian leadership reestablishes order through repression. In other cases, new leaders are installed who attempt to implement democratic processes but fail. In yet other cases, order requires external intervention (e.g., by the United Nations or another country). And there are also cases in which there is a *failed state*, a lengthy period of chaos during which no group is able to maintain political and social order. Basic order maintenance and protection from violence are too often missing from many people's lives in the Global South (Bates 2008; Sorensen 2008).

MILITARY REGIMES Until recently, the new political leadership that restored order in many developing countries often came from the military. There are three reasons the military emerges under conditions of political decay. First, a key norm within the military is a *commitment to order*, a norm that induces the military to act when the existing leadership has failed to maintain social order. Second, the military has the *capabilities to function effectively* because it is the most highly institutionalized and disciplined organizational structure in most developing countries. Third, the military has the *capacity to subdue disorder* because it usually controls the greatest concentration of force and violence in the society.

As in the examples of Ghana, Nigeria, and Congo, the emergence of strong military leadership has been a recurrent pattern in numerous Global South countries. In the early 1980s, for example, military regimes were in power in 15 of the 22 major Latin American states, 20 of the 26 major sub-Saharan African states, and many of the MENA states. The military in most developing countries now accepts the professional norm that it should support the civilian regime and prevent political decay but should not seize power. In "protected democracies," the military does not take direct political control but protects the political leadership in exchange for public policies that the military supports, such as maintaining social stability and the military's privileged status in society (Colburn 2002). There are still cases in which members of the military take political power in countries experiencing political decay (as in Honduras in 2009, Guinea-Bissau and Mali in 2012, Egypt in 2013, and Thailand in 2014). The military actors typically claim that they are restoring order, honesty, and democracy, but they usually establish an authoritarian regime.

INTERNAL WAR When political decay becomes so extensive that no groups, not even the military, can maintain order, a country is likely to become embroiled in internal war—either civil or revolutionary. Conflict is often shaped by identity politics—some combination of ethnonationalist, class, religious, and regional cleavages (Laitin 2007). In the past decade, rival groups competing for power and control of resources reduced numerous countries to near anarchy, including Afghanistan, Central African Republic, Chad, Colombia, Congo, Georgia, Iraq, Ivory Coast, Libya, Mali, Myanmar, Sudan, Sierra Leone, Somalia, Syria, and Yemen. In a few countries (e.g., Cambodia, Colombia, India, Nepal, Peru, the Philippines), variations of Marxism continue to inspire violence from frustrated groups that are persuaded their situation fits Marx's revolutionary call that the people have nothing to lose but their chains (recall the Debate in 8).

Major internal violence in Global South countries is almost always supported by other states. While different rationales are offered for intervention, these other states are usually pursuing their own national interests while providing financial or military assistance to combatants. Indeed, a key element in the pervasive insecurity *and* instability of developing countries is the ease with which other states can pursue their own policy goals within the context of internal violence in these states. Syria and Israel invade Lebanon; Uganda, Rwanda, Burundi and then the UN send troops into Congo's civil war; the Soviet Union and then the United States are major participants in the internal war in Afghanistan; NATO enters the internal war in Libya. Almost all recent uses of UN peacekeeping forces (14 of 16 active operations in 2013) have been attempts to maintain *internal* stability in a developing country (United Nations Peacekeeping 2013). From the peacekeeping operations in the Western Sahara and Darfur to those in Haiti and Kosovo, the UN efforts have focused on limiting internal conflict—both its domestic intensity and its risk of spreading across borders.

Democratization

The trend toward **democratization**, the third pillar of the stability goal, is evident in the Global South (Chapter 10). Most developing countries are under considerable pressure to shift away from authoritarian and military regimes toward regimes with an elected leadership; a multiparty system; and open, pluralist politics. Two key sources of this pressure are citizen groups demanding political rights and the governments and financial institutions of the Global North.

Figure 14.3 summarizes the levels of freedom in Global South countries, according to Freedom House (2014). A "free" country grants its citizens extensive political rights (e.g., to form political parties that represent a significant range of voter choice, to engage in vigorous political opposition) and civil liberties (e.g., protection of religious,

Figure 14.3 Levels of Freedom in the Developing Countries, by Region, Circa 2013

SOURCE: Freedom House (2014)

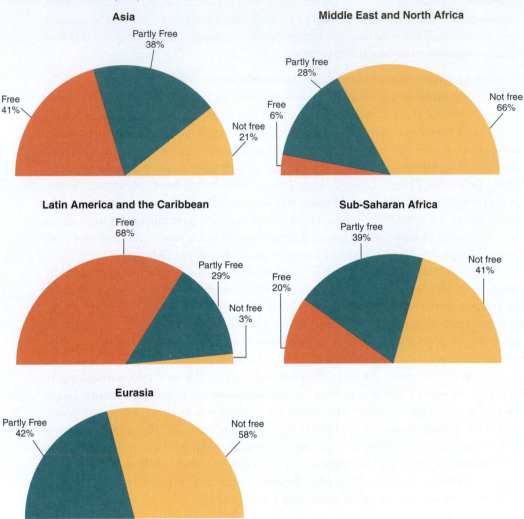

Asia

Partly Free 38%

Free 41%

Not free 21%

Middle East and North Africa

Partly free 28%

Free 6%

Not free 66%

Latin America and the Caribbean

Free 68%

Partly Free 29%

Not free 3%

Sub-Saharan Africa

Partly free 39%

Free 20%

Not free 41%

Eurasia

Partly Free 42%

Not free 58%

ethnic, economic, linguistic, and other rights). A country that is "not free" substantially limits these rights and liberties. "Partly free" means that there are significant political restrictions and violations of civil liberties, even though the country might be an electoral democracy (recall pages 170–176). To focus on some individual countries, Figure 14.3 reports the broad range of scores for selected Global South countries on the Democracy Index computed by the Economist Intelligence Unit (2013). This index combines scores on measures of the electoral process, the functioning of government, political participation, the political culture, and civil liberties.

The spread of democratization is most extensive in *Latin America and the Caribbean*. In 2014, across the entire Western Hemisphere, only Cuba was categorized as "not free" (Freedom House 2014). Recently, some countries, such as Bolivia and Ecuador, weathered serious episodes of political decay that earlier would almost certainly have resulted in a military coup. Some, including Argentina, Haiti, and Venezuela, defeated coup attempts. Freedom House (2014) classifies over two-thirds of the Latin American countries as fully "free" democracies (including Argentina, Brazil, Chile, Costa Rica, Panama, and Uruguay). Among the 10 "partly free" countries are Colombia, Honduras, Mexico, and Venezuela.

In the *Asia-Pacific region*, the spread of democratization is mixed. China emphatically crushed the prodemocracy movement in Tiananmen Square in 1989 and has strongly resisted citizen demands for increased political rights and civil liberties. Cambodia, Myanmar, North Korea, and Vietnam are also among the eight countries

Figure 14.4 Democracy Index Scores for Selected Global South Countries

SOURCE: Economist Intelligence Unit (2013)

Higher Score (10.0-0.0) denotes higher level of democracy

Notes: Egypt score prior to 2013 coup; Myanmar score prior to 2013 elections

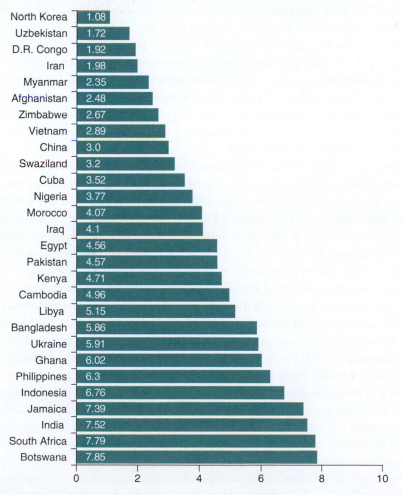

that are classified as "not free." Fifteen more (including Bangladesh, Malaysia, Pakistan, and the Philippines) are only "partly free." The 16 "free" countries include Indonesia and India, still the world's largest democracy, although it has been battered occasionally by political decay, including parliamentary deadlock, assassination, and extensive violence among Hindus, Muslims, and Sikhs. Electoral democracies are functioning in 59 percent of the Asian countries, although some are fragile and under persistent pressure from dissatisfied groups.

Freedom House concludes that *Eurasia*, composed of 12 countries, is currently the least free region in the world. It describes the "year-by-year assault on democratic freedoms through much of Eurasia," attributable to the actions of authoritarian leaders and pressures from Russia (Freedom House 2014). Fifty-eight percent of the countries, including Azerbaijan, Belarus, Kazakhstan, and Russia are "not free." The remaining 42 percent of countries, such as Armenia, Georgia, and Moldova, are only "partially free."

Although less than two-fifths of the countries in *sub-Saharan Africa* are electoral democracies, this is the region's highest level on this measure since independence. Freedom House (2014) classifies 20 percent of the countries as "free," including Botswana, Ghana, Lesotho, Senegal, and South Africa, while 39 percent are "partly free" (e.g., Kenya, Nigeria) and 41 percent are "not free" (e.g., Angola, Congo, Zimbabwe).

Many developing countries in the *Middle East* and *North Africa* have introduced elements of democratic politics, especially in response to the Arab Spring of 2011 although democratic gains have so far been modest. Morocco and Tunisia are among the five countries classified as "partly free." Sixty-six percent of the countries are still classified as "not free," although some now have multiple political parties competing in relatively open elections (e.g., Algeria, Iraq). The region is in considerable flux, as are the Freedom House classifications.

The recent wave of democracy (discussed in Chapter 10) seems to be moving in both directions in the Global South. On the one hand, increases in overall prosperity and in education levels in many countries have improved the conditions for the consolidation of democracy. Most regimes have granted some political rights to individuals and groups and have raised the level of elite accountability through elections. The percentage of electoral democracies is at an all-time high. Also, in the aftermath of questionable elections, leaders have been driven from power by popular uprisings. Such "soft coups" demanding greater democracy removed leaders from power recently in Bolivia, Egypt, Georgia, Haiti, Kyrgyzstan, Paraguay, Peru, Ukraine, and Yemen and forced concessions in countries such as Morocco and Myanmar. While such "people power" has some virtues, it offers citizens a mixed message about the range of legitimate tactics for replacing leaders.

On the other hand, Freedom House describes "authoritarian resistance," recent setbacks, and a global pushback against democracy and groups advocating political freedom and human rights (Freedom House 2014). Some regimes have increased their repression in response to popular uprisings. There are still occasional military coups. And many recent elections lack legitimacy. For example, in 2014 Syrian President Bashar al-Assad insisted on holding a sham election, despite widespread violence and the country's inability to mount a fair election. He retained the presidency without a legitimate mandate in an election many other countries described as a mockery of democracy.

The Rise of the Global South?

14.6 **Evaluate the reported "rise of the South."**

From 2008 forward, the countries in the Global North hit a rough patch in which their economies stopped growing or grew at sluggish rates. To the surprise of many, the economies of many Global South countries continued to expand during the global financial crisis. Thus the 2013 United Nations Human Development report is titled "The Rise of the South" and opens with the claim that the current period is characterized by "the striking transformation of a large number of developing countries into dynamic major economies" (UNDP 2013: iv).

Although some of the growth statistics are especially strengthened by the performance of countries highlighted in Chapter 15—the transitional developed countries, including four of the BRICS countries (Brazil, India, China, and South Africa)—more than 40 countries across the Global South have recently made significantly stronger gains on the Human Development Index (HDI) than expected, based on their previous performance. And the Global South countries have achieved a higher economic growth rate than the Global North countries for more than a decade. How can the Global South sustain this unexpected progress? The UN identifies three major drivers that facilitate effective development of Global South countries.

First, a successful strategy must be grounded in *a strong, active, and responsible state*. The UN terms this a "proactive development state." The policies of such a state must be guided by a long-range vision based on shared norms and values as well as rules and institutions that build societal and political trust and cohesion. While there are multiple paths to success, it is essential that the government's policies support the growth of key sectors of the economy, expand the number of quality jobs, and invest in "people-friendly" policies in education, health, and public services (UNDP 2013: 4).

The second driver of development is *success in tapping into global markets*. A Global South country can generate positive growth when it imports skills and knowledge from the rest of the world and then produces and exports the goods and services the rest of the world would like to purchase. This requires both private firms and the state to take actions that further the country's gradual and strategic integration into the global market. The state must also implement policies that minimize any shocks to the domestic economy that might occur as a result of global engagement (UNDP 2013: 4).

The third driver of the rise of the Global South is a *commitment to social policy innovation*. The state must make substantial investments in education, healthcare, social protection, legal empowerment, and a reduction of inequality. According to the UN, these state policies will support long-term, sustained economic growth and create a population that is both capable of contributing to that economy and supportive of political and social institutions that are fair and stable (UNDP 2013: 5).

Despite the UN's optimistic assessment and prescription, the current overall balance sheet of the Global South seems complicated in terms of the pursuit of prosperity, security, and stability. In the pursuit of prosperity, the positives include greater economic diversification, with manufactured goods now accounting for two-thirds of exports (excluding oil). The annual economic growth rate for the low-income countries has averaged 5.5 percent since 2000, which is more than triple the rate of growth of the world's high-income countries (World Bank 2013). The average person in the developing world is living longer (on average, 16 years longer than in 1960), is healthier, is better educated, and has more material possessions than at any prior time.

However, most Global South economies are still net importers of capital, technology, manufactured goods, oil, and even food, and there is considerable continued dependency on the developed countries and multinational corporations. Prosperity is very uneven, with some countries enjoying substantial economic growth while many other developing countries languish. Moreover, inequality in the distribution of prosperity is increasing within most Global South countries, particularly those with rapid growth. There are serious shortcomings in the pursuit of prosperity when 2.4 billion Global South people live on less than $2 per day.

Developing countries are spending more each year to achieve greater security, but there is little evidence that most citizens in the Global South feel more secure from violence than in the past. The spread of more deadly weapons, the increasing movements of populations across borders and within countries, the disruptive aspects of globalization, and the propensity of external actors to intervene within the borders of many Global South countries have altered the nature of insecurity but certainly have not fundamentally reduced it.

Economic underdevelopment is the main factor distinguishing the countries of the Global South from those of the Global North. But *political* underdevelopment is a pivotal problem if the political system is the crucial instrument for social and economic change, as suggested by the UN's drivers of development. Regardless of their political approach, nearly all developing countries face challenges as they attempt to use the political system to achieve prosperity, security, and stability. Most countries have valuable natural resources and a population that is willing to apply its energies to achieve these goals. However, the depth of the peoples' patience and support of specific political leaders or even of the country's current political institutions is not strong. And it is repeatedly tested in a turbulent world when there are recurrent episodes of disappointment with policy outcomes, corruption, and evident gaps between aspirations and realities.

For the leaders of many Global South countries, determining the best strategy for achieving desired outcomes might seem baffling. At every turn, the underlying political choices are fundamental: freedom versus security, economic development versus social welfare, political equality versus economic equality, democracy versus efficiency, aid versus independence, neoliberalism versus state capitalism, guns versus butter. It does seem possible that for some Global South countries, especially the low-income developing countries, *no* political approach and *no* form of political economy can simultaneously achieve all their major goals (a possibility this book first put forth in the Compare in 1 "acid test"). The leaders of any developing country might need to make very difficult decisions about how to gain even partial success on some of their goals. This view suggests that some objectives will have to be sacrificed in the quest for others, and there is no assurance that *any* objective can be fully attained. Thus the Debate in 14 asks whether there will always be a group of poor, underdeveloped countries.

The Debate in 14

Will There Always Be a Global South?

For many decades, some countries have been described as "least developed countries," "Third World," and "Global South." Such terms are meant to characterize a large number of countries that have a relatively low level of economic development, measured as GDP per capita. The label might encompass as many as 150 countries that are not yet "developed" to the level of countries in the Global North; but a more limited classification might include the 36 "low-income countries" and some or most of the 48 "lower-middle-income" countries (World Bank 2013). Some analysts predict that these less developed countries will close the gap with the more developed countries, given the homogenizing dynamics of globalization (see Chapter 11). Others claim that substantial inequality among countries is a fundamental feature of the global system and that continuing economic inequality is inevitable in a world of limited resources, free trade, disparities in technology, and hegemonic power relations. The poor countries, it might be said, will always be with us. Will there always be a Global South?

The Global South Is on a Path to Development

- Numerous social indicators reveal significant recent improvement in the life conditions of those living in the Global South. Life expectancy in low-income countries has increased from 53 years to 61 years (1990–2011); the literacy rate has increased from 69 percent to 80 percent (1990–2005); the mortality rate for children under five (per 1,000) has decreased from 164 to 95 (1990–2011) (UNDP 2008; WHO 2013; World Bank 2013).

- The proportion of people living on less than $1.25 per day in the Global South has decreased from 47 percent in 1990 to 22 percent in 2010 (UNMDG 2013).

- Overall, the countries of the Global South achieve substantially higher economic growth rates than the high-income countries. Since 2000, low-income countries have grown at an annual rate of 5.5 percent and lower-middle-income countries have grown at 6.2 percent, compared with only 1.7 percent annual growth in the high-income countries (World Bank 2013).

- The mobility of capital, the transfer of technology across borders, and the extensive outsourcing of economic activity associated with globalization are producing substantial and increasing economic and social benefits for most citizens in the developing countries (Baghwati 2007; Wolf 2004).

- The Global South has increased its share of world merchandise trade from 25 percent to 47 percent between 1980 and 2010, and its share of world output is also now 47 percent (UNDP 2013: 2). The external debt service (as a percentage of exports) that burdened most developing countries has been reduced from 16 percent in 1990 to only 3 percent in 2011 (UNMDG 2013).

- If "Global South" is merely the newest label for those countries that are *relatively* poor, even while the absolute standard of living rises to a reasonable level for most of the population in most developing countries, then there will always be a group of "least developed countries," but only because some countries will continue to be less rich than others.

The Global South Will Never Disappear

- It is likely to take generations for the "average person in the Global South" to catch up with even the current social statistics of the average Global Northerner. The Global Southerner lives 18 fewer years, has one-twentieth the yearly income, and is 30 times more likely to be illiterate. In the last two decades, 1 billion people have experienced a deterioration in their standard of living (UNDP 2010; World Bank 2013).

- There are more people in the Global South living in extreme poverty today than there were in 1981. Education is critical, yet only 36 percent of children in low-income countries attend secondary school (UNWDG 2011; World Bank 2013).

- Despite higher growth rates and claims of convergence, the absolute differences between the least developed countries and the developed countries remain huge. For example, even if economic growth in the developed countries were to stop from this moment forward, it would take Latin America until 2177 and sub-Saharan Africa until 2236 to catch up (World Bank 2005: 37).

- The developed countries continue to enjoy enormous competitive advantages over the Global South countries, in terms of their control of capital flows, their greater technological capacity and innovativeness, and their military and political power. These advantages helped generate the current vast inequalities between rich and poor countries, and there is no reason to assume that the rich countries will allow these advantages to wither.

- Powerful global institutions such as the WTO and multinational corporations generally operate in ways that favor the developed countries over the Global South. Globalization has resulted in increasing inequality between the world's rich and poor countries (Khor 2011).

- Since 1970, the value of international trade for countries in the Global North has increased significantly more than for the Global South, despite a population that is less than one-fifth as large. And the IMF reports that 40 of 62 low-income countries for which it has data are in high or moderate risk of debt distress (IMF 2013).

- A few developing countries will successfully reach a high level of development. However, there are few data or trends to suggest that there will be any dramatic reduction in the dependency or increase in the overall quality of life for the majority of people in most Global South countries relative to developed countries.

More questions …

1. Might globalization generate some hardships and greater inequalities for some Global South populations in the short run but ultimately have very positive impacts on productivity, trade, and prosperity in their countries?

2. Is it a satisfactory situation if most people in the less developed countries are increasingly better off in terms of life expectancy, literacy, caloric intake, and so forth, yet the relative disparities in quality of life between people in the Global South and in the Global North increase?

Key Concepts

democratization, p. 405
export promotion, p. 392
foreign direct investment (FDI), p. 395
Global South, p. 383

green revolution, p. 393
import substitution, p. 392
International Monetary Fund (IMF), p. 402
microcredit, p. 396

neocolonialism, p. 388
neoliberalism, p. 391
statism, p. 391

For Further Consideration

1. Assess the claim that broad labels like "Global South" have no meaning, either analytical or political, in the complicated, globalized world.

2. Are the problems in achieving economic development in the developing countries attributable primarily to the actions of the developed countries, or are they better explained by domestic circumstances in these countries?

3. Choose a real (or imaginary) developing country and specify its conditions. Given your country's conditions, what arrangements (especially political institutions and

political economy) make the most sense for progressing toward the key development goals you emphasize?

4. How do you explain the fact that some states in the Global South were able to grow even as the states in the Global North struggled?

5. Other than greater economic prosperity, what conditions seem most likely to sustain the shift to democratization in many Global South countries? In particular, what forms or arrangements of political structures are most important?

For Further Reading

Andersen, Roy, Robert Seibert, and Jon Wagner. (2012). *Politics and Change in the Middle East.* **10th ed. New York: Pearson.** A multidisciplinary, comparative introduction to the political systems in this important region, focusing on current challenges.

Arvidsson, Adam, and Nicolai Peitersen. (2013). *The Ethical Economy: Rebuilding Value After the Crisis.* **New York: Columbia University Press.** The authors present the interwoven relationship between economic development and positive social capital. They suggest paths to development that more thoroughly consider citizen-centric policies.

Barrientos, Armando. (2013). *Social Assistance in Developing Countries.* **Cambridge: Cambridge University Press.** Provides an introduction to anti-poverty programs in the Global South, including the historical and political context behind the enormous growth of social assistance programs.

Collier, Paul. (2008). *The Bottom Billion: Why the Poorest Countries are Failing and What Can be Done about It.* **New York: Oxford University Press.** A compelling analysis and set of policy prescriptions regarding the severe problems, particularly grounded in corruption, resource wealth, and subordination in the global economy, that cripple the 50 poorest, failing countries in the Global South. Also see Collier's *Wars, Guns and Votes* (2010).

Dominguez, Jorge I., and Anthony Jones, eds. (2007). *The Construction of Democracy: Lessons from Practice and Research.* **Baltimore: Johns Hopkins University Press.** Scholars and major political officials from numerous countries, mainly in the developing world, explore the necessary conditions for creating and sustaining democracy, with particular emphasis on the fit between the sociocultural nature of the country and the fostering of associational behavior and trust among the citizens.

Isbister, John. (2006). *Promises Not Kept: Poverty and the Betrayal of Third World Development.* **7th ed. Bloomfield, CT: Kumarian.** A sensible and balanced analysis of the difficulties that have prevented most developing countries from achieving sustained development, exploring both the external and the internal obstacles to prosperity.

Lomberg, Bjorn, ed. (2013). *Global Problems, Smart Solutions: Costs and Benefits.* **New York: Cambridge University Press.** How would you spend an additional $75 billion of development assistance? Here, 50 experts offer their proposals for the best use of global development dollars. The proposals are then ranked by a panel of respected senior economists.

Meadows, Donella, Jurgen Randers, and Dennis Meadows. (2004). *Limits to Growth: The 30-Year Update.* **White River, VT: Chelsea Green Publishing Company.** Updating the earlier arguments in their *Limits to Growth* studies, the authors provide a powerful case that overpopulation, overuse of resources, and the failure to respond effectively to these phenomena are dangerous challenges to prosperity and stability in all countries, with particular risks for those in the developing world.

Moyo, Dambisa. (2009). *Dead Aid: Why Aid Is Not Working and How There Is a Better Way for Africa.* **New York: Farrar, Straus and Giroux.** A controversial argument that development in many African countries has actually been harmed by the more than $1 trillion in aid, which has caused aid dependency and worsened corruption, and that different approaches are necessary to facilitate development.

Nugent, Paul. (2004). *Africa Since Independence: A Comparative History.* **New York: Palgrave Macmillan.** A richly comparative discussion of the evolution of many important African countries, covering the entire postcolonial period.

Onwumechili, Chuka. (1999). *African Democratization and Military Coups.* **Westport, CT: Praeger.** A sobering and occasionally encouraging characterization of 40 years of struggle to establish democracy in African countries and to limit the tendency toward violent takeovers and authoritarian rule by the military.

Schedler, Andreas, ed. (2013). *The Politics of Uncertainty: Sustaining and Subverting Electoral Authoritarianism.* **New York: Oxford University Press.** This analysis examines how contemporary authoritarian leaders manipulate elections and offer a guise of democracy while trying to retain their power in a context of high uncertainty.

Simon, Julian. (1998). *The Ultimate Resource 2.* **Princeton, NJ: Princeton University Press.** A powerful critique of those, like the Limits to Growth group, who predict disaster due to overpopulation and environmental degradation. It argues that the ultimate resource (people producing knowledge and then applying it as technology) will outstrip problems.

Skidmore, Thomas, Peter Smith, and James Green. (2009). *Modern Latin America.* **7th ed. New York: Oxford University Press.** A helpful comparative introduction to society, politics, and economic development in Latin America, with numerous interesting case studies.

Weatherby, Joseph N., et al., eds. (2011). *The Other World: Issues and Politics of the Developing World.* **9th ed. New York: Longman.** Thoughtful general chapters on neo/colonialism, women and development, and political economy precede informative chapters focusing on each region of developing countries.

Wiarda, Howard J., ed. (2004). *Authoritarianism and Corporatism in Latin America—Revisited.* **Gainesville: University Press of Florida.** This book argues that the apparent shift toward democratization in many Latin American countries is illusory. Rather, these countries still have strongly entrenched authoritarian and corporatist power structures.

World Bank. (Yearly). *World Development Report.* **New York: Oxford University Press.** Systematic yearly statistics on the economic, financial, and demographic aspects of development for more than 180 states. Each annual issue also emphasizes a key theme (e.g., 2009 on economic geography; 2010 on climate change; 2011 on conflict, security, and development; 2012 on gender equality; 2013 on jobs) with a strong emphasis on the developing countries.

Yunus, Muhammad. (2008). *Creating a World Without Poverty: Social Business and the Future of Capitalism.* **New York: Public Affairs Publishing.** A remarkable vision from the inspiring Nobel Prize winner who established the Grameen Bank (Focus in 14), in which he sketches a business model that would enable every family to live with dignity and security.

On the Web

http://allafrica.com

This site links to hundreds of current Africa-focused newspaper articles as well as more than 900,000 articles in a searchable archive.

http://english.aljazeera.net

An Arab world perspective (in English) on the news from arguably the most influential regional news source in the Middle East.

http://lanic.utexas.edu/index.html

The Latin American Network Information Center, hosted at the University of Texas, Austin, provides a vast number of Internet-based information sources about all countries in Latin America.

http://www.undp.org

The Web site for the United Nations Development Programme, a key unit of the United Nations that specializes in issues of economic and political development.

http://www.unohrlls.org/en/home

The site for the United Nations' Office of the High Representative for the (48) "Least Developed Countries," (31) "Landlocked Developing Countries," and (38) "Small Island Developing States" provides details of the challenges and opportunities for this almost entirely Global South group.

http://www.aseansec.org

On the official Web site of the Association of Southeast Asian Nations are information and documents relevant to ASEAN, news about countries in the region, and somewhat self-serving Web pages constructed by each member state.

http://www.unctad.org

This part of the home page of the United Nations Conference on Trade and Development focuses on issues regarding the world's least developed countries.

http://www.un.org/womenwatch

This French-based bilingual site provides links to various research, documents, organizations, and activities that concern the role of women in the development process.

http://www.twnside.org.sg

Based in Malaysia, the Third World Network provides a strong perspective through a diverse array of analyses, policy papers, and information on the full range of issues facing developing countries, including trade and development, environment, human rights, and globalization.

Chapter 15
The Transitional Developed Countries

Learning Objectives

15.1 Trace the historical, political, and economic development of the postcommunist states.

15.2 Evaluate the attempts by the postcommunist states to achieve prosperity through a transition to market economies.

15.3 Assess the efforts by postcommunist states to balance democratic freedoms and political stability.

15.4 Analyze the impact of the fall of the Soviet system on the security of postcommunist states.

15.5 Analyze the pursuit of prosperity by the Latin American transitional developed countries

15.6 Characterize the quest for stability in the Latin American Transitionals.

15.7 Describe the security goals of the Latin American Transitionals.

15.8 Explain the BRICS concept.

15.9 Analyze the pursuit of prosperity by the BRICS.

15.10 Characterize the quest for stability in the BRICS.

15.11 Describe the security goals of the BRICS.

15.12 Identify the factors associated with the prospects for further development in the transitional developed countries

It was not easy being Hungary in the twentieth century. As a landlocked country in the center of Europe, Hungary was drawn into every continental drama. It was the junior partner in the Austro-Hungarian Empire, but was on the losing side in World War I. As a result of the war, Hungary lost two-thirds of its land, and more than 5 million ethnic Hungarians found themselves living within the new borders of other countries. Communists and right-wing fascists fought for Hungary's soul between the wars.

Hungary then sided with Germany during World War II, and by the end of the war the country was physically and psychologically devastated. At this point, troops from the Soviet Union helped the communist leaders take control of the Hungarian government. By the late 1940s, Hungary was part of the Soviet Bloc of states and had one of the most repressive communist regimes in Europe. Huge numbers of the regime's critics were killed or imprisoned, and there was minimal prosperity under the rigid command political economy.

Frustrated citizens took to the streets in a 1956 rebellion and tried to set up a more democratic government; but the Soviets invaded with more than 150,000 troops and brutally crushed the "freedom fighters." Although the near-totalitarian government ruled firmly, there were experiments in the 1970s and 1980s with more private enterprise in the economy and expanded rights for workers, and Hungary was said to have established "goulash communism" (that is, combining some of every approach into the political economy pot).

Hungary was among the leading countries when the peoples of Eastern Europe were able to throw off the communist yoke in 1989. Hungary shifted immediately to democratic politics, holding its first open and competitive multiparty election in 1990. It also abandoned the command political economy, quickly privatizing almost half of the state-owned enterprises. Between 1990 and 1998, the share of GDP generated by the private sector rose rapidly, from 25 percent to 80 percent. The state also withdrew many of its communist-era human and social services to citizens.

This combination of changes resulted in a few difficult years of transition and financial hardship for most people in the society. But foreign direct investment flowed in, and Hungary became a poster child for the remarkably rapid transformation of some former Communist Bloc countries into relatively prosperous, market-based economies. It joined the European Union (EU) in 2004 and became a member of the North Atlantic Treaty Organization (NATO). Hungary's 10 million citizens enjoy strong political rights and civil liberties.

Unfortunately, extensive borrowing and the dead weight of the many state enterprises that were not sold off became a serious drag on the economy, especially when the global economic meltdown occurred in 2007 and onward. It has averaged only 1.6 percent per year economic growth since 2000. As economic conditions have again become very difficult for many citizens, confidence in political leaders and political parties has dropped significantly. A nationalist political party has dominated the last two elections, and it has cut back on democratic practices and asserted more control over the political economy. Nonetheless, Hungary has made a quite impressive transition from the oppressive life and underachieving economy of the communist era to its current state. Freedom House rates it as a free, liberal democracy with a high score (1.5). Hungary has a GDP per capita (PPP) of $19,800, is in the "very high" group on the Human Development Index (.831), and has the fourth most equal income distribution in the world. It seems more promising to be Hungary in the twenty-first century (CIA 2014; World Bank 2013).

As suggested in the discussion of Figure 10.1, Hungary is among a group of countries termed *transitional developed countries*. They are characterized by levels of economic and social development that are lower than those in the Global North but are notably higher than those of countries in the Global South. They also seem to be transitioning toward higher levels of economic and political development at rates that could result in their classification as developed countries relatively soon. Based on Figure 10.1 and these characteristics, this chapter focuses on three subsets of countries where the forces of positive development seem especially strong. These three groups are termed the postcommunist developed countries (PCDCs), the Latin American Transitionals, and the BRICS, a grouping of five special cases from the transitional and developing country categories.

An analysis of such countries in this final chapter might be helpful for enhancing our understanding of the ever-changing and dynamic world of contemporary politics. Currently, they are revealing case studies of "countries in the middle" within our framework of analysis. We consider their current situation as well as the conditions under which we would expect the transitional countries to improve. Chapter 10 indicated that positive development is not inevitable. Thus this chapter asks: What combination of factors is likely to lead to a successful transition to the Global North level of development? What factors suggest a failure to transition? Hopefully, you will be able to apply the concepts and political knowledge you have learned in earlier chapters to explore the broad patterns of change these groups are encountering and make your own assessments of how these transitional countries will cope with the challenges they face in their quest for prosperity, stability, and security. Let's examine postcommunist developed countries first.

The Postcommunist Developed Countries

15.1 Trace the historical, political, and economic development of the postcommunist developed countries.

After the Soviet Bloc broke up in the late 1980s and early 1990s, 29 new national political systems emerged, including 15 states carved out of the former Soviet Union. Many NGOs treat this set of 29 countries as a group. Freedom House (2013) clusters these countries as "Nations in Transit," and the World Bank (2011) referred to the entire group as "Emerging Europe and Central Asia" (Western Europe is part of another group of "high-income economies"). However, based on the classification scheme in Figure 10.1, our analysis excludes from the transitional group those 11 postcommunist countries that still have the characteristics of other developing countries (e.g., Albania, Armenia, Georgia, Moldova, Tajikistan, Ukraine, Uzbekistan).

Thus, this chapter focuses on the 18 countries from this group that are at moderate levels on economic and social development in Figure 10.1. This group is designated the *postcommunist developed countries (PCDCs)*. These PCDCs include some of the states that emerged from the Soviet Union (e.g., Belarus, Estonia, Kazakhstan, Latvia, Lithuania, Russia) and most of the states that evolved from the Soviet Union's previous allies in Central and Eastern Europe (e.g., Bulgaria, Croatia, the Czech Republic, Hungary, Poland, Romania, Serbia, Slovakia, Slovenia). These countries have a combined population of about 240 million.

Post-communist St. Petersburg, Russia bustles with commerce and consumerism even in the shadow of its Communist past.

Some of the PCDCs, particularly those in Central and Eastern Europe, have been engaged in a process of substantial economic and political transformation similar to that of Hungary described above. Until the late 1980s, these countries were communist states and were trying to achieve prosperity, stability, and security under the structure of a command political economy and totalitarianism (for 60 years in the Soviet Union and 40 years in Central and Eastern Europe). Since about 1990, these states have abandoned their communist ideologies and attempted to transform themselves into more market-oriented political economies and to implement democratic politics. These sweeping changes were the watershed events in the shift in the international system to the post–Cold War period (described in Chapter 13). However, a few of the PCDCs that emerged from the former Soviet Union, most notably Russia, have resisted the strongest currents of change. In these countries, the political regimes remain authoritarian and the political economies have strong elements of state capitalism (as described in Chapter 8).

Figure 10.1 reflects that these countries are relatively advanced on the social development dimension. Their populations are well educated and mainly urban, and they are incorporating advanced technologies into their economies and their private lives. The states have adopted democratic political processes and are institutionalizing them in varied degrees. The political economies in most states were significantly depressed during the economic transitions in the 1990s, but their GDP per capita measures are now increasing and nine have reached the level of high-income countries on the World Bank's

Table 15.1 Acid Test II

	Kappa	Lambda	Mu
Governmental type	Nondemocracy	Electoral Democracy	Nondemocracy
Political rights (1 [highest]–7, Freedom House)	7	4	6
Civil liberties (1 [highest]–7, Freedom House)	6	4	5
Press freedom	Not free (15th percentile)	Free (72nd percentile)	Not free (19th percentile)
Significant political parties	1	54	7
% females in legislature	37%	12%	11%
Life expectancy	71	67	70
Human Development Index	.912	.770	.788
Literacy rate	99%	98%	99%
% below poverty line	2%	44%	11%
Serious crimes/100,000	687	5,490	3,650
GDP/capita: 10 year average annual growth	2.7%	–4.7%	4.8%
Inflation	3%	68%	7%
Gini index of income inequality	21.5	48.7	42.0
Top:Bottom 20% of income distribution	5.4:1	12.6:1	7.6:1
GNI per capita (not PPP)	$3,200	$1,600	$12,700

measure (2013). Some citizens in these countries support the shift to a market economy, although others are dissatisfied with the effects of this change on themselves and on their society. Thus, the next sections explore their current quest for prosperity, stability, and security. But before you explore the details of these countries in transition, you are invited to examine Table 15.1 and then take one more "acid test" in Compare in 15.

Compare in 15

Acid Test II

Here is another acid test. Before reading further, examine Table 15.1 closely. As in the Compare in 1, assume that you were born in one of these three countries 20 years ago, but you do not know your life conditions at birth (e.g., gender, ethnicity, family wealth, intelligence, and so on). *Into which of these three countries would you prefer to have been born? Why?*

Each of the three countries seems to offer a different bundle of virtues and shortcomings, and you are forced to make trade-offs. If you especially value economic and social stability, safety, and equality, you might choose Kappa. Lambda might be your choice if individual rights and freedoms are given highest priority. And the economic vibrancy and potential of Mu might lead you to prefer to be a young adult there, despite its political and social negatives.

In this acid test, the three alternatives actually characterize the *same* country at three recent time periods. Kappa is the Soviet Union in 1989, just before it broke into multiple countries; Lambda is Russia in 1999, after 10 years of postcommunist adjustments; and Mu is Russia in 2013. Over this brief period, Russians have experienced a roller-coaster ride from a rigid and repressive totalitarian system that did provide basic economic and personal security (Kappa) to a free but impoverished, dangerous, and chaotic system of democracy and free enterprise (Lambda), and then to an authoritarian system with greater economic prosperity (Mu).

Kappa: The Russian people lived for seven decades under a system guided by the principles of Marxism–Leninism, where a commitment to equality promised everyone a decent standard of living; access to affordable education, jobs, and health care; and a safe, secure life. The political system did generally deliver on these goals, although the level of prosperity and the quality of goods were modest at best, and life was relatively dull under a repressive, one-party state that substantially limited personal freedoms. The Soviet Union was one of the world's two great military superpowers and had substantial international influence. However, shortcomings in the envisioned prosperity and quality of life led (then) president Mikhail Gorbachev to begin loosening restrictions on the political and economic systems in the late 1980s, facilitating the collapse of the Soviet Union by 1991.

Lambda: The 1990s was a period of complex transitions as the new state of Russia abandoned communism. There were efforts to establish a competitive, multiparty democracy, privatize the political economy, and severely cut the provision of communist-era services by the state. These changes were generally successful in producing a free society and market economy; but the transition also resulted in a negative growth rate, surging unemployment, hyperinflation, (e.g., prices increased twenty-six-fold in 1992 alone), a drastic increase in poverty and hardship (e.g., an increase from 2 percent in 1989 to 50 percent in 2000), a vast and widening gap between the rich and the poor, and skyrocketing crime. Amid pervasive corruption in the society, two-thirds of the lucrative enterprises moved into the hands of insiders (especially powerful entrepreneurs called oligarchs), whose agenda was to acquire the society's economic assets at bargain prices and then exploit those assets ruthlessly. This *crony capitalism—the processes enabling members of the old (Communist Party) elite to use their connections to prosper as the new economic elite—*did produce a small proportion of very wealthy people.

Mu: Since 2000, the political system has been dominated by Vladimir Putin, a former KGB (secret police) officer who has changed many aspects of the Russia of the 1990s. He has been popular among many Russians for his aggressive attempts to reassert Russia's power in regional politics. The political economy has generally been reformulated as a system of state capitalism. Economic growth has been mostly positive, benefitting from high prices for oil and other commodities. Most Russians have experienced improvements in their material prosperity, compared to the Kappa and Lambda periods. Crime rates have dropped from the Lambda period as law enforcement and security services have reestablished their traditional, heavy-handed approach toward crime. Corruption remains high, although lower than during the Lambda period. Despite a multiparty system, Putin has reasserted very strong authoritarian control of political life—jailing rivals, stifling political opposition, and muffling the media—and Russia is again "not free" according to Freedom House. The Russia-in-transition of 2013 seems to offer its citizens, especially those with entrepreneurial zeal, the promise of substantial opportunities for economic advancement. However, many Russians who valued the transition to democracy and increased civil liberties are deeply distressed by the restraints on their political and personal freedoms. And those who relied on state support or have been unable to adjust to the new political economy of state capitalism look back with some longing at the old days under communism (CIA 2014; UNDP 2013; Goldman 2003, 2008; McFaul, Stoner-Weiss, and Bunce 2010).

Further questions

1. What criteria guided your choice? Did they seem similar to the priorities you applied on Compare in 1 (Acid Test I)?

2. Is it reasonable that many Russians now say they prefer the Russia of the 1980s (Kappa) to the current conditions (Lambda)?

Goal: Prosperity

15.2 Evaluate the attempts by the postcommunist states to achieve prosperity through a transition to market economies.

Strategy

When they were communist regimes, the principal strategy for achieving the goal of the equal distribution of abundant goods and material welfare to the entire population was the *command political economy*, as detailed in Chapter 8. The state and the Communist Party, guided by a comprehensive plan, attempted to control nearly all of society's valued resources. Most citizens had access to inexpensive or free health care, education, food, and shelter, and most had economic security against such problems as illness and old age. Thus, like Kappa (in Compare in 15), these countries did reach relatively high levels on most quality of life measures (such as the Human Development Index). However, these countries' economic performance (on measures such as GDP per capita) was disappointing. As described in Chapter 8, the rigid planning and limited incentives in these command economies resulted in low productivity and poor-quality products. This caused a serious mismatch between demand and supply. That is, there was persistently more demand by the people for quality goods, from bread to housing, than there was available supply of these goods.

Since the early 1990s, most of the PCDCs have attempted to achieve a rapid transition to a market political economy. Private firms produce goods for profit, and the prices of most goods are determined by supply and demand. Central planning has been abandoned, and most state-owned enterprises have been sold to private actors (privatized) or shut down. In 1990, the average proportion of GDP in the private sector in these countries was less than 15 percent. By 2006, GDP in nearly all PCDCs was between 75 and 80 percent private (Estrin et al. 2009). Fourteen of the 18 PCDCs are now among the top half of all (177) countries in economic freedom, led by Estonia at tenth (Heritage Foundation 2014). The political economies of the others, including Belarus, Kazakhstan, and Russia, are best described as state capitalism.

Performance

During the initial years of transition, most PCDCs experienced a substantial decline in GDP and hyperinflation (inflation averaged higher than 100 percent per year in all but two of the PCDCs) (World Bank 1996: Table A3). The real income of most people dropped substantially, cuts in welfare services were deep, and unemployment soared. The number of people in absolute poverty increased enormously in less than a decade—from about 14 million people just prior to the "fall of communism" in 1988 (4 percent of the region's population) to 147 million in 1996 (40 percent of the population). This is the period of Russia-as-Lambda in Compare in 15.

Since the late 1990s, the economies and the living standards of many people in the PCDCs have improved. Eleven of the PCDCs are now among the 28 member states of

Figure 15.1 Prosperity Measures for Selected Transitional Developed Countries

SOURCE: UNDP (2013)

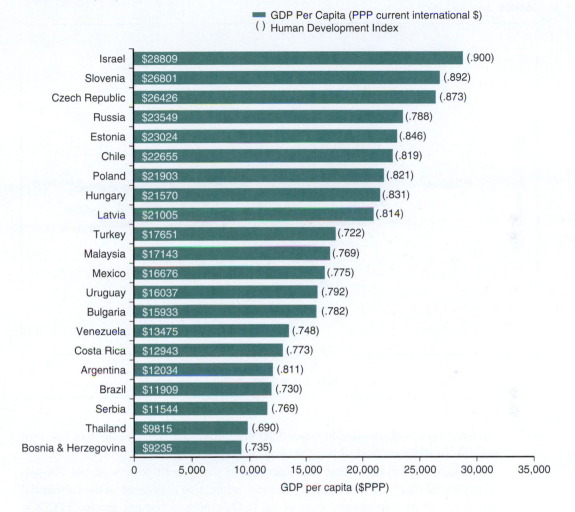

Legend:
- GDP Per Capita (PPP current international $)
- ( ) Human Development Index

Country	GDP Per Capita	Human Development Index
Israel	$28809	(.900)
Slovenia	$26801	(.892)
Czech Republic	$26426	(.873)
Russia	$23549	(.788)
Estonia	$23024	(.846)
Chile	$22655	(.819)
Poland	$21903	(.821)
Hungary	$21570	(.831)
Latvia	$21005	(.814)
Turkey	$17651	(.722)
Malaysia	$17143	(.769)
Mexico	$16676	(.775)
Uruguay	$16037	(.792)
Bulgaria	$15933	(.782)
Venezuela	$13475	(.748)
Costa Rica	$12943	(.773)
Argentina	$12034	(.811)
Brazil	$11909	(.730)
Serbia	$11544	(.769)
Thailand	$9815	(.690)
Bosnia & Herzegovina	$9235	(.735)

GDP per capita ($PPP)

the EU, and 6 others are in various stages of potential membership. As Figure 15.1 indicates, there is a relatively high level of prosperity in some PCDCs, especially Russia and most of the Central European countries, such as Slovenia, the Czech Republic, Slovakia, Hungary, and Poland. Nine of them now achieve "very high" Human Development Index scores, placing them in the range of some Global North countries.

Figure 15.2 provides information on economic growth rates in the transitional developed countries. Can you see why the most desirable location for a country in Figure 15.2 would be in the upper-right corner? Why might upper left be less impressive than it seems? Notice that for all the countries in Figure 15.2, the correlation is *negative*: That is, countries that had higher growth in one period tended to have lower growth in the other period. Looking more closely at Figure 15.2 reveals that most of the PCDCs generally had relatively low or negative economic growth rates in the 1990s

Figure 15.2 Comparative Economic Growth Rates in Selected Transitional Countries, 1990–2000 and 2000–2012

SOURCE: World Bank 2013

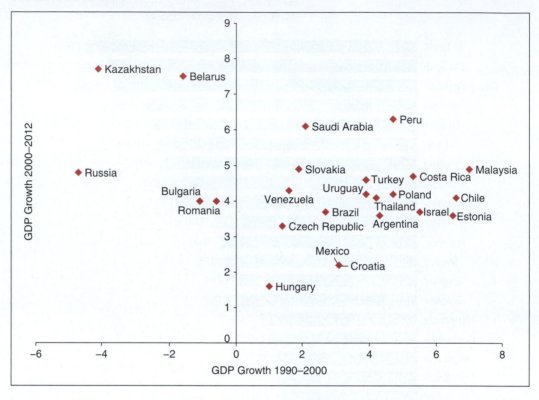

but have improved considerably since 2000, with many averaging more than 4 percent per year (well above the Eurozone average of 1.1 percent).

Moreover, it appears that the main reason the overall pattern across the two time periods for all the transitional countries is negative is because of the substantial differences in growth among many of the PCDCs. Notice that one group of PCDCs, including Kazakhstan, Belarus, and Russia, has negative average annual growth from 1990 to 2000 but high rates of positive growth since 2000. These countries experienced substantial difficulties in adjusting their political economies to the global system in the postcommunist period. However, they seem to have managed to at least stabilize their economies more recently under state capitalist systems. Another group of the PCDCs, including Estonia, Slovakia, and the Czech Republic, have transitioned to a free market economy more effectively and have sustained positive annual growth for the entire period since 1990. In general, for all of the PCDCs, prosperity and optimism about the economic future are more evident among the population living in major cities and among the younger cohorts; poverty and disillusionment are more common in nonurban areas and among the older generations, who have lost nearly all the social services and welfare they received under communism.

Challenges

Because their political economies now function like other market systems in the global economy, the postcommunist developed countries face all the formidable challenges to sustaining prosperity that confront the developed countries of the Global North, as detailed in Chapter 13. Competition for markets and resources is ruthless, flows of capital and labor are difficult to manage, and nonstate actors are hard to control. Since the global recession that began in 2008, most PCDC economies have struggled with challenges such as low economic growth and high unemployment, although not as much as the Global North.

Moreover, the ongoing transitions of their political economies generate additional challenges for the PCDCs. First, the state and key economic actors must continue to *streamline their regulatory systems* and *institutionalize free market mechanisms* (e.g., capital markets, business contracts, business law), which did not exist under the command economy. In some PCDCs, a combination of state capitalism, business cartels, and corruption inhibit economic growth. Second, these states must *establish an appropriate level of welfare distribution* for the many people whose material living conditions have declined significantly. The older cohorts in these countries were socialized to believe in their right to cradle-to-grave support from the state. Now, many face the dual hardship caused by both economic transition and their governments' drastic reductions of the large state subsidies for food, shelter, health care, education, transportation, and other benefits. Third, the PCDCs must *ensure that the vigorous new group politics does not undermine economic policymaking*. In the electoral democracies, many citizens have voted out each set of incumbent leaders and parties, whom they blame for the negative impacts from economic transitions and from the harsh effects of a turbulent global economy. This repeated turnover of government control results in substantial political instability and makes it difficult for any political leadership to implement tough economic policies and retain popular support (Bonker 2006).

Goal: Stability

15.3 Assess the efforts by postcommunist states to balance democratic freedoms and political stability.

Strategies

As communist political regimes, a basic assumption in Soviet Bloc countries was: prosperity + equality = stability. That is, social and political stability would result because the people were satisfied with the relatively equal distribution of abundant goods and services. Although these countries did have among the world's most equal distributions of wealth and did provide many inexpensive goods and services to all citizens, the major shortcoming in the stability equation was that the systems were unable to produce goods in abundance so there were chronic shortages of most goods.

The failure of the economy to provide adequate goods was a major source of citizen dissatisfaction and potential instability.

To create stability in the absence of prosperity, these authoritarian states utilized four key instruments of social control over many aspects of people's lives: (1) the *Communist Party*, whose active members, about 10 percent of population, acted as a watchdog against dissidents; (2) a huge *governmental apparatus* of administrators, police, and others who enforced obedience; (3) *rewards* (e.g., desired jobs, better housing) were allocated to those who were obedient, and *sanctions* (e.g., loss of benefits, prison) were imposed on those who resisted; and (4) extensive use of the agents of *political socialization* (e.g., schools, mass social organizations, the media) to drill in communist ideology. Overall, these social controls created a highly stable but also highly oppressive environment for most people.

During the 1980s, opposition to the Communist Party became more open and personal freedoms expanded significantly, with an enormous boost from Soviet premier Mikhail Gorbachev's policy of *glasnost*—a tolerance of public discussion and criticism of the political, economic, and social systems. Then, in 1989, the citizens in every East European country filled the streets, demanding political, economic, and human rights. After decades of repression, the Communist Party leadership capitulated in country after country, lacking either the will or the capacity to retain power. A signal moment was November 9, 1989, when the Berlin Wall, the most notorious symbol of the Iron Curtain, was opened, allowing a joyous reunion of 1 million East and West Berliners. Except in Romania (where events corresponded to a violent revolution from above), the dramatic changes occurred in these countries with so little violence that they are best described as "democratic revolutions" (see Chapter 12). By December 1991, even the Soviet Union "died" and was replaced by 15 independent countries.

These countries adopted new constitutions that established hybrid governments, with a president and a legislature–plus–prime minister selected through (mixed-member) proportional representation electoral systems (see Chapter 7). In most of the hybrids, the cabinet handles day-to-day policymaking. But the president has substantial power, including the right to dismiss the prime minister and cabinet, a power that has been exercised in response to citizen dissatisfaction with the governments' handling of the major economic and political transitions. In countries where these hybrid systems are still not fully institutionalized, there are situations in which the power relationships between president and prime minister have become very strained (Schleiter and Morgan-Jones 2009).

There is a *freedom divide* among these countries (Puddington 2011). Most of the PCDCs have institutionalized the political structures and processes of democracy. Elections are fair, open, and very competitive; multiple parties hold seats in the legislature; and there are smooth leadership turnovers. The citizens' political rights and civil liberties are extensive, and there is a vigorous political discourse. Table 15.2 shows that 13 of the PCDCs are now classified as "free" by Freedom House (2013), including 8 that have already been rated as "consolidated democracies." Macedonia is only "partly free" and is among the six PCDCs characterized as "semi-consolidated

Table 15.2 Democracy Rankings of Postcommunist Developed Countries

Country	Freedom House Ranking and Score	EIU Democracy Index Classification and Score[a]
Consolidated Democracies		
Czech Republic	Free: 1.0	Full democracy 8.19
Slovenia	Free: 1.0	Flawed democracy 7.88
Estonia	Free: 1.0	Flawed democracy 7.61
Slovakia	Free: 1.0	Flawed democracy 7.35
Lithuania	Free: 1.0	Flawed democracy 7.24
Poland	Free: 1.0	Flawed democracy 7.12
Hungary	Free: 1.5	Flawed democracy 6.96
Latvia	Free: 2.0	Flawed democracy 7.05
Semi-Consolidated Democracies		
Croatia	Free: 1.5	Flawed democracy 6.93
Bulgaria	Free: 2.0	Flawed democracy 6.72
Romania	Free: 2.0	Flawed democracy 6.54
Serbia	Free: 2.0	Flawed democracy 6.33
Montenegro	Free: 2.5	Flawed democracy 6.05
Macedonia	Partly Free: 3.0	Flawed democracy 6.16
Consolidated Authoritarian Regimes		
Russia	Not Free: 5.5	Authoritarian regime 3.74
Kazakhstan	Not Free: 5.5	Authoritarian regime 2.95
Azerbaijan	Not Free: 6.0	Authoritarian regime 3.15
Belarus	Not Free: 6.5	Authoritarian regime 3.04

[a] The EIU Democracy index ranges from high democracy (10.00) to low (0.00).

SOURCE: Freedom House (2014); Economist Intelligence Unit (2013)

democracies" at this point. On the Democracy Index from the EIU (2013), only the Czech Republic is rated as a full democracy, with most of the others ranked "free" by Freedom House scoring only as *"flawed democracies,"* usually due to lower scores on the level of political participation and the weakness of a democratic political culture, despite relatively high scores on electoral process and pluralism.

In contrast, four (Azerbaijan, Belarus, Kazakhstan, and Russia) are "consolidated authoritarian regimes" that have reverted to state repression and control mechanisms similar to those of the communist era. All are classified as "not free." Since Vladimir Putin's regime began in 2000, Russia has steadily reduced democratic practices, political rights, and civil liberties. The three other authoritarian regimes have each had only one or two entrenched leaders since 1990. Like Russia, they have reimposed Soviet-era restrictions on democratic practices such as free speech, freedom of the press, and political opposition, as well as strong state control of the economy (Freedom House 2014; Shkolnikov 2009).

Challenges

Currently, most of the PCDCs face significant destabilizing forces related to social disorder, nationality issues, and globalization. Many of these countries, including Slovenia, Hungary, Slovakia, Belarus, the Czech Republic, and Kazakhstan, still have among the highest levels of income equality in the world (measured by the Gini index of inequality; recall Table 8.1). However, *economic and social inequality* have increased since 1989 in most of these transitional countries in the absence of communist controls, and the gaps between the rich and poor have become substantial and apparent to everyone in these societies.

SOCIAL DISORDER   The combination of freewheeling capitalism, the decline in communist-era social controls, and increases in inequality has resulted in a rise in *social disorder*. This is reflected in a decline in citizens' obedience to laws and rules and is particularly evident in the high incidence of crime. In Russia, more than 4,000 mafia crime groups are engaged in widespread extortion, auto theft, drug peddling, burglary, and other criminal activities. In the first five years of postcommunism, for example, reported serious crimes increased 270 percent in Romania, 222 percent in Bulgaria, and 105 percent in Poland (Murphy 1995). While crime rates have now stabilized, countries that were accustomed to almost no violent crime under communism are now attempting to cope with distressing levels of crimes against both people and property. In the more authoritarian PCDCs, the police are either ineffective or corrupt, and citizens live in fear of organized crime, random criminal violence, and even the police (McFaul 1998).

NATIONALITY CONFLICTS   A few nationality groups, such as the Poles and the East Germans (who were reunited with their West German brothers and sisters in 1990), now live in ethnically homogeneous states. In 1993, Czechoslovakia peacefully broke into two states based on its two main ethnic groups (Czechs and Slovaks). However, *identity politics and ethnonationalism* (recall Chapter 5) threaten the stability of many PCDCs because they have significant minority populations. Marginalized nationality groups are increasingly active in demanding greater autonomy, and the majority group has often responded by aggressively asserting its domination.

Thus, internal nation-based conflict has produced disorder in many PCDCs. Yugoslavia, a complex multiethnic state under communism, became a brutal battleground as different nation-based groups killed more than 250,000 of their neighbors during the 1990s and still struggle with interethnic hostilities despite the breakup of the Balkans into six countries (recall the opening section of Chapter 12). Current nation-based hostility in several countries is particularly directed against the Roma (gypsies) and against those of Russian heritage who live in other PCDCs (because Russians were transplanted to control other parts of the Soviet Bloc during communism). Other conflicts that have exploded into separatist violence include several in highly multinational Russia (e.g., Chechnya and Ingushetia). Russia also invaded Georgia in support of the demands for autonomy by the South Ossetians and reannexed parts of Ukraine (e.g., Crimea) where most people have Russian identity.

ENTRY INTO EUROPE AND GLOBAL SOCIETY Until 1989, the Iron Curtain countries restricted their populations both physically and culturally. The people were kept in, and the world, including the many complex cultural and economic changes that were occurring, was kept out. After decades of relative isolation, most PCDCs are now fully engaged with global society. Unrestricted travel, unlimited media exposure, the huge expansion of communications technologies, and the effects of EU membership on 11 of the PCDCs have exposed the people to a dizzying array of new experiences, expectations, and cultural norms. If their political system does not deliver the material life and good governance that the people now expect, the decline in support for the country's leaders and the political institutions undermines the stability of both the state and the society. Most of the PCDCs that have attempted to institutionalize democracy and the market economy find that sustaining an effective response to these destabilizing factors has been difficult. In response, governments in some of the PCDCs have reverted to authoritarianism.

Goal: Security

15.4 **Analyze the impact of the fall of the Soviet system on the security of the postcommunist states.**

In Halford John Mackinder's (1996) famous nineteenth-century geopolitical analysis, Eastern Europe and Western Russia were the essential "heartland": Control of that region would ensure world dominance. The region has been a battlefield for the last 200 years, including devastating invasions by the French under Napoleon, during World War I, and by the Germans under Hitler during World War II.

Given this history, the Soviet Union perceived itself to be surrounded by hostile threats to its survival after World War II. To the east was capitalist Japan, a historical military adversary. To the southeast was China, with its huge population and alternative vision of communism. To the southwest, the militancy of Islamic fundamentalism presented a clear danger, given its antipathy to communism and the large population of Muslims in the Soviet Union's southwestern regions. To the west were the major capitalist powers, with their deep animosity to communist systems and with NATO's devastating military (including nuclear) capabilities stretched along almost half of the Soviet Bloc's border.

As a consequence, the Soviet Union placed exceptionally high importance on security goals and aimed for unchallengeable military power. To create a buffer zone, the Soviet Union gained control over territory on all sides, annexing some areas and creating a bloc of subservient states in Central and Eastern Europe. The Soviet Bloc built the world's most powerful military for conventional warfare, and the Soviet Union had near parity with NATO allies in air power and nuclear capabilities. From the late 1940s until the late 1980s, the Cold War rivalry between the Soviet Union and the United States dominated the bipolar international system and spawned a huge military buildup on each side. Soviet leaders from Stalin to Gorbachev opted for guns over butter, spending 9 to 15 percent of national income on defense. This high military expenditure substantially reduced the resources available for economic growth and the distribution of welfare and is a key reason for the demise of the Soviet system.

In the postcommunist period, the Soviet security system changed dramatically. Some of the countries in the bloc did not survive—either disappearing (East Germany) or splitting up (Yugoslavia, Czechoslovakia, and even the Soviet Union itself, which was replaced by 15 countries in 1991). Ten former members of the Soviet Bloc joined their old enemy NATO, despite strong opposition from Russia. For Russia under Putin, the security response to the more multipolar global system has been to strengthen ties with the enemies of its enemies (e.g., Iran, Syria, Venezuela) and to rebuild its military. In 2012, Russia increased its military spending by 16 percent, and its military budget for 2012–2015 includes a planned increase of more than 40 percent. Although diminished from its Cold War strength, Russia's military machine still includes a huge standing army and more stockpiled (6,700) and deployed (1,800) nuclear weapons than China (about 250 total) and the United States (about 5,550 stockpiled and 2,150 deployed) combined (SIPRI 2013).

While Russia, the United States, and the other major powers have undertaken some reduction in nuclear weapons, the increasing presence of weapons of mass destruction and terrorism around their borders results in significant security risks for the PCDCs (Davenport and Taylor 2013). And Russia's military resurgence, its assertive foreign policy, its reconquest of part of Ukraine, and its nuclear arsenal are viewed with alarm by most of its geopolitical neighbors, including many other PCDCs (Aslund and Kuchins 2009; McFaul, Stoner-Weiss, and Bunce 2010). Some insecurity is also associated with the decline of national identity for citizens in the PCDCs that have joined the EU and NATO. All of the postcommunist developed countries are attempting to adapt to the new global security environment.

The Latin American Transitionals

As noted in Chapter 10, there is a set of Latin American countries within the transitional developed countries classification in Figure 10.1 that also seems to form a grouping. This group includes Chile, Mexico, Uruguay, Venezuela, Costa Rica, Brazil, and Argentina. These countries generally share many aspects of culture and language, history, class structure, and, of course, region. They were colonized early, and most have been independent for more than 150 years. They transitioned from rural and agrarian systems to societies that are mainly urban, but considerable wealth is still concentrated in natural resources and agriculture. Among the well-institutionalized structures in these societies are the armed forces, the church, and an upper-class elite. Their politics has generally been elite-dominated and historically was authoritarian, often under a strong, singular leader. In recent decades, democratic practices are the norm, although political instability is not uncommon. Our examination of these *Latin American Transitionals* focuses on their contemporary quest for greater prosperity, stability, and security.

Goal: Prosperity

15.5   **Analyze the pursuit of prosperity by the Latin American transitional developed countries.**

Unlike the PCDCs, the Latin American Transitionals have not engaged in recent, rapid transformations of their political economies. However, prior to the 1970s, many of these political economies did have forms of statism, with substantial state ownership and control of the economy. Beginning with Chile, many of the Latin American Transitionals began to shift toward market economies from the 1970s forward. As the neoliberal model was embraced, state enterprises were sold off, privatization of government services was extensive, and foreign investment was encouraged. GDP per capita has risen, and nearly all have averaged annual economic growth of more than 3.5 percent since 1990 (Figure 15.2).

Las presidentes: Presidents Cristina Fernandez de Kirchner of Argentina, Michelle Bachelet of Chile, and Dilma Rousseff of Brazil (left to right) consult in Chile in 2014.

However, this growth was not consistent; it tended to occur in spurts, followed by periods of economic decline and inflation, rather like the Latin American Transitionals' less developed regional neighbors (recall Chapter 14). For example, Mexico suffered a "peso crisis" in 1994, Brazil's economy has been highly volatile (see Focus in 15), and the economies of Argentina and Uruguay dropped precipitously in 2002. Argentina is indicative of the up-and-down pattern. In 2002, Argentina was in a severe period of negative growth and unemployment, defaulted on $130 billion in bonds, devalued its currency, and was in deep economic crisis. After a bumpy decade, the economy exploded in 2010 and 2011, driven by manufacturing and food exports, and averaged about 9 percent growth. However, the economy has more recently struggled again, with very low growth and high inflation (25 percent) (Kraul 2011). Thus the average economic growth rates for the Latin American Transitionals, which seem generally positive in Figure 15.2, can be understood as masking years of high growth and years of relatively low or negative growth.

On the one hand, some citizens in the Latin American Transitionals enjoy an extremely high standard of living, many material possessions, and quality services (e.g., health care, education). Argentina and Chile (and soon Uruguay) have HDI scores above .800. On the other hand, many people across Latin American have suffered a serious reduction in their standard of living over the last three decades. Those who are very poor experience a life as harsh as that in many of the developing countries.

In addition, Panama and Chile are among the 20 countries with the world's highest levels of wealth inequality, and every Latin American Transitional except Argentina and Venezuela is among the world's one-third most unequal countries (CIA 2014).

While the reasons for these features of the Latin American economies are disputed, some analysts attribute the negative features to the same sorts of weaknesses listed above for PCDCs. Privatization, corruption, international competition, and exploitation by multinationals and "crony capitalists" within the countries have taken a severe toll on their political economies (Weintraub 2009). As the Latin American transitional economies have been buffeted by the forces of globalization and high economic volatility, their governments have implemented structural adjustment programs required by the International Monetary Fund. Cuts in government spending and restrictions on the money supply have resulted in increased unemployment and reductions in government services.

Some political elites have sought to turn frustration with these economic results of neoliberalism and globalization into political advantage for populist parties, resulting in electoral success in some countries like Bolivia and Venezuela and the implementation of extensive programs redistributing goods and money to the lower economic groups (Handlin 2013). For example, Venezuela's late president Hugo Chavez promoted "twenty-first century socialism" as an alternative development path for Latin America. The Venezuelan model emphasizes stronger state engagement in the political economy, with increased state ownership of major resources, more extensive redistribution of benefits to the less advantaged, and a resistance to key aspects of economic globalization. The issues associated with economic liberalization policies pervade not only the strategies for prosperity but also the dynamics of political stability and democratization in the Latin American Transitionals (de Cordoba and Vyas 2012; Wiarda and Kline 2007).

Focus in 15

Order and Progress in Brazil: Sometimes

The motto on the Brazilian flag is "Order and Progress." The vision of order and progress has guided much of Brazilian policy since the founding of the republic in 1889, but recent history has cast doubt on its ability to sustain this vision. Brazil is the fifth largest country (in area) in the world, is sixth largest in population (almost 203 million), and has vast natural resources. In many ways, Brazil reflects the promise of development in the twenty-first century—but it also epitomizes the troubles associated with that quest.

Progress

From the mid-1960s to the mid-1970s, the state took the lead in guiding Brazil's industrialization, emphasizing import substitution and promoting exports. The involvement of international capital and foreign corporations was encouraged. The results were impressive. Brazil's economic development was praised worldwide as a "miracle," with yearly growth averaging 10 percent. Brazil's economy is now larger than that of all the rest of South America and is the eighth largest in the world. Since 2000, its average annual growth has been a respectable 3.7 percent, with strong performance in recent years. It is a BRICS country due to its increasing impact on the global economy. It is a leader among the developing countries in the production of many goods, including agricultural exports such as coffee, sugar, and cocoa; minerals such as tin, gold, iron ore, and bauxite; and industrial goods such as textiles, cement, automobiles, weapons, and machinery. Since 1970, life expectancy has increased 14 years (to age 74), infant mortality has dropped to one-third its former level, and adult literacy has risen to 90 percent. Brazil won the global competition to host the 2014 World Cup and the 2016 Summer Olympics.

Order

Politically, Brazil is a constitutional democracy. The government is a federal republic, with an elected president who has dominant power over the bicameral National Congress. It has a multiparty system, universal and compulsory voting, an independent judiciary, and a partly free press. Its Freedom House rating is "free," and its citizens enjoy relatively high levels of political rights and civil liberties. There have been two decades of competitive and fair elections, including the smooth transition to the presidency of Dilma Rousseff in 2011 after 79 percent voter turnout. The large state bureaucracy has maintained social and political order, with minimal class-based conflict, and Brazil is often cited as one of the world's most successful multiracial societies. A strong military ensures Brazil's security and sovereignty.

Progress?

The economic miracle in the 1970s was built on a weak base of economic statism. It was fueled by debt-led growth and deeply dependent on external support for finance capital, technology, and markets. Much of the growth was in the 600 state-owned companies, many of which were extremely inefficient and eventually went bankrupt. The emphasis on industrial development has had many negative consequences, including a decline of the agricultural sector resulting in 2 million landless peasants and the need to import basic foods.

After years of miracle growth, the economy came close to collapse in the early 1980s and again in the mid-1990s. The average annual growth rate is erratic, with the last four years being –0.3, 7.5, 2.7, and 0.9 percent. During the 1990s, hyperinflation was also a problem (reaching a staggering high

of 2,864 percent in 1990). Brazil's foreign debt is the third largest among the transitional countries and Global South—more than $430 billion. Despite government aid programs, one in five Brazilians lives in poverty. Brazil has the world's sixteenth most unequal distribution of income, with wealth heavily concentrated in the urban upper and upper-middle classes.

Order?

Since 1930, the military has deposed six top political leaders. The military, supported by the middle class, seized power most recently in a 1964 coup against an elected government that was judged too sympathetic to the needs of the many rural and urban poor. The military government was repressive and ruthless, crushing leftist opposition, censoring the press, and compiling one of South America's worst records of human rights abuses. An elected president took office in 1985 after 21 years of authoritarian military rule, and a new constitution was implemented in 1988. Since that time, the recurrent economic problems have provoked a huge rise in social disorder. Crime rates are extremely high; urban riots are frequent, especially in the huge *favelas* located in the cosmopolitan cities; and there is violence between peasants and landholders, who are disputing the government's announced but unfulfilled promises of land reform.

One recent president (Collor de Mello) was forced to resign due to a massive corruption scandal. When the next president (Fernando Henrique Cardoso) was elected in 1995, the citizens reflected their disgust with government: One in three Brazilians abstained from voting in the presidential election, and blank (protest) votes outnumbered votes cast for any senate candidate in 22 of the 26 states. Brazil scores only 42 on a 100-point corruption scale (where 100 is very clean). Like prior administrations, President Rousseff's government was immediately embroiled in corruption scandals, and five Cabinet ministers were among those fired in her first nine months.

Policymaking is stymied by a fractious legislature composed of more than a dozen major political parties, many of whose members actually change parties between elections and are primarily loyal to their regional political bosses. The Brazilian flag's proud announcement of "Order and Progress" flaps ironically over the building where these politicians attempt to govern (CIA 2014; Goodwin 2008; Transparency International 2013; World Bank 2013).

Further Focus

1. Based on this account, what might be the main reason why less than one in three Brazilians is satisfied with how democracy works in their country?

2. What policies might help Brazil achieve the GDP per capita and HDI score of a developed country?

Goal: Stability

15.6 **Characterize the quest for stability in the Latin American Transitionals.**

Strong political leaders and a hegemonic class elite were also characteristic of most Latin American transitional countries in the second half of the twentieth century, apart from consistently democratic Costa Rica. Argentina, Chile, Uruguay, and Venezuela alternated between periods of rule by a civilian government and by authoritarian military regimes that, in most cases, came to power by violence and ruled repressively. Mexico was dominated nationally by a single, socially conservative political party, PRI, from 1929 until 2001.

Broadly, this political authoritarianism in Latin America has been linked with a traditional social structure that was based on hierarchical class strata and a dominant ruling class whose members controlled the economic and political systems. Political–cultural norms also included popular acceptance of leaders, often with a military background (*caudillos*) in an earlier era, who exert extremely strict control over the political system. Thus, the political cultures have typically assumed that there would be electoral democracies but that the regime would be hegemonic, involving the alternation between elites rather than open competition among truly opposing groups (Arias 2011; Castenada 2011).

Democratization?

By the late 1980s and early 1990s, most of these countries had begun a process of democratization that is proceeding at varying rates in different countries. Vigorous and competitive democratic politics reemerged in the 1990s in place of repressive regimes in Argentina, Chile, and Uruguay. With the 2000 election of Vicente Fox, even PRI in Mexico lost its one-party dominance of the national political system (recall Chapter 7). Freedom House (2014) classifies all the Latin American Transitionals except Venezuela as "free." On the EIU (2013) Democracy Index, Uruguay and Costa Rica are classified as "full democracies," and the rest (except Venezuela) are classified as "flawed democracies," with generally high scores on civil liberties and on electoral process and pluralism but more mixed scores on the effective functioning of government and on political participation.

Along with positive effects, the combination of democratization, greater prosperity, and economic volatility has generated forces of instability in many of these countries. One specific source of instability is those groups that have been most negatively affected by cutbacks in government welfare and by the recurring periods of economic crisis (Handlin

2013). A second source is the minority ethnic groups in many of these countries, who also tend to be among the poorest citizens. Thus frustration and political violence are evident from the large numbers of poor and politically marginalized groups, such as the peasants in the Chiapas region of Mexico and the Indian populations in Chile (recall the Maputo in Chapter 9). Criminal groups have also created very high levels of violence. Instability that occurs just outside the borders of a country can spill over into internal disruption and violence; for example, in Venezuela (from Colombia). The mix of economic volatility, inequality, and widespread political disillusionment continues to generate serious challenges to the stability of the Latin American Transitionals.

The probability of instability increases where the dissatisfaction of the poor is not counteracted by the middle classes who, in many Latin American countries, offer little support for their political systems (Arias 2011; Torcal and Montero 2006). There are numerous examples of this instability: an attempted coup based on middle-class unrest regarding the authoritarian style of President Hugo Chavez in Venezuela (2002); two recent Costa Rican presidents who have been jailed for corruption; rioting in Argentina (2002) resulting in the succession of five "presidents" in less than three weeks; and the middle classes' lack of enthusiasm for the political regime in countries such as Mexico and Brazil (Focus in 15; Castenada 2010). Thus, in 2013, less than half of those surveyed in Brazil, Chile, Mexico, and Venezuela indicated they were "satisfied" with the way democracy was working in their country (Latinobarometro 2013).

Goal: Security

15.7 **Describe the security goals of the Latin American Transitionals.**

The borders of Latin American states were established in the nineteenth century and have been relatively stable for more than 150 years. While there have been occasional border issues and political disagreements between these countries and their neighbors in recent decades, these rarely reach the level of militarized disputes. Interstate war involving these states was rare in the twentieth century. While the Latin American Transitionals' considerable military strength could be deployed for protection against neighboring states, it has been more actively engaged in maintaining internal order, either by supporting the political leadership or by overthrowing it and seizing political power. Costa Rica and Panama are the exceptions in that they have no standing military but rather rely on a national police force.

Some of the most significant external threats to security have been from the former colonial powers that limited the Latin American Transitionals' autonomy and freedom of action, particularly the United States, Spain, and Great Britain. Their relationships with the powerful United States, which has a strong economic and political presence over the entire hemisphere, has dominated the security concerns of many of these countries. Venezuela's late president Chavez took the lead in promoting new directions in foreign policy that involve ties with countries that are antagonistic to the United States, such as Cuba and Iran. The most notable conventional war since 1950 that involved a Latin American country is the Falklands War between Argentina

and Great Britain in 1982. This conflict resulted from the Argentine military government's attempt to seize islands off its coast that remained under the colonial dominion
of Britain. Argentina's defeat in this short war, like the deep penetration into Latin
American economies by the Global North countries and their financial institutions,
was a reminder that dependency and subordination can persist in the postcolonial
period, even for relatively strong Latin American countries.

The BRICS Countries

15.8 **Explain the BRICS concept.**

The discussion of the PCDCs and the Latin American Transitionals devoted considerable attention to Russia and Brazil. These two countries are also part of another grouping of five countries that do not cluster in Figure 10.1 or on any other concept in this
book. They do not have the same major political institutional arrangements, similar
political economies, a common culture, or a shared region. However, this set of five
countries is now widely referred to as the **BRICS**. While only two of the five are part
of the transitional developed countries group in Figure 10.1, the BRICS group has
received so much attention that it is worthwhile to consider these countries explicitly
in terms of their pursuit of prosperity, stability, and security.

Whence came the BRICS? In the first few years of the twenty-first century, senior
analysts at Goldman Sachs, a global investment firm, attempted to predict the worldwide distribution of power in 2050. They posited that a small set of countries outside
the Global North would have a huge impact on the global system. They termed these
countries the BRICs—standing for Brazil, Russia, India, and China.

The premise underlying the BRICs analysis was simple: If the BRIC countries,
with more than 2.5 billion people, embraced the modernizing economic principles
associated with global trade and globalization, their economies would become very
large and substantially shape the global economy by 2050. In 2003, the BRIC's combined GNP was only 15 percent of that of the largest economies of the Global North;
yet the BRICs could become the dominant force in shaping the global economy as
they developed, given their size, extensive resources, geostrategic locations, and the
changing conditions in Global North countries (Kowitt 2009; O'Neill 2001; Wilson and
Purushothaman 2003). In 2006, diplomats from each of the BRIC countries gathered in
New York for the first official BRIC meeting. And by 2010, the four BRICs became the
five BRICS, when they invited South Africa to join the group.

Earlier chapters in this book should alert you to the huge differences among the
BRICS. Recall, for example, the Compare in 1 that highlighted many differences between
India and China. Brazil is mostly tropical, while vast areas of Russia are covered by
permafrost. India and China each have 25 times more people than South Africa. India
is a parliamentary democracy, and Russia is an authoritarian nondemocracy. China is
a one-party state, and Brazil has more than a dozen parties competing for seats in the
legislature. Brazil has no serious military enemies on its continent, while India borders
on two major nuclear powers with which it has fought. Indeed, it might be argued that

the main commonality among the BRICS is the goal of a future global system that is not dominated by the Global North countries, especially the United States, Japan, and the EU. What development strategies do the BRICS employ to achieve this shared goal?

Goal: Prosperity

15.9 **Analyze the pursuit of prosperity by the BRICS.**

The BRICS have embraced a market- and trade-based economic strategy that enables them to compete globally with the Global North. Trade with other countries has been a crucial part of their economic development strategies. In China, this has been particularly driven by the export of manufactured goods at prices that are highly competitive in the global marketplace. Brazil and Russia have taken full advantage of exporting their abundant natural resources as well as goods from an expanded manufacturing base. South Africa and India have grown their knowledge sectors to serve clients both inside and outside their countries.

As in the earlier developmental state strategy (recall Chapter 10), the government in each of the BRICS has been an active partner with the firms that have been most effective in the production of goods and services. Public policies have favored certain actors and sectors in the attempt to facilitate export-oriented growth. Brazil is the only BRICS country that has been very supportive of production for domestic consumption, although the domestic market is becoming very important in all of the BRICS. Each state's economic policies have facilitated the emergence of an elite class that is extraordinarily wealthy.

A full house of BRICS: Top leaders of the five BRICS countries meet in Brazil in 2014. From left to right, Vladimir Putin (Russia); Narendra Modi (India); Dilma Rousseff (Brazil); Xi Jinping (China); and Jacob Zuma (South Africa).

One of the most interesting aspects of the BRICS' cooperation is the formation of the BRICS Development Bank in 2013. This bank will fund development projects in the five member states to enhance infrastructure (e.g., roads, sewers, schools) and to promote the expansion of targeted manufacturing and service sectors. It will also pool the currencies of the BRICS states to fend off any future currency or financial crisis. This bank is envisioned as a means to provide the countries with greater independence regarding monetary policy and the flow of investment and thus to limit the constraints and dependency imposed on the BRICS' economies by Global North financial institutions, especially the World Bank and the IMF. Earlier information in this book has demonstrated that each of the BRICS has enjoyed periods of notable economic growth. It has been most spectacular and sustained in China, which has averaged 10.6 percent growth per year from 1990 to 2012. India's growth has been more sporadic, averaging 6.8 percent over the same period. Years of high growth alternating with periods of low growth have been common in the other BRICS, resulting in more modest average growth rates in Brazil (3.7 percent), Russia (4.8 percent), and South Africa (3.6 percent). Analyses projecting strong, rapid growth and development in the BRICS assume that each will continue to: (1) integrate successfully into the global economy; (2) diversify its mix of goods; (3) increase the levels of prosperity and consumption for a large proportion of its population; (4) sustain a favorable balance between government revenues and government spending; and (5) maintain political and social stability, the second major goal of the BRICS.

Goal: Stability

15.10   Characterize the quest for stability in the BRICS.

The core approaches for achieving stability differ among the BRICS. China has been most aggressive in suppressing political freedoms, controlling the media and Internet, and limiting antisocial behavior through its system of security forces and prisons. Russia has pursued similar strategies, although at a less intensive level. While China has prevented almost any cracks in its one-party government system, Russia has allowed multiple parties, although it is an increasingly authoritarian illiberal democracy at best. Both countries are rated "not free" with low scores from Freedom House (2014). In contrast, India, Brazil, and South Africa operate "free" constitutional democracies, with multiparty elections, limited mandates, and relatively high levels of political, media, and personal freedoms.

Although each of the BRICS has a political system with strong capabilities, each does face serious threats to stability. Corruption is pervasive among both public sector and private sector actors, draining productive resources and undermining social and economic relations. Anger and frustration with corruption exist in all five countries and occasionally explode into protest, especially in China and India. Moreover, all BRICS have high levels of wealth inequality that are increasing with greater prosperity. This, along with ethnic, religious, and caste-based inequalities in each of the BRICS, might be a central cause of the high levels of crime. All of these factors result in low levels of support for public officials and political institutions and are potential sources of the kinds of political decay and internal political violence described in Chapters 10 and 12. The ultimate success of each of the BRICS might depend on the extent to which it can limit or mitigate the destabilizing tendencies that are associated with both the current conditions in each country and those exacerbated by development.

Goal: Security

15.11   Describe the security goals of the BRICS.

Each BRICS country faces different security challenges. Only Brazil enjoys few security risks from the other countries in its region. South Africa faces a persistent risk that regional sectarian violence across sub-Saharan Africa will lead to an influx of refugees that it cannot manage. Tribal identities within South Africa and across its borders add to the potential risks. India is a nuclear power that has ongoing conflict with another nuclear power, Pakistan; is in a volatile region drenched with violence; and could even find itself fighting again with current BRICS buddy China. China, also a nuclear power, might experience a reemergence of security issues and hostilities with either India or Russia. China also must deal with both vast borders shared with numerous countries and security threats from internal ethnic populations that militate for autonomy, particularly Tibetans and Uighurs. As noted earlier in this chapter, Russia still has a massive military machine that it is rapidly expanding and an aggressive foreign policy because it too perceives hostile countries along many of its lengthy borders.

Chapter 12 noted that countries with extensive military capability are more likely to engage in interstate conflict. Each of the five BRICS is the most militarized country in its region. Four of the five are among the world's top twelve countries in total military expenditure, led by China (second behind the United States) and Russia (third), with India eighth and Brazil twelfth. Russia, India, and South Africa rank among the lowest one-fourth of all the countries in the world on the Global Peace Index. Further, the empirical analyses about power transitions in international relations suggest that if the BRICS' global power rise is as substantial as predicted, each will increasingly be involved in open conflict with other states. The rise to the top of the global pecking order is never gentle.

The future of the BRICS might be intertwined. An emerging power center that is a rival to the economic and military might of the United States and the EU could alter political and economic relationships around the world. However, if any of the BRICS states is incapable of fully participating with the others at the international level because of economic mismanagement or political instability, the coalition might not survive. Similarly, if the BRICS cannot maintain their alliance in the face of a major global crisis, if their incentives to cooperate are swamped by their individual national interests, or if the BRICS Development Bank fails, the notion of their shared future could dissipate. Yet even if they do not sustain their shared vision, the size of their populations, the scale and complexity of their economies, and their role in the global trade regime suggest that the economist from Goldman Sachs was correct. The BRICS will be an economic and political force to reckon with for decades to come.

The Future of the Transitional Developed Countries

15.12 **Identify the factors associated with the prospects for further development of the transitional developed countries.**

While the three sets of countries in transition discussed in this chapter are quite different from one another, most share both optimism and uncertainty about their futures. They have experienced substantial, positive change in recent decades, yet these development dynamics could disrupt their quest for prosperity, stability, and security. In terms of Figure 10.1, in order to move up the scale of development a transitional country needs to achieve further improvements in three dimensions: economic development, social development, and the political system's capabilities.

First, the *economic development* to move a country up the scale requires that more value-added activity be introduced into the economy. The direct paths for upward movement include both increasing profitable exports and growing a domestic middle class that purchases more consumer goods. Also, private sector firms and the state must combine to create more jobs, especially jobs that are characterized by greater profitability in the highly competitive international marketplace. And for most of the transitional countries, the increasing global scarcity of many valued commodities and resources will present major challenges. Thus the state must respond effectively to a complex set of choices regarding its political economy, including policy decisions about how to incentivize and regulate private firms, the state's forms of involvement in the production and distribution of goods to its citizens, and state actions to further the country's economic interests in the global economy.

Second, improvements in *social development* can be difficult for the state to control. Social capital and community are created through culture and tradition as much as through government policy. While culture is globalizing in many ways, resistance to change and progress can be rooted in religious beliefs and traditional norms that are not easily overcome. Overall social development will lag if women and ethnic, religious, or sexual minorities are treated as less than full citizens. Yet the governments in some transitional countries will find it politically difficult to implement policies that deliver greater equality. Social development can also be advanced or hindered by public policies regarding the speed and trajectory of improvements in education, in the technical and communications skills its population needs for many twenty-first century jobs, and in the availability and framing of the Internet and the array of new information and communications technologies. In addition, the increasing urbanization of these countries will generate new demands in terms of the infrastructure—whether building housing, delivering clean water, transporting food and goods, or limiting environmental degradation. Given the context of globalization and the conflicting political and cultural norms among policymakers and the citizenry, the challenges to social development might constitute obstacles that prevent the rise of some transitional countries.

Third, and most broadly, the transition to higher development will be contingent on *the political system's capabilities* to deliver prosperity, stability, and security. As described in Chapter 14, successful development is served by a strong, active, and responsible state that is willing and able to tap into the opportunities in the global market and to deliver improvements in education, health, and quality of life to most of its citizens. Meeting the expectations of the citizens is critical. Some policies will face considerable citizen resistance. Some dimensions of development pay off slowly—good elementary schools, for instance, do not directly impact the economy until those students move into the workforce and find suitable jobs. Policymakers will enact a mix of effective and ineffective decisions. Most economies will have good years and bad years in the global marketplace. Some foreign policy actions will succeed, but others will fail.

In the current era, it is often the case that a population quickly loses patience with a government and its policies when there are few immediate benefits or a downturn in material conditions. If a government lacks the popular support necessary to sustain its development policies, its capacity to stay the course can be very limited, especially in a complex world made even more challenging by unexpected natural or human-made crises. The results can be government dysfunction and political instability. Yet there are encouraging examples of countries that have moved up steadily on the development scale. Singapore is a particularly striking case, along with others such as Chile, the Czech Republic, and South Korea. Many transitional developed countries clearly have the potential to achieve levels of political, economic, and social development comparable to those of some Global North countries. And, ironically, globalization might be a great equalizer because it could limit the capacity of Global North countries to maintain their competitive advantage.

It is evident that no one fully understands how to sustain positive, balanced development in the current international environment. The transitional countries are vulnerable to many forces that the state and its leaders cannot control. Most of the countries examined in this chapter are likely to confront periods when false steps, political decay, disruptions from the external environment, or bad luck will significantly challenge their pursuit of prosperity, security, and stability. Some will achieve the high levels of economic and social development of the developed countries. Each of these transitional countries strives to be in that group, sooner rather than later, later rather than never.

So ...

We have explored complex questions about politics in this book, and sometimes, despite our desire for clarity and closure, there is no straightforward answer. It is possible that this is both the best and worst of times in the political world and that there are grounds for both hope and despair. That is our Final Debate.

Many people look to their political system and its leaders to provide effective solutions in a complex world. But many also seem to think that political actions are a major source of obstacles preventing their achievement of goals. This book's central objective has been to increase your understanding of the political world through the discussions and many examples that, hopefully, have helped you (to use Popper's expression from Chapter 1) "to see more clearly than before."

Voltaire observed, "If we believe absurdities, we shall commit atrocities." The political world is full of disagreement, hyperbole, and ruthless competition. Political science cannot necessarily make the world a better place; its primary role is to increase our understanding about how politics works. Such understanding can be the basis of insights: about different conceptions of how politics should be organized, about the basis of any real political disagreements that require response, about mechanisms for conflict resolution, and about how to organize ourselves in the pursuit of specific (private, group, national, or global) interests within a framework of the common good.

As individuals, we often feel powerless in the face of the massive power mobilized in the political world. But every individual—even you!—can affect what happens. The widely celebrated democratic ideals are based on the assumption that people, individually and collectively, can make a difference. First, if you approach political questions with knowledge, insight, and sensitivity, you can better understand how to think and act in the political world. Second, you can communicate your own political demands and supports to influence the policies that are made by actors in the political system. Third, you can become a political activist—as a shaper of public opinion, a leader of a political group, or a public official.

What is your personal strategy to act in ways that increase the likelihood that this really does become "the best of times"? The American novelist F. Scott Fitzgerald observed: "One should be able to see that things are hopeless and yet be determined to make them otherwise." In the political world, things are not hopeless unless people like you fail to think, to understand, and to act.

The Final Debate

What Time Is It?

Novelist Charles Dickens opens *A Tale of Two Cities* with his famous observation: "It was the best of times, it was the worst of times. It was the age of wisdom, it was the age of foolishness.... It was the spring of hope, it was the winter of despair." Many people might consider this an apt description of the political world in the second decade of the twenty-first century. As you reach the end of this book, it is reasonable for you to consider what *you* now think about the political world. How would you characterize the political world today? How does it affect *you*?

It Is the Worst of Times

- There is now far greater possibility of the use of weapons of mass destruction than at any point in human history. Our weapons arsenals have far more power and efficiency than ever before, and a few of the 4,300 operational nukes could end most life on Earth. There is not only a proliferation of governments that can deploy dangerous weapons but also other, more reckless actors, including rogue states and terrorist groups, that are able to either steal or manufacture nuclear, chemical, or biological weapons that can do massive harm.

- Our applications of technology are out of control. The development and uses of many technologies are often driven by self-serving motives, short-term thinking, and indifference to their negative impacts. It is no coincidence that the huge expansion of technological capacity has occurred during a period in which humans have killed far more of their race than at any other time in history, environmental degradation has reached frightening levels, the loss of community and social trust is severe, and global inequalities are at their starkest levels.

- Many governments seem incapable of effective governance—that is, they seem unable to make and implement wise policy decisions that respond to the demands presented by diverse groups with conflicting agendas and different ideologies. Governments are increasingly constrained by insufficient global resources to satisfy all needs. While more countries are democracies, this situation has not led to increases in political knowledge, participation, or commitment to democratic principles. And contemporary political institutions have not changed the underlying reality that power corrupts.

- The complexity and interdependency of national economic systems have created a volatility and fragility that have resulted in economic downturns that are more rapid, deeper, and more difficult to correct. The new global economy makes it almost impossible for a government to manage its own economy or to protect it from severe disruptions.

- Globalization has also undermined the capacity of governments to protect their economies from manipulation by global capital and multinational corporations, to protect their workers from the loss of jobs, or even to protect their national cultural norms and values from being undermined by outside influences that are alien and undesirable. Both the clash of civilizations between hostile worldviews and the intolerance among nation-based identity groups seem to be generating more and more dangerous conflicts.

- *The bottom line: We live in a world of uncertainty and insecurity where the general welfare of humankind is not nurtured or protected.*

It Is the Best of Times

- The danger of a catastrophic nuclear war between the United States and the Soviet Union, whether intentional or accidental, is no longer a grave risk. All the major nuclear powers have reduced their stockpiles. Since the end of the Cold War, the United Nations has been much more active in collective peacekeeping operations, and there are now comparatively few interstate wars. The fact that democracies do not fight with one another is another positive factor as an increasing majority of countries embrace democracy.

- Technology (i.e., applied knowledge) in its many forms has vastly expanded human powers of control and production. With wise policies from our governments to guide the development and application of technologies, we have the capacity to provide sufficient resources to ensure that every human being has the food, health, knowledge, and material goods for a long and satisfying life.

- Democracy and political institutionalization have spread to more political systems than ever. As citizens experience the value of open political discussion and of selecting their leaders in fair and competitive elections, they become more engaged and take more responsibility for dealing with the political issues in their country and the world. They demand more effective governance from political actors, and they support leaders who further the goals of prosperity, stability, and security.

- The new global economy has increased the quality, affordability, and accessibility of almost every good and service that people need. Worldwide, today's "average person" enjoys a material standard of living that far surpasses that of any previous era.

- Globalization has increased the richness and breadth of our experiences and broadened our identity as citizens of the world. We share information and ideas, trade goods and services, and recognize that what happens everywhere has consequences for our own welfare. The incentives and interdependency encouraging us all to get along have never been greater.

- *The bottom line: More people live longer and with a higher quality of life than at any point in history.*

More questions …

1. If you were to judge this debate, what would be your decision on which side is more compelling?

2. *How about you?* Given the political world described in this Debate, throughout this book, and in your broader experience, do you expect that things will be better or worse for *you* over the next several decades? Why?

Key Concepts

BRICS, p. 436
crony capitalism, p. 421
flawed democracies, p. 427
freedom divide, p. 426

Latin American Transitionals,
  p. 430
postcommunist developed
  countries (PCDCs), p. 418

transitional developed
  countries, p. 417

For Further Consideration

1. Why has Russia not followed the path toward democracy that seems successful in most of the other postcommunist developed countries?

2. Under what, if any, conditions might the Cold War be revived?

3. Develop an argument for which (if any) of the BRICS countries will be the first to reach

the group of more developed countries considered in Chapter 13.

4. What do the three categories of transitional countries have in common? Are there special challenges each category faces that the other categories do not?

For Further Reading

Alexander, James. (2000). *Political Culture in Post-Communist Russia: Formlessness and Recreation in a Traumatic Transition.* **New York: St. Martin's.** From detailed studies of two Russian towns, the author offers an illuminating explanation of the difficulties associated with the "traumatic transition" from authoritarianism to a more liberal democratic political culture and the continuing impacts of broader Russian cultural traditions.

Beausang, Francesca. (2012). *Globalization and the BRICs: Why the BRICs Will Not Rule the World for Long.* **New York: Palgrave Macmillan.** As counterpoint to the arguments that the BRIC countries will be the major force at mid-century, the author (an economist) identifies many key limitations associated with these countries, especially regarding income inequality and lack of innovation.

Flynn, Norman. (2000). *Miracle to Meltdown in Asia.* **New York: Oxford University Press.** The rise and sudden crisis in the Asian countries that have passed through the transitional stage are thoughtfully analyzed, with particular attention given to the balance of power among the market, cronyism, and authoritarianism in governing the state and guiding the political economy.

Freedom House. (2011). *Nations in Transit 2011* **http://www.freedomhouse.org.** A Freedom House book with chapter-length descriptions of the politically relevant developments in each PCDC and the other countries that emerged from the Soviet Empire.

Goldman, Marshall. (2008). *Petrostate: Putin, Power, and the New Russia.* **Oxford: Oxford University Press.** An analysis of the clever actions by Vladimir Putin and other Russian leaders to renew the country's power and global position, primarily by exploiting its oil resources.

Kaplan, Stephen B. (2103). *Globalization and Austerity Politics in Latin America.* **New York: Cambridge University Press.** Explores the tension between global financial markets and the domestic politics of democracies in Latin America. Austerity measures may be pushed by the investment interests or may arise as smart domestic politics.

Mahbubani, Kishore. (2008). *The New Asian Hemisphere: the Irresistible Shift of Global Power.* **New York: Public Affairs.** A carefully developed and rather persuasive argument that the twenty-first century, like most earlier centuries before the last several, will be dominated by the countries of Asia.

Mankoff, Jeffrey. (2009). *Russian Foreign Policy: The Return to Power Politics.* **Lanham, MD: Rowman & Littlefield.** The author explores the evolving and increasingly aggressive strategy of Putin and Russia to reassert itself in its region and then globally through diplomacy, trade, and military strength.

McFaul, Michael, Kathryn Stoner-Weiss, and Valerie Bunce. (2010). *Democracy and Authoritarianism in the Postcommunist World.* **New York: Cambridge University Press.** Three leading scholars of the region provide a rich analysis of the patterns of political and social transition in the PCDCs.

North, Douglass C., John Joseph Wallis, Steven B. Webb, and Barry R. Weingast, eds. (2013). *In the Shadow of Violence: Politics, Economics and the Problems of Development.* **New York: Cambridge University Press.** The articles explore such questions as: Can political control of economic privileges be used to limit violence and build coalitions? How can countries best minimize violence while supporting economic growth?

O'Neil, Jim. (2012). *The Growth Map: Economic Opportunity in the BRICs and Beyond.* **New York: Penguin Group.** An insightful guide to the prospects for economic growth throughout the developing and developed world written by the originator of the BRICs concept.

Oppenheim, Lois Hecht. (2007). *Politics in Chile: Socialism, Authoritarianism and Market Democracy.* **3rd ed. Boulder, CO: Westview Press.** The transitions in politics and political economy in Chile, arguably the most successful Latin American Transitional, are described for the period since 1970, from Allende's socialism through Pinochet's authoritarianism to the current rise toward developed country status.

Thomas, Robert. (1999). *The Politics of Serbia in the 1990s.* **New York: Columbia University Press.** An interesting approach to understanding the political dynamics and power struggles in Serbia, the key protagonist in the chaotic Balkans, with an analysis of what was being said (as well as done) by the key actors, especially the late Slobodan Milosevic.

True, Jacqui. (2003). *Gender, Globalization, and Postsocialism: The Czech Republic After Communism.* **New York: Columbia University Press.** A rich combination of the study of the dynamics of change in a postcommunist society with the way in which gender roles are affecting those changes and being changed by them, all within the context of globalization.

Wiarda, Howard J., and Harvey Kline, eds. (2014). *Latin American Politics and Development.* **8th ed. Boulder, CO: Westview Press.** A solid and current set of readings covering exactly what the title suggests, including general chapters on the region's history, political parties and interest groups, and democratization as well as individual chapters on a dozen countries.

On the Web

http://lanic.utexas.edu

The Latin American Network Information Center, hosted by the University of Texas, Austin, provides a vast number of Internet-based information sources about the politics, economics, culture, and other areas of the Latin American NICs and other countries in the region.

http://www.tol.cz

Transitions Online provides detailed information regarding political and cultural issues relevant to these postcommunist developed states.

http://www.themoscowtimes.com/index.php

An online daily English-language newspaper published in Moscow that provides a perspective on the politics and society of Russia.

http://www.europeanforum.net

The European Forum for Democracy and Solidarity offers country-by-country information on politics and economics for various social democratic parties, including those in the postcommunist developed countries.

Appendix
Political Analysis

The mind rests in explanation.

—Aristotle

Chapter 1 suggested that you are often exposed to knowledge claims about the political world. Focus in 1 explained how you might develop a political analysis to assess the claim that younger adults have less political knowledge than older adults. Suppose you heard the claim that "in a democracy, men are more likely to vote than women." If the 1976 data in Table 1 were presented as evidence, would you be satisfied that the claim is correct?

The United States is a democracy, and a presidential election seems like a legitimate instance of voting. The table indicates that a higher proportion of men than women voted in the 1976 presidential election. But you would probably want more data—for example, from more election years in the United States. So Table 1 provides a second election for comparison. Now what do you think of the claim? Because the data from 2012 are not consistent with the pattern from 1976, you would recognize that the analysis of this knowledge claim is not straightforward. You might decide to analyze

SOURCE: Frank & Earnest reprinted by permission of Newspaper Enterprise Association, Inc.

Table 1 Participation of Eligible Voters in the 1976 and 2012 U.S. Presidential Elections, by Gender

	1976	
	Men	**Women**
Voted	a. 77%	b. 67%
Did not vote	c. 23%	d. 33%

Yule's Q = +.24

	2012	
	Men	**Women**
Voted	a. 60%	b. 64%
Did not vote	c. 40%	d. 36%

Yule's Q = −.08

---

data from more U.S. elections. You would discover that women voted at a lower rate than men in every U.S. presidential election through 1976, and that women have voted at a higher rate than men in every subsequent election. Now what? Perhaps you would decide that, to better assess the claim, it would be appropriate to examine data for other democracies. Or you might attempt to explain why the relationship between gender and voting in the United States seems to have changed.

When you explore these kinds of issues, you are engaged in political analysis. Chapter 1 defined **political analysis** as the attempt to describe and explain political phenomena. This Appendix will introduce you to some of the basic tools political scientists use for political analysis—that is, for conceptualizing, collecting, and analyzing data about political phenomena. After a brief discussion of various types of data, we shall consider how to read data like those in Table 1 and how to draw a tentative inference based on those data. Most of the Appendix describes four broad approaches used for political analysis: taxonomic analysis, formal analysis, functional analysis, and relational analysis.

Data in Political Analysis

Many political analyses rely on data assessment. *Data* can be defined as any observations, facts, statistics, or other forms of information that attempt to measure or represent some aspect of reality. The data used in political analysis can be characterized according to different dimensions, including the style of measurement, the level of analysis, the composition, and the time dimension.

1. *Style of measurement.*
   a. *Nominal data measure by applying names to phenomena that have some common characteristic.* Examples: male voters or female voters; Conservative, Labour, or Liberal Democrat parties in Britain; democratic, authoritarian, or totalitarian governments.

b. **Ordinal data** *rank phenomena,* such as from higher to lower, bigger to smaller, greater to lesser. Examples: developed countries or developing countries; voters who are older than 64, voters between ages 35 and 64, or voters younger than age 35; Canada ranked fifth in the world in 2013 on GDP per capita (PPP, excluding ministates).

c. **Interval data** *are like ordinal data, but they also have a numerically equal distance between any two adjacent measures*—the distance from 5 to 6 is the same as the distance from 81 to 82. Example: The difference on an opinion scale between 1 (= strongly agree) and 2 (= agree) is the same as the difference between 4 (= disagree) and 5 (= strongly disagree).

d. **Ratio data** *are like interval data, but they also have a real zero point.* Examples: Canada's GDP per capita PPP is $42,693; the percentage of citizens participating in boycotts for political or ethical reasons; the number of seats in the legislature held by a particular political party.

2. *Level of analysis.* Political data can be measured at different levels of combination. Examples: at the *individual* level, the strength of a particular individual's loyalty to a political party; at the *group* level, the percentage of Canadians who believe that terrorism is never justifiable; the average number of correct political knowledge answers for young adults; at the *system* level, the total number of operational nuclear weapons worldwide. (In international relations theory, the three levels are individual, state, and global system.)

3. *Composition.* Data can measure a single phenomenon, such as a political leader's age or a country's rate of inflation in a particular year, or they can aggregate phenomena, such as the percentage of total votes cast for all conservative political parties in an election or a country's average annual rate of inflation over 10 years.

4. *Time dimension.*

a. **Cross-sectional data** *measure a single point in time.* Example: a country's GDP per capita in 2014.

b. **Longitudinal data** *measure several points through time.* Example: a country's GDP per capita in 1970, 1990, and 2010.

The example of voting in the 1976 and 2012 presidential elections uses data that are nominal (men versus women), ratio (percentages), and aggregated (for many people) in a longitudinal analysis (two comparable elections). You might think of data as dry statistics, but the data in political analysis are rooted in real-world events. If properly analyzed, relevant data can increase our political knowledge on an endless list of questions. Examples: Are countries that spend the greatest amount on military preparedness more likely to avoid war? Is religion or social class a better predictor of whether a Scot will vote for the Labour Party? What characteristics of a country are most associated with the level of citizen support for democracy?

On Reading Tables

Does Table 1 help you clarify the relationship between gender and voting level in democracies? Because political analysis often includes data presented in tables, it is useful to know the basic steps for reading them. When you examine a table such as

Table 1, you should first establish precisely what the data are about. The title of the table and the names given to the variables (the key concepts measured in the table) indicate what the analyst who created the table thinks it reveals. But the analyst can be misleading or mistaken, so it is worthwhile to assess whether the phenomena measured by the data correspond to the labels given to the variables, whether the data seem relevant to the analytic question, and whether the data seem accurate.

Next you should examine the data in the table. What do the data measure? Table 1 provides data on the percentage of men and women who did or did not vote in the election of the U.S. president in 1976 and 2012. How are such tabular data read? Is either of these two statements supported by the 2012 data in the table?

1. Forty percent of those who did not vote were men.
2. Thirty-six percent of the women did not vote.

It is useful, especially when there are percentages in a table, to examine how the columns (up and down) and the rows (across) are formed. In the case of percentages, find any direction(s) in which the data total 100 percent. In this table, the columns total 100 percent. Thus, statement 2 is supported by the table and statement 1 is not. Can you see why this is so?

In many cases, the analyst uses more sophisticated techniques than tables to assess the relationships among variables. Focus in the Appendix discusses the relational modes of analysis and considers the use of statistical techniques to examine these relationships. It also helps you interpret a correlation statistic like the one in Table 1.

You can look at simple arrays of data, like those in Table 1, and draw your own conclusions. Graphical representations (like the four scattergrams in Figure 1) are another straightforward way to assess data. Each point in the figures represents one case, located at its appropriate value on each of the two variables in the analysis. This visual mapping of cases can provide useful insights about the nature of the relationship between two variables.

As the data become more complex, statistics can help inform your judgment. Table 1 indicates that the correlation between gender and voting in the 1976 election data is ±.24, using a simple correlation statistic for 2 × 2 tables called Yule's Q. The correlation of ±.24 suggests that in these data, there is a moderate systematic relationship between male gender and higher probability of voting. In the 2012 data, the relationship between gender and voting appears less pronounced, and this judgment is supported by the Yule's Q of −.08, which indicates that there is almost no systematic relationship between gender and voter turnout rate.

While most statistics of association require a calculator or a computer, you can calculate Yule's Q yourself for any 2 × 2 table: (1) Multiply the values of the two cells on each diagonal: $a \times d$ and $b \times c$; (2) subtract the two products: $ad - bc$; (3) add the two products: $ad + bc$; (4) divide $ad - bc$ by $ad + bc$; (5) the result of this division should be a correlation score, ranging between +1.00 and −1.00. The formula for Yule's Q is thus $(ad - bc)/(ad + bc)$. (In contrast to most correlation statistics, a positive Yule's Q means that the ad diagonal is stronger than the bc diagonal.) This is a simpler statistic than most analysts would use.

Focus in the Appendix

Assessing Relationships among Phenomena

To interpret most quantitative analyses in political science (and most other social sciences), you need to understand a bit about the meaning of the most commonly used statistics (e.g., Pearson's *r*, regression analysis, factor analysis). Ideally, you will take some statistics coursework so that you understand the logic and assumptions of the statistics being employed.

The simplest relational statistics (e.g., Pearson's *r, tau beta*, Spearman's *rho*) usually range in value between +1.00, which indicates a perfect positive relationship between the variables, and –1.00, which indicates a perfect negative relationship between the variables. These simple statistics (as well as more sophisticated ones) also have a *significance* level—an indication of how likely it is that the observed relationship between the variables might have occurred by chance. This is normally measured in terms of this chance probability: .05, .01, .001. The smaller the probability of a chance relationship, the greater the analyst's confidence that the variables are actually associated.

In the case of two variables, a +1.00 correlation would look like graph *A* in Figure 1: As one variable increases one unit in value, the other variable increases at a corresponding rate. For example, you would find a +1.00 correlation if each $100,000 spent on congressional political campaigns increased voter turnout by 1 percent. A –1.00 correlation would look like graph *B*. Rarely do real-world phenomena

Figure 1 Correlation Relationships between Two Hypothetical Variables, *X* and *Y*

Perfect Positive Correlation:
r = + 1.0

A

Perfect Negative Correlation:
r = − 1.0

B

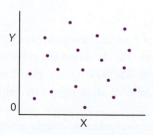

Virtually No Correlation:
r ≅ .00

C

Mild Positive Correlation:
r ≅ + .30

D

in political science even come close to a perfect positive or negative correlation.

A correlation statistic close to .00 means that there is almost no linear relationship between the two variables, as in graph *C*. For example, you might find that campaign expenditure levels have no consistent relationship with voter turnout rates. Political phenomena are often extremely complex and subject to many influences, so they typically have little or no systematic relationship with other factors that you might consider. Thus, in many political analyses, the statistical associations are low or statistically insignificant. The strongest statistical relationships for interesting political data are usually at moderate levels of correlation, in the range of ±.10 to ±.35, as in graph *D*.

Beyond simple statistics and graphs, political scientists use an array of sophisticated data analysis techniques to examine questions involving quantitative data. Most of the techniques are elaborations on the basic idea of examining whether the values on phenomena seem to be systematically related to each other, although the techniques can involve extremely complex computations that analyze the interrelated effects of many **independent variables** (*the variables that in a cause-and-effect explanation produce change in another variable*) that account for changes in the value of the **dependent variable**—*the variable whose changing value the analysis is attempting to explain.*

The use of statistics and other quantitative techniques can be helpful in political analysis. The more demanding task for the analyst is to use careful judgment to decide whether the relationship identified by such techniques has *substantive* significance. The key question is: Do the tables, statistics, and other data provide useful insights about political processes or about how political phenomena are associated?

Modes of Political Analysis

Chapter 1 indicated that political science has little theory in the strictest sense of the term; that is, it does not have a set of precise, systematically related generalizations. However, most contemporary political analysis strives to make our understanding of politics more general, precise, and systematic by ordering empirical data using one of these four modes of political analysis: taxonomic, formal, functional, or relational.

Taxonomic Analysis

Aristotle (384–322 B.C.E.), the father of political analysis, was interested in distinguishing different types of Greek city–states. He classified them by using a concept derived from earlier work by Herodotus (ca. 484–425 B.C.E.): the size of the ruling group. Aristotle defined three categories: The city–state might be ruled by one person, by a few people, or by many people.

This is an example of **taxonomic analysis**: *the orderly arrangement of some political phenomena by developing a set of distinct categories*. Most political analysis begins with a taxonomy—a set of categories that classify data into different types. The categories within a taxonomy establish the crucial concepts that define the analysis. The criteria

Table 2 Aristotle's Taxonomy of Political Systems

How Many Rule?	In Whose Interest?	
	General	Self
One	Monarchy	Tyranny
A few	Aristocracy	Oligarchy
Many	Polity	Democracy

for naming the types and for classifying phenomena into each type are arbitrary in the sense that they are established by the analyst on the basis of substantive concerns. But the categories ought to be exhaustive (all cases are classified), mutually exclusive (no case fits into more than one category), and comparable (all categories are distinguished by the same criteria). Relevant data might be of any type, although they are usually nominal or ordinal.

Aristotle's three categories of city–states are sufficient to create a taxonomy. But to enrich his analysis, Aristotle employed a second concept: the group(s) whose interests the ruler serves. His two categories were: (1) The ruler(s) could rule in the general interest or (2) the ruler(s) could rule in self-interest. Thus, Aristotle's taxonomy of governments had two central concepts, each based on nominal data, resulting in the six categories displayed in Table 2. Aristotle then provided names for each category in the taxonomy. He labeled as a **monarchy** any city–state in which one person ruled in the general interest; if a few ruled in their own interests, the system was called an **oligarchy**. Notice that Aristotle labeled the most perverse case, in which many attempt to rule in their self-interests, a **democracy**!

Aristotle used his taxonomy for political analysis by placing each Greek city–state in one of the six categories. Athens, for example, was classified as an aristocracy. Notice that a taxonomy organizes data, but it does not answer the *how* and *why* questions. To explore such questions (e.g., Is a prosperous middle class more likely in an oligarchy? Under what conditions does a polity transform into a democracy?), the analyst must move beyond taxonomic analysis.

Formal Analysis

Suppose you want to travel around New York City on the subway. If you are unfamiliar with New York, you will probably use a subway map, which indicates the spatial relationships among different subway stations and identifies the stations where one subway line connects with another.

A subway map is an example of the product of formal analysis. A **formal analysis** *specifies abstract forms that correspond to the reality in which the analyst is interested*. The analyst attempts to model reality by defining and relating concepts so that the linkages among the concepts in the formal analysis reflect the dynamics and interactions among the actual phenomena. Some formal analyses have the same physical form as the phenomena being modeled, such as a miniaturized version of an automobile engine. But most formal analyses use symbol systems as abstract representations of the phenomena, such as a subway map, a schematic drawing of the circuitry in a radio, or a mathematical formula for the trajectory of an object moving through space.

Most formal analyses of political phenomena are recent. Some political scientists have attempted to devise schematic diagrams that represent how some aspect of politics works. In one well-known example, David Easton (1965) developed an abstract diagram, composed of boxes and arrows, that attempts to characterize the flow of activities by which decision makers in the political system establish public policies. Their decisions are influenced by the resources available in the environment and the pressures they experience from various groups. This political system model is explained in detail in Chapter 5.

An array of formal analyses called **rational choice theory** (or *public choice theory*) has become an important approach in political science(recall Chapter 4). Applications of rational choice theory can be complex, but they share two basic features. First, they attempt to represent political processes primarily by means of mathematical formulations or systems of symbolic notation. From the perspective of advancing a science of politics, such formal theories are given prominence because they aim to be general, systematic, abstract, and testable in actual settings.

Second, these applications assume that political actors (e.g., voters, legislators, political parties) behave purposefully. The approach does not assume that all political actors behave with complete rationality all the time, but it does assume that their behavior is goal-oriented and calculating. Both their preferences for various outcomes and their calculations of the costs, benefits, and likely success of different strategies to achieve those outcomes can be formulated as quantified indicators or as systems of symbols (Mueller 2003).

Rational choice theory is applied to a variety of topics in the study of politics. The question of whether to vote in an election allows for a brief and simplified example. The rational choice approach suggests that a person will/should calculate whether to vote by the following sort of analysis: First, how much will it cost (in time, energy, etc.) to figure out what each candidate will do, assess how it will affect outcomes that I value, and then actually go vote? Second, how much will I benefit if a particular candidate wins? Third, what is the probability that my vote will determine if my candidate wins? By comparing the costs and benefits outlined above, an individual can decide whether it is worth it to vote. Rational choice theorists identify a "paradox of voting"—in their analytic framework, it is almost never rational to vote because the costs will far outweigh the benefits, particularly because of the extraordinarily small chance that an individual vote will make the difference in who wins (Riker and Ordeshook 1973). Of course, some might reply that there are good reasons to vote: If everyone who supports a candidate follows the same logic and decides not to vote, the candidate would lose; voting is an expression of citizenship and group solidarity; and sometimes elections are close and a few votes do make a difference (ask Al Gore about Florida in 2000).

Functional Analysis

Suppose someone asks you how a car works. You are likely to discuss the key structural components of a car's engine and power train, such as its carburetor, pistons, and driveshaft. You might then detail the processes of the internal combustion engine, noting how an ignited fuel expands in an enclosed area, pushing a series of mechanisms into directed motion. This style of description and explanation is the basis of functional analysis. *Functional analysis describes the contributions of a certain element (process or structure) to the activities of the phenomenon under study.*

In political science, one widely used form of functional analysis identifies certain functions (i.e., processes) that occur within a political system, and it describes how and by what structures the functions are performed. Some scholars (Powell, Dalton, and Strom 2012) have defined certain functions, including political communication, rule adjudication, and interest articulation, that must be performed in every political system.

Applications of functional analysis are described in Chapters 5, 10, and 11. As a brief example here of applications of functional analysis, we can consider the interest articulation function. Individuals might want their government to protect their right to own handguns. The processes by which individuals communicate this specific interest to others in the political world are called *interest articulation*. According to functional analysis, this communication of political needs and wants is a necessary function in every effective political system. Most functional analysts also describe and explain how structures perform these types of functions. Thus, interest groups emerge to amplify the shared interests of many individuals. For example, the National Rifle Association uses various strategies to promote many individuals' concerns about gun ownership to those who make and implement government policies on firearms.

Related to functional analysis is constitutive analysis. *Constitutive analysis assumes that political functions can be explained primarily in terms of one fundamental concept.* (Indeed, every scientific discipline ultimately strives to discover the fundamental structure or process that accounts for more complex phenomena.) Among the concepts that have been proposed as the central one to explain politics are the interactions among groups, classes, or roles. Constitutive theories are discussed in various chapters, especially in Chapter 9, which presents the elite, class, and pluralist approaches to explaining politics. As an example, Karl Marx's (1867) theory of politics pivots on one key concept: class. In every historical period, society is divided into a set of classes based on the distribution of economic power. The structure of classes determines political and social relations as well as economic relations. In political terms, the class structure determines who wields political power, for what purposes, and for whose benefit. The role of the state and the dynamics of political change are also explained in terms of class relations.

Relational Analysis

Table 1 considers the question of voting differences between men and women: Is there some relationship between an individual's gender and the likelihood that she or he votes? This is typical of the kinds of questions addressed by relational analysis.

The central goal of **relational analysis** is to *discover and explicate the systematic connections between phenomena*. The basic question is always: Are political phenomena linked? For example: Are democratic countries more stable than nondemocratic countries? Are older people more politically knowledgeable than younger people? Is Confucian culture more associated with higher national economic growth than Muslim culture is? What characteristics are associated with states more likely to participate in interstate wars?

Both formal analysis and functional analysis also assume connections, but relational analysis merely tries to identify the connections between phenomena. It does not attempt to model or schematize the connections, as does formal analysis. And it does not focus on crucial functions, as does functional analysis. There are two levels of relational analysis: (1) correlational analysis and (2) causal analysis. To determine whether there is a systematic association between variables, most correlational and causal analyses use various statistical techniques. These statistics provide a mathematical appraisal of the extent to which change in one phenomenon is systematically related to changes in one or more other phenomena. Focus in the Appendix provided further information about a few such statistics.

CORRELATIONAL ANALYSIS. Correlational analysis *determines whether there is a statistically probable relationship between two variables*. It does not presume, as does causal analysis (discussed in the next section), that one variable is the agent that causes change to occur in another variable. It merely assesses the strength and direction of an association between variables. Many empirical attempts to understand politics begin with the establishment of a correlation between political phenomena.

Evaluating the linkage between gender and voting in Table 1 is an example of correlational analysis. The table and the Yule's Q statistic both seem to support the tentative conclusion that, for 1976 at least, there is a modest *correlation* (i.e., *a systematic, statistically probable association*) between gender and voting. However, the correlation statistic for the 2012 election is considerably weaker (closer to .00), and it is in the opposite direction (women's participation is higher). Any generalization could also take into account empirical comparative analyses of many countries that do not find a strong correlation between gender and voting rates in most democracies (Inglehart and Norris 2003). The need for more data and more subtle analyses seems clear.

CAUSAL ANALYSIS. Causal analysis goes beyond correlational analysis because it *explicitly identifies one phenomenon as the effective agent that brings about changes in another phenomenon*. Much of the language in political analysis is loosely causal, implying that there is a cause-and-effect relationship between two variables. However, causal analysis is the only approach that attempts an explicit empirical test of cause and effect. Causal analysis presents the "If X, then Y" mode of explanation described in Chapter 1. Here X is the *independent variable* that, given a certain value, actually causes Y, the *dependent variable*, to change in a particular way.

An example of causal analysis links the electoral system and the number of political parties. In his landmark book *Political Parties*, French political scientist Maurice

Table 3 Relationship between Number of Political Parties and Type of Electoral System

Number of Parties[†]	Electoral System[*]	
	Plurality	Other
Two	23	4
More than two	7	73
Yule's $Q = +.97$		

Note: Based on data from 20 Western democracies in elections of legislative representatives between 1945 and 1965.
[*]In plurality or "first-past-the-post" systems, the party/candidate with the largest number of votes wins a seat in the legislature, and all other parties/candidates gain no seats. In "other" systems, there is some form of proportional representation or vote transfer.
[†]Number of political parties with at least 5 percent of the seats in the legislature.
SOURCE: Rae 1972.

Duverger (1954) contends that the type of electoral system *causes* the number of effective parties to increase or decrease. He offers two hypotheses:

1. Plurality electoral systems (in which the candidate who receives the most votes wins) reduce the number of major political parties toward two.
2. Electoral systems with proportional representation (in which candidates are elected to the legislature in proportion to their party's share of the total vote) and with multimember districts (more than one legislator per district) allow more than two major parties(recall Focus in 6).

Political analysts (e.g., Riker 1982; Taagepera and Shugart 1989: Ch. 13) have tested Duverger's hypotheses using data from various electoral systems. Table 3 presents data from 20 democratic countries for the period from 1945 to 1965 (Rae 1972). Do you think the data in Table 3 support Duverger's hypothesis? Why?

Drawing Conclusions from Empirical Analyses

The purpose of empirical analysis is to increase our knowledge about politics. It is especially important that the analyst draws appropriate conclusions. In political analysis, as in politics, things often are not what they seem. Let us consider some of the potential problems, using the causal analysis of electoral systems and party systems as an example. You probably concluded that the data in Table 3 support Duverger's hypothesis. The relationship seems very strong, and the correlation statistic (+.97) is extremely high. Do we now know that the electoral system causes different types of party systems? Yes, maybe.

Yes: There is certainly some persuasive empirical evidence for such a conclusion, such as this very high correlation. And, on logical grounds, it does seem reasonable that the electoral system might cause variations in the number of parties that survive over time.

Maybe: The political analyst must always be cautious in drawing conclusions and making generalizations. Several questions should be considered:

1. Are the data and methods appropriate? Did the analysis use accurate, relevant data and the correct analytic techniques? Are the sample of nations and the time period examined typical? Does this generalization hold for non-European nations? Were systems divided between "plurality" and "other" in a manner consistent with Duverger's hypothesis?

2. Are the analyst's inferences about cause and effect persuasive? Might the dependent variable (in this case, the number of political parties) actually have a significant effect on the presumed independent variable (the electoral system)? That is, because the parties in most legislatures have the power to establish the electoral system, certain parties might try to implement an electoral system that perpetuates their power via the existing party system.

3. Are there plausible rival hypotheses? Is there another independent variable, not considered in this analysis, that might better account for the pattern of values of the dependent variable? It is possible that both the number of parties and the electoral system are related primarily because each is correlated with the third variable? For example, the number of fundamental issues that divide the electorate might have the greatest effect on the number of major parties if one party emerges for each pattern of positions on the fundamental issues (Taagepera and Shugart 1989).

When political scientists use the scientific method, other analysts might raise any of these kinds of problems with a conclusion. The data, the methods, or the inferences might not stand up to such scrutiny. In our examination of Duverger's claims about the causal relationship between electoral systems and the number of parties, none of the three problems just listed seems to undermine the analysis. Until one of these types of criticisms is supported persuasively, we can have some confidence that the generalization about the causal relationship is correct—that electoral systems do seem to cause certain types of party systems to evolve over time.

The gender and voting analysis based on the 1976 election data in Table 1 can serve as an example of how an initial causal inference can be challenged. There is clearly a correlation in 1976 between gender and voter turnout. The three potential problems must be considered in an assessment of whether the data reveal that gender differences do *cause* a different probability of voting:

1. The data and methods seem appropriate. However, a generalization (even limited to the United States) certainly requires more than a single case.

2. The posited cause-and-effect relationship seems reasonable. This is the only possible direction of causality because voting certainly cannot "cause" gender. Also, there are reasonable explanations for why men might vote at higher rates than women. Can you think of at least one?

Table 4 Participation of Eligible Voters in the 1976 U.S. Presidential Election, by Gender and Education Level

Education Level	Percentage Who Voted	
	Men	Women
Grade school	72	50
High school	69	64
College	86	84

3. However, to make a compelling argument that the data reveal causality, it would be necessary to ensure that there is no other causal agent (i.e., no plausible rival hypothesis) that better explains voting levels or that creates the apparent relationship between gender and voting. While the analyst can never disprove every competing hypothesis, it is important to examine and reject the most plausible ones.

Let us reexamine the 1976 voter turnout data in Table 1. Can you propose another explanation for the incidence of voting in the United States that is as plausible as gender? Among those you might suggest are age, social class, occupation, interest in politics, identification with a political party, and education level. Table 4 provides the relevant data on one of these alternative explanations—education level—for our analysis of voting in 1976. Do these data alter your judgment about the importance of gender?

One reasonable interpretation of Table 4 is that the 1976 election revealed a considerable difference between men and women in the incidence of voting among those with minimal education, but almost no difference in the levels of voting between men and women who have a college education. In the absence of further analysis (and many further analyses could be attempted), these data about education seem to reduce the power of gender as an adequate causal explanation of voting. One might infer, at least on the basis of Table 4, that both education and gender were important in 1976 but that the impact of gender was powerfully altered by education level. Perhaps the gender gap had shifted by 2012 because the proportion of men and women with college educations had equalized. Perhaps. This closer look should suggest that if you were developing a causal theory of voter turnout, you would need to consider many variables and diverse data.

This example reveals a common challenge for most of the interesting questions addressed by causal analyses of politics: There are almost always clusters of plausible explanatory factors that seem interrelated. For example: What accounts for a person's decision to vote for the conservative National Action Party (PAN) in Mexico—class, education, family experiences, occupation, wealth, beliefs about society, attitudes toward governmental leaders, or something else? What factors lead a group to undertake revolutionary violence—political oppression, poverty, corrupt government officials, charismatic leadership, unequal distribution of wealth, foreign domination, or something else? Working on these kinds of puzzles is the stuff of political analysis.

Knowledge and Politics Revisited

Chapter 1 suggested a number of ways in which it is possible to know things about the political world. Your understanding of politics does not need to be grounded in the scientific method and in empirical analysis. Insight and understanding about politics might be based on the method of authority or the method of personal thought, or they might be derived from other sources such as literature, film, or art.

In the attempt to develop precise and valid generalizations about politics, however, most contemporary political scientists use some form of the scientific method and some of the modes of political analysis described in preceding sections. Whatever types of data and modes of analysis they use, political scientists generally accept the notion that all aspects of their research should be subject to scrutiny and challenge by other analysts. Most also agree that their hypotheses, inferences, generalizations, and theories must be subject to some empirical test of validity. Although various sources of knowledge can provide you with insights about politics, this book emphasizes the modes of political analysis described in this Appendix as the best means for a broad understanding of the political world.

Key Concepts

causal analysis, p. 456
constitutive analysis, p. 455
correlation, p. 456
correlational analysis, p. 456
cross-sectional data, p. 449
dependent variable, p. 452
formal analysis, p. 453
functional analysis, p. 455
independent variable, p. 452
interval data, p. 449

longitudinal data, p. 449
monarchy, p. 453
nominal data, p. 448
oligarchy, p. 453
ordinal data, p. 449
political analysis, p. 448
ratio data, p. 449
rational choice theory, p. 454
relational analysis, p. 456
taxonomic analysis, p. 452

Glossary

adjudication   Every society creates and enforces rules and laws regarding the proper forms of behavior for individuals and groups. The adjudication function attempts to interpret and apply the relevant rules or laws to a given situation. Most political systems have established judicial structures (e.g., criminal courts) whose primary role is adjudication.

administration   The general term used to describe the machinery and processes through which rules and policies of an organization are applied and implemented. It is a core function of political systems and is usually one of the four basic institutional structures (along with executives, legislatures, and judiciaries). (*See also* bureaucracy.)

assembly system   A form of collective leadership in which a large group, usually constituted as a legislature, is clearly dominant over the executive. Examples: the United Nations; the European Parliament.

associational interest group   A type of political interest group organized specifically to further the political objectives of its members. Examples: the British Medical Association; Common Cause. (*See also* interest group.)

authoritarianism   (1) A political system generally characterized by little or no commitment to equality or democratic participation and by a strong emphasis on order and stability. The political behavior of the population is severely constrained. In many countries, authoritarian regimes are dominated by a military elite. (2) A personality syndrome, associated particularly with political and social attitudes and behavior, in which the individual tends to revere strong leadership, draw sharp boundaries between the identity group and all others, be intolerant of unconventional behaviors, and exhibit considerable hostility toward minority groups.

authority   (1) A source of knowledge about the political world. The method of authority involves the appeal to any document, tradition, or person that is believed to possess the controlling explanation regarding a particular issue. (2) The legitimacy attached to the decisions of the political system, in the sense that people will willingly accept those decisions as binding, independent of their self-interest.

balance of power   A configuration of power among a set of states in which there is a broad equality in the power resources (political, economic, and especially military) that can be exercised by competing states. Through a system of shifting alliances, no state or group of states is able to achieve a preponderance of power. Thus, stability and the status quo are usually sustained because states will intervene to prevent a serious imbalance that might lead to domination.

BRICS   An acronym for the countries Brazil, Russia, India, China, and South Africa. These countries are projected to be major actors in the global system by 2015 and have entered into a comprehensive agreement to cooperate in the economic sphere.

bureaucracy   Though often used as a synonym for administration, bureaucracy has been defined, especially by Max Weber (1958a), as a particular structure and style through which administration can operate. Structurally, bureaucracy is characterized by hierarchical organization and a highly specialized division of labor. Members of the bureaucracy behave according to specific rules of action so that treatment of each case is relatively predictable and nondiscriminatory. (*See also* administration.)

capitalism   One of the great "isms," explicitly linking politics to political economy, capitalism is a system that corresponds loosely to a market economy. In this system, private economic actors are generally free from state constraints and the state engages in only limited efforts to shift resources among private actors. Capitalism is founded on the philosophy of laissez-faire economics. There is no assumption that capitalism requires a particular form of political processes to function efficiently.

causal analysis   A type of relational analysis, causal analysis goes beyond correlational analysis because it explicitly identifies one phenomenon as the effective agent that brings about changes in another phenomenon. Causal analysis presents the "If X, then Y" mode of explanation, where X is the independent variable that, given a certain value, actually causes Y, the dependent variable, to change in a particular way.

civil law   A system of law in which the central principle is to apply a very precise, detailed set of existing legal codes to the current case. Sometimes termed "scholar-made law," it evolved from Roman law and the Napoleonic codes and is common in many countries influenced by continental European legal forms.

civil war   A form of political violence that occurs when a significant proportion of the population within a region actively supports a separatist movement and political violence emerges on a large scale. Examples: Syria (2011—   ); U.S. Civil War (1861–1865).

class approach An analytic explanation of the value allocation process (politics) based on a core notion of stratification—structured inequality in the distribution of key values in society. The class approach centers on an examination of the tactics of class domination and the dynamics of class struggle. Class theory is particularly associated with the writings of Karl Marx (1867/1981) and later forms of Marxist theories.

classical liberalism One of the major Western political ideologies. In classical liberalism, the highest value is placed on each individual's natural rights to life, liberty, and property and the freedom of the individual to pursue these rights as an independent actor. Government plays a very limited role under classical liberalism, which celebrates a laissez-faire economy and discourages government attempts to create material equality (although equality of opportunity is important). Political thinkers associated with classical liberal thought include John Locke (1632–1704), Adam Smith (1723–1790), and John Stuart Mill (1806–1873).

colonialism A situation of dominance and subordination in the relations between two states. One state asserts substantial power and control over the other, based on military, economic, and/or political power. The goals of the dominant state might include: to extract resources, to control a market for its products, to use the strategic location, to instill its own values into members of the subordinate state, or to obtain international prestige. Most areas that were colonial holdings became independent in the decades after 1945. (*See also* neocolonialism.)

command economy An ideal-type political economy in which the state assumes total control of almost all significant factors of production. The state replaces or eliminates the role of private owners of land, labor, and capital; makes all production decisions; and determines the value of all goods. The state owns, plans, controls, and regulates all major economic activity. (*Compare with* market economy.)

common law A legal system that is grounded in general laws that have been promulgated over time. It relies on precedents, based on earlier judicial decisions, to guide current adjudication. Sometimes referred to as "judge-made law," it is the dominant form of jurisprudence in the United States, Great Britain, and numerous other countries.

communism One of the major "isms" linking politics and political economy, communism is a system that is closely associated with the command political economy. Based on the theories of Karl Marx (1867/1981) and others, the key to communism is the socialization of resources—the notion that the state must maintain control of society's land, labor, and capital. Although it is primarily an economic system, communism also emphasizes an ideological commitment to economic and social equality among all of its citizens. It also posits that until such equality is achieved, government and politics must be guided powerfully by a unified leadership. Examples: Cuba; the former Soviet Union.

confederation A loose association of states. In a confederation, each state delegates some power to a supranational central government but still retains primary power, and its compliance is always conditional. Confederations are usually created when states decide that the performance of certain functions is enhanced by structured cooperation with other states. Example: the United Nations.

conservatism One of the major Western political ideologies, at the core of conservatism is the commitment to sustain traditional values and forms of behavior and to maintain social order. Tradition and religion, rather than reason, are viewed as the most reliable sources for guiding society. There is loyalty to the nation and antipathy to egalitarianism. The writings of Edmund Burke (1790/1955) provide a good example of conservative thought.

constitution A set of statements that describes the fundamental rules of a political system, including a characterization of the core activities of major political structures. Most constitutions are a single, written document, such as the U.S. Constitution, but some are embedded primarily in major statutes, precedents, and legal decisions.

constitutional regime A political system that operates in terms of the rule of law, as defined in the constitution, and that ensures effective restraints on the power holders. The defining feature of a constitutional regime is that the state does attempt to fulfill the provisions of its constitution.

core Refers to the set of states, firms (especially multinational firms), and financial institutions that have enormous power and influence in the global system and the international political economy. The core, primarily located in the developed countries, dominates the world's "periphery," composed of institutions and peoples that have minimal power and are primarily located in the developing countries. Core is a crucial concept of the dependency approach, which is an explanation of both the relations between states and the development process.

corporatism A corporatist state is characterized by extensive economic cooperation between an activist state and a set of large organizations that represent actors who control major productive resources. In the hope that there will be cooperation and consultation (rather than conflict) among the state, big capital, big owners, and big labor, the leaders of these groups are given great influence in working with the state to make and implement policy on key political economy issues.

correlational analysis A form of relational analysis that determines whether there is a statistically probable relationship between two variables. The analysis does not conclude that one variable is actually the agent that causes change to occur in another variable (as in causal analysis) but merely assesses the strength and direction of the association between variables. Correlational analysis is often a key step in any empirical attempt to understand politics.

council system   A political system in which a small group shares collective leadership and is responsible for both executive and legislative functions. All members of the council have relatively equal power, so decisions and actions are based on the will of the council majority or council consensus. Examples: mayor–council systems and boards of supervisors in many U.S. local governments; Switzerland.

coup   Occurs when the top political leader or leadership group is replaced by violence or the explicit threat of violence. A coup is a common form of leadership turnover in political systems that have no accepted and enforceable procedures for leadership succession. Examples: ouster of Morsi in Egypt (2013); elimination of Gaddafi in Libya (2011).

democracy   A political system in which governance is accomplished by leaders whose authority is based on a limited mandate and who are elected by a universal electorate. Such an "electoral" democracy becomes a "liberal" democracy when the population selects among genuine alternatives and also has significant rights to political participation, expression, and opposition.

democratic socialism   A variation of socialist ideology that treats greater egalitarianism as its primary goal but also assumes that its goals can and should be implemented by a government that comes to power and rules by democratic means, not by violence and repression. Under democratic socialism, the government might own some of the major economic resources and regulate much of the economy, but it does not attempt to plan and control all aspects of the economic system. (*See also* socialism.)

democratization   The effort to institutionalize democratic political regimes more fully and deeply, especially in countries with limited democratic processes. Analyses often try to measure the extent of democratic consolidation and to specify the political, economic, and social conditions conducive to further democratization.

dependency approach   This claims that an economic and political hierarchy exists in which many actors take advantage of those with less power and resources. At the top are the most developed countries, and the poor people and the villages of the developing countries are at the bottom. Some analysts claim that many of the difficulties facing the less developed countries stem from their vulnerability to, and dependence on, the more highly developed countries and the transnational institutions they control.

dependent variable   The Y variable whose value changes as a result of changes in some other specified (independent) variables. Causal analysis presents the "If X, then Y" mode of explanation, where X is the independent variable that, given a certain value, actually causes Y, the dependent variable, to alter in value in a particular way.

dictatorship   A political system in which political leaders are not subject to a limited mandate but have absolute power and authority. The citizens have no regular and realistic opportunity to replace such political leadership in a nonviolent manner.

dual executive   A political system in which one actor, the head of state, performs the more ceremonial aspects of top leadership and embodies the nation, while another actor, the head of government, is responsible for the more political aspects of the executive role. (*See also* executive.) Example: The United Kingdom has Queen Elizabeth II (head of state) and Prime Minister David Cameron (head of government).

economic development   This occurs as more and more households and firms within a country are engaged in ever-higher levels of production and consumption. Based on greater control of the environment and resources, more (and more complex) goods are produced and exchanged, and the gross domestic product (GDP) gets larger relative to the number of people sharing in the market.

electoral system   The framework by which the votes of citizens are converted to specific selections of candidates who have a mandate to hold office. There are many variations, some based on selection proportional to votes cast (forms of PR) and others based on the selection of the candidate with most (plurality) or at least half (majority) of the votes.

elite approach   An analytic explanation of the value allocation process (politics) in which the political world is characterized by political stratification, the segmentation of the population into separate groups with greater or less power. There are only two major strata—those that do more of what there is to do (in the policy process) and that get more of the resources that are available, and those that do less and get less. These two groups are called the political elite and the mass, respectively. Key elite theorists include Gaetano Mosca (1896/1939) and C. Wright Mills (1956).

executive   The branch of the political system composed of a leader or group of leaders who are responsible for defining and managing the implementation of public policy. A broad definition of the executive includes not only the chief executive (e.g., mayor, governor, prime minister, president, queen) but also the entire administrative system.

fascism   A political ideology that places fundamental importance on the unity and harmony of government and society and is defined particularly by its opposition to forces that might weaken that collective unity. It further assumes that the top leader is the embodiment of the natural will and that all individuals and groups must obey the will of the leader. It is both antisocialist and antidemocratic. Fascism had a major impact on twentieth-century history and is particularly associated with regimes such as those of Adolf Hitler ("Nazism") in Germany (1932–1945) and Benito Mussolini in Italy (1922–1943).

federation   A political system in which there is a constitutional division of power and functions between a central government and a set of regional governments, usually known as states, provinces, or cantons. Power is shared among the levels of government, and no level has legal power to dominate any other level in all policy domains. Examples: Brazil; Canada; Mexico; the United States.

formal analysis   Specifies abstract forms that correspond to the reality in which the analyst is interested. The formal analyst attempts to "model" reality. Most formal analyses use symbol systems as abstract representations of the phenomenon under study, such as a subway map or David Easton's (1965) political system model.

functional analysis   Describes the contributions of a certain element (process or structure) to the activities of the phenomenon under study. For example, one form of functional analysis identifies certain functions or processes (e.g., political communication, rule adjudication) that occur within a political system and describes how and by what structures the functions are performed.

geopolitics   An analytical method that assumes that the geography of a state—its particular geographical location and also its physical characteristics, natural resources, and human resources—can significantly affect the domestic and foreign policy actions of the state.

globalization   The increasing integration of diverse economic, sociocultural, military, and environmental phenomena by means of dense networks of action and information that span vast distances around the world. These networks dramatically increase interdependence among actors within the international system and within environments such as the economic system and the environmental system.

guerrilla war   Violent opposition to an existing regime by means of a long, protracted campaign primarily from rural bases. Fighting is typically in a hit-and-run style, with extensive efforts to win the support of the peasants and the creation of new political institutions prior to collapse of the old regime. Example: FARC's lengthy campaign against the Colombian government.

hegemony   The existence of an extraordinarily powerful group (a "hegemonic elite") or country ("hegemon") that sustains its domination over other actors for a long period of time.

hybrid system   A political system that attempts to blend the desirable aspects of both the presidential and cabinet systems of government. Hybrid systems have a prime minister and an elected legislature that can both enact and implement policies, but they also have a president who may have relatively equal power with the cabinet or may have key specific, but limited, powers. Examples: France; Russia.

ideal types   An analytic construct that defines "pure forms" of a phenomenon (e.g., ideal types of political economies). These forms are distinguished by the configuration of key characteristics. Few, if any, real-world cases are identical to an ideal type, which is a means to facilitate comparative analysis.

independent variable   The variable in a cause-and-effect hypothesis or explanation that produces change in another variable. In the "If X, then Y" mode of explanation, X is the independent variable that, given a certain value, actually causes Y, the dependent variable, to change in a particular way.

interest group   A group that directly attempts to influence the allocation of public values or other actions of those in the political system. It may undertake political action, provide goods or services to political actors, or provide data and information to those within the political system in its attempts to achieve its political objectives. It may also exert influence through compliance or noncompliance with the government policy process.

intergovernmental organizations (IGOs)   Political actors whose members are states, not private groups or individuals. IGOs can shape the cooperative relations among states, some or all of whom are their members. States form IGOs to provide a forum of communication among states, to enact multinational laws and treaties, and to intervene in disputes between states. Examples: European Union; NAFTA; NATO.

international law   A broad attempt to establish principles and rules that formalize and constrain the interactions among states. Positivist law, or written agreements between states in the form of international treaties or conventions, is the basis for international law.

international organization   A broad term that refers to many of the crossnational institutions whose objectives are to influence the behavior and policies of states. The two primary forms are nongovernmental organizations (NGOs) and intergovernmental organizations (IGOs). Examples: Amnesty International; the United Nations.

international regime   A set of norms, rules, and procedures that are accepted by many countries and guide their behavior with one another in a particular issue domain. Examples: the World Trade Organization on trade relations; the Nuclear Nonproliferation Treaty.

international relations   One of the four major subfields within political science, "IR" examines the interactions among states and other transnational actors as they pursue political goals. Subjects of analysis include foreign policy, interstate conflict, globalization, and international law.

judicial review   In political systems where the judiciary is relatively independent, the judiciary can interpret or even revoke the policy decisions and actions taken by the other political structures, thus exercising the power of judicial review. In the United States, for example, the Supreme Court exercises the power of judicial review when it decides whether a law passed by Congress is unconstitutional.

judiciary   An important branch of most political systems, the system of courts and personnel that determine whether the laws of the society have been transgressed, and if so, whether and what type of sanctions ought to be imposed on the transgressor.

legislature   The political structure in which, typically, policy issues are discussed and assessed and public policies are enacted by a set of elected or appointed legislators. Although a particular legislature may not exercise these powers, most have three broad roles: (1) enacting legislation; (2) representing the citizenry; and (3) overseeing the executive.

liberal democracy   A political system that not only is an electoral democracy (periodic elections, limited mandate) but also ensures extensive political rights (e.g., parties promoting genuine alternatives, opposition) and civil liberties (e.g., freedom of expression, religion, and the media).

liberalism   In international relations theory, liberalism assumes that states can cooperate in mutually beneficial ways. Liberalism expects the state to make decisions and act in the international system based on its own mix of normative principles that might encourage cooperation. Conflict can be avoided through the construction of international institutions based on mutually acceptable principles.

market economy   An ideal-type political economy in which there is near-total private control of land, labor, and capital. Every actor has direct control over his or her own factors of production, and production decisions are essentially the sum of all private actors' decisions. The exchange value of goods is decided by the market. The state is generally quite passive in a market economy, simply enforcing rules and providing minimal protection to economic actors. (*Compare with* command economy.)

Marxist–Leninist socialism   A variant of socialist ideology heavily influenced by the writings of Karl Marx and the interpretations by V. I. Lenin. It begins with three assumptions regarding the changes necessary to produce the key goals of equality and social justice: (1) it might be necessary to use violence to overthrow the old economic order; (2) a powerful government is necessary

to restructure the economic system; and (3) a small dictatorial leadership group must manage the government and effect the economic and social changes. This group will be unnecessary when equality is achieved and can be replaced by decentralized citizen-run politics. (*See also* socialism.)

micropolitics   An analytic focus on individual and small-group political processes, with a particular emphasis on how the individual understands the political world and how the individual acts politically.

mixed economy   A political economy that attempts to combine the strengths of both market and command economies while also minimizing their shortcomings. Control of the means of production is shared between the state and private actors. The state's rules, actions, and direct involvement in the economic system guide some production, distribution, and pricing decisions and also moderate and limit the market behavior of private households and firms.

monarchy   (1) A political system with a hereditary sovereign, often called a king or queen, as in United Kingdom of Great Britain and Northern Ireland. (2) Analytically, a political system in which one person exercises a very large proportion of political control, which can also be termed an "autocracy."

nation   A sociopolitical unit defined by a deeply shared fundamental identification among a set of people based on shared ethnicity, language, descent, culture, religion, and/or geographic space. The nation is a major group, beyond the family, with whom the individual identifies very powerfully.

nationalism   A strong affection and commitment to the well-being of the nation with which one identifies, in comparison with minimal concern for those outside the nation. Nationalism can become the underlying principle shaping people's loyalty and willingness to make sacrifices for the protection and enhancement of the nation and its collective interests.

natural law   Sensible, widely accepted (universal?) norms of behavior that direct us to act with goodness and are recognizable through human reason. They should guide the relations among states and individuals and should restrain hostile or destructive interactions.

neocolonialism   New forms of domination and dependence between states that have emerged in the decades since the end of colonialism (after World War II). Although direct occupation by colonial powers was ended at independence, domination has been extended in some cases by the manipulation of power resources such as economic aid, technology transfer, military support, and economic intervention. (*See also* colonialism.)

neoliberalism   An approach to economic development that emphasizes a reliance on a local and global free market that is guided by entrepreneurs who shape decisions about the production and distribution of goods. The state plays a minimal role in the political economy, and public spending is focused on infrastructure support (e.g., transportation, education) rather than welfare distribution.

nonconstitutional regime A political system in which there is persistent nonenforcement of crucial limits on the rulers and/or protection of the rights of the ruled, especially those limits and rights specified in a constitution and other key legal documents. Most authoritarian or totalitarian regimes are nonconstitutional.

nongovernmental organizations (NGOs) National or transnational associations that are not part of the governmental/state apparatus but are committed to the promotion of an issue with national or international policy dimensions. (In the latter case, the association is called an international nongovernmental organization.) Members are groups and individuals who combine their knowledge and financial and political resources to pursue a shared objective. Examples: Amnesty International's monitoring of human rights; Médecins sans Frontières (Doctors Without Borders) provisions of medical assistance.

normative political knowledge Answers questions about what ought to be rather than simply providing descriptions and explanations of what is. Examples of normative questions: What are the appropriate domains of state action? Should there be limits on free speech? How much and what types of health care should the state provide?

oligarchy Literally, rule by the few. Hence, a political system in which a small number of actors dominate the resource allocation process, usually serving their own interests.

parliamentary government A political system in which the executive and legislative functions and structures are fused. The people elect the legislature (parliament), whose majority empowers a cabinet, which then empowers one of its members to be the chief executive, usually called a prime minister or premier. The cabinet devises, drafts, and implements most policies, although they must be enacted by the legislative majority. Examples: Italy; the United Kingdom.

participatory democracy Democracy in its classic sense as government of and by all the people. There is active, direct participation by all citizens in the policy process.

party system The configuration of political parties in a political system. Party systems are generally classified according to the number of political parties and the nature of the interactions among the parties in the governing process.

pluralism An analytic explanation of the value allocation process (politics) that is grounded in the concept of the group—any aggregate of individuals who interact to pursue a common interest. Within this approach, politics can be understood as the interaction among groups that are pursuing their political interests, and policy decisions are the outcome of that group process. It is assumed that any particular individual can belong to many different groups and has some political resources that can be used in an attempt to influence policy decisions.

political analysis The attempt to describe and explain political phenomena that strives to make understanding of politics more general, precise, and systematic, and ultimately to generate and test theories.

political belief system The configuration of an individual's political orientations across an array of political issues. Many political beliefs are evaluative orientations, which synthesize facts (cognitive orientations) and feelings (affective orientations) into a judgment (evaluative orientation) about some political phenomena.

political culture The general configuration of a particular people's (e.g., a nation's or a country's) political beliefs. It characterizes those cognitive, affective, and evaluative orientations that are dominant among those people. Many explanations of political behavior and political processes are grounded in interpretations of political culture.

political decay The phenomena that occur when there is a decline in the capacity of the political system, especially its effectiveness in maintaining order. It can be manifest in collective behavior such as demonstrations, protests, rebellion, and other forms of political violence. It is often associated with extensive demands that the political system cannot meet and with the loss of citizen support for the political system. According to Samuel Huntington (1968), the probability of political decay increases as a state has a lower level of political institutionalization.

political development The specifically political aspects of development and modernization. It can refer either to a set of characteristics of the political system or to the process through which those characteristics are increased. The key characteristics of more developed political systems can include: (1) the concentration of power in the central state; (2) "modern" forms of political organization, such as institutionalized party systems and effective bureaucracies; (3) complex and extensive forms of individual and group political behavior; and (4) expanded capabilities of the political system to maintain order, manage the environment, meet the demands of the citizens, and so on.

political economy The combination, in theory or in practice, of politics and economics. The political system and the economic system are inextricably intertwined because many of the decisions made by the political system have significant effects on the economy, and activities within the economic system have major effects on the state. Two ideal-type political economies are the market economy and the command economy.

political elite   A general term for those individuals who have relatively high levels of power, influence, interest, knowledge, and involvement in political life. It is the stratum of the population that does more of what there is to do (in the policy process) and gets more of what there is to get (in the allocation of values).

political ideology   A comprehensive set of beliefs about the political world, including a specification of desirable political goals and the best way to achieve those goals, based on particular assumptions about human nature, the relation of the individual to the state and society, and the desirability of equality.

political institutions   The established roles, rules, procedures, and structures through which government operates (e.g., the electoral college, parliament, the bureaucracy, and the military).

political institutionalization   The extent to which political organizations and procedures have acquired value in the eyes of the population and the stability to withstand significant pressure. It is measured by the political system's capacity to regulate its citizens, respond flexibly to citizen demands, extract and distribute resources efficiently, and adapt to changing circumstances.

political participation   The term applied to all modes of the political actions by individuals and groups. The broad goal is to influence the actions or selection of political rulers. Modes of political participation for an individual range from listening to political discourse, to voting, to taking part in a demonstration, to holding political office.

political party   An organized group that attempts to capture political power directly by placing its members in government office. The political party is the broadest institution in most political systems that links individuals and groups to the state, and it can organize the activities of those participating in government. It also aggregates political interests into a comprehensible set of policy goals.

political resources   Something that can influence the actions and decisions of political actors, such as social status, money, legality, special knowledge or skills, ability to mobilize large numbers of people, visibility in the media, and control of productive capabilities. According to the pluralist approach, political resources are of many forms and widely distributed. According to the class and elite approaches, one or a few types of political resources are critical, and control of those resources tends to be concentrated in a limited group.

political science   A set of techniques, concepts, and approaches whose objective is to increase the clarity and accuracy of understandings about political phenomena. This academic discipline is labeled a "science" in many countries because most political scientists use the scientific method to establish shared knowledge about the political world.

political socialization   The process through which individuals acquire their cognitive, affective, and evaluative orientations toward the political world. Some of the most important agents (sources) are the family, the schools, peer groups, the media, religion, and culture.

political society   Formed when individuals cede to the state a monopoly over the legitimate use of violence, sacrificing their own right to do violence to others in exchange for a similar sacrifice from others. Thomas Hobbes (1651) called this agreement among individuals the *social contract*.

political system   A (formal) theoretical concept that attempts to model the fundamental structures, processes, and institutions of politics. According to David Easton (1965), the defining feature is its authoritative allocation of values for the collectivity.

political violence   The use of physical violence, or very serious threats of such violence, to achieve political goals. The modes range from nuclear war, to assassination, to riots. Some analysts define as political violence other activities that do not entail physical violence, such as racial epithets or ethnic discrimination.

politics   The processes through which power and influence are used to promote certain values and interests and to determine who gets what, when, and how in a given social system.

positivist law   Explicit written agreements, often enacted by legislatures and interpreted by judiciaries, that specify appropriate and unlawful behaviors as well as the sanctions for the latter. In the form of treaties or conventions between states, positivist law is the basis of international law.

power   Exercised when A (one actor) induces B (another actor) to behave in a manner in which B would not otherwise behave. One taxonomy classifying the forms of power includes force (coercive power), exchange (economic power), and mutuality (integrative power).

presidential government   A political system in which there is a separation of executive and legislative power and structures. This is meant to ensure a system of checks and balances in the policy process, with the legislature taking primary responsibility for policymaking and the president (the executive) taking primary responsibility for policy implementation (although in practice these distinctions may be blurred). The president and the members of the legislature are elected independently, for fixed terms. Examples: Mexico; the United States.

privatization   The selling off of state-owned firms to private actors and/or the use of private firms to provide public goods and services.

prosperity   A fundamental goal for a state and its citizens, with key subgoals including the capacity of the political economy to control resources in order to produce and distribute desired goods and to provide for adequate material well-being for its population (see Figure 5.1).

public policy   Any decision or action by a governmental authority that results in the allocation of a value. A taxonomy of public policies could be based on the functional area of the policy (e.g., environmental, trade), the overall effects of the policy (e.g., redistributive, symbolic), or the stages of the policy process (e.g., problem definition, evaluation).

rational choice theory   An array of formal analyses that share two basic features: (1) they are attempts to represent political processes primarily by means of mathematical formulations or systems of symbolic notation; and (2) it is assumed that the behavior of political actors is goal-oriented, based on self-interest, and calculating. Examples: game theory; minimum winning coalition theory.

realism   A perspective, especially in international relations theory, that assumes that people are naturally disposed to behave selfishly and that this self-interested orientation extends to the behavior of states. The fundamental goal of each state is to ensure its own security and survival by maximizing its power. Interstate conflict is likely to be a recurring event, and states sometimes use balance-of-power strategies to limit the frequency of major conflicts.

relational analysis   Approaches to political analysis that specify the systematic connections between sets of phenomena, revealing either patterns of association (correlation) or causality.

representative democracy   A form of electoral democracy in which citizens elect people to represent them in the governing process and to allocate values on their behalf for the collectivity. Also known as a republic.

revolution   A rapid and fundamental transformation of the state organization and of the allocation of values in a society. A revolution often involves the use of force and violence to destroy the existing political system.

security   A fundamental goal of a government and society, with key subgoals including the capacity to survive and to protect its borders from unwanted external intervention (see Figure 5.1).

security dilemma   The situation in the politics across borders in which every state is concerned about its security goals because there is no overarching authority that can necessarily enforce a violation of a state's sovereignty.

social democracy   A political system with strong, institutionalized democratic politics; a mixed political economy with both considerable free market activity and regulation; and substantial policies of social welfare distribution to all citizens. Examples: Belgium; Sweden.

social market system   A political–economic system in which the state encourages the operation of an extensive free-market economy but is also committed to social welfare distribution and some income redistribution, within the context of a democratic political process. Contemporary examples: Germany; Sweden.

social networks   The group of people, including friends, family members, peers, and colleagues from work, school, clubs, churches, or other groups, that may exercise significant influence on a person's attitudes and values.

socialism   One of the major Western political ideologies, in which the most important goal is to provide a high-quality, relatively equal standard of living for all. Each individual is encouraged to enhance the collective good of all in an environment that encourages cooperation and sharing. Government plays a crucial role as it attempts to use its allocation of values and control of resources to increase the material, social, and political equality of all citizens. Two major variations are Marxist–Leninist socialism and democratic socialism.

soft power   A form of power exercise in which actor B is persuaded to agree to what another actor (A) wants because B greatly admires A's qualities, culture, or ideals, even if the agreement is not in B's evident self-interest. In this situation, there is no explicit use of either force or economic inducement, the "hard" forms of power.

sovereignty   The premise that each state has complete authority and is the ultimate source of law within its own borders. It assumes that all states are equal before the law and that each state has the right to protect its territory against any aggression or intervention.

stability   A fundamental goal of a government, with key subgoals including the capacity to maintain public order and to manage public institutions with adequate capabilities to function effectively in pursuing its policy objectives (see Figure 5.1).

state   (1) The legal notion of the state is that it is a "territorially bound sovereign entity." (2) In the general language of political science, the word *state* usually refers to the organizational units, institutions, and individuals that perform the political functions for a national territorial entity, such as France or Nigeria. (3) The state can also be defined as the entity with a monopoly on the legitimate use of violence to enforce the laws and decisions of the society.

state capitalism   A political economy in which the leaders of the political system assert extensive control over who is allowed to compete in key sectors of the economy and in which the primary goal of the economy is to serve state power.

statism   A state-centered strategy for facilitating economic development. The statist approach emphasizes the importance of strong state action to support and guide the production and distribution of goods by the political economy. The state typically plans and regulates major aspects of the political economy and might own and operate key economic sectors.

taxonomic analysis   Approaches to political analysis that establish the orderly arrangement of phenomena into a set of categories that classify those phenomena/data into different types. Categories should be exhaustive, mutually exclusive, and differentiated by consistent criteria. The categories of a taxonomy establish the crucial concepts that structure the analysis.

territorial integrity   A concept closely associated with sovereignty, it is a premise of international law that holds that a state has the right to resist and reject any aggression, invasion, or intervention within its territorial borders.

terrorism   Premeditated violence serving an underlying political objective, in which the target of violence is a "noncombatant." Those engaged in terrorism can have a variety of political objectives, such as promotion of a cause, revenge, or extraction of resources. As a revolutionary strategy, terrorism involves selective acts of violence, usually by small, organized cells of political activists.

totalitarianism   A political regime that demands complete obedience to its extensive rules regarding not only politics but also nearly all aspects of life, including culture, economics, religion, and morality. It might prescribe and proscribe the behavior and thoughts of its population in every domain of existence. Examples: contemporary North Korea; the Soviet Union under Joseph Stalin.

transnationalism   A system of institutions and relationships in which key actors' loyalties and identities are not linked to any particular country. Many of these powerful actors are multinational corporations (MNCs) such as General Motors, Exxon, and Sony, and other important transnational actors include the International Monetary Fund, OPEC, NATO, and other IGOs and NGOs. Increasingly, MNCs and other transnational actors hold international economic power, shape global culture and communications, and operate outside the legal control of states.

treaty   A formal agreement between states that they will cooperate or assist each other militarily, economically, and/or politically. A treaty carries a stronger expectation of compliance than an alliance. Examples: NATO; Nuclear Nonproliferation Treaty.

unitary state   A political system in which the central government holds all legitimate power. The central government may delegate power or functional responsibilities to territorial units (often called departments, regions, or prefectures), but those delegated powers and functions can be revoked at any time. Examples: China; France; Japan; Philippines.

war   Interstate violence that is sustained, organized, and usually involves hostilities between the regular military forces of the states. War is the ultimate mechanism for attempting to resolve power struggles and conflict between states. Examples: Iran–Iraq War (1980–1988); Korean War (1950–1953).

welfare state   A system of state interventions in the political economy whose goal is to implement public policies that provide all citizens with an adequate quality of life in domains such as education, health care, housing, and employment opportunities. Usually characterized by relatively high taxes, more extensive resource allocations (e.g., transfer payments or subsidized goods and services), and more active state intervention to protect citizens against the behaviors of those firms or others whose actions reduce the quality of life. Example: Sweden.

References

Abadie, Alberto. (2004). "Poverty, Political Freedom, and the Roots of Terrorism." Cambridge, MA: KSG Working Paper 04–043 (October).

Abdallah, Saaman, Sam Thompson, Juliet Michaelson, Nic Marks, and Nicole Steuer. (2011). *The Happy Planet Index*. http://www.happyplanetindex.org/data/

Acemoglu, Daron, and James A. Robinson. (2009). *Economic Origins of Dictatorship and Democracy*. New York: Cambridge University Press.

Acemoglu, Daron, and James A. Robinson. (2012). *Why Nations Fail: The Origins of Power, Prosperity, and Poverty*. New York: Random House.

Agnew, John. (2003). *Geopolitics: Re-Visioning World Politics*. London: Routledge.

Agnew, John. (2009). *Globalization and Sovereignty*. Rowman & Littlefield.

Aguilar, Francesco, and Mauro Galluccio, eds. (2011). *Psychological and Political Strategies for Peace Negotiation: A Cognitive Approach*. New York: Springer.

Almond, Gabriel, and Sidney Verba. (1963). *The Civic Culture*. Princeton, NJ: Princeton University Press.

Amnesty International. (2014). *Amnesty International Report 2013*, https://www.amnesty.org/en/annual-report/2014

Anderson, James E. (2011). *Public Policymaking: An Introduction*. 7th ed. Independence, KY: Cengage.

Anduiza, Eva, Michael Jensen, and Laia Jorba, eds. (2012). *Digital Media and Political Engagement Worldwide: A Comparative Study*. New York: Cambridge University Press.

Ardrey, Robert. (1966). *The Territorial Imperative*. New York: Atheneum.

Arendt, Hannah. (1963). *On Revolution*. New York: Viking Press.

Arias, Oscar. (2011). "Culture Matters: The Real Obstacles to Latin American Development." *Foreign Affairs* (February): 2–6.

Armijo, Leslie Elliott. (2007). "The BRICs Countries (Brazil, Russia, India, and China) As Analytical Category: Mirage or Insight?" *Asian Perspectives* 31(4): 7–42.

Aslund, Anders, and Andrew Kuchins. (2009). *The Russia Balance Sheet*. Washington, DC: Peterson Institute for International Economics.

Bachrach, Peter, and Morton Baratz. (1962). "The Two Faces of Power." *American Political Science Review* 56 (December): 947–952.

Bagdikian, Ben. (2004). *The New Media Monopoly*. Boston: Beacon Press.

Baghwati, Jagdish. (2007). *In Defense of Globalization*. New York: Oxford University Press.

Bajoria, Jayshree, and Robert McMahon. (2013). *The Dilemma of Humanitarian Intervention*. Council on Foreign Relations. http://www.cfr.org/humanitarian-intervention/dilemma-humanitarian-intervention/p16524

Barber, Benjamin R. (1996). *Jihad vs. McWorld*. New York: Random House.

Barber, Benjamin R. (2004). *Strong Democracy: Participatory Politics for a New Age*. 20th anniv. ed. Berkeley: University of California Press.

Bardach, Eugene. (2011). *A Practical Guide for Policy Analysis: The Eightfold Path to More Effective Problem Solving*. 4th ed. Washington, DC: CQ Press.

Barnet, Richard J., and John Cavanagh. (1994). *Global Dreams: Imperial Corporations and the New World Order*. New York: Simon and Schuster.

Barnett, Michael N., and Martha Finnemore. (2004). *Rules for the World: International Organizations in Global Politics*. Ithaca, NY: Cornell University Press.

Basic, Nedzad, David Goetze, and Charles Anthony Smith. (2003). "Secession Crises, Human Welfare, and Conflict Resolution." *Conflict, Security, & Development* 3(2): 185–209.

Basu, Soumita. (2013). "Emancipatory Potential in Feminist Security Studies." *International Studies Perspectives* 14: 455–458.

Bates, Robert H. (2008). *When Things Fell Apart: State Failure in Late Twentieth Century Africa.* Cambridge: Cambridge University Press.

Baumol, William, and Alan Blinder. (2012). *Economics.* 12th ed. Independence, KY: Cengage.

Baumgartner, Frank, Jeffrey Berry, Marie Hojnacki, David Kimball, and Beth L. Leech. (2009). *Lobbying and Policy Change: Who Wins, Who Loses, and Why.* Chicago: University of Chicago Press.

Baumgartner, Frank, and Beth Leech. (1998). *Basic Interests: The Importance of Groups in Politics and Political Science.* Princeton, NJ: Princeton University Press.

Bell, Stephen. (2011). "Do We Really Need a New 'Constructivist Institutionalism' to Explain Institutional Change?" *British Journal of Political Science* 41(4): 883–906.

Bennett, W. Lance. (2012). *News: The Politics of Illusion.* 9th ed. New York: Pearson.

Bentley, Arthur. (1908/1967). *The Process of Government.* Cambridge, MA: Harvard University Press.

Berenskoetter, Felix, and M. J. Williams, eds. (2007). *Power in World Politics.* New York: Routledge.

Berrebi, Claude. (2007). "Evidence About the Link Between Education, Poverty, and Terrorism Among Palestinians." *Peace Economics, Peace Science, and Public Policy* 13(1): article 2.

Berry, Jeffrey. (2000). *The New Liberalism: The Rising Power of Citizen Groups.* Washington, DC: Brookings Press.

Betts, Richard K. (2010). "Conflict or Cooperation?: Three Visions Revisited." *Foreign Affairs* 89 (November/December): http://www.foreignaffairs.com/articles/66802/richard-k-betts/conflict-or-cooperation?page=show

Bickel, Alexander M. (1962). *The Least Dangerous Branch: The Supreme Court at the Bar of Politics.* New Haven: Yale University Press.

Bill, James, and Robert Hardgrave. (1981). *Comparative Politics: Quest for Theory.* Lanham, MD: University Press of America.

Bimber, Bruce. (2003). *Information and American Democracy: Technology and the Evolution of Political Power.* New York: Cambridge University Press.

Binningsbo, Helga Malmin. (2013). "Power Sharing, Peace and Democracy: Any Obvious Relationships?" *International Area Studies Review* 16(1): 89–112.

Birnbaum, David. (2005). "The Road to Riches is Called K Street," *Washington Post* (June 22, 2005): A01. http://www.washingtonpost.com/wp-dyn/content/article/2005/06/21/AR2005062101632.html

Black, Cyril. (1966). *The Dynamics of Modernization.* New York: Harper and Row.

Blank, Grant, and William H. Dutton. (2014). "Next Generation Internet Users: Digital Divides, Choices, and Inequalities." In *Society and the Internet: How Information and Social Networks are Changing Our Lives,* edited by M. Graham and W. H. Dutton. Oxford: Oxford University Press.

Bloomberg.com (2009). http://www.bloomberg.com/apps/news?pid=20601109&refer=home&sid=aH3aDwXXnvqc

Blustein, Paul. (2006). *And the Money Kept Rolling In (and Out): Wall Street, the IMF, and the Bankruptcy of Argentina.* New York: Public Affairs.

Bongar, Bruce, Lisa Brown, Larry Beutler, James Breckenridge, and Philip Zimbardo, eds. (2006). *Psychology of Terrorism.* New York: Oxford University Press.

Bonker, Frank. (2006). *The Political Economy of Fiscal Reform in Central-Eastern Europe.* Northampton, MA: Edward Elgar Publishing.

Boulding, Kenneth E. (1989). *Three Faces of Power.* Newbury Park, CA: Sage.

Boulding, Kenneth E. (1993). "Power." In *The Oxford Companion to Politics of the World,* edited by Joel Krieger, 739–740. New York: Oxford University Press.

Boulianne, S. (2009). "Does Internet Use Affect Engagement? A Meta-Analysis of Research." *Political Communication,* 26(2): 193–211.

Brandal, Nik, Oivind Bratberg, and Dag Einar Thorsen. (2013). *The Nordic Model of Social Democracy.* New York: Palgrave Macmillan.

Bratton, Michael, and Nicholas Van de Walle. (1997). *Democratic Experiments in Africa: Regime Transitions in Comparative Perspective.* Cambridge: Cambridge University Press.

Brecher, Michael, and Jonathan Wilkenfeld. (2000). *A Study of Crisis.* Ann Arbor: University of Michigan Press.

Bremmer, Ian. (2010). *The End of the Free Market: Who Wins the War Between States and Corporations?* New York: Portfolio Penguin.

Bremmer, Ian. (2013). *Every Nation for Itself: What Happens When No One Leads the World.* New York: Portfolio Penguin.

Bremer, Stuart. (1980). "National Capabilities and War Proneness." In *Correlates of War II,* edited by J. David Singer, 57–82. New York: Free Press.

Brinton, Crane. (1957). *The Anatomy of Revolution.* Rev. ed. New York: Vintage.

The Brookings Institution. (2011). "How Social Networking can Reinvigorate American Democracy and Civic Participation." Washington, DC. (June 28, 2011). http://www.pewinternet.org/Presentations/2011/Jun/~/media/Files/Presentations/2011/Jun/Brookings_social_media.pdf

Brownlee, Jason, Tarek Masoud, and Andrew Reynolds. (2013). "Why the Modest Harvest?" *Journal of Democracy* 24(4): 29–44.

Brzezinski, Zbigniew. (2004). *The Choice: Global Domination or Global Leadership.* New York: Basic Books.

Bueno de Mesquita, Bruce, and George Downs. (2005). "Development and Democracy." *Foreign Affairs* 84 (September/October): 77–86.

Burke, Edmund. (1790/1955). *The Works of Edmund Burke.* New York: Harper and Row.

Calderisi, Robert. (2007). *The Trouble with Africa: Why Foreign Aid Isn't Working.* New York: Palgrave.

Campbell, Arthur. (2013). "Word-of-Mouth Communication and Percolation in Social Networks." *The American Economic Review,* 103(6): 2466–2498.

Cantril, Hadley. (1965). *The Pattern of Human Concerns.* New Brunswick: Rutgers University Press.

Carden, James W. (2013). "Why Russians Still Don't Hate Communism." *The National Interest* (October 23, 2013). http://nationalinterest.org/commentary/why-russians-still-dont-hate-communism-9294

Carruthers, David and Patricia Rodriguez. (2009). "Mapuche Protest, Environmental Conflict and Social Movement Linkage in Chile." *Third World Quarterly* 30(4): 743–760.

Castells, Manuel. (2009). *Communication Power.* New York: Oxford University Press.

Castells, Manuel. (2012). *Networks of Outrage and Hope: Social Movements in the Internet Age.* New York: Polity Press.

Castenada, Jorge G. (2011). *Manana Forever?: Mexico and the Mexicans.* New York: Alfred Knopf.

Castles, Francis G. (2004). *The Future of the Welfare State: Crisis Myths and Crisis Realities.* New York: Oxford University Press.

Castles, Francis G., Stephan Leibfried, Jane Lewis, Herbert Obinger, and Christopher Pierson, eds. (2010). *The Oxford Handbook of the Welfare State.* New York: Oxford University Press.

Ceka, Besir. (2012). "The Perils of Political Competition: Explaining Participation and Trust in Political Parties in Eastern Europe." *Comparative Political Studies* 46(12): 1610–1635.

Center for Responsive Politics. (2013). http://www.opensecrets.org.

Central Intelligence Agency. (2013). *World Factbook 2013.* http://www.odci.gov/cia/ciahome.html

Central Intelligence Agency. (2014). *World Factbook 2014.* https://www.cia.gov/library/publications/the-world-factbook

Chadwick, Andrew. (2013). *The Hybrid Media System: Politics and Power.* New York: Oxford University Press.

Chadwick, Andrew, and Philip Howard. (2009). *Routledge Handbook of Internet Politics.* New York: Routledge.

Chamie, Joseph. (2014). "Israeli Palestinian Population Growth and Its Impact on Peace." *PassBlue Covering the UN* passblue.com/2014/02/02israeli-palestinian-population-growth

Cheibub, Jose Antonio. (2007). *Presidentialism, Parliamentarianism, and Democracy.* New York: Cambridge University Press.

Chin, Gregory T. (2010). "Remaking the Architecture: The Emerging Powers, Self-insuring, and Regional Insulation." *International Affairs* 86(3): 693–715.

Cigler, Allan. (2013). "Interest Group Money in the 2008 Federal Election." In *Interest Group Politics,* 8th ed., edited by Allan Cigler and Burdett Loomis. Washington, DC: CQ Press.

Cigler, Allan, and Burdett A. Loomis, eds. (2013). *Interest Group Politics.* 8th ed. Washington, DC: CQ Press.

Clausewitz, Karl von. (1833/1967). *On War.* Edited and translated by Michael Howard and Peter Paret. Princeton, NJ: Princeton University Press.

Compton, Jr., Robert W. (2000). *East Asian Democratization: Impact of Globalization, Culture, and Economy.* Westport, CT: Praeger Publishers.

CNA Corporation. (2007). *National Security and the Threat of Climate Change.* Alexandria, VA: CNA Corporation.

Cronin, James, George Ross, and James Shoch, eds. (2011). *What's Left of the Left: Social Democrats in Challenging Times.* Durham, NC: Duke University Press.

Cohen, Saul Bernard. (2008). *Geopolitics of the World System.* 2nd ed. Rowan & Littlefield.

Colburn, Forrest. (2002). *Latin America at the End of Politics.* Princeton, NJ: Princeton University Press.

Coles, Robert. (2003). *Bruce Springsteen's America: The People Listening, a Poet Singing.* New York: Random House.

Collier, Paul. (2008). *The Bottom Billion: Why the Poorest Countries are Failing and What Can Be Done about It.* New York: Oxford University Press.

Collier, Paul. (2010). *Wars, Guns and Votes: Democracy in Dangerous Places.* New York: Harper.

Collier, Paul, and Anke Hoeffler. (2007). "Unintended Consequences: Does Aid Promote Arms Races?" *Oxford Bulletin of Economics and Statistics* 69(1): 1–27.

Collier, Paul and Anthony J. Venables. (2010). *Natural Resources and State Fragility.* EUI Working Paper RSCAS 2010/36

Compton, Robert W. (2000). *East Asian Democratization: The Impact of Globalization, Culture, and Economy,* Westport, CT: Greenwood Publishing Group.

Connor, Walker. (1994). *Ethnonationalism: The Quest for Understanding.* Princeton, NJ: Princeton University Press.

Converse, Philip. (1964). "The Nature of Belief Systems in Mass Publics." In *Ideology and Discontent,* edited by David Apter, 224–240. Glencoe, IL: Free Press.

Cortright, David, and George Lopez, eds. (2002). *Smart Sanctions: Toward Effective and Humane Sanctions Reform.* Lanham, MD: Rowan and Littlefield.

Costanza, Robert. (2008). "Stewardship for a 'Full' World." *Current History* (January): 30–35.

Council on Foreign Relations. (2005). *What Is Terrorism?* http://cfrterrorism.org/terrorism/introduction.html.

Crenshaw, Martha. (2000). "An Agenda for the 21st Century." *Political Psychology* 21: 405–420.

Cropf, Robert A., and William S. Krummenacher, eds. (2011). *Information Communication Technologies and the Virtual Public Sphere: Impacts of Network Structures on Civil Society.* Hershey, PA: IGI Global.

Crouch, Colin, and Wolfgang Streeck, eds. (2006). *The Diversity of Democracy: Corporatism, Social Order and Political Conflict.* Cheltenham, UK: Edward Elgar.

Cutright, Phillips. (1963). "National Political Development: Measurement and Analysis." *American Sociological Review* 20: 253–264.

Dafoe, Allan, John R. Oneal, and Bruce Russett. (2013). "The Democratic Peace: Weighing the Evidence and Cautious Inference." *International Studies Quarterly* 57(1): 201–214.

Dahl, Robert. (1961). *Who Governs? Democracy in an American City.* New Haven, CT: Yale University Press.

Dahl, Robert. (1971). *Polyarchy: Participation and Opposition.* New Haven, CT: Yale University Press.

Dahl, Robert. (1991). *Democracy and Its Critics.* New Haven, CT: Yale University Press.

Dahl, Robert. (2006). *A Preface to Democratic Theory.* Expanded ed. Chicago: University of Chicago Press.

Dahl, Robert, and Bruce Stinebrickner. (2003). *Modern Political Analysis.* 6th ed. New York: Pearson.

Dahlstrom, Carl, Victor Lapuente, and Jan Teorell. (2012). "The Merit of Meritocratization: Politics, Bureaucracy, and the Institutional Deterrents of Corruption." *Political Research Quarterly* 65(3): 656–668.

Dahrendorf, Ralf. (1959). *Class and Class Conflict in Industrial Society*. Stanford, CA: Stanford University Press.

Dalby, Simon. (2008). "Imperialism, Domination, Culture: The Continued Relevance of Critical Geopolitics." *Geopolitics* 13.3 http://www.informaworld.com/10.1080/14650040802203679

Dalton, Russell. (2013). *Citizen Politics: Public Opinion and Political Parties in Advanced Industrial Democracies*. 6th ed. Washington, DC: CQ Press.

Dalton, Russell. (2009). *The Good Citizen*. Washington, DC: CQ Press.

Davenport, Kelsey, and Marcus Taylor. (2013). *Assessing Progress on Nuclear Nonproliferation and Disarmament* Washington, DC: Arms Control Association.

Davies, James C. (1971). "Toward a Theory of Revolution." In *When Men Revolt and Why,* edited by James C. Davies, 134–147. New York: Free Press.

Davis, Winston. (1987). "Religion and Development: Weber and the East Asian Experience." In *Understanding Political Development,* edited by Myron Weiner and Samuel Huntington, 221–280. Boston: Little, Brown.

De Cordoba, Jose, and Kejal Vyas. (2012). "Henrique Capriles Representa la Primera Gran Amenaza Para Chavez." *Wall Street Journal Americas* (October 2, 2012).

Delli Carpini, Michael X., and Scott Keeter. (1996). *What Americans Know about Politics and Why It Matters.* New Haven, CT: Yale University Press.

Demick, Barbara. (2003). "U.S. Gets a Bad Name in South Korea." *Los Angeles Times,* July 12, A3.

Deng, Kent G. (2010). "Globalisation, China's Recent Miracle Growth and Its Limits." In *China's Globalization—Today, Tomorrow,* edited by Kent Deng, 139–160.. Rijeka: IntechOpen.

Derbyshire, Denis, and Ian Derbyshire. (2000). *Encyclopedia of World Political Systems*. New York: M. E. Sharpe.

Diamond, Larry. (2008). *The Spirit of Democracy: The Struggle to Build Free Societies Throughout the World*. New York: Holt.

Diamond, Larry, and Marc F. Plattner. (2001). *The Global Divergence of Democracies*. Baltimore: Johns Hopkins University Press.

Diamond, Larry, Marc F. Plattner, and Daniel Brumberg. (2003). *Islam and Democracy in the Middle East.* Baltimore: Johns Hopkins University Press.

Diamond, Larry, and Marc F. Plattner. (2009). *Democracy: A Reader.* Baltimore: Johns Hopkins University Press.

DiPaolo, Amanda. (2010). *Zones of Twilight: Wartime Presidential Powers and Federal Court Decision Making.* Lanham, MD: Lexington Books.

Dolan, Julie Ann, Melissa Deckman, and Michele Swers. (2007). *Women and Politics: Paths to Power and Influence*. New York: Prentice Hall.

Domhoff, G. William. (2005). "Social Cohesion & the Bohemian Grove: The Power Elite at Summer Camp." http://sociology.ucsc.edu/whorulesamerica/power/bohemian_grove.html

Domhoff, G. William. (2013). *Who Rules America? The Triumph of the Corporate Rich*. 7th ed. Boston: McGraw-Hill.

Downs, Anthony. (1957). *An Economic Theory of Voting*. New York: Harper and Row.

Doyle, Michael W., and Nicholas Sambanis. (2000). "International Peacebuilding: A Theoretical and Quantitative Analysis." *American Political Science Review* 94 (December): 779–801.

Drezner, Daniel. (2008). *All Politics Is Global: Explaining International Regulatory Regimes* Princeton, NJ: Princeton University Press.

Duverger, Maurice. (1954). *Political Parties*. New York: Wiley.

Dwyer, Michael B. (2013). "Micro-Geopolitics: Capitalising Security in Laos's Golden Quadrangle." *Geopolitics* doi: 10.1080/14650045.2013.780033

Easterlin, Richard. (2006). "Building a Better Theory of Well-Being." In *Economics and Happiness: Framing the Analysis,* edited by Luigino Bruni and Pier Luigi Porta, 29–64. New York: Oxford University Press.

Easton, David. (1965). *A Framework for Political Analysis*. Englewood Cliffs, NJ: Prentice Hall.

Ebenstein, William, and Alan O. Ebenstein. (2001). *Introduction to Political Thinkers*. 2nd ed. Florence, KY: Wadsworth.

Eckstein, Harry. (1966). *Division and Cohesion in Democracy: A Study of Norway*. Princeton, NJ: Princeton University Press.

Economic Policy Institute. (2011). *The State of Working America.* http://www.stateofworkingamerica.org/

EIU. (2013). The Economist Intelligence Unit. Democracy Index 2013. www.academia.edu/3312471/The_Economist_Democracy_Index.html

Edwards, George, Martin Wattenberg, and Robert Lineberry. (2014). *Government in America.* 16th ed. New York: Pearson.

Elgie, Robert. (2004). "Semi-presidentialism: Concepts, Consequences and Contesting Explanations." *Political Studies Review* 2(3).

Elkington, John, and Seb Beloe. (2003). *The 21st Century NGO: In the Market for Change.* London: SustainAbility.

Enders, Walter, and Todd Sandler. (2012). *The Political Economy of Terrorism.* 2nd ed. New York: Cambridge University Press.

Enloe, Cynthia. (2001). *Bananas, Beaches and Bases: Making Feminist Sense of International Politics.* Berkeley: University of California Press.

Eriksson, Mikael, Peter Wallensteen, and Margareta Sollenberg. (2003). "Armed Conflict, 1989–2002." *Journal of Peace Research* 40: 593–607.

Erikson, Erik. (1969). *Gandhi's Truth.* New York: W. W. Norton.

Escriba-Folch, Abel. (2013). "Accountable for What? Regime Types, Performance, and the Fate of Outgoing Dictators, 1946–2004." *Democratization* doi: 10.1080/13510347.2013.738866

Esping-Andersen, Gosta. (1990). *The Three Worlds of Welfare Capitalism.* Princeton, NJ: Princeton University Press.

Estrin, Saul, Jan Honousek, Evzen Kocenda, and Jan Svejnar. (2009). "Effects of Privatization and Ownership in Transition Economies." *Policy Research Working Paper 4811.* New York: World Bank.

Europa: Gateway to the European Union. (2011). http://europa.eu.int/index_en.htm

Evans, Gareth. (2009). *The Responsibility to Protect: Ending Mass Atrocity Crimes Once and for All.* Washington, DC: Brookings.

Fagen, Richard. (1964). *Cuba: The Political Content of Adult Education.* Stanford, CA: Hoover Institute.

Fallows, James. (1995). *Looking at the Sun: The Rise of the New East Asian Economic and Political System.* New York: Random House.

Farrell, Henry. (2012). "The Consequences of the Internet for Politics." *Annual Review of Politics* 15: 35–52.

Federation of American Scientists. (2014). http://www.fas.org/.

Feldman, Stanley, and Karen Stenner. (1997). "Perceived Threat and Authoritarianism." *Political Psychology* 18: 741–770.

Fendrich, James. (1993). *Ideal Citizen: The Legacy of the Civil Rights Movement.* Albany, NY: SUNY Press.

Ferguson, Niall. (2012). "We Are All State Capitalists Now." *Foreign Policy.* (February 10, 2010).

Fick, Paul. (2000). *The Dysfunctional President: Understanding the Compulsions of Bill Clinton.* Rev. updated ed. New York: Citadel Press.

Fisher, Joseph P., and Brian Flota (2013). *The Politics of Post-9/11 Music: Sound Trauma and the Music Industry.* Burlington, VT: Ashgate Publishing, Ltd.

Folkenflik, David. (2013). *Murdoch's World: The Last of the Old Media Empires.* New York: PublicAffairs.

Fowler, James, and Christopher Dawes (2009). "Partisanship, Voting, and the Dopamine D2 Receptor Gene." *Journal of Politics* 71(3) (July 2009): 1157–1171.

Franko, Patrice. (2007). *The Puzzle of Latin American Economic Development.* 3rd ed. Lanham, MD: Rowman & Littlefield.

Fraser, Matthew. (2005). *Weapons of Mass Distraction: Soft Power and American Empire.* New York: St. Martin's Press.

Freedom House. (2013). *Freedom of the World.* http://www.freedomhouse.org

Freedom House. (2014). *Freedom of the World 2014.* www.freedomhouse.org/repport/freedom-world/freedom-world-2014

Friedman, Thomas L. (1999). "DOScapital." *Foreign Policy* 113 (Fall): 110–127.

Friedman, Thomas L. (2007). *The World Is Flat: A Brief History of the Twenty-first Century.* 2nd revised ed. New York: Farrar, Straus and Giroux.

Friedman, Jonathan and Kajsa Friedman. (2013). "Globalization as a Discourse of Hegemonic Crisis: A Global Systemic Analysis." *American Ethnologist* 40(2): 244–257.

Fukuyama, Francis. (1992). *The End of History and the Last Man*. New York: Free Press.

Fukuyama, Francis. (1999). *The Great Disruption: Human Nature and the Reconstitution of Social Order*. New York: Free Press.

Fukuyama, Francis. "Confucianism and Democracy." (2009). In *Democracy: A Reader*, edited by Robert Putnam and Marc Plattner. Baltimore: John Hopkins University Press.

Fund for Peace. (2014). *The Failed States Index 2014*. www.fundforpeace.org.

Garrett, R. Kelly, and James N. Danziger. (2011). "The Internet Electorate." *Communications of the ACM* 54(3) (March): 117–123.

Gartner, John D. (2009). *In Search of Bill Clinton: A Psychological Biography*. New York: St. Martin's Griffin.

George, Alexander L., and Juliette L. George. (1956). *Woodrow Wilson and Colonel House: A Personality Study*. New York: Dover.

Givan, Rebecca Kolins, Sarah Anne Soule, and Kenneth Roberts, eds. (2010). *The Diffusion of Social Movements: Actors, Mechanisms, and Political Effects.* New York: Cambridge University Press.

Gladwell, Malcolm. (2010). "Why the Revolution Will Not Be." *The New Yorker*. (October 4, 2010). Retrieved from http://www.newyorker.com/reporting/2010/10/04/ 101004fa_fact_gladwell

Glanville, Luke. (2013). "The Myth of 'Traditional' Sovereignty." *International Studies Quarterly* 57: 79–90.

Gledhill, John. (2013). "Assessing (In)security after the Arab Spring." *PS: Political Science and Politics* 46(4): 709–720.

Gleditsch, Nils Petter, Lene Siljeholm Christiansen, and Håvard Hegre. (2007). *Democratic Jihad? Military Intervention and Democracy*. World Bank Policy Research Working Paper 4242.

Global Exchange. (2009). "Top Reasons to Oppose the World Trade Organization." http://www.globalexchange.org

Glosney, Michael A. (2010). "China and the BRICs: A Real (but limited) Partnership in a Unipolar World." *Polity* 42(1): 100–129.

Gochman, Charles S., and Zeev Maoz. (1984). "Militarized Interstate Disputes, 1816–1976." *Journal of Conflict Resolution* 18 (December): 588–615.

Goldman, Marshall I. (2003). *The Piratization of Russia*. New York: Routledge.

Goldman, Marshall I. (2008). *Petrostate: Putin, Power, and the New Russia*. Oxford: Oxford University Press.

Goldstein, Joshua S. (2003). *War and Gender: How Gender Shapes the War System and Vice Versa*. Cambridge: Cambridge University Press.

Goldstein, Joshua S. (2012). *Winning the War on War: The Decline of Armed Conflict Worldwide*. New York: Dutton.

Goodin, Robert, and Philip Pettit, eds. (2006). *Contemporary Political Philosophy: An Anthology*. 2nd ed. Oxford: Blackwell.

Goodwin, Paul. (2008). *Latin America*. 13th ed. New York: McGraw-Hill.

Gowa, Joanne. (2000). *Ballots and Bullets: The Elusive Democratic Peace*. Princeton, NJ: Princeton University Press.

Graber, Doris A. (2009). *Mass Media and American Politics*. 8th ed. Washington, DC: CQ Press.

Graham, Mark, and William H. Dutton, eds. (2014). *Society and the Internet: How Information and Social Networks Are Changing Our Lives*. Oxford: Oxford University Press.

Grameen Bank. (2011). http://www.grameen-info.org

Grameen Foundation. (2014). *Microfinance: A Poverty Lens on Financial Inclusion*. Gurgaon, India: Grameen Foundation.

Green, Donald P., and Ian Shapiro. (1994). *Pathologies of Rational Choice Theory: A Critique of Applications in Political Science*. New Haven, CT: Yale University Press.

Green, Eva G. T., et al. (2009). "Reactions to Crime as Hierarchy-regulating Strategy: The Moderating Role of Social Dominance Orientation." *Social Justice Research* 22(4): 416–436.

Grossmann, Matt. (2012). *The Not-So-Special Interests: Interest Groups, Public Representation, and American Governance.* Stanford, CA: Stanford University Press.

Grotius, Hugo. (1625/1957). *De Jure Belli et Pacis [On the Laws of War and Peace].* New York: Macmillan.

Hall, Peter A., and Michele Lamont. (2013). "Why Social Relations Matter for Politics and Successful Societies." *Annual Review of Political Science* 16: 49–71.

Hamilton, Alexander, James Madison, and John Jay (2007). *The Federalist Papers.* Minneapolis, MN: Filiquarian Publishing, LLC.

Handlin, Samuel. (2012). "Social Protection and the Politicization of Class Cleavages During Latin America's Left Turn." *Comparative Political Studies* 46(12): 1582–1609.

Handlin, Samuel. (2013). "Survey Research and Social Class in Venezuela: Evaluating Alternative Measures and Their Impact on Assessments of Class Voting." *Latin American Politics and Society* 55(1): 141–167.

Hansen, Nina, and Tom Postmes. (2013). "Broadening the Scope of Societal Change Research: Psychological, Cultural, and Political Impacts of Development Aid." *Journal of Social and Political Psychology* 1(1): 273–292.

Happy Planet Index. (2013). http://www.happyplanetindex.org/data/

Harm, Marie, and Hermann Wiehle. (1942). *Lebenskunde für Mittelschulen. Fünfter Teil. Klasse 5 für Mädchen.* (Halle: Hermann Schroedel Verlag), pp. 168–173. http://www.calvin.edu/academic/cas/gpa/textbk01.htm

Haynes, Jeffrey, ed. (2010). *Religion and Politics in Europe, the Middle East and North Africa.* London: Routledge/ECPR Studies in European Political Science.

Haynes, Jeffrey, ed. (2007). *An Introduction to International Relations and Religion.* Essex: Pearson.

Hayoun, Massoud. (2013). "Bo Xilai Trial May Shake China's Economy for Years." *AlJazeera America.* (August 26, 2013). http://america.aljazeera.com/articles/2013/8/26/as-bo-xilai-trialendsantigraftcampaignwillrearon.html

Hearnshaw, F. J. C. (1933). *Conservatism in England.* London: Macmillan.

Heilbroner, Robert. (1993). "The Multinational Corporation and the Nation-State." In *At Issue:*

Politics in the World Arena, edited by Steven L. Speigel, 338–352. New York: St. Martin's Press.

Heilbroner, Robert. (1994). *Twenty-First Century Capitalism.* New York: W. W. Norton.

Henao, Luis Andres. (2013). "Chile Mapuche Conflict Fueled By Deadly Attacks Against Indian Activists." Huffington Post.com (May 30, 2013). http://www.huffingtonpost.com/2013/05/31/chile-mapuche-conflict_n_3366970.html

Heritage Foundation. (2013). *Index of Economic Freedom 2013.* http://www.heritage.org/research/features/index/countries.cfm

Heritage Foundation (2014). *Economic Freedom Index 2014.* http://www.heritage.org/index/ranking

Herman, Dan, and Andrew F. Cooper. (2013). "Between Collective Action and a Fragmented Political Economy: The G20 and the Return of Protectionist Impulses." *Contemporary Politics* 19(4): 399–410.

Heyne, Paul, Peter Boettke, and David Prychitko. (2013). *The Economic Way of Thinking.* 13th ed. New York: Pearson.

Hibbing, John, and Kevin Smith, eds. (2007). *The Biology of Political Behavior.* The Annals of the American Academy of Political and Social Science, 614 (1).

Hibbing, John, Kevin Smith, and John Alford. (2013). *Predisposed: Liberals, Conservatives and the Biology of Political Differences.* New York: Routledge.

Higley, John, and Michael Burton. (2006). *Elite Foundations of Liberal Democracy.* Lanham, MD: Rowman & Littlefield.

Hill, Stephen. (2010). *Europe's Promise: Why the European Way Is the Best Hope for an Insecure Age.* Berkeley: University of California Press.

Hobbes, Thomas. (1651/1958). *Leviathan.* Oxford, England: Clarendon.

Hoffman, John, and Paul Graham. (2009). *An Introduction to Political Theory.* 2nd ed. Essex, England: Pearson Educational.

Holzgrefe, J. L., and Robert Keohane, eds. (2003). *Humanitarian Intervention: Ethical, Legal, and Political Dilemmas.* New York: Cambridge University Press.

Hoover, Kenneth, James Marcia, and Kristen Parris. (1997). *The Power of Identity: Politics in a New Key.* Chatham, NJ: Chatham House.

Horowitz, Donald L. (1990). "Comparing Democratic Systems." *Journal of Democracy* 1(4): 73–79.

Huber, Evelyne, and Fred Solt. (2004). "Successes and Failures of Neoliberalism." *Latin American Research Review* 39: 150–164.

Huddy, Leonie, David O. Sears, and Jack Levy, eds. (2013). *The Oxford Handbook of Political Psychology.* New York: Oxford University Press.

Hunter, Floyd. (1953). *Community Power Structure.* Chapel Hill: University of North Carolina Press.

Huntington, Samuel P. (1968). *Political Order in Changing Societies.* New Haven, CT: Yale University Press.

Huntington, Samuel P. (1991). *The Third Wave: Democratization in the Late Twentieth Century.* Norman, OK: University of Oklahoma Press.

Huntington, Samuel P. (1998). *Clash of Civilizations and the Remaking of the World Order.* New York: Simon and Schuster.

Huxley, Aldous. (1932). *Brave New World.* London: Chatto and Windus.

IDMC (Internal Displacement Monitoring Center). (2011). http://www.internal-displacement.org

Ikeda, Maki, and Atsushi Tago. (2014). "Winning over Foreign Domestic Support for Use of Force: Power of Diplomatic and Operational Multilateralism." *International Relations of the Asia-Pacific.* DOI: 10.1093/irap/lcu003.

Ikenberry, G. John. (2011). *Liberal Leviathan: The Origins, Crisis, and Transformation of the American World Order.* Princeton, NJ: Princeton University Press.

IMF. (2013). International Monetary Fund List of LIC DSAs. (November 13, 2013). http://www.imf.org/external/pubs/ft/dsa/dsalist.pdf

Inglehart, Ronald, and Pippa Norris. (2003). *Rising Tide: Gender Equality and Cultural Change Around the World.* New York: Cambridge University Press.

Inglehart, Ronald, and Christian Welzel. (2005). *Modernization, Cultural Change, and Democracy: The Human Development Sequence.* New York: Cambridge University Press.

Inglehart, Ronald, and Christian Welzel. (2010). "Changing Mass Priorities: The Link Between Modernization and Democracy." *Perspectives on Politics* 8(2) (June 2010): 554.

Inkeles, Alex. (1997). *National Character: A Psycho-Social Perspective.* New Brunswick, NJ: Transaction.

Inkeles, Alex, and David Smith. (1999). *Becoming Modern: Individual Change in Six Developing Countries.* Cambridge, MA: Harvard University Press.

Innes, Abby. (2014). "The Political Economy of State Capture in Central Europe." *JCMS: Journal of Comparative Market Studies* 52(1): 88–104.

Institute for Economics and Peace. (2014). *Global Peace Index 2014.* http://www.visionofhumanity.org/pdf/gpi/2014_Global_Peace_Index_Report.pdf

International Institute for Democracy and Electoral Assistance. (2014). www.idea.int/vt

International Food Policy Research Institute. (2013). www.ifpri.org/

International Social Survey Program. (2004). http://www.gesis.org/en/services/data/survey-data/issp/modules-study-overview/citizenship/

Isbister, John. (2006). *Promises Not Kept: Poverty and the Betrayal of Third World Development.* 7th ed. Bloomfield, CT: Kumarian Press.

Iyengar, Shanto, and Kyu S. Hahn. (2009). "Red Media, Blue Media: Evidence of Ideological Selectivity in Media Use." *Journal of Communication* 59(1): 19–39.

Iyengar, Shanto. (2011). *Media Politics.* 2nd ed. New York: Norton.

Jackson, Robert. (2007). *Sovereignty: The Evolution of an Idea.* Malden, MA: Polity Press.

Jenkins, Barbara. (1993). "Multinational Corporations." In *The Oxford Companion to Politics of the World,* edited by Joel Krieger, 606–608. New York: Oxford University Press.

Jennings, M. Kent, Gregory Markus, and Richard Niemi. (1991). *Youth-Parent Socialization Panel Study, 1965–1982.* Ann Arbor, MI: Interuniversity Consortium for Political Research.

Jennings, M. Kent, Laura Stoker, and Jake Bowers. (2009). "Politics Across Generations: Family Transmission Reexamined." *The Journal of Politics* 71(3): 782–799.

Jensen, Jane. (2008). *Women Political Leaders: Breaking the Glass Ceiling*. New York: Palgrave Macmillan.

Johnson, Chalmers. (1983). *Revolutionary Change*. 2nd ed. London: Pearson.

Johnson, Chalmers. (1995). *Japan: Who Governs?: The Rise of the Developmental State*. New York: W. W. Norton.

Johnson, Simon. (2009). "The Quiet Coup." *The Atlantic*. (May 2009). http://www.theatlantic.com/doc/200905/imf-advice

Johnson, Tyler, and Paul M. Kellstedt. (2013). "Media Consumption and the Dynamics of Policy Mood." *Political Behavior* 36(2): 377–399.

Johnston, Michael. (2006). *Syndromes of Corruption: Wealth, Power, and Democracy*. New York: Cambridge University Press.

Juergensmeyer, Mark. (2003). *Terror in the Mind of God: The Global Rise of Religious Violence*. Rev. ed. Berkeley: University of California Press.

Juergensmeyer, Mark. (2008). *Global Rebellion: Religious Challenges to the Secular State*. Berkeley: University of California Press.

Jung, Jai Kwan, and Christopher Deering. (2013). "Constitutional Choices: Uncertainty and Institutional Design in Democratizing Nations." *International Political Science Review* doi: 10.1177/0192512113503929

Kahler, Miles. (2003). "The State of the State in World Politics." In *Political Science: State of the Discipline*, edited by Ira Katznelson and Helen Milner, 56–83. New York: W. W. Norton.

Kaplan, Robert D. (2009). "The Revenge of Geography." *Foreign Policy* (May/June): 96–105.

Karatnycky, Adrian, and Peter Ackerman. (2006). "How Freedom Is Won: From Civic Struggle to Durable Democracy." http://www.freedomhouse.org/template.cfm?page=137

Karlekar, Karin. (2009). "Freedom of the Press." http://www.freedomhouse.org

Katz, E., and Paul Lazarsfeld. (1955). *Personal Influence*. New York: Free Press.

Kegley, Charles W., Jr. (2011). *World Politics: Trend and Transformation*. 13th ed. New York: Thompson Wadsworth.

Kegley, Charles W., Jr., and Eugene Wittkopf. (2004). *World Politics: Trend and Transformation*. 9th ed. New York: Thomson Wadsworth.

Kennedy, Paul. (2006). *The Parliament of Man: The Past, Present, and Future of the United Nations*. New York: Random House.

Kenny, Sue, Ismet Fanany, and Sutria Rahayu. (2012). "Community Development in Indonesia: Westernization or Doing it Their Way?" *Community Development Journal* 48(2): 280–297.

Keohane, Robert O. (2005). *After Hegemony: Cooperation and Discord in the World Political Economy*. Princeton, NJ: Princeton University Press.

Keohane, Robert O., and Joseph Nye. (2000). "Globalization: What's New. And What's Not. (And So What?)" *Foreign Affairs* (Spring): 104–119.

Keohane, Robert O., and Joseph Nye. (2011). *Power and Interdependence: World Politics in Transition*, 4th ed. New York: Pearson.

Khor, Martin. (2011). "Developing a Global Partnership for Development: Critical Issues and Proposals for Trade and Finance." http://www.twnside.org.sg/crisis_2.htm

Kinder, Donald R., and David O. Sears. (1981). "Prejudice and Politics: Symbolic Racism versus Racial Threats to the Good Life." *Journal of Personality and Social Psychology* 40(3): 414–431.

King, Gary, Kay Scholzman, and Norman Nie, eds. (2009). *The Future of Political Science: 100 Perspectives*. New York: Routledge.

King, Michael, and Donald M. Taylor. (2011). "The Radicalization of Homegrown Jihadists: A Review of Theoretical Models of Social Psychological Evidence." *Terrorism and Political Violence* 23(4): 602–622.

Klare, Michael T. (1997). "The New Arms Race: Light Weapons and International Security." *Current History* 96 (April): 173–178.

Klare, Michael. (2002). *Resource Wars: The New Landscape of Global Conflict*. New York: Henry Holt.

Klare, Michael. (2007). "Global Warming Battlefields: How Climate Change Threatens Security." *Current History* (November): 355–361.

Klare, Michael. (2009). *Rising Powers, Shrinking Planet: The New Geopolitics of Energy*. New York: Holt.

Klare, Michael. (2012). *The Race for What's Left: The Global Scramble for the World's Last Resources*. New York: Metropolitan Books.

Klein, Naomi. (2008). *The Shock Doctrine: The Rise of Disaster Capitalism*. New York: Metropolitan Books.

Klingemann, Hans Dieter. (2009). *The Comparative Study of Electoral Systems*. New York: Oxford University Press.

Koopmans, Tim. (2003). *Courts and Political Institutions: A Comparative View*. Cambridge: Cambridge University Press.

Kowitt, Beth. (2009) "For Mr. BRIC, Nations Meeting a Milestone." CNNMoney.com 6/17/2009.

Kraul, Chris. (2011). "Are Argentina's Good Times an Illusion?" *Los Angeles Times*, August 2, 2011: B1, B5.

Kuhn, Thomas. (1996). *The Structure of Scientific Revolutions*. 3rd ed. Chicago: University of Chicago Press.

Kurian, George, James E. Alt, Simone Chambers, Geoffrey Garrett, Margaret Levi, and Paula D. McClain, eds. (2011). *The Encyclopedia of Political Science*. Washington, DC: CQ Press.

Kurzban, Robert, Peter DeScioli, and Daniel Fenn. (2012). "*Hamilton v. Kant*: Pitting Adaptations for Altruism against Adaptations for Moral Judgment." *Evolution and Human Behavior* 33(4): 323–333.

Laitin, David D. (2007). *Nations, States, and Violence*. New York: Oxford University Press.

Lanchester, John. (2010). *I. O. U.: Why Everyone Owes Everyone and No One Can Pay*. New York: Simon & Schuster.

Laquer, Walter. (2009). *The Last Days of Europe: Epitaph for an Old Continent*. New York: St. Martin's Griffin.

Larkey, Edward. (1990). "Rock Music and Cultural Theory in the German Democratic Republic." In *Politics in Familiar Contexts*, edited by Robert L. Savage and Dan Nimmo, 215–224. Norwood, NJ: Ablex.

Lasswell, Harold. (1960). *Psychopathology and Politics*. New York: Viking.

Latinobarometro. (2013). http://www.latinobarometro.org

Lau, Richard R., and David P. Redlawsk. (1997). "Voting Correctly." *The American Political Science Review* 91(3): 585–598.

Lau, Richard, and David Redlawsk. (2008). "Older but Wiser? Effects of Age on Political Cognition." *The Journal of Politics* 70 (January): 168–185.

Law, David S., and Mila Versteeg. (2011). "The Evolution and Ideology of Global Constitutionalism." *California Law Review* 99(5): 1163–1259.

Layard, Richard. (2011). *Happiness: Lessons from a New Science*. 2nd ed. New York: Penguin.

Lebow, Richard Ned. (2012). *The Politics and Ethics of Identity: In Search of Ourselves*. New York: Cambridge University Press.

Leiken, Robert S. (2009). "The Menace in Europe's Midst." *Current History* 108(717): 186–188.

Lenski, Gerhard. (1984). *Power and Privilege: A Theory of Social Stratification*. Chapel Hill, NC: University of North Carolina Press.

Lenz, Gabriel, and Chappell Lawson. (2011). "Looking the Part: Television Leads Less Informed Citizens to Vote Based on Candidates' Appearance." *American Journal of Political Science* 55(3): 574–589.

Lenz, Gabriel, Chappell Lawson, Andy Baker, and Michael Myers. (2010). "Looking Like a Winner: Candidate Appearance and Electoral Success in New Democracies." *World Politics* 64: 561–593.

Lerner, Jennifer, Roxana Gonzalez, Deborah Small, and Baruch Fischoff. (2003). "Effects of Fear and Anger on Perceived Risks of Terrorism: A National Field Experiment." *Psychological Science* 14(2): 144–150.

Lewis, Orion A., and Sven Steinmo. (2012). "How Institutions Evolve: Evolutionary theory and institutional change." *Polity* 44(3): 314–339.

Levi, Margaret. (2002). "The State of the Study of the State." In *Political Science: State of the Discipline*, edited by Ira Katznelson and Helen Milner. New York: W. W. Norton.

Levy, Francesca. (2010). "The World's Happiest Places." *Forbes.com*. http://www.forbes.com/2010/07/14/world-happiest-countries-lifestyle

Levy, Jonah, ed. (2006). *The State after Statism*. Cambridge, MA: Harvard University Press.

Lijphart, Arend. (1984). *Democracies: Patterns of Majoritarian and Consensual Government in Twenty-One Countries*. New Haven, CT: Yale University Press.

Lijphart, Arend. (2007). *Thinking about Democracy: Power Sharing and Majority Rule in Theory and Practice.* New York: Routledge.

Lindblom, Charles E. (1977). *Politics and Markets: The World's Political-Economic Systems.* New York: Basic Books.

Lindblom, Charles E. (2003). *The Market System: What It Is, How It Works, and What to Make of It.* New Haven, CT: Yale University Press.

Linz, Juan J. (1990a). "The Perils of Presidentialism." *Journal of Democracy* 1(1): 51–69.

Linz, Juan J. (1990b). "The Virtues of Parliamentarism." *Journal of Democracy* 1(4): 84–91.

Linz, Juan J. (1993). "Authoritarianism." In *The Oxford Companion to Politics of the World,* edited by Joel Krieger, 60–64. New York: Oxford University Press.

Linz, Juan J. (1994). "Presidential or Parliamentary Democracy: Does it Make a Difference?" In *The Failure of Presidential Democracy,* edited by Juan J. Linz and Arturo Valenzuela, 3–87. Baltimore: Johns Hopkins University Press.

Linz, Juan J., and Alfred Stepan. (1996). *Problems of Democratic Transition and Consolidation: Southern Europe, South America, and Post-Communist Europe.* Baltimore: Johns Hopkins University Press.

Lipset, Seymour Martin. (1959). "Some Social Requisites of Democracy: Economic Development and Political Legitimacy." *American Political Science Review* 53 (March): 69–105.

Little, Richard. (2007). *The Balance of Power in International Relations: Metaphors, Myths, and Models.* New York: Cambridge University Press.

Loader, Brian D., and Dan Mercea, eds. (2012). *Social Media and Democracy: Innovations in Participatory Politics.* New York: Routledge.

Locke, John. (1690/1963). *Two Treatises on Government.* New York: New American Library.

Love, Nancy S., ed. (2010). *Dogmas and Dreams: A Reader in Modern Political Ideologies.* 4th ed. New York: Seven Bridges Press.

Luke, Timothy W. (2013). "Corporate Social Responsibility: An Uneasy Merger of Sustainability and Development." *Sustainable Development* 21: 83–91.

Lukes, Steven. (2005). *Power: A Radical Review.* 2nd ed. London: Palgrave-Macmillan.

Lundberg, Erik. (2013). "Does the Government Selection Process Promote or Hinder Pluralism? Exploring the Characteristics of Voluntary Organizations Invited to Public Consultations." *Journal of Civil Society* 9: 58–77.

Lupia, Arthur, and Mathew McCubbins. (1998). *The Democratic Dilemma: Can Citizens Learn What They Need to Know?* Cambridge: Cambridge University Press.

Machiavelli, Niccolò. (1517/1977). *The Prince.* Translated and edited by Robert M. Adams. New York: W. W. Norton.

Mackinder, Halford John. (1996). *Democratic Ideals and Reality.* Washington, DC: U.S. Government Printing Office.

Mahbubani, Kishore. (2008). *The New Asian Hemisphere: The Irresistible Shift of Global Power.* New York: PublicAffairs.

Mainwaring, Scott, and Matthew S. Shugart, eds. (1997). *Presidentialism and Democracy in Latin America.* Cambridge: Cambridge University Press.

Malcolm, Jeremy. (2013). "Internet Freedom in a World of States." *Digital News Asia* 18 (February).

Malloch-Brown, Mark. (2002). "The Millennium Development Goals and Africa: A New Framework." Address at Makerere University, Uganda. November 12, 2002. http://content. undp.org/go/newsroom/2002/november/ mmb-uganda

.en;jsessionid=axbWzt8vXD9

Malloch-Brown, Mark. (2012). *The Unfinished Revolution: The Road to International Cooperation.* New York: Penguin Books.

Mander, Jerry. (1999). "Regarding the WTO." *International Forum on Globalization.* http://www. ifg.org/media.html

Mandelbaum, Michael. (2004). *The Ideas That Conquered the World: Peace, Democracy, and Free Markets in the Twenty-first Century.* New York: PublicAffairs.

March, James G., and Johan P. Olsen. (1989). *Rediscovering Institutions: The Organizational Basis of Politics.* New York: Free Press.

March, James G., and Johan P. Olsen. (2006). "Elaborating the 'New Institutionalism.'" In *The*

Oxford Handbook of Political Institutions, edited by R. A. W. Rhodes, Sarah Binder, and Bert Rockman. Oxford: Oxford University Press.

Marien, Sofie, Marc Hooghe, and Ellen Quintelier. (2010). "Inequalities in Non-institutionalised Forms of Political Participation: A Multi-level Analysis of 25 Countries." *Political Studies* 58(1): 187–213.

Marinov, Nikolay, and Hein Goemans. (2008)."What Happened to the Coup d'Etat?: International Responses to the Seizure of Executive Power." Paper presented at the Midwest Political Science Association Annual Conference, Chicago, IL, April 3, 2008.

Marshall, Monty G., and Benjamin Cole. (2011). *Global Report 2011: Conflict, Governance and State Fragility.* http://www.systemicpeace.org/GlobalReport 2011

Martin, Shane, Thomas Saalfeld, and Kaare Strøm, eds. (2013*). The Oxford Handbook of Legislative Studies.* Oxford: Oxford University Press.

Marsteintredet, Leiv, and Einar Berntzen. (2008). "Reducing the Perils of Presidentialism in Latin America through Presidential Interruptions." *Comparative Politics* 41(1): 83–101.

Marx, Karl. (1867/1981). *Capital*: *A Critique of Political Economy* Translated by David Fernbach. New York: Vintage.

Marx, Karl, and Friedrich Engels. (1848/1978). "The Communist Manifesto." In *The Marx–Engels Reader,* 2nd ed., edited by Robert Tucker, 482–500. New York: W. W. Norton.

Maslow, Abraham. (1954). *Motivation and Personality.* New York: Harper and Row.

Maxfield, Sylvia. (1997). *Gatekeepers of Growth: The International Political Economy of Central Banking in Developing Countries.* Princeton, NJ: Princeton University Press.

McCormick, John. (2006). *The European Superpower.* New York: Palgrave.

McCormick, John, and Jonathan Olsen. (2013). *The European Union.* 5th ed. Boulder, CO: Westview Press.

McDuie-Ra, Duncan, and John A. Rees. (2010). "Religious Actors, Civil Society, and the Development Agenda: The Dynamics of Inclusion and Exclusion." *Journal of International Development* 22(1): 20–36.

McFaul, Michael. (1998). "Russia's Summer of Discontent." *Current History* 97 (October): 307–312.

McFaul, Michael. (2007). "New Russia, New Threat." *Los Angeles Times*, September 2, M8.

McFaul, Michael, Kathryn Stoner-Weiss, and Valerie Bunce. (2010). *Democracy and Authoritarianism in the Postcommunist World.* New York: Cambridge University Press.

McLellan, David. (1983). "Marx in England." *History Today* 33(3). http://www.historytoday.com/MainArticle.aspx?m=12568&amid=12568

McLellan, David., ed. (2007). *Marxism after Marx.* 4th ed. New York: Palgrave.

Meadowcroft, James. (2013). "Reaching the Limits? Developed Country Engagement with Sustainable Development in a Challenging Juncture." *Environment and Planning C: Government and Policy* 31: 988–1002.

Mearsheimer, John J. (2001). *The Tragedy of Great Power Politics.* New York: W. W. Norton.

Mearsheimer, John J. (2011). *Why Leaders Lie: The Truth about Lying in International Politics.* New York: Oxford University Press.

Meckled-Garcia, Saladin. (2013). "Does the WTO Violate Human Rights (and Do I Help It?): Beyond the Metaphor of Culpability for Systemic Global Poverty." *Political Studies* doi: 10.1111/1467–9248.12036.

Meisner, Maurice. (1999). *Mao's China and After.* 3rd ed. New York: Free Press.

Meisner, Maurice. (2006). *Mao Zedong: A Political and Intellectual Portrait.* London: Polity Press.

Mencken, Henry Louis. (1916). *A Little Book in C Major.* New York: John Lane Company.

Meyer, Josh. (2007). "Small Groups Now a Large Threat." *Los Angeles Times*, August 16, A1, A10.

Microcredit Summit Conference. (2006). http://www.microcreditsummit.org

Microcredit Summit Conference. (2013). *Vulnerability: The State of Microcredit.* http://www.microcreditsummit.

Miller, Benjamin. (2007). *States, Nations, and the Great Powers: The Sources of Regional War and Peace.* New York: Cambridge University Press.

Miller, Roger LeRoy. (2014). *Economics Today.* 17th ed. New York: Pearson.

Mills, C. Wright. (1956/2000). *The Power Elite*. New York: Oxford University Press.

Moisi, Dominique. (2009). *The Geopolitics of Emotion: How Fear, Humiliation, and Hope are Reshaping the World*. New York: Random House.

Molina, Oscar, and Martin Rhodes. (2002). "Corporatism: The Past, Present, and Future of a Concept." *Annual Review of Political Science* 5: 305–331.

Monroe, Kristen. (2011). *Ethics in an Age of Terror and Genocide: Identity and Moral Choice.* Princeton, NJ: Princeton University Press.

Montgomery, Evan Braden. (2013). "Competitive Strategies against Continental Powers: The Geopolitics of Sino-Indian-American Relations." *Journal of Strategic Studies* doi: 10.1080/01402390.2012736383

Moore, Barrington. (1966). *The Social Origins of Dictatorship and Democracy*. Cambridge, MA: Harvard University Press.

Morales, Evo. (2006). Quoted in *La Prensa* (September 10, 2006). http://en.wikipedia.org/wiki/Domestic_policy_of_Evo_Morales

Moravcsik, Andrew. (2012). "Europe After the Crisis: How to Sustain a Common Currency." *Foreign Affairs* 91(3): 54–68.

Morgenthau, Hans J. (2005). *Politics among Nations*. 7th brief ed. Revised by Kenneth W. Thompson with David Clinton. New York: McGraw Hill.

Mosca, Gaetano. (1896/2011). *The Ruling Class*. Translated by Hannah Kahn. Charleston, SC: Nabu Press.

Mossberger, Karen, Caroline Tolbert, and Ramona McNeal. (2008). *Digital Citizenship: The Internet, Society, and Participation*. Cambridge, MA: MIT Press.

Moyo, Dambisa. (2012). *Winner Take All: China's Race for Resources and What It Means for the World*. New York: Basic Books.

Mueller, Dennis. (2003). *Public Choice III*. New York: Cambridge University Press.

Murphy, Dean. (1995). "East Europe P.D. Blues." *Los Angeles Times*, February 28, H1, H4.

Murray, Charles. (1984). *Losing Ground: American Social Policy, 1950–1980*. New York: Basic Books.

Nadiri, Khalid. (2007). "Of Note: China's Peasant Populism: A Look Inland." *SAIS Review* 27(1) (Winter–Spring): 125–126.

NCTC (National Counterterrorism Center). (2011). *A Chronology of Significant International Terrorism for 2009*. http://www.NCTC.gov

Niemi, Richard G., and Mary A. Hepburn. (1995). "The Rebirth of Political Socialization." *Perspectives on Political Science* 24(1): 7–16.

Niemi, Richard G., Herbert Weissberg, and David Kimball, eds. (2011). *Controversies in Voting Behavior*. 5th ed. Washington, DC: CQ Press.

Nimmo, Dan, and James E. Combs. (1990). *Mediated Political Realities*. 2nd ed. White Plains, NY: Pearson.

Norpoth, Helmut. (1987). "Guns and Butter and Government Popularity in Britain." *American Political Science Review* 81(3): 949–959.

Norris, Pippa. (2003). *Institutions Matter*. London: Cambridge University Press.

Norris, Pippa. (2004). *Electoral Engineering: Voting Rules and Political Behavior*. Cambridge: Cambridge University Press.

Norris, Pippa, and Ronald Inglehart. (2012). *Sacred and Secular: Religion and Politics Worldwide*. 2nd ed. New York: Cambridge University Press.

Norris, Pippa, and Ronald Inglehart. (2009). *Cosmopolitan Communications: Cultural Diversity in a Globalized World.* New York: Cambridge University Press.

Nugent, Neill. (2008). *The Government and Politics of the European Union*. 6th ed. Durham, NC: Duke University Press.

Nye, Joseph S. (2009). *Soft Power: The Means to Success in World Politics*. Washington, DC: Public Affairs.

Nye, Joseph S. (2011). *The Future of Power*. New York: PublicAffairs.

O'Connor, Karen, and Larry Sabato. (2007). *The Essentials of American Government*. 8th ed. New York: Pearson.

OECD. (2011). Organization of Economic Cooperation and Development. *Main Economic Indicators*. http://www.oecdilibrary.org/economics/main-economic-indicators_22195009

O'Farcheallaigh, Ciaran. (2013). "IR Theory and Domestic Adoption of International Norms." *International Politics* doi: 10.1057/ip.2013.23

O'Neill, Jim. (2001). *Building Better Global Economic BRICs*. Global Economics Paper No. 66. New York: Goldman Sachs & Co.

Organski, A. F. K. (1968). *World Politics*. New York: Alfred Knopf.

Orwell, George. (1945/1964). *Animal Farm*. Middlesex, England: Penguin.

Orwell, George. (1949/1967). *1984*. Middlesex, England: Penguin.

Ozzano, Luca. (2013). "The Many Faces of the Political God: A Typology of Religiously-oriented Parties." *Democratization* 20(5): 807–830.

Packenham, Robert. (1998). *The Dependency Movement: Scholarship and Politics in Development Studies*. Cambridge, MA: Harvard University Press.

Panitch, Leo. (2009). *Renewing Socialism: Democracy, Strategy, and Imagination*. London: Merlin Press.

Papacharissi, Z. (2010). *A Private Sphere: Democracy in a Digital Age*. Cambridge: Polity Press.

Parenti, Michael. (2010). *Democracy for the Few*. 9th ed. New York: Wadsworth.

Parker, Richard D. (2005). "Five Theses on Identity Politics." *Harvard Journal of Law and Public Policy* 29(1) (Fall): 53–59.

Pattison, James. (2012). *Humanitarian Intervention and the Responsibility to Protect: Who Should Intervene?* New York: Oxford University Press.

PERC [Political and Economic Risk Consulting]. (2011). http://www.asiarisk.com/

Peterson, Scott. (2001). "Jaded Hope: Russia 10 Years Later." *Christian Science Monitor,* August 17, 1, 7–8.

Petrik, Will. (2009). "International Monetary Fund and the Inter-American Development Bank: A History of Limited Choices and Broken Promises." Council on Hemispheric Affairs. http://www.coha.org/2009/04/international-monetary-fund-and-the-inter-american-devel-opment-bank-a-history-of- limited-choices-and-broken-promises/

Pew. (2011). *Pew Internet and American Life Project*. http://www.pewinternet.org/

Pew Foundation. (2009). *Global Restrictions on Religion*. http://www.pewforum.org/files/2009/12/restrictions-fullreport.pdf

Pew Research Center. (2010). "Public Knows Basic Facts about Politics, Economics, but Struggles with Specifics." http://www.pewresearch.org/2010/11/18/public-knows-basic-facts-about-politics-economics-but-struggles-with-specifics

Pharr, Susan J., and Robert D. Putnam, eds. (2000). *Disaffected Democracies: What's Troubling the Trilateral Countries?* Princeton, NJ: Princeton University Press.

Phillips, Kevin. (2003). *Wealth and Democracy: A Political History of the American Rich*. New York: Broadway Books.

Pickering, Jeffrey, and Mark Peceny. (2006). "Forging Democracy at Gunpoint." *International Studies Quarterly* 50(3): 539–60.

Pinker, Steven. (2011). *The Better Angels of Our Nature: Why Violence Has Declined*. New York: Viking.

Plant, E. Ashby, and Patricia Devine. (2003). "The Antecedents and Implications of Interracial Anxiety." *Personality and Social Psychology Bulletin* 29(6): 790–801.

Plasser, Gunda. (2002). *Global Political Campaigning*. Westport, CT: Greenwood Publishing.

Popper, Karl. (1963). *The Open Society and Its Enemies*. Vol. 2. New York: Harper and Row.

Population Reference Bureau. (2013). *2013 World Population Data Sheet*. Washington, DC: PRB.

Posen, Barry. (2003). "Command of the Commons: The Military Foundation of U.S. Hegemony." *International Security* 28 (Summer 2003): 5–46.

Post, Jerrold. (2004). *Leaders and their Followers in a Dangerous World: The Psychology of Political Behavior*. Ithaca, NY: Cornell University Press.

Post, Jerrold. (2008). *The Mind of the Terrorist: The Psychology of Terrorism from the IRA to al-Qaeda*. London: Palgrave Macmillan.

Poulantzas, Nicos. (1973). *Political Power and Social Classes*. London: Sheed and Ward.

Powell, G. Bingham, Kaare Strom, and Russell Dalton, eds. (2012). *Comparative Politics Today: A Theoretical Framework*. 6th ed. New York: Pearson.

Pratto, Felicia, et al. (1994). "Social Dominance Orientation: A Personality Variable Predicting Social and Political Attitudes." *Journal of Personality and Social Psychology* 67(4): 741–763.

Prior, Markus. (2010). "You've Either Got It Or You Don't? The Stability of Political Interest over the Life Cycle." *The Journal of Politics* 72(3): 747–766.

Prunier, Gerard. (2008). *Africa's World War: Congo, the Rwandan Genocide, and the Making of a Continental Disaster.* New York: Oxford University Press.

Przeworski, Adam. (1985). *Capitalism and Social Democracy.* Cambridge: Cambridge University Press.

Przeworski, Adam. (1993). "Socialism and Social Democracy." In *The Oxford Companion to Politics of the World,* edited by Joel Krieger, 832–838. New York: Oxford University Press.

Przeworski, Adam. (2004). "Democracy and Economic Development." In *The Evolution of Political Knowledge,* edited by Edward D. Mansfield and Richard Sisson. Columbus: Ohio State University Press.

Przeworski, Adam. (2010). *Democracy and the Limits of Self-Government.* New York: Cambridge University Press.

Przeworski, Adam, Michael Alvarez, Jose Antonio Cheibub, and Fernando Limongi. (2000). *Democracy and Development: Political Institutions and Well-Being in the World, 1950–1990.* New York: Cambridge University Press.

Puddington, Arch. (2011). "Democracy under Duress." *Journal of Democracy* 22(2): 17–31.

Putnam, Robert. (1993). *Making Democracy Work: Civic Traditions in Modern Italy.* Princeton, NJ: Princeton University Press.

Putnam, Robert. (2001). *Bowling Alone: The Collapse and Revival of American Community.* New York: Simon & Schuster.

Putnam, Robert D., and David E. Campbell. (2012). *American Grace: How Religion Divides and Unites Us.* New York: Simon & Schuster.

Putnam, Robert, and Marc Plattner, eds. (2009). *Democracy: A Reader.* Baltimore: John Hopkins University Press.

Pye, Lucian W. (1962). *Politics, Personality, and Nation-Building.* New Haven, CT: Yale University Press.

Quaranta, Mario. (2013). "The Impact of Institutional Decentralization on Protest in Western Europe." *International Political Science Review* 34(50): 502–518.

Rae, Douglas. (1972). *The Political Consequences of Electoral Laws.* New Haven, CT: Yale University Press.

Rajan, Raghuram. (2010). *Fault Lines: How Hidden Fractures Still Threaten the World Economy.* Princeton, NJ: Princeton University Press.

Rasler, Karen, and William R. Thompson. (2005). *Puzzles of the Democratic Peace: Theory, Geopolitics, and the Transformation of World Politics.* New York: Palgrave Macmillan.

Redefining Progress. (2007). "Genuine Progress Indicator." www.rprogress.org.

Reppy, Susan. (1984). "The Automobile Air Bag." In *Controversy,* 2nd ed., edited by Dorothy Nelkin, 161–174. Beverly Hills, CA: Sage.

Reynolds, Andrew, Ben Reilly, and Andrew Ellis. (2005). *Electoral System Design: The New International IDEA Handbook.* http://www.idea.int/publications/esd/

Rhoden, T. F. (2013). "The Liberal in Liberal Democracy." *Democratization* doi: 10.1080/13510347.2013.851672

Richards, Andrew. (2007). "Economic Challenges for New Democracies." In *The Construction of Democracy: Lessons from Practice and Research,* edited by Jorge Dominguez and Anthony Jones, 45–76. Baltimore: Johns Hopkins University Press.

Riek, Blake M., Eric W. Mania, and Samuel L. Gaertner. (2006). "Intergroup Threat and Outgroup Attitudes: A Meta-Analytic Review." *Personality and Social Psychology Review* 10(4): 336–353.

Riker, William. (1962). *The Theory of Political Coalitions.* New Haven, CT: Yale University Press.

Riker, William. (1982). "The Two Party System and Duverger's Law." *American Political Science Review* 76(4): 753–766.

Riker, William, and Peter Ordeshook. (1973). *An Introduction to Positive Political Theory.* Englewood Cliffs, NJ: Prentice Hall.

Ritholtz, Barry. (2009). *Bailout Nation: How Greed and Easy Money Corrupted Wall Street and Shook the World Economy.* New York: Wiley.

Ritter, Daniel, and Alex Trechsel. (2011). "Revolutionary Cells: On the Role of Texts, Tweets, and Status Updates in Nonviolent Revolutions." Paper presented at the Conference on the Internet, Voting, and Democracy. Laguna Beach, CA. May 15, 2011.

Robinson, Matthew (2009). *Justice Blind? Ideals and Realities of American Criminal Justice.* 3rd ed. Upper Saddle River, NJ: Prentice-Hall.

Robinson, Simon. (2003). "Iraqi Textbooks: X-ing Out Saddam." *Time,* July 21: 18.

Robinson, William I. (1998). *Promoting Polyarchy: Globalization, U.S. Intervention, and Hegemony.* Cambridge: Cambridge University Press.

Rodrik, Dani, ed. (2003). *In Search of Prosperity: Analytic Narratives on Economic Growth.* Princeton, NJ: Princeton University Press.

Rodrik, Dani, ed. (2011). *The Globalization Paradox: Democracy and the Future of the World Economy.* New York: W. W. Norton.

Rolfe, Meredith. (2012). *Voter Turnout: A Social Theory of Political Participation.* Cambridge: Cambridge University Press.

Roodman, David. (2012). "Think Again: Microfinance." *Foreign Policy.* foreignpolicy.com/articles/2012/02/01/think_again_microfinance

Rosenberg, Shawn. (1988). *Reason, Ideology, and Politics.* Cambridge: Polity.

Rosenberg, Shawn. (2002). *The Not So Common Sense: Differences in How People Judge Social and Political Life.* New Haven, CT: Yale University Press.

Rostow, W. W. (1960). *The Stages of Economic Growth: A Non-Communist Manifesto.* Cambridge: Cambridge University Press.

Rotberg, Robert I., ed. (2003). *When States Fail: Causes and Consequences.* Princeton, NJ: Princeton University Press.

Roubini, Nouriel, and Stephen Mihm. (2011). *Crisis Economics: A Crash Course in the Future of Economics.* New York: Penguin.

Rubenfeld, Samuel. (2011). "Egypt Requests Freeze on Mubarak's Assets." *Wall Street Journal* (February 22, 2011).

Rummel, R. J. (2014). *Death by Government.* http://www.hawaii.edu/powerkills/20TH.HTM

Russett, Bruce. (2010). "Peace in the Twenty-First Century." *Current History* 109 (January 2010): 11–16.

Russett, Bruce, John R. Oneal, and Michaelene Cox. (2000). "Clash of Civilizations, or Realism and Liberalism Déjá Vu?: Some Evidence." *Journal of Peace Research,*37: 583–608.

Russett, Bruce, Harvey Starr, and David Kinsella. (2009). *World Politics: The Menu for Choice.* 9th ed. New York: Thomson Wadsworth.

Rustow, Dankwart. (1967). *A World of Nations: Problems of Political Modernization.* Washington, DC: Brookings Institution.

Ryan, Alan. (2012). *On Politics: A History of Political Thought: From Herodotus to the Present.* New York: Liveright.

Safran, William. (2008). *The French Polity.* 7th ed. London: Pearson.

Sageman, Marc. (2008). *Leaderless Jihad: Terror Networks in the Twenty-First Century.* Philadelphia: University of Pennsylvania Press.

Sahoo, Sarbeswar. (2013). "Rethinking Secularism." *Contemproary South Asia* 21(3): 348–349.

Said, Edward. (2001). "The Clash of Ignorance." *Nation* (October). http://www.thenation.com/doc/20011022/said

Salisbury, Robert H. (1990). "The Paradox of Interest Groups in Washington, DC: More Groups and Less Clout." In *The New American Political System,* rev. ed., edited by Anthony King. Washington, DC: American Enterprise Institute.

Salisbury, Robert H., John P. Heinz, Robert L. Nelson, and Edward O. Laumann. (1991). "Triangles, Networks, and Hollow Cores: The Complex Geometry of Washington Interest Representation." In *The Politics of Interests,* edited by Mark P. Petracca, 130–149. Boulder, CO: Westview.

Samuels, David J., and Matthew S. Shugart. (2013). "Party 'Capacity' in New Democracies: How Executive Format Affects the Recruitment of Presidents and Prime Ministers." *Democratization* doi: 10.1080/13510347.2012.757695

Sassen, Saskia. (1996). *Losing Control? Sovereignty in the Age of Globalization.* New York: Columbia University Press.

Sassen, Saskia. (2008). *Territory, Authority, Rights: From Medieval to Global Assemblages.* 2nd ed. Princeton, NJ: Princeton University Press.

Schain, Martin, Aristide Zolberg, and Patrick Hossay, eds. (2002). *Shadows Over Europe: The Development and Impact of the Extreme Right in Europe.* New York: Palgrave Macmillan.

Shambaugh, David. (2013). *China Goes Global: The Partial Power.* New York: Oxford University Press.

Schedler, Andreas, ed. (2006). *Electoral Authoritarianism: The Dynamics of Unfree Competition.* Boulder, CO: Lynne Reinner.

Schedler, Andreas, ed. (2013). *The Politics of Uncertainty: Sustaining and Subverting Electoral*

Authoritarianism. New York: Oxford University Press.

Schelling, Thomas. (1960). *The Strategy of Conflict.* Cambridge, MA: Harvard University Press.

Scherer, Andreas Georg, Guido Palazzo, and David Seidl. (2013). "Managing Legitimacy in Complex and Heterogeneous Environments: Sustainable Development in a Globalized World." *Journal of Management Studies* 50(2): 259–284.

Schick, Allen. (2012). "Can National Legislatures Regain an Effective Voice in Budget Policy?" *OECD Journal on Budgeting* 1(3): 15–42.

Schleiter, Petra, and Edward Morgan-Jones. (2009). "Constitutional Power and Competing Risks: Monarchs, Presidents, Prime Ministers, and the Termination of East and West European Cabinets." *American Political Science Review* 103(3) (August): 496–512.

Schlozman, Kay, Sidney Verba, and Henry Brady. (2013). *The Unheavenly Chorus: Unequal Political Voice and the Broken Promise of American Democracy.* Princeton, NJ: Princeton University Press.

Schmalleger, Frank J. (2011). *Criminal Justice: A Brief Introduction.* 9th ed. Englewood Cliffs, NJ: Prentice Hall.

Schmidt, Eric, and Jared Cohen. (2010). "The Digital Disruption: Connectivity and the Diffusion of Power." *Foreign Affairs* 89 (November/December): 75–85.

Schmitter, Phillippe C. (1989). "Corporatism is Dead! Long Live Corporatism!" *Government and Opposition* 24(1) (January): 54–73.

Schmitter, Phillippe C. (1993). "Corporatism." In *The Oxford Companion to Politics of the World*, edited by Joel Krieger, 195–198. New York: Oxford University Press.

Schneider, Carsten. (2011). *The Consolidation of Democracy: Comparing Europe and Latin America.* London: Routledge.

Schultz, William Todd, ed. (2005). *Handbook of Psychobiography.* New York: Oxford University Press.

Schumpeter, Joseph. (1950). *Capitalism, Socialism, and Democracy.* 3rd ed. New York: Harper and Row.

Sen, Amartya. (2006). *Identity and Violence: The Illusion of Destiny.* New York: W. W. Norton.

Sesser, Stan. (1992). "A Nation of Contradictions." *New Yorker*, January 13, 37–68.

Sharp, Gene. (2010). *From Dictatorship to Democracy: A Conceptual Framework for Liberation.* 4th U.S. ed. http://www.aeinstein.org/organizations/org/FDTD.pdf

Shaw, George Bernard. (1903/2001). "Maxims for Revolutionists." In *Man and Superman.* New York: Penguin Classics.

Shepsle, Kenneth A. (2010). *Analyzing Politics: Rationality, Behavior, and Institutions.* 2nd ed. New York: W. W. Norton.

Shirky, C. (2011). "The Political Power of Social Media." *Foreign Affairs* (January/February). http://www.foreignaffairs.com/articles/67038/clay-shirky/the-political-power-of-social-media

Shkolnikov, Vladimir. (2009). "Nations in Transit: Democracy's Dark Year." In *Nations in Transit,* 13th ed, 1–9. New York: Freedom House.

Shniderman, Adam, and Charles A. Smith. (2015). "Towards Justice: Neuroscience and Affirmative Defenses at the ICC." *Studies in Law Politics and Society* 66, pp.tbd.

Shugart, Matthew, and John M. Carey. (1992). *Presidents and Assemblies: Constitutional Design and Electoral Dynamics.* New York: Cambridge University Press.

Siegal, David A. (2011). "When Does Repression Work? Collective Action in Social Networks." *Journal of Politics* 73(1): 232–247.

Silone, Ignazio. (1937). *Bread and Wine.* Translated by Gwenda David. New York: Harper and Row.

Simone, Vera. (2001). *The Asian Pacific: Political and Economic Development in a Global Context.* 2nd ed. New York: Pearson.

Singh, Inderjit. "China and India: Comparative Transition to Modernization." Paper presented at the annual meeting of the International Studies Association, Hilton Hawaiian Village, Honolulu, Hawaii, March 5, 2005, http://www.allacademic.com/meta/p71394_index.html

SIPRI (Stockholm International Peace Research Institute). (2013). *The SIPRI Yearbook.* http://www.sipri.org

Sivard, Ruth Leger. (1996). *World Military and Social Expenditures 1996.* Washington, DC: World Priorities.

Skinner, B. F. (1948). *Walden Two*. New York: Macmillan.

Skocpol, Theda. (1979). *States and Social Revolutions: A Comparative Analysis of France, Russia, and China*. New York: Cambridge University Press.

Smelser, Neil. (2007). *The Faces of Terrorism: Social and Psychological Dimensions*. Princeton, NJ: Princeton University Press.

Smick, David. (2008). *The World Is Curved: Hidden Dangers to the World Economy*. New York: Penguin.

Smith, Adam. (1776/2009). *An Inquiry into the Nature and Causes of the Wealth of Nations*. http://www.adamsmith.org/smith/won-intro.htm

Smith, Anthony D. (2010). *Nationalism.* New York: Polity Press.

Smith, Charles A. (2012). *The Rise and Fall of War Crimes Trials: from Charles I to Bush the II*. New York: Cambridge University Press

Smith, Charles A., and Antonio Gonzalez. (2013) "The Role of the International Court in Globalizing Human Rights; Peace or Justice?" In *The Politics of the Globalization of Law, Getting from Rights to Justice*, edited by Alison Brysk, 47–62. New York: Routledge.

Smith, Charles A., and Brandon Miller-de la Cuesta. (2011). "The Role of Peacekeepers in the Formation of Networks." *Human Rights Review* 12(3): 287–299.

Smith, Charles A., and Heather M. Smith. (2011). "Human Trafficking: The Unintended Consequences of United Nations Intervention." *International Political Science Review* 32(2): 139–160.

Smith, Ian. (2013). "Election Boycotts and Hybrid Regime Survival." *Comparative Political Studies* doi: 10.1177/001040134885448

Smith, Jackie. (2007). *Social Movements for Global Democracy*. Baltimore: Johns Hopkins University Press.

Sniderman, Paul. (1975). *Personality and Democratic Politics*. Berkeley: University of California Press.

Sniderman, Paul M., Richard Brody, and Phillip Tetlock. (1993). *Reasoning and Choice: Explorations in Political Psychology*. New York: Cambridge University Press.

Sniderman, Paul M., et al. (1991). "The Fallacy of Democratic Elitism: Elite Competition and Commitment to Civil Liberties." *British Journal of Political Science* 21 (August): 349–370.

Sniderman, Paul M., Louk Hagendoorn, and Markus Prior. (2004), "Predisposing Factors and Situational Triggers: Exclusionary Reactions to Immigrant Minorities." *American Political Science Review* 98(1): 35–49.

Sniderman, Paul M., and Louk Hagendoorn. (2009). *When Ways of Life Collide: Multiculturalism and Its Discontents in the Netherlands*. Princeton, NJ: Princeton University Press.

Sniderman, Paul, and Edward H. Stiglitz. (2012). *The Reputational Premium: A Theory of Party Identification and Policy Reasoning*. Princeton, NJ: Princeton University Press.

Social Progress Imperative. (2014). *Social Progress Index 2014*. http://www.socialprogressimperative.org/data/spi

Sophocles. (1967). *Antigone*. Translated by E. F. Watling. Middlesex, England: Penguin.

Sorensen, Georg. (2008). *Democracy and Democratization: Processes and Prospects in a Changing World*. 3rd ed. Boulder, CO: Westview.

Spagnoli, Filip. (2003). *Homo-Democraticus: On the Universal Desirability and the Not So Universal Possibility of Democracy and Human Rights*. Cambridge: Cambridge Scholars.

Starrs, Sean. (2013). "American Economic Power Hasn't Declined—It Globalized!: Summoning the Data and Taking Globalization Seriously." *International Studies Quarterly* 57: 817–830.

Staub, Ervin. (2011). *Overcoming Evil: Genocide, Violent Conflict, and Terrorism*. New York: Oxford University Press.

Stein, Howard. (2006). "The World Bank and the Application of Asian Industrial Policy to Africa: Theoretical Considerations." *Journal of International Development* 6(3): 287–305.

Steans, Jill. (2013). *Gender and International Relations*. 3rd ed. Malden, MA: Polity Press.

Stepan, Alfred. (2009). "Religion, Democracy, and the 'Twin Tolerations.'" In *Democracy: A Reader,* edited by Robert Putnam and Marc Plattner, 117–138. Baltimore: John Hopkins University Press.

Stephan, Walter G., and Cookie W. Stephan. (1996). "Predicting Prejudice." *International Journal of Intercultural Relations* 20(3–4): 409–426.

Stevens, Charles E., and Joseph T. Cooper. (2010). "A Behavioral Theory of Governments' Ability to Make Credible Commitments to Firms: The Case of the East Asian Paradox." *Asia Pacific Journal of Management* 27: 587–610.

Stiglitz, Joseph. (2006). *Making Globalization Work.* New York: W. W. Norton.

Stiglitz, Joseph. (2003) *Globalization and Its Discontents.* New York: W. W. Norton.

Stiglitz, Joseph. (2010). *Free Fall: America, Free Markets, and the Sinking of the World Economy.* New York: W. W. Norton.

Stoessinger, John G. (2010). *Why Nations Go to War.* 11th ed. Boston: Wadsworth.

Stojanovic, Nenad. (2010). "Mononational and Multinational States: A Valid Dichotomy?" Paper presented at the European University Institute (May 21, 2010). http://www.eui.eu/documents/mwp/conferences/neilmaccormick/paperstojanovic.pdf

Stone, Clarence. (1989). *Regime Politics.* Lawrence, KS: University Press of Kansas.

Stone, Deborah. (2011). *Policy Paradox: The Art of Political Decision Making.* 3rd ed. New York: Norton.

Stone Sweet, Alec. (2004). *The Judicial Construction of Europe.* Oxford: Oxford University Press.

Strøm, Kaare. (2004). "Parliamentary Democracy and Delegation." In Kaare Strøm, Wolfgang C. Müller, and Torbjörn Bergman (eds.), *Delegation and Accountability in Parliamentary Democracies.* Oxford: Oxford University Press: 55–106.

Strauss, Leo. (1959). *What Is Political Philosophy?* New York: Free Press.

Stone, Clarence. (1989). *Regime Politics.* University of Kansas Press.

Sullivan, Brandon, Mark Snyder and John L. Sullivan, eds. (2007). *Cooperation: The Political Psychology of Effective Human Interaction.* New York: Wiley-Blackwell.

Sunstein, Cass. (2001). *Designing Democracy: What Constitutions Do.* New York: Oxford University Press.

Sunstein, Cass. (2009). *On Rumors: How Falsehoods Spread, Why We Believe Them, What Can be Done.* New York: Farrar, Straus & Giroux.

Svolik, Milan W. (2013). "Learning to Love Democracy: Electoral Accountability and the Success of Democracy." *American Journal of Political Science* 57(3): 685–702.

Szabo, Stephen. (2011). "Welcome to the Post-Western World." *Current History* 110 (January 2011): 9–13.

Taagepera, Rein, and Matthew S. Shugart. (1989). *Seats and Votes.* New Haven, CT: Yale University Press.

Taras, Raymond, and Rajat Ganguly. (2010). *Understanding Ethnic Conflict: The International Dimension.* 4th ed. New York: Pearson.

Tawney, R. H. (1938). *Religion and the Rise of Capitalism: A Historical Study.* Middlesex, England: Penguin.

Tesler, Michael, and David O. Sears (2010). *Obama's Race: the 2008 Election and the Dream of a Post-Racial America.* Chicago: University of Chicago Press.

Thompson, Leonard. (1966). *Politics in the Republic of South Africa.* Boston: Little, Brown.

Thompson, Mark R. (2003). *Democratic Revolutions: Asia and Eastern Europe.* London: Routledge.

Thoreau, Henry David. (1849/1981). *Walden and Other Writings.* Edited by J. W. Krutch. New York: Bantam.

Thurow, Lester C. (1997). *The Future of Capitalism.* New York: Penguin.

Tickner, J. Ann. (2001). *Gendering World Politics.* New York: Columbia University Press.

Tilly, Charles. (2007). *Democracy.* New York: Cambridge University Press.

Tocqueville, Alexis de. (1835/1945). *Democracy in America.* New York: Knopf.

Torcal, Mariano, and Jose Ramon Montero. (2006). *Political Disaffection in Contemporary Democracies: Social Capital, Institutions, and Politics.* London: Routledge.

Transparency International. (2013). http://www.transparency.org

Triesman, Daniel. (2004). "Stabilization Tactics in Latin America: Menem, Cardosa, and the Politics of Low Inflation." *Comparative Politics* 36 (July): 399–419.

True, Jacqui, and Brooke Ackerly. (2010). *Doing Feminist Research in Political and Social Sciences.* New York: Palgrave.

Truman, David. (1951). *The Governmental Process.* New York: Knopf.

Tsebelis, George. (2002). *Veto Players: How Political Institutions Work.* Princeton, NJ: Princeton University Press.

Turner, Thomas. (2011). "Kabila's Congo: Hardly 'Post-Conflict'." *Current History* 110 (May 2011): 196–201.

Union of International Associations. (2011). http://www.uia.be/

UNCTAD. (2011). *Commodities at a Glance.* http://www.unctad.org/en/docs/1suc20112_en.pdf

UNCTAD. (2013). *UNCTAD Statistics* UNCTAD.org/en/pages/statistics.aspx

UNDA. (2011). *The United Nations Development Agenda: Development for All—Goals, Commitments, and Strategies Agreed at the United Nations World Conferences and Summits since 1990.* New York: United Nations.

UNDP (United Nations Development Programme). (2001). *Human Development Report 2001.*

UNDP (United Nations Development Programme). (2005). *Human Development Report 2006.* http://www.hdr.undp.org/reports

UNDP (United Nations Development Programme). (2006). *Human Development Report 2006.* http://www.hdr.undp.org/reports

UNDP (United Nations Development Programme). (2007). *Human Development Report 2007.* http://www.hdr.undp.org/reports

UNDP (United Nations Development Programme). (2008). *Human Development Report 2008.* http://www.hdr.undp.org/reports

UNDP (United Nations Development Programme). (2011). *Human Development Report 2010/2011.* http://www.hdr.undp.org/reports.

UNDP (United Nations Development Programme). (2013). *Human Development Report 2013.* http://www.hdr.undp.org/reports.

UNHCR. (2011). *United Nations High Commissioner for Refugees.* www.unhcr.org

UNHCR. (2013). United Nations High Commissioner for Refugees. Displacement: the 21st Century Challenge. http://www.unhcr.org.uk/fileadmin/user_upload/pdf/UNHCR_Global_Trends_2012.pdf

UNICEF. (2011). *Global Inequality: Beyond the Bottom Billion—A Rapid Review of Income Distribution in 141 Countries.* New York: UNICEF.

UNMDG. (2013). *United Nations Millennium Development Goals.* http://www.un.org/millenniumgoals/13_MDG%20Report_EN.pdf

United Nations Peacekeeping Operations. (2013). http://www.un.org/Depts/dpko/dpko/home.shtml

UNMDG. (2011). *United Nations Millenium Goals.* http://www.un.org/milleniumgoals/

UNWFP. (2013). United Nations World Food Programme. http://www.wfp.org

United States State Department (2014). *National Consortium for the Study of Terrorism and Responses to Terrorism: Annex of Statistical Information.* http://www.state.gov/j/ct/rls/crt/2012/210017.htm

Uppsala. (2013). *Uppsala Conflict Data Program.* http://www.pcr.uu.se/research/UCDP/

USDOJ. (2008). "Former Officer and Director of Global Engineering and Construction Company Pleads Guilty to Foreign Bribery and Kickback Charges." September 3, 2008 www.justice.gov/archive/opa/pr/2008/September/08-crm-772.htl

Verba, Sidney, Norman Nie, and Jae-on Kim. (1978). *Participation and Political Equality: A Seven-Nation Comparison.* Cambridge: Cambridge University Press.

Verba, Sidney, Kay Schlozman, and Henry Brady. (1995). *Voice and Equality: Civic Voluntarism in American Politics.* Cambridge, MA: Harvard University Press.

Vision of Humanity (2011). http://www.visionofhumanity.org/gpi/home.php

Victoroff, Jeff. (2005). "The Mind of the Terrorist: A Review and Critique of Psychological Approaches." *Journal of Conflict Resolution* 49 (February): 3–42.

von Braun, Joachim. (2008). "Food and Financial Crises: Implications for Agriculture and the Poor." International Food Policy Research Institute: *Food Policy Report No. 20.* http://www.ifpri.org/pubs/fpr/pr20all.asp

von Hau, Matthias, James Scott, and David Hulme. (2012). "Beyond the BRICs: Alternative Strategies of Influence in the Global Politics of Development." *European Journal of Development Research* 24(2): 187–204.

Waldron, Jeremy. (2006). "The Core of the Case Against Judicial Review." *Yale Law Journal* 115 (2006): 1346–1406.

Wallerstein, Immanuel. (1974). *The Modern World System*. New York: Academic Press.

Wallerstein, Immanuel. (1980). *The World System II*. New York: Academic Press.

Wallerstein, Immanuel. (2004). *World-Systems Analysis: An Introduction*. Raleigh, NC: Duke University Press.

Wallerstein, Immanuel. (2005). "After Developmentalism and Globalization, What?" *Social Forces* 83(3) (March): 1263–1278.

Wallerstein, Immanuel, Charles Lemert, and Carlos Aguirre Rojas. (2013). *Uncertain Worlds: World-Systems Analysis in Changing Times*. Boulder, CO: Paradigm Publishers.

Walt, Stephen M. (1997). "Building Up a New Bogeyman." *Foreign Policy* 106: 176–89.

Walt, Stephen M. (2006). *Taming American Power: The Global Response to U.S. Primacy*. New York: W. W. Norton.

Walzer, Michael. (2006). *Just and Unjust Wars*. 4th ed. New York: Basic Books.

Weatherby, Joseph. (2011). "The Old and the New: Colonialism, Neocolonialism, and Nationalism and the War on Terror." In *The Other World: Issues and Politics of the Developing World*, 9th ed., edited by Joseph Weatherby et al., Ch. 2. New York: Pearson.

Weatherby, Joseph, et al. (2011). *The Other World: Issues and Politics of the Developing World*. 9th ed. New York: Pearson.

Webber, Douglas. (2013). "How Likely Is It that the European Union Will Disintegrate? A Critical Analysis of Competing Theoretical Perspectives." *European Journal of International Relations* doi: 10.1177/1354066112461286

Weber, Martin. (2013). "Between 'Isses' and 'Oughts': IR Constructivism, Critical Theory, and the Challenge of Political Philosophy." *European Journal of International Relations* doi: 10.1177/1354066112466573

Weber, Max. (1951). *The Religion of China: Confucianism and Taoism*. Edited by Hans H. Gerth. New York: Free Press.

Weber, Max. (1958a). *From Max Weber: Essays in Sociology*. Edited by Hans H. Gerth and C. Wright Mills. New York: Oxford University Press.

Weber, Max. (1958b). *The Religion of India: The Sociology of Hinduism and Buddhism*. Translated by Hans Gerth and Don Martindale. New York: Free Press.

Weintraub, Sidney. (2009). "An Economic Storm Hits Latin America." *Current History* 108: 58–64.

Weiss, Thomas, ed. (1996). *NGOs, the UN, and Global Governance*. Boulder, CO: Lynne Rienner.

Weiss, Thomas. (2012). *Humanitarian Intervention*. 2nd ed. New York: Polity Press.

Weiss, Thomas, and Sam Daws, eds. (2009). *The Oxford Handbook on the United Nations*. Oxford: Oxford University Press.

Weitz, Eric D. (2005). *A Century of Genocide: Utopias of Race and Nation*. Princeton, NJ: Princeton University Press.

Welzel, Christian. (2007). "A Human Development View on Value Change." http://margaux.grandvinum.se/SebTest/wvs/articles/folder_published/article_base_83

Wendt, Alexander. (1995). "Constructing International Politics." *International Security* 20(1): 71–81.

Wendt, Alexander. (1999). *Social Theory of International Politics*. Cambridge: Cambridge University Press.

Whang, Taehee, Elena V. McLean, and Douglas W. Kuberski. (2013). "Coercion, Information, and the Success of Sanction Threats." *American Journal of Political Science* 57(1): 65–81.

White, Stephen. (2012). *The Top 175 Global Economic Entities 2011*. dstevenwhite.com/2012/08/11

Wiarda, Howard J. (1997). *Corporatism and Comparative Politics: The Other Great "Ism."* Armonk, NY: M. E. Sharpe.

Wiarda, Howard J. (2003). *Political Development in Emerging Countries*. Belmont, CA: Wadsworth.

Wiarda, Howard J. ed., (2004). *Authoritarianism and Corporatism in Latin America—Revisited*. Gainesville: University Press of Florida.

Wiarda, Howard J. (2013). *Culture and Foreign Policy: The Neglected Factor in International Relations*. Ashgate Publishing Company.

Wiarda, Howard J., and Harvey Kline. (2007). *A Concise Introduction to Latin American Politics and Development.* 2nd ed. Boulder, CO: Westview Press.

Wilensky, Harold. (2002). *Rich Democracies.* Berkeley: University of California Press.

Williams, Michelle. (2008). *The Roots of Participatory Democracy: Democratic Communists in South Africa and Kerala, India.* New York: Palgrave Macmillan.

Wilson, Dominic, and Roopa Purushothaman. (2003). *Dreaming with BRICs: The Path to 2050.* Global Economics Paper No.: 99. New York: Goldman Sachs & Co.

Wilson, Edward O. (1978). *On Human Nature.* Cambridge, MA: Harvard University Press.

Wilson, William Julius. (1990). *The Truly Disadvantaged.* Chicago: University of Chicago Press.

Wilson, William Julius. (1997). *When Work Disappears.* New York: Knopf.

Winters, Jeffrey A. (1998). "Asia and the 'Magic' of the Marketplace." *Current History* 97 (December): 418–425.

Wolf, Martin. (2004). *Why Globalization Works.* New Haven, CT: Yale University Press.

Wolfers, Justin, and Betsey Stevenson. (2013). "Subjective Well-Being and Income: Is There Any Evidence of Satiation?" *American Economic Review* 101(3) (May 2013): 598–604.

World Economic Forum. (2013). *Global Competitiveness Report 2013–2014.* http://www.weforum.org/issues/global-competitiveness

World Wildlife Federation (2013). "Farming Impacts." http://wwf.panda.org/what_we_do/footprint/agriculture/impacts/soil_erosion/

Woo-Cumings, Meredith, ed. (1999). *The Developmental State.* New York: Cornell University Press.

World Bank. (1996). *World Development Report 1996.* New York: Oxford University Press.

World Bank. (2005). *World Development Report 2004–2005.* New York: Oxford University Press.

World Bank. (2011). *World Development Report 2011.* New York: Oxford University Press.

World Bank. (2013). *World Development Report 2013.* New York: Oxford University Press.

World Trade Organization. (2011). *What Is the World Trade Organization?* http://www.wto.org.

World Values Survey. (2006). http://www.worldvaluessurvey.org.

Woshinsky, Oliver. (1995). *Culture and Politics.* Englewood Cliffs, NJ: Prentice Hall.

Wright, Erik Olin, ed. (2005). *Approaches to Class Analysis.* Cambridge: Cambridge University Press.

Wright, Erik Olin, and Joel Rogers. (2010). *American Society: How It Actually Works.* New York: W. W. Norton.

Wrong, Dennis. (1996). *Power: Its Forms, Bases, and Uses.* Brunswick, NJ: Transaction.

Yan, Zhang. (2010). "Bribery Cases on Rise in China." *China Daily* (September 8, 2010). http://www.chinadaily.com.cn/china/2010-09/08/content_11271378.htm

Yunus, Muhammad. (2011). *Building Social Business: The New Kind of Capitalism that Serves Humanity's Most Pressing Needs.* New York: Public Affairs Publishing.

Zakaria, Fareed. (2007). *The Future of Freedom: Illiberal Democracy at Home and Abroad.* Rev. ed. New York: W. W. Norton.

Zakaria, Fareed. (2009). *The Post-American World.* New York: W. W. Norton & Company.

Zaller, John R. (1992). *The Nature and Origins of Mass Opinion.* New York: Cambridge University Press.

Zukin, Cliff, et al. (2006). *A New Engagement? Political Participation, Civic Life, and the Changing American Citizen.* New York: Oxford University Press.

Credits

Chapter 1 Page 2: Cindy Charles/Photoedit; 10: Hulton Archive/Getty Images; 12: Pablo Martinez Monsivais/AFP/Getty Images/Newscom

Chapter 2 Page 26: David Grossman/Alamy; 40: akg-images/Newscom; 42: Matthew Chattle/Alamy

Chapter 3 Page 56: Altsean-Burma/AFP/Getty Images/Newscom; 61: Jose Luis Magana/AP Images; 73: Sakchai Lalit/AP Images

Chapter 4 Page 83: Viktor Drachev/AFP/Getty Images; 100 (left): AP Images; 100 (right): Time & Life Pictures/Getty Images; 104: Anthony Taber/The Cartoon Bank

Chapter 5 Page 112: STRINGER Iraq/Reuters; 116: LEGNAN KOULA/EPA/Newscom; 128: George Booth The New Yorker Collection/The Cartoon Bank

Chapter 6 Page 136: Francis Miller/Time & Life Pictures/Getty Images; 140: Max Nash/Pool/AP Images; 146: Denis Farrell/AP Images

Chapter 7 Page 164: Karim Kadim/AP Images; 172: Philimon Bulawayo /Reuters /Landov; 183: Alexander Zemlianichenko/AP Images

Chapter 8 Page 198: AFP/Stringer/Getty Images; 203: Mimi Mann/AP Images; 216: Julio Etchart/Alamy

Chapter 9 Page 232: Roberto Candia/Candr/AP Images; 243: AP Images; 249: NOREEN AHMED-ULLAH/KRT/Newscom

Chapter 10 Page 258: feiyuezhangjie/Shutterstock.com; 275: Sezayi Erken/AFP/Getty Images/Newscom; 282: Chor Sokunthea/Reuters /Landov

Chapter 11 Page 289: Sergei Chuzavkov/AP Images; 303: THONY BELIZAIRE/Getty Images; 312: Bullit Marquez/AP Images

Chapter 12 Page 321: Ron Haviv; 329: Suzanne Plunkett/AP Images; 338: peter jordan / Alamy

Chapter 13 Page 356: Jon-Pierre Lasseigne/AP Images; 361: Ulrich Liechti-VBS/Reuters; 369: Mike Luckovich/Creators Syndicate, Inc

Chapter 14 Page 380: The Granger Collection, NYC; 386: AP Photo/Sunday Alamba; 393: U.S. Agency for International Development

Chapter 15 Page 419: James Dazinger; 431: Mario Ruiz/EPA/Newscom; 437: Kyodo Extra/AP Images

Appendix Page 447: Tom Thaves/Universal Uclick

Index